American Liberty & Justice

Lone Star Law

A LEGAL HISTORY OF TEXAS

MICHAEL ARIENS

FOREWORD BY GORDON MORRIS BAKKEN

TEXAS TECH UNIVERSITY PRESS

★

This book is typeset in Minion Pro. The paper used
in this book meets the minimum requirements
of ANSI/NISO Z39.48-1992 (R1997). ∞

Typesetting: StudioKaelin

Printed in the United States of America
11 12 13 14 15 16 17 18 19 / 9 8 7 6 5 4 3 2 1

Texas Tech University Press
Box 41037
Lubbock, Texas 79409-1037 USA
800.832.4042
ttup@ttu.edu
www.ttupress.org

Library of Congress Cataloging-in-Publication Data

Ariens, Michael S., 1957–

Lone star law : a legal history of Texas / Michael
Ariens ; foreword by Gordon Morris Bakken.

p. cm.—(American liberty & justice)

Summary: "An overarching history of the law and legal
culture of Texas, particularly investigating the days of
early settlement through 1920; Texas's law of property,
families, and businesses; criminal law and tort law; and
the Texas legal profession"-—Provided by publisher.

Includes bibliographical references and index.

ISBN 978-0-89672-695-6 (hardback)

1. Law—Texas—History. I. Title.

KFT1278.A75 2011
349.764—dc23   2011030194

For Renée

CONTENTS

★

ILLUSTRATIONS

★

FOREWORD

★

Michael Ariens's *Lone Star Law: A Legal History of Texas* is an exciting, comprehensive analysis of the law of America's most diverse and significant state. Diversity of population and legal heritage make explaining Texas challenging, but Ariens has triumphed in this book. He clearly explains the multinational legal heritage of Texas, the challenges of the Republic, and the accomplishments of statehood. He surveys a legislative past as well as the judicial heritage that confronted problems of land, water, crime, and industrial revolution amid an agricultural and ranching economy.

This book is more than a celebration of judicial wisdom and legislative foresight. Ariens critically analyzes both cases and statutes in their historical context. He puts governors in that context as Texas molds a heritage of the rule of law. The rule of law had many predecessors. Spanish and Mexican law prevailed with early settlement, but colonists imported English common law as well as state law learned and practiced in their states of origin. Legislators and judges sorted out the conflicts and built a society based on the rule of law with special Texas flavoring. Reading about the origins and public policy positions of legislators and judges may be as intellectually challenging as determining the ingredients of the chopped beef sandwiches at Angelo's Texas Bar-B-Que in Fort Worth. The sandwiches are made of many ingredients, such as mustard, pickles, onions, and barbecue sauce. You know you are tasting Texas-style barbecue wherever it is served, but the sauce varies regionally. Likewise, the law had many ingredients, but you will know that it was distinctively and uniquely Texan. Texas is large, diverse, and nationally significant. Law in action has much to do with place, and like a Texas barbeque sandwich it can be enjoyed with Shiner or Lone Star depending upon location. Ariens puts plenty of Texas flavoring on his interpretations, and they must be savored for their time and place.

Texas produced presidents, senators, and representatives for the national political and legal system, but in Texas law, people in local and state politics mattered. Michael Ariens gives the reader a sense of how people mattered in the evolution of the rule of law. Remember, the chef knows what went into the sauce. That is the secret of place, but in *Lone Star Law*

Ariens excises the ingredients of law and makes the recipes of time and place clear.

Enjoy the read and savor it Texas-style.

GORDON MORRIS BAKKEN, *Series Editor*
California State University, Fullerton

PREFACE

★

THIS BOOK offers an overarching history of the law and legal culture of Texas. My reach has certainly exceeded my grasp. The shelves of law school libraries groan with reports, statutes, descriptions, and assessments of the legal world of Texas. In the 1960s and 1970s the Texas Court of Criminal Appeals routinely decided or dismissed twenty-five hundred cases each year. The Texas Supreme Court, the Texas Commission of Appeals, and Texas courts of appeals have combined to issue more than one hundred thousand opinions. Federal courts have also issued many important opinions concerning Texas law. And every two years the Texas legislature meets and adopts hundreds of statutes. This one-volume history will discuss just a small number of those decisions and statutes. Because each case that reaches an appellate court tells a story, most of those stories are left untold. The stories I tell are intended to serve as a representative glimpse of the legal history of the people of Texas.

This book has taken a long time to finish. I have been aided by a number of talented and dedicated persons whose assistance has been invaluable.

Thanks to Noel Parsons, retired director of Texas Tech University Press, for encouraging me to write this book.

My thanks to the research assistants over the years who aided me, including Christine Hortick, Joseph Hoffer, Kimberly Phillips, James Rodriguez, Alexis Lorick, Jason Petty, Benjamin Slawson, Andrew Edelman, Nishma Shah, Ryan Cox, Gabe Hughes, and Andrew Skemp. Thanks to Stacy Fowler for filling several hundred requests for materials located elsewhere. Thanks also to Katy Stein for gathering nearly hidden information.

My deepest thanks to Associate Dean Vicki Mather for providing me a teaching leave to complete the book and for her constant support. Thanks also to Dean Charles Cantú and Associate Dean Reynaldo Valencia for fostering a scholarly atmosphere at the law school. Thanks to my colleagues Mark Cochran, Richard Flint, Doug Haddock, Dorie Klein, Vincent Johnson, Victoria Mather, Ana Novoa, Geary

Reamey, Bernard Reams, John Schmolesky, and Wayne Scott for their critical comments and suggestions. Their assistance makes it crucial for me to acknowledge that all remaining mistakes are my responsibility.

The work of the two deans of Texas legal history, Joseph W. McKnight and Hans W. Baade, made it possible for me to write this book. Their deep knowledge of the pathways of the law, their understanding of comparative law as well as legal history, and their love of scholarship are inspiring. This work is my acknowledgment of the debt I owe them.[1]

Texas has long been blessed with extraordinary historians, and the careful work of modern Texas historians provides enormous insight into Texas's political and legal history. The existence of many strong graduate history programs at universities in Texas, which have resulted in a number of dissertations and theses on aspects of Texas history, has been tremendously helpful.

The Internet provides opportunities for many to say almost anything, or even nothing, but it also provides the opportunity to make historical records widely available. The University of North Texas's Portal to Texas History has digitized Gammel's *Laws of Texas*, and its searchable function allows one to perceive the shape of legislative developments in a way unavailable even a decade ago. The digitization of the historic *Dallas Morning News* allows one to learn how journalists understood events as they happened. The Texas State Historical Association has created the Handbook of Texas Online and placed all of the volumes of the *Southwestern Historical Quarterly* on the Internet. All of these developments made my research much easier.[2]

Finally, thanks to my wife Renée, to whom this book is dedicated, and without whose support and love this book would not have been written, and to our children, Stephanie, Caitlin, and John.

This book is written for the interested lay reader. I avoid legal jargon as much as possible and explain legal concepts as simply as possible. Those interested in the sources used to construct this book may consult the end notes and bibliography.

LONE STAR LAW

★

Introduction

★

THE DECEMBER 20, 1999, issue of *Texas Lawyer* anticipated the new century a year early with a thoughtful retrospective, "*Texas Lawyer*'s 20th Century in Review." One article listed twenty-one landmark cases of Texas, "cases that rocked the century." It chose wisely, and most are discussed in this book. The article's premise is, however, wrong. A list of cases that "rocked the century" is offered on the assumption that law is more important than culture in shaping and arranging the course of history. One goal of this book is to argue that although law affects culture, it cannot shape culture. Harmful or deleterious societal trends can be meliorated by judicial decisions or statutes, and ideas about what "the law" dictates can temper the intemperate passions of the people. Society's general acceptance of the ideal of the rule of law lessens societal acceptance of extralegal action (such as lynching) and enhances acceptance of legal declarations with which many may disagree (such as prayer in public schools). Ideas about law matter in American and Texan culture. But law, particu-

larly judge-made law, cannot lead the way to a more just and civil society. If the law is contrary to public consensus, it will be the law, and not the consensus, that gives way. Law may reflect what society values, but the pronouncements of judges and legislators do not declare the moral worth of a society. This may be particularly true in a state in which judges are elected to office in partisan races. This book examines the interplay between Texas culture and law, the varying impact of national culture on Texas cultural trends as reflected in law, and the impact of the laws of other states and the national government on Texas law.[1]

Texas possesses a rich history that allows one to evaluate the formation of its legal culture within a broader social culture. A *legal* history of Texas offers a slightly different vantage point to assess a place both southern and western, a colony and a Republic, a state of the Union and a Confederate state, and a borderland. Declarations of law by courts and legislatures are rarely the final word. How a society reacts to those pronouncements is the story after the story and may give the reader some sense of how a society accepts, rejects, or modifies formal law.[2]

In addition to assessing the relationship between Texas law and its culture, I have three other goals. First, I examine the influence of Texas's exceptional history on its law. Texas, like the United States, was born of revolution, and like many Americans, Texans have historically viewed themselves as exceptional. American exceptionalism can describe traits both positive (an optimism about the future, an ideology that allows anyone to dream of succeeding, the protection of an individual's right to pursue happiness) and negative (violence in society, racism, and a narcissism reflective of a solitary pursuit of individual desire). Texas exceptionalism frames the history of the Texas Revolution, including the surprise victory in the Battle of San Jacinto. That exceptionalism also applied to the Canary Islanders who risked their lives to move to the remotest part of New Spain. "Only in Texas" described the oil wildcatters and speculators who made the state the center of the twentieth-century American oil exploration industry. Its statewide peace officers, the Texas Rangers, were burnished in legend ("one riot, one Ranger"), one that often ignored the very human failures of the Rangers.[3]

Those making Texas law have hewed often to an exceptionalist view of the foundations and development of Texas law. Texas law was exceptional in part because it melded Spanish (or Castilian) civil law with American common law. Defenders of the Texas legal system claimed its unique amalgamation more fully protected the liberty of its citizens than either system alone. Structurally, the Texas legal system was exceptional in creating two separate but equal appellate courts, one (the supreme court) limited to hearing appeals in civil cases and the other (the court of criminal appeals) limited to hearing appeals in criminal cases. Despite a number of unusual aspects in its legal culture, the idea of exceptionalism fits poorly in the history of Texas law. The extent to which Texas lawmakers relied on law found in other states to shape Texas law is a constant theme. Texas differed economically and demographically from many other states for much of its history, and its variety of geographies enhanced those differences. Yet those differences should not hide the important influences the law of other states and of the federal government had on Texas law. Texas was always part of a larger social and legal whole, and how others understood law affected the choices made in Texas legal policy. Early attempts to explain Texas's legal history focused on uniquely Texas laws, such as its homestead act. This aspect of Texas legal exceptionalism has on some occasions led Texas judges astray, to reach for a distinctive Texas law when either none exists or when it does not properly reflect Texas's legal history.[4]

Second, following the approach taken by Walter A. McDougall in the first two volumes of his history of America, I discuss the commonality of Texans and Americans as "hustlers," both in a positive and a negative sense. McDougall notes that the diaspora from England was based in part on economic, religious, and political changes, joined by "the fourth spirit of English colonization, the racial and legal one." The first three concerned individual liberty, for each change unshackled the individual from the crown, choosing what to make and sell, what to profess as a matter of faith, and how to organize a polity beyond hereditary monarchy. Americans used these "original spirits" to justify their revolution. Anglo-Texans ("Texians") used the same spirits to justify their own revolution. The fourth spirit, the racial and legal one, both reflected ideas of individual liberty (the rule of law protected the individual from corruption in government) and was contrary to them, for it allowed American colonists to justify displacing those already living on the newly colonized land and to enslave imported Africans. In Texas, hustlers developed the land and later cities that propelled much of its economy. Hustlers also celebrated the displacement of Mexican rule for a republic, a republic that both embraced African slavery and made second-class citizens of those non-Anglo Mexicans who now lived in the republic. Hustling also led to shortcuts to prosperity. Hustlers used violence to obtain wealth and power—wealth to corrupt governors and power to nullify impartial justice. In addition to the settlers from the Canary Islands, who found opportunities in Texas unavailable to them in Spain, early European settlers of Texas flocked there both to leave other places (and sometimes people) behind and to make something of themselves. Hustling had a substantial and continuing impact on the development of Texas law.[5]

Third, I avoid mythologizing Texas law in the tradition of the earliest Texas historians. The stories that follow present the flawed and heroic Texan. The work of modern Texas historians on myth and memory has guided my approach concerning a legal history of Texas.[6]

Although this legal history discusses hundreds of cases and statutes, they are discussed and evaluated as they reflect jurisprudential and cultural changes in Texas since its settlement by Spanish subjects. This law offers a story about the state of Texas, its residents, and its legal system beyond any doctrinal point (for example, when is the defendant liable in contract or tort?). The life of the dead letter of the law is what sparks an interest in any legal history, and the life of the law in Texas has been dynamic and tragic.

The subtitle of this book is *A Legal History of Texas*. Many particular topics of interest to historians of Texas and to legal historians may be touched upon only briefly, if at all. Decades of doctrine are occasionally collapsed into one or two paragraphs, and some legal topics are only lightly noted. This book is a starting point for those interested in developing further one or more of the topics discussed in these pages.

ONE

Creating Texas Law, 1718–1864

★

SPANISH EXPLORERS sailed the entire Texas coast in 1519. However, it took nearly two centuries for Spain to settle this part of northern New Spain permanently. Spaniards founded a settlement in 1716 in present-day East Texas, and two years later, Mission San Antonio de Valero, Presidio San Antonio de Béxar, and Villa de Béxar were located near the San Antonio River's headwaters. In 1731, three missions were moved from East Texas to the San Antonio River valley, and emigrants from the Canary Islands arrived and settled what they called San Fernando de Béxar. The population in the area grew slowly. Residents of San Fernando de Béxar numbered about five hundred by 1750 and fifteen hundred by 1800. The entire Spanish population in Texas by the early nineteenth century was approximately four thousand. As late as 1820, as Moses Austin readied his petition to settle three hundred families in Texas, only about two thousand residents lived in San Fernando, of a total population in Texas of about seven thousand,

excluding most indigenous tribal members. By 1860, as the nation readied for the possibility of civil war, the U.S. Census Bureau calculated that 604,215 persons lived in Texas, including 182,921 slaves.[1]

Nearly all of Spanish and Mexican Texas was a frontier, a status that continued through the existence of the Republic (1836–45) and antebellum state (1845–60). Laws developed by central authorities in Mexico City, Monclova, San Antonio, San Felipe de Austin, Washington-on-the-Brazos, Houston, or Austin were only slowly communicated. Consequently, decisions by magistrates when Texas was a province of Spain (1718–1821) and Mexico (1821–36) were made less in reliance on the formal Spanish (Castilian) or Mexican law and more on the felt needs of the people living in small communities. The resolution of civil and criminal disputes might vary significantly from the formally stated law developed by the sovereign. The effective operation of the laws through 1860 (and indeed afterward) was subject to a more than occasional willingness of Texans to take the law into their own hands, because of either a disregard of the legal system or an inability of officers of the law to enforce it.

The law applicable in Texas during nearly all of Spanish and Mexican rule was based on the civil law system, traced to early Roman law, including the Justinian Code (AD 529–34). The civil law system (also known as *ius commune*) was adopted in most of continental Europe and is distinguished as a legal system from the English common law system transplanted to English colonies in America. One distinctive difference between civil law and common law was that the former usually codified large aspects of private law through legislation, while the latter developed private law through decisions by judges in particular cases.[2]

The assertion of independence by Texians from Mexico in 1835–36 did not lead to a wholesale rejection of Mexican law. Instead, it led to an amalgam of Spanish civil law and English common law. On January 20, 1840, the fourth congress of the Republic of Texas adopted a law providing that "the Common Law of England (so far as it is not inconsistent with the Constitution or the Acts of congress now in force) . . . shall continue in full force until altered or repealed by Congress." Despite this declaration, the major purpose of this statute was to retain the civil law rules concerning marital property. In addition to the retention of the civil law of marital property, some aspects of the law of civil procedure remained based on Spanish law (see chapter 8). Some water rights existed pursuant to Spanish and Mexican law, and the Congress of the Republic modified or rejected other common law doctrines in light of civil law alternatives.[3]

LAW IN NORTHERN NEW SPAIN

From the founding of the presidio at San Antonio in 1718 to the Mexican war of independence from Spain beginning in 1810, what was to become part of Texas was a modest slice of northern New Spain sparsely settled by Spanish subjects. The Alamo and other missions near San Fernando de Béxar (San Antonio) were designed to protect the heart of New Spain in present-day Mexico from a hostile attack on its perimeter. The population was largely poor, with most eking out a living as farmers. Few colonists in northern New Spain possessed the resources to take legal disputes from the local judges (*alcaldes ordinarios*) to the provincial governor and then to the *audiencia* (royal appellate court) in Guadalajara.[4]

No trained lawyer could make a living practicing law in San Fernando de Béxar through the first decades of the nineteenth century. Despite these substantial obstacles, the residents "found the time and energy to sue each other." A few self-trained legal writers assisted claimants in San Antonio during this time. The absence of lawyers was felt throughout the region, not just in San Fernando de Béxar. The governor of the region encompassing Texas lacked an *asesor* (legal assistant) on hand to provide immediate legal advice. One trained *asesor* was assigned to the commandant general of the interior provinces during the late eighteenth century, and he gave legal opinions to the governors of Texas, New Mexico, and Alta California. This *asesor*, Pedro Galindo Navarro, possessed a "small library." Joseph McKnight notes that "in the western provinces [of New Spain], judicial proceedings were almost always handled wholly without in their initial stages and often without any trained lawyer's intervention in the matter's completion."[5]

The law of the New World was called *derecho indiano* (the law of the Indies). As Charles Cutter notes, *derecho indiano* comprised law from Castile and law created in the New World. The former was, in order of importance, legislation from Castile, municipal laws applicable if royal law was silent, and finally, Las Siete Partidas, a code of laws compiled during the thirteenth century. The law of the New World consisted of laws crafted by Spanish officials serving in the New World as well as laws adopted by local governments. One of the most important legal texts of New World law was the *Recopilación de Indias*, published in 1681 and available to the *alcaldes ordinarios* in San Antonio. Formal law modified by local authorities was called *derecho vulgar*. Although some law books could be purchased in the New World in the seventeenth century, eighteenth-century law in northern New Spain was less influenced by the formal law in the *Recopilación de Indias* than by custom, by notions of equitable fairness (*equidad*), and by local interpretations, all of which were necessary to lessen disharmony raised by disputes in these small outposts. Local interpretation was crucial and "perhaps the most overlooked dimension of the Spanish colonial legal system." Local interpretation was necessary because of the absence of any law-trained lawyers and judges; in San Antonio, not only were the first two *alcaldes ordinarios* not trained in law, but neither was well educated by the standards of the time. Northern New Spain remained a class-based society modeled on the Old World, but fairness in the handling of disputes was an essential aspect of its legal system. This sensible approach cemented bonds in a remote frontier whose residents were subject to attack by outsiders and who were tied together by blood and shared economic interests.[6]

The criminal law system of northern New Spain followed the inquisitorial method of the continental European civil law system, as distinguished from the accusative method found in the common law system developed in England. The common law system made the trial judge an impartial, disinterested and largely passive observer. The role of lawyers was enhanced in the common law system by the adoption of the adversarial system of proof, under which the parties were responsible for providing evidence proving the party's case. Proof consisted in part in the examination of

witnesses by questions from the lawyers. The proof offered by the parties was then evaluated by the jury, ordinary men in the community who together determined whether the accused was guilty of the crime charged. In the inquisitorial system, the magistrate or judge enjoyed an active role in the investigation and gathering of evidence and proof. The role of lawyers in the inquisitorial system was secondary, with the judge asking most of the questions at different times during the various proceedings. Juries were, for the most part, unheard of in the civil law system in northern New Spain, and the judge determined the guilt of the criminal defendant.[7]

After a person was accused of a crime in northern New Spain, a fact-finding inquiry called a *sumaria* commenced. It was conducted by the magistrate who eventually heard the case. The *sumaria* built the case against the accused, who took no part in determining the facts. Near the completion of the *sumaria*, and after the accused was imprisoned (which meant little given the absence of any jail in San Antonio during that time), the accused was given a chance to confess, claim his innocence, or explain the circumstances of his crime. This *confesión* ordinarily completed the *sumaria*. The record in the *sumaria* constituted the bulk of the proceedings in the case.

The second step in the process was the *plenario*, at which the parties offered proofs. The *plenario*, Cutter informs us, was a "haphazard" affair, a result in great part of the judge's lack of legal training, a condition that also afflicted any lawyers involved in the case. Witnesses might be called, and witnesses might be disqualified. The accused was allowed to ratify his *confesión*, and the matter was sometimes dropped without explanation, likely due to the agreement by the parties concerning appropriate compensation. The final phase of the proceeding was the *sentencia*, the punishment phase. Because prisons did not exist in northern New Spain, the goal of punishment was to ensure that the community's needs for order and fairness were met. The magistrate was given a large measure of discretion to assess the appropriate punishment. Any case that reached the *sentencia* stage presumed the guilt of the accused. Consequently, the judge would not declare the accused innocent of the crime at the *sentencia*; he might, however, absolve the accused. Punishments often involved shaming, designed to return a straying sheep to the flock, or banishment, to excise the sinner from the community. Fines and enforced work on public projects were also notable punishments. Cutter notes only a few cases in which the sentence was death, and no death sentence could be carried out without some overview of the proceedings beyond the local magistrate.[8]

LAW IN AUSTIN'S COLONY

In 1821, after the death of his father, Moses, Stephen F. Austin became *empresario*, the entrepreneurial leader of what would become Austin's Colony. In March 1822, Austin traveled to San Antonio to apprise the governor of the progress made in settling the colony. The transition of sovereignty from Spain to Mexico led the local governor to demand that Austin obtain approval of his grant in Mexico City. Austin finally accomplished this task by the middle of 1823, after nearly a year's absence from Texas.[9]

As *empresario*, Austin possessed the duty to administer the system of legal justice for his colonists. After his return Austin held elections for one *alcalde* to preside in each of the two colonies then in existence. Josiah Bell, who had served as justice of the peace during Austin's absence, was elected, as was John Tumlinson. (That same year, on his way to San Antonio to discuss the problem of crime plaguing Austin's colony, Tumlinson was murdered.) Neither Bell nor Tumlinson read Spanish, the only language in which Mexican law was printed, and neither was trained in law, making the administration

of justice in Austin's colony uneven at best. The decisions of the *alcaldes* were subject to the *empresario*'s approval. Austin's decisions in turn were sometimes subject to approval by the provincial governor or by authorities in Mexico.[10]

In January 1824, as competing groups in Mexico struggled over the proper organization of that country's government, Austin published his Civil Regulations and Criminal Regulations for the administration of justice in his colony. The Civil Regulations were initially thirty in number (two articles on animals were added in May 1824) and were written in English. The Civil Regulations spoke specifically only of judgments in the private law subjects of contracts and property (Art. 18). The absence of any Civil Regulations on the private law subject of torts is not surprising, for the law of accidental harms was in its infancy, and the criminal law was used to remedy intentional harms. Article 5 of the Civil Regulations accounted for the illiterate by requiring the constable to read the defendant the complaint and summons (an order requiring the defendant to appear in court) and made provisions for the itinerant nature of the residents of the colony, allowing a copy of the summons to be left at the defendant's house or "with some one of his white family" if the defendant was not at home (Art. 6). A civil case began with a written petition to the *alcalde* "stating in a short but clear manner the cause and nature of his complaint" (Art. 3). Austin adopted the sensible Spanish/Mexican tradition of encouraging the *alcalde* first to "effect an amicable compromise between" the parties (Art. 9) and by allowing parties to ask for arbitrators (Arts. 9–14) to attempt to resolve the dispute before it reached the *alcalde*. In a small community, continued good relations with one another were essential to the community's survival and growth, and lawsuits needed to be settled with as little rancor as possible. Austin allowed appeals only if the sum was for more than twenty-five dollars (Art. 20). A defendant appealing a judgment was required to give as security "double the amount of the judgment and costs"; a plaintiff appealing a case was required to post a security valued at double the amount of the costs incurred. The extensive cost of posting security in order to appeal created a strong disincentive for parties who lost at trial, allowing disputes to be quickly resolved.[11]

Most cases in Austin's colony were heard by the *alcaldes*. Austin served as the initial judge only when the issue was financially significant, a claim in excess of two hundred dollars (Art. 16). Some cases were appealed to Austin. Civil suits were sufficiently numerous that in 1826 Austin created an appellate court of *alcaldes* to relieve him of that duty. This appellate court was replaced after the adoption of the Constitution of Coahuila and Texas (1827) and legislation (through decrees) implementing the constitution. It was not until mid-1834 that provincial legislation was adopted locating an appellate court in Texas. Before Decree 277 was adopted in April 1834, all civil appeals beyond Austin or the group of *alcaldes* were sent to Saltillo; that distance, combined with the expense of the posted security, made an appeal merely an abstract possibility. Despite the absence of trained lawyers (Austin was modestly trained in law), as Joseph McKnight notes, "[a]mong Austin's colonists there does not appear to have been any serious dissatisfaction with the administration of civil justice."[12]

Austin's Criminal Regulations totaled twenty-six. The adoption of the Criminal Regulations was necessary, Austin wrote, to protect "public peace and safety of the settlers" against "pilfering depredations of strolling parties of Indians and robbers" and the "transit of men of bad character." The first five articles established the relationship of settlers with Indians: the Criminal Regulations required settlers to act as militia members, allowed the punishment of "rude" or "suspicious" Indians, and criminalized the abuse or ill treatment of Indians

by settlers. Articles 7–9 concerned "morals" offenses, prohibiting gambling, "profane swearing and drunkenness," and living as a couple without the benefit of marriage. (Enforcement of this last law was stayed until sixty days after the arrival of a priest to marry couples living together.) Articles 10–14 concerned the interaction of criminal law and slavery, including the crimes of stealing slaves and harboring fugitive slaves. It also described the penalty for the crime of theft committed by a slave (whipping, which, because it was a punishment different from that for theft by a free person, was contrary to Mexican law). Articles 15–18 spoke of the punishments for theft, assault, slander, and counterfeiting. In all cases the primary punishment was a fine, but "hard labor on public works" was also possible.

The colony lacked a jail, and the local government failed to raise money to build one. Settlers accused of a crime were sometimes ordered shackled before trial to limit their liberty. This proved a failure. Article 19 stated the process of the criminal trial, including the "verdict of a jury of six disinterested and honest men." Austin's decision to give a jury of one's peers the power to issue verdicts in criminal cases was clearly contrary to Mexican law. Its inclusion suggests the value Texians accorded trial by jury—the belief that trial by jury was central in protecting individual liberty against government tyranny. The remaining articles largely concerned issues of process, including what to do if a fine or costs of the trial were not paid and the permissible purposes for using collected fines.

As noted by Marvin Schultz, "felony trials proved to be rare events in Austin's colony." In part this was because of the general safety of the residents of the colony. Another reason related to Mexican law: before any person could be subject to corporal or capital punishment, the case was subject to review by trained magistrates in Saltillo, hundreds of miles distant from

Austin's colony. The practical effect of such a requirement was a substantial delay in felony trials and punishments. The absence of a jail and the ineffectiveness of shackling in deterring escape by an accused made it nearly impossible to prosecute felonies in a timely fashion. For example, a defendant named Parker was accused of murdering a man named Early in 1828. The circumstantial evidence was strong, and Parker was found guilty and sentenced to death. He was shackled and placed in the care of a custodian while local authorities waited to hear from Saltillo. Before the magistrates in Saltillo determined whether the sentence should be carried out, Parker allegedly died from disease. After his "death," Texians learned that Parker's real name was Isaac Desha and that he was wanted for murder in Kentucky. Whether Parker/Desha actually died while in custody remains unknown; some accounts relate that the custodian freed Parker and allowed him to escape. In 1830, a scandalous murder was never tried, largely because of the necessity of notices and appeals to Saltillo as well as demands in the community for a jury trial in English. Unlike their attitude about the administration of civil justice, Texians were dissatisfied with the administration of criminal justice in Coahuila and Texas.[13]

THE CONSTITUTION OF COAHUILA AND TEXAS AND THE ADMINISTRATION OF JUSTICE

The 1827 constitution of the joined Mexican states of Coahuila and Texas divided the branches of government into executive, legislative, and judicial branches. The judicial branch was based on the Spanish civil-law system. For example, Article 172 of the constitution stated, "The tribunals and courts of justice, being authorized solely for applying the laws, shall never interpret the same, or suspend their execution." This was consonant with the civil-law view of magistrates. Judges in the civil-law system were understood as functionaries different from common-law judges. In the civil-law system, particularly after the adoption in France of the *Code Civil* (1804), the magistrate's duty was to apply the codified law, not interpret it. In the common-law tradition, much law was a product of prior decisions (precedent) of common-law judges and not a product of statutory legislation. The magistrate had no authority to "interpret" the law in the sense of making it up in either system. However, the civil-law tradition made the law stated in the code the focus of lawyers and judges, not any decision of the magistrate. A civil-law judge would never look at a prior judge's understanding of a code provision when applying it. He would look solely at the code provision itself. In the common-law tradition, the judge applied the already existing (even if never before articulated) common law to the case before him. He did not invent law but used reason and any analogous prior (precedential) cases to elucidate the law applicable to the present case. Article 180 followed the Spanish tradition of requiring conciliation before any trial. The same article indicated that a trial was "by writing," contrary to the common-law system of trial by the oral testimony of witnesses subject to cross-examination by counsel.[14]

The judicial provisions in the 1827 constitution reflected some aspects of the common law. For example, Article 191 limited the authority of state officials to search the houses, papers, and effects of an inhabitant. The exception to this prohibition, unlike that of the Fourth Amendment in the United States Constitution, which also protected persons from government searches and seizures, was not a requirement that the government show "probable cause" but, "except in those cases, and in the form, the law provide," an exception consonant with codified law. More importantly to Anglo-Texans, Article 192 declared as "one of the main objects of attention of congress" the establishment of "trial by jury in criminal cases" and gradually "even to adopt it in civil cases in proportion as the advantages of this valuable institution become practically known."[15]

Decree 39, adopted by the legislature of the state of Coahuila and Texas on June 21, 1827, supplanted much of Austin's Civil and Criminal Regulations. Decree 39 focused on procedure and structure, largely avoiding specific declarations on the substantive civil or criminal law. Decree 39 was divided into six sections. The first detailed the administration of justice by "inferior magistrates," the *alcaldes*. Section II listed the process by which civil lawsuits began, focusing on the Mexican goal of conciliation of disputes. Section III discussed the duties of justices of the peace and general assessors. Section IV, the longest, elaborately listed the responsibilities of the appellate court, the Supreme Tribunal of Justice, and practice before it. Section V concerned the execution of judgments in civil and criminal cases and appeals from those judgments, and Section VI was limited to prison issues. Although adopted in the aftermath of the 1827 constitution, Decree 39 ignored trial by jury and assumed rather than noted the three stages of the criminal trial under Mexican law. Further, although titled a "Code of Laws for the Administration of Justice," it did not declare the substantive law of property or contracts in the decree, an ordinary aspect of the civil-law system of codification.[16]

On April 6, 1830, the national government of Mexico issued a decree prohibiting the continued immigration into Texas of Anglo-Americans and their slaves. In time the law would represent a "turning point" in the history of Texas. Just two weeks later, the congress of the state of Coahuila and Texas issued abortive Decree 136, which attempted to implement trial by jury in criminal cases. The decree may have been an effort to placate Texians concerned

about the meaning of the April 6 law. Although the congress adopted the decree, the governor returned it unsigned for revisions. Under the decree between twenty-one and eighty-four jurors were elected to a year-long term. At trial, in the presence of counsel for the accused, the defendant was shown the list of jurors, from which he picked seven men. The government was permitted to make only two objections to prospective jurors. A majority vote sufficed for decision. One difficulty with the insertion of the jury into the Mexican criminal trial was that the trial otherwise remained unaffected. A criminal case commenced with the *sumaria*, in which the magistrate gathered evidence of the guilt of the accused in the absence of the lawyer for the accused. If the magistrate continued the matter at the end of the *sumaria*, he had decided the defendant had committed the crime. The jury was inserted into the *plenario*, something of an equivalent to a trial as understood in the common law, but operated under a quite different set of assumptions about the role of the parties and the duty of the court. Adding a jury to the proceedings after the judge had collected sufficient evidence of the guilt of the accused simply created a possible conflict between the judge and the jury.[17]

One difference between the *plenario* and the common law jury trial is found in Article 13 of Decree 136. That article gave the jury the opportunity to ask questions of the "prisoner and his counsel," which they "shall answer." In 1830 the common law in England and the United States prohibited parties from testifying, based on the belief that a party might have to choose between telling the truth at the possible cost to his case or lie under oath to benefit his case at the cost of eternal damnation. Both options exacted a significant cost to the party, so the common law eliminated that decision. Further, the Fifth Amendment to the U.S. Constitution, largely adopted by American states in their own constitutions, prevented the govern-

*Stephen F. Austin, 1836.
Courtesy Texas State Library
and Archives Commission.*

ment from compelling a defendant accused of a crime "to be a witness against himself" (for example, by coercing a confession outside of the trial). Finally, the questioning of witnesses in the common law was undertaken by counsel for the parties; the members of the jury in the common-law system heard testimony but were prohibited from asking questions of any witness. The approach as outlined in Decree 136 was consistent with the civil-law tradition, and an engrafted common-law jury had relatively little to recommend it. Even so, the enthusiasm of Texians for trial by jury led them to conduct such a trial in June 1830, on the mistaken assumption that the decree had been made effective as law.[18]

Although no provision in Mexican law allowed for it, civil matters were tried before juries in Austin's colony upon the request of one of the parties. In 1826, Austin heard a case involving a claim of more than two hundred dollars with the assistance of a jury of twelve men. Eleven jurors held for the plaintiff, and Austin issued a judgment in his favor.[19]

The promise of Article 192 of the 1827 Constitution of Coahuila and Texas was not kept until the adoption in April 1834 of Decree 277, by which time it was too late to assuage the fears of many Texians. Decree 277 was adopted at a time of rapprochement between Mexican officials and Anglo-Texans. In 1833, Austin left his colonies to promote support of an autonomous Texas state. He found most Tejanos in San Antonio and Goliad unsupportive. He

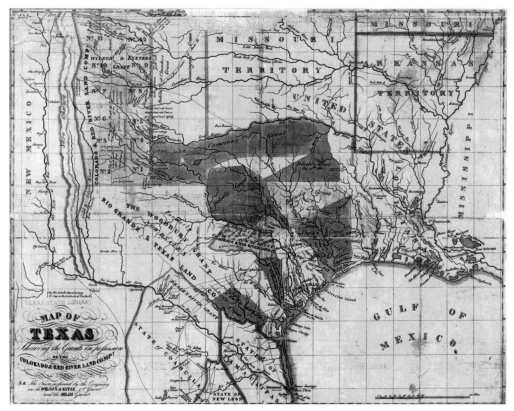

Texas in 1832. Courtesy Texas State Library and Archives Commission.

then traveled to Mexico City to make his case. In October, after surviving a cholera outbreak, he wrote to the *ayuntamiento* (city council) in San Antonio urging the separation of Coahuila and Texas. Biographer Gregg Cantrell notes that Austin "was counseling sedition, or nearly so." Austin left Mexico City in December to return to Texas. In early January 1834, he was arrested on a charge of sedition in Saltillo. He was sent back to Mexico City and remained in prison there until Christmas Day 1834, when he was released on bail on the condition that he remain there until his seemingly interminable case was resolved.[20]

Sterling Robertson and Thomas Jefferson Chambers used Austin's arrest and imprisonment to curry favor with the Coahuila and Texas and national governments as well as to disparage Austin. Robertson managed to have the state congress make him an *empresario*,

awarding him a contract that had been Austin's. Chambers, Robertson's attorney, aided in the slander of Austin to Mexican authorities. In the spring of 1834, as Austin languished in prison, Chambers was admitted to the practice of law in Mexico, and in March he was appointed attorney general (*asesor general*) for Texas (although he remained in Coahuila). In order to calm restless Anglo-Texans, General Antonio López de Santa Anna recommended that the Coahuila and Texas congress adopt several liberal laws. It complied. These laws included making English one of the two official languages in the state (Decree 270, Art. 11, adopted March 18, 1834); allowing the sale of public lands to foreigners (Decree 272, Art. 8, March 26, 1834), that is, Anglo-American Texans; appointing a general commissioner for Texas (Decree 272, Art. 13); adding two professors of law to aid the *asesor general*, the state's attorney, in clearing the case load (Decree 273, adopted between March 26 and April 19, 1834); spending money to defend "the lives and property of the citizens" from the "perfidy, rage, and barbarity of the hostile Indians" (Decree 278, April 19, 1834); and adopting a law, Decree 277 (April 17, 1834), allowing for jury trial in criminal cases. This last law was known as the Chambers Jury Law because of Chambers's influence as state attorney.

Decree 277 consists of 140 articles. It amended the administration of justice in Texas by adopting some common-law provisions and by providing Texians greater access to the courts to resolve disputes. In addition to creating an appellate court in Texas, Decree 277 formally allowed trial by jury in all civil and criminal cases (Art. 2). As in the common law, the jury consisted of twelve men (Art. 7), although, unlike the common law, merely eight and not all twelve were necessary for a verdict. Article 24 made juries the "judges of all the facts in controversy" and explicitly made "conclusive" any factual decision reached by it. These provisions were part of the common law but were unheard of in Spanish and Mexican law. Article 30 required the trial to be held in the language of the accused, and a criminal defendant was appointed an attorney if he could not afford one (Art. 32). In addition, testimony by witnesses was made at the time of the trial before the court, not beforehand, as was customary in the Spanish/Mexican tradition (Art. 39), and lawyers for both parties were permitted to ask questions of the witnesses (Art. 69). But by the time Decree 277 was adopted, a more efficient and "Americanized" administration of the law appeared insufficient to end complaints from Texians about Mexican rule. When Texians drafted the Consultation of 1835 and the Declaration of Independence and Constitution of 1836, they listed the absence of trial by jury in criminal cases as one of the reasons justifying their rebellion. Chambers, who attempted to play both the Mexican and Texian

angles, eventually became a Texan but failed in his regular attempts at election to public office.

THE CONSULTATION OF 1835

The October 1835 Consultation declared a state of war between Texians and the general government in Mexico. It did not recommend independence. Instead, officers of the provisional government were to swear fealty to the Mexican Constitution of 1824. The participants in the Consultation proposed a provisional plan of government. After creating a provisional judiciary in Article V, Article VI gave judges jurisdiction of all "crimes and misdemeanors recognized and known to the common law of England." Some civil matters (for example, issuing writs of attachment) were based on the civil code of Louisiana, itself adopted from the French Code Civil. Article VII required that "[a]ll trials shall be by jury" and that criminal cases be regulated pursuant to the common law of England. Little else was said about the judicial system, which largely ground to a halt as the issue of who was to govern Texas moved from dispute to resolution.[21]

THE TEXAS CONSTITUTION OF 1836

As the Battle of the Alamo reached its end, a group of delegates met at Washington-on-the-Brazos at a previously called Plenary Convention. Most of the delegates were men under the age of forty, and a large majority of the fifty-eight delegates were emigrants from other southern states. On the second day of the convention, March 2, 1836, the delegates declared independence from Mexico and adopted the Texas Declaration of Independence, which claimed that the "centralized military despotism" of General Santa Anna ignored all interests "but that of the army and the priesthood, both the eternal enemies of civil liberty." The declaration then cited thirteen particular grievances, including the Mexican government's failure "to secure, on a firm basis, the right of trial by jury." These grievances required Texians to enforce, by violence if necessary, "political separation" from Mexico. A motion to appoint a committee to draft a constitution was also approved that day.[22]

Delegates immediately began working on a constitution, wary of the possibility that Santa Anna's army was on the march east from San Antonio. The first draft of the Constitution of the Republic of Texas was completed on March 9 and adopted late during the night of March 16–17. As written, it is a pastiche, drawn from the Constitution of the United States and a number of state constitutions. The first two articles concerned legislative power, the third executive power, and the fourth judicial power. Article V declared the conditions for eligibility for public service. Article VI discussed eligibility for and the compensation and duties of the president of the republic, as well as impeachment of officers. The remainder of the constitution included eight sections of a Schedule, eleven General Provisions, and a Declaration of Rights consisting of seventeen sections.

The drafters of the constitution feared the abuse of power by the executive and limited the president to one term in office. One constitutional oddity was a limit on congress's power, related to a fear of unchecked legislative power. Article II consisted of seven sections: the first six gave congress specific powers similar to grants given the U.S. Congress in Article I, section 8 of the U.S. Constitution, such as the authority to declare war (Art. II, § 4), to "regulate commerce" (Art. II, § 2), and to "establish post offices and post roads" (Art. II, § 3). In Article II, section 7, the Texas congress was given the power to "make all laws which shall be deemed necessary and proper to carry into effect the foregoing express grants of power," similar to the power granted the U.S. Congress in Article I, section 8, clause 18 of the U.S. Constitution. But the difference between the U.S. Congress and the Congress of the Republic

of Texas was that the former was developed in light of the existence of states, requiring a federal system dividing power between the federal government (legislature, executive, and judiciary) and the states. Limiting the power of the Congress of the Republic in the absence of "states" simply created a likelihood of legislative weakness and ineptitude.

The Schedule incorporated all existing law unless expressly repealed and demanded that law enforcement officers remain in office unless and until others were appointed. Section 7 of the General Provisions declared that "so soon as convenience will permit, there shall be a penal code formed on principles of reformation, and not of vindictive justice." The same section also required that "all laws relating to land titles shall be translated, revised and promulgated." Section 9 stated the rule on slaves and slavery: all slaves remained in a state of slavery, and congress had no authority to emancipate slaves or prohibit persons from bringing their slaves into the Republic. No slaveowner was permitted to free a slave without congress's consent, unless the slave was sent out of the Republic to live. Finally, no free person of African descent was permitted to reside in the Republic without the consent of congress. Section 10 barred "Africans, the descendants of Africans and Indians" from citizenship in the Republic. Together, these provisions were intended to prevent free blacks from settling in Texas, and the number of free blacks counted in the 1850 and 1860 censuses was under four hundred (although this may have missed half of the free blacks living in Texas).

The Declaration of Rights, similar to the Bill of Rights in the U.S. Constitution, lacks both the brevity and clarity of the latter. The most unusual aspect of the seventeen provisions of the Declaration of Rights is that it does not explicitly provide for a right to trial by jury in civil cases, a right provided for in the Seventh Amendment to the U.S. Constitution. The Ninth Declaration declares that "No person, for the same offence, shall be twice put in jeopardy of life or limbs. And the right of trial by jury shall remain inviolate." This language somewhat follows Article VII of the Plans and Powers of the Provisional Government of Texas in the Consultation of 1835, which declared "all trials shall be by jury."

Three other provisions in the 1836 constitution deserve some attention. First, Article IV, section 13 requires congress to introduce by statute "the common law of England, with such modifications as our circumstances, in their judgment, may require." This grant of power allows congress to decide when the common law of England shall apply, and when that law shall be modified (the following sentence of this provision requires that the "common law shall be the rule of decision" in all criminal law matters). It should have been located in Article II. Similarly, section 7 of the General Provisions requires congress to form a penal code and translate, revise, and promulgate "all laws relating to land titles." These are both grants of power and duties imposed on the congress, also appropriate for inclusion in Article II. Second, section 10 of the Declaration of Rights takes up an inordinate amount of space on the subject of land. It purported to grant every head of family a league and a *labor* of land (a total of approximately 4,600 acres, for a square league consisted of 4,428.4 acres and a *labor*, 177.14 acres). It also barred aliens (particularly Americans) from holding land in Texas and specifically declared void the grants of land to John T. Mason in 1834 and to others by act in March 1835. The opportunity to own land was the greatest selling point Texas possessed. The divestment of land awarded in the 1834 and 1835 acts was one attempt to ensure that the right Texans owned vast amounts of land in the Republic. Third, section 12 of the Declaration of Rights barred imprisonment "for debt in consequence of ability to pay." Texas would soon adopt laws on homesteads and bankruptcy that further protected debtors.

President Sam Houston, 1837 or 1838. Courtesy Texas State Library and Archives Commission.

After Santa Anna was captured by Sam Houston's army in the Battle of San Jacinto, Houston agreed to send him back to Mexico on the condition that the Mexican army leave Texas permanently. The temporary withdrawal of Mexican troops led in September 1836 to a vote on ratification of the constitution. The vote was positive, and the first congress of the Republic of Texas opened on October 3, 1836.

LAW IN THE REPUBLIC OF TEXAS, 1836–1845

As an embryonic nation, Texas appeared emblematic of Thomas Hobbes's view of man's life in a state of nature: poor, solitary, nasty, brutish, and short. Texas had no money in its treasury, a "bedraggled army on the lookout for excitement [that] constituted a danger to law and order," and existential threats from both indigenous tribes and the Mexican army. The first congress spent most of its energy on military matters. Near the end of the session in December, it organized the Supreme Court of the Republic of Texas and divided the republic into four judicial districts. The Texas Supreme Court thus consisted of a chief justice and the four district court judges. The constitution disqualified from any case heard by the supreme court the district judge who signed the judgment after the trial. That meant that each appealed case would be heard by the remaining four justices, creating possible quorum problems, given the difficulties of travel. This was a distant problem, however, for the Texas Supreme Court did not meet until early 1840.[23]

The first congress also discussed three other items of legal interest. First, it several times voted, over President Sam Houston's veto, to create a general land office as a way to generate revenue for the bankrupt republic. Second, it adopted a law allowing the incorporation of the Texas Rail Road, Navigation, and Banking Company. This corporation proposed connecting the Rio Grande and the Sabine River by canals and railroads and creating a bank. Its banking authority permitted it to issue notes that served as paper money. Although the act was not strongly opposed when adopted, it became a contentious issue in the 1837 elections. The Jacksonian opposition to banks (in 1832, as president of the United States, Andrew Jackson had vetoed the continuing existence of the Second Bank of the United States, which went out of business in 1837), a view adopted by many Texans, along with the Panic of 1837 doomed the company. This was the first of many attacks in Texas against corporations as monopolies (see chapter 4). Third, congress adopted a criminal law code as mandated by the constitution. However, the constitution ordered a penal code "formed on principles of reformation, and not of vindictive justice," and the 1836 law was decidedly harsh and draconian. Making death the punishment for a wide variety of crimes was a plausible but horribly incomplete answer to the problem of what to do with convicts when no prison existed.[24]

Through the end of 1839 the republic

John Hemphill, undated. Courtesy Texas State Library and Archives Commission.

struggled to organize itself, and its leaders hoped either for annexation to the United States or official recognition by England and France. Texas remained unstable, contentious, and poor. It issued paper money that quickly lost its value. Mirabeau Lamar succeeded Sam Houston as president and created an army to initiate a campaign that forcibly removed the Cherokees from their lands.

In March 1840, Comanches traveled to San Antonio to discuss a treaty and ransom for Anglo-Texans held by them. The parties met in the district courthouse. When the Texas commissioners and the Comanches disagreed about the number of prisoners being held, the commissioners had the interpreter inform the Comanches that they would be held hostage until the captives were released. The Council House Fight resulted in the deaths of thirty-five Comanches, including several women and children. District Court Judge John Hemphill, who had been holding one of the semiannual court sessions in San Antonio, disemboweled one of the Comanches "but declared that he did so under a sense of duty, while he had no personal acquaintance with nor ill-will toward his antag-

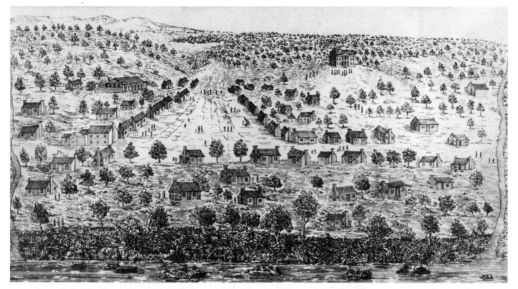

Drawing of Austin, Texas, in 1844. Courtesy Texas State Library and Archives Commission.

onist." The fight, or massacre, made the term *Texan* "anathema in Plains Indian camps." Two years later, in September 1842, shortly after District Judge Anderson Hutchinson opened a session of the Fourth District Court in San Antonio, Mexican general Adrian Woll led fourteen hundred soldiers in capturing San Antonio. Woll imprisoned Hutchinson and a number of lawyers. Woll's troops retreated a week later, beneficiaries of indecisive and possibly incompetent Texas military leadership. Among those chasing Woll was the chief justice of the Texas Supreme Court, Hemphill, who was serving as acting adjutant general. Hutchinson remained in Woll's custody for months. He was released in mid-1843, at which time he resigned from office and moved back to Mississippi. Because the supreme court did not meet between January 1842 and June 1843, Hemphill did not miss any session of the court while in military service.[25]

The 1839 congress adopted an act protecting the homestead of a family from seizure by creditors. This law did more than merely protect the family home; it also protected fifty acres of land or "one town lot," improvements up to

five hundred dollars, furniture up to two hundred dollars, tools, books, and "all implements of husbandry," plus five milk cows, one horse, one ox, and twenty hogs. Spanish/Castilian law provided debtors some protections from creditors in the seizure of personal property, as did some states. But neither Spanish nor American law exempted a debtor's land from debt enforcement. This homestead act was drawn particularly from Decree 70 of the 1829 Coahuila and Texas legislature, which protected residents from debt collectors for a period of twelve years and which provided that even after the expiration of the term, no debt could be ordered paid by the sale of lands, tools, or implements of husbandry but only "in fruits or money in a manner not to affect their attention to the families, to their husbandry, or art they profess." Two years later, the congress of Coahuila and Texas repealed this act. The repeal, McKnight notes, had absolutely no impact in Texas. Although published and distributed, it was as if it never existed. Texans and those writing about Texas continued to believe that property was strongly protected or even exempt from debt collection in the colony. Similarly, the 1839 homestead act was almost immediately repealed. On February 5, 1840, the fourth congress of Texas adopted An Act Concerning Executions, which provided that satisfaction of a judgment on a debt could include "the improved lands and home-stead of the defendant." Within a year, this act was curtailed. The fifth congress adopted a law repealing parts of An Act Concerning Executions and stated that the 1839 homestead law "is hereby declared to be in full force and effect." The homestead law was constitutionalized in the 1845 constitution, where it remains. In a republic likely containing a "debtor-fugitive element" that was "substantially greater than that of mature communities," a slew of laws protecting debtors from creditors is not surprising. What is surprising is that the Congress of the Republic was of two minds in 1840, which was not the case by 1845.[26]

American debtors fled to Texas when Texas was a colony of Mexico. The Panic of 1837 created even greater incentives for Americans to flee to the republic. The 1839 homestead law protected from seizure by creditors the lands and implements of work and home of Texans. It did not wipe out those debts; it merely prevented a creditor from seizing those assets in satisfaction of those debts. In August 1841, the U.S. Congress adopted a national bankruptcy law. Seven months earlier, the Congress of the Republic of Texas had adopted a bankruptcy system despite the absence of any explicit constitutional authority to do so. The Texas bankruptcy act allowed a debtor to petition for bankruptcy (the U.S. bankruptcy law allowed creditors to force a debtor into involuntary bankruptcy). If a Texas debtor chose to enter bankruptcy and either was married, supported a child or grandchild, or was a *feme sole* (an unmarried woman), the debtor was able to reserve from sale his or her homestead and up to fifty acres of land (or one town lot). If, however, the bankrupt was a single man, he was allowed only "one year's occupation of his homestead." As was true of the homestead

law, the bankrupt petitioner also kept his or her horse, tools, books, and implements of trade. The homestead law, combined with the bankruptcy law, offered strong protections to debtors. Both laws protected a debtor who supported a family by exempting from debt collection the debtor's home, land, and tools. The constitutional prohibition on imprisonment for debt made the Republic of Texas a haven (in both a positive and negative sense) for those encumbered by debts.[27]

The Texas Constitution's demand that congress adopt the common law, with such exceptions as they might create, was fulfilled by the fourth congress in January 1840. A December 20, 1836, law organizing the district courts required those courts to apply the common law of England in reference to juries and the law of evidence. The January 1840 act, although it declared the adoption of the common law by the republic, was largely focused on an exception to the common law, the system of community property within a marriage. Community property originated in the civil law (see chapter 5). The 1840 act allocated ownership of property by the parties as they entered marriage, and the ownership of property accrued during the marriage. For example, all land and slaves owned by a woman entering marriage remained her separate property during the marriage. Although the husband had the sole authority to manage her land and slaves, he lacked any ownership interest. Further, all property other than land and slaves acquired during the marriage was the "common property of the husband and wife." Two weeks after "adopting" the common law, the Congress of the Republic declared that "the adoption of the common law shall not be construed to adopt the common law system of pleading." Instead, Texas adopted a version of the Spanish/Mexican system of pleading in civil cases, a system that focused on substance and downplayed the importance of form, a system of pleading unheard of in the common law system (see chapter 8). The fourth congress of the Republic of Texas adopted several additional laws rejecting the common law in favor of the civil law, including laws on who took a decedent's property (the law of succession), laws rejecting the common-law formalities of conveying real property, and laws rejecting common-law rules related to mortgages.[28]

THE SUPREME COURT OF THE REPUBLIC OF TEXAS

The 1836 Constitution created a supreme court consisting of a chief justice and a minimum of three and a maximum of eight district judges, who also served as associate justices.[29] The court's jurisdiction was limited to appeals. A majority of the associate justices and the chief justice constituted a quorum. The supreme court initially comprised five members. A fifth district court was created by the congress in May 1838, and the sixth and seventh district courts were created in late January 1840. The chief justice and district court judges were elected through a joint ballot of both houses of congress. The first chief justice of the Republic of Texas was James Collinsworth. At the time he committed suicide in 1838, the court had not yet met. John Birdsall was appointed chief justice by President Sam Houston and served temporarily while congress was not in session. When congress returned, it rejected Birdsall's nomination. In late 1838, Thomas Jefferson Rusk, formerly a general in the Army of the Republic of Texas, was elected chief justice. Rusk learned of his election after the January 1839 term of the supreme court was to have been held. On January 13, 1840, the first session of the Supreme Court of the Republic of Texas opened.[30]

The work of the supreme court of the republic is largely found in a single volume of reports collected and published by James Wilmer Dallam and known as *Dallam's*, which published the opinions of the supreme court from 1840 to 1844. *Dallam's* consists of 140 opinions. Thirty additional opinions were issued in 1845, and the seventeen "missing cases" and two dissenting opinions of the republic were officially published in the *Texas Law Review* in 1986. The first session of the court disposed of forty-nine cases. It wrote brief decisions in eighteen cases and concluded its work in two weeks. In mid-1840, Rusk resigned as chief justice, and at the end of the year congress elected John Hemphill to succeed Rusk.[31]

Like Rusk, Hemphill was born in 1803 in South Carolina and learned law there. Hemphill moved to Texas in 1838 and began practicing law and learning Spanish. Less than two years after his arrival, Hemphill was elected a district judge. Even though he was elected after the brief first session of the supreme court had begun, he wrote two opinions of the court and one concurring opinion. Hemphill served as chief justice of the Supreme Court of Texas until 1858, when he resigned to become U.S. senator. Hemphill was a strong proponent of the civil-law system who brought to the court a deep knowledge of Spanish law.[32]

From the inception of the state of Texas through 1856, the supreme court consisted of three men: Hemphill and Associate Justices Royall T. Wheeler and Abner Lipscomb. Although they occasionally disagreed, the jurisprudence of the initial Supreme Court of the State of Texas was substantially enhanced by stability in membership. This starkly contrasted with membership in the supreme court of the republic. By the time the January 1841 term began, Hemphill was its fourth chief justice. In early 1841 three new district judges were elected, continuing a pattern of rapid turnover in the judiciary. This instability in the district courts generated instability in the supreme court. Although the president had the authority to appoint district judges, only congress possessed the authority to elect them, and several district court appointees were passed over. Twenty-six men served as district judges in the seven districts created by the republic. Several never participated in a session of the supreme court because it did not meet until 1840, and several others failed to make sessions between 1840 and 1845.[33]

The opinions of the Supreme Court of the Republic of Texas are short, plainly written, and usually though not always devoid of citations to decisions of U.S. courts or the courts of the American states or to secondary works such as Joseph Story's *Commentaries on the Constitution* (1833). The court, like the lawyers who practiced before it, possessed relatively few legal works, whether of the common law or the civil law. It wrote many more opinions in civil cases than criminal cases. As might be expected of a newly created court, a substantial number of opinions concerned issues defining the authority of the judicial branch, including rights to appeal, the extent of the supreme court's reviewing authority, and the extent of congress's authority to broaden the jurisdiction of the court. One of the court's longest and most important opinions (spanning seventeen printed pages) concerned the constitutionality of an act creating the territory of Ward. This case required the court to assess its power of judicial review, the power to declare unconstitutional an act of congress. In an earlier case, *Morton v. Gordon* (1841), the supreme court first declared unconstitutional an act of congress that restricted appeals. In *Stockton v. Montgomery* (1842), the court held unconstitutional the act creating the territory of Ward. It declared, "If a legislative act impugn its principles the act must yield; and whenever it is brought before the court it must be declared void. Nay, the act is inherently nothing." The court then cited "2 Dal. 304; 1 Cran. 175." The former citation was to *VanHorne's Lessee v. Dorrance* (1795), a decision by the Circuit Court of Pennsylvania holding unconstitutional a Pennsylvania law on the ground that it violated the contracts clause of the U.S. Constitution. The second citation was to *Marbury v. Madison* (1803), the famous decision of the Supreme

Court of the United States written by Chief Justice John Marshall declaring that the court possessed the power of judicial review. In *Allen v. Scott* (1844), the Texas Supreme Court again held unconstitutional an act of congress, this time a law creating a southern division of the Red River County judicial district. The law was unconstitutional "because it violates the spirit of the constitution and is at war with its plain meaning and intent." The act was unconstitutional, apparently, because it offended the court's sensibilities, not because it offended any clear textual provision of the 1836 constitution.[34]

The absence of a clear constitutional provision guaranteeing a right to trial by jury in civil cases did not affect the court's broad adoption of that right. In *McGill v. Delaplain* (1843), Rebecca Pincena sued Delaplain, the administrator of the estate of William Brisbone, for monies allegedly owed her by the estate. The trial court dismissed her claim. Delaplain argued that the case was properly dismissed because it was heard under Mexican civil law, and the court had the power to dismiss cases under civil law. The Texas Supreme Court reversed, noting that "by our constitution and laws, we think the trial by jury was secured to the plaintiffs, if they chose to persist in it." In *Bailey v. Haddy* (1840), the supreme court cobbled together the rather vague provisions in the Declaration of Rights in the constitution with the acts of congress creating a supreme court and the district courts, the act applying the common law to juries and evidence, and the 1840 act adopting the common law to conclude that a right to trial by jury in civil cases was protected.[35]

Finally, the supreme court of the republic noted the applicability of Spanish law whenever appropriate. In *Scott v. Maynard* (1843), Hemphill discussed what constituted community property under Spanish civil law and explained that the district court's ignorance of community property law led it astray: "Throughout the progress of this cause in the court below, as well as before this tribunal, there has been a strange compound of error, and a mixture of the different systems of jurisprudence, springing originally from this mistake." This was in part a result of the "scarcity of books or authorities on questions arising under the former laws of the country." However, it remained the duty of the lawyers "to exhaust all which may be accessible to them before they turn for assistance to the common or any other system of law." In *Mills v. Waller* (1841), Hemphill discussed the Spanish law concerning land fraud, and in *Garret v. Nash* (1843), Hemphill discussed a widow's right to one-quarter of her husband's estate under Spanish law.[36]

THE REGULATOR-MODERATOR WAR AND THE RULE OF LAW

In the Regulator-Moderator War of 1839–44, two factions battled over control of the "Neutral Ground," land originally claimed by the United States as part of Louisiana and by Spain as part of Texas. Both nations had agreed not to exercise dominion over the area in the early nineteenth century, which made it perfect for those fleeing the law or contemptuous of it. The Neutral Ground was then claimed (although nearly disclaimed as well) by the Republic of Texas. The theft of official Mexican land certificates, which could be used to claim thousands of acres of land in the Neutral Ground, was the biggest business over which the contestants fought. The possessors of the certificates were deemed outlaws by a group that considered themselves "regulators" of the area. In 1840, Charles W. Jackson, a leader of the Regulators, shot and killed Joseph Goodbread, aligned with a group involved in fraudulent land transactions. Jackson was no hero, for he was wanted in Louisiana for murder. Because he was working with the then sheriff, Jackson agreed to be "arrested." Somewhat surprisingly to Jackson, a grand jury indicted him, and he went to trial

in July 1841. District Judge John Hansford presided. Hansford was allied with the Moderators, who took their name because they wished to "moderate" the actions of the Regulators. The trial was quickly aborted after Hansford noted the presence of a significant number of armed men in court to support Jackson. (Jackson was also armed.) Hansford left town that evening and ordered the sheriff (again, aligned with the Regulators) to adjourn the court. The sheriff apparently disobeyed Hansford, and the trial continued without the judge. The prosecutor offered no evidence, and Jackson was acquitted. In January 1842, congress initiated impeachment proceedings against Hansford, accusing him not only of misbehavior in Jackson's case but also for holding court while drunk. Hansford resigned to avoid impeachment. Two years later, Hansford was shot and killed by Regulators after he refused to hand over slaves he was holding pursuant to a court order.[37]

Regulators claimed victory after Jackson's acquittal and moved to consolidate power, burning the homes of the McFadden (also spelled McFaddin) family and others. Moderators sought revenge, gaining it when they killed Jackson and another man, an innocent bystander named Lauer. Several McFadden brothers and others were captured by Regulators, given an irregular "trial," convicted by the mob, and hung. When Watt Moorman, Jackson's successor as leader of the Regulators, was arrested for murder, he agreed to be tried only by John Ingram, who, sympathetic to the Regulators, held the indictment invalid. When several Moderators were arrested as accessories to murder, they agreed to be tried by a Judge Lister, a Moderator. Lister, like Ingram before him, found the arrest of the Moderators invalid.[38]

Regulators and Moderators formed not only in Shelby County, where the war was centered, but also elsewhere in East Texas. In Harrison County, about seventy-five miles north of Shelby County, other murders were committed.

In March 1842, Regulators attacked Robert Potter at his home. Potter was infamous in North Carolina for "Potterizing," that is, castrating, his then-wife's cousins in the 1830s, a crime for which he was convicted. Potter left North Carolina in disgrace and moved to northeast Texas, where he arrived in time to serve as a delegate at the March 1836 convention, signing the Texas Declaration of Independence and serving as a draftsman of the Texas Constitution. The immediate cause of Potter's murder was because Potter had requested that the Texas Congress urge citizens of the republic to bring William Pinkney Rose to justice. Rose was accused of murdering John B. Campbell, the Panola County sheriff. Potter had Rose declared an outlaw and sought to arrest Rose to obtain the five-hundred-dollar reward. When Potter went to Rose's home, Rose successfully hid under a brush pile. Potter then went home to sleep while Rose gathered a group to attack him. Potter fled his home upon Rose's arrival, leaving Harriet Ames, his "wife" (their marriage was eventually held invalid), and ran to Caddo Lake. Rose and other Regulators followed, and they killed Potter when he came up for air. Although Rose was arrested, he was never tried for Potter's murder.[39]

In mid-1844, President Sam Houston sent the militia to effect an agreement terminating the war, and after even more skirmishes and deaths, the war wound down. Those with a need for violent action found an outlet shortly thereafter by the onset in 1846 of the Mexican-American War, in which both Regulators and Moderators fought, this time on the same side.

A Stray Yankee in Texas was published in 1853. The book's author was Samuel A. Hammett, who wrote the book under the pseudonym Philip Paxton. Hammett had served as the clerk for the district court in Montgomery County, Texas (just north of Houston), in the 1840s. He then moved to New York and began writing about his experiences in Texas. *A Stray Yankee in Texas* is a travelogue, a study of

Texas law, and a repository of tall tales, all written for northern tastes. Hammett's portrayal of law in Texas is in turn caustic and comical, and occasionally both. Exaggerating to make his point, Hammett declared "lawsuits have no limits" in Texas. The second section of his book, a discussion of the willingness of some Texans to take the law into their own hands, is titled "Lynch Law" and presented in a deliberate and sober manner. Hammett discussed the Regulators and Moderators and then examined why the guilty so often were not brought to justice on the frontier. The weakness of the legal system meant outlaws "may completely set the law of the land at defiance." If a case managed to reach trial, witnesses and jurors were often amenable to bribes; if that failed, criminals were protected by "*judges, lawyers, clergymen, militia officers of high rank*, planters and merchants," often because of common membership in secret societies (at this point Hammett cited an 1848 *Galveston News* article for support of his claim). Texas historian C. L. Sonnichsen concluded that Hammett's report reflected the position that Texas "justice was a farce. If the judge happened to be honest, the jury could be tied up, witnesses killed or intimidated, and the whole body of law-abiding men overawed. And there was nothing anybody could do about it." Lynchings in antebellum Texas were largely linked to a disregard of or frustration with Texas criminal justice, although some race-based lynchings occurred in pre–Civil War Texas.[40]

In a 1941 essay, Texas historian William Hogan discussed the relation between "rampant individualism" and the law in antebellum Texas. Hogan noted that fights were common, including in the Congress of the Republic, and few such altercations were considered sufficiently serious to become the subject of a grand jury investigation or indictment. Hogan also found that "[l]ess than twelve per cent of the murder and assault with intent to kill cases culminated in convictions," for much of the populace believed that some Texans simply needed killin'. Other killings never reached trial. The first governor of the state of Texas, James Pinckney Henderson, a lawyer, wrote about killing a man, N. B. Garner, who had threatened and indeed tried (according to Henderson) to kill him. Henderson noted that "I demanded an investigation of the affair after I killed Garner & the court of inquiry declared me fully justified." In a frontier society with little effective law enforcement, self-help was common, and society made contextualized determinations how to characterize deaths: Hogan noted that a "murder" differed from a "killing" which differed from a "difficulty." The Regulators and Moderators both made part of their appeal a claim to return the community to law-abidingness, but both did so outside the channels of the law. In an era in which the revered (by southerners) former president of the United States Andrew Jackson often disregarded the rule of law, it is unsurprising that Texans took the law into their own hands.[41]

The struggle to maintain a rule of law is a persistent theme in Texas legal history. The rule of law is designed to constrain the exercise of power, exemplified by Lord Acton's adage, "Power tends to corrupt, and absolute power corrupts absolutely." The rule of law is also designed to protect the legal stranger to a community to the same extent as its most prominent citizen. And it rejects the notion that the people can simply act contrary to the law whenever they believe the law is wrong. Both the "peopling" of Texas and its development have made the quest for an embedded rule of law more complex and difficult. That striving has been an important part of Texas legal history.

THE CONSTITUTION OF 1845

Lame-duck U.S. president Martin Van Buren fostered annexation of Texas into the United States in March 1845. By the end of 1845, annexation was largely complete, and the Republic of Texas was no more. Annexation required the adoption of a constitution for the state of Texas. The 1845 Constitutional Convention of sixty-one elected members officially began in Austin on July 4. The chairman of the convention, former chief justice Thomas Jefferson Rusk, who "considered the Judicial Department the most important branch of the government" because it was independent of the passions of the people, appointed the fifteen members to the Committee on the Judiciary. The draftsman of the judiciary section was Chief Justice John Hemphill.[42]

On July 11, 1845, Hemphill proposed the judiciary article, which eventually became Article IV. This article provided for a supreme court consisting of three members, a chief justice and two associate justices, none of whom had the additional duty of serving as district judges. The justices of the Texas Supreme Court were nominated by the governor, subject to confirmation by the senate. District courts remained trial courts, but the constitution permitted the legislature to create inferior courts with limited jurisdiction to relieve the district courts of congested court dockets.

On July 28, 1845, the convention, meeting as a committee of the whole, discussed whether to grant a right to trial by jury in matters of "law or equity." In the common-law system, only matters of "law" were subject to trial by jury. Matters of equity were decided by the court of chancery in England, and the jury was foreign to that court. During this discussion, Hemphill spoke against adding the right of trial by jury to matters in equity, in order to speak well of the civil law system: "I cannot say that I am very much in favor of either chancery or the common law system. I should much have preferred the civil law to have continued in force for years to come. But inasmuch as the chancery system, together with the common law, has been saddled upon us, the question is now, whether we shall keep up the chancery system or blend them together."[43]

After Rusk spoke in favor of creating a right to jury trial in matters in equity, the convention voted to amend the judiciary article, and Article IV, section 16 created a right to a jury trial upon demand by one of the parties in any case in equity. By the end of the 1840s, New York adopted a statutory system of pleading in civil cases (known as the Field Code after the commissioner who wrote it, David Dudley Field) that abolished the distinction between law and equity. However, abolition in the Field Code did not abolish all distinctions between law and equity, including when trial by jury was available. In Texas, however, the adoption of the Spanish system of initiating a civil (that is, noncriminal) case eliminated any need for a distinction of law and equity. Granting a right to trial by jury in equity matters was simply part of working out a mixed system of resolving civil disputes, a system traced to both common-law and civil-law origins.[44]

The 1845 constitution attempted to resolve four other crucial issues. It returned to the issue of land titles issued by Mexico in the early 1830s. The 1836 constitution spoke specifically about the land titles held by John T. Mason and others, and the 1845 constitution again held void the grant by Mexico to Mason. Second, the deputies to the convention, possibly reflecting the creation and dissolution in 1836–37 of the Texas Rail Road, Navigation, and Banking Company and certainly reflecting the Jacksonian hatred of banks, forbade the creation of any corporation "with banking or discounting privileges" (Art. VII, § 30). Relatedly, the fear of corporations led to the adoption of the requirement that no corporation could be created unless approved by two-thirds of each house (Art. VII, § 31). Third, the homestead law, adopted in 1839, which exempted from debt collection the debtor's home and land, was constitutionalized. A family's homestead, "not to exceed two hundred acres of land, (not included in a town or city, or any town or city lot or lots,) in value not to exceed two thousand dollars, shall not be subject to forced sale for any debts hereafter contracted; nor shall the owner, if a married man, be at liberty to alienate the same, unless by the consent of the wife, in such manner as the legislature may hereafter point out" (Art. VII, § 22). Fourth, the 1840 act that provided for the adoption of a variant of the Spanish law system of community property for married couples was constitutionalized. The constitution made all property brought by the wife into the marriage her separate property, which limited (although it did not defeat) a spendthrift husband's ability to drain her property (Art. VII, § 19).

THE STATE OF THE LAW IN THE STATE OF TEXAS

Hemphill was continued in office as chief justice by the senate, which possessed the constitutional authority to confirm the governor's nominees. He was joined by Abner S. Lipscomb and a holdover from the Supreme Court of the Republic of Texas, Royall T. Wheeler. Lipscomb, a native South Carolinian like Hemphill, apprenticed in the law office of South Carolina senator John C. Calhoun. Calhoun is known best for his Nullification Doctrine, which claimed the states could nullify federal laws with which they disagreed. Advocacy of this doctrine peaked in 1832–33, by which time Lipscomb had moved to Alabama and had become chief justice of its supreme court. Hemphill was living in South Carolina during the Nullification Crisis and was an ardent Nullifier. Lipscomb served as a member of the 1845 constitutional convention, and was nominated to the supreme court by Governor Henderson. He remained an associate justice until his death in November 1856. Wheeler was born in Vermont. He learned law in Ohio and moved to Arkansas in 1837. By the end of the decade Wheeler had moved to Nacogdoches and was elected district judge on January 1, 1845. After Hemphill's resignation to serve as U.S. senator,

Members of the Texas Supreme Court's "Old Court," 1864.
Courtesy Texas State Library and Archives Commission.

Wheeler became chief justice, a position he held until his death in 1864.[45]

Whether the three members of what was called the "Old Court" got along well is unclear. Some friction existed between Wheeler and Lipscomb, who were born nearly a generation apart. In 1849, Wheeler wrote to his future supreme court colleague Oran M. Roberts complaining that Lipscomb's opinions were "crude, superficial, partial, and totally defective in legal accuracy and precision and habitually so." Lipscomb was noted for his plainly written opinions, many of which were free of citation to any legal authorities. Wheeler wrote the most opinions of the three, with Lipscomb shortly behind. Hemphill wrote only about a quarter of the opinions of the court. Of the more than two thousand opinions published by the Old Court, only seventy-one, or 3 percent, included either a concurrence or a dissent. Some dissents, such as Wheeler's in *Coles v. Kelsey* (1847), were lengthy and repetitive. Others were brief or simply noted without opinion. The lack of dissents, like the absence of dissents in the Supreme Court of the United States when John Marshall was chief justice (1801–35), may not indicate agreement among the members of the court. Both the press of time (the court averaged about two hundred published opinions per year while traveling to three cities in a circuit in hearing and deciding cases) and the interest in speaking as uniformly as possible likely reduced the number of published dissenting opinions.[46]

The division of labor among the three was as follows: Wheeler wrote most of the court's opinions in criminal cases, while Lipscomb wrote most opinions in matters of procedure. Hemphill wrote most of the court's decisions that reflected Spanish legal roots, including a number of decisions broadly interpreting the law of community property and homesteads.[47]

The Supreme Court of the State of Texas first met in December 1846. It issued opinions in just under one hundred cases. Most of the cases are civil cases concerning issues of debt, land titles, and procedure. The court was not fixated on form to the exclusion of substance. For example, in *Foster v. Van Norman* (1846) the judgment was issued for more money than the plaintiff claimed. This mistake, held the court, was amenable to correction, and thus "no injustice has been done" to the defendant in this error. In addition, the record reflected the names of only eleven jurors, but also indicated that the jury consisted of "*twelve* good and lawful men." Because the defendant did not object at the time the verdict was rendered, "it will not be noticed in this court." Several other cases were a consequence of the transformation of Texas from an independent republic to a state. For example, in *Cocke v. Calkin & Co.* (1846), the issue was whether the collector of customs for the republic was liable for holding merchandise brought from New Orleans to Galveston for failure to pay customs duties. As a republic, Texas possessed the authority to adopt a tariff for any goods coming from outside the republic. As a state, Texas was constitutionally prohibited from imposing a tariff on goods from another state. The goods landed in Galveston on January 30, 1846. Annexation occurred on December 29, 1845, but the government of the republic continued in office until February 16, 1846. In a lengthy opinion by Hemphill, the court held that the "admission of a State is one act, and the extension of the laws and jurisdiction of the Union, is another and distinct exercise of authority." Thus, the laws of the republic remained in force until February 16, 1846, and the collector was not liable for holding the goods. Hemphill's opinion is couched broadly in terms of the compact theory of the constitution. Like John C. Calhoun, Hemphill concluded that the United States was created by a compact or agreement of the states. He thus disagreed with the opinion of Chief Justice John Marshall, who declared in *McCulloch v. Maryland* (1819) that the United States was created by the people. Without touching on the issue of the origins of the United States, the Supreme Court of the United States reversed in *Calkin v. Cocke* (1852). It concluded that on the date of annexation all laws of the Union immediately became effective.[48]

J. H. Davenport's *History of the Supreme Court of the State of Texas* (1917) rarely spoke ill of any Texas Supreme Court justice and often spoke well of justices whose work product or judicial behavior deserved little if any commendation. But his praise of the triumvirate of Hemphill, Lipscomb, and Wheeler demands some attention: "It is generally conceded by the most capable and conservative authorities that to this court is due the honor and distinction of having been one of the greatest tribunals in the history of the American judiciary." Davenport's lavish praise simply echoed the view

of both contemporaries and later commentators. Should the work of the antebellum Texas Supreme Court be so favorably viewed?[49]

Hemphill's desire for a strong homestead exemption led him to interpret broadly the protections given debtors from creditors, adding a judicial "gloss" to the protections for debtors found in the constitution and statutes. In *Wood v. Wheeler* (1851), the issue was whether the widow Wheeler could keep the homestead secure from her deceased husband's creditors. The homestead was a city lot valued at two thousand dollars. The homestead law of 1839 protected improvements to a homestead up to five hundred dollars, and the 1845 constitutional provision protected lots up to a valuation to two thousand dollars. The debts Wheeler contracted were made before February 16, 1846, when the state constitution became operative. Hemphill concluded that the debts could not be collected through the forced sale of the home, even if the widow was given five hundred dollars from the sale as the value of her homestead. The point of the homestead provision was to protect a family from being forced from their home due to indebtedness. In *Sampson and Keene v. Williamson* (1851), the court interpreted the homestead provision as barring the sale of any home under a court order, for such a sale was a "forced sale" barred by the constitution. In *Cobbs v. Coleman* (1855), the court held that the 1839 homestead law, which spoke of both families and single men, remained in force even after the adoption of the constitutional provision protecting homesteads. The interpretive difficulty was that the constitutional provision on homesteads was limited to families, declaring in part: "The legislature shall have power to protect by law, from forced sale, a certain portion of the property of all heads of families. The homestead of a family . . . shall not be subject to forced sale for any debts hereafter contracted." In *Pryor v. Stone* (1857), Hemphill protected as a homestead a widower's law office/home, even though his children lived elsewhere, and in dictum the court stated that the lot would be exempt from debts even if merely used as an office. As noted by Paul Goodman, "Homestead exemption aimed at providing a measure of security in an increasingly insecure, volatile economy." Texas law, as interpreted by the Old Court, "tilted the scales in favor of security against market freedom, of debtors against creditors." Although described as "Texas's most significant contribution to American jurisprudence," the homestead provision was not without cost to Texans. The more difficult it was for a creditor to satisfy a debt, the more expensive credit became. In antebellum Texas, this was perhaps not a significant problem; in the late nineteenth and early twentieth centuries the problem of finding a balance between debtor and creditor in Texas would arise again.[50]

During the last quarter of the nineteenth century the Texas Court of Appeals, which decided all criminal appeals between 1876 and 1891, gained a reputation for foolish exactitude. The Old Court eschewed the formalities of the common law. In *State v. Odum* (1853), the defendant challenged his indictment for theft on the ground that it stated that he stole a "bolt of domestic" (a bolt of cotton with which to make clothes) and did not state that the bolt of domestic constituted "goods." The district court agreed and dismissed the indictment. The state appealed, and the supreme court reversed. Chief Justice Hemphill made the following comments about formalism in the criminal law:

> Much has been said in the books, relative to the requisite certainty in criminal pleading; and many niceties and distinctions have been indulged in, the effect of which, on the one hand, has been to permit offenders to escape and crime to go unpunished, and on the other, to artfully conceal from the defendants the real nature of the charges against them.
>
> The rules relative to certainty are admirable; but, in their practical operation, they are frequently incumbered [*sic*] with such a mass of superfluity and fiction, as to defeat their own purposes, and to engender obscurity, instead of producing light and distinctness.
>
> The spirit of reform which has pervaded our civil system of procedure, has not as yet reached our criminal pleading. Its excrescences still deform our jurisprudence; and I will proceed to consider, whether, under this ancient system, such as it is, the judgment under revision can be sustained.
>
> The offense is stated to be the stealing of a bolt of domestic, the property of another. Is not this plain? Can any one of common understanding doubt that this is a crime prohibited and punishable by law? Does it require any special astuteness to ascertain that a bolt of domestic is goods or a chattel, and consequently the subject of larceny? It is assumed in the motion, that the domestic should be described to be goods. Would this convey any information to the defendant or the Court, of which they were not apprised? Neither the one nor the other can doubt, but that a piece of domestic is goods. There is no possibility of their misapprehending it to be land and not a chattel. To impute such incapacity to a Court, would be highly indecorous; and it could not exist in the defendant, without an imbecility which would render him, legally, incapable of crime.[51]

The court adopted the following rule in questions of the sufficiency of the indictment: "And though it is not in general necessary to follow the exact words of the statute, yet where a word not in the statute is substituted in the indictment for one that is, the word thus substituted must be equivalent to the word used in the statute, or of a more extensive signification than it, and include it, or it will not be sufficient." This allowed the court to refuse in several cases to overturn a murder conviction on the ground that the indictment failed to follow the language of the statute and state that the murder was committed "premeditately [*sic*] and deliberately." An indictment that the murder was committed "feloniously, maliciously, wilfully, premeditatedly and of his malice aforethought" was also found sufficient.[52]

In some cases the court declared indictments defective. When doing so it acted reluctantly. In *Cain v. State* (1857), the court reversed Cain's conviction for enticing away a slave. In reversing because the indictment failed to indicate that Cain acted "feloniously," the court, in an opinion by Justice Wheeler, wrote, "However little apparent reason there may be for still adhering to the technical language of the common law in framing indictments, or applying its strict rules of construction to criminal proceedings, the courts have not felt at liberty to depart from or disregard them, without legislative sanction." The court took pains not to find the indictment defective when the defendant was suitably apprised of the charges against him. When the legislature adopted the penal code of 1856 (effective in 1857), the court concluded that the code dispensed with the common-law requirement that an indictment include the word "feloniously."[53]

TEXAS LAW, FREE PERSONS OF COLOR, AND SLAVERY

The institution of African slavery required official acknowledgment in the criminal law that slaves were persons. Because slavery in Western and American thought was linked closely with race or color, the presence in Texas of "free persons of color" (the phrasing regularly used in antebellum legislation) constituted a category of persons that confounded the legislature. Section 9 of the General Provisions of the 1836 Texas constitution declared, "No free person of African descent, either in whole or in part, shall be permitted to reside permanently in the Republic, without the consent of Congress." This perceived solution, emigration, was, like African recolonization efforts, doomed to fail.

For example, the 1837 legislature permitted all free persons of color residing in Texas at independence to remain in the state as long as they obeyed the laws. The legislature demanded the removal of all free Negroes in an act of February 5, 1840, but President Sam Houston proclaimed a two-year grace period for all free persons of color in December 1842. Although intermittent efforts were made to remove free persons of color, a small number (officially 355 persons in 1860, though it may have been twice that) remained in the state.[54]

What legal protections or disabilities accompanied free persons of color and slaves in the criminal law? The Penal Act of 1836, adopted by the first congress, did not separately list punishments for slaves or indicate that slaves were subject to criminal sanction for a broader range of actions than free persons. Although the constitution limited the ability of a free person of color to remain in the republic, section 31 of the 1836 act criminalized the action of stealing or selling any free person as a slave, setting the punishment at death. An act of December 14, 1837, adopted six months after the joint resolution allowing "all free Africans or descendants of Africans" to remain, specifically provided for punishments of slaves and free persons of color for the violation of criminal laws peculiar to them. It made a crime the use of "insulting or abusive language" by a slave or free person of color upon a white person (section 6) and punished by death the attempted murder or maiming of a white person (section 1) by a slave or free person of color. A free person of color who aided a slave in escaping the bonds of slavery was sentenced, upon conviction, to the value of the slave. If the free person of color was unable to pay this fine, he "shall be sold as a slave for life."[55]

The Penal Act of 1848 did not specifically distinguish between acts committed by free white persons, free persons of color, and slaves. It readopted a version of the prohibition on the sale of a free person as a slave in a broader kidnapping provision. The 1854 penal act differed greatly from the 1848 act, though not as one might think. Despite the heightened sectional tension by the early 1850s over the issue of allowing slavery in the territories acquired by the United States after the Mexican-American War (exacerbated by the adoption in May 1854 by the U.S. Congress of the Kansas-Nebraska Act), the 1854 act reinforced as "Offences Against the Person" the sale or holding of a free person as a slave. This was in great part a result of the high demand for slave labor in Texas in the 1850s, which increased the incentive to kidnap and sell free persons of color into slavery. More interestingly, and again in the section of the act concerning "Offences Against the Person," it declared that the "murder or manslaughter committed upon the body of a slave shall be punished in the same manner as murder or manslaughter upon the body of a free white person." This prohibition was based on a provision in the 1798 Georgia constitution, adopted by Alabama (1819) and Missouri (1820) and carried to Texas from Alabama by Justice Abner Lipscomb. As early as 1847 the supreme court upheld the manslaughter conviction of a white man for killing a slave, a possibility rejected by some slave states. However, in a rural, underpoliced society such as Texas, the discipline and punishment of slaves was common and ordinarily outside the purview of the criminal justice system.[56]

Article 674 of the 1856 penal code rephrased the 1854 language regarding murder of a slave, declaring it murder for one to cause the death of a slave "by reason of abuse or cruel treatment." Article 564 of the 1856 penal code listed five occasions when the murder of a slave was justifiable and thus not proscribed by Article 674. In general, a person could murder a slave only when the murderer was in "reasonable fear of loss of life." Articles 670–78 prohibited the "cruel treatment of slaves." Article 670 prohibited anyone, including the owner of a slave, from unreasonably abusing or cruelly treating

a slave. Articles 795–801 equated slaves and free persons of color for purposes of prosecution and punishment. Although Article 801 acknowledged that "[a] slave or free person of color when tried for a penal offence, is in law a person," "his personal rights . . . are subject to rules different from those which would be applied in the case of a free white person, arising from the peculiar position of these classes of persons in society."

The 1858 amendments to the penal code suggest a deepening fear of slave insurrection and revolt. For example, the penalty range for inciting an insurrection of slaves was raised from three to fifteen years to ten to thirty years. The punishment range for stealing or enticing a slave was increased from one to seven years to five to fifteen years. Although the minimum fine for cruelly abusing a slave was reduced from $250 to $100, "cruel treatment" was amended to include failing to provide the slave with "comfortable clothing or a sufficient quantity of wholesome food." Most importantly, a new section, Article 802, was adopted. It granted considerably more authority to the master over the slave:

> 1st. The right of the master to the obedience and submission of his slave, in all lawful things, is perfect, and the power belongs to the master to inflict any punishment upon the slave not affecting life or limb, and not coming within the definition of cruel treatment, or unreasonable abuse, which he may consider necessary for the purpose of keeping him in such submission, and enforcing such submission to his commands; and if, in the exercise of this right, with or without cause, the slave resists and slays his master, it is murder.

Although the second provision of Article 802 continued to bar the master from killing or maiming his slave, the third provision stated that the master was the "exclusive judge" of the necessity for moderate correction of his slave.

The remainder of Article 802 set forth, in great detail, when moderate correction was permissible and forbade violent responses by slaves that were justifiable in law if made by free white persons.[57]

Finally, new Article 819 defined eight different crimes as death penalty offenses. These included not only murder and insurrection, but also four crimes if committed on a white person: "rape upon a free white woman," "robbery when committed upon a free white person," "assault with intent to commit murder, rape or robbery upon a free white person," and "assault with a deadly weapon upon a free white person."[58]

The February 1860 amendment to the insurrection statute indicated an even more frenzied effort to maintain slavery. Article 653 was amended to criminalize any public statement by a free person that "masters have not the right of property in their slaves," or any statement "calculated to produce in slaves a spirit of insubordination." And any private statement to "bring the institution of slavery (African) into dispute in the mind of any free inhabitant" was punishable by imprisonment between two and five years. In summer 1860 the fear of insurrection caused many Texans to claim an abolitionist plot was behind a series of fires that occurred in many parts of the state. Before these fears were calmed, as many as eighty slaves and thirty-seven whites alleged as plotters may have been murdered by mobs. Evidence of an insurrection plot was sparse but sufficient for many. One of the victims, a Methodist minister named Anthony Bewley, was hanged after receiving the benefits of "lynch law," including a parody of a trial. One contemporary speaking of the Bewley murder declared, "The time had come that ninety-nine innocent men had better suffer than let one guilty escape." This reversed the common law adage of English judge Sir William Blackstone that "better that ten guilty persons escape than

that one innocent suffer." A recent history concludes, "[T]he total absence of any convincing evidence that there *was* a plot, together with much circumstantial evidence and testimony indicating that none existed, strongly suggests that there was no conspiracy." The fear of Texas citizens of a slave insurrection generated a passion that overtook the reason of the law.[59]

The Texas Code of Criminal Procedure of 1856 made a fervent effort to solve the free person of color "problem." Not only were free persons of color incompetent to testify under the code (as were slaves), except when the defendant was also a slave or free person of color, but the code of criminal procedure also permitted any magistrate to take any free person of color without special permission to reside in Texas and have him hired out for six months to the highest bidder. After completing this term, if the free person of color did not leave Texas within thirty days, he was to be arrested and hired out for five years. If he still refused to leave Texas, he was to be sold as a slave. The 1858 legislature also permitted free persons of color to voluntarily enslave themselves. The supreme court interpreted this last provision strictly, holding that a free person of color was not permitted to enslave himself before the adoption of the law.[60]

Whether the antebellum law on the books was reflected in the law in action is unclear. Four nonslaveowners were convicted of mistreatment of slaves owned by others. Slaveowners were not subject to the same rules concerning mistreatment as nonslaveowners, making these convictions more about protecting the property rights of slaveowners than protecting slaves. Moreover, "[w]hites who attacked or mistreated slaves generally went free since slaves could not testify against them in court." Not only did internal legal limitations (the incompetence of slaves to testify) affect the implementation of the law on the books, so too did external factors that were cultural (the belief in the inferiority of slaves), political (as sectional tension grew, so too did the insistence in the South on maintaining the "peculiar" institution), structural (Texas had relatively little law enforcement), and geographic (in a rural state violence against slaves in the countryside was nearly impossible to detect).[61]

The Old Court's slave law jurisprudence regularly considered the humanity of the slave in the various cases that came before it, and its decisions were part of its efforts to craft a rule of law in Texas. It did so within the context of fully supporting the institution of slavery, for acknowledging the humanity of slaves did not necessitate their emancipation. One of the court's earliest decisions was an appeal from a murder conviction of a slave named Nels. The court reversed the conviction on the ground that it appeared from the written record of the case that the jury was not sworn in. This was a technicality that might have been simply the failure of the clerk to include the swearing of the jury in the record. But it allowed the court to avoid a more sensitive and difficult issue: did the trial court err in informing the members of the jury that Nels's lawyer had confessed a fact harmful to Nels's case? Whether the lawyer had utterly failed to represent Nels or whether the trial judge had failed to understand that any statement made by the lawyer for the accused is not evidence was unimportant once the court found another reason to reverse the conviction. Article VII, section 2 of the 1845 constitution guaranteed to any slave the right to trial by jury for any crime greater than petit larceny. *Nels* encouraged trial courts to effectuate the right to trial by jury, to provide something more than mere formal adherence to it. (Of course, Nels's jury consisted solely of white males.)[62]

The slave's humanity was also addressed in cases in which a white man was convicted of manslaughter in the killing of a slave. In *Chandler v. State* (1847), the court rejected the defendant's contention that the murder of a slave

was not subject to the criminal laws because a slave was subject to the absolute dominion of his master. The court noted that in legislative acts concerning slavery, "slaves have uniformly been treated as *persons,* in the contemplation of those laws." (Article VII, section 3 of the 1845 constitution also declared that "[a]ny person who shall maliciously dismember, or deprive a slave of life, shall suffer such punishment as would be inflicted in case the like offence had been committed upon a free white person.") The court reiterated its conclusion in *Chandler* eight years later in *Nix v. State* (1855). Finally, in an 1857 case the supreme court reversed the district court's dismissal of the indictment of a white man for whipping a slave, again citing *Chandler* with approval and concluding that the district court failed to acknowledge that "an assault and battery, by one not the owner, is *prima facie* an invasion of" the slave's personal rights as a human being.[63]

A final issue concerned manumission of slaves by owners. The 1836 constitution declared, "nor shall any slave-holder be allowed to emancipate his or her slave or slaves, without the consent of Congress, unless he or she shall send his or her slave or slaves without the limits of the Republic." During the republic, only two of fifteen requests by owners to manumit slaves were granted. The 1845 constitution omitted this provision, although it is unclear why. It permitted the legislature to determine whether to allow owners to free their slaves. No law was ever passed on the subject. In several cases the Texas Supreme Court interpreted the law to favor manumission and liberty, even as other states began restricting manumission. For example, in *Moore v. Minerva* (1856), the court held that a former slave who accompanied her former master from Ohio to Texas remained free because she had been freed before she came to Texas. That she had moved to Texas in violation of the act of February 5, 1840, was irrelevant, for that law was limited to the forfeiture of freedom, not a person's state of freedom. In *Jones v. Laney* (1847), the court held that "the right of property connects with it the right of relinquishing that property." It affirmed the district court's decision declaring Laney free. Similarly, in *Purvis v. Sherrod* (1854), the court allowed the owner of slaves to free them through his will. If Texas law required their removal from the state, the former slaves, along with the owner's sister (who was given the power to resolve the issue), would decide where they would settle. As Timothy Huebner notes, the court's opinion by Abner Lipscomb, the former Alabama supreme court justice, "overlooked an important fact. At the time Lipscomb cited these precedents from other states [allowing emancipation of slaves outside of the state], all had either been overruled or had received heavy criticism in more recent opinions from state courts." It also ignored Alabama law, from which Texas had taken its 1836 constitution's ban on manumission. The same result was reached by the court when the owner of a slave gave the slave as a conditional gift to another, with the condition being manumission of the slave upon reaching maturity. Only when the owner attempted to manumit a slave in Texas did the court declare it unlawful.[64]

THE SUPREME COURT AFTER THE OLD COURT

The death of Lipscomb in late 1856 and the resignation of Hemphill in 1858 to serve in the U.S. Senate created the first changes to the court's membership since Texas became a state. Lipscomb was replaced by Oran M. Roberts, like Lipscomb a native South Carolinian and formerly a lawyer in Alabama. Wheeler replaced Hemphill as chief justice, and James Bell, son of Josiah Bell, an *alcalde* in Austin's Colony, took Wheeler's seat. Bell was thirty-three, the youngest person to serve on the Texas Supreme Court.[65]

The court's jurisprudence changed little during the brief period before the outbreak of the Civil War in April 1861. Without Hemphill's presence, the court referred less and less to civil-law antecedents; by the end of the nineteenth century, the court's use of Spanish law texts was minimal, even though Texas continued its use of aspects of the civil-law system.

TEXAS ON THE BRINK OF CIVIL WAR

The claimed slave insurrection in 1860 largely ended the debate on the future course of Texas despite the public opposition of Governor Sam Houston to secession. South Carolina seceded in December, a month after Abraham Lincoln won election as president. The supreme court was itself badly split. Wheeler, though a native of Vermont and a Whig, quietly supported secession. His brother justices were vociferous and on opposite sides of the question. On December 1, 1860, Associate Justices Oran M. Roberts and James Bell publicly debated whether Texas should secede. Bell, a Unionist and the first native Texan to serve on the court, concluded that only the governor had the authority to call a convention on secession and warned strongly against separation from the United States. Roberts was, in the words of Unionist and lawyer George W. Paschal, "a zealous leader" of the movement for secession. He wrote the initial call for a convention on secession. Roberts argued that the people have the procedural right to convene to determine whether to secede without the permission of the governor. He substantively argued that Texas should secede. In early January 1861, Texans voted to send representatives to a convention to determine whether to secede. The convention began at the end of the month, and Roberts served as its presiding officer. On February 1, 1861, delegates voted 166 to 8 in favor of seceding from the United States. The convention's decision was approved by three-quarters of all voters (46,153 to 14,747), and Texas left

U.S. Senator Sam Houston, ca. 1859–1860. Courtesy Texas State Library and Archives Commission. Oran M. Roberts, proponent of secession while serving as a judge of the Texas Supreme Court, undated. Courtesy Texas State Library and Archives Commission.

the United States for the Confederate States of America.[66]

THE SUPREME COURT DURING THE CIVIL WAR

In *Parker v. State* (1862), Bell noted that a "public place" may be public at some times and private at others. To make his point, he gave as an example a lawyer's office. A lawyer's office could be a public place and "may, also, and in times like the present, many doubtless are very private and quiet and undisturbed places at all hours." This nod to the legal quietude caused by the Civil War also reflected the reduction in the work of the court. Justice James Norvell's 1966 essay on the Civil War court valiantly attempted to demonstrate the significance of the court's work, but his most damning compliment was that "the decisions of the Civil War court are not mere dead letters of the law."[67]

In early 1862, Roberts left the court to serve as an officer in the Confederate Army. In April, the Confederate congress adopted the Confederate Conscription Act, and on May 30, Brigadier General P. O. Hebert declared martial law in Texas, in part to enforce the act. The court's most important decision during the war was *Ex Parte Coupland* (1862), arising from these two actions. *Coupland* was the first case in the Confederacy to assess the constitutionality of the Conscription Act. Coupland was in the custody of the military pursuant to the Conscription Act when he petitioned Chief Justice Wheeler for a writ of habeas corpus ("you have the body," which detention, the writ claims, is illegal). The case was apparently brought to Wheeler by George Paschal, who was adamantly opposed to martial law: "I brought it before the chief justice to test the constitutionality of this declaration of military power over a State, in which there was not one soldier hostile to the Confederate cause." Wheeler denied the petition (the court was not

Proclamation by Governor Sam Houston, March 4, 1861, Secession Vote. Courtesy Texas State Library and Archives Commission.

in session, so Wheeler alone decided). Coupland appealed to the entire three-member court. By the time the case reached the court, it was a "fictional" case, for Coupland had disappeared to parts unknown after his release from military custody. Paschal was also no longer counsel of record for Coupland. Justice George Fleming Moore, who replaced Roberts, wrote the opinion for a majority of the court (himself and Wheeler), and held the draft law constitutional. Moore concluded the power to wage war implicitly included the power to draft soldiers to fight the war. In the view of Unionist and Texas loyalist Bell, the act was unconstitutional because congress's explicit constitutional power to raise armies was limited by the requirement that it use only necessary and proper means to effectuate its explicit powers, and conscription was not a necessary means to raise an army. Although he cited the case as support, Bell's conclusion stood Marshall's decision in *McCulloch v. Maryland* (1819) on its head, for

that decision interpreted the "necessary and proper" clause of the American constitution in a broad rather than a narrow manner.[68]

As Paschal notes in an 1869 preface to volume 28 of the *Texas Reports*, the consequences of *Coupland* were baneful for Texans devoted to the rule of law. Paschal himself was arrested by military authorities shortly after Coupland's case was tried by Wheeler. He was released shortly thereafter but was again arrested late in the war. Of Wheeler's opinion in *Coupland*, Paschal wrote, "[I]n this crisis, the conviction that our liberties were being lost was intensified when I saw such a law student as Chief Justice Wheeler bow to the storm and abdicate the civil law." Even accounting for Paschal's Unionist prejudice, his conclusion speaks to the stresses facing any legal system at a time of war.

The helplessness of the court to effectuate a rule of law was demonstrated two years later when military authorities refused to subject themselves to the law. In late October 1863, five persons were arrested and held by the Confederate army for calling for "Common Sense," which questioned the Confederate justification for continuing to wage war. One of the five was Richard Peebles, a veteran of the Texas Revolution. Peebles and the others petitioned the supreme court for a writ of habeas corpus. The court ordered the men be placed in the temporary custody of the Travis County sheriff, a civil officer. General John Magruder ordered Major J. H. Sparks to take custody of the men, and Magruder refused to acknowledge the court's authority to hear the petition. Two opinions written by Justice Moore in the spring of 1864 fulminated against Magruder's actions and offered "our most decided condemnation" of his actions. But this condemnation was a paper tiger. Although the court managed initially to win the unconditional release of the prisoners, the five "political prisoners" were immediately rearrested. Three, including Peebles, were sent to Mexico after ten months' confinement. The court refrained from punishing either Sparks or Magruder, resting its conclusion on the belief that the demands of the war effort ruled out imprisonment and that a fine was inappropriate. Of course, it was unlikely that any punishment would have been accepted by military officers. This made the court's decision its least unattractive option to maintain its integrity.[69]

Coupland had other personal and institutional consequences. The twenty-year friendship between Paschal and Wheeler was irretrievably broken. Wheeler, subject to depression, committed suicide in April 1864. Four months later, Bell was denied renomination to his position as associate justice because of his well-known Unionist views, including his dissent in *Coupland*. Paschal eventually moved to Washington, D.C., and became a disillusioned intermittent counsel for Texas in its postwar attempt to recoup its bonds (see chapter 2).

The end of the Civil War in 1865 led to several new Texas constitutions as well as turmoil in its supreme court. Reconstruction attempted and failed to bring transformative political and social reform. Slavery was constitutionally outlawed (Thirteenth Amendment (1865)), Confederate officials were barred from public office (Fourteenth Amendment (1868)), and the *Dred Scott v. Sandford* (1857) decision holding that Negroes could not be citizens was overturned (same amendment). Finally, freedmen were granted the right to vote (Fifteenth Amendment (1870)). The consequences of and reactions to Reconstruction reverberated in Texas for the next sixty years, as legal and extralegal issues concerning race formed a central part of Texas's legal history.

TWO

Law and Crises, 1865–1920

★

THE ARRIVAL of Union soldiers in Texas in June 1865 symbolized a turn in Texas history, including Texas legal history. The aftereffects of war and Reconstruction, an expanding population, and new economic opportunities all combined to make this period one of turbulence and growth. The liberty granted former slaves ensured a dramatic shift in the relationship between whites and freedmen, "resolved" a generation later by the adoption of Jim Crow laws mandating legal segregation of whites and blacks. Violence wracked the state throughout the post–Civil War era, and lynchings became a tool of white terror against African Americans from the 1880s through the first decades of the twentieth century. Beginning in the 1870s railroads became a powerful (and to many, a baneful) influence in Texas politics, leading to the creation of the Texas Railroad Commission in 1891. Texas was an early proponent of regulating corporations, adopting an antitrust law in 1889 and enforcing it rigorously (see chapter 4). The settlement of

West Texas was promoted by the sale of vast tracts of state land, leading to battles over property rights and use of public lands by private landowners (see chapter 3). At the beginning of the new century, the discovery of oil at Spindletop initiated a restructuring of the economy of Texas, eventually making energy a prominent and even quintessential part of Texas economic life. The nineteenth-century debate over prohibition continued and intensified during the first two decades of the twentieth century, creating a host of unintended consequences affecting law in Texas. Women, a number of whom led the fight for prohibition, proselytized for the right to vote, finally gaining it at the end of this period. Texas during these decades changed greatly in economic, cultural, and demographic terms. It became both a southern and western state. Texas judges and lawyers, as well as law enforcement officers, struggled mightily to create a stable and solid rule of law, but repeated legal and political crises made this effort nearly insuperable.[1]

LEGAL REVERBERATIONS IN A POST–SLAVERY STATE

In Texas, the end of slavery is known as Juneteenth, for in Galveston on June 19, 1865, Union general Gordon Granger read Lincoln's Emancipation Proclamation freeing slaves in the rebellious states. Texas was largely untouched materially by the Civil War, and General Granger's arrival in Galveston in June 1865 represented neither defeat nor a conquering of the state, but a Confederate surrender. Psychologically, defeat and return to the Union left many in Texas unsettled, from freedman to Confederate army conscript. Many families had lost men fighting for the Confederacy (and occasionally for the Union) for a cause that was now "lost." Former slaves were now free but owned nothing. Wealthy planters lost much of their wealth when slavery was abolished.

Decrees by President Andrew Johnson began presidential reconstruction of the former Confederate states. Johnson appointed Unionist A. J. Hamilton provisional governor of Texas and introduced an amnesty proclamation allowing many southerners to return with full privileges to public life in the South (leaders of the Confederacy were excluded). Johnson's proclamation for Texas also asked Hamilton to call a convention at which it would consider ratifying the Thirteenth Amendment abolishing slavery, declare loyalty to the Union, and repudiate the debt of the Confederacy. Hamilton returned to Texas and on August 2 walked two miles from his burned-down home to the capitol for inauguration.[2]

The end of slavery had not ended the legal consequences arising from the peculiar institution. In 1866, Maria, now a freedwoman, was indicted for and convicted of murdering Mary, another slave, in 1863. The Texas Supreme Court reversed Maria's conviction on the ground that the trial court failed to instruct the jury correctly on the "legal provocation or passion" that may have reduced her crime

from murder to manslaughter. As noted by the reporter of the court's opinions, George W. Paschal, a Unionist during the Civil War, the court had completely overlooked a crucial issue: was Maria subject to the punishments listed in the Texas code of criminal law for her crime? A slave convicted of a crime in Texas was subject to one of two possible punishments, whipping or death. For example, a slave convicted of manslaughter was subject to a public whipping by the sheriff. In contrast, a free person convicted of manslaughter was subject to possible imprisonment. As provisional governor, A. J. Hamilton "subjected the freedmen to the same mode of trial and punishment as white persons," a standard also adopted in Art. VIII of the 1866 Texas Constitution. Was Maria, a slave when she killed Mary and a freedwoman when tried for murder, punishable by the law in effect when the act was committed, or by the law in effect when she was tried?[3]

In 1867 the supreme court heard the appeal by William Wilson of his conviction for cruel treatment of his slave. Wilson was accused in 1861 of inflicting "six hundred stripes with a gutta-percha strap" on his slave Nat, who died from the beating. Indicted for murder, Wilson was not tried until May 8, 1865. Wilson's trial took place a month after Confederate Army general Robert E. Lee surrendered to Union Army general Ulysses S. Grant at Appomattox, but before the June 2 surrender by Confederate general E. Kirby Smith of the Trans-Mississippi Department in Galveston harbor. The trial court gave the jury the option of finding Wilson guilty of murder or of cruel treatment of a slave, or acquitting him altogether. The jury found Wilson guilty of cruel treatment and fined him the maximum amount, two thousand dollars. The jury clearly believed Wilson's abhorrent actions deserved some punishment, but the trial's timing may have led it to settle on this "just right" solution. The supreme court acknowledged that the jury had concluded Wilson deserved punishment for his actions:

"The fine being the highest punishment that could be inflicted upon the defendant for the offense of which he is convicted . . . induces the belief that the acts of the defendant were in gross violation of the law, probably meriting a much higher penalty than was adjudged against him." But the supreme court reversed Wilson's conviction, holding that cruel treatment of a slave and murder were wholly separate crimes. A person charged with murder might be not guilty of murder because the jury concluded he lacked the required intent to kill, but his reckless actions in disregard of human life made him guilty of the lesser included offense of manslaughter. By declaring murder and cruel treatment of a slave separate crimes, a jury could not conclude that the defendant's lack of an intent to kill made him guilty of cruel treatment rather than murder. With this interpretation, the court reversed Wilson's conviction.[4]

The legacy of slavery also raised civil-law issues. Were contracts for the sale or lease of slaves made after the Emancipation Proclamation void or enforceable? Every southern state faced this issue, and all but Louisiana held that such contracts were enforceable. In *Hall v. Kease* (1868), the Texas Supreme Court held the answer was contingent on the effective date of the end of slavery. The contracts upon which the lawsuit was brought had been made in January 1865, after the Emancipation Proclamation (effective on January 1, 1863) but before Juneteenth or the ratification of the Thirteenth Amendment in December 1865. The court was divided. Speaking for the three-person majority, Chief Justice Amos Morrill concluded that slavery was not abolished in Texas by the Emancipation Proclamation but by ratification of the Thirteenth Amendment. Thus, the sale was lawful when made, and the buyer (or lessor) was liable on the contract even though he could no longer benefit from the contract once slavery was prohibited. The two dissenters concluded that slavery ended on January 1, 1863, making the contract void. Their conclusion was

premised on the rationale that enforcing such contracts was against public policy.[5]

THE CONSTITUTION OF 1866

The election of convention delegates to write the new constitution to replace the discredited Confederate Constitution of 1861 took place on January 7, 1866. By that time the battle over the rights accorded freedmen had coalesced. Hamilton presciently believed Texas needed to recognize the civil liberties of the freedmen in order to return fully to the Union. His opponents believed acceding to Andrew Johnson's modest demands was sufficient to readmit Texas into the Union. Conservative Unionists and secessionists achieved a majority in the constitutional convention. Among the secessionists elected to the convention was Texas Supreme Court chief justice Oran M. Roberts, the leader of the 1861 secession convention. About one-third of the delegates had served as officers in the Confederate Army, and another third may have served as enlisted men.[6]

The convention adopted provisions taking care of most of President Johnson's requests: It renounced secession (Ordinance No. 1), repudiated debt accrued from the Civil War (Ordinance No. 2), arranged for elections of representatives (Ordinance No. 3), and even acknowledged the end of slavery (reluctantly stating, "African slavery, as it heretofore existed, having been terminated within this State, by the Government of the United States, by force of arms, and its re-establishment being prohibited, by the amendment to the Constitution of the United States, it is declared that neither slavery nor involuntary servitude . . . shall exist in this State"). It did not, however, ratify the Thirteenth Amendment.[7]

The great fear of white southerners in the aftermath of the Civil War was racial equality. And they believed racial equality could arrive stealthily. Carl Moneyhon has noted that white southerners feared that "[a]llowing blacks to testify in court would lead to blacks sitting on juries, then to suffrage, and finally to total social and political equality." The convention attempted to placate this fear by limiting freedmen to testifying only in cases in which freedman were involved in both sides of the matter (as victim in a criminal case when the defendant was a freedman, or in a civil case when both plaintiff and defendant were freedmen). The constitution prohibited a free person of color from testifying in any case in which a white person was a party, though it gave the legislature the authority to allow freedmen to testify in all other cases. As was true in all other southern states in 1866 (and in most northern states as well), freedmen were given neither the right to vote nor the right to sit on juries.[8]

Although the constitutional convention met the terms and conditions set forth by President Johnson for the readmission of Texas into the Union, many Republican congressmen opposed admission to Congress of representatives from southern states unless the freedmen's civil liberties were more fully protected by former Confederate states. After all, the Thirteenth Amendment eliminated the three-fifths clause of the U.S. Constitution, which counted every five slaves as three persons for purposes of allocating membership in the House of Representatives. Now those five former slaves counted as five persons, increasing the number of congressional representatives from former Confederate states. Unless Congress acted, this increase in southern representation would occur without any corresponding right of the freedmen to vote. Further, the relationship between Johnson and Congress was rapidly deteriorating. As the members of the Texas constitutional convention met, so too did Congress, which on March 15 passed the Civil Rights Bill of 1866. The bill was vetoed by Johnson on March 27, and Johnson's veto was overridden by two-thirds of both houses of Congress by April 9, 1866. The Civil Rights Act of 1866 allowed freedmen to sue, be sued, testify, make contracts, and enjoy all

the laws protecting their security and property as enjoyed by white citizens. Near the end of June the proposed Fourteenth Amendment was sent to the states for ratification. This proposed amendment reversed the notorious *Dred Scott* (1857) decision by making all persons born in the United States citizens, barring any state from interfering with the privileges or immunities of those citizens, and guaranteeing to all persons due process of law and the equal protection of the laws. Section 2 of the amendment prohibited states from counting freedmen for purposes of representation and electoral votes if they were not allowed to vote. Section 3 barred from office anyone who swore to uphold the Constitution and who then "shall have engaged in insurrection or rebellion against the same, or given aid or comfort to the enemies thereof." Section 4 repudiated any Confederate war debt. Finally, in July 1866 a revised Freedmen's Bureau bill was also adopted by Congress over a veto by Johnson.[9]

The Texas Constitution of 1866 was ratified by a vote in late June, and in August the new Democratic governor, James Throckmorton, and the legislature were sworn into office. The eleventh legislature adopted a series of acts known as the Black Code, laws that would be overturned by the initiation by Congress of Reconstruction in 1867.

THE TEXAS BLACK CODE AND THE FREEDMEN'S BUREAU IN TEXAS

The Black Codes were a series of laws adopted in the former Confederate states intended to regulate the life and work of former slaves. The first series of Black Codes was adopted by several former Confederate states in 1865. A second series was adopted by other such states in 1866, including Texas. Among the laws passed by the eleventh legislature were laws barring a person of color from testifying in any criminal prosecution except "where the prosecution is against a person who is a person of color";

regulating contracts for labor, which restricted the ability of freedmen to leave employment by making it a crime to entice a contracted laborer into leaving his employment; and segregating passengers in railroad cars by race. The legislature also adopted a law titled An Act to Define and Declare the Rights of Persons Lately Known as Slaves, and Free Persons of Color, the last of the Black Code laws. Despite its title and section 1, which granted the right of freedmen to sue and be sued, to make contracts, and to own property, this act was designed to ensure a subordinated legal place for persons of color in Texas. Section 2 of the act declared, "[N]othing herein shall be so construed as to repeal any law prohibiting the intermarriage of the white and black races, nor to permit any other than white men to serve on juries, hold office, or vote at any election," and it reiterated the limitations on testifying by freedmen. Most of these statutes and others related to these statutes, such as laws on vagrancy and crime, were adopted within a two-week period. Barry Crouch concludes that the view that Texas's Black Code was more lenient and less restrictive than the black codes of other southern states is wrong, for "the Texas black codes are interchangeable with those enacted by any other Southern state." In addition to adopting the Black Code, the eleventh legislature refused to ratify the Fourteenth Amendment.[10]

As the Texas legislature completed its work on the Black Code, biennial congressional elections took place. Andrew Johnson campaigned against "Radical Republicans" in the U.S. House and Senate; the result was a landslide victory for Republicans. The election of this new Congress, which would not begin its first session for thirteen months, energized the outgoing Congress, which adopted congressional reconstruction.[11]

The Bureau of Refugees, Freedmen, and Abandoned Lands, known as the Freedmen's Bureau, was intended to offer opportunities for the freedmen to make their way in a postslavery world. Texas was the last former Confederate state in which the Freedmen's Bureau was organized. In a state the size of Texas, the employees of the bureau were limited in their ability to effect any change in the status of the freedmen. By early 1867, Assistant Commissioner and General Charles Griffin wrote that he believed the Texas judicial system had collapsed, and in much of the state "murder is bold and unchecked—in those parts the life of a white man is worth but little, the life of a freedman is worth nothing." Indeed, between the end of the Civil War in June 1865 and the summer of 1868, 509 whites and 468 blacks were murdered. The annual report by Governor E. M. Pease in early 1868 claimed 411 unsolved murders and assaults, 188 of which were apparently by white men upon freedmen. Further, the Texas criminal justice system was used, in the late 1867 view of a later assistant commissioner of the bureau, Joseph J. Reynolds, "rigorously, cruelly and unjustly" by whites against freedmen.[12]

A study of the Freedmen's Bureau in Texas by Barry Crouch concluded that freedmen used the bureau's legal processes (in lieu of the Texas judicial system) regularly and effectively. The freedmen "pressed their legal rights aggressively and with an awareness of what the law should do for them." However, the bureau essentially left Texas by the end of 1868, making it much more difficult for freedmen to obtain legal justice in much of the state.[13]

CONGRESSIONAL RECONSTRUCTION AND TEXAS LAW

On March 2, 1867, Congress overrode three vetoes of President Andrew Johnson and introduced congressional reconstruction. The former Confederate states were divided by law into five military districts, and any existing state government in those states was declared provisional. The Reconstruction Act required these states, including Texas, to draft and ratify by popular vote a new constitution and mandated that this constitution include a provision allowing suffrage for all freedmen. In addition, the former Confederate states were required to ratify the Fourteenth Amendment, which Texas and all other Confederate states save Tennessee had refused to do.

In April 1867, General Charles Griffin issued two edicts: Circular No. 10 permitted military authorities to ensure that civil courts decided cases impartially, "but where it is evident that local civil tribunals will not impartially try cases brought before them, and render decisions according to law and evidence, the immediate military commander" would have the offenders arrested and tried by a military commission or tribunal. Circular No. 13, issued on April 27, required all jurors to swear an "Ironclad Oath" of loyalty, which required the oath taker to swear he had never "voluntarily borne arms against the United States" and that he had never "yielded a voluntary support to any pretended government." This disabled many white Texans from serving as jurors. In addition, this circular, known as the Jury Order, barred the exclusion in Texas courts of freedmen to sit as jurors, a civil liberty denied them in the 1866 Black Code.[14]

In July, Griffin removed Governor Throckmorton from office and replaced him with Elisha M. Pease. Pease asked Griffin to replace all officeholders who opposed the policies of the federal government. Several district judges were removed from office in August, and on September 10 the five members of the Texas Supreme Court, three more district judges, and other executive officials were displaced as "impediments to reconstruction." Writing in 1917, lawyer J. H. Davenport concluded that "[t]his was the culminating act of a despotic regime in the subversion of constitutional government and the destruction of the liberties of a defenseless people by an ignoble conqueror." Davenport's *History of the Supreme Court of Texas* neglected to mention the continuing violence committed against the freedman, violence left

unchecked and unabated by local law enforcement officials.[15]

In the fall of 1867, violence against freedmen increased dramatically. Even so, 89 percent (49,550) of eligible freedmen registered to vote by early 1868. About 50 percent (60,445) of white Texans registered to vote, and enough of them were Republicans, making it likely that Republicans would comprise a majority of the constitutional convention writing the new constitution. The vote on whether to call for a constitutional convention passed handily, and the newly formed Republican Party claimed a dominant majority of the delegates to the convention.[16]

THE CONSTITUTION OF 1869

The Reconstruction constitutional convention began on June 1, 1868. It continued, in a desultory and fractious fashion, until February 1869, with a break resulting from a lack of funds. It ended with a whimper, failing to complete its work. Military authorities cobbled together the records of the convention to complete the constitution in order to bring it to the voters for adoption. During the convention, groups allying themselves with or declaring themselves a part of the Ku Klux Klan killed up to twenty-five freedmen at Millican. Republicans were assaulted and murdered across southeast and east Texas, Freedmen's Bureau schools were burned, and one convention delegate, George W. Smith, was assassinated. In the November 1868 presidential election, Republican Ulysses S. Grant, commanding general of the armies of the Union during the Civil War, won election (no votes were counted from the reconstructed states, including Texas). Shortly after the constitutional convention disbanded, and just before Grant's inauguration, Congress proposed the Fifteenth Amendment for ratification. The Fifteenth Amendment declared that the "right of citizens of the United States to vote shall not be denied or abridged by the United

States or by any state on account of race, color, or previous condition of servitude."[17]

The 1869 Texas constitution, adopted by voters in July, protected the civil rights of the freedmen by recognizing "equality of all persons before the law" and by declaring that no Texan shall "ever be deprived of any right, privilege, or immunity, nor be exempted from any burdens, or duty, on account of race, color, or previous condition" (Art. I, § 21). Article VI guaranteed the right of freedmen (males only) to vote, and section 27 of the General Provisions legitimized the marriages of former slave couples and made their children legitimate under the law. The supreme court was reduced from five members to three. All supreme court justices were appointed with the advice and consent of the senate for nine-year terms (Art. V § 2); district judges were similarly appointed for eight-year terms (Art. V § 6).

In February 1870 the elected members of the twelfth legislature were called to session as a provisional legislature to ratify the Thirteenth, Fourteenth, and Fifteenth amendments and to elect Texas's senators in Congress. The legislature did so. On March 30, 1870, Texas was readmitted into the Union, and military government ended the next month. The twelfth legislature was then called into special session by Reconstruction governor Edmund Davis as Texas returned to civil rule.[18]

TEXAS V. WHITE AND THE CONSTITUTIONALITY OF SECESSION

Not only, therefore, can there be no loss of separate and independent autonomy to the States, through their union under the Constitution, but it may be not unreasonably said that the preservation of the States, and the maintenance of their governments, are as much within the design and care of the Constitution as the preservation of the Union and the maintenance of the National government. The Constitution, in all its provisions, looks to an indestructible Union, composed of indestructible States.[19]

Chief Justice Salmon P. Chase of the U.S. Supreme Court asserted as a matter of law what the Union had asserted as a matter of fact during the Civil War: the states were indestructibly a part of an indestructible Union. Secession was unlawful and ineffectual, unrecognized in any court of law.[20]

In 1850, Texas agreed to forfeit its claims to western lands in exchange for $10 million in United States bonds, issued in $1,000 increments, which paid annual interest at a rate of 5 percent (see chapter 3). These bonds were redeemable after December 31, 1864. Half of those bonds were delivered to Texas, made payable to it, and half remained with the federal government. When Texas initially received the bonds in 1851, the legislature adopted a law requiring an endorsement of the bonds by the governor before anyone else could claim lawful ownership. In 1862, after seceding from the Union, the Texas legislature repealed this provision. On the same day, it created a military board to sell the bonds to pay for the war. In early 1865 the board sold 135 bonds (76 other bonds located in England were also promised) to George White and John Chiles. Including interest, the bonds were worth $156,200. White and Chiles agreed to provide the Texas military board with cotton cards (an important tool used to comb cotton fibers) and medicine in exchange for the bonds. If White and Chiles failed to fulfill their obligations, they were required to pay back Texas by giving Texas state bonds, not United States bonds. As White and Chiles knew, United States bonds were redeemable in gold at face value with interest. Texas state bonds were redeemable at about eight cents on the dollar, allowing White and Chiles to make an exorbitant profit even if they failed to deliver the promised goods. As White wrote one member of the military board, "It is important that the feds should not get possession of this contract." White and Chiles failed to deliver the requested goods.[21]

Governor A. J. Hamilton learned about this corrupt bargain shortly after he entered office. He appointed George W. Paschal agent of Texas to recover the bonds and to sue any bondholders (such as White and Chiles) who failed or refused to return them. Salmon P. Chase, when secretary of the treasury, had ordered the Treasury Department not to redeem the bonds. But since the end of the war, this order had been rescinded, and several persons, including John P. White, George's brother, had redeemed some of the bonds (John redeemed ten thousand dollars in bonds).

Events in Texas then intervened. James Throckmorton was elected governor and took office in August 1866. Paschal, a Unionist, was removed as agent and replaced by lawyers in Washington who were given a contingent fee of 25 percent of the value of whatever bonds they recovered. On February 15, 1867, Texas sued White and Chiles in the Supreme Court of the United States. Congress adopted reconstruction in March, and in the summer Throckmorton was removed from office. The newly appointed governor of Reconstruction Texas, Elisha M. Pease, reappointed Paschal as agent for Texas. Washington counsel remained on the case.

The case was initially argued to the Supreme Court in February 1868. The most important issue was whether Texas could sue in federal court. This raised the issue of the status of Texas in the United States in 1868 (it was subject to military rule and without representatives in Congress), as well as the issue of what effect, if any, secession had on the states in relation to the Constitution and the United States. The Supreme Court reserved argument on the latter issue and in early 1869 heard both the jurisdictional claim (did Texas have the right to sue in federal court?) and the substantive claim (did Texas have a right to claim the bonds, or was the contract made by the military board with White and Chiles in 1865 enforceable?).

Chase concluded that the states remained part of the Union during the Civil War. He noted that even the March 2, 1867, Reconstruction Acts "necessarily imply recognition of existing governments." The states and the United States remained indestructible. Texas thus enjoyed the jurisdictional right to sue in the Supreme Court. On the substantive issue, the Court held that the contract of White and Chiles was unenforceable because they had notice the state had imposed a restriction on the transfer of the bonds. That restriction was the 1851 law requiring the governor to endorse these bonds to transfer ownership from the State of Texas. The 1862 law repealing that endorsement requirement was of no effect, Chase concluded, because it was "intended to aid the rebellion." Notice of this defect was sufficiently broad that innocent third party purchasers of the bonds were not protected against a suit by Texas for recovery of those bonds.

The search for the bonds continued. For the second time Paschal was removed as agent, again as a result of changing fortunes in Texas state government. Texas filed more suits against other bondholders, and the difficulty of tracing which bonds went to White and Chiles, and whether other such bonds were subject to the decision in *Texas v. White*, made for much additional litigation. Chase's substantive legal conclusion came under attack (it was finally overruled in *Morgan v. United States* (1885)). Paschal held money collected from his successful lawsuit and claimed authority to hold it until the state had paid him his fee, which Paschal set at $20,000 (out of $47,325 then collected, minus $11,738 to the Washington attorneys and $1,626 for costs). Paschal also claimed a contingent fee in bonds currently held in Europe and then the subject of ongoing litigation. Texas demanded he turn over all remaining monies. Paschal refused. In *In re Paschal* (1871), the Supreme Court declined to hold Paschal in contempt, concluding he was permitted to hold the money and any papers of the client (Texas) when he possessed "a fair and honest set-off, which ought in equity be allowed by the complainant." If Paschal returned the money, he was wholly at the mercy of the legislature in awarding him his fees, for Texas was immune from any lawsuit. Because Paschal's

Unionist sympathies were well known in Texas during the Civil War, if Paschal returned the collected monies he was not going to be paid. The Court was well aware that Paschal's only leverage was to retain the funds and force Texas to sue him. As Paschal lived in Washington, D.C., that would give Paschal a fair jury trial on the claims by the parties. Additionally, the Supreme Court held Chiles in contempt for disobeying the Court's order in *Texas v. White*.[22]

Texas eventually recovered $339,000 from bonds held in Europe. Of that total, $300,000 went into the state treasury, $8,000 was paid to the Washington lawyers, and the remainder to Jabez and DeWitt Clinton Giddings, who had been named agents for Texas by Governor Richard Coke in 1873. This $31,000 payment to the Giddings brothers might never have been possible but for the work of their brother George, who served as a representative of the Military Board in the capital of the Confederacy, Richmond—the board that began the process of unlawfully selling the bonds.[23]

STATE POLICE AND MILITIA

In 1870 the first Texas legislature since the imposition of congressional reconstruction agreed, after a long and contentious debate, that one approach to attacking the continued rise in violence in the state was the creation of a militia and a state police. The Committee on Lawlessness and Violence of the Constitutional Convention of 1868–69 issued two reports on violent crime, compiled from local sources (though not all violent crimes were reported). The initial report indicated that, of the 939 homicides listed, 373 were committed by whites against blacks, while 10 were committed by freedmen against whites. The second report increased the number of murders from 1865 to mid-1868 to 1,035. Yet only 279 indictments and five convictions for murder were reported during this same time frame. Indeed, the 1870 census reported 323 homicides in Texas in one year, the most of any state. Texas was part of a "staggeringly violent" Southwest.[24]

Even though the need for greater policing was evident to all Texans, the Texas State Police existed for just three years, when the thirteenth legislature repealed the 1870 act over the governor's veto. Levels of violence had not dropped significantly during that time. In just the first three months of 1873, seventy-eight murders were reported from just fifty-four counties. The number of arrests effected by the State Police during its existence was astonishing. In the first month of its existence it made 109 arrests for murder and 130 arrests for assault with intent to murder. Through 1872 the State Police had made 581 arrests for murder and another 27 arrests from January through March 1873. But although these data were significant, another datum was more significant. About 40 percent of the State Police were African Americans, and many white Texans were simply unwilling to be policed by freedmen. After the State Police were disbanded, some of its former members joined the Texas Rangers, an all-white law enforcement body.[25]

THE SEMICOLON COURT, *EX PARTE RODRIGUEZ*, AND THE END OF RECONSTRUCTION

The return of Texas to the Union portended a return to power by the Democratic Party. Elections in 1871 and 1872 indicated that it was merely a matter of time before the party controlled both the legislative and executive branches. When the thirteenth legislature opened in January 1873, Republicans held twelve seats in the Texas House, compared with fifty-five in the previous legislature. The Texas Senate had a majority (although not a veto-proof majority) of Democrats. The incumbent Republican governor of Texas, Edmund J. Davis, faced reelection in 1873. His Democratic opponent, Richard Coke, had been a member of the Texas Supreme Court when congressional reconstruction was instituted and was one of those removed from office as an impediment to Reconstruction. The race for governor led to one of the most well-known cases decided by the Texas Supreme Court, *Ex parte Rodriguez*, also known as the Semicolon Case.[26]

Before the gubernatorial election the legislature repealed the act creating the State Police, reorganized the militia, and adopted the Act Regulating Juries, which heightened juror qualifications in an initial attempt to reduce the number of possible African American jurors. The legislature also proposed three amendments to the constitution, one of which was to restructure the supreme court to consist of five judges appointed by the governor. On March 31 (as amended the next day) the legislature adopted an act regulating elections, which altered the voting place from the county seat to election precincts contiguous with the precinct of each justice of the peace. Section 12 of this act declared that all elections "shall be held for one day only." On May 26, 1873, the thirteenth legislature adopted a law providing for a general election on the first Tuesday of December 1873 (December 2) and every two years afterward. Article II, section 6 of the 1869 Reconstruction constitution stated, "All elections for State, district, and county officers shall be held at the county seats of the several counties, until otherwise provided by law; and the polls shall be opened for four days, from eight o'clock A.M. until four o'clock P.M. of each day." The constitution clearly allowed the legislature to alter by law the location of the election, such as altering polling places from the county seat to election precincts. Did it also allow the legislature to alter the length of time of polling from four days to one day?[27]

At the December 2, 1873, election, Coke defeated Davis in the gubernatorial race by a two-to-one margin. Democrats won massive victories in the house and senate, and the three amendments to the constitution were all adopted by the voters, requiring only adoption

by the incoming legislature to become part of the constitution. Then a defeated incumbent running for reelection as sheriff of Harris County, A. B. Hall, arrested Joseph Rodriguez on December 15 for allegedly voting twice in the election of December 2, a crime under an act of March 31, 1873.[28]

Because Rodriguez was arrested for the crime, he was permitted by law to seek a writ of habeas corpus from the supreme court. His lawyers requested the writ the next day, December 16, 1873. His argument that his arrest was unlawful depended on a court's concluding that the election laws were unconstitutional because they provided for an election of just one day, while the constitutional language in Article III, section 6 after the semicolon appeared to require all elections to take place over a four-day period. But though arrested, Rodriguez had not been indicted, as was required in felony cases. For those ready to oust Republicans from public office based on the election results, this case was a legal fiction, a contrivance designed to declare the election unconstitutional so Republicans could illegally maintain power. Further, because the constitutional amendment restructuring the supreme court had been approved by voters on December 2, and because incumbent supreme court justices were unlikely to retain their places if Coke became governor (because they had been appointed by the hated Republican Davis), any decision in *Rodriguez* declaring the election unconstitutional (thus eliminating the constitutional amendment restructuring the membership in the supreme court) represented a conflict of interest in the supreme court.

Presiding judge Wesley Ogden issued the writ the day it was requested, December 16, and the case was initially argued in the supreme court beginning on December 22. The court refused to dismiss the case as requested by the state, which signaled its likely conclusion. (Only if a case existed could the court declare the May 26 act unconstitutional.) It issued its decision on January 6, 1874. A unanimous court, in an opinion by Moses Walker, a Union soldier during the Civil War who came from Ohio to Texas as part of military reconstruction, held that the election law of 1873 was unconstitutional. It was unconstitutional because the language "until otherwise provided by law" applied only to the first clause of Article III, section 6. Thus, the second clause, which required the polls to remain open for "four days," could not be reduced by legislative action. If the "until otherwise" language applied to both clauses, the court mused, why was it found only at the end of the first clause and not again (or solely) at the end of the second clause? As noted by Lance Cooper in his revisionist history of the case, the creation of the semicolon itself was a mystery. The proponent of Article III, section 6 was A. J. Hamilton, one of Rodriguez's attorneys, and his version in the records of the 1868–69 constitutional convention contained a comma, not a semicolon, after "until otherwise provided by law." Cooper makes clear that the convention delegates did not insert the semicolon; it was added by one of the members of a military committee created to piece together a constitution after the convention adjourned without completing its work. Had the court checked the *Journal of the Reconstruction Convention*, it would have found a comma, not a semicolon. That *should* have made all the difference to the court. Whether it *would* have led the court to interpret Article III, section 6 differently is, of course, unknown.[29]

For once and future justice Oran Roberts; for Alexander W. Terrell, lawyer for the state arguing the constitutionality of the election law; and for others apoplectic that the court would take this case, the court's reasoning was an invalid political ploy. The vitriolic rejection of *Ex parte Rodriguez* gave rise to the epithet "Semicolon Court" to describe both this court and the case. For those who rejected Reconstruction, or who wished for a "redeemed" state cleansed of Reconstruction, the court's decision was but a glaring example of the absence of a rule of law, part of a quest for political power by northern carpetbaggers and their southern allies, the scalawags. The problem with this view was that the court's interpretation was perfectly acceptable as a constitutional matter. Although the language of Article III, section 6 was unclear, a semicolon is regularly used to separate topics. The bigger problems were that (1) the case was wholly fictitious, which the court surely knew but refused to acknowledge; (2) the members of the court had a conflict of interest in deciding the case, for to decide as they did seemed an effort to save their jobs (because the decision then implicitly negated the constitutional amendment restructuring the supreme court); (3) the Constitutional Convention of 1868–69 had ended in chaos, without a completed document or vote by members of the convention on a document, making it even more important that the court take care in interpreting it; and (4) the court lacked the power to override the will of a majority of the people as expressed in the December 1873 election, as it would soon learn.[30]

The court's decision did not prevent Coke from becoming governor or the legislature from adopting the constitutional amendment restructuring the supreme court. The legislature elected in December 1873 met in Austin in January 1874, daring Davis, whose term ended in April, to stop them. When the legislature challenged Davis to use the militia to prevent them from meeting, Davis hesitated and wrote to President Grant for assistance. Grant refused to become involved, and the legislature took the additional step of immediately inaugurating Coke, which Davis futilely protested. By January 24, 1874, the house agreed with the senate to adopt the constitutional amendments of 1873, and three days later Governor Coke appointed five new members to the court, including Oran M. Roberts as chief justice. The members of the

Oran M. Roberts, as Professor of the newly-created University of Texas law department, 1884. Reprinted by permission of the Tarlton Law Library, Jamail Center for Legal Research, University of Texas School of Law.

Semicolon Court were outcasts, and Reconstruction was firmly at an end in Texas.[31]

THE CONSTITUTION OF 1876

In addition to the changes made by the 1873 thirteenth legislature discussed above, members proposed the drafting of a new constitution to replace the 1869 Reconstruction constitution. Somewhat surprisingly, these efforts failed, as Democrats found themselves divided on issues of procedure (Should the constitution be amended by a convention of elected members or by an appointed commission of experts?) and possibly substance (What should the constitution say about pay of government officials, finances, public education, and other topics?). The Democratic-dominant fourteenth legislature agreed with Governor Coke's call for a new constitution but was divided on how a new constitution should be undertaken. The senate called for a constitutional convention,

while the house called for a commission. Coke attempted to breach the impasse by suggesting a revision of the constitution through a special joint committee of house and senate members. By mid-April that committee completed a new constitution, which, John Mauer notes, "was a liberal document tending to increase rather than decrease governmental power." This document never reached the voters, for the house delayed consideration, which killed it.[32]

The public cry for a constitutional convention increased. On March 13, 1875, the legislature adopted a joint resolution calling for vote by the people on whether to call a constitutional convention. The election, scheduled for August 1, included votes on both the delegates to the convention and whether the voter favored or opposed the call. If a majority opposed the call, the proposed amended constitution of the legislature would be submitted to the people for a ratification vote.[33]

Voters approved the call for a constitutional convention, and the ninety delegates began meeting in Austin in September 1875. Thirty-eight delegates were members of the Texas State Grange, an organization of farmers who opposed government favoritism and financial largesse toward large corporate interests, particularly railroads and banks. Another thirty-three were lawyers.[34]

The 1876 constitution differed from previous Texas constitutions as well as the U.S. Constitution both in length and particularity. The traditional American view of a constitution was stated by Chief Justice John Marshall in *McCulloch v. Maryland* (1819): "A constitution, to contain an accurate detail of all the subdivisions of which its great powers will admit, and of all the means by which they may be carried into execution, would partake of the prolixity of a legal code, and could scarcely be embraced by the human mind." The 1876 constitution, consisting of over 63,000 words, embraced the "prolixity of a legal code." Among its many provisions it continued the protection of a homestead from debt collection (Art. XVI, §§ 50–52) and instructed the legislature to protect a "certain" portion of personal property from forced sale (Art. XVI, § 49). The state was strictly limited in its fiscal expenditures and in undertaking debt, and the judicial department was restructured with an eye to creating a greater financial efficiency in the administration of justice.[35]

REFORMING THE APPELLATE COURT SYSTEM IN THE 1876 CONSTITUTION

By the time the constitutional convention met in 1875, the supreme court, consisting of five members, had a massive sixteen hundred cases pending before it. It was hopelessly behind. The solution of the constitutional convention offered the court only a slight reprieve. Article V, section 5 created a court of appeals consisting of three members. The court of appeals was given jurisdiction to hear all appeals in criminal cases (the government was forbidden to appeal in criminal cases, Art. V, § 26) and any appeals in a civil case from a county court. Ratification of the 1876 constitution thus permanently stripped the supreme court of jurisdiction in criminal appeals. This did not enable the supreme court to keep abreast of its docket.[36]

The 1876 constitution mandated an annual salary of $3,550 (Art. V, §§ 2, 5) for members of the supreme court and the court of appeals. This was less than the $4,500 salary of appellate judges in the 1866 (Art. IV, § 2) and 1869 (Art. V, § 13) constitutions. When the appellate judiciary was reorganized by constitutional amendment and implementing legislation in 1891–92, the salary of the members of the supreme court was constitutionally set at $4,000. That remained the salary until 1913, when the salaries were raised to $5,000. Thus, the salary of members of the supreme court increased nominally by $500 between 1866 and 1913.[37]

THE SALT WAR OF 1877

No one was punished; no one was tried; no one was even arrested.[38]

The unhappy story of the El Paso Salt War of 1877 offers a sense of the ways in which law was both used and understood in nineteenth-century West Texas and the different ways in which historical events are interpreted.[39]

In far West Texas, salt beds located roughly one hundred miles east of El Paso (then known as Franklin) were mined by local Mexican Americans from at least the time of the Civil War, and likely earlier. Salt from the Guadalupe Salt Lakes was available to anyone who would make the dangerous and arduous journey and undertake the labor to gather the salt for sale or use (some of the salt miners traveled directly to Mexico to sell it after filling their *carretas* (wagons), extending the time of their journey from the El Paso area). In 1866 Samuel Maverick attempted to claim ownership of the salt lakes. The survey he ordered to gain title encompassed some of the area but missed much of the salt lakes. Although Maverick's effort failed, it also acted as a wake-up call to area residents and others interested in the possible profits found in the salt. When Anglo-Texans (numbering less than one hundred of the twelve thousand or so residents in the valley) in El Paso realized Maverick had failed to secure title to much of the salt beds, several formed the Salt Ring to gain title to this unclaimed public land. In 1868 the Salt Ring resurveyed the area and filed a certificate. This claim of title to the salt lakes angered local Mexican Americans, but the certificate was later found defective, and the Salt Ring halted its efforts. In late 1869, Albert Jennings Fountain, running for state senator as part of the Radical wing of the Republican Party, needed a campaign issue. He was elected after settling on protecting the salt lakes from the depredations of the Salt Ring. After election Fountain claimed he was approached by the influential Father Antonio Borrajo, who had supported Fountain's election bid, with a proposition to share ownership of the salt lakes. Fountain rejected this offer as contrary to his campaign promise to allow anyone to gather the salt for free. A second offer by Borrajo included a third partner, an Italian immigrant named Louis Cardis. Fountain rejected that offer as well. When Fountain introduced legislation to make part of the salt lake beds property owned in trust for the area's residents, Borrajo and Cardis helped sabotage the bill. They then continued their effort to discredit Fountain, an effort joined by other Anglo residents of El Paso. The campaign was successful: Fountain was indicted on seventeen charges, including fraud and embezzlement. Cardis and another traveled to Austin to testify falsely against Fountain. Fountain was acquitted, but his Texas political career ended as Republicans were swept out of office.[40]

In 1872, the year Fountain was tried and acquitted, Charles Howard moved to El Paso. A staunch Democrat and former soldier in the Confederate Army, Howard saw part of his mission as turning El Paso from a Republican to a Democratic stronghold. His arrival, joined by internal political intrigues in El Paso, set in motion the events that led to the Salt War of 1877. If the enemy of my enemy is my friend, then Howard's enmity toward the Radical Republican Fountain drew Cardis, nominally a Conservative Republican, to Howard. Cardis spoke Spanish well and possessed a strong influence with the Mexican American population. Howard was an articulate orator in English, with an overweening confidence in his abilities and his plan for El Paso. Both were ambitious and sought a mutually profitable alliance. Their initial goal was to wrest control of local political offices from Radical Republicans in the 1872 election.[41]

This joint ticket won handily, only to have their victory taken away by the Texas secretary of state, a Radical Republican. In the 1873 elections that wholly ended Reconstruction in Texas, Cardis greatly aided the Democratic Party's victory in El Paso. Howard was elected district attorney. Within four months the incumbent Republican district judge was ousted, and Howard was named to replace him. Cardis won election to the position of state representative as a Democrat. And the two men, "alike ambitious, and alike unscrupulous," began to battle one another over control of political offices in El Paso.[42]

The relationship between Howard and Cardis soured dramatically. Howard apparently beat Cardis with a cane in 1875, and by 1876 Howard and Cardis supported opposing slates for election. Cardis was reelected state representative, but otherwise his candidates were defeated. Howard did not run for reelection as district judge, but his hand-picked successor won after Cardis's effort to stuff the ballot box failed.

On the last day of 1875 Howard married Austinite Sarah "Lou" Zimpelman. Her father, George Zimpelman, began lending money to Howard, whose business efforts, including a government contract to supply grains to Fort Davis and Fort Stockton, were financial disasters. In June 1877 Lou Howard died. During her illness Zimpelman spent a substantial amount of time in El Paso tending to her. At this time Zimpelman and Howard decided to claim title to the salt lakes, which promised great wealth. Zimpelman purchased the Maverick certificates as well as certificates from the Memphis and El Paso Railroad. If they surveyed the remaining land, they could obtain certificates of title to the entire Guadalupe Salt Lakes.[43]

Shortly after his wife's death Howard began his travels to survey the salt lakes and land near Quitman that might possess silver. His first stop was Quitman, where Howard found Cardis inspecting his stage coach station. Howard assaulted Cardis but claimed that Cardis's cowardly behavior caused him to decide not to shoot him. The surveying party later went to the salt lakes and measured three 640-acre sections of land contiguous with the Maverick lands. The survey materials were then sent to the Texas General Land Office. Before the office issued title to Zimpelman, Howard posted notices claiming the land and barring anyone from mining salt there without first obtaining Howard's permission and agreeing to transport it on his behalf for a set rate. Then Howard decided to demand the arrest of several local residents, including José María Juárez and Macedonia Gandara, after they allegedly declared publicly they would take salt from the lakes.[44]

Both Gandara and Juárez were arrested on September 29, 1877, and brought to court. Gandara claimed that he had no intention to mine salt, and the matter was dismissed at Howard's request. When no evidence was presented against Juárez, Howard stood up and said, "I guess we will have to dismiss the case against him too." Howard's tone when making this statement is described as "a scornful laugh." Juárez, who did not understand English, reacted to Howard's apparent mocking tone by reaffirming his intent to travel to the lakes. He further declared "he did not care about the law." Juárez was placed under a peace bond by the sheriff, but whether he was taken to jail is unclear. By ten o'clock that same night, a group of armed men demanded that the judge who heard the earlier matters issue a warrant for Howard's arrest. The judge, Gregorio N. García, told them to file a complaint. A little while later, García left his home to investigate noise in the plaza. Both García and his brother Porfirio, also a judge, were taken captive by the group.[45]

What the historian calls this group of armed men may signal how he or she views the El Paso Salt War. Testimony by Anglos the following year used the word *mob* to describe

the group, a word exclusively used by Walter Prescott Webb in *Texas Rangers*. C. L. Sonnichsen also used the word *mob*, but he framed the issue as one involving a claim in justice to the salt beds: "True, they had no claim which would have stood up in an American court—but they had a claim. From their point of view, they had about as much on their side as our forefathers did in resenting the Stamp Act." The revisionist history by Mary Romero notes that Chicano writers accurately called these events a "people's revolt" and names the revolutionaries a "group." A 2004 *Harvard Law Review* "Note" describes these men as "mexicano rioters," "residents," indicating the "local Mexican and Mexican-American population," and "group," but also uses "mob," sometimes within quote marks and sometimes without. The "Note" also uses "vigilante actions" in quote marks. Paul Cool's 2008 book *Salt Warriors* variously uses "armed men," "armed Paseños," "insurgents" and "insurgent force," "restive assembly," and once "mob" in quote marks. These men could be described as a body, vigilance committee, rioters, irregular posse, or even concerned citizens. A declaration that those who took Howard and others captive were a mob suggests they acted outside the law. Calling Howard's captors residents or locals portrays Howard as disturbing the customs of the area, customs that may have been a type of law. *Insurgency* is defined as a rebellion against the organized government, but Cool portrays the insurgents as a body of residents seeking justice when the law was found wanting. No matter what nomenclature is used, this body of persons eventually took Howard captive and later killed him.[46]

On Monday, October 1, Howard was taken prisoner along with his salt lake agent, John McBride, joining the García brothers. After a number of threats to kill Howard were made by members of the group, the leaders of this loosely organized body agreed to a written settlement signed by Howard. Howard would renounce any claim to the salt lakes, decline to prosecute his captors, and leave the county forever. To ensure he left permanently, the committee demanded a twelve-thousand-dollar bond that would be forfeited if he returned. Finally, Howard confessed that his demand that Gandara and Juárez be arrested and prosecuted "is unjust, improper and without cause and that the people of the county aforesaid have had just cause to raise against him." On October 4, Howard was escorted out of El Paso County, and the judges were released.

Less than a week later, Howard returned to El Paso, entered a local store, and shot and killed Louis Cardis. In Howard's view, the trouble caused him by Cardis had directly led to his recent imprisonment, making the murder self-defense. Although armed, Cardis neither fired his gun nor apparently drew his weapon. Howard again left town for New Mexico, but not until he first attempted to turn himself in to a customs inspector. On November 15, 1877, Major John Jones coaxed Howard to return to Texas. Early the next day, a complaint for murder was written out, and Jones had a justice of the peace release Howard on a bond of four thousand dollars. The case would be heard in March. Jones then returned to Austin, leaving behind a hastily gathered group of Texas Rangers who would fail in their duty to keep the peace and obey the law, shaming the reputation of the organization.

In early December, Howard returned to El Paso for the last time. He still maintained that salt was being stolen from salt beds owned by his father-in-law. Lieutenant John Tays of the Rangers agreed to escort Howard to the nearby town of San Elizario to take control of the "stolen" salt. Howard and eighteen Rangers arrived in San Elizario on the afternoon of December 12. The next day a gunfight began between insurgents and the Rangers. It continued for four days. On the fifth day Howard agreed to surrender. So did the Texas Rangers. Howard, McBride, and a quarrelsome local named

John Atkinson were executed by the mob. The captured Texas Rangers were allowed to leave without their weapons. Although there were cries for the deaths of more Anglos, the insurgency's leader, Francisco Barela, prevented further homicides.[47]

This shamed group of Texas Rangers and a sheriff's posse of violent, lawless volunteers (bad men behaving badly) from New Mexico left from El Paso to San Elizario shortly before Christmas 1877. Federal troops left for San Elizario from the other direction. On their way, some of the Rangers and the posse murdered several residents, including two men taken prisoner who were shot at close range after having "escaped," stole what they could, and destroyed much of the rest. Some of the federal soldiers later joined in looting homes in San Elizario.

No insurgent was ever tried; neither was any Ranger or sheriff's posse member. Title to much of the salt lakes was awarded to Zimpelman, although 2,240 acres were eventually determined as remaining within the state's possession. Some efforts to gather salt without paying were made, but most Paseños eventually paid.[48]

The El Paso Salt War suggests much about the use (or misuse) of the law: Howard, a former district judge, used the law to exert power. He had Gandara and Juárez arrested knowing that his demand was unlawful. Howard also knew his initial claim of ownership (as agent of Zimpelman) of the salt beds was legally indefensible. He agreed to dismiss both cases because the law was a tool to be used as a bullying tactic, to intimidate Mexican Americans into obeying not the law, but Howard himself. Similarly, Howard's assault and later murder of Cardis, the latter of which was justified by Howard as self-defense, exhibits his disdain for law in a quest for wealth. The actions of the Mexican American insurgents also reflect a selective acceptance of law. The request by its members to obtain a warrant for Howard's arrest after the Gandara/Juárez incident suggests their respect for the law, but imprisoning the two judges García after the group's demand was denied indicates both a frustration with the law and a desire to obtain vengeance even when the law forbids it. The initial capture of Howard, with the cries to kill him and others taken prisoner, is uneasily juxtaposed with the very legalistic negotiations and attempted settlement of the dispute. The demand for a "bond" payable if Howard returned to El Paso, along with the demand that Howard confess his abuse of the legal system in arresting Gandara and Juárez is very lawlike. The requirement that Howard sign the settlement is a strange combination of law (it is a contract, so it must be signed) and violence (Howard is surely coerced into signing). The later capture and execution of Howard, McBride, and Atkinson was murder, but the insistence by some of the group's leaders that no others (the Texas Rangers) be killed required some sense of order, if not law.

The El Paso County sheriff's use of lawless men to "enforce" the law provides another perspective on the use of law. The sheriff was motivated by blood-lust, and the Rangers were motivated by shame. Neither was interested in a lawful resolution to lawlessness, and if violent men used violence to quell this disturbance, so be it. The murder of the two "escaped" prisoners barely amounted to a coverup; even so, no Ranger or member of the posse was indicted. The rule of law remained an abstract and even incoherent concept for many late nineteenth-century Texans. The personification of the law, in the sheriff and his posse, Texas Rangers, and judges, as demonstrated in the Salt War, brought little solace and much fear to local residents. Mao Zedong's assertion that "political power grows out of the barrel of a gun" often proved true in late nineteenth-century Texas. In the Salt War violence replaced law.[49]

LAWLESSNESS IN LATER NINETEENTH-CENTURY TEXAS

The people, too, are not content with the slow but sure workings of the law, but must violate the law by lynch law. . . . Northern journals comment in severe terms upon us as a community of murderers and robbers, and can we with truth deny the accusation? We dare not do it, for our State press would be sufficient evidence to condemn us.[50]

Crime increased in Texas during the late nineteenth century for several commonplace reasons: law enforcement personnel were few in number and often untrained in either the prevention or investigation of crimes; young, transient men of little means and often without family envisioned the possibility of wealth in the theft of others' goods; men were willing to use violence to repel any perceived threat to their honor; many distrusted government; and the existence of a strong sense of white supremacy allowed for violent correction of "impudent" freedmen. In addition, Texas suffered from an ineffective criminal justice system, leading the *Frontier Echo* to acknowledge that citizens had resorted to lynching. From the end of the Civil War through the first two decades of the twentieth century Texans engaged in an odd dance of rejecting and embracing law, including justifying lynching by resort to claims of law. For many Texans, the end (combating violence) justified the means (engaging in violence). Lynching was also a tool of racial terror, as Anglos lynched hundreds of freedmen and Mexicans, often in the name of law and order.[51]

Murders in Texas increased steeply after the Civil War. At least 1,035 murders had been committed in the three years between the end of the Civil War and mid-1868. Yet only 279 indictments and five convictions for murder were reported. The 1870 census reported Texas had the highest number of homicides in the nation, 323. This was 195 more homicides than recorded by any other state. The number of Texans reported in the 1870 census was 818,579; just under 4.4 million people lived in New York in 1870, yet only slightly more than 100 murders were committed there.[52]

The abolition of the State Police in 1873 was followed by a "surge" in lawlessness. Author H. V. Redfield counted 401 murders reported in the *Galveston News* in 1878. He also noted reports that 148 more persons were "severely or dangerously wounded" that year. More than two dozen murders were reported in February 1880 in Texas, more than occurred annually in Massachusetts, home to 200,000 more people than Texas. Redfield declared a Texas newspaper claimed at least 800 murderers were at large in the state. Most murders were intraracial (in 1878, 269 were white-on-white murders and 27 were black-on-black murders). But when the murders were known to be interracial, the disparity in whites murdering blacks was astonishing. In 1878, fifty-three African Americans were murdered by whites, compared with six whites murdered by blacks.[53]

A study of criminal justice in Washington County between 1868 and 1884 offers evidence of a halting respect for the operation of the law when justice was sure. In December 1880 a Negro laborer named Alexander Mason killed a white shopkeeper named Ferdinand Bohnenstengel. Bohnenstengel had demanded a retraction from Mason and ejected him from his store when Mason refused. Mason stood outside the shop daring Bohnenstengel to "come after him." When the storekeeper did with a buggy whip in hand, Mason hit him with a board. Mason fled but returned after two months. A month after surrendering, Mason was tried and acquitted by a jury consisting of seven African Americans and five whites. Mason's case is remarkable in several respects: first, Mason was acquitted despite having committed the murder as a matter of honor; second, Mason was not lynched, something

that had begun to occur in a number of cases in Texas; and third, Mason was tried before an interracial jury, which occurred less often after the 1876 legislature required that jurors be literate. Donald Nieman's study of Washington County notes that Mason's case was not singular. Ten African Americans were accused of murder of a white person, but only six were tried and only three convicted. During the same time frame, four white persons were charged with murder for killing blacks. It appears that no white person was convicted of murder or manslaughter in the death of an African American. However, in cases in which a white person was accused of assault with intent to kill a black person, jurors might convict (three of five cases), but they would convict on the lesser offense of aggravated assault and impose a fine rather than sentence the defendant to imprisonment.[54]

Tangled political and race relations in Washington County led to the end of the use of law to mediate disputes. In 1886 several blacks believed the son of a Democratic Party candidate for office intended to steal a ballot box to tilt the election, and in the fracas that followed they killed him. Three men were arrested. A lynch mob took them from jail and murdered them. The Washington County lynchings, in an area that had earlier reached some accommodation of power between blacks and whites, were but a minor event in a decades-long era of terror. Lawrence Rice estimates that "between 1870 and 1900, no fewer than 500 Negroes met death by lynching or some other form of mob violence."[55]

The reasons for lynchings changed during the last decades of the nineteenth century in Texas. In 1876 the West Texas *Frontier Echo* suggested lynchings were more often a reaction to a broken or sputtering criminal justice system than a method by whites to intimidate and terrorize blacks or Mexicans. This was not the case in most of Texas. Lawlessness in the Nueces Strip in South Texas was rampant, and many Mexican Americans were lynched by Anglos. By the mid-1870s lynchings in Texas and nationwide were predominantly used as a terror tactic against blacks and, in South Texas, Mexicanos—lynchings that grew in number and brazenness in the 1880s. Efforts to harness lynchings through use of the criminal law went unavailing. A mid-1880s grand jury investigation of the lynching of an African American resulted in no indictments; in another event at about the same time, the governor's request that a sheriff gather a posse to prevent the lynching of a black man accused of murder was made too late to be effective. Lynching became the dominant mode of execution in Texas. In 1891, Governor Jim Hogg noted that twenty-seven persons were hung by law that year for their murders, while 140 Texans were lynched.[56]

The legislature adopted an antilynching law in 1897, following the lead of several other Southern states, after two notorious lynchings. In 1893, Henry Smith, a seventeen-year-old African American, was accused of raping a young white girl. Smith was captured in Arkansas and returned by rail to Texas. He was brought back to be lynched in Paris, Texas, where the alleged assault occurred. With Smith bound to a chair, the girl's father tortured Smith with a hot iron. Smith was then burned at the stake while thousands watched, a crime that made the front page of the *New York Times*. Four years later, as Robert Hillard was publicly lynched, an enterprising photographer sold pictures. Again, a large crowd gathered to watch. The Hillard lynching was the specific impetus for the legislature to adopt an antilynching law. The law punished "murder by mob violence" with death or life in prison and permanently banned from office any peace officer who allowed mob violence in his jurisdiction. Lynchings declined to a yearly average of thirty-nine for the five-year period from 1899 to 1903. This was a substantial decline from an average of seventy-one (1889–93) and seventy-

two (1894–98) lynchings each year during the two previous five-year periods. However, mob violence against African Americans remained a significant problem in 1900.[57]

The shooting of Sheriff Garrett Scott in 1900 represents the willingness of some Texans to embrace lawlessness in a quest for power. Scott was elected sheriff of Grimes County in East Texas in 1882 through a combination of white and black support as an Independent Greenbacker. After the collapse of this third party, Scott joined the People's Party (known as the Populists) and was regularly reelected. In 1899, disgruntled Democrats unable to win local elections quietly created the White Man's Union, which went public in the spring of 1900. In July a black man named Jim Kennard, the district clerk, was murdered on Main Street in Anderson, the county seat of Grimes County. His alleged killer, J. G. McDonald, had helped organize the union. The union demanded the end of "Negro rule," and in late September someone killed Jack Haynes, a black leader of the Populists. By the time of the November elections, at least one People's Party candidate had withdrawn his candidacy because of fear of violent reprisals. The number of Grimes County voters in 1900 was just 40 percent of the number two years earlier, as many Populists either left the county or refused to vote. Scott lost his reelection bid for sheriff as White Man's Union candidates won election to all local offices. The day after the election, men began arriving at the courthouse on Main Street in Anderson and went to the second floor. Emmett Scott, Garrett's brother, came to town and went to a friend's store. He was shot and killed there by a union member, who also died after being shot with his own gun by Emmett Scott as the latter was dying. Garrett Scott heard the shots. As he rushed to the store, he was shot by the men gathered at the courthouse. He lay wounded in the street until his sister dragged him to safety. The fighting at Anderson lasted five days, as Scott's family attempted to figure out a way to

Texas Rangers Frontier Battalion, late nineteenth century.
Courtesy Texas State Library and Archives Commission.

get Garrett out of town for medical attention. Finally, a company of the Texas Voluntary State Guard traveled from Houston to remove Scott. A substantial number of black residents subsequently abandoned Grimes County, and the People's Party was finished there. McDonald was never tried for Kennard's death, nor was anyone tried for the attempted murder of Garrett Scott.[58]

The Grimes County affair suggests the ineffectiveness of the criminal justice system in late nineteenth-century Texas. The arrest of violent offenders was spotty. Even if arrested, some were never indicted by the grand jury. Even when the grand jury found sufficient evidence existed to indict the defendant, many were never tried. Donald G. Nieman's Washington County study (1868–84) states that of the seventy-seven blacks indicted for murder, only fifty-six (73 percent) were tried. Only thirty-three (59 percent) were found guilty of first or second degree murder. Thirty-three whites

were indicted for murder during the same time, and just twenty (60 percent) were tried. Only seven (35 percent) were convicted. A similar story was found for those accused of assault with intent to kill. Just 73 percent (sixty-five out of ninety) of blacks and 55 percent (thirty-five of sixty-four) of whites were tried, and 40 percent (thirty-six) and 37.5 percent (twenty-four) were convicted, respectively.[59]

After conviction, an appeal to the Texas Court of Appeals (1876–91) was likely to result in a reversal of the conviction, particularly beginning in the early 1880s. An editorial in the July–August 1887 issue of the Saint Louis–based *American Law Review* excoriated that court's work. The *Review* noted that the court of appeals affirmed in 882 cases and reversed in 1,604 cases, a reversal rate of 65 percent between 1876 and 1891. The editorial actually understated the problem. The reversal rate accelerated beginning with volume 11 of the *Texas Court of Appeals Reports*, which is dated from 1881. In volumes 11–21 (1886) the court of appeals reversed four cases for every case it affirmed, an almost unbelievable ratio. Many reversals were for trivial reasons, and a defendant with an attorney of any legal ability was unlikely to spend any time in prison for a crime. For example, the court reversed for misspellings ("guity" rather than "guilty") and declared defective any indictment that did not end exactly with the words "against the peace and dignity of the State" (see chapter 7). The Texas Court of Appeals was infected by a kind of fealty to an idealized version of law that ignored the reality of trials in Texas. This legal formalism accepted a view of law as rules that were followed for their own sake, no matter their importance or the reason for their existence.[60]

THE 1891 CONSTITUTIONAL AMENDMENT OF THE JUDICIAL BRANCH AND CASE OVERLOAD

Between 1870 and 1890 the number of Texans nearly tripled to over 2.2 million. More people meant more legal business for the courts, from disputes about land and contracts to criminal prosecutions. Further, the rise of the railroad generated a tremendous increase in personal injury cases in late nineteenth-century Texas. The increased press of legal business in the district courts is shown by the rapid creation and reorganization of judicial districts. The 28th, 29th, and 30th Judicial Districts were created in 1879. By 1885, the 39th Judicial District was created by the legislature; only six years later, it created the 51st Judicial District. The increase in the number of district courts resulted in more judgments subject to appeal to the supreme court and court of appeals, quickly overwhelming them. As early as 1879 the legislature adopted a law creating the Texas Commission of Appeals. This commission consisted of three persons "learned in the law" to hear cases appealed to the supreme court if both parties agreed. Two years later, an amended

act allowed the supreme court to send cases to the commission without consent of the parties. Although the commission reduced the burden on the supreme court, the tsunami of appealed cases left it with a massive backlog. The solution of the legislature was to reorganize the judicial department by constitutional amendment.[61]

The 1891 legislature proposed amending Article V of the 1876 constitution organizing the judicial branch of government. The supreme court would remain a body of three members, and its jurisdiction would be largely limited "to questions of law arising in cases of which the Courts of Civil Appeals have appellate jurisdiction." The Texas Court of Appeals would be renamed the Texas Court of Criminal Appeals, with jurisdiction "in all criminal cases." It, too, would consist of three members. Its minor civil appellate jurisdiction would be taken over by the newly created Texas Courts of Civil Appeals, which would hear appeals in "all civil cases of which the District Courts or county Courts have original or appellate jurisdiction." The legislature was given the authority to determine whether to create two or three courts of civil appeals (each with three members) and to create as many judicial districts as warranted.[62]

The 1891 amendment was controversial. It was fairly criticized as poorly written. For example, the supreme court was given jurisdiction in any case in which a state statute was held unconstitutional by a court of civil appeals, but not if that court held the statute constitutional; the amendment failed specifically to declare what constituted a quorum in the court of civil appeals. And it was unfairly criticized as creating a judicial system that would uphold unconstitutional acts of the legislature and create different laws for different parts of the state. Voters adopted the amendment, and in April 1892 the legislature reorganized the appellate judiciary of Texas. Texas became the only state to create two appellate courts of equal stature, one concerned with civil cases and one concerned with criminal cases.[63]

The 1891 amendment was designed to reduce the clogged docket of the appellate courts. It failed to accomplish this goal in the supreme court, the newly constituted court of criminal appeals, or the several courts of civil appeals. The constitution limited each of these courts to three members, and Texas's judicial needs far exceeded the capacity of those three-person courts to decide and write opinions in all the cases appealed each year. Each court resolved this problem differently: the court of criminal appeals wrote very brief opinions, and when affirming a conviction did so summarily and often without any opinion. Even so, during the first decade of the twentieth century the court of criminal appeals reversed 59 percent of appealed cases. Between 1908 and 1917 its docket grew, and the percentage of reversals in the court of criminal appeals declined to 34 percent. The several courts of civil appeals tore through their dockets by quickly summarizing the facts and offering a limited and superficial evaluation of each appellant's claims in their written opinions. Doing so allowed those courts to issue several hundred opinions annually. From 1892 through the first decade of the twentieth century, the members of the Texas Supreme Court tried to keep abreast of the docket by rarely writing concurring or dissenting opinions. From 1900 to 1910, the supreme court issued slightly fewer than 120 opinions per year. The membership of the Texas Supreme Court from 1892 through 1910 was extraordinarily stable; only four persons sat on the three-member court. This familiarity among its members allowed the supreme court to act more efficiently, but it was slowly drowning in a mass of cases generated by a tremendous increase in population. Texas's population rose to over 3 million in 1900 and nearly 3.9 million in 1910, and the legislature helped sabotage the court by creating additional courts of civil appeals, which generated more cases for the supreme court to hear. The number of courts of civil appeals grew from the original three in 1892 to eight in 1911.[64]

By 1911 the Texas Bar Association, looking at the data provided by the supreme court, concluded that the court was "about one year behind in its work." At the same time, the issue of prohibition began to dominate all Texas political races, including races for the supreme court. Membership in the supreme court changed regularly between 1911 and 1920, in part a result of the politics of prohibition. These changes led the court to fall further behind. By July 1914, Chief Justice Thomas Jefferson Brown admitted the court was at least three years behind in its work. In the 1917 term (October 1917–June 1918), the court issued only twenty-nine opinions as tensions among the judges increased. The court was now five years behind in its work. As the court's productivity waned, the legislature vainly attempted to find a remedy.[65]

In 1915 the legislature sent to the voters an amendment to the constitution increasing membership in the supreme court from three to five. The amendment failed. The 1917 legislature created the Committee of Judges, a body of judges selected from the courts of civil appeals, to determine whether a request by a party for supreme court review should be granted. A year later, the same legislature, in a special session, revived the commission of appeals, this time consisting of six members divided into two panels, prosaically named Section A and Section B. The commission of appeals remained in existence until the supreme court was expanded to nine members by constitutional amendment in 1945.[66]

The crisis in the supreme court ended not only because the commission of appeals decided a large number of pending cases in a short period of time, but because the court found stability again as a result of the 1920 elections. The loss in the primary of William E. Hawkins, the court's main impediment to clearing its docket, and the arrival of three justices who remained on the court together for thirteen years depoliticized the court, allowing it to perform its job more efficiently. The court would, however, suffer from a crowded docket through much of the twentieth century, as the spare resources given the judicial system made it nearly impossible for courts to keep up (see chapter 6).

THE TEXAS RAILROAD COMMISSION

The economic power of the railroads and the schemes of robber barons Jay Gould and Collis Huntington, who controlled most Texas railroads by the early 1880s, led farmers and others to demand more regulation of railroads. They were unhappy with price discrimination in the transportation of different goods, the power of railroads in the legislature (created in part by the granting of "passes" allowing legislators to ride the rails for free), and pooling arrangements among railroads that eliminated price competition. Railroads successfully fought off efforts in 1881 to create a railroad regulatory agency, but that was just the first skirmish. As attorney general from 1887 to 1891, James Hogg made a name for himself by using his position to litigate the schemes of the railroads to agree on rates and engage in other anticompetitive practices. Efforts to regulate railroads were bolstered by similar national efforts. In 1887 the U.S. Congress, led by House Commerce Committee chairman John H. Reagan of Texas, adopted a law creating the Interstate Commerce Commission (ICC) with the power to regulate railroads engaged in interstate commerce. In the 1889 Texas legislative session, after the two houses at first disagreed on whether to create a railroad commission to regulate railroads, they at last agreed on a joint resolution to propose a constitutional amendment to allow the creation of such a commission. Thomas Jefferson Brown, then in the legislature, where he had proposed the commission bill, wrote a series of newspaper articles explaining why voters should support the amendment. Most critically, Brown argued,

railroad commissions in other states had effectively set reasonable rates, providing a sufficient reason to support the amendment. (Brown became a member of the Supreme Court of Texas in 1893, where he remained until his death in 1915.)[67]

The 1890 race for governor was dominated by the positions of the contenders on the amendment. Hogg's support helped him win the Democratic Party nomination, and he won easily in November. The proposed amendment was approved by over 70 percent of the voters, and the Texas Railroad Commission was created at the next legislative session.[68]

One of the Railroad Commission's first actions was to issue an order setting rates that different railroads could charge for the transportation of goods. Several railroads sued, claiming that the Railroad Commission's action was unconstitutional. The plaintiffs claimed that the commission's decision to set by maximum rates took the company's property in violation of the due process clause of the Fourteenth Amendment. A federal district court issued an injunction barring the commission from enforcing its order. The case was then heard by the Supreme Court of the United States. It held that Texas possessed the constitutional authority to prescribe the rates charged by railroads through a railroad commission. However, the Court also held that Texas could not take a railroad's property, which it defined to include some profit. Consequently, the Railroad Commission was permitted to set rates as authorized by law, but the injunction remained with respect to enforcing on the railroads the rates initially set by the commission. The Supreme Court's decision in *Farmers' Loan & Trust v. Reagan* (1894) is one of the earliest examples in which the Court accepted the doctrine of substantive due process, a belief that the due process clause was not limited to matters of process, but contained a substantive element. The Texas Railroad Commission could continue to set rates, but its decisions were subject to judicial oversight, limiting its authority.[69]

The commission's power was sharply curtailed by the Supreme Court twenty years later. In the *Shreveport Rate Cases* (1914) the issue was whether the ICC possessed the authority to regulate intrastate railroad rates as part of its authority to regulate interstate rates. Transportation rates within Texas and between Texas and Louisiana varied sharply: "The first-class rate from Houston to Lufkin, Texas, 118.2 miles, was 50 cents per 100 pounds, while the rate from Shreveport to the same point, 112.5 miles, was 69 cents. The rate on wagons from Dallas to Marshall, Texas, 147.7 miles was 36.8 cents, and from Shreveport to Marshall, 42 miles, 56 cents." The ICC found that the interstate shipment rate was a reasonable rate, and ordered the railroads to abide by that rate when shipping goods wholly within Texas. The ICC's regulation of *intrastate* rates was challenged as unconstitutional because it was claimed the ICC acted beyond its authority to regulate *interstate* commerce. The Court upheld the order, concluding that Congress may "prevent the common instrumentalities of interstate and intrastate commercial intercourse from being used in their intrastate operations to the injury of interstate commerce." Although the ICC lacked the authority directly to regulate intrastate commerce, it could regulate indirectly those rates to protect interstate commerce. This left little for the Texas Railroad Commission to regulate in the railroad transportation business. By 1920, however, the commission had begun another chapter in its regulatory history when it was given the authority to regulate the oil and gas industry.[70]

THE RISE OF JIM CROW

Laws segregating Texans on the basis of race existed since the Texas Revolution. After the Texas Black Code was eliminated by congressional reconstruction, the constitution of 1869, and implementing legislation, laws officially segregating whites and blacks, known as Jim Crow laws, were not adopted by Texas until 1889. Segregation as a matter of custom, sometimes enforced by violence, continued without the sanction of law and occasionally in the face of contrary law during those two decades. For example, an 1866 law mandating segregated passenger seating on railroad cars was repealed by legislation in 1871. The 1871 law also made punishable by a fine any effort by a person to enforce segregation in railroad passenger cars. Yet Texans remained largely segregated in railroad cars as a matter of custom, and no actions appear to have been taken to enforce the law that barred segregated seating in railroad transportation. Many whites believed no freedman was his social equal. Consequently, law or no law, segregation in railroad car seating was a customary norm that was disobeyed at the peril of the freedman. Many freedmen believed that even if social equality was not possible, equality in terms of civil and political rights should be actively sought. Jury service was a highly prized civil right. Interracial juries existed in Washington County from the late 1860s through the early 1880s. That the racial composition of juries often mirrored the race of the parties in intraracial disputes (black victim and black defendant often meant black jury and white victim and white defendant meant white jury) was of less concern to the freedmen than formally protecting the right to serve on juries.[71]

Those freedmen who attempted to alter customary segregation in social settings found the task daunting. The federal Civil Rights Act of 1875 attempted to protect social rights by granting to all persons "the full and equal enjoyment of the accommodations, advantages, facilities, and privileges of inns, public conveyances on land or water, theaters, and other places of public amusement." Before the Supreme Court of the United States held the act unconstitutional in the Civil Rights Cases (1883), some African Americans in Texas entered "white" bars and other places of public accommodation pursuant to the act. They were nearly always given a hostile reception. Blacks who sued, claiming discrimination in violation of the Civil Rights Act, rarely succeeded. The United States alleged that Milly Anderson, a black woman, was denied admission to a passenger car reserved for women because she was of African descent. The government prosecuted three officers as well as an employee of the Houston & Texas Central Railway Company with violating the 1875 Civil Rights Act. In charging the jury, the federal district court judge declared that if Anderson was denied a seat in the only passenger car for females because of her race, the defendants should be found guilty, but "if the jury believe from the evidence that there were two cars on this occasion, and that they were equally used and appropriated for the carriage of ladies and gentlemen who had first-class tickets, without distinction of race or color, and that they afforded the same advantages, comforts, conveniences, and enjoyments," then the defendants should be found not guilty.[72]

The movement toward official acknowledgment of segregation gained momentum in the 1880s, particularly after the Civil Rights Act of 1875 was declared unconstitutional. Several Texas cities adopted ordinances creating separate waiting areas for black and white railroad passengers during the decade. The state legislature then moved to make segregation on the basis of race a matter of law, not merely custom. Texas's first Jim Crow law, adopted in 1889, concerned racial segregation in railroad passenger cars. Unlike the 1866 law, this law did not mandate segregated seating in passenger cars, but merely "authorized and empowered" railroads to do so. Two years later the legislature required railroads to provide separate coaches and threatened railroads with a fine of between one hundred and one thousand dollars for every trip made without segregated passenger cars. In both instances, and in the case of an amendment to this later act during

the same session, Governor Jim Hogg allowed the bill to become law without his signature, although he encouraged the legislature to adopt such a law.[73]

The separate coach law was indirectly challenged in *Pullman Palace-Car Co. v. Cain* (1897). Thomas Cain, a Methodist church bishop, was traveling from Saint Louis to Galveston on a first-class ticket. In addition, Cain purchased a berth in a Pullman sleeping car. When the train reached Texas, he was removed from the sleeping car and placed "in a separate apartment set apart for negroes under the separate coach law of this state." For his trouble Cain was given a two-dollar rebate, which he accepted under protest. He sued both the Pullman Company, which owned the sleeping car, and the International & Great Northern Railway Company, from which he purchased his initial ticket. Pullman claimed it was not liable because the railroad controlled all events on the train. The Galveston jury found in his favor and awarded him one hundred dollars in damages from both defendants. A divided court of civil appeals affirmed the judgment, concluding that Cain "did not contract for anything that was unlawful." Cain "did not contract that he should be carried in the same car with white people," but assumed that upon reaching Texas, he would be placed in a similar coach separate from white passengers. The decision in *Cain* was issued by the court of civil appeals eleven months after the Supreme Court of the United States upheld the doctrine of "separate but equal" in *Plessy v. Ferguson* (1896). *Cain* followed that doctrine but upheld the judgment in Cain's favor because no separate coach had been made available to him. The reasoning in *Cain* offered a small opening to those attacking Jim Crow: make separate but equal so expensive that railroads would demand a change in the law. It was not economically efficient for a railroad or Pullman to offer two separate Pullman sleeping cars, and a legally enforceable insistence on this point would have led either to

Francis Lubbock, John H. Reagan, A. W. Terrell, and James Hogg, circa 1890s. Courtesy Texas State Library and Archives Commission.

economic ruin for the railroads or a demand to abolish separate but equal. This approach was eventually taken in the 1930s when the National Association for the Advancement of Colored People (NAACP) sued to enforce the "equal" aspect of "separate but equal." But *Cain* was never cited by another Texas court; it was an outlier, a decision whose significance was its insignificance.[74]

In 1907 the legislature adopted laws expanding the separate coaches law to streetcar and interurban railways, and in 1909 it adopted a statewide law mandating separate depots for black and white train passengers. The Texas streetcar law followed laws passed by other southern states, beginning with Louisiana in

1902, and merely applied statewide what many cities had already created locally. By the time of the 1907 act, only Galveston among the major cities in Texas lacked an ordinance requiring separate seating by race on streetcars. Local ordinances were met with resistance by blacks in Houston and San Antonio, where boycotts of the streetcars followed their adoption. The Houston boycott lasted at least eight months, and the one in San Antonio at least three. But with Jim Crow becoming more powerful during the first decade of the twentieth century, the legislature found every reason to make rigid the segregation of the races in public transportation.[75]

The state's criminal prohibition against

marriage between two persons of different races (which meant marriage between persons who were defined as white and black) was first adopted in 1837. It was readopted in 1854 and was part of Texas's Black Code of 1866. In *Frasher v. State* (1877), the newly formed court of appeals held that a criminal prosecution of Frasher, a white man, for marrying a woman of mixed race violated neither the Fourteenth Amendment nor the Civil Rights Act of 1875. The court nevertheless reversed Charles Frasher's conviction on the ground that the judge misled the jury by instructing it that "[t]he allegation that the defendant married a negro is not sustained by evidence that he married a person of mixed blood, unless it is shown that she comes within the class designated in the law as negroes." How this instruction was misleading was left wholly unclear by the court of appeals. Under Texas law, a "Negro" was defined as a person with one-eighth "African blood." Frasher's wife, Lettuce Bell, was of mixed race. To convict Frasher, the jury had to determine whether Lettuce Bell was a person of at least one-eighth "African blood." The trial court's instruction to the jury favored Frasher, for the court instructed the jury it could not convict Frasher without first determining whether Lettuce Bell was a Negro. Even though Frasher's conviction was reversed, the appellate court reaffirmed the law prohibiting interracial marriages. *Frasher* thus encouraged other prosecutions of white men for marrying black women (only whites were subject to prosecution before 1879).[76]

Emile François married an African American woman. He was prosecuted by the state. After his conviction in 1879, François requested Judge Thomas Howard Duval, the federal district judge for the Western District of Texas, grant him a writ of habeas corpus based on the same arguments made by Frasher. In 1877, Judge Duval had issued a writ in a similar unpublished case (*Ex parte Brown*) concluding that the Texas miscegenation law was no longer valid since the end of slavery. The opinion of the court of appeals in *Frasher* caused him to change his mind: "That the law in question is unwise and unjust—that it is repugnant to the spirit of the constitution, and of the civil rights bill, both of which contemplate the equality of all persons before the law, and the equal protection of the law to all—I have no doubt. At the same time, I am not satisfied that it violates the letter of either." The law was unjust not because Duval accepted interracial marriages, but because it discriminated against whites. Duval found such marriages "unnatural," with whites "mainly to blame" for their existence due to their "influence" over the former slaves. When François appealed his conviction to the Texas Court of Appeals, he argued that the law violated his rights under the Texas constitution. The court rejected his contention and affirmed his conviction. In 1884, François was pardoned by the governor after serving much of his five-year sentence.[77]

Prosecutions continued. Katie Bell was alleged to be a white woman who married a black man. Both were indicted. Her husband was tried and acquitted. At her trial, Bell offered evidence of his acquittal, which the trial court rejected. She was convicted and sentenced to two years in prison. The newly created Texas Court of Criminal Appeals held that the trial court did not err in barring evidence of her husband's acquittal or in admitting evidence that she testified she was white in a civil case and that her first husband was a white man who served in the Confederate Army. (Evidence that the first husband served in the Confederate Army was harmless error because Bell received the minimum sentence.) Marriage between a black person and a white person remained unlawful in Texas until the Supreme Court of the United States in *Loving v. Virginia* (1967) held miscegenation laws unconstitutional.[78]

A miscegenation law only prohibited marriage between whites and blacks; it did not criminalize sexual relations between persons of different races. In 1909, Fort Worth adopted an ordinance making it a misdemeanor for an interracial couple to engage in sexual relations. Minnie Strauss, an African American, was charged with and convicted of having sexual intercourse with a white man, W. A. Randall. (Randall testified on her behalf at trial.) She could not be tried under state law because it did not prohibit "simple" acts of sexual intercourse outside of marriage; only "habitual" acts of sexual intercourse between unmarried persons constituted a crime. Strauss made several sophisticated arguments on appeal, claiming not only that the ordinance interfered with state law, an act beyond the city's authority, but that it also violated the Texas and American constitutions by creating a crime based solely on the color of one's skin. The court of criminal appeals was divided, with each of the three judges writing a separate opinion. Presiding Judge Albert Prendergast rejected each legal claim, in particular rejecting the claim that the law was unconstitutionally predicated on the color of the parties: "Our laws have all the time recognized, and legislated upon, the difference between negroes and whites." But he reversed the conviction for evidentiary reasons. During the direct examination of Randall, Strauss's lawyer asked Randall why he was putting on his pants when the officers of the law entered the room. The prosecution objected, and the trial court sustained the objection. Prendergast declared that the trial court erred in barring the answer, which would have been that the parties intended to have sexual intercourse but had not yet done so when they were interrupted. Judge Alfred Harper would have affirmed the conviction. Judge William Davidson, concurring in the result, concluded that the Fort Worth law was unconstitutional because municipalities had no authority to adopt criminal laws.[79]

From the late 1880s and through the late 1890s local Democratic Party officials created in several counties the "white primary," which excluded blacks from voting. In 1902 the Texas legislature sent to the voters a proposed amendment to the constitution allowing the state to adopt a poll tax of $1.50, which was used to keep the poor, and poor minorities in particular, from voting. It passed, 200,650 to 107,748. The next year, Alexander W. Terrell, the proponent of the poll tax and a prominent Texas lawyer-legislator, proposed effectively requiring the Democratic Party to hold a primary. A primary law was adopted on April 1, 1903. (An amended election statute was adopted in 1905, and both were known as the Terrell Election Laws.) A month later the legislature adopted a law amending the qualifications of jurors, which required (unless excused) all prospective jurors to have paid their poll taxes. In 1900 the Supreme Court of the United States reversed the conviction of Texan Seth Carter, a black man convicted of murder, because blacks were unconstitutionally excluded from his jury. But by the end of the decade, the Supreme Court had affirmed convictions from Texas in two other very similar cases, and Texas counties began systematically to exclude African Americans from grand juries and trial juries.[80]

Public education was segregated by race in 1893, a law modified and reenacted in 1905. In 1907, interracial adoptions were prohibited, and places of public accommodation were permitted to "refuse admission to objectionable characters," a thinly disguised nod to discrimination. The 1909 legislature came near to closing the circle by mandating that white males under age sixteen be sent to the State Institution for the Training of Juveniles and "kept, worked and educated entirely separate from the inmates of other races, and shall be kept apart in all respects."[81]

The lynching of Jesse Washington on May 15, 1916, in Waco may suggest the struggle in Texas to accept the workings of the criminal justice system and the depth to which race relations had fallen. Washington, a seventeen-year-old Negro farmhand, was charged with the May 8, 1916, murder of a white woman, Lucy Fryer. After giving several inconsistent statements, Washington confessed to murdering Fryer, and the murder weapon was found where Washington told them it would be. Washington was indicted on May 11. The district court appointed several young, inexperienced attorneys to represent him at trial, which began on Monday, May 15. Washington pled guilty. At the sentencing phase, the defense attorney asked one question on cross-examination and called only Washington to the stand. The attorney's question showed little effort and had no effect. The jury was out for four minutes before deciding Washington should hang for his offense. Spectators then rushed toward Washington and dragged him from the courthouse. Washington was beaten and hanged from a tree in the center of town before he was burned alive. A large crowd watched and then ghoulishly sought mementos of the lynching, including parts of Washington's body. A photographer had sufficient time before the lynching occurred to set up his camera in order to take photos he would later sell. The mayor and chief of police watched the lynching from the mayor's office. No one was charged with murder by mob violence in what became known as the Waco Horror.[82]

SPINDLETOP

The discovery of oil at Spindletop on January 10, 1901, was the initial catalyst transforming Texas from a rural, agrarian society dominated by cotton farming and cattle ranching to an urban society dominated, at times, by the energy industry. Although the number of manufacturing concerns had grown by 400 percent between 1880 and 1900, the Texas economy depended on the cotton trade and, to a lesser extent, stock raising (mostly cattle) at the turn of the century and through the first several decades of the twentieth century. Spindletop slowly changed all that. In the first nine days after erupting, Spindletop produced eight hundred thousand barrels of oil, the largest amount of oil then found. The result was a free-for-all, with speculators and landowners drilling wells

as fast as they could. That frenzy, combined with fraud, gave rise to the name "Swindletop." This frenzy existed in part because Texas had adopted the common law rule of capture applicable to oil found at Spindletop and elsewhere: what oil you captured was yours, and what your neighbor captured was his (see chapter 3). Hustling for oil was everywhere, and those who had the most moxie and power made handsome profits.[83]

The discovery of oil at Spindletop did not immediately launch the legislature into action. A 1905 law made any person liable if he caused water to escape and damage an already existing oil well, enforceable by a fine of up to five thousand dollars through a lawsuit filed in district court. The legislature noted that "the rich oil and gas fields in the State of Texas . . . are capable of supplying to the people of Texas for many years a long felt want for cheap fuel." The "long felt want" for cheap fuel drove the nation's oil industry for decades. Despite its concern, the legislature did not legislate against "waste" for some time. In 1913 the legislature allowed a suit to be filed to restrain the waste of natural gas, but it was not until 1919 that Texas began more serious regulatory efforts. The thirty-sixth legislature banned the production of oil and gas in a manner that constituted waste, defined the term, and gave to the Texas Railroad Commission the authority "to make and enforce rules and regulations for the conservation of oil and gas." During the 1920s, and particular with the discovery of oil in East Texas in 1930, additional oil finds made Texas the preeminent oil and gas state in the nation.[84]

THE CONTINUING CALL FOR PROHIBITION

The 1876 constitution required the legislature to "enact a law whereby the qualified voters of any county, justice's precinct, town or city, by a majority vote, from time to time, may determine whether the sale of intoxicating liquors

Prohibition rally in Nacogdoches, Texas, 1904. Courtesy Dolph Briscoe Center for American History, University of Texas at Austin (di 06790).

shall be prohibited within the prescribed limits" (Art. XVI, § 20). The legislature did so that year. For many prohibitionists ("drys" or "pros"), banning the consumption of alcohol was a moral crusade, and local-option elections making the state a patchwork of dry and "wet" jurisdictions was insufficient. By the early 1880s the movement for a statewide ban on alcohol was in full swing. The legislature debated in 1881 whether to place before voters a prohibition amendment to the constitution. In doing so, Texas reflected the second national prohibition movement in the United States, which peaked by the end of the 1880s. In 1887 the twentieth legislature finally sent an amendment to the voters, which was rejected. Prohibitionists immediately claimed their opponents ("antis" or "wets") "had imported Mexicans, Negroes, and Indians from outside the state" to vote against prohibition, had stuffed the ballot box, and even had used "Negro women" disguised as men to vote (women lacked the right to vote).[85]

The defeat of the prohibition amendment in Texas foreshadowed the end of this second movement nationwide. But a third and nationally successful prohibition movement began again shortly after the turn of the century. Texas again followed this national trend. In 1903 the Texas Local Option Association was formed, and a second prohibitionist body, the Anti-Saloon League, entered Texas in 1907. They were opposed by the Texas Brewers Association and the Retail Dealers Association. In 1908 prohibitionists revived the campaign for a vote to amend the Texas constitution to permit statewide prohibition. A slight majority (145,130 to 141,441) of Democratic primary voters that year urged the legislature to place the issue before the voters. The legislature avoided the issue during its 1909 and 1910 legislative sessions. In 1911 the legislature acquiesced after a larger majority of Democratic Party primary voters had urged such an amendment the year before. A statewide prohibition amendment was placed on the July 1911 ballot. This generated the then-largest turnout in Texas election history. The amendment failed by a vote of 237,393 to 231,096. Once again, prohibitionists made a race-based claim for the amendment's failure. Drys claimed that the liquor interests had unlawfully paid the poll taxes of minority voters who then voted wet. They were also convinced that corporate liquor interests had unlawfully spent money to influence the election, a claim that subsequent investigation found true.[86]

The failure of pros to obtain statewide prohibition in 1911 significantly affected the Texas Supreme Court. The 1910 gubernatorial election was a race among four Democratic candidates, two pros and two antis. One of the antis, Oscar Colquitt, was elected. In short succession, resignations from the court by two members gave Colquitt the opportunity to appoint a majority of the court, persons the pros believed were opposed to prohibition. That the court had little to do with prohibition was inconsequential. Prohibitionists quickly lined up to challenge Colquitt's supreme court appointees in the 1912 Democratic Party primary. One of the challengers, William E. Hawkins, defeated one incumbent. The other incumbent, Nelson Phillips, managed to survive despite winning only 30 percent of the popular vote. His four opponents, all prohibitionists, split the remainder of the vote, and because the election law did not require that any candidate obtain a majority, Phillips won.[87]

Prohibitionists in Texas finally succeeded in 1918. The legislature passed laws limiting the manufacture of alcohol and ratified the Eighteenth Amendment creating national prohibition.[88]

GREGORIO CORTEZ,
THE TEXAS RANGERS,
AND THE BANDIT WAR OF 1915

The Mexican Revolution beginning in 1910 unsettled and destabilized a border area already in transition after an influx of Anglos during the previous two decades. The revolution further strained the uneasy relationship between the Texas Rangers and Mexican American residents along the border. Even before the revolution, Rangers had shot and killed several border-area residents either in claimed self-

defense or while the Mexican American was trying to "escape." The revolution unleashed a lawlessness on the border that was both exacerbated and finally quelled by the extralegal violence committed by Rangers upon both bandits and innocent residents of the area. The Bandit War stained the reputation of the Rangers.[89]

On June 12, 1901, Gregorio Cortez and his brother Romaldo were questioned by the Karnes County sheriff about a stolen horse. Cortez spoke Spanish and the sheriff English. The inability of the translator to interpret correctly or fully the statements made by the Cortez brothers led the sheriff to conclude they were involved in horse theft (and they may have been, but their answers did not disclose guilt), a serious crime. Sheriff Brack Morris pulled his gun and shot Romaldo. Gregorio then fatally shot Morris and fled to a friend's home on land owned by a man named Henry Schnabel. When Gonzales County sheriff Richard Glover learned Cortez's location, he and a posse went there on the evening of June 14 either to arrest or to kill Cortez, and a gun battle erupted. Cortez shot and killed Glover, and Schnabel was shot from close range by one of the members of the posse. The aftermath was a manhunt that enveloped innocent Mexican American residents of Gonzales County. During the next eight days "one of the most intensive manhunts in the history of Texas" occurred. Nine Mexican Americans were killed, three were wounded, and seven others were arrested by those searching for Cortez. Cortez was finally captured near Laredo. He became a folk hero in South Texas, and money was raised for his defense.[90]

The trial for the Gonzales County killings took place in late July, and Cortez was found guilty of second degree murder (one juror held out against eleven ready to convict of first degree murder) and sentenced to a long prison term. Cortez was tried shortly thereafter for the killing of Morris. This time he was convicted

Texas Rangers posing on horseback for a photo, upon which is written, "Mexican Bandits Killed at North [?]." Courtesy Texas State Library and Archives Commission.

of first degree murder and sentenced to death. Cortez appealed both convictions, and in decisions released in January and June 1902 the Texas Court of Criminal Appeals reversed. In the Gonzales County case, the court of criminal appeals held the trial court should have continued the case to allow a defense witness time to appear to testify; it also held it was error to allow a prisoner to testify that he heard Cortez's confession when he could not state what Cortez had said in Spanish. The court reversed Cortez's conviction for Morris's death because he could not receive a fair trial in Karnes County due to the prejudice of its residents. It required the trial be moved. A lynch mob unsuccessfully tried to murder Cortez during that time. Cortez was not retried in Schnabel's death. In the second trial for Morris's death, the jury could not agree on a verdict. In the third trial, the jury found Cortez not guilty. In between the first and second trials for the death of Gonzales County sheriff Glover, Cortez was tried and found guilty of horse theft, a conviction the court of criminal appeals also reversed. At the second trial for the murder of Glover, Cortez was convicted of first degree murder and sentenced to life in prison. The court of criminal appeals affirmed this conviction. Cortez's law-

yer, R. A. Abernethy (also spelled Abernathy), zealously and effectively represented his client at both the trials and appeals. Cortez was conditionally pardoned in 1913. He fought briefly in the Mexican Revolution and died in Texas in 1916 of natural causes.[91]

The Bandit War of 1915 was a response by some Mexicanos to long-standing political, social, and economic subordination in South Texas, a social protest that resorted to violence. For others, material gain and revenge were reasons for the war. Revenge was a response to violence committed by law enforcement or Anglos against Mexicano families. Criminal activity had been on the rise from the beginning of the year. In late June, however, events turned more violent. Carlos Esparza, the Cameron County sheriff, was murdered by bandits crossing over from Mexico. As noted by Rodolfo Rocha, eight separate incidents of violence took place in July in the Rio Grande Valley, including murder, kidnapping, and assault. Both Anglos and Mexicanos were killed in July by bandits. Over two dozen incidents occurred in August, including several gun battles with local law enforcement officers and federal soldiers. Sporadic conflicts occurred through mid-November. Murders by Mexicano bandits were reciprocated by Texas Rangers, and the cycle of violence became more vicious as vengeance and cruelty on both sides intensified. As noted by Rocha, "[E]very Latin became a suspect, either as a raider or sympathizer [and] law officers offered no quarter to either." At least 20 percent of the 222 Mexicanos killed during the Bandit War were lynched, and the Texas Rangers were accountable for a significant number of those lynchings. The justification for killing alleged bandits was, according to Texas Ranger captain Henry Ransom, because "very few Mexicans had been convicted of crimes in the County." That these victims may have had nothing to do with the bandit raids was unimportant to Ransom. In one instance, even though it was clear the actual criminals had long since skipped back to Mexico, Ransom rounded up four "suspects," took them into the woods, and killed them. He also wanted custody of two "suspects" captured by the local sheriff, W. T. Vann. Vann refused and took the two men into custody despite Ransom's insistence on shooting them. Vann later determined the two men were innocent and released them from jail. In the opinion of Texas Rangers historian Robert Utley, "[t]he 'bandit war' of 1915 tainted the Ranger image more blackly than any episode in their history."[92]

Of the thirty men indicted for crimes during the bandit war, twelve were arrested and tried. Five were convicted, one of whom had his conviction overturned by the court of criminal appeals. Thousands of Mexican Americans left the Rio Grande Valley for Mexico, fearful of the Texas Rangers who violated their oath to uphold the law.[93]

WOMEN AND SUFFRAGE

In the debates at the constitutional conventions that produced the 1869 and 1876 Texas constitutions, very modest efforts were made to consider allowing women to vote, efforts that quickly failed. The Fifteenth Amendment to the U.S. Constitution granted "citizens" the right to vote, yet despite that language the Supreme Court in *Minor v. Happersett* (1875) held that the amendment was intended to grant the right to vote only to male "citizens," based on a nearly uniform historical and contemporary consensus among the states denying women the right to vote.[94]

Nearly two decades later, after a few western states granted women the right to vote in state elections, the Texas Equal Rights Association was formed to advocate for the right of women to vote. The association lasted from 1893 to 1896. A second suffrage organization, called the Texas Woman Suffrage Association, was formed in 1903, and, like its predecessor, it existed for just a short time, but a revived association met in 1913, and its members gathered through the remainder of the decade. Its name was changed in 1916 to the Texas Equal Suffrage Association. Another women's suffrage organization, a branch of the National Woman's Party, was created in Texas in 1916. The movement to give women the right to vote in Texas was gaining momentum.

A proposal to allow women the right to vote in Texas passed the house but not the senate in the 1915 legislative session. At the next legislative session, a constitutional amendment allowing women to vote was introduced, but it failed to obtain the necessary two-thirds majority in the house. The next step taken by suffragists was ingenious. Texas was a one-party state, making the general election less important than the primary election. Giving women the right to vote in a primary was within the authority of a simple majority of the legislature. Suffragists urged adoption of such a law. Governor William Hobby called a special session in spring 1918 to work on amending election laws as well as adopting prohibition legislation. At its fourth called session the legislature granted women the right to vote in all primaries and nominating conventions. The act also exempted women from paying the poll tax. Women were thus eligible to vote in the July 1918 primary. Not surprisingly, they supported their supporter, Hobby, in the Democratic primary race for governor.[95]

Before the primary election one tax collector refused to issue a poll tax receipt to Alma Koy, preventing her from voting. Koy sued, and the district court held the suffrage law unconstitutional. As this case was appealed, the successful introduction of women into the voting booth led the legislature in 1919 to propose amending the constitution to allow women who were citizens (the vote was concomitantly taken from aliens) the right to vote in all elections. Despite unanimous support for this measure in the legislature, the amendment was disapproved of by a majority of (male) voters in the May 1919 election. The next month the federal suffrage amendment was sent to the states for ratification. Before the end of June, this amendment was ratified in Texas, the first southern state to do so. In January 1920 a divided Texas Supreme Court, relying in great part on decisions in other states and on the proposition that judicial review should be sparingly exercised, in *Koy v. Schneider* held that the 1918 act was constitutional. By the end of 1920 the Nineteenth Amendment, granting women the right to vote in all federal and state elections, had become part of the U.S. Constitution.[96]

CONCLUSION

Much of Texas in 1920 echoed the state of Texas in 1866. Texas remained a predominantly rural state in 1920, although the energy industry was poised to transform its economy in the next two decades. Morals legislation had become a more prominent feature of Texas law by 1920, but the difference was largely one of degree, not kind. This emphasis, from prohibition to restrictions on bawdy houses and brothels to initial efforts to control the use of narcotics such as cocaine (first outlawed in 1905), was the beginning of a concerted effort

in the twentieth century to regulate human behavior through law. Mob violence by 1920 had dissipated, though the last public lynching in Texas was not until 1942. A resurgence of the Ku Klux Klan in the 1920s nationally and in Texas reinforced Jim Crow, the legally enforced system subordinating African Americans. The worst features of the criminal justice system had been cured, although procedural fairness in criminal trials was often lacking, in part because of a policy of excluding blacks from most juries and winnowing Mexican Americans from juries in parts of South Texas between 1900 and 1920. In 1919 a joint committee of the Texas legislature investigated the conduct of the Texas Rangers in South Texas. The investigation found, according to the *Dallas Morning News*, "evidence of a shocking and intolerable condition," but legislation reorganizing the Rangers that year was largely bereft of reform. The Rangers were finally restructured in 1935. The appellate courts by 1920 had matured in part, though all of them still suffered from an onslaught of cases.[97]

The Longview riot of 1919, during what became known as Red Summer in the United States (for all the blood spilled during the riots against African Americans by whites), was evidence that the issue of race and racism remained a central aspect of early twentieth-century Texas. Lemuel Walters was arrested after he was allegedly found in the bedroom of a white woman in Longview, or after he allegedly propositioned the woman, depending on which set of facts one accepts. In one view he was then taken from jail by masked men, who possessed a key to the cell, and lynched. Another version claims that Walters was taken by the sheriff to the train station to get him out of town to avoid lynching, but somehow (this is unclear in this second factual recitation) Walters was found after the train left Longview and lynched. In either case, Walters was dead, and when local African American residents asked the county judge whether he would make sure these killers were apprehended by the authorities, the judge, an executive officer of the county, said he would do so but asked the delegation to keep quiet.

Two weeks later, the *Chicago Defender*, a weekly newspaper published for blacks, was delivered in Longview. It contained a story on the lynching of Walters. Two prominent black residents of Longview, Dr. C. P. Davis and Samuel L. Jones, were believed by whites to be involved in the reporting of this event. On July 10, 1919, Jones was attacked and beaten by several white residents of Longview, including brothers of the woman in whose bedroom Walters may have been found. Jones finally escaped and went to the office of Dr. Davis for treatment. After midnight, whites attacked Jones's house, which was defended by a substantial number of black residents. Four whites were injured during the thirty-minute pitched battle. The next morning, more whites gathered, returned to Jones's now abandoned house, and set it afire. They then went to Davis's office, and later his house, and burned both. Some white men went to the house of Marion Bush, Jones's father-in-law. (Were they the sheriff and another man intent on protecting the black residents from violent whites? Other men going to Bush's home intent on finding Jones to harm him and ready to harm Bush as well? The facts are disputed.) At some point after the men arrived, Bush became involved in a shoot-out with them and then left Longview. The next day, while still seeking refuge, Bush was killed. The Texas Rangers and National Guard were called in, and Governor Hobby declared martial law. The riot ended. Seventeen white men were arrested for murder, and nine were charged with arson. About twenty black men were arrested and later sent to Austin for their safety. The former were never tried for their crimes. The latter returned to Longview several weeks later and were not tried. Longview was the site of the first of three race riots in Texas that summer.

A month after the Longview riot, the white executive secretary of the NAACP, John Shillady, traveled to Austin to complain about the government's efforts to drive the NAACP out of Texas. As he was walking to his hotel, he was accosted by a handful of men, including the county judge, Dave J. Pickle, and a constable. The constable, Charles Hamby, began to beat Shillady. Others joined in. When they finished, they took him to the train station, forced him to buy a ticket, and warned him not to return to Texas. No one was prosecuted, for Hobby wrote the NAACP informing it that "the only offender in connection with the matter" was Shillady. Shillady, emotionally shattered by the experience, resigned from the NAACP a year later.[98]

THREE

Land, Oil, Water, and Sea

THE LAW OF TEXAS PROPERTY

★

THE LURE of Texas was its vast expanses of land, millions and millions of acres of land available for settlers. The opening of Texas to Americans in the early 1820s offered settlers the opportunity to purchase some of that land more cheaply than comparable land in the United States. Eighty acres of public land in America in 1820 sold for $100, payable in cash. The 1825 colonization law of the Mexican state of Coahuila and Texas allowed a person settling in Texas to obtain a league (4,428.4 acres) of land for about $117, a cost of about 2.6 cents per acre. By the time of the Texas Revolution in 1835–36, Spanish and Mexican land grants totaled slightly more than 26 million acres. As a nascent nation, the Republic of Texas claimed as public lands more than 216 million acres, nearly the only asset it held. The Republic of Texas not only asserted control (actual control by the republic was largely nonexistent) of an extraordinary amount of land, but it also claimed ownership of all mineral estates pursuant to Spanish law, of all land off the shore of the Gulf of Mexico for three leagues (more than ten miles), and of the land over which rivers passed. It would take several generations before the wealth created through minerals, particularly oil and gas, would be known, and by that time the state of Texas eschewed its claims to most minerals found on lands once part of the public domain. For most of Texas history, wealth has come from ownership of land.[1]

Access to land drove the settlement of Texas throughout the nineteenth century, and offers by the government of low-cost public land available for private purchase and settlement were a constant if only intermittently successful fiscal policy of the state. Some of the land distributed by the state was impossible to use for farming or ranching without access to water, making the allocation of surface water rights (such as rivers) essential to make that and other land habitable and profitable. Despite the importance of the issue, the legislature and courts took nearly eighty years to create an efficient and rational system of surface water rights. The law of groundwater (such as aquifers) has been consistent, but consistently attacked as insufficient to meet the needs of farmers, ranchers, and urban consumers of water.

The land grab of the nineteenth century ended just before the rise of the oil and gas industry, an industry that generated much of the economic growth enjoyed by Texans during the twentieth century. The manner in which Texas courts developed the law of ownership of oil and gas directly affected the manner in which both independents (or wildcatters) and major oil companies sought oil and developed their finds. The law of capture (a type of "finders, keepers"), which allowed an oil producer to take oil under common land and own it, created a chaotic situation as applied to the largest oil discovery in the United States in the early 1930s. This situation was not resolved until Texas abandoned the law of capture. The restructuring of the law of oil and gas both stabilized the oil and gas industry and increased the power of the Texas Railroad Commission well beyond its jurisdictional boundaries.

The curious nature of the 1845 annexation of Texas by the United States also led to two of the three important cases styled *United States v. Texas*. In 1896 the Supreme Court of the United States decided the boundary of Texas and "Indian territory" (soon to become the state of Oklahoma) based on Texas's agreement to cede its 1850 land claim for ten million dollars. (A series of cases between Texas and Oklahoma during the 1920s were needed to settle finally the boundary between the two states.) A second case styled *United States v. Texas* (1950), and known as the Tidelands Controversy, concerned title to 2.4 million acres at the bottom of the Gulf of Mexico. Public officials in Texas concluded that the oil underneath the floor of the Gulf made it crucial for the state to claim ownership. The United States also claimed ownership of these lands, and the Supreme Court resolved the dispute in favor of the national government. The decision was roundly condemned in Texas and became a crucial issue in the 1952 elections, and the decision was later revised by an act of Congress. The conclusion of the Tidelands dispute offers a cautionary tale of getting what you wish for. That Texas politicians sought a congressional victory rather than a compromise was a product of political attacks on the Supreme Court for holding unconstitutional the admission of whites only to the University of Texas Law School.[2]

THE LAW OF LAND DISTRIBUTION IN SPANISH AND MEXICAN TEXAS

The policy of land distribution during Mexican rule was to give land away as long as those who received it settled on it. The 1823 colonization act granted to married settlers a league (4,428.4 acres) to use for grazing and a *labor* (177.1 acres) to use for farming. Two years later, an act of the legislature of Coahuila and Texas granted to married settlers a *labor* for farming and 24 *labor*s (4,251 acres, one *labor* shy of a league) for grazing. Single men received substantially less than married men, but if a man married a Mexican woman, he received 6.25 *labor*s in addition to the league and *labor* to which he was entitled. The cost to obtain this land included thirty dollars to the Mexican government, payable in four years' time; fees to the land commissioner (fifteen dollars) and clerk (ten dollars); two dollars for stamped paper for title to the land; and about sixty dollars to the *empresario*, the organizer who marketed the land and who contracted with the Mexican government to bring families to settle Texas. The *empresario* was paid by Mexico in land; some contracts called for the *empresario* to receive about 23,000 acres of government land for each hundred families brought to Texas. Thomas Lloyd Miller estimates that during Spanish and Mexican rule of Texas, slightly more than 26 million acres were awarded to private parties.[3]

Section 11 of the national Mexican law of April 6, 1830, halted legal emigration from the United States to Texas by prohibiting "the citizens of foreign countries, lying adjacent to the Mexican territory," from "settling as colonists in the states or territories of the republic adjoining such countries" (that is, Texas). Although the act was repealed by a national law of November 25, 1833, followed on March 26, 1834, by Decree 272 of the Coahuila and Texas legislature, which allowed foreigners to purchase public land, the act of April 6 represented a transformative event in Texas history. Halting the immigration of Americans into Texas made very clear to Texians that they were subject to the decrees of the heretofore distant central government, one in which Roman Catholicism was the official religion and Spanish the official language. Stephen F. Austin interpreted the law of April 6 in a light most favorable to settlers (for example, section 10 of the law declared that no change in the colonies already established was to be made, including ownership of slaves then held by colonists in Texas) and to the *empresarios* (including himself) interested in encouraging immigration in order to fulfill their contracts and obtain more land. But for three years the immigration into Texas of Americans was officially prohibited.[4]

The 1833 repeal of the law of April 6 and the adoption of Decree 272 led almost immediately to the "making [of] excessively large and fraudulent land grants" by the Coahuila and Texas legislature. Two of those grants were to John T. Mason and to a group of speculators; the former was alleged to amount to more than 20 million acres. These were not, however, the only large land grants that upset Texans. The law of Coahuila and Texas allowed the government to sell to Mexican citizens grants of land

in the amount of eleven leagues, over 48,000 acres. In 1830, Jim Bowie traveled to Saltillo and induced a number of Mexican citizens to purchase eleven-league grants and sell them to him. Bowie obtained fifteen or sixteen of these grants, which began the traffic by straw purchasers (persons whose purchase was funded or supported by someone ineligible to make the purchase) in such grants. Many Anglo Texans concluded that vast swaths of Texas were being handed over to a small number of "speculators."[5]

Decree 272 was the impetus for John Mason to attempt to purchase millions of acres of land. Eugene Barker notes that Mason obtained a large grant of land during the 1834 Coahuila and Texas legislative session, when on April 19, 1834, Decree 278 was adopted, allowing the governor, in order to protect Texans on the frontier from "hostile Indians," to distribute 400 leagues, over 1.7 million acres. These lands were to be limited to those serving in the militia, but the order was written in a way that allowed the governor to "distribut[e] them agreeably to the rules and conditions he shall establish." On March 14, 1835, in Decree 293 (as modified by Decree 295, adopted on March 30, 1835), another 400 leagues were subject to sale by the governor of Coahuila and Texas "on the basis and conditions he shall judge proper." Through this decree Samuel Williams and John Durst received 124 leagues (over 500,000 acres), nearly all of which they immediately resold in 10–league increments. The act of March 14 of the provincial legislature was annulled by the federal government in April, too late to halt the distribution of much of this land. The "federalists" in the Coahuila and Texas legislature regretfully rejected the claim of authority by "centralists" in Mexico City; this regret lasted until the arrival of soldiers of the central government caused provincial legislators to flee. Although land speculation was not a cause of the Texas Revolution, it was surely on the minds of the delegates to the Constitutional

Convention in March 1836. When the Texas Constitution was adopted, the delegates noted the perceived corrupt bargains obtained in the grants of land to Mason in 1834 and to "sundry individuals" through the act of March 14, 1835, by which "eleven hundred leagues of land has been claimed." The constitution specifically disavowed the grants of land to Mason and to those whose claims were based on the March 14 act.[6]

The delegates of the Consultation of Texans who drafted the Plans and Powers of the Provisional Government of Texas in the fall of 1835 considered, among other subjects, ownership of land in Texas. Article XIV of the Plans and Powers ordered all land commissioners and *empresarios* to halt operations "during the unsettled and agitated state of the country." Article XVIII declared null and void all grants "illegally and fraudulently made" by the Coahuila and Texas legislature. Article XV guaranteed to all "persons now in Texas" the "quantum of land" they were entitled to when they came to Texas, and Article XIX forfeited lands of those who left Texas to avoid participating in the coming "struggle." The Plans and Powers, adopted on November 13, 1835, also purported to invalidate any Texas land titles issued by Mexico after that date.[7]

Once Texas became a nation, the nagging question of who owned what land resurfaced. In 1837 the Congress of the Republic, in conjunction with the creation of the Texas General Land Office, included a provision allowing all *empresarios* to file suit against the president of the republic for their land claims. These cases took years to conclude. In *Houston v. Perry* (1848), the Texas Supreme Court held in favor of the premium land claims of the heirs of Stephen F. Austin on "principles of justice." A decade later, John T. Mason's claim, purportedly extinguished by the 1836 constitution, was the subject of a lawsuit appealed to the Texas Supreme Court. In *Rose v. Governor* (1859), the court noted that Rose took his claim for premium lands from Mason in 1843. Rose filed suit in December 1857. The court held that the act of December 14, 1837, which allowed *empresarios* to sue, did not allow Rose to sue because of the proviso in the statute that "neither aliens, nor the assignees of aliens, shall be entitled to the benefits of this act." Thus, Rose's claim through Mason, an "alien," failed.[8]

LAND GRANTS IN THE REPUBLIC OF TEXAS

Like the government of Mexico, the government of the Republic of Texas was all but bankrupt. Land was the only asset available for it to replenish its coffers. As a result, congress moved quickly to sell land in order to obtain revenue. In addition, the delegates to the Texas constitutional convention made sure that land would be made available freely to those who aided the cause of the revolution. Section 10 of the General Provisions of the 1836 constitution granted as of right a league and a labor to every head of family and guaranteed to any male seventeen or older "now living in Texas" one-third of a league of land.

Fraudulent land certificates flooded Texas shortly before the Texas Revolution and continued to do so during the existence of the republic. The delegates to the constitutional convention were aware of this fraud and believed the creation of a General Land Office was necessary to combat it. The constitution required congress to create a land office to settle land title disputes, and the first congress created that office in December 1836. President Sam Houston, who feared congress's action would increase rather than reduce land fraud, vetoed the bill. Congress overrode his veto. Six months later, the legislature adopted a "supplementary act" on the General Land Office. Again Houston vetoed the bill, and again congress overrode it. Houston still refused to open the office, believing that it would be flooded by fraudulent claims that it would not be able to discover. Finally, in December 1837, a third act "to reduce into one act, and to amend the several acts relating to the establishment of a General Land Office," was adopted. For the third time Houston vetoed a General Land Office bill, and for the third time the bill was adopted over Houston's veto. Shortly thereafter, the General Land Office opened.[9]

Despite the efforts of the General Land Office, fraudulent land certificates threatened the stability of the Republic of Texas during its existence. As Thomas Lloyd Miller noted, "The words 'land' and 'fraud' were almost synonymous in Texas." On January 29, 1840, the Texas Congress adopted another act to limit fraud, this time over the veto of President Mirabeau Lamar. The act created two boards of land commissioners, one each for counties east and west of the Brazos River, each consisting of three members elected by congress. These boards were to travel to each county, in tandem with a body of three county commissioners, also elected by congress, to inspect and determine which certificates of title were genuine. This law was reinforced by a criminal act, adopted on February 5, 1840, sentencing those involved in fraud to receive thirty-nine lashes and to serve between three and twelve months in jail (no state prison existed). Another act adopted the same day provided for a civil claim allowing one to sue in trespass to try title to land. Although Texas rejected the common law of pleading in favor of a system influenced by Spanish law (see chapter 8), it created the action for trespass to try title to land in order to create some order in landownership. The law was no match for those whose wealth was generated through the sale of fraudulent certificates. The Regulator-Moderator War during the early 1840s resulted in large part from sales of fake land grant certificates (see chapter 1).[10]

The desperate financial condition of the republic made its survival unlikely. It continued to use the lure of land to stave off financial ruin. In February 1841 congress revived the *empresario* system, granting to William S. Peters and others the right to settle lands on the frontier. The Peters contract was followed by contracts with Henry Castro in 1842, the German Emigration Company in 1843, and Charles Mercer in 1844. In each instance the *empresario* was granted land once a sufficient number of families settled on land Texas wished to sell. Just one day after the Virginian Charles Mercer signed an *empresario* contract with President Sam Houston, the legislature adopted a law stripping the president of the power to enter into such contracts and declared forfeit any contracts that were not "strictly and rigidly complied with." The legislature's action was generated by the incorrect belief that Mercer had somehow tricked the republic and its president into granting him a favorable contract. The contract granted Mercer land for each family settled and a premium of ten sections (6,400 acres) of land for every hundred families annually settled in what is now northern Texas. The legislature's demand that all such contracts be strictly and rigidly complied with was to avoid complying with the terms of *empresario* contracts.[11]

Litigation and legislation concerning the Mercer *empresario* contract reflects something about both the poverty of the republic and the passions of those seeking land within it. Shortly after Mercer obtained his *empresario* contract, he organized the Texas Association to raise capital to meet the annual quota of one hundred families to settle in his reserved lands. Mercer's efforts conflicted not only with a majority of the legislature, but also with those who held much of Texas's debt. To survive, Texas had borrowed money by securing it with land scrip. The creditor could sell the scrip to those interested in settling in Texas. Those persons holding scrip would stake a claim to public land, send their claim to the General Land Office, and receive certificates of title to the land. Some of those settlers were interested in settling on land reserved by contract to the *empresario* of Mercer's colony. The republic was unable to survey the public domain in a way that clarified who owned what land. The surveys by Mercer's own surveyors and agents were plagued with threats of violence by Texans who had already settled on land reserved for Mercer's settlers. An additional complication was the inaccuracy of some surveying, resulting in an overlapping border between the Mercer and Peters colonies.

The debate by the framers of the 1845 constitution included vituperative comments about the *empresario* system and suggestions to negate *empresario* contracts. Instead of including such a provision in the 1845 constitution, the drafters approved an ordinance calling for the people to vote (at the same time they voted on ratification of the constitution) on approving a statement ordering the attorney general to sue the *empresarios*. The ordinance passed, and the first legislature of the state of Texas ordered the attorney general to commence suit against the *empresarios*. In October 1848, District Judge Robert Emmett Bledsoe Baylor, who helped found the university that bears his name, held that the Mercer colonization contract was void. Baylor did not abrogate the contract on the ground that Mercer had not complied with its terms, but on the ground that the initial contract itself was unlawful. While this decision may have salved a populist urge, it merely created more chaos regarding landownership in Mercer Colony. The legislature, in 1850, adopted a law guaranteeing a remedy for every colonist who had settled in the colony before Baylor's decision was issued. A second law protecting settlers in Mercer Colony was adopted in January 1852. Both laws pointedly excluded any benefits for the *empresario*. A month after this second law was adopted, Mercer sold his interest in the Texas Association.[12]

The dispute continued for another thirty years. Petitions to the legislature allowing the Texas Association to sue the state (necessary because Texas was immune from a lawsuit) failed. The Supreme Court of Texas, in *Melton v. Cobb* (1858), heard competing claims to land within Mercer Colony. Melton possessed a headright certificate granted by the state and located his land within Mercer Colony. (Under the Mercer Colony contract, land within the colony was reserved for settlers brought in by the company, so this public land was not available to those who held certificates.) Cobb took possession of part of the same land through the colonization contract with Mercer. If the republic's contract with Mercer was unconstitutional, as Judge Baylor had earlier concluded, then Cobb's claim through the *empresario* contract with Mercer was invalid. The supreme court upheld the district court's conclusion in favor of Cobb. The court noted that even if the contract with Mercer was invalid, the legislature had validated it by subsequent action. In 1875 the Texas Association, through George Hancock, Mercer's successor, sued John Groos, the commissioner of the General Land Office, in federal court for an injunction barring Groos from opening Mercer Colony land to general settlers. The circuit court granted the injunction. By the time the case reached the Supreme Court of the United States in 1883, both named parties were substituted, and in *Walsh v. Preston* (1883) the Supreme Court held in favor of land office commissioner W. C. Walsh. In the majority's view, neither Mercer nor his successors had offered proof that they had brought into the colony immigrants from outside of Texas as required by the *empresario* contract. In dissent, Justice John Marshall Harlan criticized the court for applying to the association's evidence "the same rules of strictness and technicality which would be applied to an indictment for a criminal offense." He pointed to *Melton v. Cobb* to support his conclusion, a case the majority ignored. The Texas Asso-

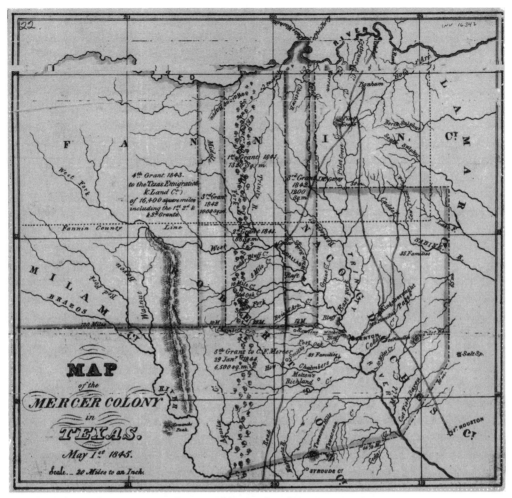

Mercer's Colony, 1845. Courtesy Texas State Library and Archives Commission.

ciation thus received no land for its efforts to populate the Mercer Colony.[13]

The continuing problem of fraud in land titles and the difficulty of assessing who owned title to which lands led the Texas legislature in August 1856 to create a Commission of Claims, also known as the Court of Claims. The previous October the office of the adjutant general was destroyed by fire, apparently set intentionally. This meant the loss of the names of the soldiers who were eligible to receive land for their service and the soldiers who had already claimed their land. The legislature created the Commission of Claims in part to compile a list of those who had obtained land certificates, to compile a list of those eligible to receive lands, and to ferret out forged certificates. The commissioner of claims was appointed by a joint vote of the legislature. Although the 1856 act was to expire in two years, the legislature renewed its existence in 1858 and 1860. The position of commissioner of claims ended on December 31, 1861. During its existence the commission approved 7,942 land certificates. Thomas Lloyd Miller's history of the public lands of Texas indicates that in the "dockets" of applications for land, only about 1,000 of 3,348 applications were approved, about 30 percent.[14]

The proposed 1844 treaty of annexation by the United States exchanged the public land of Texas for the assumption of Texas's ten-million-dollar debt. The U.S. Congress rejected this proposal in June, in part because Texas would become another slave state in the Union. The advisability of annexing Texas became an important issue in the 1844 presidential election. Democratic candidate James Polk consistently favored it; Whig Henry Clay engaged in a "consistent straddle." After Polk eked out a victory, outgoing Democratic President Martin Van Buren, determined to revive Manifest Destiny, urged Congress to resolve to admit Texas. It did so on March 1, 1845, three days before Van Buren's presidency ended. The joint resolution admitting Texas to the Union assumed neither the debts of the republic nor ownership of its public lands. Texas "shall also retain all the vacant and unappropriated lands lying within its limits, to be applied to the payment of the debts and liabilities" of the republic. The very next year, a Texas Senate committee suggested the sale of the state's public lands to the United States, but again no transfer took place. By the end of the republic, the *empresario* system alone had transferred about 4.5 million acres to private hands. Still, the state of Texas claimed ownership of approximately 182 million acres of land. Thus, unlike other states entering the Union, Texas retained its public lands, a decision that in time would benefit it greatly.[15]

THE BORDER OF
THE STATE OF TEXAS

The joint resolution admitting Texas to the Union allowed it to be formed "subject to the adjustment by this government of all questions of boundary that may arise with other government." The annexation of Texas by the United States was the catalyst for the Mexican-American War of 1846–48, which in turn was the catalyst for the clarification of the boundaries of the state of Texas, in part through the Compromise of 1850.

The first congress of the republic claimed its southern and western boundaries ran to the Rio Grande. If Mexico laid claim to less than all of Texas, it surely claimed sovereignty to all land between the Rio Grande (called the Río Bravo del Norte in Mexico) and the Nueces River. The Treaty of Guadalupe Hidalgo, concluded by the United States and Mexico on February 2, 1848 (and proclaimed on July 2, 1848, by the United States), and which formally ended the Mexican-American War, acknowledged that the border between the United States (and thus Texas) and Mexico was the middle of the Rio Grande. The inclusion of much of South Texas as part of the United States raised concerns by residents of the area about the validity of their land titles. The land held by Tejanos in South Texas was now clearly in American and Texas territory. In addition to making the Rio Grande the border, Mexico ceded its claims to much of the land that became New Mexico, Arizona, Colorado, and Nevada in the Treaty of Guadalupe Hidalgo. Texas claimed ownership of all land within the Rio Grande and south of the Arkansas River, plus a thin, rectangular strip north and west of the Arkansas River. Texas thus claimed Santa Fe and much of present-day New Mexico. The land in dispute totaled about sixty-seven million acres.[16]

Because Texas owned its own public land, it was responsible for determining who owned what land within its territory. In late 1849 Governor Peter Bell urged the legislature to create a "secure and permanent basis" for land titles in South Texas by creating a board of commissioners, and in February 1850 the legislature adopted Bell's suggestion. The commission that resulted is known by the names of its two commissioners, William H. Bourland and James B. Miller. Bourland and Miller traveled through the Trans-Nueces to investigate titles in South

Texas claimed through Spanish and Mexican land grants. After receiving evidence from the claimants, Bourland and Miller were authorized to report on the state of each title to the governor, who would then ask the legislature to act to regularize the titles. The first commission hearing took place in Laredo in July 1850, and claimants initially refused to make their claims before the commission. After they were assured of the good faith of Bourland and Miller, several *rancheros* made their claims, and the Texas legislature confirmed some land titles on September 4, 1850. This early action by the legislature made a number of landowners more amenable to the commission, although in the interim residents near Rio Grande City had refused to make any claims.[17]

In Brownsville, a number of titles were pressed upon the commission, and Miller decided to travel by ship to Galveston before returning to Austin overland. On the way, the ship sank. Miller survived, but the original titles (and fees) he carried with him were lost in the Gulf of Mexico. The commission's subsequent request that the law be amended to make the decision of the commissioners final was rejected, and they had to return to Brownsville and again undertake the entire process.

Bourland continued to make stops in South Texas during the first nine months of 1851. The final report of the commission was issued to the governor on November 11, 1851, and the legislature confirmed 234 claims on February 10, 1852, which "followed closely the recommendations of the commissioners." In all, the Miller-Bourland Commission recommended 76 percent of the claims presented to it. Because it did not investigate all such titles, the Texas legislature created another board in 1854, but that one accomplished little. By an act of 1860, the legislature gave the courts authority to adjudicate land claims. A final law, adopted in 1901, concerned the validity of claims based on grants made between the time of Texas independence and the adoption of the Treaty of Guadalupe

Hidalgo, when both Texas and Mexico claimed sovereignty over the area.[18]

In general, the Miller-Bourland Commission and the Texas legislature held valid most of the original Spanish and Mexican land grants and did so in a fair and reasoned fashion. When these decisions were made, titles to the lands in the Trans-Nueces were claimed not only by the original Mexican grantees but also by Anglo-Texans who had purchased their titles from original Mexican grantees, a fact that may have influenced the decisions by the commission and the legislature. The relative fairness undertaken in adjudicating land titles in South Texas was in stark contrast with the efforts of the United States in adjudicating similar land claims in New Mexico.

As the Miller-Bourland Commission began its work on establishing land titles in South Texas, the U.S. Congress debated the proper western and northern borders of Texas as part of the discussion of what came to be known as the Compromise of 1850. The victory over Mexico in the Mexican-American War gave the United States vast new territories, and organizing those territories was halted by the question of the legality of slavery. The Missouri Compromise of 1820 declared that slavery was prohibited in any territory or state north of latitude 36° 30′, with the exception of Missouri. Much of the land ceded by Mexico to the United States was south of that latitude. And slavery was prohibited in this new American territory when it belonged to Mexico. Well before the end of the war, antislavery members of Congress proposed the Wilmot Proviso, which banned slavery in any territory obtained by the United States from Mexico. Although the proviso failed, it was a warning concerning the organization of the Mexican Cession.

The sectional conflict over the issue of slavery had by late 1849 reached a level that suggested the possibility of disunion. Even though slavery was the predominant issue, Kentucky senator Henry Clay wrote in a June

1849 letter that "more difficulty will be encountered in fixing the boundaries of Texas than in deciding the question of the introduction of Slavery in the new territories." This difficulty was due in part to the federal government's military occupation of Santa Fe and its initiation of a civil government. Texas claimed Santa Fe and hastened to organize the "county" of Santa Fe at the close of the Mexican-American War. President Zachary Taylor believed that organizing New Mexico would allow the courts to decide the boundary of Texas. At the end of January and in early February 1850, Clay offered a compromise to avert secession. Clay proposed that the Mexican ban on slavery continue in the unorganized territories won from Mexico. In addition to pressing for adoption of an enforceable fugitive slave act, Clay's compromise included two resolutions concerning Texas, following up on a bill offered by Missouri senator Thomas Hart Benton: The first made the Rio Grande the western border of Texas but removed from the state much of its northern territory, including Dallas and Fort Worth, and shifted that land to the Mexican Cession. The second provided for the U.S. government to assume the debt held by Texas. Although northerners appreciated the first resolution concerning Texas, the state was adamantly opposed to it. The second was rejected by many northerners.[19]

In April 1850 the Senate created a Committee of Thirteen, which reported the next month on an omnibus bill that included provisions on the boundary of Texas and its debt but that did not include a fugitive slave law or the issue of slave trade in the District of Columbia. After President Taylor's death on July 9, 1850, the crisis over the Texas boundary intensified, with an increasing possibility of a clash between federal troops and Texas soldiers. Despite the efforts of Massachusetts senator Daniel Webster and others, including new president Millard Fillmore, the omnibus bill concerning the compromise failed at the end of July. On August 5 a revived bill concerning the Texas boundary was offered. It excluded Santa Fe and much of New Mexico from Texas, but it gave Texas the Panhandle, the eastern border of which was designated as the one-hundredth meridian and the northern border of which was 36° 30′ latitude. In the view of antislavery Whigs, this new bill gave Texas "70,000 square miles more than it deserved." The bill also gave Texas respite from its debt, in exchange for Texas's claim to Santa Fe and elsewhere north and west of present-day Texas.

The following day, President Fillmore sent a letter to Texas governor Peter Bell concerning the boundary dispute. Fillmore declared that the western lands claimed by Texas belonged to the United States, which intended to defend that territory through the use of troops, if necessary. After this saber-rattling, Fillmore then offered a sweetener for the state. Texas should have its boundary settled quickly by Congress, and Fillmore made this issue his highest priority. On August 9, three days before a special session of the Texas legislature was to convene, the Texas bill passed the Senate by a vote of thirty to twenty. As noted by Michael Holt, the vote on Texas was "extraordinary," for among the parts of the Compromise of 1850, this was the only bill that required both the North and the South to compromise their interests. The remainder of the compromise was passed by the U.S. Senate in August. The U.S. House then moved the Texas boundary bill to the top of its agenda, and an amended bill was adopted in early September, to which the Senate agreed. After a special election approving the state's cession of this land to the federal government, the Texas legislature adopted a bill on November 25, 1850, agreeing to cede 67,000,000 acres of land in exchange for ten million dollars in "stock" (actually bonds) and avoiding a military clash with the federal government. Despite ceding this land, Texas received about 33,000 square miles more than was initially approved by the Committee of Thirteen.[20]

Texas Boundaries, 1850–53. Courtesy Texas State Library and Archives Commission.

When Texas became a state in 1845, its debt had totaled $9,949,007. It had no intention of paying that amount, having little ability to pay even a modest fraction of what it owed. A report issued on January 1, 1850, listed a total state debt of $11,055,694.70, which was discounted in value to $5,600,696. Texas bonds accruing at 10 percent interest were sold for twenty-nine cents on the dollar in February 1850, but the possibility of a compromise allowing Texas to pay its debt pushed the value of those bonds to fifty-four cents on the dollar by May. Texas passed a law giving creditors land valued at fifty cents per acre in payment, and the legislature refused to pay interest after July 1, 1850, in order to coerce creditors to accept. Creditors disparaged the offer. They supported the compromise by which Texas would cede land to the federal government for $10 million in United States bonds, which gave creditors the hope of receiving cash rather than land. The Boundary Bill withheld $5 million in bonds until creditors released their claims in exchange for the bonds. Five million dollars in U.S. bonds went to Texas, and those bonds became the focus of the post–Civil War case of *Texas v. White* (1869) (see chapter 2). After much discussion, Congress appropriated a total of $7.75 million for the payment of creditors of the state. Texas voters rejected this offer, but this act of Congress gave the Texas legislature the sole authority to accept it. After extensive debate concerning the overall cost to Texas in accepting this proposal, a bill accepting the offer was narrowly approved in 1856. This $7.75 million paid creditors holding over $10 million in Texas debt. By the time the Civil War began, Texas was largely free of debt.[21]

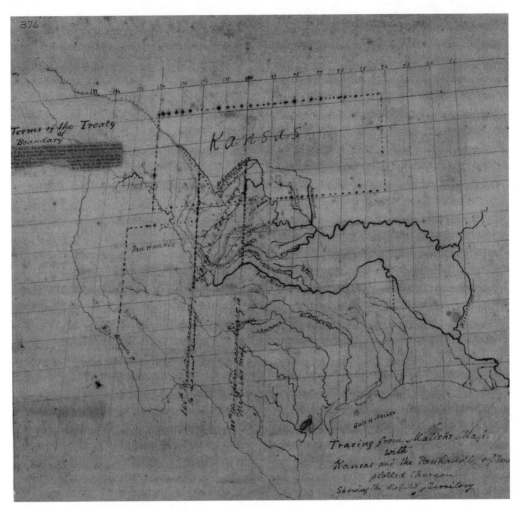

Tracing of the Melish Map, ca. 1818. Courtesy Texas State Library and Archives Commission.

The Compromise of 1850 did not fully resolve the dispute concerning Texas's boundary, particularly along borders with what became Oklahoma but also with New Mexico. Texas and the United States contested the line where the one-hundredth meridian, the eastern boundary of the Panhandle, crossed the Red River. An 1885 act of Congress created a commission of members appointed by the president to fix this boundary, which eventually led to litigation. Texas claimed it owned Greer County, while the federal government claimed it was part of Indian Territory (Oklahoma). The

1819 Adams-Onís Treaty between the United States and Spain indicated that an 1818 "Melish map" fixed the boundaries between the two. Part of that treaty declared that the hundredth meridian was to constitute one boundary between the two nations. The Texas boundary bill of 1850 also declared the eastern border of the Texas Panhandle was the hundredth meridian. The conflict existed in part because the Melish map fixed the hundredth meridian about one hundred miles east of its actual geographical location. Texas had claimed this land as early as 1860. The U.S. Supreme Court held that because the boundary fixed by the treaty and the boundary bill was intended to be the true hundredth meridian, the boundary as stated in the Melish map was inapt. Over 1.5 million acres were transferred from Texas to Indian Territory as a result of *United States v. Texas* (1896).[22]

It took three more decades before the true hundredth meridian was ascertained. During the 1920s Oklahoma and Texas engaged in a decade-long dispute in the Supreme Court of the United States concerning both the location of the hundredth meridian and the border between the two states on the Red River. The location of the Red River border intensified after oil was found there. The Supreme Court held that the border ran along the southern border of the Red River, not the middle, as Texas claimed. This decision was again based on the 1819 treaty with Spain. The next issue was how one determined what constituted the "south bank" of the Red River. The Court again held against Texas's position that the south bank was marked as its "low water line." Instead, the Court held that the boundary was "at the outer line of the river bed which separates the bed from the adjacent upland." Finally, the Court affirmed the finding of the geographically correct location of the hundredth meridian. This decision awarded to Texas some land that earlier had been awarded to Oklahoma. The question then was what happened to ownership of the land now that it was in Texas. After the final decision of the Supreme Court, a suit was filed in Texas seeking an order that the commissioner of the General Land Office classify the land formerly in dispute. The Texas Supreme Court held the case for seven years, finally deciding in 1939 that it was "without power to convert a writ of mandamus into an adjudication of a doubtful claim" and dismissing the claim. Later that year the Texas legislature declared that the public lands found to be in Texas would be sold based

on a law from 1931, which Oklahoma politicians found acceptable.[23]

POST–CIVIL WAR LAND GRAB

At the end of the Civil War, approximately 90 million acres, or more than half of Texas, consisted of unclaimed public land. Most of that land was west of the ninety-eighth meridian, which bisected Texas. As noted by Texas historian Walter Prescott Webb, the land west of the ninety-eighth meridian met the three criteria for a Great Plains environment. The land was level, treeless, and semiarid. The absence of trees meant there were no logs for cabins and no rails for fences. Rain was much more sparse west of the ninety-eighth meridian than in eastern or southeastern Texas. Running streams and waters were largely absent. Plains grass grew there, but it grew on a thin topsoil. In the 1860s buffalo numbering in the millions thrived on the plains grass, and the presence of buffalo meant the presence of Indian tribes that hunted buffalo. Despite the forbidding nature of the Great Plains, Texans began to move west after the Civil War.[24]

By the time the 1876 constitution was ratified, the public domain had been reduced to about 59,000,000 acres, including 3,000,000 acres set aside as consideration for the building of the capitol and 1,000,000 acres set aside for the benefit of the state university. Half of the remainder was reserved for the school fund. By 1882 the unreserved public domain was apparently exhausted, having been sold or, more often, given away to settlers, speculators, and railroads. In less than two decades Texas gave away 36,876,492 acres of land to settlers (and speculators who had "settlers" claim land and transfer their title to the speculators for resale). Another 10,000,000 acres were given to veterans, and 3,050,000 acres were eventually given in exchange for the building of the capitol. To railroads, the state gave 32,153,878 acres. A March 1873 amendment (approved by the people in the November 1872 elections) to the 1869 constitution allowed the legislature to grant up to twenty sections (12,800 acres) per mile of railroad track. By early January 1874, Democrats controlled the legislative and executive branches. The fourteenth legislature chartered forty-two railroads, of which just twelve constructed railroad track. The ordinary incentive given these railroads was sixteen sections (10,240 acres) of land for each mile of railroad track.[25]

In 1898 a settler claiming his right to homestead land under the 1876 constitution was turned away by the Texas Supreme Court, which held that unclaimed public lands were exhausted. The court's decision in *Hogue v. Baker* caused the legislature to adopt a law auditing all lands granted since 1876. The legislature found that the transfers of public domain land had left the public school fund almost 6 million acres shy of what it was due to receive. But the auditors also "found" 4.4 million acres of unappropriated public land and 1.4 million acres of excess land given to the railroads. This land, plus $17,180.27 (representing the shortage of acreage valued at $1.00 per acre), was given to the public school fund. The end of homestead land limited a prospective settler to the options of purchasing land from another private owner or purchasing land from the public school fund, land that was often inhospitable to either farming or ranching. The Texas frontier was no longer by 1900, and land law largely passed into the law of transfers of property between private parties.[26]

FRAUD, SPECULATION,
AND THE FIFTY CENT LAW OF 1879

Fraud in land titles was a persistent problem in nineteenth-century Texas. A July 14, 1879, act allowed a person to buy up to 640 acres of public land in West Texas for fifty cents per acre. The act did not require the purchaser to settle on the land, nor did it limit the resale of the land to another. Another law adopted six days earlier allowed the sale of school lands in organized counties. School lands were sections of land that alternated with formerly public land awarded to railroads. This July 8, 1879, law allowed the sale of 160 acres of land if the land was arable, and up to three sections (1,920 acres) if the land was suitable only for grazing. The minimum fee was one dollar per acre, and the actual cost was its appraised value, if higher than one dollar per acre. The problem, as noted in an 1882 report by Land Commissioner W. C. Walsh, was that fewer than one hundred of the more than twenty-five thousand surveyed sections of land had appraised land valued at more than the minimum. The July 14 act was adopted just as investment in cattle ranching began to offer a substantial annual return to investors, including foreign investors, and the act encouraged speculation in landholdings. The Fifty Cent Law allowed any "person, firm or corporation" to purchase the land. Although the July 8 law allowing the sale of school lands was amended in 1881 to increase the minimum purchase price to two dollars per acre if the land possessed fresh water and one dollar if it did not, speculation and fraud in public land purchases continued.[27]

In 1883 the legislature created two land boards. The first, the State Land Board, regulated the sale and leasing of school lands, including increasing the price of such lands. The second, the Land Fraud Board, was created to investigate fraud in public land sales and given the authority to initiate prosecutions. It was also given the authority to annul purchases made in violation of the land laws. The Land Fraud Board referred for prosecution by the attorney general the sale of about 750,000 acres of land in violation of the 1879 and 1881 acts. It also concluded that much land acquired in violation of the statutes was purchased by foreign corporations and speculators. How much land was reclaimed for the state by the attorney general is unclear. An estimate made in 1941 suggested that 163,200 acres were returned to the state through the efforts of the Land Fraud Board.[28]

GRASS LAWS AND THE FENCE WARS

The opening of West Texas and the Panhandle to cattle ranching was a product of several developments. First, the arrival of the railroad in Abilene, Kansas, in 1867 made the raising of cattle much more profitable than it had been, for it opened up markets in the midwest and east. Within five years 1,460,000 cattle were driven from Texas to Kansas, including 700,000 Texas cattle in 1871 alone. Between 1875 and 1885, more than three million cattle were driven from Texas for sale and slaughter. Second, in 1875 the benefits of barbed wire were first demonstrated in Texas, although it was not until an 1878 demonstration in San Antonio by John Warne "Bet-a-Million" Gates that its properties were fully recognized. Its impact, however, was tremendous. As noted by John Stricklin Spratt, "in less than half a decade barbed wire changed the entire system of western agriculture." Third, the slaughter and extermination of buffalo in Texas and elsewhere in the Great Plains (over 4.3 million buffalo were killed between 1872 and 1874) by the end of the winter of 1876–77 not only eliminated the danger of the buffalo for those who wanted to raise cattle, but it eliminated from the area Native Americans who hunted buffalo.[29]

When Charles Goodnight decided to operate a cattle ranch in Palo Duro Canyon in the Panhandle in mid-1877, he was apparently its first white settler. Goodnight and his men killed the remaining buffalo that ate the plains grass he wanted for his cattle, giving them a store of buffalo meat that lasted two years. The last Native Americans who roamed the area were moved out of the Panhandle in 1879. Soon other cattle ranchers had moved to the Panhandle to enter the burgeoning cattle business. They were joined by farmers (derogatorily called "nesters" by the ranchers), a situation that caused much consternation to both groups.[30]

The development of cattle ranching between 1870 and 1900 in West Texas is astonishing. No cattle grazed in the Panhandle in 1870. By 1900, more than 256,000 cattle were there. More than 900,000 cattle were counted in twenty West Texas counties. Goodnight operated the JA Ranch, named after his financier, John Adair. During the five-year existence of the contract between Goodnight and Adair, profits totaled an extraordinary $512,000. In 1881, only two cattle companies obtained charters to do business in Texas, but the outsized return on investment by the JA Ranch quickly drew investors to the business. In 1883–84, 104 land and cattle companies filed charters to do business in Texas.[31]

The beginning of the transformation of cattle ranching in the Panhandle occurred as early as 1880. Cattle from central Texas carried tick fever, which Panhandle cattle had not contracted. As cattle were driven from central Texas to Kansas, Goodnight and others used fences to keep the tick-fevered cattle away from their herds and warned cattle drivers to avoid the JA Ranch on pain of violence. That same year, Goodnight and others formed the Panhandle Stockmen's Association. One reason for its creation (formalized the next year) was to lobby for a leasing act, for the large cattle ranchers preferred to pay for use of the unoccupied public school lands rather than take their chances on finding free grass on which their cattle could graze. Smaller ranchers, many of whom had little capital to purchase land and cattle, supported "free grass," the free use of public lands on which cattle could graze. They could purchase more cattle without incurring the capital expenditure of buying land. The legislature avoided the issue in 1881.

The free grass issue was complicated by the state's system of designating public and railroad land. The state kept one section (640 acres, a square mile) of land for the benefit of the public schools (school land) for every section taken by the railroads. This created a patchwork. Goodnight and others in the Panhandle Stockmen's Association had purchased much of the range land they used, lessening their interest in open-range cattle ranching. As an economic matter, the competition created by smaller cattle ranchers using free grass created the possibility of too many cattle feeding on too little land. Leasing land, which monopolized the use of that land, offered the large cattle ranches a competitive advantage over smaller operations. Further, the arrival of farmers and barbed wire, and the envy of Texans in the eastern part of the state, quickly changed the politics of free grass. Farmers opposed free grass because cattle not penned in could drift onto their land and destroy their crops. Barbed wire made efficient the use of fencing to keep one's own animals in and the animals of others out, but only when used on a large scale. Envy was a result of the bubble in cattle prices in the early 1880s, which led many Texans to conclude that ranchers were becoming wealthy off land owned by the state.[32]

The 1876 Texas Constitution was greatly influenced by farming interests. A plurality of delegates were members of the Grange (or Patrons of Husbandry), an organization of farmers supportive of farming interests, including government assistance to farmers. Farmers believed fences would keep grazing animals such as cattle from damaging their crops. The constitution granted the legislature "the power to pass such fence laws, applicable to any subdivision of the State, or counties, as may be needed to meet the wants of the people." The 1876 legislature adopted a law allowing for county-wide elections to determine whether animal stock would be allowed to run free. The issue for farmers was, Who should bear the cost of fencing? Should they be required to fence their lands to keep cattle out, or should ranchers be required to fence their lands to keep their cattle in? For large cattle ranchers, the cost of barbed wire was modest. On a large ranch, the cost might be as low as 2¢ per acre. But fencing in a farm of 160 acres might cost a hundred dollars, or 62.5¢ per acre. The initial response after barbed wire came to the attention of Texas farmers and ranchers was a legislative effort to outlaw it. That effort failed, and two laws were adopted in 1879 making barbed wire a lawful fence if built to the legislature's specifications. But some ranchers fenced not just the land they owned, but also school land on which their cattle had traditionally ranged, effectively declaring dominion over public lands. Not surprisingly, this outraged many. By the early 1880s, cattle ranchers faced both the end of the open range and the beginning of the fence-cutting war.[33]

The cattle industry's profits continued to increase during the first half of the 1880s. In 1881 and 1882, the Fifty Cent Law was now a bargain for the larger cattle ranchers, and purchases created a small land boom. The sale of school lands, allowed by laws in 1879 and 1881, also contributed to the land boom. In 1882 and 1883 land laws granting railroads land for construction of track were repealed, and public land sales were halted as the state's public domain was exhausted. Cattle prices increased during both 1883 and 1884, the key years in the grass lease and fence-cutting fights. The boom caused more money to be invested in cattle; seventeen new cattle companies were chartered in Texas in just one week in 1885. In 1883, during the cattle boom and in light of the diminishment of public lands for settlement, the Texas legislature acted to amend the school law, increasing the sale price of land and allowing the lease of school land. Section 16 of the act required competitive bidding to lease a section of school land and imposed a minimum fee of four cents an acre. The sale and leasing arrangements were to be administered by a State Land Board that included the governor, attorney general, comptroller, treasurer, and General

Land Office commissioner, all elected officials. The large ranchers, as was customary, simply bid on the land they had formerly used for free, at the minimum price of four cents per acre. None bid on public range land regularly used by other ranchers. In reaction to this concerted action, the Land Board declared that no state land would be leased for less than eight cents per acre. In Charles Goodnight's view, the State Land Board had exceeded its authority. In the state's view, Goodnight and others had improperly used school lands as their own to produce enormous profits.[34]

The grass lease fight quickly shifted to a fence-cutting fight in 1883. Following great losses in cattle during the winter of 1882–83, barbed wire reached the Panhandle. It had already proved popular in much of the rest of Texas cattle country. Drought then came to much of Texas in the summer of 1883, even as prices for cattle continued to increase. That year, "[f]ence-cutting was reported in more than half the Texas counties." By the end of 1883, the cost of fence cutting was estimated at twenty million dollars. Governor John Ireland called a special session in early 1884 to make fence cutting a felony. The legislature did so, but also made it a misdemeanor for anyone knowingly to put a fence around another's property or around the school lands.[35]

In the winter of 1884, a two-hundred-mile-long drift fence that spanned the Panhandle in an east-west direction did too well its job of protecting the grass of the ranchers living south of the fence. During the severe winter, the drift fence created "a chain of carcasses where entire herds drifted into it to starve and freeze to death." By mid-1885 the boom in cattle prices became a bust. The weather then exacerbated the difficulty in the cattle ranching business. A second consecutive severe winter hit the Panhandle, and a drought in Texas from 1885 to 1887 "bankrupted many Texas cattlemen." The continuing fear of tick fever also led Panhandle cattlemen to attempt to bar central Texas

cattlemen from driving their herds through the Panhandle in 1885.[36]

The grass lease fight continued even as the cattle industry foundered. Goodnight and other ranchers continued to claim a right to use the "leased" school lands to graze their cattle. The state disagreed. In late 1885, Texas attorney general John D. Templeton instructed the local district attorney to convene a grand jury to indict Goodnight and others for illegally enclosing school lands in violation of the 1884 law. In January 1886 Templeton did so. The grand jury consisted of men called to perform their service in July 1885, well before Templeton had made his request. The foreman of the grand jury was none other than Charles Goodnight. He was not the only rancher accused of illegal fencing on the grand jury, and the grand jury issued seventy-six indictments against more than fifty cowmen, including Goodnight. Goodnight's biographer, J. Evetts Haley, notes correctly that the number of eligible grand jurors in the sparsely populated Panhandle was insufficient to avoid conflicts of interest, but he does not examine the possibility that Goodnight and others agreed to indict themselves because they knew they would not be convicted by a local jury. An acquittal would bar a second trial under the principle of double jeopardy. Goodnight's lawyers argued at trial that he and other defendants had made the minimum required bid of four cents per acre, that the leases had been awarded them by the local surveyor, and that the lease payments had been tendered yearly to the Land Board, which had refused to accept them. The jury declared Goodnight not guilty, as juries did in fifty-four of the fifty-six illegal enclosure cases.[37]

The 1886 acquittal did not end the fight between Goodnight and Templeton. In April 1886, Goodnight and several others appeared before the Land Board and urged it to accept their lease tender. The cattlemen eventually obtained over one hundred thousand dollars in cash, placed it in a wheelbarrow, and rolled it

James Hogg, undated. Courtesy Texas State Library and Archives Commission.

James S. Hogg began efforts to remove from office Frank Willis, the district judge in Goodnight's cases. In Hogg's view Willis was unfit for office. Willis had wrongly allowed Goodnight to serve on the grand jury that considered Goodnight's case. He had also ignored the conflict of interest in the employment of the district attorney and sheriff by the Panhandle Stockmen's Association. Hogg suggested that the legislature remove Willis through address, an alternative to impeachment. The biographers of Goodnight and Hogg offer two decidedly different pictures of the Willis affair. Goodnight's biographer concludes Willis was unfairly subject to a "vigorous prosecution" by Hogg. Hogg's biographer believes Willis was used by Goodnight, and the large cattle owners used "henchmen" as well as their power in the legislature to obtain a legislative acquittal of Willis.[39]

Goodnight continued his lobbying efforts on the grass lease fight in the 1887 legislature. Cattle prices continued their decline since 1885, even with drought and severe winters reducing cattle stock in Texas. Estimates at the time indicated a depreciation in the value of cattle of one hundred million dollars. To assist some struggling cattle ranchers the legislature considered a bill requiring an open range. The open range bill was led by Temple Lea Houston, Sam Houston's son. Houston had served as the first district attorney in the unorganized counties of the Panhandle in 1882 and was elected senator from the Panhandle in 1884. Goodnight was convinced that a law requiring an open range would cause further economic ruin, but the bill seemed on the verge of passing. Goodnight called on George Clark, former judge of the court of appeals and legal fixer extraordinaire. Goodnight agreed to pay Clark a fee of five thousand dollars if he killed the bill. Clark halted the free grass bill by falsely telling other legislators that Houston and Goodnight were secretly working together to ensure an open range. That Houston was working for small

down Austin's Congress Avenue. They offered the money to the state treasurer, who refused to accept it. Templeton's biannual attorney general's report for 1885–86 falsely (or at least incompletely) declared that "there is a sentiment hostile to the idea of paying for the use of the lands." Templeton then attacked the "farcical judicial proceedings" held in Donley County against Goodnight and others and suggested that the legislature should amend the law to allow these cases be tried in Austin. On May 5, 1886, Templeton filed a petition asking the court to issue an injunction against Goodnight compelling him to remove fences around public lands and barring him from constructing any new fences enclosing public lands. Although the district court issued a temporary injunction, in July it dismissed the petition and awarded Goodnight costs. The state appealed.[38]

In early 1887 newly elected attorney general

cattle ranchers in opposition to large ranchers such as Goodnight was lost on many senators. Clark received his fee. Shortly after Houston's bill died, the legislature adopted a bill allowing leases of school lands for up to five years, at a price of four cents per acre, exactly what Goodnight wanted. It also abolished the Land Board and gave to the commissioner of the General Land Office the power to issue leases on school lands.[40]

In mid-1888 the Texas Supreme Court issued its opinion in *State ex rel. Templeton v. Goodnight*. It held that dismissing the petition for an injunction was error, and noted that Goodnight had enclosed over six hundred thousand acres of public school lands as well as fourteen thousand additional acres of unappropriated public domain. The case was reversed and remanded for a new trial. But through the 1887 act Goodnight now lawfully leased the land that he had earlier enclosed. No trial took place.

The grass lease fight ended with victory for large cattle ranchers at the expense of open range enthusiasts. The five-year lease payable annually at the beginning of the lease term created price certainty among large ranchers, allowing them to bear the price decline in the cattle market while their more leveraged competitors fell by the wayside. Whether the initial four cents per acre lease amount was fair is unclear. What was clear was that the State Land Board had no legal authority to refuse to accept the lease tenders. In addition, Texas lawmakers lacked an understanding of the limits of the land in the Panhandle, making arguments over free grass less about either the economics of cattle ranching or the long-term consequences of grazing and more about populist interests against corporate "monopolies," including large cattle organizations. Hogg's biographer, Robert Cotner, concludes that the failed effort to remove Judge Willis from office demonstrated Hogg's fidelity to the law. Hogg's first test as attorney general was evidence of his desire that

Texas "emerge from a state of rampant lawlessness and lax enforcement in all areas." Finally, the employment of George Clark to "fix" the free grass bill portended a new stream of business for the modern lawyer. Influence peddling would become a tradition in Texas, and lawyers often led the way.[41]

ALIEN LAND LAW

The boom in cattle ranching led those with capital to invest in the industry. A number of those investment syndicates were foreign owned and purchased wide swaths of public domain land. The building of the capitol in the mid-1880s, in exchange for 3,050,000 acres of land, was but one example. The Chicago-based Capitol Syndicate financing the capitol building was aided by the Capitol Freehold Land and Investment Company, an investment group based in London. The syndicate's expenses totaled $3,244,593.45, making the effective purchase price of the land about $1.06 per acre, roughly twice the existing price of western lands with water. The land created the XIT Ranch, "generally recognized as the largest in the United States." In 1886 the Grand State Farmers' Alliance, which had supplanted the Grange, attacked the "monopoly" of landownership in Texas, particularly land monopolies of foreign syndicates. The alliance believed that corporate land monopolies left little or no land for the individual farmer, and landownership was the key to individual prosperity. The alliance also believed Texas should remain an agrarian state in which farmers owned their own land.[42]

If the alliance was to achieve its goals, it believed it crucial to alter Texas's land policy. In addition to demanding that fences be removed from school lands and that settlers be allowed easy purchase of public lands, the alliance urged that aliens be prohibited from owning lands and that any lands owned by aliens be forcibly sold "to actual settlers and citizens of the United States." The 1887 lease law enhanced the power of the land and cattle ranching corporations by giving them five-year leases, and the law forbade the state from selling leased land during the lease term. Still, an estimated 3.5 million acres of public lands were illegally fenced in 1887, costing the state $567,000 in revenue. By 1890, over 7 million acres of school land were leased, and sales of public lands had increased to $540,735 from $187,235 just two years earlier.[43]

Attorney General Jim Hogg, the leading candidate for governor in 1890, tied the issue of land monopolies to foreign corporations that had rushed into Texas in the 1880s. Hogg's biographer argued that the "barbed-wire barriers thrown around millions of acres by cattlemen and foreign corporations—barriers that sent the on-rushing land seekers swirling in circles, frantically looking for places to homestead, with or without water and trees," necessitated a solution benefiting farmers, which Hogg was going to find. And as far as votes went, small Texas farmers voted in much greater quantity than did foreign corporations.[44]

Three months after Hogg's inauguration, the Alien Land Law was adopted. The 1891 act began with the soothing declaration that the personal property rights of aliens were protected to the same extent as such property held by citizens of the United States. The next section then barred any alien from owning "any interest in the lands within the State of Texas." More importantly, the act barred the conveyance of title to land to "any firm, company, or corporation composed of such in whole or in part."[45]

The constitutionality of the Alien Land Law was quickly challenged in court, in at least two test cases. A test case is a lawsuit created between parties only nominally adverse to one another, often to challenge a statute's validity in court. One concern of those opposed to the law was that liens taken by aliens might not be enforceable if taken after adoption of the bill. In an interview published in the *Dallas Morning News* on July 24, 1891, one of the proponents of the bill disclaimed that possibility, declaring that the law was merely intended to stop aliens "from taking permanent title to Texas lands without becoming citizens of the United States." Six days later, Texas Land & Mortgage Company, a foreign corporation incorporated in Great Britain and doing business in Texas, entered into an agreement with one Gunter (no first name given). The company lent Gunter money secured by a mortgage on his property. Gunter immediately conveyed the mortgaged property to Henry Coke, which made his note of indebtedness due to Texas Land & Mortgage. Gunter refused to pay. The company then sued Gunter, who defended on the ground that the company lacked the authority to do business in Texas. It was a mortgage lending company incorporated in London, and the alien land law barred it from taking a mortgage lien and foreclosing on the property, for that would make it the owner of the property. The case was tried on an agreed set of facts, and the district court held the alien land law unconstitutional on the ground that the legislature failed to declare the subject of the act in its title. Gunter appealed. Although the supreme court was badly behind on its docket, the court took and decided the case in near record time. It affirmed the decision of the district court holding the law unconstitutional. It did the same in a second, similar case.[46]

Hogg then called the legislature into special session to reenact an alien land law. A law limiting alien ownership of Texas land was adopted, satisfying populist sentiment. However, it was written in a way that blunted its impact. The 1892 act did not apply to any alien who currently owned land; it excepted from the ban any alien who became a "bona fide inhabitant" of Texas; it did not apply to land in any town; it specifically allowed any alien to take a mortgage lien and to enforce such lien; and it excluded any mention of "alien" corporations. Corporate owners of Texas land were ignored in the 1892 act, possibly in part because the cattle boom was over and British cattle companies were on the verge of failure. This law, unlike the 1891 law, was not challenged in court, for it had little or no effect on landownership in Texas. It was passed in the spring of 1892 to stymie the development of the People's Party. For populists, the land issue "had no rival." The gubernatorial candidate of the People's Party, Thomas Nugent, declared that land was "nature's divinely given opportunity to work." In addition to the challenge from Nugent, Hogg faced another opponent, George Clark, Charles Goodnight's erstwhile lawyer. Clark was known as a "railroad" lawyer, a lawyer for corporate interests (in perceived contrast to the "people's" interests). Although Clark lost the Democratic nomination, he campaigned on a fusion ticket of conservative Democrats and Republicans. Hogg, the incumbent Democratic governor in a Democratic stronghold, won the gubernatorial election with about 44 percent of the vote, much less than the 76 percent with which he had won in 1890.[47]

In 1893 the legislature adopted the Perpetuities and Corporation Land Law, which declared that any private corporation "whose main purpose of business is the acquisition or ownership of land" shall be prohibited from acquiring any land. It gave those corporations fifteen years to make an actual sale of those lands. The law failed to divest large landowners of their land. By 1910, Texas had 11,123 farms of one thousand acres or more, and the percentage of tenant farmers rose from 37.6 percent in 1880 to 52.6 percent in 1910. Under this land law, as was the case with the Alien Land Law, only the attorney general had the authority to initiate a lawsuit for forfeiture of ownership. The Alien Land Law of 1892 remained in effect until 1921, when it was slightly amended. It had little effect in transferring land from large corporate landholders to landless farmers.[48]

The decades-long project of transferring land from the public to private interests ended by 1900. The populist effort to divest large corporations, particularly foreign corporations, of extensive landholdings failed to create an abundance of small farmers who owned their own land. Texas wealth would soon shift from land to the minerals found underneath the land. Discoveries of oil and gas transformed the Texas economy and much of its legal system.

OWNERSHIP OF MINERALS

Under Spanish law all minerals were owned by the king, and a grant of land to an individual did not convey ownership of minerals on the land unless expressly granted. The earliest Texas constitutions and statutes implicitly or explicitly retained this rule. For example, when Texas adopted the common law in 1840, it did not repeal the laws concerning "mines and minerals of every description." When the state confirmed Spanish and Mexican land grants pursuant to the Miller-Bourland Commission, it explicitly reserved its rights to the salt lakes. The supreme court in 1862 (formally reported in 1867) reaffirmed the reservation to the state of minerals of formerly public land. It was not until the adoption of Article VII, section 39 of the 1866 constitution that Texas released to private landowners "all mines and mineral substances" found under the soil. This rejection of Spanish law was, in slightly modified language, readopted in both the 1869 (Art. X, § 9) and 1876 (Art. XIV, § 7) constitutions. The privatization of ownership of minerals underneath one's land in the 1866 constitution was a result of a long dispute regarding title to El Sal del Rey, a salt lake in Hidalgo County.[49]

El Sal del Rey was located within San Salvador del Tule, a large grant of land in present-day South Texas awarded by the King of Spain to Juan José Ballí in 1798. By the time the Civil War began in 1861, the dispute over the ownership of the salt in El Sal del Rey had become enmeshed in the efforts to impeach John Watrous, the first federal judge in Texas.

Watrous was accused in 1858 by then U.S. senator Sam Houston of conspiring to take over El Sal del Rey, which Houston claimed was owned by Texas. At the same time, the issue of the ownership of minerals located on private land was presented to the supreme court in *Cowan v. Hardman*. Changes in the composition of the court and difficulties in resolving the issue caused the case to remain on the court's docket through January 1862, when the Confederate state of Texas decided to assert control over El Sal del Rey by statute. (In November 1862 the supreme court held in *Cowan* that the state owned minerals located on private land.) The taking of El Sal del Rey was justified as necessary because of the Civil War. Texas controlled El Sal del Rey until late 1863, when Union troops raided it. Ownership of El Sal del Rey was discussed in the Constitutional Convention of 1866. The initial proposal was to continue government possession and control of El Sal del Rey, a proposal that would have quieted title to it, for litigation over ownership was then seventeen years old. The same day, a proposal was made to give to all landowners minerals that were later discovered. The eventual provision adopted by the voters released the state's claim to all minerals, whether already known or undiscovered. This provision was continued in similar form in the 1876 constitution. Thus, when oil and gas were discovered on private land, they were owned by the landowners, not Texas.[50]

OIL AND GAS

[I]t appears that a fascinating study of modern legal, political, and economic trends may be made from the otherwise uninteresting story of the regulation of the oil industry in Texas.

So Robert E. Hardwicke, an early chronicler of the legal history of oil and gas in Texas, wrote in 1938. This history is a history of both the limits of the use of law and of the importance of

law in providing a framework for the resolution of difficult political and economic problems. The resolution in the 1930s of the crisis of too much oil ended with a centralization of power in the Texas Railroad Commission, originally created in 1891 to regulate railroads. A long-fought struggle concerning the regulation of oil and gas during the 1930s ended with Texas courts and the Supreme Court of the United States enhancing the broad exercise of authority by the commission. The Railroad Commission largely set oil prices in the United States through the 1960s, when its power was supplanted by OPEC, the Organization of Petroleum Exporting Countries. By 1972 the commission no longer limited oil production, as the industry entered an era of massive structural change, including several oil shocks. The commission's authority to regulate oil production required both a change in the understanding of the rights of persons in property and the understanding of modern constitutional law.[51]

From the time oil was discovered in 1859 in Pennsylvania through the end of the nineteenth century, the quest for oil in the United States became increasingly more intense and more profitable. Its primary use during the nineteenth century was as kerosene for illumination. The development of the internal combustion engine and the radical increase in automobile ownership in the United States altered the major use of oil from kerosene to gasoline during the twentieth century. Although Texas was a minuscule actor in the efforts to discover oil in the nineteenth century, two of the large oil fields discovered in Texas during the twentieth century made Texas a central participant in the business of oil production and thus the law of oil and gas. In particular, the discovery of oil in East Texas in 1930 precipitated a legal battle over regulatory control of oil production between the United States and Texas, a battle eventually ending in favor of the latter.[52]

A small amount of oil was found in Texas

before 1894, but the first sustainable discovery of oil was in Corsicana that year. Although the Corsicana discovery was modest, it led the 1899 legislature to allow corporations to organize to transport, sell, buy, and store oil, gas, and other minerals and gave those organizations the state's power of eminent domain. A grant of the state's power of eminent domain allowed private corporations to buy another's land to lay pipes and pipelines, as long as the pipeline did not go underneath a home or other occupied building, if they paid the landowner just compensation. Pipeline corporations were limited in purpose. They were barred from engaging in oil production or exploration, thus preventing the integrated (producing, transporting, refining, and marketing) oil company from incorporating as a Texas corporation (see chapter 4). The same legislature adopted Texas's first oil and gas conservation act, following the lead of Pennsylvania and other oil producing states.[53]

Patillo Higgins, although largely alone in his view, was convinced that the hill called Spindletop (Higgins called it "Big Hill") near Beaumont was the crest of an oil field. In 1899 he hired Anthony Lucas to drill there. Their initial efforts failed, and Higgins was out of money. Lucas traveled to Pittsburgh to see James Guffey and John Galey, successful independent oil men. Guffey and Galey agreed to fund Lucas's effort, taking seven-eighths ownership for themselves. Higgins would receive whatever fraction of the one-eighth granted Lucas as Lucas wished. On January 10, 1901, drillers struck a huge gusher of oil that spewed between 75,000 and 100,000 barrels per day during its initial nine-day flow. The Spindletop find dwarfed other American oil fields. Before Spindletop, the largest flow of oil discovered in the United States produced about 6,000 barrels per day. In 1902 alone, 17.4 million barrels of oil were recovered from the Spindletop field. After a relatively fallow period of discovery, large pools of oil and gas were found in North Texas in the 1910s and in West Texas and the Panhandle in the 1920s. The largest discovery of all was in East Texas in 1930. Although the discovery of oil transformed the Texas economy during the twentieth century, it did not do so immediately. Texas remained a state dominated by cotton during the first forty or so years of the twentieth century. However, as noted by John Stricklin Spratt, "[o]il brought into existence an entire new field of law," the law of oil and gas, a hybrid of the private law of property and the public law of constitutional rights, federalism (the division of power between the federal and state governments), and administrative law.[54]

A 1905 statute regulated the drilling and operation of oil wells, replacing the 1899 law. The modern regulatory (administrative) state was then in its infancy. The federal government had created the Interstate Commerce Commission in 1887, and several states created railroad commissions before Texas did so in 1891. However, the power and authority of regulatory bodies in the government was uncertain. To whom was the power to enforce this law given? The 1905 act gave to the district courts the power to enforce the act, "upon the application of any person . . . interested either as land owners, lessees of land or as well owners." A jury could fine those violating the law between five hundred and five thousand dollars. The legislature concluded by noting that oil and gas fields were being operated in "a wasteful and reckless manner as is dangerous to human life and property." Yet the legislature did not act again until 1913, this time to regulate the escape of natural gas. These laws were not enforced. The incentives for landowners and others to apply to the district court for a remedy were minimal, and no one else had any authority to do so.[55]

The first modest change in this enforcement structure was a 1917 law giving the Texas Railroad Commission the power to regulate pipelines carrying petroleum. In August of that year voters amended the Texas constitution to conserve the state's natural resources. Although the amendment specifically mentioned just water, it broadly declared that the conservation of all natural resources was a public right and duty and provided the legislature with the authority to pass all laws to conserve such resources. In 1917 the United States entered World War I. Texas suffered that year from a cold winter and a shortage of coal and natural gas even as gas was wasted by oil men who saw little or no market for it. The visible waste of natural gas was an immediate impetus for the 1919 legislation that gave the Texas Railroad Commission the authority to regulate the oil and gas industry. The commission was the only notable regulatory agency in the state with any expertise and standing at the time, and given the restriction of its authority over railroads by decisions of the Supreme Court of the United States, it possessed the time to undertake such work.[56]

Despite oil finds in other areas of Southeast Texas during the first decade of the twentieth century, most oil in the United States during that time came from California. In 1909 Texas was just the sixth largest producer of oil in the United States, which caused a lag in the development of oil and gas law in Texas. The first major decision of the Texas Supreme Court on oil and gas was *Texas Co. v. Daugherty* (1915). The issue in *Daugherty* was whether an oil lease taken by the Texas Company conferred to it a property interest subject to taxation. The court held that a property interest was conveyed, and thus the company was subject to the tax. The result was adoption of a legal theory known as "ownership in place," in contrast with the concept in states such as Illinois, which adopted an "exclusive right to take" theory. Ownership in place meant that one possessed a property right in the minerals underneath one's land. A related question was whether ownership in place affected the common law rule of capture with regard to oil and gas. In the late nineteenth century, state courts in Pennsylvania and Ohio analogized oil and gas (and water) to

ferae naturae (of a wild nature, applied in law to untamed animals). Under the common law, because a wild animal could escape, the mere fact that such an animal was on one's property did not convey ownership of that animal. Capture of the animal was necessary to convey ownership. The Texas Supreme Court noted that the analogy to wild animals was "at best, a limited one," for wild animals were public property, while the ownership of oil and gas was "an exclusive and private property right" of the landowner. Despite recognizing the limitations of the analogy, Texas, like all other states to confront the question, adopted the rule of capture as applied to oil and gas. Even though the right to take the oil and gas was a private property right in Texas, the rule of capture still applied to the production of the oil and gas. Consequently, title to oil and gas could be lost through legitimate drainage by another through the rule of capture.

The result of the adoption of the rule of capture as applicable to oil and gas made drilling a zero-sum game. The idea is that what I took was mine and what you took was yours, no matter where the oil was originally located. Oil located beneath one person's land could "escape" or "migrate" to that of another, who was permitted to capture it. Nearly all oil fields were located under land owned by many. Application of the rule of capture to oil and gas resulted in a battle among landowners for the oil located under the property of all. Under the rule of capture, a property owner lacked the option to choose not to drill and sue for the "loss" of oil suffered as a result of drilling undertaken by another landowner. The property owner (or leaseholder, as was more common) drilled for oil; so did his neighbor and his neighbor's neighbor. Whoever brought oil to the surface became its owner, even if the oil was originally located under another's land. Geologically, the greater the number of oil wells producing from the same field, the greater the likelihood of a rapid loss of pressure, which led to a quicker exhaustion of the oil field and a lesser recovery of the oil in the ground. (In the early twentieth century "an average of less than 25 percent of the oil in place underground was recovered" because of poor drilling practices, including overdrilling.) Fewer wells allowed for greater capture of the oil in the field. Thus, as noted by oil and gas lawyer Robert Hardwicke in the 1930s, "[t]he rule of capture is frequently and scornfully called 'the law of piracy' or 'the law of the jungle.'" But as Hardwicke argued, it was too simple merely to place the blame for oil and gas production problems on the common-law rule of capture. In Hardwicke's view, the real doctrinal villain was the "offset drilling" rule. By barring an owner of land from suing for an injunction against his neighbor whose wells drained the owner's property, the rule required the owner to protect his property in minerals by drilling his own wells, which would "offset" the drainage occurring by the actions of his neighbor. The offset drilling rule, then, was the rule that Hardwicke believed resulted in both physical waste (the operation of too many wells, creating inefficient production of oil, leading to excessive storage and evaporation and a loss in recovery amounts) and economic waste (too much money spent on too many wells for the amount of oil in the field, leading to both excessive capital expenditures and a surplus of oil, leading to a decline in prices).[57]

By 1919 oil had been discovered in the northern part of the state, in Electra (1911), Ranger (1917), Burkburnett (1919), and elsewhere. The discovery of oil in Burkburnett predated the assumption of conservation regulatory authority by the Railroad Commission. However, the commission possessed authority over pipelines. The Burkburnett discovery created two problems: first, the rule of capture encouraged more rather than less drilling, and second, pipelines were incapable of transporting all of the oil produced at Burkburnett. The Railroad Commission ordered a five-day shutdown of the Burkburnett wells. This order

was declared invalid by Attorney General C. M. Cureton, who issued his own order requiring pipeline operators to take oil from each operator. If the operator could not handle all the oil produced, then each oil producer was given a proportionate share of pipeline capacity. This was the first proration (allocating a percentage to each operator) order in Texas. This "proration order" concerned pipeline use; later, proration orders capping and allocating production would apply to oil and gas production itself.[58]

The authority given the Texas Railroad Commission in 1919 led to the promulgation of rules regarding oil and gas production, made more imperative by the problems encountered in production and transportation at the Burkburnett field. The commission hired University of Texas law professor George Butte to craft those rules. Butte, an unsuccessful Republican candidate for governor in 1924 (and apparently the first Republican ever hired by the commission), was a progressive Republican in the mold of future president Herbert Hoover. The most contentious and important of the thirty-eight rules proposed by Butte and adopted by the commission was Rule 37, which prohibited a well from being drilled within 150 feet of an existing well and within 300 feet of a lease boundary. This spacing rule was intended to limit the rapid dissipation of pressure and reduce the need for offset drilling. It was joined by Rule 38, a density rule that limited producers to no more than one well for every two acres. Although Rule 37 was challenged in several cases, each Texas court assessing its validity concluded in favor of the Railroad Commission's exercise of power. The need for judicial assessment of the application of Rule 37 was lessened by the ability of operators to obtain an exception to its enforcement. In some cases operators simply ignored it. The opportunity to obtain exceptions to the spacing rule were a result of a program of cooperation between oil producers and the commission. This cooperative model included early voluntary proration efforts in 1927 and 1928, including in the Yates field in West Texas, the largest oil field in the United States in the 1920s, with 392 wells on twenty thousand acres able to produce up to 5.25 million barrels per day. Early proration efforts were fostered by major oil companies, which possessed an interest in sustaining the productive capacity of an oil field as long as possible. What was unclear was the legal authority of the Railroad Commission to impose proration if an operator refused to agree to be bound by such an order. The authority of the commission would be severely tested by the 1930 Black Giant find in East Texas.[59]

A constitutional challenge to the authority of the Railroad Commission to regulate oil and gas was rejected by the Texas Supreme Court in 1928, providing the commission greater legitimacy. The next year the legislature adopted a law titled Conservation of Oil and Gas. It prohibited the production, transportation, storage, or use of oil or gas "as to constitute waste; provided, however, this shall not be construed to mean economic waste." The Railroad Commission was permitted to regulate oil and gas to prevent physical waste. On August 14, 1930, the commission issued its first statewide proration order pursuant to this grant of authority. It limited the production of oil in Texas to 750,000 barrels per day. The order was the calm before the storm, for the commission was about to face the greatest challenge to its authority in its existence.

Like Patillo Higgins before him, Columbus "Dad" Joiner was confident he would find oil where all others had declared no oil existed. And like Higgins, Joiner was both correct and unable to reap the enormous riches that followed a large oil discovery. Joiner believed oil was in Rusk County in East Texas. On October 3, 1930, as the Great Depression settled in across the country, Joiner's Daisy Bradford Number 3 well blew. Disbelief among oil men dissipated as more independent oil operators soon found

more oil in the area. The East Texas discoveries overshadowed the other oil fields in Texas. The "Black Giant" was forty-five miles long and between five and ten miles wide. The find was devastating to other oil producers, for the production of crude oil in the United States had reached a billion barrels that year, already more than necessary to fulfill all petroleum needs of the country. The discovery of a massive oil pool in East Texas exacerbated the problem of excessive supply, which meant a decline in prices. From an average price of one dollar a barrel in 1930, prices dropped to fifteen cents a barrel by May 1931. By June 1931, one thousand wells had been installed at the Black Giant, producing 500,000 barrels per day. In 1932 the field produced 109,561,000 barrels, and the following year 204,954,000 barrels were produced. Dad Joiner had, in his quest for financing, sold more interests than existed. His misfortune eventually became the source of H. L. Hunt's great wealth, as Hunt bought out Joiner's interests for $30,000 in cash and eventually $1.305 million after production commenced. Hunt then settled the many claims against Joiner.[60]

Major oil companies had concluded no oil was in East Texas, and they had relatively few oil leases in the area. The Black Giant was dominated by independent oil men whose desire to capture whatever oil they could created the likelihood of physical and economic waste. The short-term interest of independent oil men was in capturing and selling as much oil as possible, even as the price collapsed, for what they did not take another would capture and sell as his own. Large operators argued this made long-term planning of production of oil impossible.

The commission issued another proration order in January 1931. It was quickly challenged as unconstitutional. The next month, as the extent of the East Texas oil field was becoming more clear, the Travis County district court heard the claims attacking the proration order. Danciger Oil & Refining Company directly challenged the constitutional authority of the Railroad Commission to set limits on oil production in the state. At the conclusion of the hearing, the district court dissolved the temporary injunction barring the commission from enforcing the proration order. It rejected the argument that the actions of the commission were either an impermissible attempt to control oil prices (that is, to prevent economic waste) contrary to the 1929 act or an unconstitutional taking of the plaintiff's property. This decision had little practical effect. The Railroad Commission did not issue orders regulating the production of oil in the Black Giant until May 1, 1931, orders that were routinely ignored or evaded. However, *Danciger* had a legal impact. Because the proper place (venue) for challenges to the commission's orders was in Travis County, and a court in that county had already decided *Danciger* in favor of the commission, those opposed to production limits in East Texas avoided state court and filed suit in federal court. A three-judge panel heard *Macmillan v. Railroad Commission* in late June 1931.[61]

Meanwhile, conditions in East Texas were becoming more chaotic, as most ignored the proration order of the commission and produced as much oil as possible. By July, Governor Ross Sterling called the legislature into special session to pass a conservation act clearly granting the commission the power to prohibit economic waste. While factions of the legislature battled over whether to allow the commission to prevent economic waste, the federal court on July 28 issued its opinion in *Macmillan*. It held that the proration order for the Black Giant "was fixed at an arbitrary basis." The commission had attempted to prevent economic waste under the "thinly veiled pretense of going about to prevent physical waste." This was beyond the commission's power, making its orders void. Those legislators supportive of independent oil men used the language in *Macmillan* to adopt, on

August 12, 1931, the Anti-Market Demand Act, which expressly prohibited the Texas Railroad Commission from considering economic waste in its proration orders. By that time the East Texas field was producing a million barrels of oil a day, more than one-third of the demand for oil in the United States. The price of oil had dropped to ten cents or less a barrel. Five days after the legislature acted, Governor Sterling, former president of Humble Oil & Refining Company, declared martial law in the East Texas oil field.[62]

After martial law was imposed, the commission issued an order limiting production in East Texas to 400,000 barrels per day. The order also imposed a limit of 225 barrels per day for each well, no matter its producing capacity or the character of the land on which the well was located. Though this order was immediately challenged, it raised the price of oil to eighty-five cents per barrel by the end of the year. A three-judge federal panel heard the challenge to the order limit and to the actions of Sterling and General Jacob Wolters, a lawyer for the Texas Company charged with enforcing martial law in East Texas. On February 19, 1932, the federal district court, again in an opinion by Judge Joseph C. Hutcheson, Jr., held Sterling's actions unlawful in *Constantin v. Smith*. The court did not rule on the commission's proration order because it had already expired. Sterling appealed the decision to the Supreme Court of the United States and maintained the production quota during the appeal.[63]

In March 1932, the Texas Court of Civil Appeals affirmed the district court's decision in *Danciger*, upholding the authority of the Railroad Commission to issue a statewide production limit to conserve oil from physical waste. This court rejected the reasoning of the federal court's opinion in *Macmillan*. Two months later, the Supreme Court of the United States upheld Oklahoma proration orders in *Champlin v. Corporation Commission of Oklahoma*. That decision strongly suggests that *Macmillan* was wrongly decided. However, neither decision affected the claims by oil producers that the Railroad Commission had acted beyond the scope of its authority by regulating to prevent economic waste. In July 1932, in *People's Petroleum Producers, Inc. v. Sterling*, Judge Hutcheson read his opinion in *Macmillan* as support for the position of the Railroad Commission in limiting production, an unusual if not odd interpretation. He expressed doubt whether the orders of the commission were constitutional against a challenge that its actions were "so unreasonably and drastically restrictive" as to take the property of the oil producers, but he avoided deciding that issue. *People's Petroleum* suggested the federal courts would be more deferential in evaluating the orders of the commission. That hope was dashed with the court's decision on the merits in *People's Petroleum v. Smith* on October 24, 1932, that the commission's orders restricting production in East Texas were unreasonable because they were designed to limit economic waste. The court also concluded that the per-well allotment provided for by the commission was unreasonable. The Texas legislature then took the step it had refused to take a year earlier. It adopted the Market Demand Act, which permitted the Railroad Commission to regulate to prevent both economic and physical waste. A month after the adoption of the Market Demand Act, the U.S. Supreme Court upheld the three-judge district court's opinion in *Constantin*.[64]

The Market Demand Act did not lessen litigation concerning proration orders of the Railroad Commission during 1933, particularly in federal court. The Texas Supreme Court reversed on procedural grounds the lower court decisions in *Danciger* and offered no opinion on the constitutionality of the commission's actions. After adoption of the Market Demand Act, the Railroad Commission set the allowable production in East Texas at 290,000 barrels. This was immediately challenged in federal court. In *People's Petroleum Producers, Inc. v. Smith* (1933), a three-judge panel held the per-well proration order unconstitutional. In response, the commission on April 22, 1933, increased the East Texas quota to 750,000 barrels per day and later to 1,000,000 barrels per day, an astonishing amount considering American demand was about 2.7 million barrels per day. By May 5 the price of East Texas oil had dropped to four cents a barrel. Shortly after the Texas Supreme Court's decision in *Danciger* was issued, John Danciger filed suit in federal court challenging the Market Demand Act and the commission's actions. The court initially issued a temporary restraining order, but on June 25, 1933, it ordered the restraining order dissolved and the suit dismissed. This opinion by Judge Hutcheson offers an early reorienting of the role of the courts in assessing administrative action. He focused on a standard of review that included an assessment whether the commission's action "has no foundation in reason, [or] is a mere arbitrary exercise of power having no substantial relation to the authority justly conferred." This was more deferential than the "unreasonableness" standard offered in Hutcheson's earlier opinions. The large allowance to East Texas oil producers depressed prices, which were ten cents a barrel in the middle of the year. This price was also caused by the running of "hot oil," oil produced in defiance of and contrary to the orders of Railroad Commission.[65]

President Franklin Delano Roosevelt commenced a broad if often incoherent effort to combat the Great Depression upon inauguration on March 4, 1933. During Roosevelt's first hundred days in office, he proposed fifteen bills. Each was approved by Congress, including the National Industrial Recovery Act (NIRA), adopted on June 16. One amendment to the NIRA, section 9(c), gave the president the discretionary authority to limit the interstate transportation of hot oil by criminalizing such action. By mid-July Secretary of the Interior

Harold Ickes began requiring producers to file affidavits that they were not producing or shipping hot oil pursuant to an executive order issued based on 9(c). Federal employees were sent to East Texas to enforce this executive order, immediately leading to a production decline of over 22 percent. The NIRA also allowed the president to create and enforce codes of competition to lessen price wars. On August 19, 1933, the Code of Fair Competition for the Petroleum Industry, promulgated pursuant to the NIRA, was adopted (a revised code was adopted in mid-September) by presidential executive order. By late 1933, two sets of special agents of the Department of the Interior were in Texas to enforce the hot oil provisions, including a Tyler division consisting of sixty-seven agents. Hot oil continued to flow out of East Texas, despite fines, as the price of East Texas oil slowly increased, increasing profits for hot oil sellers. The Interior Department quickly filed fifty lawsuits claiming a violation of the hot oil regulations. As noted by historian Nicholas Malavis, "[a]ll 50 defendants were released on bond and resumed their illicit activities." In October 1933 two lawsuits were filed in federal court, one challenging the Railroad Commission's new orders reducing to four hundred thousand barrels the daily limit for East Texas, and the other claiming the NIRA was unconstitutional.[66]

Both cases were initially tried together at the end of December 1933. The three-judge panel, again led by Hutcheson, upheld the four-hundred-thousand-barrel limit in *Amazon Petroleum Corp. v. Railroad Commission* (1934). In the companion case of *Panama Refining Co. v. Ryan* (1934), the federal district court held that the codes of competition regulated intrastate commerce beyond Congress's authority to regulate commerce "among the several states." The codes were thus inapplicable to the plaintiffs, who "have not subscribed to such code and are not engaged in interstate commerce." This allowed the district court to avoid deciding

the constitutionality of section 9(c). Writing in February 1934, the district court offered a standard interpretation of interstate commerce. Issues of production and manufacture were ordinarily understood as intrastate activities outside of congressional regulatory authority, a view accepted by the Supreme Court as late as mid-1936. This view abruptly came to an end in mid-1937.[67]

Three months later, the U.S. Court of Appeals for the Fifth Circuit reversed the district court's decision in *Panama Refining*. It rejected the oil company's commerce clause argument and quickly dismissed the claim that the NIRA unconstitutionally delegated legislative power to the executive. The Supreme Court of the United States granted certiorari. In *Panama Refining Co. v. Ryan*, issued on January 7, 1935, the Court, by a vote of eight to one, held that section 9(c) of the NIRA was an unconstitutional delegation of Congress's power to the president.[68]

Panama Refining, also known as the *Hot Oil Case*, is one of just two cases (both decided in 1935 and both concerning the NIRA) in which the Supreme Court has held Congress unconstitutionally delegated its legislative power to the president. Much of the modern American administrative state consists of broad statutes adopted by Congress, enforced through the adoption and implementation by administrative bodies of detailed regulatory rules. Persons are punished by fines for violating regulations that have never been specifically adopted by Congress. And a party who violates those properly promulgated regulations will not prevail in court by claiming Congress unconstitutionally delegated its legislative power. *Panama Refining* was the first decision by the Supreme Court holding a New Deal law unconstitutional, and it signaled the beginning of a constitutional crisis. The Supreme Court issued several other decisions in 1935 holding unconstitutional New Deal laws, including a decision declaring unconstitutional the NIRA. Similar holdings followed in 1936. After winning reelection in 1936, Roosevelt in February 1937 offered a court "reorganization" plan, called a "court-packing" plan by his opponents. Roosevelt lost the battle (legislation eventually failed) but won the war. In March 1937 the Supreme Court broadened its understanding of interstate commerce in *NLRB v. Jones & Laughlin Steel Corp.* Its reasoning allowed the federal government to control oil production directly. But by the time *Jones & Laughlin Steel* was decided, Texas and other states had gained congressional approval to regulate oil production through an interstate oil compact.[69]

In the middle of 1934, as the appeals in the *Amazon* and *Panama Refining* cases were taken, bills were filed in Congress allowing the secretary of the interior to establish national mandatory production quotas on petroleum. The reaction by at least one Texas congressman was to compare national control of oil production (derisively called the Ickes Oil Dictatorship Bill) to Reconstruction, "where soldiers undertook to make . . . white people subject to Negro people." The Supreme Court's decision in *Panama Refining* created an instant fear that the production of hot oil would again depress oil prices. Within six weeks of the decision, Congress adopted the Connally Hot Oil Act. The act prohibited the transportation in interstate commerce of "contraband oil," which was defined as oil produced in contravention to state proration orders. The act thus avoided national regulation of oil production but allowed national prosecution of hot oil producers. It also gave states, particularly the Texas Railroad Commission, the power to issue proration orders enforceable by either state or federal authorities. The Hot Oil Act was held constitutional by Judge Hutcheson. Several oil-producing states, including Texas, entered into the Interstate Oil Compact, ratified by Congress in August 1935. Finally, in June 1935 the Texas Supreme Court recognized the doctrine of correlative rights, which limited the

rule of capture, allowing each landowner the opportunity to obtain a fair share of oil found in a reservoir common to several landowners. The court declared that "when an oil field has been fairly tested and developed, experts can determine approximately the amount of oil and gas in place in a common pool, and can also equitably determine the amount of oil and gas recoverable by the owner of each tract of land under certain operating conditions." The Railroad Commission now possessed the authority under the spacing requirements of Rule 37 to limit a property owner's common law right of capture to protect the correlative rights of another landowner in possession of part of the common oil pool.[70]

Writing in late 1938, Robert Hardwicke noted that "about one-half of the known oil reserves of the United States are located in Texas," and Texas produced 42 percent of the oil in the United States. By 1948 Texas produced about half of the crude oil in the United States. Through the mid-1950s Texas produced over 40 percent of all American-based oil. The aftermath of the East Texas oil crisis resulted in an extensive increase in the power of the Railroad Commission, both as a consequence of greater judicial deference to administrative and legislative bodies beginning in 1937 and because of Texas's predominance in oil production. Oil producers continued to challenge the commission's Rule 37 decisions (Hardwicke counted more than one hundred appellate decisions on Rule 37 in the years 1938–48), but they were largely unsuccessful. In 1939 the Texas Supreme Court adopted the "substantial evidence" rule now commonplace in administrative law. The substantial evidence rule gave courts the authority to overturn an order of the Railroad Commission only if the order was "illegal, unreasonable, or arbitrary." In making this determination, the commission's interpretation of the facts would be accepted as long as those facts were "reasonably supported by substantial evidence." Although it vacillated on this standard, the court reaffirmed the substantial evidence rule in 1946, enhancing greatly the commission's power by making judicial challenges to its actions unlikely to succeed.[71]

The Supreme Court of the United States also severely limited constitutional challenges based on the due process clause of the Fourteenth Amendment. In *Railroad Comm'n of Texas v. Rowan & Nichols Oil Co.* (1940), an oil company challenged proration orders of the Railroad Commission on grounds of both reasonableness and due process. The company won at the federal district court and in the Fifth Circuit on the ground that the commission's order was "confiscatory," taking the company's property (oil in the ground) contrary to the due process clause of the Fourteenth Amendment. The Supreme Court rejected the challenge and deferred to administrative expertise: "It is not for the federal courts to supplant the Commission's judgment even in the face of convincing proof that a different result would have been better." The company's claim that the commission was taking its private property by limiting extraction of its oil was also dismissed by the Court. After 1937 a person's claim that a regulation of private property violated the due process clause of the Fourteenth Amendment was a lost cause.

The Court followed up *Rowan & Nichols* with a 1941 opinion concerning the Railroad Commission. The Pullman Company, which owned sleeping cars attached to passenger trains, challenged the decision of the commission that required the use of a conductor or his equivalent when just one sleeping car was attached to the train. Pullman ordinarily used porters if one sleeping car was attached and a conductor only if two or more sleeping cars were attached. The commission's rule appears to have been based on reasons of race: conductors were white, and porters were black. Requiring a conductor thus required the use of a white employee in a sleeping car. Texas segregated train cars on the basis of race, and its

rule was intended to ensure that whites in the sleeping car were not subject to orders given by a black employee. The Court created the *Pullman* "abstention" doctrine in its decision. It suggested that federal courts abstain from determining the constitutionality of a matter of state law if the state's highest court had not yet definitively interpreted it and the state court could resolve the constitutional issue by doing so. *Pullman* abstention is not constitutionally mandatory, and as the civil rights movement came to the fore of judicial consciousness during the 1950s, abstention was rejected in matters of civil rights. However, these decisions limited the ability of oil producers to challenge decisions of the commission in federal court. Those objecting to commission orders were sent to state courts and the deferential substantial evidence rule.[72]

The post–World War II history of the relation between the doctrine of ownership in place and small tracts of land took one major turn. In 1946, in *Railroad Commission v. Humble Oil & Refining Co.* (known as the *Hawkins Case*), the Court of Civil Appeals suggested that every landowner possessed a right to an individual well. This was necessary, stated a later court, "to prevent the confiscation of the gas underlying his tract, he, therefore, becomes entitled to confiscate gas from adjacent properties sufficient to pay the cost of his drilling operations and return a reasonable profit." If a small landowner could not profitably take just the gas from his property, he could claim a right to take gas from his neighbor's property to make his well profitable. Given the ownership in place doctrine, by what right did one small landowner take another's property to guarantee a profit? Small landowners were voters. Large tract owners were often major oil companies, many of which were headquartered outside the state. The populist history of Texas favoring the "little guy" against the large, faceless foreign (out-of-state) corporation also suggested why small landowners were protected in obtaining not only their minerals, but the minerals of others as well. On the other hand, if the small landowner was prevented by commission regulations from putting even one well on his property, other landowners would end up taking (through the rule of capture) the small landowner's minerals, which also seemed unfair. The Railroad Commission thus often granted Rule 37 spacing exceptions to small producers. By 1960, however, Texas oil producers were subject to greater economic pressure from cheap foreign oil, particularly from the Middle East but also from Mexico and Venezuela. Greater competition forced the Texas oil industry to become more efficient in oil production. However, neither the legislature nor the elected Railroad Commission was willing to alter the economically inefficient but politically potent right of small landowners to take another's oil. In two cases decided in 1961 and 1962, a divided Texas Supreme Court limited the practice by which small landowners were allowed to take more than their "fair share" through Rule 37 exception requests. It did so in a less than forthright fashion, for the members of the court were also elected officials. The *Port Acres* and *Normanna* decisions explicitly noted that the only way to make these small areas profitable was to allow them to take gas from the property of others. Even so, the ability of a small landowner to take another's gas in order to make his well economically sustainable violated the property rights of the other landowner. The commission's orders benefiting small landowners were thus invalid, because they did not "afford an opportunity to all of the parties to produce and save their fair share of the minerals or their equivalent." The dissent stated what the court was unwilling to declare directly: "When I wrote the dissent in *Normanna*, it was my deliberate purpose to guard against compulsory pooling by judicial decree. I find the Court now following the advocates of compulsory pooling in the present case." This policy, the dissent argued with much justifica-

tion, was solely within the legislature's purview. The court's oblique decisions led the commission to begin to apply new spacing rules to make oil and gas production more efficient. The court made it clear by 1964 that the commission could no longer favor small landowners. In 1965, nudged by the court, the legislature adopted a law providing for limited compulsory pooling to protect small landowners, a populist response to the court's decisions.[73]

The history of the regulation of gas was not as tortured as that of oil, but extensive litigation occurred, and the result favored federal regulatory power over gas. After early skirmishing concerning the validity of the commission's orders, the 1935 Texas legislature adopted a comprehensive gas regulation bill, known as House Bill 266. After adoption, a question before the commission was the regulation of gas in the Panhandle Gas Field. The commission's order dividing the field into east and west fields was challenged in federal court on the ground that it was beyond the authority granted by House Bill 266. The three-judge court barred enforcement of the order, concluding that House Bill 266 was a statute prohibiting waste, not a statute allowing the commission to prevent drainage or to modify the common law rule of capture. One commentator declared this conclusion did "violence to the legislative history of the act." The Supreme Court of the United States upheld that conclusion in *Consolidated Gas Utilities Co. v. Thompson*. Even so, the Supreme Court doubted the trial court's finding that correlative rights could not be protected by the commission other than to prevent physical waste.[74]

One difficulty in regulating gas was the nature of the resource. A second difficulty was a lack of a commercial market for it. Throughout the 1930s operators flared billions of cubic feet of casinghead gas (gas produced from an oil well as opposed to gas produced from a gas well), a tremendous physical waste. The commission refused to prohibit this practice until

World War II, when the need for oil and gas for war operations prioritized resource conservation. In 1947 the commission issued an order shutting down any oil well until its casinghead gas could be saved for lawful use. It did so in light of a federal threat to exercise control over gas for conservation purposes issued by the Federal Power Commission (FPC) in its 1946 hearings on gas waste. The commission's order was immediately challenged. Although the Texas Supreme Court upheld the district court's temporary injunction barring enforcement of the shutdown order, it broadly held in favor of the commission's power to prevent flaring of casinghead gas. By 1949 the commission's power to regulate the waste of gas was clear.[75]

The legislature never gave the commission the authority to issue proration orders concerning the statewide production of gas. Further, the supreme court's 1937 *Thompson* decision, which held that the commission lacked the authority to prorate gas production, remained in effect until after the end of World War II. In *Corzelius v. Harrell* (1945) the supreme court ordered the commission to allocate gas production among competitors in the same field. Through the end of the 1940s, the commission allocated gas production within fields if requested by producers. It did not, however, attempt to create any statewide proration efforts.[76]

Construing the federal Natural Gas Act of 1938, the Supreme Court of the United States held in 1954 that the FPC possessed the authority and duty to regulate gas sold for interstate transportation and resale, despite the fact that the FPC disclaimed such authority. By 1963 the Supreme Court declared that orders of a state regulatory body requiring an interstate pipeline company to purchase gas ratably (that is, equitably rather than discriminatorily) from all wells connecting with its pipeline system interfered with the exclusive regulatory jurisdiction of the FPC. This was because state orders doing so would indirectly regulate the price of interstate gas. Because FPC prices for gas were lower than Texas prices, gas producers attempted to insulate themselves from interstate regulation by selling only within the state. By the mid-1970s, as the first energy shock hit the United States, a surplus of gas existed in Texas, while the rest of the United States suffered a shortfall. By 1978 the Railroad Commission, which had attempted to reduce gas production to lessen the Texas surplus, was accused of price fixing. The adoption by Congress of the National Gas Policy Act of 1978 temporarily ended the difficulty by allowing intrastate gas to be sold to interstate pipelines without coming under the permanent regulatory authority of the Department of Energy.[77]

WATER LAW

Water is separated into three recognized types in Texas: (1) surface water found in lakes and rivers; (2) diffused water, ordinarily created by precipitation and also called sheet flow; and (3) groundwater. Surface water is owned by the state, which regulates the manner in which a person may take state-owned water. Diffused water and groundwater are owned by private landowners, who are permitted to capture and control that water for their use with relatively little interference by the state. This section focuses on the development of the law of surface water and groundwater.[78]

Surface water law has undergone four distinct phases: a Spanish and Mexican legal system in effect to 1840, when the Congress of the Republic of Texas adopted the common law of England; a "western" modification of the English riparian rights system until 1889; a dual system combining riparian rights law with a system of prior appropriation law until 1967; and a licensing system since 1967. The law regarding ownership of groundwater has, for over one hundred years, been based on the "absolute ownership" or "rule of capture" of the English common law. The different legal approaches to different types of water, in light of the very different geological formations in Texas, as well as the manner in which Texas was populated, offers a striking perspective on the manner in which courts and the legislature work together or in opposition to fashion (or avoid fashioning) law.[79]

Texas courts and legislatures have historically been strongly influenced by the common-law doctrine of vested rights. Once a right (often a property right) exists (has vested, rather than being contingent), that right cannot be taken away without due process and just compensation. One difficulty with this doctrine in nineteenth-century American legal history was in determining the difference between impairment of a vested right and alteration of the legal remedy available when a vested right was impaired. For example, state laws allowing for the discharge of debts impaired a contractual vested right, the right to be repaid. Were such state laws constitutional? The Supreme Court of the United States eventually held constitutional such laws, if prospective, because they affected only the remedy and not the right. This is called the right/remedy distinction. In Texas law, vested property rights gave a citizen the rights that existed when that citizen or the citizen's predecessor took the land from the sovereign. Thus, determining the landowner's vested water rights largely depended on which sovereign (Spain, Mexico, Republic of Texas, or state of Texas) originally granted the land.[80]

The Spanish and Mexican system of water law applied to lands granted by those sovereigns, slightly more than twenty-six million acres in Texas. In *Motl v. Boyd* (1926), the Texas Supreme Court declared in dictum that the Spanish law of water rights was similar to the English common law of riparian water rights. Riparian water rights allowed a landowner whose land encompassed or bordered a flowing stream to take water from the stream for the landowner's use. The landowner did

not have an ownership interest in the water but a right to reasonable use of that water, a right also enjoyed by other landowners, including those downstream. If the reasonable use of the water for natural purposes (water for animals and residents, but ordinarily not for irrigation) diverted all of the water to the upstream owner, leaving nothing for the downstream user, that remained a lawful reasonable use. Thirty years after *Motl* was decided, it was clear that its conclusion was based on an incorrect understanding of a Mexican legal treatise. Peter Reich has concluded that the *Motl* court "was aware of the distortion." The court allegedly fostered this distortion because "the riparian irrigation doctrine facilitated water monopolization, in this case by the owners of large riparian estates." Joseph McKnight's explanation was more benign, concluding that *Motl* was a result of a loss of "the thread of Hispanic learning" after the Civil War. A 2003 *Baylor Law Review* article alternatively suggests that Texas courts in the 1920s "appeared sincerely unfamiliar with Spanish law." The legal reassessment of *Motl* occurred as a result of another long drought in Texas during the 1950s. In *State v. Valmont Plantations* (1961), the Texas Court of Civil Appeals rejected the dictum in *Motl* and concluded that Spanish and Mexican law did not allow a riparian right of irrigation, an opinion adopted by the Texas Supreme Court.[81]

When Texas adopted the common law of England in 1840 it adopted English water law. In *Hans v. Choussard* (1856), Chief Justice John Hemphill, who preferred Spanish civil law to the common law, recognized that Texas had adopted the common law doctrine of riparian rights. Although irrigation was traditionally understood as an "artificial" use rather than a "natural" use in riparian rights law, the Texas Supreme Court in dictum in 1863 and in a holding in 1868 stated irrigation was a "natural use." In 1872, the reviled Semicolon Court (see chapter 2) rejected the claim that irrigation was a natural use and suggested that the legislature remedy the issue by statute. The Semicolon Court's decisions were anathema in post–Reconstruction Texas and were sparingly cited as precedent. The court's suggestion was largely ignored. At the same time, the Texas legislature adopted a number of laws suggesting that it controlled the use of surface water and that riparian owners lacked a right to use surface water to irrigate. The privatization of most of Texas public lands between 1840 and 1889 gave landowners vested riparian rights, including the right to use water for all natural uses. Whether a riparian right to irrigate was a natural use remained unclear.[82]

In 1889 the legislature adopted its first prior appropriation act for water, applicable to arid and semiarid West Texas. Prior appropriation created a system granting water rights to those who used it for "beneficial purposes," including irrigation, and was the water law system used in arid western states. Several factors coalesced to bring about the legislation. Texas had suffered from a severe drought beginning in 1883. Railroads had received from the state millions of acres in arid and semiarid West Texas during the 1870s and wanted to sell that land. Further, Texas had in 1879 and 1883 begun to sell its school land, much of which was in West Texas. That land was difficult to sell to farmers if irrigation was not clearly permitted. Irrigation canal companies were unwilling to spend capital unless secure water supplies existed. By 1889, most western states had adopted the prior appropriation system of water rights instead of the common law riparian system, which offered a guide to restructuring water law in arid Texas. Finally, the confused state of the law of water rights as contradictorily declared in the courts and the legislature made clarity an important concern for settlers and sellers of land.[83]

The 1889 act did not create clarity. Although it borrowed prior appropriation law from Wyoming, Nebraska, and Oregon for unappropriated waters, it did not define the term *unappropriated water*. (It did declare that such

waters were the property of the state.) The act acknowledged that some existing landowners maintained riparian rights that were not to be prejudiced by the act. For example, a landowner with land lying along a riverbank was not to be deprived by an appropriator of flowing water "for his own domestic use." One who wished to take "unappropriated" water was required to file an affidavit with the county clerk regarding the amount of water claimed. Two months after the law was adopted, in construing an 1875 law creating an irrigation canal company, the Texas Supreme Court held the legislature did not have the authority to regulate the use of water for irrigation if it affected riparian owners: "[T]he legislature had no power to take away or impair the vested rights of riparian owners without providing for the payment of a just compensation." Vested rights were now a constitutional rule. The 1889 law was amended in 1893, and in 1895 the legislature adopted another appropriation act applicable to the entire state. The 1895 law divided surface water into the ordinary flow and the storm and rain waters, the latter of which were declared the state's water. In *Barrett v. Metcalfe* (1896), the Court of Civil Appeals held unconstitutional the act of 1889 if it deprived riparian owners of the right to irrigate, a reinforcement of the vested rights doctrine and an apparent expansion of riparian rights.[84]

In 1905 the supreme court declared irrigation an artificial use, but it permitted riparian owners to a reasonable use for irrigation (meaning they could not take all of the water in order to irrigate, as they were allowed to do for natural uses). However, the court limited its opinion to lands granted by the state before the 1889 and 1895 acts, which declared water was publicly owned. This was a pyrrhic victory, for nearly all of the state's land had been sold or given away before those acts became law. The result was an unwieldy system after 1895: Water rights depended on the law in existence at the time it was granted. Lands granted before 1840 were subject to Spanish and Mexican law, lands granted between 1840 and 1895 were subject to the doctrine of riparian rights, and a combined system of prior appropriation and riparian rights applied to lands granted after 1895 (and sometimes after 1889). In addition, the extent to which riparian rights included the right to irrigate was unclear for those public lands privatized before 1895. The law was a confused mass of legislatively and judicially declared rights and limitations, both limited by the court's constitutionalization of the vested rights of riparian owners.[85]

Another drought led to an act in 1913 that denied recognition of any riparian right to land granted by Texas after July 1, 1895. The adoption in 1917 of the Irrigation Act, along with the Conservation Amendment to the Texas Constitution, was in part a response to another drought that year. The 1917 act created a Board of Water Engineers to decide conflicting water rights claims. The legislature again followed the path of Wyoming and Nebraska, both of which had created such a board. Although courts in those states had upheld these administrative bodies against a constitutional attack, the Texas Supreme Court rejected that conclusion. The board's authority to make such decisions, the court declared in *Board of Engineers v. McKnight* (1921), violated separation of powers, for the executive branch (through the board) impermissibly encroached on the judicial power to adjudicate disputes. The board continued in existence, capable of giving permits for water use if the applicant promised development, but unable to take away any water rights. The state of water law was a mess, and the judiciary attempted to reconcile a conflict it had created.[86]

The holding (not the dictum) of *Motl v. Boyd* (1926) was an attempted compromise between riparian rights holders and prior appropriation rights holders, structured in part on the legislature's irrigation acts. The court declared that normal and ordinary flow of streams was subject to riparian rights, a conclusion that followed the express statement in the 1913 act that riparian owners could not be prejudiced in their use of water without their consent. However, storm waters and flood waters in streams were not subject to riparian rights, a conclusion that followed the legislature's 1895 conclusion declaring state ownership of such water. Unfortunately, *Motl v. Boyd* failed to reflect scientific understanding. The distinction between normal and ordinary flow and storm waters made little sense to hydrologists. In general, the difficulty was that, as stated much later by Justice Jack Pope, "the concepts basic to the two systems [riparian rights and prior appropriation] were hostile to each other." Riparian rights existed as part of the land grant, existing only if the landowner owned land adjacent to the stream; appropriation rights existed as a matter of state grant, and a landowner far from the stream could obtain such rights. Riparian rights continued to exist even when the landowner took no water; appropriation rights could lapse if unused. Consequently, water law in Texas "was in a chaotic state prior to the enactment of the Water Rights Adjudication Act of 1967."[87]

During the 1950s Texas suffered from another multiyear drought, which led to claims of water rights in the Rio Grande Valley that far exceeded the amount of water available. The lawsuit filed by the state in 1956 to adjudicate these rights took over thirteen years and "cost an estimated $10 million in court costs and attorneys fees." Because the Texas Supreme Court had declared the 1917 act unconstitutional, only courts were permitted to resolve disputes among water rights holders with conflicting claims. The 1953 legislature created a nonjudicial forum to resolve competing water claims, but it was held void in 1958. The University of Texas School of Law sponsored water law conferences in 1952, 1954, 1955, 1956, and 1959. The proper resolution to the oversubscription of prior appropriation rights, the extent to which riparian rights extended before the adoption of the common law of England in 1840, and the rights in groundwater and other topics were analyzed, and proposed solutions were offered. One initial breakthrough was a brief paper given in 1955 by Will Wilson, an associate justice of the supreme court, titled *A Reappraisal of Motl v. Boyd.* Justice Wilson and University of Houston Law School dean A. R. White in a separate paper suggested that the dictum in *Motl* that Spanish law included riparian rights with a power to irrigate was incorrect. Six years later, then Court of Civil Appeals justice Jack Pope wrote the opinion in *State v. Valmont Plantations* (1961), one of the cases arising from the South Texas water claims. Pope's history of Spanish and Mexican land grants conclusively demonstrated that a specific grant was necessary in order to claim a right to irrigate. No implicit grant of riparian rights existed under Spanish or Mexican law. Pope's conclusion was adopted by the supreme court the following year. This breakthrough, which affected the law applicable to many important Texas waterways, generated momentum for the legislature to adopt the Water Rights Adjudication Act in 1967, which gave the Texas Water Commission authority to resolve water claims for surface waters.[88]

By 1982, Jack Pope was a member of the Texas Supreme Court. The Water Rights Adjudication Act was challenged both as violating separation of powers and as an unconstitutional taking, a claim rooted in the vested rights doctrine. Pope first rejected the claim that the act violated separation of powers as decided in *McKnight*. He noted that the act was drafted specifically to remedy the constitutional infirmities declared in *McKnight*. The Water Rights Adjudication Act provided for judicial review of the administrative decisions of the Water Commission, making *McKnight* inapt. The court also rejected the takings claim of riparian owners. The act limited riparian owners to receive the "maximum beneficial

use" of water taken between 1963 and 1967. This was a limitation of the traditional common-law riparian right to all "reasonable use." Because the court noted that a riparian right was not a right of ownership of the water, but a right to use nonflood waters (called a usufructory use), the abrogation of a "continued non-use of the usufructory right" was not a taking. This conclusion conflicted with common-law doctrine, which did not require a riparian rights owner to use the water in order to maintain the common-law right. The court carefully distinguished between a common-law right to use water and a constitutional right barring a taking of property. The limitation of the riparian user to "maximum beneficial use" did not take any property and thus did not violate the Texas constitution. The court mentioned that the 1967 act was modeled after Oregon's law, which had been upheld by Oregon courts as early as 1914. The act was a reasonable exercise of the state's powers.

The history of the use and ownership of groundwater has been less confusing but of increasing concern as the population of Texas boomed during the twentieth century. In *Houston & Texas Central Railway Co. v. East* (1904), the Texas Supreme Court adopted the absolute ownership rule for groundwater. Under this rule the owner of the surface land also owned the water percolating underneath that land, creating a vested property right in the water. As was true of oil pools, groundwater generally was found underneath the land of more than one owner. In such a case, each owner was permitted to capture the groundwater as the owner saw fit. This was permitted even if one owner's capture of the groundwater lessened the ability of a second owner to capture groundwater located beneath the second owner's land. The rule of capture did not recognize any correlative rights among owners of a common pool of water. In *East*, the supreme court noted that "probably" every American court other than New Hampshire's had adopted the rule of capture, and it followed suit. The court additionally noted that the defendant railroad's use of twenty-five thousand gallons of water daily for its trains was "a reasonable and legitimate use of the water." Finally, it held the railroad was not acting with malice or wantonly in taking the water, and therefore "[n]o reason exists why the general doctrine should not govern this case."[89]

Numerous efforts were made over the decades to abrogate the rule of capture for groundwater. The 1917 Conservation Amendment to the Texas Constitution required the state to conserve water as a matter of public right and duty. By later statute an owner was limited to using groundwater for a "beneficial use," a modest limitation on the rule of capture. In 1949 the Texas legislature adopted the Water Control and Improvement District Act, which permitted the formation of local conservation districts for underground water. It was the first state to create local districts to attempt to control the use of groundwater. Litigation proposing abrogation of the rule of capture failed in 1955 and in 1978. In the first case, the court declared the legislature was given the "exclusive" duty to regulate groundwater. In the latter case, the court modified the common law rule by allowing a plaintiff to make a claim that a defendant's negligence in taking water caused subsidence in the plaintiff's land. In 1996, the court, in rejecting a facial constitutional challenge to a statute creating the Edwards Aquifer Authority, restated the authority of the legislature to regulate groundwater. Finally, in 1999 the supreme court declined to limit the rule of capture to reasonable use, despite "compelling reasons for groundwater use to be regulated."[90]

The concurring opinion of Justice Nathan Hecht noted that by 1963 Texas was the only western state to continue to follow the rule of capture. Groundwater supplied 56 percent of all water needs in Texas by 1992, and twenty-nine different aquifers were underneath 81 percent of the state, making groundwater a crucial aspect of Texas water needs. Although Justice Hecht concluded that a provision in the Restatement (Second) of Torts offered a model rule to replace the rule of capture, he concurred because a 1997 statute regulating some water use was sufficient to give the legislature time to create a "fair, effective, and comprehensive regulation of water use." Thus, "for now—but I think only for now—*East* should not be overruled." The rule of capture remained law in Texas not because it remained law elsewhere but because the court wanted to force an unwilling legislature to fulfill its duty to regulate water use. Of course, the court itself possessed the authority to overrule *East*. Neither branch of government was willing to take the first step, apparently to avoid possible political repercussions for initiating such a change.[91]

Since Hecht's warning, the legislature has acted on several occasions to further regulate water rights. In 1997 the legislature adopted Senate Bill 1, initially hailed as a major effort to protect the water supply in Texas but not the comprehensive bill claimed by its sponsors. In 2001, in response to a judicial decision holding that a groundwater district lacked the authority to limit groundwater recovery based on land area, and giving the legislature forty days to remedy this statutory gap, the legislature adopted Senate Bill 2, which expressly authorized limitations on water production based on "acreage or tract size." This limitation on water production by statute may lead to the adoption of a correlative rights approach to groundwater, as happened with oil many decades earlier. The legislature also acted in 2005. About 90 percent of the aquifers designated by the Texas Water Development Board are covered by local groundwater conservation districts, and most of those local districts have adopted rules regulating water production. The legislature resisted creating a statewide system of groundwater regulation in favor of local district regulation. However, it has declared that the "ownership and rights of the owners of the land and their lessees and assigns in groundwater are hereby recognized." What those rights constitute, however, remains uncertain. Further, the legislature has permitted the local districts to limit or alter those rights as long as they do not discriminate in doing so. Litigation attempting to clarify the legislature's language will again send the issue to the courts.[92]

THE TIDELANDS CONTROVERSY (*UNITED STATES V. TEXAS (1950)*)

In April 1945, three months into his fourth term of office, President Franklin D. Roosevelt died. He was succeeded by Harry S Truman, the unprepossessing Missourian. The presidency of FDR had greatly shifted the balance of political power from the states to the federal government. This change in the nature of federalism was worrisome for both good and ill reasons. For some, the accumulation of power by the federal government at the expense of state governments portended corruption. For others, particularly some southern Democratic politicians, a shift in power to the federal government threatened to upset the system of *de jure* (by law) racial segregation. Roosevelt's death, followed quickly by the end of World War II, offered the possibility to rectify this perceived imbalance, for either or both of these reasons. The Tidelands Controversy was portrayed by proponents of federal power as a story about limiting the baneful influence of oil men. Those who opposed the assertion of federal power over the tidelands argued that the story was about the defense of the interests of the states and reviving federalism in the face of a continuing federal grab for power. But the Tidelands Controversy also served as a proxy for the upcoming battle over the role of the federal government in protecting and advancing civil rights.

Shortly before Roosevelt's death, Secretary of the Interior Harold Ickes persuaded him to order Attorney General Francis Biddle to sue for title to the submerged lands off the coast of California. Biddle did so by suing an oil company leasing submerged land from California. This frustrated Ickes, who wanted Biddle to sue California itself in the Supreme Court of the United States. On September 28, 1945, President Truman issued an executive order claiming that all minerals in the seabed were subject to the jurisdiction and control of the United States. Three weeks later, the new attorney general, Tom Clark, a Texan and future Supreme Court justice, abandoned Biddle's suit and sued California in the Supreme Court. Clark did so only after receiving a second order from Truman to settle the issue nationwide. The battle over title to the California tidelands led indirectly to the resignation of Ickes in February 1946, which gave the issue more prominent news coverage. In mid-1946 Congress sent a joint resolution to Truman disclaiming any right, title, interest, or claim in the submerged lands (a quitclaim bill) within three miles of the coast of any state. Truman vetoed the joint resolution. *United States v. California* (1947) was argued in March 1947, and in May the Supreme Court held in favor of the United States.[93]

The Court did not distinguish itself in its decision, nor in its aftermath, for it expressly refused to declare that the United States owned the submerged lands, even though the decision held that California did not own those lands. Its inconclusiveness meant both more litigation and a political firestorm. *United States v. California* did not, contrary to Attorney General Clark's hopes, resolve the tidelands issue.

The 1948 presidential election was notable for at least two events: First, the Democratic National Convention was the subject of a protest and departure by a number of so-called Dixiecrats, who left the convention after a strong civil rights statement was made part of the Democratic Party's platform. These southern Democrats talked of "secession" from the Democratic Party, and some supported the presidential candidate of the States' Rights

Party, South Carolina senator J. Strom Thurmond, an erstwhile Democrat. Thurmond won thirty-nine electoral votes and over one million popular votes. Second, Truman, seemingly against all odds, was elected president, ensuring that the Tidelands Controversy would not be resolved in favor of the states through political action.

In a few circumstances a lawsuit may be filed in the Supreme Court using the original jurisdiction of the Court, as occurred in *United States v. California*. After Truman's election Attorney General Clark asked the Supreme Court to allow the United States to file suit there against Texas and Louisiana. The Court granted the petition in mid-1949 and heard argument in both cases in late March 1950. Many Texans concluded that the Tidelands Controversy was about the federal government's excessive exercise of power; others believed the controversy was about protecting the oil industry, upon which a significant portion of the economy of Texas depended. These interests converged in the Tidelands Controversy, and politicians were acutely aware of the anger of most Texans toward the federal government on the issue. Consequently, many Texans viewed Tom Clark's actions advocating the federal government's claim as betraying his home state of Texas.

For Texas attorney general Price Daniel, Sr., the Tidelands Controversy was a political winner, for it was one of a pair of 1950 cases in which Texas claimed the mantle of states' rights against federal "interference." Less than a week after the Supreme Court heard arguments in *United States v. Texas*, it heard oral argument in *Sweatt v. Painter* (1950). Heman Sweatt was denied admission to the University of Texas Law School solely because he was African American, and he challenged the law that prohibited the admission of blacks to the University of Texas (see chapter 6). Texas opposed civil rights claims by resorting to claims of federalism, or, more notoriously, states' rights,

the same argument made by Texas in the Tidelands Controversy. These cases were also a reminder to some Texans of the Supreme Court's 1944 decision holding unconstitutional the "white primary" used in Texas to bar blacks from voting in the Democratic Party primary (see chapter 7). Whether Daniel won or lost these cases in the Supreme Court, he was a hero to many white Texans, for he was battling for Texas against the powerful federal government. If Daniel lost, it was because of the Supreme Court's "prejudice" against claims of states rights. Politically Daniel was in a no-lose position, a position rarely enjoyed by politicians and one Daniel could exploit.[94]

It was cold political calculation that led Daniel to reject compromises promoted by the speaker of the U.S. House, Texan Sam Rayburn, before the Supreme Court issued its opinion. Rayburn proposed that ownership of the minerals under the seabed be divided between the state and federal governments. Within three leagues (approximately ten miles) of the shoreline, over 60 percent of the minerals would be owned by Texas and other coastal states, with the remainder owned by the federal government. From three leagues offshore to the edge of the continental shelf, approximately 125 miles from shore, the federal government would receive the majority of the mineral interest, but the states would receive about one-third ownership. A second proposed compromise adjusted the ownership interests of the federal government and the states, with Texas reducing its claim of ownership from three leagues to three miles offshore. Rayburn knew that Truman would veto any bill granting complete control of submerged lands to the states; he also believed that more oil was likely to be found beyond the three-league limit, and cutting the state in for a smaller part of a much larger pie made this compromise beneficial to Texas. Texas political officials rejected each.[95]

The Tidelands Controversy not only was a political winner for Daniel, but Texas's unique history also made it plausible that the state had a winning legal argument despite *United States v. California*. When Texas became a republic, it claimed ownership of all submerged land in the Gulf of Mexico lying within three leagues of the shore. The Republic of Texas was diplomatically recognized by the United States. Recognition implicitly accepted the republic's claim to submerged lands three leagues from shore. Texas also argued that the unique treaty annexing it into the United States distinguished its case from that of other states. Because the United States implicitly recognized Texas's ownership of its tidelands, Texas argued it maintained ownership of the tidelands unless it ceded them to the United States. In the treaty of annexation, Texas ceded "all public edifices, fortifications, barracks, ports and harbors, navy and navy yards, docks, magazines and armaments, and all other means pertaining to the public defense." It remained responsible for its debt, and as a result "shall also retain all the vacant and unappropriated lands lying within its limits." The former provision did not explicitly cede its claim to the tidelands, and the latter implicitly suggested Texas maintained ownership of the tidelands as vacant and unappropriated land.

The four-person plurality opinion (Justice Tom Clark recused himself) first rejected Texas's claim that the Court did not possess original jurisdiction to hear this case. It then held that the "equal footing" clause in the treaty, by which Texas was admitted to the Union "on an equal footing with the existing States," not only gave Texas the same powers and position as other states, but negatively took from Texas any special powers or rights not held by other states. The equal footing clause "negates any implied, special limitation of any of the paramount powers of the United States in favor of a State." Because the Court in *United States v. California* rested its conclusion on the "paramount powers" of the national government without declaring the United States owned the tidelands, it avoided the messy problem that the republic and the state of Texas possessed never-ceded title to the tidelands. The "equal footing" provision implicitly meant that the federal government's paramount powers could not be limited by an assertion peculiar to Texas. Because no other state owned its offshore land, neither did Texas. The dissenters noted, "'Equal footing' has heretofore brought to a state the ownership of river beds, but never before has that phrase been interpreted to take away from a newly admitted state property that it had theretofore owned." The dissent concluded that the treaty of annexation granted the state of Texas all vacant lands, which included its tidelands. Although concurring in the result for reasons of precedent, Justice Felix Frankfurter noted, "How that shift [in ownership] came to pass remains for me a puzzle."[96]

Texas's request for a rehearing was rejected. The issue then returned to Congress. In summer 1952, Rayburn and Senator Lyndon Baines Johnson managed to shepherd through Congress a bill granting Texas and other coastal states ownership of three leagues of sea bed. As expected, Truman vetoed the bill, claiming that the states were engaged in "robbery in broad daylight." During the 1952 presidential election campaign, Democratic nominee Adlai Stevenson voiced support for Truman's view and the Court's decision. Republican candidate Dwight D. Eisenhower promised to sign a tidelands bill giving the states ownership if it reached his desk. Nearly all Texas statewide Democratic officials up for reelection ran also as Republicans and railed against the federal "seizure" of the tidelands. Price Daniel ran for the U.S. Senate as a Democrat, but he, too, actively supported Eisenhower's candidacy. Both Daniel and Eisenhower won election. On entering office, Daniel immediately proposed a bill granting the tidelands to the states. Eisenhower signed the Federal Submerged Lands Act of 1953 in May. This pleased Texas oil men, for the royalty paid for producing minerals from state lands was 12.5 percent, while the federal government charged a 37.5 percent royalty.[97]

The act relinquished the federal government's claim to lands within three miles of shore. In addition, if a state upon entering the United States owned more than three miles, it owned that additional submerged land, up to three leagues. When the federal government later challenged Texas's claim to three leagues, the Supreme Court held that the Annexation Resolution meant "Texas' maritime boundary was established at three leagues from its coast for domestic purposes." Thus, Texas received ownership of its original three leagues of sub-merged land in the 1953 Act. But it received no ownership of any minerals beyond that limit to the continental shelf. By 1961 the United States had entered into oil leases beyond Texas's three-league limit. Those leases, through which Texas would have earned revenue had it embraced one of Sam Rayburn's proposed compromises, earned the United States over thirty-five million dollars. As noted by Rayburn biographer C. Dwight Dorough, writing in 1962, "Under Rayburn's bill Texas would have received more income than under the 1953 law which now exists."[98]

FOUR

The Railroad and Other Corporations

★

Today's Texas is hailed and decried for its business-friendly environment. State officials offer out-of-state corporations aggressive economic incentives to operate in Texas. These efforts would have stunned many nineteenth- and early twentieth-century Texans, who viewed corporations with distrust. Many believed corporations acted to the detriment of ordinary citizens, and Texas sought to limit the accumulation and exercise of corporate power through its constitutions and legislative acts. The suspicion that corporations continually grasped for power peaked at the end of the nineteenth century. However, attacks on corporations, particularly claims of monopoly, remained politically popular through the first half of the twentieth century.

Texas became a republic while Andrew Jackson was president of the United States, and most Texans were deeply influenced by Jackson's anticorporate populism. An early corporate entity, banks were feared in part because they issued notes used as currency (gold was

both heavy and scarce)—notes that often fell in value. A ten-dollar note issued by a bank might depreciate to the extent that it was worth two dollars or less in gold, and it was worth nothing if the bank failed. Further, banks and other financial institutions earned profits by lending money with interest, and nineteenth-century Texas was largely populated by farmers and stock raisers often burdened by onerous debt. During most of the nineteenth century banks were not permitted to incorporate under state law, limiting Texas to national banks (banks incorporated by federal law) and unincorporated private banks.

Texans not only feared banking corporations, but they also perceived most corporations as harmful monopolies. Texas agrarians thought of railroads as both the lifeblood of post–Civil War Texas economic development and as rapacious corporate entities ready to impose monopolistic rates unless restrained by law. Even before any railroad tracks were built, the 1853 Texas legislature adopted a stiff regulatory regime for railroad corporations. The 1876 constitution, strongly influenced by farmers, included an entire article (Art. X) on railroads, adopted to limit the power railroads might exercise.

The rise of large corporate entities, including railroads, and cries of monopoly led Texas in 1889 to become the second state to adopt an antitrust law, doing so even before the federal government acted. Indicia of ambivalence toward the corporation were the adoption in 1874 of a general incorporation law and a prohibition in the 1876 constitution on creating a corporation through private act of the Texas legislature. Even though "there existed a genuine feeling of hostility toward the corporate form of business enterprise" when the general incorporation law was adopted, Texas, joining most other states, saw this law as the lesser of the two evils of increased legislative corruption and increased corporate power. That Texas was willing to countenance the arrival of the corporation did not lessen its interest in regulating businesses. The 1874 law substantially restricted the activities of corporations, and though most other states amended their incorporation laws by the first third of the twentieth century, Texas did not do so until 1955. Texas also regularly used its antitrust laws to regulate the activities of corporations through 1950, although the effectiveness of such action appears slight.[1]

The discovery of oil at Spindletop in January 1901 led to the creation of several large oil corporations chartered in Texas, financed by capital from New York and Pennsylvania but also in substantial part by Texans. Those new oil corporations, particularly Gulf Oil and Texaco, found it difficult to compete with Standard Oil under the state's restrictive corporation laws. Although Texas antitrust law indirectly facilitated the growth of Gulf Oil and Texaco by shielding them from Standard Oil, both Texas corporations eventually reincorporated elsewhere because of the inadequacies of Texas corporate law. Gulf Oil was a Texas-chartered

corporation for less than six years. Even Texaco, chartered as a Texas corporation in April 1902 by both native and adopted Texans, was reorganized as the Texas Corporation in 1926 under the laws of Delaware and headquartered in New York, a direct result of Texas's inflexible corporation laws. By the early 1950s, a business lawyer advised his clients "not to incorporate as a Texas corporation, but to organize under the laws of some other state, usually Delaware," because of the illiberality of Texas corporation law and its lack of responsiveness to twentieth-century business methods and concerns.[2]

Texas maintained varied and contradictory policies toward business and corporations until the late 1950s. After Reconstruction, Texans desired development, which meant enticing railroad corporations to lay track. Those enticements included giving away more than thirty-two million acres of public land by 1882 (see chapter 3). At the same time, politicians portrayed railroads as monopolistic predators whose machinations were inimical to the interests of Texas farmers. Alien (that is, non-Texan) land corporations fostered economic development and were despised. The legislature attempted to outlaw such corporations and severely restricted the amount of land other corporations could own, efforts that were largely unsuccessful but not officially ended until 1981. Oil companies, including Standard Oil, brought both well-paying jobs and allegedly monopolistic business practices to Texas during the first half of the twentieth century. How Texans viewed Standard Oil and other oil companies during that time depended less on the particular "monopolistic" practice challenged by the Texas attorney general than on the existing need for jobs. The result was that antitrust actions from 1910 through the early 1960s were more often a matter of politics (including the political ambition of the attorney general) than law.

In 1937, in the midst of the Great Depression, Texas historian Walter Prescott Webb wrote a populist denunciation of the rise of the American corporation. The corporation, in Webb's telling, had allowed the North to conquer and rule the South and West. The North was home to nearly all large corporations and "80 or 90 per cent of the wealth in the United States." This concentration of wealth existed even though the South and West were the homes of "most of the natural wealth of America." Most insidiously, the control of American wealth by corporations meant wealth moved from the South and West to the North. The absence of capital in the South and West limited the ability of those regions to establish thriving local industries, and when such industry was created, it was crushed by monopolistic northern corporations. The 1944 edition of Webb's book included a chapter on the destruction of a Texas milk bottle manufacturer by a rapacious northern corporate patent holder, a chapter omitted from the initial 1937 edition for fear that the patent holder would sue Webb's publisher. For Webb, this one example demonstrated the evil nature of large corporations. One solution Webb proposed was to abolish the legal fiction that a corporation was a "person" for purposes of American constitutional law. Webb also suggested a national system of chartering corporations to replace the system of state charters. Finally, Webb believed the end of the frontier in 1890 also represented the beginning of the rise of the modern corporation in America. In a "frontierless" America, the corporation represented the greatest threat to democracy.[3]

This chapter suggests a different view. Texas often relied on outside capital in its economic development. It was not, however, a "colony" exploited for its natural resources. Instead, Texas used eastern (or northern, in Webb's parlance) capital to its benefit. In addition, the power of corporations was regularly checked by the Texas government. The Supreme Court's decisions that included corporations as "persons" for purposes of the Fourteenth

Amendment did not leave Texans powerless against large corporations, and the presence in Texas of "foreign" (non-Texas) corporations did not weaken the state's considerable power to regulate them. Still, Webb's cri de coeur represents a substantial Texas sentiment, one with a strong and long historical pedigree. For much of the past fifty years, Texas has rearranged its laws to draw business to the state, although occasional waves of fear of foreign corporations still surface.[4]

THE REPUBLIC AND BUSINESS

In December 1836 the first congress of the Republic of Texas created the Texas Rail Road, Navigation, and Canal Company pursuant to its constitutional authority (Art. II, § 3) to "grant charters of incorporation." The law was unusual, for the first congress spent most of its time organizing its government and preparing itself against possible attack from Mexico and indigenous tribes. Indeed, this was the only act of the first congress creating a private business. As suggested by its name, the company was permitted to lay tracks and dig canals, particularly to connect the Sabine River and the Rio Grande, the claimed eastern and western borders of the republic. The company also possessed the power to create a bank, which was not suggested by its name. Indeed, the major purpose of the company was to act as a bank. Herbert Gambrell states the "primary interest" of the incorporators "was banking—the kind of banking done by the Bank of England and the late Bank of the United States." The company was allowed to issue currency and open as many branches of the bank as permitted by a future congress. The company could purchase and sell land, exercise the state's power of eminent domain (taking private property by paying just compensation), and occupy public lands by paying "the minimum price of such lands." The company was given a "life" of forty-nine years, with the privilege of extending its life by another forty-nine years by paying the government one-half million dollars in gold or silver. The company proposed raising the astonishing amount of five million dollars in capital, in shares valued at one hundred dollars each. Two directors named in the act were Branch T. Archer and James Collinsworth, both of whom served in the first congress. A corporation the size of the proposed company in the republic would have exercised a great deal of power, for its capital accumulation, aided by the ability to issue currency, would have given it the ability to purchase vast swaths of land and control a significant part of the Texas economy.[5]

In July 1837, before the company had obtained the capital necessary to begin its existence, the *Telegraph and Texas Register* charged that the company was a hated monopoly. The furor about the company's perceived power was such that the second congress began looking at whether it could repeal the charter act, but the company failed before congress acted. The Panic of 1837, generated by transfers of public monies and an increased demand for the "hard" money of gold and silver necessary to purchase public lands, began in May. The company found it impossible to raise the one million dollars in capital or even the twenty-five thousand dollars in gold or silver required to open the bank. Instead, the incorporators offered the republic promissory notes as payment in lieu of gold or silver. Attorney General John Birdsall, apparently prodded by President Sam Houston, rejected the notes and declared that only gold or silver payment would suffice to permit the company to open a bank. It then collapsed.[6]

The perception that the incorporators of the company had used their influence in congress to gain a profitable concession from the republic made Texans even more wary of corporations. The fear that corporations were powerful and unscrupulous predators who sought government-granted monopolies gained ascendancy during the existence of the republic. Despite this fear the Congress of the Republic chartered a number of companies, including three more railroads. However, no railroad track was built by any of these corporations by the time Texas was annexed. Other chartered corporations made little impression on the Texas economy. The Panic of 1837 not only long affected development of the Texas economy, but it further prejudiced Texans against banks.[7]

REGULATING CORPORATIONS IN ANTEBELLUM TEXAS

The 1845 constitution of the state of Texas restricted the legislature's ability to issue corporate charters. In a nod to the Jacksonian fear of banks, it simply prohibited the creation of any "corporate body . . . with banking or discounting privileges" (Art. VII, § 30). Second, to avoid the possibility of another Texas Rail Road, Navigation, and Canal Company Act scandal, the constitution made it difficult for the legislature to create any private corporations. A private corporation could not be created unless supported by a two-thirds majority of each house (Art. VII, § 31). Once created, the continued existence of the corporation was subject to the judgment of any future legislature: "[T]wo-thirds of the legislature shall have power to revoke and repeal all private corporations, by making compensation for the franchise." Consequently, all Texas corporations lacked a secure existence. The necessity that the legislature make "compensation" to the shareholders of any Texas corporation whose existence it annulled was a relatively thin protection for those investors. First, the absence of a modifier before "compensation" was telling. In another provision of the constitution the government could take a person's property only when the person was given "adequate" compensation (Art. I, § 14). The Fifth Amendment to the U.S. Constitution prohibited the federal government from taking private property without the payment of "just" compensation. The absence of either word put corporate shareholders in a tenuous position. Second, even though the contracts clause of the federal constitution limited the extent to which Texas could eliminate chartered corporations, Texas minimized this risk by requiring the legislature to make some compensation.[8]

The provisions on corporations and banks in the 1845 constitution were included despite efforts by some delegates less hostile to them. A motion was made to exclude the antibanking provision from the constitution on the ground that banks had aided in the economic prosperity of many in the "mother country" (the United States). That effort failed. Several days later, a proposal to reconsider the banking provision demonstrated the anger toward banks possessed by many Texans. Convention president Thomas Jefferson Rusk declared:

> The gentleman from San Patricio says that many individuals have been benefitted by banks. Thousands upon thousands, sir, have been ruined by them. I consider it a bright page in the history of General [Andrew] Jackson that he had the honor of giving the blow which will eventually destroy them upon this continent. And I wish by no vote of mine, here or elsewhere, to authorize the institution of a bank, which may benefit a few individuals, but will carry, here as elsewhere, ruin, want, misery and degradation in its train.[9]

The constitution gave the legislature the exclusive authority to create a private corporation. No corporation could be created outside of a specific legislative grant. A general incorporation law lessened the control of the legislature over the creation of corporations by allowing individuals to create a corporation. Such a law also lessened the possibility of efforts to bribe legislators to obtain a corporate charter. A proposal to allow the legislature to adopt a general incorporation law was defeated

by the Constitutional Convention. While the extent of the constitution's hostility to the corporation was unusual compared with that of many other states, only three states had passed a general incorporation law by 1845. In 1846, New York's new constitution limited the legislature's power to grant corporate charters to cases in which "the objects of the corporation cannot be attained under general laws." Texas adopted a similar provision in its 1876 constitution, by which time many other states had followed New York's approach.[10]

The first legislature of the state of Texas, following the trend of other American states, allowed Texans to create limited partnerships for any business other than banking. A limited partnership consisted of at least one general partner, who was liable personally for all debts of the limited partnership, and one or more "special partners," who contributed cash and whose liability was limited to the extent of their capital contributions. The limited partnership was recognized only after all partners signed a certificate before a judge or notary public and filed that certificate with the clerk of the county court where the partnership was located. The name of the partnership could not include the name of any special partner. The limitation of liability given special partners, a limitation unavailable to any partner in a general partnership, caused the legislature to include several provisions requiring the partnership to provide public notice of the manner of its existence. In addition, the statute lifted the limits on the special partner's liability if he transferred partnership property to favor any particular creditor or partner at the expense of other creditors. These notice and fraud provisions protected creditors who might lend money mistakenly assuming the partnership was a general partnership. Limited liability gave an investor protection from personal liability through the limited partnership, making it a valid option when considering what business form to adopt.[11]

The first major corporate charters granted

by the Texas state legislature were for railroads. By 1850 it had chartered nine railroad corporations. None had begun laying track by 1852, when the legislature offered eight sections of state land per mile of track laid. The next year, the first railroad began its operations, and in 1854 and 1856 the legislature sweetened the incentives to railroad entrepreneurs by offering sixteen sections of land (10,240 acres) per mile of track laid. The enhancement of incentives was accompanied by a large increase in railroad charters. Between 1846 and 1861, fifty-eight railroad charters were granted; other charters adopted by the legislature were vetoed by the governor. Few corporations built any railroad track.[12]

Even before the first railroad track was laid, the fourth legislature adopted in February 1853 a significant law regulating all incorporated railroads. The immediate cause of the act was speculation in railway stocks and the issuing of "large amounts of fictitious stocks and bonds" by two early railroad companies. The act prohibited a corporation's directors from paying any dividends "when the company is insolvent" and made them liable for the company's debts if they did so. A railroad corporation was also required to establish a principal office and inform the public of its location so notice of any lawsuit could be served upon it there. The company's operations were strongly regulated, and the legislature declared it would prescribe passenger and freight rates "should they be deemed too high," with the limitation that such rates would not reduce net profits less than "to a sum equal to twelve per centum per annum upon its capital stock." Railroads were required to provide, in an annual report to the Texas comptroller of public accounts, information about the railroad's stock, construction expenses, income, debt, dividends, and other information, including numbers of persons injured and the "sales of lands donated by the State, and the quantity remaining unsold." Finally, the legislature included a provision

allowing the state to repay a railroad the amount it had expended in constructing its line and to pay it for its railroad cars, real property, and other assets, along with interest at 12 percent, and take title to the railroad (§ 17). The state never exercised this authority, and in 1860 it was legislatively rescinded.[13]

The legislature twice amended the 1853 Railroad Regulation Act before the Civil War. It did so in part to create financial incentives for railroads to construct lines. An 1857 amendment focused on the manner in which railroad debts would be paid (the Panic of 1857 had begun in the middle of the year, and nationwide several railroads had failed) and how to protect the state's investment against a railroad creditor intending to make Texas a party to litigation. An 1860 law limited the ability of the railroad to condemn private property and imposed additional duties on railroads. For example, railroads whose tracks passed through a field or enclosure were required to build a sufficient cattle guard. Any company failing to make an annual report to the comptroller and commissioner of the General Land Office "shall forfeit all right to receive any lands which may have been granted to them by their charter." Finally, a company that completed twenty-five miles of track but failed to add twenty-five more miles annually no longer forfeited its corporate charter.[14]

The goal of the law of corporations in antebellum Texas was to regulate the railroads. Corporations were fitfully located in a society dominated by transplanted Southern farmers. Railroads were crucial to broadening the markets available to farmers. They were also capital-intensive businesses that obtained state subsidies (mainly land but also money) to build track. Between 1856 and the start of the Civil War in 1861, twenty-one new corporate charters were granted by the state, and a number of other railroad charters were amended. In the 1850s most new Texans settled near railroad lines or where such lines were projected. But

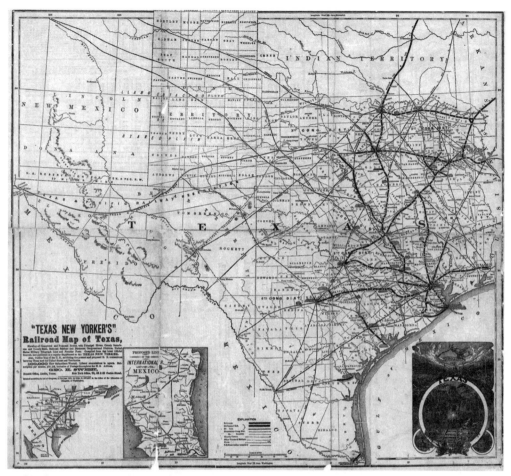

Railroads in Texas, 1874. Courtesy Texas State Library and Archives Commission.

Texas track mileage in 1860 was just 404 miles. The onset of the Civil War in 1861 effectively halted all railroad building for a decade.[15]

THE POST–CIVIL WAR CONSTITUTIONS AND CORPORATIONS

The 1866 Texas Constitution readopted earlier constitutional limitations on corporations and banks. These restrictions were lessened by the Reconstruction constitution of 1869. This constitution, completed by federal military officers, lacked any provisions restricting the creation of corporations or banks. Consequently, some state-chartered banks (fewer than twenty)

opened between 1869 and 1876, joining some federally chartered banks in Texas created as a result of Civil War–era federal laws. State-chartered banks were again banned by the 1876 constitution, although nationally chartered banks remained. Fourteen nationally chartered banks were operating in Texas by 1880, joined by eighty-five unincorporated private banks. Only one state-chartered bank remained open by 1886.[16]

The 1876 constitution reflected Texas's traditional opposition to corporations and banks, joined by a concern regarding legislative corruption. Article XII regulated private corporations. Section 1 prohibited the legislature from chartering a corporation by private legislation.

Instead, all private corporations were created through a general law designed to prevent legislative favoritism toward particular corporations. Section 6, barring a corporation from any "fictitious increase of stock or indebtedness," was designed to prevent frauds of "watered" (diluted) stock, as had occurred in New York in the Erie Railway Wars of the late 1860s. At least three of the seven sections in Article XII, as well as a fourth more general statement, protected the absolute authority of the state to regulate freights and tolls charged by persons and corporations "for the use of highways, landings, wharves, bridges and ferries, devoted to public use." Such regulatory authority "has never been and shall never be relinquished or abandoned by the State, but shall always be under legislative control" (§ 3). Article XVI, section 16 renewed the ban on any corporation "with banking or discounting privileges."[17]

The 1876 constitution was strongly influenced by farmers. Farmers and their representatives were suspicious of the power that large corporate interests might wield. In addition to banning corporate banks and restricting corporations, the 1876 constitution also regulated the role of railroads. Article X allowed the legislature to regulate rates, including "establishing reasonable maximum rates of charges for the transportation of passengers and freight," as well as the power "to correct abuses and prevent unjust discrimination and extortion in the rates of freight and passenger tariffs on the different railroads in this State" (§ 2). Although the statutory limits of maximum rate charges were often much higher than actual charges, the legislature jealously enforced its power to regulate rates. It never simply allowed railroads to determine rates by resorting to the law of supply and demand. The constitution also declared railroads "common carriers," subjecting their actions to close regulation for the benefit of the people. In the early 1890s Texas moved from legislative regulation of railroads to administrative regulation through the Texas Railroad Commission.[18]

Article X was adopted after passage of an orgy of legislation heavily subsidizing railroad construction in Texas. A March 1873 amendment to the 1869 constitution allowed the legislature to grant up to twenty sections (12,800 acres) per mile of railroad track, substituting the cash grant awarded to several railroads during Republican rule during Reconstruction. The post-Reconstruction fourteenth legislature chartered forty-two railroads, granting most sixteen sections of land for each completed mile of railroad track. Only fourteen of those railroads laid any track. However, the continued subsidies offered railroads helped increase railroad track from 591 miles in 1870 to 3,244 miles in 1880 and 8,710 miles by 1890. The cost to the state was 32,153,878 acres granted to railroads. Even at the modest price of fifty cents an acre (a price then used for the sale of some arid or semiarid public land in West Texas), the subsidy represented the substantial amount of over $16 million. For this Texas generated 2,928 additional miles of railroad track, a cost of $5,464 per mile of track. How well railroads did for themselves during the 1870s and 1880s led to greater regulation in the form of the Texas Railroad Commission.[19]

TEXAS GENERAL INCORPORATION ACT OF 1874

In December 1871 the Republican-controlled twelfth legislature adopted a law allowing corporations to incorporate without legislative permission. This general incorporation law, however, lacked the opening phrase, "Be it enacted by the Legislature of the State of Texas," making the law inoperative. The 1873 legislature, in which Democrats held a legislative majority, attempted to remedy this fatal flaw by simply amending section 1 of the 1871 act to include that introduction. This act then recognized all corporations created under the 1871 act. This, too, was insufficient, for the law failed specifically to reenact all of the sections of the 1871 act. On April 23, 1874, the fourteenth legislature largely readopted the entire 1871 act. The Texas general incorporation act was taken from the 1859 general incorporation law of Kansas. The 1874 act allowed incorporators the option of using the provisions of the act or obtaining a special charter from the legislature to create the corporation. For example, the forty-two railroad corporations chartered by the fourteenth legislature were all created by special acts. This option was eliminated in the 1876 constitution (Art. XII, § 1). Ratification of the 1876 constitution made the 1874 general incorporation act the sole manner by which private corporations could be created in Texas. The 1874 act, as regularly amended, remained the Texas law of corporations until 1955.[20]

When Texas adopted its 1874 general incorporation law, it was the forty-second jurisdiction (of forty-seven states and territories) to do so. It was the twentieth state to prohibit the legislature from creating corporations by special charter, placing Texas among the broad middle of this transformation.[21]

The 1874 law divided corporations into public and private corporations and subdivided private corporations into religious, charitable, and for-profit corporations. It listed twenty-seven separate purposes for which a corporation might be formed, the last of which allowed incorporation "[f]or any other purpose intended for mutual profit or benefit not otherwise especially provided for." A stockholder was liable for the debts of the corporation only to the extent of the value of the stock he owned, thus barring a creditor from seizing a stockholder's personal assets to satisfy the company's debt (§ 42).

This listing of purposes for which a corporation could exist, even with a catch-all provision (repealed in 1885), suggested an effort to bind corporations within narrow straits. Corporate charters were limited to a life of twenty years (§ 11). The assets of a corporation could be used only "to accomplish the legitimate objects of the creation," although this was broadly interpreted as an initial matter. For example, an 1889

Texas Supreme Court decision allowed a corporation under the catch-all provision to invest in real estate, commodities, stocks, and bonds. The 1885 repeal of the catch-all was alleviated in part by the regular addition by the legislature of further purposes for which to incorporate. By the time the 1874 law was replaced in 1955, more than one hundred particular purposes were acknowledged as permissible corporate efforts. However, legislative limitations on corporate purposes created difficult problems of organization after the discovery of oil at Spindletop in 1901.[22]

In *Ramsey v. Tod* (1902), the issue was whether Texas secretary of state John G. Tod was justified in refusing to file a corporate charter. (Until the charter was filed, the entity did not possess a legal existence in Texas.) The proposed corporation existed for two purposes: buying and selling goods and merchandise involving agricultural and farm products, and accumulating and lending out money for that purpose. Tod refused to file the charter on the ground that the 1874 law prohibited incorporation of a business engaged in more than one purpose allowed by law. Even though both purposes for which the corporation was organized were permitted by law, those purposes were found in different statutory provisions. The Texas Supreme Court held that Tod had properly interpreted the law in refusing to file the corporate charter. It declared a corporation "could be created under one subdivision only." A corporation could exist to fulfill more than one purpose only if more than one purpose was "named in the same subdivision, but in that case only." This limitation was based on the court's focus on the use of the word "purpose" in singular form, not plural, when listing in section 6 of the act what the corporate charter must declare. Section 5 of the act listed the "purposes" (plural) for which a corporation might be created, which seemed to indicate that a corporation might exist for more than one purpose. The court rejected this interpretation on the ground that this language was indeterminate and concluded that the numbering of permissible business purposes from one to twenty-seven indicated the importance of limiting corporations to no more than one numbered purpose. Finally, although the court noted that Texas had borrowed its general incorporation law from Kansas, it relied on evidence that the law "was thoroughly considered and carefully prepared by a person or persons learned in the law" as support for its conclusion that a corporation could exist for just one listed purpose.

This reliance on expertise in draftsmanship is odd for three reasons. First, the court's conclusion that other language in the statute was indeterminate indicated that the experts failed the test of drafting a clear and complete statute. To justify a conclusion by relying on the careful preparation of the act by experts, while criticizing the act for its careless use of language elsewhere, is to have it both ways. Second, the Texas legislature altered several provisions of law between 1871 and 1874 and in doing so may have unintentionally altered the earlier language of the statute. For example, both sections 4 and 5 of the failed 1871 general incorporation act noted the "purposes" for which corporations might be created. In the 1874 act, section 5 still listed "purposes," which the court in *Ramsey* declared indeterminate. But section 4 of the 1874 act used the singular "purpose" for which private corporations might be created. Whether this change from the plural "purposes" in the 1871 act to the singular "purpose" in the 1874 act was intentional or inadvertent was wholly unknown. This ambiguity alone argued against a reliance on expertise as indicating whether a corporation may incorporate for more than one listed purpose, for even after experts draft a bill, legislators often alter it, sometimes knowingly and sometimes carelessly. Third, the court's unwillingness to cite to any Kansas case or to any scholar supporting its conclusion makes it difficult to accept the court's claim that the 1871, 1873, or 1874 legislatures intended to restrict

corporations to one listed purpose. The consequence of *Ramsey* was a severe restriction on the activities of a corporation, a restriction that eventually drove major Texas oil corporations to reincorporate in other states. *Ramsey* was clear and stringent: A corporation was legally permitted to engage in only the purpose or purposes allowed in any one numbered section.[23]

"FOREIGN" CORPORATIONS

The Supreme Court of the United States held in *Bank of Augusta v. Earle* (1839) that a corporation was an artificial being created by law. Consequently, it "can have no legal existence out of the boundaries of the sovereignty by which it is created." A corporation created in one state thus had no right to engage in business in a second state, for it was "foreign" to any state other than the state that created it. A foreign corporation was able to engage in business in a second state only with that state's consent. In the last quarter of the nineteenth century, this view changed dramatically. In *Paul v. Virginia* (1869), the Supreme Court upheld a Virginia law that required any foreign insurance corporation to obtain a license to do business and deposit with the state bonds ranging from $35,000 to $50,000 in value. Domestic insurance corporations were not required to make any similar deposit. The Court concluded that a corporation was not a "citizen" for purposes of the privileges and immunities clause of Article IV, section 2 of the U.S. Constitution, which barred a state from discriminating against citizens of other states. Further, the Court held that the insurance business was not the subject of interstate commerce, and Virginia possessed the power to bar a foreign corporation from engaging in intrastate business in Virginia. Even though *Paul* was consonant with the Court's decision in *Earle*, it implicitly altered the ability of states to prohibit foreign corporations from doing business. The negative implication of the Supreme Court's conclusion in *Paul* was that Virginia lacked the power to bar a foreign corporation from engaging in *interstate* business in Virginia. Only Congress, with its power to regulate commerce "among the several states," was permitted to regulate the manner in which a corporation undertook commerce among the states.[24]

In 1879 the Supreme Court suggested that neither the federal government nor state governments could take the property of a person or a corporation without due process of law. Because the Fourteenth Amendment required a state to provide due process of law to any "person" before taking that person's life, liberty, or property, this conclusion indicated that the Court believed a corporation was a constitutional "person." In the late 1880s, the Court in two cases confirmed this belief. It declared that a corporation was a "person" protected by the equal protection clause of the Fourteenth Amendment. The result of these cases was that a foreign corporation could constitutionally challenge state laws that treated them less favorably than domestic corporations. The federal Jurisdiction and Removal Act of 1875 also gave federal courts jurisdiction to hear cases challenging the constitutionality of state laws, allowing a corporation to sue in federal court rather than in state court and, when a defendant in a case "arising under the Constitution," to remove the case from state court to federal court.[25]

If a state could not prohibit a foreign corporation from engaging in *interstate* commerce within its boundaries, but could prohibit it from engaging in *intrastate* business, then a major point of contention was the proper categorization of the commerce engaged in by the foreign corporation. Another regulatory option was to require the foreign corporation and/or its agents to obtain a state permit or license to enter the state to engage in intrastate business. If the foreign corporation did not obtain a permit from the state and subsequently engaged in intrastate business,

the state could provide for criminal penalties for failing to do so. In 1882, Texas adopted an occupation tax on a variety of workers, from lawyers (five dollars) and doctors (forty dollars) to drummers, itinerant manufacturers' representatives who showed samples of goods available for purchase (thirty-five dollars, payable in advance). Unlike peddlers, drummers did not make direct sales of the offered goods, but solicited orders for purchase, which is one reason they merely carried samples rather than the goods themselves. Many drummers worked for businesses located outside of Texas, including foreign corporations that operated in Texas only through their drummers. Neither the foreign corporations nor the drummers obtained a permit or license to do business in Texas or paid the occupation tax.

A drummer named William G. Asher was charged with the crime of failing to pay Texas's occupation tax. He sued for a writ of habeas corpus, claiming the charge against him violated the commerce clause of the U.S. Constitution. Asher was a drummer for a Louisiana manufacturer of rubber stamps and stencils. The parties agreed he was a citizen of Louisiana, even though much of his time was spent in Texas. The Texas Court of Appeals denied Asher's request despite a United States Supreme Court decision that clearly supported Asher's claim. The court of appeals rejected the Supreme Court's decision in *Robbins v. Taxing District* (1887) because *Robbins* was based on "unwarranted assumptions of constitutional authority,-invocations [*sic*] of the federal power, where such power does not and was never intended to apply and operate." Further, *Robbins* was "directly in conflict with well-adjudicated cases of the same court, which are not overruled, and which, in addition to their equal authority, are based upon fundamental and eternal principles of reason, justice, and right." The court of appeals also claimed the writings of legal commentators and other judicial decisions agreed that *Robbins* was wrongly decided.

The Supreme Court of the United States heard Asher's case and in short work reversed the court of appeals. It specifically responded to the contention of the court of appeals that *Robbins* was contrary to previous decisions of the Supreme Court: "Even if it were true that the decision referred to was not in harmony, with some of the previous decisions, we had supposed that a later decision in conflict with prior ones had the effect to overrule them, whether mentioned and commented on or not."[26]

A related approach to regulating foreign corporations was to condition the grant of a permit to do business in Texas. A foreign corporation desiring to "transact business in this State" was required to file its articles of incorporation with the secretary of state and request a permit to do business there. The application required each for-profit foreign corporation to authorize service of process against any agent of the corporation. Thus, if a Texan was injured by the actions of a foreign railroad corporation, he could with relative ease initiate a lawsuit by serving the petition on any agent of the railroad doing business in Texas. But Texas, which adopted its permit scheme "almost literally" from an 1886 Iowa statute, included a provision (§ 3) barring a foreign corporation sued in Texas state court from removing the case to federal court. In order to protect out-of-state residents from possible prejudice in state courts, federal law generally permitted a nonresident defendant to remove the case to federal court because the parties were residents of different states (known as diversity of citizenship jurisdiction). This provision in federal law allowed a foreign corporation, when sued by a Texan, to have the case overseen by a federal judge rather than a state judge. The former was appointed for a term of good behavior (that is, he served unless he was impeached and convicted of "high crimes and misdemeanors," a rare event), while the latter was subject to reelection by neighbors of the injured Texan who had filed the lawsuit. Removal was primarily justified on the belief that the federal judge might be less subject to possible prejudice against the corporate defendant than a state judge. Texas adopted its permit law on April 2, 1887. Nine days later, the Supreme Court held unconstitutional this provision in the Iowa law. The Texas law was subsequently declared unconstitutional by the Texas Supreme Court in 1890. Anticipating this, the legislature adopted an amended foreign corporations act in 1889 eliminating the ban on foreign corporations suing in federal court.[27]

The revised 1889 statute eliminated the prohibition on foreign corporations from suing in federal court but added a different condition. It barred a foreign corporation from suing in Texas courts if it did not possess a permit to do business in Texas. The provision placed foreign corporations in the delicate position of choosing either to forego obtaining a permit from Texas on the ground that its business was wholly interstate commerce, or to obtain a permit, thus implicitly acknowledging that some of its business might be intrastate business and subjecting itself to litigation in state courts. A number of foreign corporations chose the first option. If that corporation subsequently initiated a lawsuit in Texas state court, could its case be heard? The Texas Supreme Court, noting the right of companies to engage in interstate business without obtaining permission from Texas to do so, looked closely at the activities of the foreign corporation in determining whether it possessed a right to sue in state court. In a number of cases, the courts dismissed the case filed by a foreign corporation on the ground that it was engaged in intrastate business and lacked a permit to do business in Texas. This close consideration of interstate and intrastate commerce offered foreign corporations a strong incentive to obtain a permit to do business in Texas.[28]

Another way to limit the power of foreign corporations was to vest greater authority in the attorney general. Article IV, section 22 of the 1876 constitution gave the attorney general the power to "inquire into the charter rights of all private corporations." In the late 1880s Attorney General James Hogg used this authority to assess charters of railroads and insurance companies, as well as "wildcat" companies neither incorporated in Texas nor licensed to do business in the state. Hogg most broadly used this authority to evaluate articles of incorporation of railroads intent on doing business in Texas. During his first two-year term, Hogg certified twenty-three charters and approved the amended charters of ten other companies. Forty-three new charters were approved by Hogg during his second term, as well as eleven amended charters. Hogg required all these corporations to include a provision declaring that it "shall be forever subject to all the changes, rules, and regulations that may be prescribed by the laws of Texas." If they did not, he refused to certify the charter, thus preventing the corporation from lawfully engaging in business in Texas. Although Hogg initiated suits in a few cases, his persuasive authority was ordinarily sufficient to obtain compliance by the corporation. No case challenging Hogg's exercise of authority over corporations was heard by the Texas Supreme Court.[29]

The assertion of some state authority over foreign corporations at the end of the 1880s was closely related to a rising fear in Texas of the power exerted by corporations. Railroads remained the lifeblood of farmers, and rates for carrying freight were crucial in determining a farmer's yearly profits. In late 1881, railroad magnates Jay Gould and Collis P. Huntington secretly divided Texas in half, with Gould controlling North Texas and Huntington controlling South Texas. Even with this monopolistic division by Gould and Huntington, 1881 and 1882 were the two biggest years for laying railroad track in Texas. Track mileage increased from 6,009 miles in 1882 to 8,710 miles in 1890. But many farmers believed foreign railroads enjoyed unseemly profits at the expense of

those who tilled the soil and harvested the crops. A second threat to farmers was the rise of cattle ranching in the Panhandle in the 1880s, aided in major part by capital from foreign corporations. In 1883 and 1884, a total of 104 land and cattle companies received charters from Texas, with an aggregate capital of over thirty-seven million dollars, substantially more than the capital of railroads created at the same time. Those large land and cattle corporations had vast landholdings and were unwilling to use barbed wire to keep their cattle out of the land tilled by farmers.[30]

During the mid-1880s Texas suffered from a severe multiyear drought, a steep decline in cattle and commodity prices, and a reduction in the percentage of farms operated by their owners. Although a minor part of the Texas economy, the number and value of manufacturing and mechanical businesses increased in overall value from $9.2 million in 1880 to $46.8 million in 1890. Populists and others increasingly demanded that the power of corporations be curbed by the federal and state governments. The men who managed large corporations did not help their own cause, making it easier for the legislature and judiciary to limit by law perceived or actual corporate excesses.[31]

The first concerted effort against railroads was the dismantling of the Texas Traffic Association, a combination of railroads intent on stabilizing rates and profits. A second effort against all corporations, including railroads, was the adoption in 1889 by Texas of an antitrust act. The third was the creation of the Texas Railroad Commission in 1891 (see chapter 2).

THE TEXAS TRAFFIC ASSOCIATION

Jim Hogg was elected attorney general in 1886. His term began in early 1887 with a bang when he became involved in the legislature's investigation of Donley County district judge Frank Willis and his relationship with the Pan-

Austin, Texas, train depot, 1884. Courtesy Texas State Library and Archives Commission.

handle Stockmen's Association (see chapter 3). Although Hogg's effort failed, he soon thereafter was given another opportunity to demonstrate his willingness to fight large business entities in behalf of the people.

In mid-1885, representatives of five railroads operating in Texas met "to establish and maintain equitable and uniform rates upon traffic having origin and destination within the State of Texas." By the time the agreement was made effective, all major Texas railroads had joined the Texas Traffic Association. The purpose of the association was to avoid "extreme fluctuations in Texas rates." The members of the association elected a commissioner and provided for an executive committee that approved the "rates, classifications, rules and practices" of each railroad by a required unanimous vote. The requirement of unanimous approval of rates was in part an effort to avoid rebates or special arrangements (including underbilling) offered to those who regularly transported goods by railroad. Rate approval by the association was thus a defense to a claim of "unjust discrimination and extortion in the rates of freight and passenger tariffs on the different railroads in this State," barred by Article X, section 2 of the 1876 constitution. Rate approval created another benefit: it limited—indeed, eliminated—price competition among railroads, thereby enhancing the

likelihood of profitability of each road. The association also banned railroads from issuing passes (allowing a person to ride without paying a fare), which were used to curry favor with those who influenced possible legislative action and those who decided which railroad should be favored with shipments of freight. The association fined those railroads that violated the association's rules. About the time the association was formed, the Texas legislature adopted a law granting the attorney general the authority to "institute legal proceedings against corporations doing business within this State in violation of sections 5 and 6 of Article 10 of the Constitution of Texas."[32]

Section 5 of Article X stated in part: "No railroad . . . or managers of any railroad corporation, shall consolidate the stock, property or franchises of such corporation, with . . . or in any way control any railroad corporation owning or having under its control a parallel or competing line." Section 6 barred any railroad incorporated in Texas from consolidating with any railroad company.

The initial investigation by Attorney General John D. Templeton had concluded that the railroads had not engaged in illegal "pooling" (combining to share costs and revenues to the detriment of consumers). Templeton had determined that because the rates the railroads charged were below the maximum rates

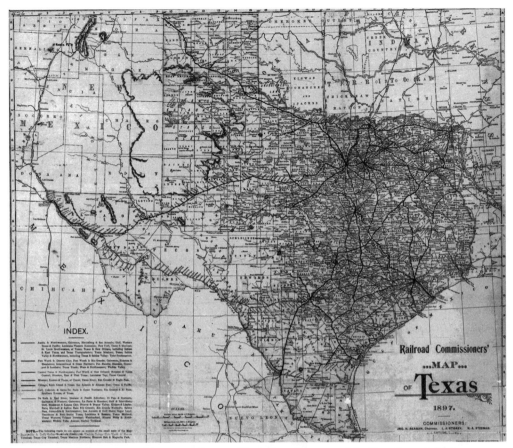

Texas Railroad Commission Map, 1892. Courtesy Texas State Library and Archives Commission.

imposed by the legislature, those members of the association had not violated any law, including Article X, sections 5 and 6. Hogg disagreed. Based on his legislatively granted authority, Hogg sued to dissolve the association, claiming its operation violated Article X, section 5. A state district court issued an injunction against the railroads as Hogg requested. On appeal, the Texas Supreme Court held that "it [is] apparent that a leading object, if not the sole object, of the association is by the appointment of a common governing committee to fix rates of transportation so as to prevent competition among the several parties to the contract." Because Article X, section 5 barred competing railroads from acting in such a way "so as to stifle competition for the traffic of the state," the association's purpose conflicted with the Texas Constitution. The supreme court affirmed. In the view of Texas railroad historian S. G. Reed, Hogg and the courts misunderstood the value of the association to ordinary Texans. The "Association functioned for three years most efficiently and to the satisfaction of its members and the public. Rates were lower and more stable than ever known." It may have been efficient, but the association violated Texas law.[33]

The railroads argued that the agreement creating the Texas Traffic Association concerned interstate commerce, over which the state lacked jurisdiction. The Texas Supreme Court's response was subtly powerful. The court first noted that the agreement involved no limitation to interstate commerce; the association applied the rate agreement to both interstate and intrastate commerce. The court then suggested the state's power might be limited if all of the corporations that entered the association were created outside of Texas. But several had been incorporated within the state, and "the association, being illegal as to some of the defendants, is illegal as to all." This opinion thus nicely insisted that foreign corporations could not find shelter from the state's regulatory authority merely through an invocation of Congress's exclusive constitutional power to regulate interstate commerce. The federal constitution protected the right of a foreign corporation to enter a state to engage in interstate commerce, but that protection did not extend to immunity when entering into illegal agreements affecting intrastate commerce, particularly when those agreements were made with Texas corporations.

ANTITRUST

One can read in the successive enactments [of the antitrust law] the story of an honest and determined attempt to regulate objectionable business activity, constantly aspiring but always short of the goal.[34]

The Texas Supreme Court's decision on the Texas Traffic Association was issued on December 21, 1888, shortly after Hogg was reelected attorney general. Regulating railroad and other monopolies by statute and by administrative regulation was in the air. At the 1888 national Democratic convention, Texas Democrats resolved that the state legislature adopt a law at the next legislative session declaring unlawful combinations in restraint of trade. The Texas Democratic Party platform opposed monopolies and supported regulating railroad rates, issues on which everyone agreed. The particular manner in which this was to be accomplished was less clear. The Non-Partisan

Party campaigned in part on a platform against monopolies and trusts, and the Farmers' Alliance and other organizations pressed for regulations against "big business." By the time the legislature met in January 1889, "it had to deal with increased interest in legislation to regulate trusts and railroads." Congress had been debating an antitrust act for a year, and although both national parties opposed trusts and monopolies of all types, nothing happened in the election year of 1888. The Texas Traffic Association case was one catalyst for the filing of several antitrust bills when the Texas legislative session opened. As the members of the twenty-first legislature discussed how to regulate trusts, the governor of Kansas wrote to Texas governor Sul Ross and seven other governors to invite legislators to meet in Saint Louis in early March to discuss the "beef combine." On March 13 the delegates adopted a resolution that the legislatures in the other states adopt the antitrust bill "recently passed by the Texas Legislature." Kansas had adopted an antitrust act on March 9, shortly before the meeting of delegates and after the Texas antitrust bill had been passed by the house. On March 22 the Texas senate passed the bill, which became the nation's second antitrust law on March 30, 1889.[35]

The Texas law was titled "Trusts—Conspiracies against Trade." It defined a trust as a "combination of capital, skill, or acts by two or more persons [or] corporations" to restrict trade, limit production, control prices, prevent competition, or refuse to sell or ship goods. The Sherman Antitrust Act, adopted in 1890 by Congress, barred combinations, by trust or otherwise, that restrained trade. The Standard Oil Trust of 1882 was the trust legislators thought of when both antitrust acts were adopted. An ordinary trust is a device separating legal and equitable title to property. A trustee holds legal title to the property. The trustee has the complete power to manage the property, but is under a strict duty (known in law as a fiduciary duty) to manage the property solely for the beneficiaries of the trust. The beneficiaries of the trust hold equitable title to the property. Trusts are often used by the wealthy for purposes of estate planning. Lawyers took the idea of the individual trust and applied it to combine corporations in order to monopolize commercial markets. In the 1882 Standard Oil Trust, fourteen corporations and partnerships surrendered legal control of their assets to a board of trustees. These "beneficiaries" received trust certificates based on the proportional value of their property. The trustees maintained complete control of the combined assets and managed that property for the benefit of the beneficiaries. The Standard Oil Trust "even at the outset dominated the oil-refining industry of the country and most of the pipe lines for the transportation of oil." It controlled 90 percent of the market and had the extraordinary amount of $70 million in capital. Even so, the trust device was rarely used and was largely unsuccessful, as several state courts declared it unlawful for a corporation to enter a trust. Despite the fleeting use of the trust device, legislative efforts to control these combinations of former competitors became known as antitrust laws. A major goal of these laws was to prevent monopolization in a market, although Texas's antitrust law did not require proof of a monopoly in order to win a case. An additional goal of antitrust laws was to limit the size of corporations, for large corporations were viewed by many in the late nineteenth century as a threat both economically and politically to states and to the nation.[36]

Tennessee and Michigan joined Kansas and Texas in adopting antitrust laws in 1889. Congress adopted the Sherman Antitrust Act the next year. The catalyst for action was fear: "The formation of gigantic combinations for these purposes in late years has created alarm and excited the liveliest interest in the public mind."[37]

The 1889 Texas antitrust law focused on railroads; land corporations, most of which were foreign corporations; and the cotton bagging market. In addition to defining a trust and what acts were unlawful, the act declared that any domestic corporation forfeited its Texas corporate charter if it violated the law (§ 2). A foreign corporation that violated the law was barred from "doing any business within this state" (§ 4). In addition to those civil penalties, violation of the act was also subject to criminal prosecution (§ 6). Any person who violated the trust law had engaged in a "conspiracy against trade" and could be punished by a fine of between fifty dollars and five thousand dollars or criminally by imprisonment from one to ten years. Section 13 of the Texas act exempted from its provisions persons who produced agricultural goods or raised livestock. This provision was added to the bill to satisfy the concerns of farmers, who feared the law would be used against them if they attempted to act together to obtain a "fair price for their products." The Texas Supreme Court held this act constitutional in 1895.[38]

The caption of the Texas trust law did not clearly state a person was subject to criminal sanction. This failure might have made those sanctions unconstitutional, because the law failed to provide fair notice of its penalties. In 1893 the Texas Supreme Court declared the antitrust law inapplicable to insurance contracts, relying in part on *Paul v. Virginia* (1869). The conclusion that an insurance contract was neither an article of commerce nor a commodity allowed the court to state its concerns about the constitutionality of the act as a criminal measure without declaring it unconstitutional. At the next regular session of the legislature, the antitrust bill was amended to mollify the court's concerns.[39]

The 1895 act was merely titled "Trusts," and largely reiterated the language of the 1889 act. Differences included encompassing insurance companies by prohibiting restrictions in "aids to commerce" and any effort to restrict "the full and free pursuit" of any business authorized by Texas law. Section 6 of the act defined more clearly and in more detail what actions were unlawful, and section 12 reiterated the exemptions to commodities producers and stock raisers formerly found in section 13. New section 12 also added an exemption for any "organization of laborers for the purpose of maintaining any standard of wages." This provision was a reaction to the application of the Sherman Act to the American Railway Union and its leader, Eugene V. Debs, in the disastrous Pullman strike of 1894. The exemption to any organization of laborers obviated the problem of the "labor injunction," by which concerted action of a labor union, an association of workers, was enjoined as an unlawful "combination" of persons acting to restrain the trade of the commercial business the labor union was protesting.[40]

The Texas trusts act was again amended in 1899. This time the law's title reflected the neologism, for it became the Anti-Trust Law. This third act was the first to proffer a definition of monopoly (§ 2). As noted by Tom Finty, the act was also "extremely lengthy and verbose. It abounded in long, violent and inflammatory sentences, evidencing either excitement of mind or intent to terrify." One substantial change from the earlier laws was the inclusion of an affidavit requirement borrowed from the law of Arkansas. The secretary of state was ordered to send annually (or more often as necessary) a letter of inquiry to the president of every "incorporated company doing business in this State." The letter required the president to file a sworn affidavit denying that the corporation had engaged in any action that violated the Texas antitrust law. The 1899 law also eliminated the exemption to farmers and stock raisers, for that exemption was under a constitutional challenge in courts outside of Texas. In a separate act by the same legislature, the provisions of the antitrust act were declared inapplicable to labor organizations.[41]

In 1902 the Supreme Court of the United States declared unconstitutional the antitrust law of Illinois in *Connolly v. Union Sewer Pipe Co.* The Court held the law violated the Fourteenth Amendment's equal protection clause by exempting farmers and stock raisers from its provisions. The court held the distinction between those subject to the act and those exempted from the act was arbitrary and unreasonable and thus unconstitutional. The Illinois antitrust law was modeled after the Texas trust law, including the language exempting farmers and stock raisers. Although the 1899 antitrust law eliminated the provision exempting farmers and stock raisers, section 14 of that act retained all provisions of the 1889 and 1895 acts that were not contrary to the 1899 act. A month later the Texas Court of Civil Appeals, in *State ex rel. Attorney General v. Shippers' Compress & Warehouse Co.* (1902), held the 1899 act implicitly included the exemption for farmers and stock raisers. Based on the Supreme Court's decision in *Connolly*, that made the 1899 law unconstitutional. On rehearing two weeks later, the Court of Civil Appeals noted that the case was not brought pursuant to the 1899 act, but the 1895 act. Because the 1895 statute explicitly included the exemption for farmers and stock raisers, the court reiterated its original conclusion, a conclusion the Court of Civil Appeals had also adopted in *State ex rel. Attorney General v. Waters-Pierce Oil Co.* (1902). It expressly declared that it was deferring to the conclusion reached by the United States Supreme Court in *Connolly*. The Texas Supreme Court affirmed *Shippers' Compress* in a June 1902 decision, also in deference to *Connolly*. But it limited its conclusion "in so far as the law of 1895 comes within the terms of the *Connolly* case." The Texas Supreme Court also noted that the Supreme Court of the United States, in *Waters-Pierce Oil Co. v. Texas* (1900), upheld the constitutionality of Texas's antitrust law and allowed Texas to revoke the permit of Waters-Pierce to do business. Thus, the Texas Supreme Court declared that the 1895 trust law was constitutional "to the extent that it authorizes the state to revoke the license of a foreign corporation or to forfeit the charter of a domestic corporation for acts done which are forbidden by the antitrust law."[42]

Despite the Texas Supreme Court's narrow interpretation of *Connolly*, the legislature's response to *Connolly* was to adopt the fourth antitrust law in fourteen years, with amendments made to the law in 1907 and 1909. The 1903 law expressly repealed all previous legislation on antitrust, thus eliminating the issue whether the exemption for farmers and stock raisers made the law unconstitutional. The law eliminated the Arkansas affidavit. However, in acts adopted in 1907 and 1909, the affidavit was revived as applied solely to foreign corporations requesting a permit to do business in Texas. Two new sections of the 1903 act, both related to the most extensive antitrust litigation arising out of Texas, were of some importance. Section 7 barred a corporation from doing business in Texas if it took the assets of a Texas corporation whose charter had been forfeited as a result of a violation of antitrust laws. Section 9 did the same for foreign corporations. These provisions were a result of the *Waters-Pierce* antitrust cases. After the Waters-Pierce Oil Company, a foreign corporation, was barred from doing business in Texas because it violated Texas antitrust law, a new corporation obtaining the assets of the old Waters-Pierce Oil Company asked for and received a license to do business in Texas. That new business would also be charged with violating Texas antitrust law. The fifteen-year saga of Waters-Pierce offers several lessons about the possibilities of and limitations on antitrust enforcement on a statewide basis.[43]

WATERS-PIERCE

The Waters-Pierce Oil Company sold kerosene, lubricating oil, grease, and harness oil in Texas and Missouri and elsewhere in the Southwest. The company was driven by Henry Clay Pierce, who created the firm in Saint Louis, Missouri,

in 1873. In 1878, Pierce sold three 20–percent interests in the company to two executives of Ohio Standard and another seller of kerosene. When the first Standard Oil Trust was created in 1882, those ownership interests were placed in the trust, making Standard Oil the majority owner of Waters-Pierce, a fact that was then publicly unknown. Pierce sent 60 percent of the profits of Waters-Pierce to Standard Oil and kept the rest. Pierce was solely responsible for the company's management. From the late 1870s for the next twenty years, the Waters-Pierce Oil Company was the dominant and sometimes sole seller of kerosene and other oils in much of the Southwest, including Texas. It controlled between 90 percent and 98 percent of the oil sales market in the Southwest during the last two decades of the nineteenth century. Its profits totaled over five million dollars between 1895 and 1900 alone.[44]

In September 1894, Attorney General Charles Culberson filed suit in McLennan County district court against more than eighty corporations and persons alleged to be engaged in monopolizing cotton seed. The court issued temporary injunctions against all the defendants. The injunctions were made permanent after the defendants decided not to contest Culberson's suit in order to avoid a forfeiture of their corporate charters. Two months later, the McLennan County attorney, Joseph W. Taylor, obtained an indictment against executives from Standard Oil and Waters-Pierce, including John D. Rockefeller, Sr. Taylor was encouraged to do so by Governor Jim Hogg, who then unsuccessfully attempted to have Rockefeller extradited from New York. No executive of either Standard Oil or Waters-Pierce was brought to trial, which left only Texas-based employees of Waters-Pierce subject to prosecution. The trial court scheduled trial for December 1895. The 1894 election moved Hogg out of the office of governor and Culberson into it. As governor, Culberson lost interest in the antitrust case. Defendant E. T. Hathaway, an employee of Waters-Pierce, was eventually convicted and fined. His lawyers, paid by Waters-Pierce, urged Hathaway to appeal rather than pay the fine. Waters-Pierce hired corporate lawyer George Clark, the conservative fusion candidate for governor who lost to Hogg in 1892, to handle the appeal. Clark worked with John D. Johnson, a lawyer from Saint Louis who regularly represented Waters-Pierce, in fashioning a constitutional challenge to the 1889 antitrust act. Hathaway spent the year after his conviction in jail while remaining on the Waters-Pierce payroll. In 1896 the court of criminal appeals reversed Hathaway's conviction on the ground that the indictment was defective and that insufficient evidence had been offered to prove Hathaway had engaged in a conspiracy to restrain trade. The court's conclusions allowed it to note but avoid Hathaway's constitutional argument. Hathaway was a free man, but the case was remanded for possible reindictment and retrial of Hathaway.[45]

Hathaway voluntarily remained in jail so his (and Waters-Pierce's) lawyers could seek a writ of habeas corpus in federal court. The request for the writ would place the issue of the law's constitutionality before the court. Before a hearing took place, the charges against Hathaway were dropped. For some reason, possibly including changes in the position of county attorney, criminal charges against the other Texas defendants remained, and Clark and Johnson decided to challenge the constitutionality of the act by requesting a writ of habeas corpus in federal court for those other defendants. In February 1897 the federal court held the act unconstitutional in *In re Grice*: "The vice of the act in question is that it attempts to prevent too much. It does not stop at reasonable limits. It is not content with making criminal general restraint of trade, but it makes criminal all restrictions of trade." In addition to violating the due process clause, the act violated the equal protection clause because it exempted farmers and stock raisers from its dictates. That

decision was appealed to the Supreme Court of the United States.[46]

Before Hathaway was prosecuted for a second time, McLennan County attorney Joseph W. Taylor, at the suggestion of Waco attorney Robert "Bob" Henry, filed a civil antitrust suit against Waters-Pierce. The goal of the civil suit was to take advantage of the incentive in the 1889 act allowing a district or county attorney to collect the penalty of fifty dollars per day of antitrust violation. A local county attorney would receive 10 percent of the penalties adjudged. This economic incentive for government attorneys to file suit led Henry to reach an agreement with Taylor, by which the former handled the matter in exchange for two-thirds of the penalty. This case was held in abeyance, however, as Martin M. Crane, Culberson's successor as Texas attorney general, initiated a civil lawsuit against Waters-Pierce in February 1896.

Johnson and Clark again represented Waters-Pierce and again challenged the constitutionality of the 1889 act and its successor, the 1895 act. After a lengthy trial, the jury held that Waters-Pierce, but not the individual defendants, had violated Texas trust law. The jury's verdict was based on its finding that Waters-Pierce had entered into illegal contracts, not that Waters-Pierce had monopolized oil sales in Texas. The district court ordered cancellation of Waters-Pierce's permit to do business in Texas but did not impose a fine. The court also noted that Waters-Pierce could continue to engage in interstate business in Texas.

While this decision was on appeal, Texas argued *In re Grice* before the Supreme Court of the United States. The Court unanimously held in favor of Texas. The case against Grice was to be tried in state court. The efforts by Clark and Johnson to obtain a federal ruling on the constitutionality of the state's antitrust statute "is clearly nothing but an attempt to obtain the interference of a court of the United States when no extraordinary or peculiar circumstances exist in favor of such interference."[47]

The Supreme Court issued its decision in *Grice* on February 21, 1898, and less than three weeks later the Texas Court of Civil Appeals issued its opinion in the appeal of Waters-Pierce concerning the cancellation of its permit to do business in Texas. The Texas court affirmed the forfeiture of the permit as required by the antitrust law. It rejected the claims by Waters-Pierce that the law was unconstitutional. The court noted that Texas possessed a general power to regulate for the benefit of the health, safety, and welfare of its residents. When a person used his property to harm another by restraining trade, the state possessed the authority to halt such harm. Regulating the use of that property did not "deprive" a person (corporation) of its property without due process of law. The court also rejected the argument that the law was unconstitutional "class" legislation because it exempted farmers and stock raisers from the act. It concluded that this policy was not arbitrary and thus not unconstitutional, even though that exemption covered about 80 percent of the state's residents. The distinction between those subject to the act and those exempted from the act was based on a well-known history of harm caused by the former, and the legislature was permitted to take into account the fact that, unlike the harm created by those subject to the law, "the danger in these respects from the excluded classes may be inappreciable." The opinion of the Texas Court of Civil Appeals, although consonant with modern constitutional law, was contrary to a then emerging analysis known as substantive due process. When the Texas Court of Civil Appeals heard *Waters-Pierce*, the Supreme Court of the United States was in the midst of creating its substantive due process edifice.[48]

The Texas Supreme Court rejected the request by Waters-Pierce for a writ of error. The company then took its case to the Supreme Court of the United States, which also affirmed the cancellation of the Waters-Pierce permit. The Supreme Court ignored the exemption for farmers and stock raisers. It did speak of the exemption for laborers added in 1895 and accepted the conclusion of the Texas Court of Civil Appeals that even if the 1895 laborers' exemption was unconstitutional, that did not affect the constitutionality of the 1889 act. Thus, Waters-Pierce was subject to a loss of its permit to do business under either the 1889 or 1895 antitrust act.[49]

The decision of the Supreme Court was released on March 19, 1900. Attorney General "Honest" Tom Smith gave Waters-Pierce until the end of May to conclude its business in Texas. Henry Pierce was urged to meet with Texas congressman (and soon to be senator) Joseph Weldon Bailey to discuss how to remain in business in Texas. Bailey refused to serve as Waters-Pierce's lawyer but agreed to assist the company, after which Pierce "lent" Bailey five thousand dollars and paid him thirty-three hundred dollars, the latter conveniently an amount Bailey owed to keep current on his debts. Bailey called in favors in Austin, and Pierce was informed that he could continue to do business in Texas, but only if the old Waters-Pierce Oil Company was dissolved and a new Waters-Pierce was incorporated. A new Waters-Pierce was incorporated, and Pierce claimed he owned 3,996 of the 4,000 shares issued by the new corporation. In fact, Standard Oil effectively owned 2,747 of those shares. On May 31, 1900, Pierce and lawyer John Johnson arrived at the office of the Texas secretary of state and requested a permit be issued allowing the new Waters-Pierce to do business in Texas. Secretary Dermot Hardy agreed to issue the permit as long as Pierce signed the required "Arkansas" affidavit included in the 1899 antitrust act, by which Pierce was to deny on oath that Waters-Pierce had violated any provision of the Texas antitrust law or was part of any trust or combination. Pierce signed the affidavit pursuant to Johnson's advice. Although the continuation of Waters-Pierce as an ongoing business concern in Texas caused an outcry among trustbusters,

Waters-Pierce faced no new obstacles in making enormous profits in Texas.[50]

The only remaining "old" obstacles were the long-dormant civil antitrust lawsuit filed in McLennan County at the behest of attorney Bob Henry, now a member of the House of Representatives in Congress, and the outstanding criminal cases that had never been tried. Bailey met with Henry to resolve these matters, which Henry was quite happy to do. The county attorney for McLennan County, Cullen Thomas, was less willing to settle the civil suit, for he saw the division of the proposed settlement of thirteen thousand dollars, with ten thousand dollars paid to the government and three thousand to Henry and his partner, as too generous to Henry. Further, the 1899 antitrust act increased the percentage received by the county or district attorney to 25 percent from 10 percent in the earlier acts, which Thomas believed the government should receive. No settlement was reached, and the case went to trial. The trial court dismissed the matter on the ground that the old Waters-Pierce Oil Company was dissolved, making the matter moot. The government appealed. The state court of civil appeals, following *Connolly* (1902), held that the 1899 antitrust law was unconstitutional because it exempted farmers and stock raisers from the act in violation of the equal protection clause. Despite the failure of the lawsuit, Henry's law partner, O. L. Stribling, received a three-thousand-dollar payment from Waters-Pierce for legal work. Whether this payment was for actual legal work performed by Stribling or simply a payoff to Stribling and Congressman Henry was never clarified, even after it came to light during a 1907 investigation of Senator Bailey by the Texas Senate.[51]

In April 1902, then, Waters-Pierce was doing business in Texas as it had for nearly thirty years. The 1889, 1895, and 1899 antitrust acts appeared to be unconstitutional, at least in some respects. No criminal conviction against an employee of Waters-Pierce had been

successfully maintained, and the civil action against Waters-Pierce for penalties had been lost. Texas remained a profitable territory for Waters-Pierce, with annual profits of the company ranging from $1,813,032.88 in 1900 to $2,790,981.87 in 1904. Waters-Pierce was capitalized at $400,000 and earned profits in the years 1900–1904 of about $11.3 million, making it an extraordinarily profitable investment. With the discovery of oil at Spindletop in 1901, the oil business became more prominent in the state's present and future. The entanglement of Waters-Pierce with the Texas antitrust laws was not, however, at an end.[52]

In 1906, Texas filed an antitrust lawsuit against the new Waters-Pierce. Several investigations into the conduct of Standard Oil had occurred since 1900, and after a report concerning a federal investigation into the oil industry and the practices of Standard Oil was released in mid-1906, several states filed antitrust suits against Standard Oil. That investigation assailed not only the practices of Standard Oil, but those of Waters-Pierce as well. An investigation by Missouri attorney general Herbert Hadley begun in 1905 focused on the monopolistic practices of Waters-Pierce. In mid-1906 the Texas and Missouri attorneys general began collaborating regarding the actions of Waters-Pierce. In a deposition conducted by Hadley, Pierce acknowledged that his lawyer, John Johnson, had agreed that Standard Oil would receive the same ownership of the new Waters-Pierce as it owned of the old Waters-Pierce. With the assistance of outside counsel, Texas filed suit against Waters-Pierce in September 1906, asking that its permit be forfeited and that Waters-Pierce pay penalties totaling $5,228,000 for daily violations of the antitrust laws since May 31, 1900.[53]

On June 1, 1907, the jury found that Waters-Pierce had violated the Texas antitrust laws of 1899 and 1903 and had done so since it was granted its permit to do business in Texas. It fined Waters-Pierce $1,500 per day for 1,033 days (May 31, 1900–March 31, 1903) under the 1899 act and the statutory amount of $50 per day for 1,488 days (April 1, 1903–April 29, 1907) under the 1903 act. The fine assessed by the jury was $1,623,900, "more than the federal Justice Department had recovered in all of its antitrust actions since 1890 combined." The new Waters-Pierce, like the old Waters-Pierce, was barred from doing business in Texas. Of the $1.6 million penalty, approximately one-quarter was to be divided among the county attorney of Travis County, special counsel hired to prosecute the case, and John Gruet, a former Waters-Pierce employee with an ax to grind. Gruet had taken confidential documents of Waters-Pierce since 1903. When he was demoted in 1905, Gruet quit and sued Waters-Pierce for $28,000 in alleged back pay. An alcoholic, Gruet altered company documents to make Waters-Pierce look even worse than it was. He used them to attempt to blackmail Senator Bailey, who had been paid a substantial sum of money by Waters-Pierce since he first intervened in its behalf in 1900. The blackmail attempt failed, and Gruet then agreed with the county attorney that he would be paid one-third of the 25 percent commission given the successful prosecutor. Gruet performed so poorly as a witness in the Texas senate's investigation of Bailey in early 1907 that he was not called as a witness in the subsequent Waters-Pierce trial. Even so, Gruet received a fee, but the amount was taken from a total award of $90,000 to the county attorney for Travis County. The remainder was awarded to Texas. The good news for Waters-Pierce, such as it was, was that the jury fined it $1,500 per day under the 1899 act, much less than the $5,000 maximum daily penalty available.[54]

Much like the 1980s *Texaco v. Pennzoil* case (see chapter 8), the losing side found it difficult to provide a *supersedeas* bond sufficient to allow it to appeal the judgment of the district court. A *supersedeas* bond ensured that the party that won at trial would be paid if the judgment of the district court was affirmed on

appeal. The first proffered bond was rejected because the company that insured the bond (a surety) lacked sufficient assets in Texas to cover the amount. A bond was finally secured, although Waters-Pierce avoided state supervision of its business by obtaining an order from a federal court appointing as the receiver of its assets someone friendly to the company's (not Texas's) interests.

The Court of Civil Appeals affirmed the jury's verdict and the trial court judgment in December 1907. The Texas Supreme Court denied the writ of error requested by Waters-Pierce, but the Supreme Court of the United States agreed to hear the matter, along with the propriety of the federal court's decision to appoint a receiver for Waters-Pierce. The U.S. Supreme Court unanimously held in favor of Texas in January 1909, rejecting Waters-Pierce's constitutional claim and concluding that the penalty decided by the jury was within the state's power.[55]

In late April 1909 the federal district court ordered the federally appointed receiver to turn over the Texas assets of Waters-Pierce to the state receiver. On April 24, Waters-Pierce paid its fine of $1,808,753.95, including interest. This massive sum was still less than the ordinary annual profits of Waters-Pierce.

A separate Texas antitrust matter against several corporations tied to Standard Oil was filed in November 1907. The case languished, with neither side apparently interested in resolving it. Shortly before the federal antitrust suit against Standard Oil was to be decided, the parties agreed to an immediate trial in October 1909. The three corporate defendants admitted guilt and paid modest fines under the 1903 act, which limited fines to $50 per day. The companies also immediately forfeited their charters and placed their assets in the hands of a friendly receiver, actions that benefited the major stockholder of the companies, Standard Oil. On December 7, 1909, the assets of these three companies were sold to John Sealy, a

Waters-Pierce pays its antitrust fine, 1909. Courtesy Texas State Library and Archives Commission.

member of a partnership and the only bidder on the property. One of these companies, Security Oil, was valued at $1.5 million by the receiver. It was sold for $85,000, just enough to pay Security's fine. On the same day at about the same time in a different room at the Driskill Hotel in Austin, the assets of Waters-Pierce were sold to Sam Fordyce, a Saint Louis businessman, also the only bidder. Fordyce bid $1,431,741.78. In neither case did the bidders name their partners. Both denied that they were acting as an agent for Standard Oil when asked by Assistant Attorney General Jewel Lightfoot. In fact, Sealy's partnership consisted of persons with long ties to Standard Oil, and Sealy retained the same managers and officers of the now-defunct corporations. Fordyce and Henry Pierce immediately formed the Pierce-Fordyce Oil Association, an unincorporated entity. Pierce owned a majority interest in the association, which simply continued the business formerly done by Waters-Pierce.[56]

On that same day, December 7, 1909, the three-year-long effort to prosecute Henry Pierce for false swearing or perjury in the May 31, 1900, "Arkansas" affidavit abruptly ended. The district court instructed the jury to return a not guilty verdict on the ground that Pierce's testimony in Missouri, during which he acknowledged that Standard Oil owned a majority interest in the new Waters-Pierce, was given under a grant of immunity applicable to any criminal prosecution initiated by Texas,

not just Missouri. Without this evidence, Texas could not prove that Pierce's affidavit, which allowed the second Waters-Pierce to do business in Texas, was made falsely.[57]

Waters-Pierce, despite being a two-time antitrust loser, provided an important and possibly crucial service to Texans. The importance of the Texas market to Waters-Pierce was clear: it spent three million dollars in penalties and legal fees between 1906 and 1909 to remain in business in Texas. Waters-Pierce, like the Standard Oil–affiliated companies sold to John Sealy, also provided jobs to Texans, highly valued since the Panic of 1907. The desire of Texas attorney general Robert V. Davidson to run for governor in 1910 led him, like past attorneys general turned governor, to consider the antitrust fight less important than encouraging companies to enter Texas, bringing needed capital and jobs.[58]

Fordyce-Pierce succeeded in Texas until Pierce tried to free himself and Waters-Pierce from Standard Oil. John Sealy and Company, which received its oil supplies from Standard Oil, was similarly situated. In 1911, John Sealy and Company became Magnolia Petroleum Company, an unincorporated joint stock association. A month later, the Supreme Court of the United States affirmed the federal antitrust ruling against Standard Oil Company of New Jersey, carving numerous companies from its control. Waters-Pierce, trying to maintain its corporate charter in Missouri, contested the effort of Standard Oil officers to assert control over it in February 1912, claiming that this would violate Missouri's antitrust law and leave Waters-Pierce subject to dissolution.[59]

Through Magnolia Petroleum, Standard Oil cut off Waters-Pierce's oil supply. Now Waters-Pierce was the apparent "victim" of monopolization by Standard Oil. Two new antitrust investigations in Texas against Standard Oil, one federal and one state, were both stillborn. The federal investigation, which included indictments, was ordered dismissed by the attorney general of the United States in February 1913. The 1912 Texas investigation by Attorney General Jewel Lightfoot, who had been closely involved in the Waters-Pierce litigation, ended with Lightfoot giving Standard Oil a clean bill of health, which many disbelieved. In late 1912, Henry Pierce purchased Standard Oil's shares in Waters-Pierce, lessening his interest in this latest antitrust matter. However, newly elected Texas attorney general Benjamin F. Looney revived the allegations against Magnolia and Standard in 1913, claiming $99,275,000 in damages. The case was settled five months later for $500,000, with Standard Oil of New Jersey agreeing only that it had violated Texas antitrust laws before October 26, 1909. Magnolia was declared not guilty. Pierce Oil Corporation, the successor to Waters-Pierce, requested a permit to do business in Texas in 1913. The secretary of state's decision denying the application was affirmed by the Texas Supreme Court, but by 1918, "[i]n some manner not clear," Pierce Oil "had cleared itself of this taint" and was the owner of Texas real estate conveyed to it by Fordyce-Pierce.[60]

After the *Waters-Pierce* case, Texas gained a national reputation for stringent antitrust enforcement. Was this reputation deserved, either then or later? Writing in 1916, Tom Finty concluded that Texas antitrust law "represents almost exclusively the legalistic view—an antiquated legalistic view, at that—and is very little tempered by the knowledge of men in business, nor by the knowledge of economists." The law,

Finty believed, was "unreasonable and unjust, for timid business men and those who believe in obeying all laws regardless of their merit," but not for the "bold," who would "tak[e] chances of the law." A University of Texas law professor's conclusion a decade later was more desultory: antitrust law ignored important matters and applied instead to a "few patent medicine" cases, in which defendants were offered "a somewhat ignoble escape which the judges themselves do not approve by a policy of supposedly overriding importance derived from the Anti-Trust Law." Consequently, "a statute aimed at great, sinister monopolistic aggregations of capital, which exact the last farthing from the common people, [is] deflected to a picayunish target—the resale and territorial arrangements between manufacturers and dealers . . . who have not the remotest hope of a monopolistic position in their field." Historian Bruce Bringhurst concludes that Texas officials "succeeded to a remarkable extent in disguising the ineffectuality of their antimonopoly activities." Lawyer and historian Jonathan Singer believes Bringhurst's conclusion is too severe: although Texas did not drive guilty companies out of the state, its antitrust actions did "gain general compliance with the antitrust laws and consideration of those laws in making business decisions." For Joseph Pratt and Mark Steiner, Texas antitrust law was largely beneficial to the infant Texas oil industry, for the "'intent to terrify' that lay behind the Texas antitrust laws helped shape the structure of the modern oil industry." Those laws ensured that Standard Oil faced more and stronger competitors, including Gulf Oil and Texaco.[61]

Texas antitrust law was applied regularly to oil companies during the first half of the twentieth century, when Texas was one of four states to enforce its antitrust laws. But writing in 1957, former governor and attorney general Dan Moody and lawyer Charles Wallace declared *Waters-Pierce* still "the biggest Texas antitrust case of all." In making a case for the enforcement of state antitrust laws, Texas attorney general Will Wilson discussed in 1961 the history of Texas antitrust enforcement since *Waters-Pierce*. He noted that Texas had successfully closed antitrust cases in 1938 for a $450,000 penalty and in 1943 for $50,000. In addition, a late 1950s Texas antitrust matter against a number of road material companies resulted in a penalty of $120,000. None of these cases, even without accounting for inflation, was similar in kind to *Waters-Pierce*, and Wilson, like many attorneys general before him, used his enforcement of Texas antitrust law to bolster his chances of gaining another political office. Wilson's history of antitrust enforcement in Texas indicated that the antitrust law was useful for two reasons: it could be used as a tool to terrorize corporations, particularly oil companies such as Standard Oil, and it could be used by a politically ambitious attorney general to remind voters of his populist bona fides. It did little else. Its *in terrorem* effect may be shown by the investigations initiated when Price Daniel was attorney general. Between 1947 and 1952 about a thousand preliminary investigations were opened, one for just about every working day. From that massive number, thirty-three lawsuits were brought, none of any lasting significance. Daniel became a United States senator from Texas in the 1952 election and was elected governor in 1956. He, Jim Hogg, Charles Culberson, and others found antitrust law useful for those hoping to move from the attorney general's office to the governor's but a hindrance to them after they won election. The Texas antitrust law was finally repealed in 1983 and replaced with a law consistent with the Sherman Antitrust Act.[62]

CORPORATIONS, CAPITAL, AND THE REINCORPORATION OF GULF AND TEXACO

The Texas Stock and Bond Law of 1893 was adopted to limit the issuance of railroad stocks and bonds secured by liens or mortgages on railroad property in Texas. Separately, the Texas Railroad Commission was given the power to regulate rates charged by railroads in Texas. The Farmers' Loan and Trust Company sued the commission, claiming its authority to regulate rates was an unconstitutional taking of property, for the rates were set so low that the railroad had insufficient capital to pay interest on its outstanding bonds. The federal circuit court agreed, and Texas successfully appealed to the Supreme Court of the United States. Before the Supreme Court issued its opinion in 1894, Governor Jim Hogg demanded the legislature adopt a stock and bond law limiting the issuance of fictitious bonds that Hogg believed might mislead investors and the public concerning the financial health of the railroad. The Stock and Bond Law was adopted in April. It reduced the indebtedness of Texas railroads slightly and reduced substantially the value of the railroad stock on a per-mile basis. Writing in 1913 about the law's effectiveness, Charles Shirley Potts concluded, "It is always a matter of great difficulty to say positively what the results of any given piece of legislation have been." Potts believed the law "has accomplished good results," but he also suggested several amendments allowing railroads to issue more bonds and revalue its assets. Edmund Miller's view was more melancholy: "It can be said with a reasonable degree of certainty that the law as it has been administered has afforded no encouragement to railroad building for large speculative gains." Further, improvements in the rails, bridges, stations, and rolling stock amounted to "a paltry sum," largely because of the commission's low estimate of the capitalization of the railroad, which artificially lowered the amount the railroad could borrow from bondholders, even with liberalized amendments to the law in 1901 and 1907. A different story was told by Texas railroad historian S. G. Reed, who, writing in 1941, noted that the law was still in effect and "has on the whole been beneficial" by allowing the issuance of stock and bonds that accurately reflected the value in the railroads.[63]

In 1899 the Texas legislature adopted the Pipeline Act, which effectively prohibited vertically integrated oil companies chartered in Texas—companies that explored and produced oil, shipped it, refined it, and marketed it. And the broadly worded 1899 antitrust law was directed in particular at Standard Oil Company, the only existing vertically integrated oil corporation chartered elsewhere. The Pipeline Act allowed a corporation to exist to store and transport oil, and under the 1874 general incorporation law, a company was forbidden to engage in more than one lawful purpose. The amount of oil discovered at Spindletop created an opportunity in Texas to develop integrated oil companies able to compete with Standard Oil, which officially avoided Texas. For Gulf Oil and Texaco, one early avenue around these restrictive laws was to have large individual shareholders take significant ownership of producing companies, which sold their oil to Gulf and Texaco, which refined it. Gulf Refining Company aligned itself with J. M. Guffey Petroleum Company. Texaco was aligned with Producers Oil Company, owned by Joseph Cullinan. This action may have violated the spirit of the law, but both companies early sought and found political protection by entering into favorable agreements with former governor Jim Hogg and the Hogg-Swayne Syndicate (Swayne was a Fort Worth lawyer and former legislator). J. M. Guffey sold to the Hogg-Swayne Syndicate fifteen prime acres of Spindletop land for $180,000, a sweetheart deal, to gain political influence in Texas. In 1902 the syndicate, now in debt, sold some of its holdings to Joseph Cullinan's Texas Fuel Company for $25,000 worth of stock.[64]

Cullinan's firm was soon incorporated as the Texas Company, known as Texaco. The April 7, 1902, charter of the Texas Company indicated that its purpose was to produce petroleum and to "construct, maintain and operate pipe lines," a combination of purposes that appeared to violate the Texas general incorporation statute. Secretary of State John G. Tod accepted the charter conditionally, awaiting the Texas Supreme Court's decision in *Ramsey v. Tod*. The court's decision, in June 1902, forbade a corporation from engaging in both producing and transporting oil, which made the Texas Company charter unlawful. The charter was amended, but Cullinan integrated operations through companies closely associated with the Texas Company.[65]

In 1903, representatives of Gulf and Texaco began discussing a possible merger initiated by the Mellon family of Pittsburgh, which controlled Gulf. Those discussions were fruitless, but a year later they were renewed. The proposal was to create a new corporation consistent with the laws of Texas, with Gulf shareholders taking 60 percent of the shares in the new corporation and Texaco shareholders taking the remainder. One initial difficulty, according to Texaco general counsel James L. Autry, was that a corporate charter creating an integrated oil company violated the 1874 general incorporation act and the 1899 pipeline act. The proposed solution was to have the legislature amend the pipeline act. The bill was derailed for two related reasons: First, sensational disclosures of monopolistic action by Standard Oil by the Kansas attorney general made headlines in Texas and raised the specter of another giant oil trust if Gulf and Texaco combined. Second, small Texas oil operators used their local presence to sway legislators to reject the bill.[66]

The legislature's inaction contributed to the collapse of the proposed Gulf-Texaco merger. It also led to the reincorporation of Gulf. In order to become a lawfully integrated oil company, Gulf reincorporated in New Jersey in 1907, acquiring the stock of J. M. Guffey Petroleum Company (the producing company), Gulf Refining Company (the "original" entity), and Gulf Pipe Line Company. The new Gulf now produced, transported, and refined oil, doing business in Texas and elsewhere as a New Jersey corporation. Texaco tried another strategy. It acted as an integrated oil company without

*Hogg-Swayne Tract,
Spindletop oil field, 1903.
Courtesy Texas Energy
Museum, Beaumont, Texas.*

reincorporating outside of Texas. In a 1907 ad Texaco proclaimed itself, "The Texas Company, Producers, Refiners and Distributors; Texas Petroleum and Its Products." The ownership interest in Texaco by Hogg and other Texans (Texans initially owned a controlling amount of stock in the corporation) may have offered some protection against possible threats that its charter might be revoked, but by the early 1910s Texaco again desired legislative authorization for its operations. By 1913, eastern investors owned 83 percent of Texaco stock, with Texans owning the remainder. Joseph Cullinan, the adopted Texan who ran Texaco, was ousted from his position that year. Despite suggestions that the state investigate the taking of a Texas corporation and making it one operated by "New York ideas," nothing materialized.[67]

In 1915 the general incorporation law was amended to allow companies to store, transport, purchase, and sell petroleum outside of Texas, as Texaco had been doing since constructing a pipeline to Oklahoma in 1908. The 1917 legislature allowed a corporation to engage in both the oil and gas producing business and the pipeline business as long as they were separately incorporated. An "organizing company" was permitted to own the stock of both a

producing company and a pipeline corporation as long as it owned only one of each. It was also permitted to own oil pipelines outside of Texas through a separate corporation. The price of this beneficence was the adoption, the same day, of a law that made pipeline companies carrying petroleum common carriers. These common carriers, like the railroads before them, were subject to close regulation by the Texas Railroad Commission. Pipeline corporations were subject to the commission's authority to decide what rates the pipeline corporations could charge. Texaco's interests in this legislation were advanced by its general counsel, Amos L. Beaty, a Texas lawyer. By 1925, Beaty was president of Texaco. He concluded that Texaco needed to reincorporate in Delaware, for, in the understated words of the company's historian, "[u]nder the corporation laws of Texas, it was difficult to achieve the flexibility needed for a necessarily complex enterprise doing business over most of the world."[68]

Throughout the last three decades of the nineteenth century, Texas suffered from a dearth of capital. Only a few banks and building and loan companies existed. Interest rates for farmers, the vast majority of Texas workers, were regularly between 12 percent and 15 percent, with an 8 percent rate sufficiently unusual to be reported. These interest rates existed at a time when agricultural prices fluctuated greatly but trended downward. Capital for oil exploration and timber in the early twentieth century ordinarily came from large investment companies in New York. This scarcity of capital was exacerbated by the absence of state-chartered banks. By 1900, calls to amend the constitution to allow state bank corporations became more prevalent. The 1902 Democratic Party platform supported a constitutional amendment to allow the incorporation of state banks, "similar to those governing national banks." This platform implicitly acknowledged inroads made by national banks into Texas. By 1900 the amount of capital required to create a national bank was just twenty-five thousand dollars. Consequently, the number of national banks in Texas increased from 198 in 1898 to 420 in 1904. Voters approved an amendment allowing the incorporation of state banks in 1904, and in 1905 the Texas legislature adopted a law, borrowed from Missouri (which borrowed from New York), allowing banks to incorporate subject to state regulation. The constitutional amendment limited a bank to no "more than one place," thus banning branch banking, and barred all foreign corporations, other than national banks, from banking in Texas. Two reasons to incorporate as a state bank rather than as a national bank were that a state bank was permitted to lend more money when the borrower used real estate as collateral, and more of the state bank's overall capital could be lent to one person. After the first five years of state banking, 584 state banks existed with capital totaling more than twenty-one million dollars. By 1920, more than 1,000 state banks were operating. Allowing state banks to incorporate not only generated more capital within the state, but it also enhanced local control of that capital. For example, the first bank chartered under the 1905 law, Union Bank and Trust, was capitalized at five hundred thousand dollars,

nearly all through local funds. In 1943, borrowing from the best features of the banking laws of other states, Texas adopted a banking code to replace the 1905 law. The 1943 code created a finance commission that appointed the banking commissioner for the state.[69]

The 1907 Robertson Insurance Law, named after Governor Jim Hogg's former law partner, James H. Robertson, required that any company engaged in the life insurance business in Texas keep 75 percent of its Texas reserves in Texas securities and Texas real estate. "Securities" included state and municipal bonds, stock in any national bank doing business in Texas or in any Texas state bank, and mortgage bonds of any Texas-chartered corporation doing business in Texas and paying a dividend. The Robertson Insurance Law was adopted during a progressive era "revolt against the evils of corporate business and the industrial society," and Texas joined other Southern states in "a sharp struggle between reformers and big business." Between 1888 and 1907, the three large New York life insurance companies collected $52 million in premiums from Texans while paying out only $16.5 million in benefits. Further, those companies invested less than $11 million in Texas securities and just $180,000 in real estate mortgages in the state. The goals of the Robertson Insurance Law included limiting the power of foreign insurance corporations, keeping capital in the state to finance Texas business initiatives, and aiding the competitiveness of local insurance companies. Additional laws adopted in 1909 furthered these goals. Although twenty-one of the forty-six foreign life insurance companies withdrew from Texas after the act was adopted, mortgages on Texas real estate tripled to over $1.125 million by 1908, "$256,675.94 more than the twenty-one companies which left the state had loaned during the thirty years they had done business in this State."[70]

MODERNIZING BUSINESS LAW

In 1949, Edmund Belsheim concluded that the absence of any major revision of the 1874 law of corporations had made Texas an outlier among the states. He noted:

> In all states except two, Montana and Texas, corporations may be formed for any lawful purpose subject to specified exclusions. In all states except thirteen, Arizona, Georgia, Kansas, Louisiana, Michigan, Mississippi, Montana, New Mexico, North Dakota, Oklahoma, Texas, Utah and Wyoming, the duration of the corporation may be perpetual. In all states except three, South Carolina, Texas and Utah, no part of the authorized capital need be subscribed or paid in prior to incorporation. In all states except seven, New York, North Dakota, South Dakota, Texas, Utah, Vermont and Wisconsin, none of the incorporators is required to be a citizen or resident of the state.[71]

University of Texas Law School dean Ira Hildebrand had called for the revision of the general incorporation law patterned after the Model Business Corporation Act in his 1942 legal treatise on Texas corporations. His call followed the "modernization" of corporation law in numerous states between 1920 and 1940, a modernization that included allowing a corporation to form for any legal purpose, permitting corporations to exist in perpetuity, and acknowledging that the capital of a corporation need not be paid in before the company was incorporated. Edward Bailey joined Belsheim's call. By late 1950 this academic momentum had been transformed into political momentum. Texas secretary of state John Ben Shepperd gave a speech making the instrumental argument that failing to revise its corporate law might cost Texans "hundreds of jobs and millions of dollars in industrial pay rolls and state revenue." For a state rapidly moving from an agricultural to an industrial economy, this was sobering news.[72]

In spring 1950 the University of Texas Law School held an all-day institute on Texas corporation laws to honor the memory of Dean Hildebrand. One commentator was Paul Carrington, a Dallas lawyer who, more than anyone else, drove the adoption of the Texas Business Corporations Act of 1955. Carrington was a member of the American Bar Association committee that revised the 1950 Model Business Corporations Act. At his urging, the State Bar of Texas resolved that the law of corporations in Texas was "unsatisfactory" and in 1950 created the Committee on Revision of Corporation Laws, on which Carrington served as chairman. The committee published a first draft of a Business Corporations Act in the May 1951 *Texas Bar Journal*. It organized an institute on the draft the day before the state bar convention began to consider changes and amendments. A second draft was almost immediately proposed and offered for sale and study. A meeting of ABA and Texas drafters to discuss the Texas draft took place at Southern Methodist University Law School in spring 1952, and the revised draft was also discussed at a second Hildebrand Conference at the University of Texas in April 1952. A third and final draft was approved by the assembly of the state bar convention in summer 1952. The state bar recommended legislative approval in its 1953 session. Without some investment from the legislature, however, the proposed reform by the state bar would likely have failed. At the 1953 legislative session, the house added sixty-five amendments to the bill. By the time the bill was sent to the senate, it had insufficient time in the limited Texas legislative session to consider it.[73]

The 1953 setback was temporary. The Section on Corporation, Banking, and Business Law of the State Bar of Texas was created before the legislature met in January 1955, and its members asked their local representatives to support the act. A new corporation code was adopted. The Texas act was predominantly based on the Model Business Corporations Act, not on Delaware's law of corporations and not on Texas's prior law of corporations. Of the 288 sections in the act, 226 were taken all or in part from the model act. Only 39 were taken all or in part from earlier Texas statutes. The act's adoption was a result of both great legal drafting skills and sublime political skills. Carrington's committee carefully wove together model act and Texas provisions as well as ninety-five sections taken from other sources. This, of course, was merely the beginning. The committee and state bar then had to convince a majority of lawyers, many of whom rarely did corporate law work, of the need and value of the revision. Finally, these "amateur draftsmen" needed to convince legislators of the value of the revision and to discourage amendments to it. The passage of the Business Corporations Act was a model of legal reform and demonstrated the influence of lawyers in mid-twentieth-century America.[74]

The act created perpetual existence for Texas corporations and changed the law regarding the transfer, restriction, and sale of shares. Texas also largely abolished the *ultra vires* doctrine, which permitted a state to revoke the charter of a corporation that acted beyond its authority, including acting beyond the purpose for which it was created. Abolishing *ultra vires* signaled that Texas was also ready to abandon the single-purpose limitation for corporations. The act explicitly permitted a corporation to exist for multiple purposes. Even so, Texas law still required that a corporation list all of its business purposes in its corporate charter. This provision was later amended to allow the charter to state that the corporation existed "for the transaction of all lawful business."[75]

The momentum generated by the adoption of the Business Corporations Act was used by the state bar to propose, and by the legislature to adopt, acts for nonprofit corporations and miscellaneous corporations in 1959 and 1961. The legislature also adopted a limited partnership act in 1955 (revised in 1987) based on the Uniform Limited Partnership Act, and a partnership act based on the Uniform Partnership Act in 1961. With the continuing assistance of the Business Law Section of the State Bar of Texas and the Texas Business Law Foundation, the legislature has regularly amended these acts to account for changes in the operations of businesses.[76]

The mid-twentieth-century modernization of Texas business law marked a significant turning point. Texas now actively sought to attract business corporations. Amendments to the Business Corporations Act were designed to make Texas "a desirable place in which to incorporate." These efforts were "not merely an accident of nature," but also a concerted approach of the legislature over time. Over the next several decades the Texas legislature regularly amended its business codes to account for new issues arising in the operation of businesses. Two examples may suffice. In 1991, in response to a perceived liability threat to professionals such as lawyers and accountants, Texas became the first state to pass a law allowing a general partnership to limit the liability of its partners for the actions of other partners through the creation of the LLP, a type of limited liability partnership. It was the fourth state to allow the creation of an LLC, an entity that legally limited the personal liability of LLC owners in the same fashion enjoyed by shareholders in a corporation. However, both the LLP and LLC remained a partnership for federal tax purposes, thus avoiding double taxation when a corporation paid its shareholders dividends. Second, in *Castleberry v. Branscum* (1986), the Texas Supreme Court held a party could pierce the corporate veil and make shareholders personally liable for the corporation's action when "individuals abuse the corporate privilege." The court, quoting a corporation law treatise, also indicated that it would allow a party to look beyond the corporation to shareholders for liability when recognizing a separate corporate existence would lead to an inequitable result. This statement generated an instant outcry from business law attorneys. The standard of avoiding "an inequitable result" made legal advice mere speculation and created substantial incentives for aggrieved persons to sue. Almost immediately the legislature adopted Article 2.21 of the Texas Business and Commerce Code, intended to strictly limit the ability of a litigant to pierce the corporate veil and make shareholders personally liable for the corporation's actions.[77]

In 2003, after eight years of work, Texas adopted the Texas Business Organizations Act. This act encompassed within one code all organizational forms, from for-profit business corporations to nonprofit unincorporated associations. This was yet another indication that Texas intended to move to the forefront of business-friendly states. Unlike Paul Carrington in the early 1950s, twenty-first-century Texas lawyers could advise clients to incorporate in Texas rather than follow tradition and incorporate in Delaware.[78]

SHARPSTOWN SCANDAL

On Monday, January 18, 1971, the day before the reinauguration of Governor Preston Smith, the Fort Worth office of the Securities and Exchange Commission (SEC) filed a civil lawsuit alleging that Frank Sharp, his associates, and several others had defrauded the public by manipulating the stock price in several companies owned substantially by Sharp. The SEC additionally charged that some of the defendants had obtained the money to purchase these stocks through loans from the Sharpstown State Bank, also owned by Sharp. With the exception of former Texas attorney general Waggoner Carr, the defendants in the SEC case were unknown to the public. What made this stock fraud a continuing story on the front pages of Texas newspapers for much of the next two years was an aside made in the SEC complaint. The SEC alleged that the

> defendants even attempted to avoid further regulation of the . . . banks by the Federal Deposit Insurance Corporation by attempt-

ing to have legislation introduced and passed by the Texas Legislature that would enable state banks to be insured by a state-chartered insurance company, and in furtherance of this proposed legislation caused large sums of money to be loaned to certain legislators, legislative employees, and members of the executive branch and arranged for them to acquire stock . . . which defendants then sold for these persons at a price greater than the amount of the loans.

The complaint did not name those allegedly bribed. In time, the public learned that Speaker of the House Gus Mutscher and Governor Preston Smith, among others, had bought and swiftly sold, at a significant profit, stock in a company controlled by Frank Sharp. The scandal eventually resulted in a guilty plea in federal court by Sharp, who turned government witness, and the conviction in state court of Mutscher and two coconspirators. Governor Smith was named an unindicted coconspirator. The scandal led to a wholesale remaking of the executive and legislative branches of the state in the 1972 election. Smith sought a third term as governor, an effort that failed spectacularly. Texas elected a new governor, lieutenant governor, and attorney general. The turnover of members in the house (77 out of 150) and senate (15 out of 31) was extraordinary. One consequence of this transformation of the Texas governing class was a legislative session in 1973 that dramatically altered Texas law and implemented the state's first substantial ethics legislation. The laws adopted during this session make the sixty-third legislature one of the most significant in Texas legal history.

Several reasons can be given for the Sharpstown scandal. A major reason was the casual culture of corruption in Austin, in which cash and other gifts were commonly bestowed on legislators by lobbyists and others interested in pending legislation. Another significant reason was the manner in which Texas banking

Gus Mutscher, Preston Smith, Lyndon Baines Johnson, and Ben Barnes (from left to right), Brenham, Texas, 1970. Courtesy Texas State Library and Archives Commisson.

laws regulated the creation and operation of banks. Banking regulation favored a banking cartel that enhanced profits at the expense of consumers and increased the possibility of legislative corruption.[79]

Frank Sharp received a charter for the Sharpstown State Bank in 1961 following a divided vote of the state's banking board. Although the 1905 state bank incorporation law allowed any set of incorporators to incorporate, provided sufficient capital was put in the bank, later legislation required that each proposed bank receive approval from the State Banking Board before beginning operations. One of the board's responsibilities was to determine whether a "public necessity of the business in the community" existed. The board in 1961 consisted of the attorney general, the state treasurer, and the state banking commissioner. One result of Texas's long-standing fear of banks was the prohibition on branch banking. For persons living in the growing suburbs of urbanizing Texas, the absence of branch banking required them either to travel downtown to bank or find a small suburban bank near home or work. Existing banks regularly urged the state's banking regulators to restrict

the number of banks chartered by the state, as a licensing system that barred branches encouraged banks to find ways to restrict the number of competitors and maintain a cartel. Throughout the 1960s existing banks facing greater competition sued the board, challenging its decisions to grant another charter. In addition, the requirement that the banking board approve all proposed bank charters led to cronyism and favoritism. In the mid-1950s, Secretary of State Howard Carney wrote Governor Allan Shivers that a pending banking charter application for "our friends in Hooks" had the approval of State Treasurer Jesse James. Carney asked Shivers to request that Attorney General John Ben Shepperd vote in favor of the charter. When Sharp applied for a bank charter, the deputy state banking commissioner voted against approving the application, apparently in service of the interests of existing banks. However, both the state treasurer and Attorney General Will Wilson voted to approve.[80]

Sharpstown State Bank was located in a growing suburban area of Houston and grew as Houston's suburban population rapidly increased. The growth rate of the bank was insufficient to fuel Frank Sharp's desire to build his financial empire, however, because Texas law limited deposits (which are liabilities to banks) to the value of the capital stock of the bank plus its certified cash surplus. Unless he increased deposits, the bank was limited in the loans (which are assets to banks) it could make. Sharp evaded this restriction by using a $3 million loan from the Sharpstown State Bank itself through a third party (the Jesuit Fathers of Houston) to increase the capital stock of the bank by $3 million. In essence, Sharp had the bank lend money to increase its own capital stock, allowing it to take in more deposits, which allowed it to lend more money—a tactic which, if discovered, is greatly frowned upon by banking regulators because it is illegal. It is illegal because it may lead to fraud and the collapse of the bank. Sharp was a sharp businessman, and the battle to obtain a corporate charter for Sharpstown State Bank may have led him to consider cutting regulatory corners. In 1963, former attorney general Will Wilson returned to private practice and became Frank Sharp's attorney. Whether Sharp believed Wilson's influence as a former Texas attorney general and Texas Supreme Court justice would aid him in his empire-building efforts is unclear. Wilson was known as incorruptible, but he was politically ambitious, having run unsuccessfully for governor in 1962. And Wilson did very well in private practice, increasing his net worth between 1963 and 1969 from $500,000 to $1.3 million. In the late 1960s, Sharp wanted to lend money through the Sharpstown State Bank without the fear that the Federal Deposit Insurance Corporation (FDIC), which insured bank deposits up to $15,000, would limit his ability to do so. Sharp's reckless banking practices were the precipitating reason for the bribery scandal.[81]

In mid-1968, Sharp took control of two insurance companies, including National Bankers Life Insurance Company (NBL). Sharp used loans from banks he controlled to finance these acquisitions. The assets of the insurance companies were then used to pay off the loans. In addition, Sharp used funds of the nonprofit Jesuit Fathers of Houston to fund his purchases. The Jesuit Fathers had received several significant charitable gifts from Sharp. Because of his donations, Sharp was received by Pope Paul VI at the Vatican in August 1969. A month after his trip to Rome, in attempting to facilitate the bribery of Mutscher and others, Sharp strongly encouraged the Jesuit Fathers to purchase large amounts of NBL stock at inflated prices, with dire financial consequences for the Jesuit Fathers.

In early 1969 Sharp created a small market in NBL stock through a brokerage house. As a publicly traded stock, NBL was required to register with the SEC. It did not. A federal district court later noted that Sharp and other defendants "accomplished the manipulation of the stock of NBL [and other companies controlled by Sharp] by causing selective purchases calculated to decrease the 'floating' supply with the market maker, Ling & Co., resulting in a corresponding rise in the value of the stocks." NBL stock more than doubled to twenty dollars per share, in part by having friends of Sharp purchase the stock with money lent by Sharpstown State Bank. A similar effort was used to pump the price of another Sharp-owned company, which increased from two dollars to sixteen dollars per share in less than three months.[82]

The Sharpstown State Bank had made a number of impermissible loans that allowed Sharp to gain control of additional companies. Other loans made by it increased the risk that the bank would fall out of compliance with FDIC regulations. Those regulations limiting the bank's risk in making loans existed in part to limit the possibility of the bank's failure should those loans not be repaid. Sharp believed that freeing Sharpstown State Bank from the FDIC's regulatory oversight would allow the bank to survive despite the bad loans it had made. Relatedly, Sharp believed that increasing the maximum amount of deposit insurance from fifteen thousand dollars to one hundred thousand would allow Sharpstown State Bank to attract money from large depositors, which would then allow the bank to increase its overall lending amounts. This increase in loans made possible by greater insured deposits in the bank would presumably lead to bank profits, as long as those loans were repaid. At the very least, the increase in lending authority would allow the bank to mask its losses on its bad loans. Sharp's solution was to have the legislature adopt a law allowing the formation of private Texas deposit insurance corporations insuring bank deposits up to one hundred thousand dollars. Sharpstown State Bank would then leave FDIC deposit insurance protection (and oversight) for private deposit insurance protection from a state-based corporation. The assumption was that this private deposit insurance corporation, in its desire to gain business, might not look at the bank's balance sheet as closely as the FDIC might. This would give Sharp some time and breathing room to continue to operate his "sick" bank.

In mid-1969 Sharp met with Speaker of the House Gus Mutscher at the Rice Hotel in Houston. The two men had a "long but somewhat casual and interrupted relationship," and in fall 1968 Sharp had told Mutscher about his idea for Texas-based bank insurance, which he proposed as beneficial to small banks. Sharp now requested passage of a private deposit insurance bill, which became House Bill 73, and a companion bill, House Bill 72, "to allow incorporation of a corporation whose purpose is to insure deposits for the benefit of bank depositors." With a literal wink and a nod, in Sharp's later testimony, Mutscher suggested that the bill might become law at a soon-to-be-announced special session of the legislature if Sharp and Mutscher could agree on a good investment, for Mutscher had suffered recent investment losses. In order to facilitate passage of the legislation, Sharp agreed in late July 1969 to sell NBL stock to Mutscher, Governor Smith,

and the head of the Texas Democratic Party, an osteopath named Elmer Baum (Smith's investment partner and personal doctor), State Representative Tommy Shannon, and others. The first three men, along with House Appropriations Chairman Bill Heatly, purchased about ten thousand NBL shares each, at prices between ten dollars and fourteen dollars per share. (Shannon purchased slightly more than four thousand shares.) The purchases were wholly funded by loans from the Sharpstown State Bank in a manner that strongly suggested the loans were made outside the ordinary course of business. Sharp never met with Smith. He spoke only with Smith's investment partner, Baum, before he sold them the stock they purchased with money lent them by Sharp's bank.[83]

On September 9, 1969, the legislature adopted the two banking bills just four days after they were introduced by Rep. Shannon and without any significant debate. Because this was not a regular session but a called session, the legislature was permitted to adopt only those bills included in the governor's "call." On September 8, Governor Smith added to the call "legislation providing for additional insurance on bank deposits." On September 10, Mutscher called Sharp and told him he wanted to sell his NBL stock. On September 11, Mutscher and two others involved in the conspiracy sold much of their NBL stock for $20 per share to the Jesuit Fathers, who were persuaded by Sharp to purchase this stock, even though stock was available on the market for about $14. (The head of the Jesuit Fathers testified that he had bought the stock at $20 per share because Sharp told him it was a good investment to do so.) In a mere six weeks Mutscher earned $18,365 on the sale of seventy-five hundred shares (out of the ten thousand shares he initially purchased). The Jesuit Fathers also purchased the stock held by Smith and Baum on September 12, giving Smith and Baum a total profit of about $125,000, again in just six weeks. On September

11, 1969, Governor Smith appointed Baum to the three-member State Banking Board, which regulated Sharpstown and other state-chartered banks. In large part because of the machinations of Sharp, the Jesuit Fathers of Houston went bankrupt in 1971, when Sharpstown State Bank stock became worthless.[84]

After the bills were sent to Governor Smith for signature, banking lobbyists and former governor Allan Shivers, now a banker and the person who sold NBL to Sharp, protested the bills. On September 29, the last day on which he was permitted to act, Smith vetoed both bills. He did so, his veto stated, because although he supported the legislation, he was "not satisfied that the approach taken by these bills is the proper one." Sharp's bribery of Mutscher and others had not gained him his deposit insurance bills. Smith collected his NBL profits and vetoed the bill. Sharp's luck had run out.[85]

The SEC's civil lawsuit included as defendants a former Texas commissioner of insurance, John Osorio, former attorney general Carr, and more than two dozen others. The federal district judge assigned to the case, Sarah Hughes, issued a temporary injunction against all defendants other than Carr. On September 16, 1971, Judge Hughes issued a permanent injunction against all defendants, including Carr. A group of house members known as the "Dirty Thirty" increased the pressure on Mutscher concerning his involvement in the Sharpstown scandal, but Mutscher remained speaker of the house through the 1971 legislative session.[86]

The SEC's lawsuit was simply the first step in unraveling the relationship between Mutscher, Sharp, and their associates. A week after the SEC lawsuit was filed, the Sharpstown State Bank failed, costing the FDIC twenty million dollars, then the largest bank failure in the FDIC's history. Sharp's lawyer sent out feelers about a plea to the U.S. attorney for the Southern District of Texas, Anthony Farris. Farris forwarded the proposals to the Department

of Justice for approval. In another twist, the information went to the head of the Criminal Division of the Department of Justice, Assistant Attorney General Will Wilson. Wilson had become a Republican and had joined the Department of Justice when Richard Nixon became president in January 1969. Wilson properly recused himself from consideration of the matter because he had represented Sharp in private practice. However, in 1970, while assistant attorney general, Wilson borrowed thirty thousand dollars from Sharp, and as a private lawyer during the 1960s Wilson had borrowed over a quarter of a million dollars from entities controlled by Sharp. His entanglements with Sharp led to his resignation from the Department of Justice in October 1971. In June 1971, after the Department of Justice accepted the proposed plea agreement, Sharp agreed to plead guilty to two felonies in federal court. He was fined and sentenced to three years' probation. Sharp was given immunity from further prosecution and agreed to testify against others involved in the bribery of state officials.[87]

Mutscher, Shannon, the legislative sponsor of the banking bills, and Rush McGinty, an executive assistant to Mutscher, were indicted. Six days later, on September 29, 1971, bank examiners who had received improper benefits from Sharp were indicted. On March 15, 1972, Mutscher, Shannon, and McGinty were convicted of conspiracy to accept a bribe. The convictions were affirmed on appeal.[88]

During Mutscher's trial, but outside the presence of the jury, the prosecution declared Governor Smith an unindicted coconspirator. Smith's response was to run for a third term as governor. He lost to both other major candidates in the Democratic Party primary. Voter resentment also led to the ouster of Lieutenant Governor Ben Barnes and Attorney General Crawford Martin, as well as to the massive turnover in the legislature.

The sixty-third legislature was one of the most influential legislatures in Texas legal history. Texas adopted both an open meetings and open records act, revised its laws regarding campaign finance and fundraising, and required the registration of lobbyists. It made sweeping amendments to the Texas penal code and adopted new laws criminalizing bribery and corruption of government officials. It also readopted the death penalty. The sixty-third legislature also modified tort law in two major respects, creating modified comparative negligence and adopting the Deceptive Trade Practices Act (see chapter 8). Its most audacious effort was to convene a constitutional convention to rewrite the Texas Constitution. The convention was three votes short of a two-thirds majority allowing a proposed constitution to be sent to the voters for ratification. Whether the open government provisions have been sufficient to reduce or even end corruption in state government is unclear. Subsequent scandals in Texas politics have included claims of judicial impropriety (see chapter 6) and the felony conviction of an attorney general (see chapter 8). No legislative scandals on a par with Sharpstown have occurred.[89]

Although the legislature adopted ethics provisions intended to curb the culture of corruption, it neither changed the law that made branch banking illegal nor altered the authority of the State Banking Board to decide which banks would be granted charters. Preston Smith's appointment of Elmer Baum to the State Banking Board surely suggested to Frank Sharp the value of buying influence. Sharp reciprocated by having the Jesuit Fathers purchase Smith and Baum's NBL shares at a stunning profit, thus tying the three men closer together. Baum's position on the banking board was a clear signal to Sharp that the Sharpstown State Bank would be protected from indelicate inquiries by state banking regulators. The power held by the banking board over state banks invited both influence peddling and attempts by the regulated (banks) to "capture" the regulatory agency.

BANKING AT THE END OF THE TWENTIETH CENTURY

Substantial changes to the Texas banking system have occurred since Sharpstown. In 1986, shortly after the savings and loan scandal of the early 1980s emerged in Texas and nationally, the Texas Constitution was amended to allow branch banking by Texas-based banks. This amendment increased the competition for business among local banks, particularly those banks located in suburban areas. The legislature subsequently implemented a law providing for branch banking. The State Banking Board was eliminated by the Texas Banking Act of 1995, which transferred from the dissolved banking board to the banking commissioner the power to approve or deny an application for a bank charter. Under the revised banking act of 1995, the "public necessity" requirement remained. That requirement was finally eliminated in 2001, replaced with the much less stringent "public convenience" standard.[90]

Echoes of the traditional Texas ambivalence toward foreign capital, even in a "business-friendly" environment, are found in the legislature's decision in 1999 to allow out-of-state banks to establish branches and own Texas bank holding companies. In 1994 Congress adopted the Riegle-Neal Interstate Banking and Efficiency Act, which generally permitted banks in different states to merge "without regard to whether such transaction is prohibited under the law of any State." However, the act allowed the states to enact a law to opt out of interstate banking mergers involving a bank located in their state as long as the law (1) applied equally to all out-of-state banks and (2) expressly prohibited merger transactions involving out-of-state banks. Texas adopted a law in 1995 intending to opt out. The 1995 law barred any Texas bank from merging with an out-of-state bank, and no Texas bank could establish a branch in another state. If a Texas bank was prohibited from establishing an out-of-state branch, no out-of-state bank could establish a branch in Texas. Similarly, no out-of-state bank could merge with a Texas bank unless that bank created an in-state corporation possessing a board of directors and capital, requirements that harkened back to the fears of outside capital expressed at the beginning of the twentieth century.[91]

Texas was one of just four states to opt out of the Riegle-Neal Act. After Riegle-Neal went into effect on June 1, 1997, NationsBank of North Carolina gained a banking presence in Texas by merging with a New Mexico bank, Sun World, that had branches in Texas. The North Carolina NationsBank then merged with NationsBank of Texas, a merger that Texas banking commissioner Catherine A. Ghiglieri challenged. The federal Office of the Comptroller of the Currency (OCC) approved the merger, and Ghiglieri sued. The federal District Court for the Northern District of Texas upheld the OCC's approval of the merger on the ground that the two banks were both Texas banks. It did not decide whether Texas's opt-out law was sufficient to prevent interstate banking mergers. But a week after the decision was issued, Ghiglieri concluded that the "Texas opt-out statute was fatally flawed under Riegle-Neal, and on that basis invited state-chartered institutions to submit applications for interstate merger and branching transactions." In 1999, faced with the involuntary arrival of interstate branch banking, the legislature adopted a law formally acknowledging and regulating it. The act was based on a model statute crafted by the Conference of State Banking Supervisors.[92]

FIVE

Family Law and Cultural Change

★

FAMILY LAW CASES, including both divorce actions and "all other family law matters," regularly constitute more than half of the civil cases filed annually in Texas district courts. Indeed, Texas family law cases exceeded the number of felony criminal cases by nearly ninety-five thousand in 2006–2007.[1]

The reasons for the number of family law matters in Texas courts include the relatively high number of marriages and divorces of Texans and an increased emphasis on judicial protection of children. From 1971 through 1998 the rate of marriages and divorces in Texas per thousand persons was higher than the national rate. Although the data are unclear, it appears that for much of American history, Texans have married and divorced more than the national population. An indirect reason for the increase in family law matters is federal law. Congress's adoption of the Child Support Enforcement Amendments of 1984, the Family Support Act of 1988, and the Child Support Recovery Act of 1992, known as the Deadbeat

Dads Act, provided financial and political incentives for all states to initiate child support actions. Finally, the Texas Department of Protective and Regulatory Services substantially increased the number of its investigations of child neglect and abuse cases in the mid-1990s.[2]

The laws of marriage, divorce, and community property have changed dramatically in Texas since the 1960s. Most of these changes reflect the improved social and economic position of women in Texas and the United States. Some change reflects a cultural shift, one that emphasizes the interests of the individual above all others. In legal historian Lawrence Friedman's view, "Family law has come to reflect, as it must, the central postulates of the republic of choice and the growing influence of expressive individualism." The culture of choice, in Friedman's telling, is about a person's right to choose how to live his or her own life, even or especially when that choice may conflict with social norms. A culture of choice reshapes law to protect the primacy of individual rights by ensuring that law remains vigilant to possible impingements on those rights.[3]

The emergence of a culture of choice is found in the changing understanding of American marriage. When Sam Houston was faced in the early 1830s with the impossibility of obtaining a divorce under Mexican law, he railed against that law and declared, "The law givers of the most enlightened communities now look upon the contract of marriage in no other light than a civil contract." Although an occasional lawyer, Houston's view of the law of marriage was in the minority. The dominant perspective was that marriage might begin as a contract, but it was more; it was a status protected by law. The Supreme Court of the United States, in *Maynard v. Hill* (1888), stated that while "[o]ther contracts may be modified, restricted, or enlarged, or entirely released upon the consent of the parties," that was "[n]ot so with marriage." The state was deeply vested in maintaining the institution of marriage, "for it is the foundation of the family and of society, without which there would be neither civilization nor progress." The belief that marriage is the foundation of family, which is the foundation of a civilization, is no longer uncritically accepted. The view that the parties to a marriage may not consent to end the marriage is wholly rejected in law. Marriage is now, as Sam Houston once fulminated, a contract that may be ended by the parties when either one so desires. It is a contract because a marriage means a partnership of two individuals, individuals whose choices about how to live a life may lead them to remain married or divorce as they choose.[4]

As long as marriage is recognized in law, the republic of choice mandates that law provide an individual a path to leave a marriage. An increase in the divorce rate, joined by an increase in the percentage of births of children to unmarried women, fosters greater judicial involvement in child support, child custody, and other matters. This chapter surveys the transformation of family law in Texas and the social movements that have fostered this transformation.

MARRIAGE IN TEXAS

The occasional arrival of Father Michael (Miguel) Muldoon to frontier Mexican Texas offered the opportunity for those betrothed through marriage bonds to marry. The officially Roman Catholic country of Mexico did not acknowledge marriages in Texas celebrated by a Protestant minister. Because Muldoon was seldom in Texas, the practice of marriage by bond became common there. A couple living in the same household outside of marriage was in "gross violation of the laws of this nation." To ameliorate the stringency of the law, it was made effective only sixty days after the arrival of a priest to solemnize such relationships. To allow couples to live together as a husband and wife before the arrival of a priest, Stephen F. Austin suggested marriage by bond, by which a couple contracted to agree to marry once a priest arrived. If either refused to complete the contract by marrying at that time, that party to the agreement forfeited the bond, a fixed amount stated in the contract. Forfeitures ranged from two thousand to sixty thousand dollars. Despite the harshness of the penalty in a society with little in assets and less in gold, it appears that marriage by bond worked fairly well. As a contract, marriage by bond was ideologically comforting. Although Sam Houston considered marriage a private act of individuals rather than a public act involving the state, this view was not the norm. Marriage by bond allowed those who wished to cohabit to do so while avoiding the legal threat of criminal punishment for fornication. For those couples who agreed to part ways before a priest arrived, it was relatively easy to retrieve the bond and dispose of it. For those who quietly rejected the public act of Roman Catholic marriage rites, marriage by bond offered legitimacy to their relationship, and the distances between settlements and farms in colonial Texas made it possible to avoid Father Muldoon if they so desired. For those who desired to solemnize their marriage pursuant to Mexican law, the appearance of Muldoon offered the chance to strengthen communal bonds by making the marriage (occasionally marriage of a number of couples at one time) a communal celebration. As noted by Mark Carroll, marriage by bond also generated economic order by allowing the couple to qualify for the larger land grant available to families in Mexican Texas.[5]

The incipient revolutionary government of 1835–36 reformed the law of marriage by authorizing any judge, *alcalde*, or regular accredited minister of the gospel to conduct marriages. The first congress of the republic reiterated this authorization in its marriage law of 1837, as did the 1866 legislature. The 1837 act also ended marriage by bond and required those couples to solemnize their marriage within six months. This admonition apparently failed to work as intended, for in 1841 the Texas Congress amended the law by legitimizing all marriages by bond and any children born to those marriages.[6]

The 1837 act forbade marriages between "any person of European descent or their descendants" and "Africans, or the descendants of Africans," a provision that remained a part of Texas marriage law until the Supreme Court of the United States declared such laws unconstitutional in 1967. As the prospect of Civil War became more likely, Texas reiterated in greater detail its criminal law sanction for marriages between persons of European and African descent. An 1854 law specifically made it a felony for a white person knowingly to marry a person of African descent, a law readopted in 1856. The felony applied only to a person of European descent who knowingly married a person of African descent. The law did not define those categories. The 1858 legislature defined a "negro" (no capital letter was used by the Texas legislature) as any person "descended

from negro ancestry" to the third generation inclusive. This circular definition meant to define a Negro as any person who had one-eighth or more African ancestry, or "blood," in the language of the statute. A white person was defined in the negative, as someone who was not a Negro.[7]

Only one significant change in the Texas law of marriage occurred between the 1830s and the 1969 adoption of the Family Code. Slaves were not permitted to marry, and in the immediate aftermath of its abolition, no particular law existed concerning marriages of former slaves and the legitimation of their children, allowing them to inherit. This was remedied by the Reconstruction constitution of 1869. Article XII, section 27 provided that "[a]ll persons who, at any time heretofore, lived together as husband and wife, and both of whom, by the law of bondage, were precluded from the rites of matrimony, and continued to live together until the death of one of the parties, shall be considered as having been legally married; and the issue of such cohabitation shall be deemed legitimate. And all such persons as may be now living together, in such relation, shall be considered as having been legally married; and the children heretofore, or hereafter, born of such cohabitations, shall be deemed legitimate." The following year the same provision was adopted by the twelfth legislature. The act also barred from prosecution for bigamy or adultery any cohabitation of slaves or former slaves that occurred before the law was adopted.[8]

Shortly thereafter the Texas Supreme Court was asked to decide whether Leah Bishop, a former slave, and A. H. Foster, her former master, were husband and wife when Foster died. Bishop claimed that after Foster moved her and their children from Louisiana to Cincinnati, Ohio, he freed her. After four years, they moved to Texas, where they lived together as man and wife "until after the law prohibiting such a marriage had been abrogated by the 14th Amendment to the Constitution." Their cohabitation gave rise to a presumption of marriage in Texas. The trial court held in favor of Bishop and against the executor who sold the homestead to pay Foster's creditors. The supreme court affirmed, deferring to the district court's assessment of the evidence. Although the court suggested the prohibition against interracial marriage was "abrogated" by the ratification of the Fourteenth Amendment, it did not hold unconstitutional Texas's antimiscegenation law. (*Miscegenation* was a word coined during the Civil War to mean interracial marriage.)[9]

Article XII, section 27 of the 1869 constitution was the subject of the court's subsequent decision in *Honey v. Clark* (1872–73). John Clark cohabited in Wharton County with a woman named Sobrina, a slave, beginning sometime in the early 1830s. Clark died without a will in 1861, leaving about $500,000 in assets, including slaves valued at about $270,000. The administrator of the estate found no heirs and gave the assets to the state as required by law. In 1871 the three adult children of Clark and Sobrina sued, demanding their share of his estate. If the children were illegitimate, they did not take as Clark's heirs. They were legitimate if Clark and Sobrina, who died in 1869, were married at the time of Clark's death. At trial, white neighbors testified that Clark did not hold out Sobrina as his wife. A number of former slaves who lived on the Clark plantation testified that Clark had made a number of statements indicating that he considered Sobrina his wife. The jury, which likely consisted in some part of former slaves (its composition is unclear, although most persons called to serve when the case was tried were freedmen), held in favor of the plaintiffs, declaring them the lawful heirs of Clark and Sobrina. In so concluding, the jury found that Clark and Sobrina were married in 1833. When the case reached the Texas Supreme Court, it noted that Mexican marriage law, applicable in Texas between 1828 and 1837, did not prohibit the marriage of persons of different races. Because Mexican law did not forbid interracial marriage, and because "a moral observance of the matrimonial condition" existed for those not allowed to marry because they were slaves, Article XII, section 27 was applicable to this case. The judgment was affirmed, and the children were awarded their share of the estate.[10]

Honey v. Clark was law for less than three years. The Reconstruction court that decided in favor of Leah Foster and the Clark heirs was roundly condemned in post–Reconstruction Texas (see chapter 2). The "Redeemer" Texas Supreme Court overruled *Honey* in *Clements v. Crawford* (1875), in which the issue was again whether an interracial couple was married under the laws of Texas. The *Clements* court held that Article XII, section 27 legitimized as marriages only those relationships in which both persons were barred from entering a marriage. George Clements was a white man and thus eligible to marry in 1868, when he and Mary Clements began living together. Mary Clements, a former slave, was not eligible to marry before the adoption of the 1869 constitution. The *Clements* court interpreted the word *both* in Article XII, section 27 to mean that both parties to the marriage had been in a state of slavery (or bondage) and thus unable to marry.[11]

The contrary conclusions reached in the two cases reflected not only race subordination but also a reframing of the language of Article XII, section 27 in light of society's norms. The *Clements* court held the constitution could not possibly countenance interracial marriages: "It is not the letter of the Constitution, nor is it believed to be its intention, to confer on any parties, white or black, whose intercourse was illegal and immoral, the rights and benefits of lawful wedlock." Only in a marriage of two former slaves was there "no violation of either law or good morals." The *Honey* court framed the issue by focusing on the eligibility of the *couple* to marry, and the law of bondage made the couple unable to marry. *Clements* was reaffirmed three years later. By then, the 1876 constitution was the fundamental law of Texas, and it eliminated the provision in the former constitution on marriages involving former slaves.[12]

The state's antebellum prohibition against interracial marriage may have been the subject of at least one questionable fornication prosecution that reached the Texas Supreme Court. In *Ashworth v. State* (1853), Henderson Ashworth, a "free person of color," was convicted of living in fornication with a "spinstress" named Lititia Stewart. Ashworth defended on the ground that he and Stewart were married and that the state offered no evidence "to prove the descent of Lititia Stewart." Although section 23 of the 1836 penal law of the Congress of the Republic made fornication a crime, and interracial marriage was banned by the congress, neither provision was explicitly adopted in the 1848 penal laws of Texas. That law also rejected the common law of English crimes, which banned fornication. Ashworth had committed no statutory crime. Despite this, the supreme court affirmed his conviction on procedural grounds and concluded vaguely that the charge was "an offense known to our laws." Ashworth's case may have been the catalyst for the legislature's decision to add the crimes of fornication and interracial marriage in 1854.[13]

Texas's 1866 Black Code renewed the ban on interracial marriage. Two years later, John Smelser and Mary Ann Fraulis were indicted and convicted of fornication. The state offered evidence that the couple lived in the same house "but occupied different rooms." It also noted that Fraulis was Smelser's former slave, "was nearly white, and wore short hair." The military Texas Supreme Court reversed, holding that the prosecution offered insufficient evidence to convict.[14]

Despite the result, *Smelser* was a harbinger of things to come. As discussed in chapter 2, a white man named Charles Frasher was charged with marrying Lettuce Bell, a woman of mixed

race, in 1875. The case was not tried for two years. When it finally was tried, Frasher was convicted and sentenced to four years' imprisonment. He appealed, challenging the constitutionality of the law. The Texas Court of Appeals dismissed Frasher's arguments. Despite that rejection, the court reversed Frasher's conviction on the ground that the instructions to the jury were misleading. The court of appeals reversed a second conviction for unlawful marriage in 1880. It held impermissible the conviction of a white woman, Mary Moore, for violating the antimiscegenation statute, using a technical interpretation of the law of indictments to conclude that the indictment was defective.[15]

The declaration by the court of appeals that Texas's antimiscegenation law was constitutional as well as a cultural change more rigidly separating persons on the basis of race encouraged other criminal prosecutions of white persons (almost always men) for marrying black persons (almost always women). Emile François married an African American woman and was prosecuted by the state and convicted by a jury. Like Frasher, François claimed Texas's antimiscegenation law violated the federal constitution and the Civil Rights Act of 1875. François's request for federal relief was denied, and his conviction was later affirmed by the Texas Court of Appeals.[16]

In 1893, Katie Bell and her husband, Calvin, were indicted for unlawfully entering into an interracial marriage. Calvin was tried and acquitted. At her trial, Bell offered evidence of his acquittal, which the trial court refused to let the jury hear. The court allowed the prosecution to offer evidence that Bell had testified in an earlier civil case that she was white and that her first husband was a white man who had served in the Confederate Army. Bell was convicted and sentenced to two years in prison. The court of criminal appeals held that excluding evidence of the husband's acquittal was not error. Evidence that she had earlier testified that she and her first husband were white was erroneously admitted, but that error was harmless because Bell received the minimum sentence. Although they had been a couple for thirty years, she and Calvin separated several months after Katie was released from prison, living in houses several hundred yards apart. Calvin provided Katie some monetary support.[17]

Katie later was engaged in litigation over the ten acres of land on which she was living. She was declared the owner of the land, possibly as a gift of the landowner. She paid an agent, who retained a lawyer for her, half of what she won. She later gave the other five acres to her son William, who then sold it to Maco Stewart. After her death in 1911, Calvin Bell and their children sued for title to this final five acres. Stewart offered evidence through the testimony of three witnesses that the general reputation in La Marque was that Katie Bell was a white woman. The trial court rejected such evidence on the grounds that the witnesses lacked the knowledge to testify to Katie Bell's reputation. The trial court instructed the jury to find in favor of Stewart if it concluded Katie Bell was a white woman and for Calvin if she was not a white woman. The jury issued a verdict in favor of Calvin. The Court of Civil Appeals reversed. It upheld the trial court's decision to exclude evidence of Katie Bell's conviction for violating the state's antimiscegenation law but found two evidentiary errors necessitating reversal. First, it concluded that the testimony of the last two reputation witnesses should have been admitted, for although they did not live in La Marque, they "had about as good opportunity to learn the general reputation of Katie Bell, in respect to being a white person, as though they lived at La Marque." Second, the Court of Civil Appeals held that the trial court's refusal to instruct the jury on the possible abandonment of Katie Bell by Calvin Bell was error. If abandoned, Katie then acted as a *feme sole*, a single woman, with a right to sell her separate prop-

erty. The court reversed the judgment in favor of Calvin and remanded the case for another trial. On rehearing, the court abandoned its decision to remand the case and issued a judgment in favor of Stewart. It concluded that because Katie and Calvin had not lived together but for a few months after her release from prison, Calvin Bell was barred (estopped, in the language of the law) from claiming that he was married to Katie Bell.[18]

Between 1870 and 1900, twenty-five persons, divided almost evenly by race, were convicted of miscegenation and spent time in prison and jail. The last recorded Texas appellate decision on the crime of interracial marriage is *State v. Flores* (1910). Flores "was a Mexican, or of Spanish extraction," which made him white under Texas law. He married Ellen Dukes, who testified that her mother was Mexican and her father "had some negro blood." The state offered testimony that Ellen looked "like a negro" based on "her physical make-up, and especially her face and hair," but no evidence was offered concerning the "quantum" of her Negro ancestry. The trial court refused to instruct the jury that the burden of proof remained on the state to show that Ellen was a Negro. Flores was convicted. The court of criminal appeals reversed, holding the trial court erred in failing to give an instruction that the state had the burden of proof to show the marriage was between a white person and a Negro as defined by law. It also commented on the lack of evidence concerning Dukes's race: "The testimony is very indefinite, and is more than unsatisfactory as to whether the woman had a sufficient amount of negro blood in her veins to come within the inhibited degree."[19]

COMMON-LAW MARRIAGE

Since 1847 Texas has permitted those eligible to marry to do so either formally through vows made before a member of the clergy or a judge or informally, by agreeing to become husband and wife, cohabiting and representing themselves to the public as married. A formal marriage meets the requirements of the marriage statute. An informal marriage, known as common-law marriage, is a marriage acknowledged after the fact by a court. Common-law marriage remains recognized in Texas law. The adoption of common-law marriage was a consequence of both Texas's 1840 adoption of the common law of England and an apparent misreading of that common law by a New York court in *Fenton v. Reed* (1809). *Fenton* held that common-law marriages were allowed in England, and because New York adopted the common law, such marriages were also lawful marriages in New York. The *Fenton* court was mistaken about English law. The Texas Supreme Court in *Tarpley v. Poage's Administrator* (1847) adopted common-law marriage, citing *Fenton* and other cases in support of its conclusion. As discussed by the court in *Grigsby v. Reib* (1913), common-law marriage no longer existed in England when Texas adopted the common law of England in 1840. But the *Grigsby* court interpreted the legislative adoption of the English common law to mean Texas adopted the common law of the *United States* as of 1840, not the common law of *England* in 1840, allowing the court to continue to recognize common-law marriage.[20]

The purpose for recognizing common-law marriage was to provide legal and social legitimation of the couple and their children and to maintain public order in the varied sexual relationships that existed in frontier Texas. No nineteenth-century government would publicly legitimize continuing sexual relationships outside of marriage. Turning a sexual relationship into a common-law marriage avoided fornication prosecutions; legitimized children from the relationship, permitting them to inherit from their fathers; and suggested a civilizing of the otherwise "primitive" frontier. Recognizing common-law marriages also limited social and economic disruption and offered recompense

to those partners (largely women) who were central to building the couple's estate.

Whether a couple was married under the common law arose only if one or both became entangled in the legal system. If the couple was not married, no issue of community property arose, and the survivor could not claim a homestead exemption from debt collectors of the deceased. The death of one might also raise issues concerning who became the lawful heirs of the property owned by the deceased. If no marriage existed, their children were illegitimate (bastards, in the language of the time) and not legal heirs of the father.

Grigsby v. Reib (1913) offered one example of the difficulties raised by common-law marriage. Jessie Stallcup Grigsby (Stallcup) was involved in a sexual relationship with G. M. D. Grigsby, a childless widower. After he died, she sued to recover a marital community property share of his estate. Stallcup claimed that they orally agreed to become husband and wife, a claim the deceased could neither confirm nor deny. They did not cohabit, but regularly engaged in sexual intercourse. The jury was instructed by the court that the couple must "cohabit together as husband and wife" to be married. The jury decided against Stallcup. The supreme court affirmed, concluding that cohabitation was a requirement for common-law marriage, along with consent by the parties and public acknowledgment of the marriage.

Common-law or informal marriage has survived the many efforts to kill it. Since the early 1960s some legislators and scholars have urged its elimination. All have failed. Court of Civil Appeals justice Jack Pope urged the 1963 legislature to "re-examine the dangers of common-law marriage in our present society." Instead, the drafters of the 1969 Family Code decided to channel its recognition in the courts. The existence of a common-law marriage could be proved in two ways: a couple could execute a document acknowledging they were married and file it with the county clerk, or prove their marriage by agreeing to marry, by living together as husband and wife, and by publicly representing they were married. In 1989 another legislative effort to abolish common-law marriage failed. Legislation was adopted making it more difficult to prove such a marriage. The legislature eliminated the statutory language allowing courts to infer the existence of an agreement to marry. It additionally required that any person who wished to prove an informal marriage begin an action within one year (later modified to two years) of the time the couple stopped living together. If the person waited more than two years to begin this action, a rebuttable presumption arose that no marriage existed.[21]

Since the adoption of the Family Code in 1969, the most significant change to the law of marriage is a constitutional amendment, adopted by voters in 2005, making marriage a "union of one man and one woman" (Art. I, § 32).

BIGAMY AND BASTARDY

The legal recognition of common-law marriage requires those who wish to end an informal marriage do so by obtaining a divorce from the district court. Failing to obtain a divorce subjects the person to a charge of bigamy if he or she marries another. Similarly, a person who leaves his or her ceremonial spouse, fails to obtain a divorce, and then enters into a common-law marriage with another is subject to prosecution for bigamy. After the Civil War, bigamy prosecutions increased substantially, with at least eighteen appeals of bigamy convictions heard by the appellate criminal courts in Texas between 1877 and 1900. In slightly more than half the cases, the conviction was overturned, often because proof of the first marriage was legally insufficient. Those cases indicate a willingness to enforce social norms through the criminal law. That willingness did not exist in antebellum Texas, as the courts shaped the law

to legitimize relationships that were arguably bigamous. The manner in which those courts avoided declaring a relationship bigamous illustrates how culture influences law.[22]

The 1837 Marriage Act reiterated the commonplace opposition to bigamy, a common-law crime under the 1836 act defining crimes. Just one bigamy prosecution was heard by the Supreme Court of the Republic. In *Republic of Texas v. Mumford* (1840), the court dismissed a prosecution for bigamy against a woman on the ground that testimony from the alleged first husband was erroneously offered against her. The court dismissed the case because no evidence existed of another marriage.[23]

The 1848 Texas penal code made any incestuous relationship a misdemeanor, but no law concerning bigamy or fornication was adopted, and a common law of crimes was rejected. It was not until 1854 that Texas explicitly made "polygamy," interracial marriage, incest, and sodomy crimes against public peace. Bigamy was a felony punishable by a prison term of up to three years. However, a prosecution was impermissible if the accused was abandoned by the first spouse for five years and did not know whether the first spouse was living (Art. 385). The bigamy ban was continued by the 1856 penal code. Just one conviction for bigamy was heard on appeal by the Supreme Court of the State of Texas before the Civil War. The court affirmed, holding that it could presume the first wife was alive when the defendant married in October 1857 because she was alive five months earlier and because the defendant later declared he had two wives.[24]

Although bigamy convictions were rare before the Civil War, a series of probate/property rights cases decided by the Texas Supreme Court between 1845 and 1860 required it to face the issue in another context. In these cases the court avoided condemning a person for what may have constituted bigamy. The Texas legislature also limited the adverse legal impact of bigamous relationships by allowing the children born to such relationships to inherit from their father. Even when a marriage was "null in law," the children were declared legitimate, making them their father's heirs.[25]

In *Smith v. Smith* (1846), the court, in an opinion by Chief Justice John Hemphill, held that a wife who innocently married an already married man retained the benefits of marriage even if the first marriage was proved and no divorce had occurred. In *Yates v. Houston* (1848), the Texas Supreme Court, again in an opinion by Hemphill, created a legal presumption that a man who remarried informally without first having obtained a divorce, was presumed to have married innocently. This presumption, called the presumption of innocence, was made primary to another evidentiary presumption, the presumption that a living person was, if no evidence existed to the contrary, considered alive: "The ordinary presumption in favor of the continuance of human life should not, under the facts of the case, outweigh the presumption in favor of the innocence of their cohabitation, and that there was no legal impediment to their contracting the matrimonial relation." The *Yates* court accepted that Tabitha Kinkaid had likely known that her husband had not obtained a divorce before she moved with him to Texas. But her error in judgment, the court noted, was all too human, and it was unwilling to "presume that erring humanity would not repent and reform." Any legal system that did not acknowledge Kinkaid's hard work in making a prosperous farm with her (likely) bigamous husband "is too harsh to have place in any beneficent system of law, and we cannot yield our assent to any such doctrine."[26]

The court's third decision on the subject, *Carroll v. Carroll* (1858), was again written by Hemphill. In *Carroll* the court created another evidentiary presumption, the presumption of divorce. Both Susan and Nathaniel were married to others when they came to Texas. They married ceremonially and began to farm. He

died, and his son from a previous marriage sued Susan for a share of his father's estate. The basis for this claim was that Susan was ineligible to receive a community property share of the farm because the marriage was bigamous and thus unlawful. The court used the presumption of innocence to declare Susan was free to marry, on the ground that it was eight years between the time of her separation from her first husband and her marriage to Nathaniel. That presumption was unavailable to Nathaniel, for evidence was presented that his first wife was alive in 1837, when Susan and Nathaniel married. The court, noting Nathaniel's first wife had remarried in 1835, subsumed within the presumption of innocence a presumption that a divorce had taken place between Nathaniel and his first wife, making him eligible to marry Susan and giving Susan a community property share in the farm. As in *Yates*, the *Carroll* court noted the strong equitable position of the second wife to community property given the extent of her contribution to the community.[27]

The legitimacy of a marriage also affected the heirship of children of that relationship. A narrow interpretation of what constituted bigamy and a liberal understanding of marriage allowed more children to be declared legitimate. In *Nichols v. Stewart* (1855), the issue was the legitimacy of the marriage of William Sowell and Sarah Grogan. Grogan entered into a bond marriage with Frederick Roe in Mexican Texas. They parted ways, ignoring the bond. Grogan then began a relationship with Sowell. Grogan became pregnant by either Roe or Sowell. She gave birth to a daughter, Rachel Turner, in December 1833. Sowell and Grogan decided to marry, which required her to obtain her release from the bond. She paid Roe and shortly thereafter entered into a bond marriage with Sowell, who died of illness soon after. The legitimacy of Grogan's marriage to Sowell determined in part the distribution of the property of Sowell's father, who died a few weeks after Sowell. At trial the jury found that Rachel Turner was the legitimate daughter of Grogan and Sowell, and thus the legitimate heir of Sowell's father. The Supreme Court of Texas, broadly interpreting the marriage act of 1837, held that a child born before the marriage was a legitimate child of the subsequent marriage.[28]

Mark Carroll notes that these and other decisions of the Texas Supreme Court were at the forefront of national changes to the law of bigamy and bastardy. Other state courts began following the Texas presumption of innocence, refashioned as a presumption of death of the first spouse, decades after it was introduced in Texas law. Those courts also adopted the Texas presumption of divorce. These opinions, concludes Carroll, "departed radically from traditional law" and reflected "enlightened judicial innovation that discounted doctrinal continuity and mainstream social policy." Hemphill's opinions were built on strands found in the civil law. That they differed from the harshness found in the common law likely delighted him. Texas marriage and illegitimacy law, though based in part on their instrumental value in a frontier society, were also founded on an ideological vision of how the law might expand the definition of marriage to account for the work performed by women on the Texas frontier.[29]

ADULTERY

From 1836 to 1848 and again from 1856 until the revision of the penal code in 1973, Texas criminalized adultery, defined as sexual relations between two persons, one of whom was married to a third person. Like fornication (sexual relations between two unmarried persons), a single act of intercourse was not defined as adultery (see chapter 7). The parties committed a crime only if they "cohabit together." The state was further required to prove the parties engaged in "habitual" sexual intercourse. Although a number of appellate decisions on adultery convictions are recorded, and

although circumstantial evidence was admissible to prove adultery, such proof was difficult in any case until the parties lived together openly and notoriously outside the bonds of marriage. Many convictions were reversed on the ground that two, three, and more acts of sexual intercourse did not constitute "habitual" carnal intercourse. By 1920 the court of criminal appeals resignedly wrote, "As to just what constitutes habitual carnal intercourse within the meaning of the statute, this court has never been able to lay down any hard and fast rule regarding it." Other Texas law made the crime more difficult to prove. In 1882 the court of appeals held that a wife could not testify against her husband when he was charged with incest against her daughter. This was later interpreted to bar a husband from filing charges against his wife in an adultery prosecution because only credible witnesses were permitted to file charges. The husband was not a credible witness because he was not a competent witness (that is, legally permitted to testify) against his wife because the crime was not one "committed by one against the other." Because both parties to the adulterous conduct were subject to prosecution, either could refuse to testify in a criminal case against the other to avoid self-incrimination. Finally, Texas, like most states, held that an adultery conviction must be set aside if the only evidence of the adultery was a confession by the accused.[30]

MARITAL STATUS
AND THE CRIMINAL LAW

Even though a wife could be convicted of adultery, Texas criminal law provided cuckolded husbands (but not wives) an additional remedy traceable through Spanish law to early Roman civil law. The 1856 penal code codified the "unwritten law" allowing a husband to kill his wife's lover (see chapter 7). The code declared as justifiable homicide the action of a husband in killing a man engaged "in the act of adultery with the wife, provided the killing take place before the parties to the act have separated." During the nineteenth century and the first several decades of the twentieth century, when the parties "separated" was broadly interpreted, providing a husband with substantial leeway in killing his wife's paramour. And from 1914 until 1925 the Texas Court of Criminal Appeals allowed the husband to kill his wife as well as her lover, an unwarranted extension of the unwritten law that was later rectified. This written version of the unwritten law remained a part of Texas law until it was repealed in the legislature's 1973 recodification of the penal code.[31]

For most of Texas and American history, a husband could not be prosecuted for the crime of rape (sexual assault) of his wife. The 1973 penal code explicitly barred such a prosecution. However, a national debate on making marital rape a crime began in the late 1970s, an offshoot of the larger women's liberation movement of the late 1960s and 1970s. This debate commenced as rape prosecutions increased and as evidence rules altered and limited defenses to charges of rape.

One example of this change was found in the Federal Rules of Evidence (FRE), which were proposed by the Supreme Court of the United States in 1973 and became law in all federal courts in 1975. In its original form, the FRE included no specific limitations on a defendant's proof that he was not guilty of sexual assault. Thus, a woman's entire past sexual conduct was possibly subject to wide-ranging examination by defense counsel. The possibility of having one's entire sexual past placed publicly on trial and the callous behavior occasionally exhibited by law enforcement towards women who attempted to file sexual assault complaints were two significant reasons why just a small percentage of estimated sexual assaults were reported and a smaller number prosecuted. In 1978 an alliance of political conservatives and supporters of women's liberation joined together to amend the FRE to include a rape shield provision (FRE 412). This evidentiary rule strictly limited the scope of the defendant's cross-examination about the complainant's sexual past.

Texas law on the complainant's reputation for "unchastity" and specific acts of her sexual history was similar to, though somewhat more restrictive than, that of other states. Texas appellate courts were inconsistent concerning whether a defendant could offer evidence of sexual acts between the complainant (victim) and a third person. However, evidence of the victim's reputation for an absence of chastity was admissible. One study of rape trials prosecuted in Travis County from 1970 to 1976 found that "[i]n the trials studied, however, defendants rarely succeeded in introducing such proof." Whether that study was replicable in other parts of the state is unclear. However, in 1975, before Congress acted to add FRE 412, Texas amended its penal code to restrict the introduction of evidence of the complainant's past sexual history in state sexual assault prosecutions. The law required the trial court to determine that the evidence was relevant and its value was not outweighed by its "inflammatory or prejudicial nature" before admitting evidence of the complainant's reputation concerning sexual matters or specific incidents of sexual behavior. Further, defense counsel was required to inform the court out of the hearing of the jury of any such questions before asking them. When Texas adopted its Rules of Criminal Evidence in 1985, it included an amalgamation of its 1975 code provision and FRE 412. This shift in the manner in which rape prosecutions were tried was a signal of further changes concerning marital status and the criminal law.[32]

By the 1980s several states amended their laws allowing the prosecution of a husband for sexual assault, although marital rape prosecutions often differed legally from other sexual assault cases. For example, a state might require the husband and wife to be living apart or to be legally separated in order to prosecute a marital rape. Texas repealed its sexual assault "spousal exemption" from rape prosecutions in 1991. One element to a charge of sexual assault of a spouse not required in other Texas sexual assault cases was that it be "accompanied by bodily injury or the threat of bodily injury."[33]

A final change in the relation of marriage and the criminal law concerns the ability of a spouse (witness-spouse) to testify against a defendant-spouse in a criminal case. In early nineteenth-century common law, no party was allowed to testify, and neither was a spouse of a party. In the last half of the century, parties were made competent witnesses. In criminal cases a husband or wife was allowed to testify on behalf of the spouse accused of a crime, but a witness-spouse was not permitted to testify *against* the defendant-spouse. The Texas Code of Criminal Procedure, adopted in 1856, rejected the common law disqualification of spousal witnesses. It eventually divided the limitation on spousal testimony into two separate privileges. The marital communications privilege barred with some exceptions a spouse or former spouse from testifying about confidential communications between husband and wife made during the marriage. The testimonial privilege continued to exist, but it changed over time in Texas. Article 648 of the code of criminal procedure barred a husband or wife from testifying against the other in a criminal case except "in a criminal prosecution for an offence committed by one against the other." In any other case a witness-spouse could not testify against a defendant-spouse even when the defendant waived any objection to the testimony of the witness-spouse. This rule was unchanged until 1965. The legislature then permitted but did not require the witness-spouse to testify against the defendant-spouse if the crime was committed against the spouse or a child of either. If the defendant-spouse was charged with a crime not involving the spouse

or child, the witness-spouse remained disqualified from testifying against the accused.[34]

This again changed when the Texas Rules of Criminal Evidence were promulgated in 1985. The witness-spouse was given the privilege to decide whether to testify against a defendant-spouse in *any* criminal case. In some cases the state could force the witness-spouse to testify against the defendant-spouse. For example, if a husband was charged with a crime against a minor child of either spouse or member of the household, his wife could be forced to testify against her husband about anything other than confidential communications between them. On the other hand, if the husband was charged with assaulting his wife, she could refuse to testify against him. More domestic violence cases were prosecuted beginning in the late 1970s, and by the late 1980s domestic assault was perceived more gravely by society than it had been two decades earlier. Further, the Texas Court of Criminal Appeals accepted expert testimony on battered woman syndrome in 1988, evidence offered to explain why an abused wife (later any abused partner) would remain in a marriage (or relationship) in which the husband (partner) was physically abusive. The rule allowing an allegedly battered wife to refuse to testify against her allegedly abusive husband was regularly attacked as bad public policy. In 1995 the Texas legislature amended the evidentiary rule, requiring a spouse to testify against the defendant when the latter was "charged with a crime committed against the person's spouse."[35]

MARITAL STATUS AND TORT LAW

The common law permitted a husband to sue for injuries caused him as a result of harm suffered by his wife. For example, if a wife was injured as a result of the intentional acts of the defendant, her husband could sue the defendant, claiming a loss of consortium (loss of a wife's affection, fellowship, and sexual relations). Most states later expanded this rule to allow a husband to sue for a loss of consortium for negligent as well as intentional actions by the defendant. The common-law rule discriminated on the basis of gender, for a wife was not permitted to sue for a loss of consortium (also called a loss of companionship when claimed by the wife) when her husband was injured. This discriminatory common-law rule was accepted by the Texas Court of Civil Appeals in 1954. Nationwide, allowing a wife to claim a loss of companionship began to change in the 1950s. In 1978, after the 1972 adoption of the Equal Rights Amendment to the Texas constitution, the Supreme Court of Texas recognized an action for a loss of consortium for a bodily injury caused by a defendant's negligence, and it did so for both spouses. The court rejected the suggestion that the claim not be acknowledged until adopted by the legislature: "Such an abdication of judicial responsibility is no longer called for in light of present social realities. The law is not static; and the courts, whenever reason and equity demand, have been the primary instruments for changing the common law through a continual re-evaluation of common law concepts in light of current conditions."[36]

The relation between the courts and the legislature regarding spousal torts was complicated throughout the 1970s. The 1969 Family Code included a provision on no-fault divorce, discussed below. Did the torts of alienation of affections and criminal conversation continue? If so, could either spouse sue? As under the common-law rule on consortium, a husband but not a wife was permitted to sue a third party for intentional actions by the third party alienating the affections between the husband and his wife. The tort of criminal conversation was also available only to the husband. If a third party engaged in sexual intercourse with a married woman, he was liable to the woman's husband for harming the husband's "legally protected marital interests." This was called the tort of *criminal* conversation because sexual intercourse between a married woman and a

man other than her husband constituted either the crime of rape (if the wife did not consent) or the crime of adultery (if the wife consented). The two torts often overlapped. In two cases decided soon after no-fault divorce was permitted in Texas, the supreme court held that alienation of affections and criminal conversation were recognized in law. In *Felsenthal v. McMillan* (1973) the supreme court encouraged the legislature to consider whether to abolish the tort of criminal conversation.[37]

In 1975 and 1987, respectively, the legislature abolished the torts of criminal conversation and alienation of affections. In *Smith v. Smith* (2004) the plaintiff sued the defendant alleging the commission of both torts. He claimed the legislature's abolition of these marital torts was unconstitutional. In an unsatisfying opinion, the court of appeals held that both torts were constitutionally abolished. The opinion failed to explain whether an extensive pre–1971 law concerning the tort of alienation of affections affected its reasoning. Although the Supreme Court of Texas had never discussed the tort, it was well recognized by a number of courts of civil appeals from the 1930s onward, and no Texas appellate court ever suggested the tort was not recognized in Texas law between the 1930s and 1971. What *Smith* signaled was a decisive shift in the understanding of the state's role in protecting marriages. Marital torts gave legal recognition to a person's interest in marriage, a status the state worked to maintain. Once the state's interest in marriage was reduced to providing for a fair division of the community property of the couple and the "best interests" of the children of the marriage, it was unpalatable that the state would allow a suit against a person involved with the husband or wife. A third party could harm a marriage by enticing a spouse to leave the marriage, but that harm was not legally cognizable in a culture that focused on self-fulfillment.[38]

The *Smith* court's decision was, by its own admission, tempered by the ability of an emotionally harmed husband or wife to sue the other spouse for intentional infliction of emotional distress. In *Twyman v. Twyman* (1993), a fractured Texas Supreme Court held a husband and wife were not immune from suit by the other for intentionally inflicting emotional distress. The court required that the conduct of the defendant-spouse be intentional, not merely negligent, and determined that the tort was complete if the plaintiff-spouse suffered severe emotional injuries. A plurality allowed this tort claim to be made in a divorce proceeding, but a double recovery (that is, a recovery for the tort of intentional infliction of emotional distress and a recovery for a disproportionate amount of the marital estate upon divorce) was prohibited.[39]

Twyman was one of a trio of cases by the Texas Supreme Court that abolished the doctrine of interspousal immunity from tort lawsuits. In 1977 it held that a husband who allegedly murdered his wife could be sued by her children. Ten years later, the court held one spouse could sue the other for negligence.[40]

Changes in the law in both criminal and civil matters from the 1970s through the end of the century were premised on a new definition of marriage. The eighteenth-century understanding expressed by the English legal writer William Blackstone that "by marriage, the husband and wife are one person in law" had long been rejected. But cultural changes from the 1960s onward promoting expressive individualism in law have fostered the view of marriage championed by Sam Houston. Marriage today is largely perceived as a contract from which either party may extract him- or herself when it no longer suits his or her needs. The spouse looking to leave the marriage may pay a price in an unequal division of the community property, but that spouse will be granted a divorce. Because marriage and divorce are about the individual's needs, laws that sheltered the married couple, whether concerning testimony by one spouse against the other or immunity from

harms caused to one spouse by the negligence of the other, no longer fit the culture. And when the culture changes, law follows culture, not the other way around.[41]

DIVORCE IN TEXAS

In 1837, President Sam Houston issued a proclamation granting a judge the jurisdiction to hear his case for divorce. Not surprisingly, the court granted him a divorce, even though the Congress of the Republic of Texas had not adopted any law allowing divorce, and Mexican law forbade it. Several months later, the congress gave district courts the jurisdiction to hear divorce matters and to issue a decree of divorce. But it was not until 1841 that Texas adopted a divorce act, which copied Alabama's 1820 divorce law. The court was permitted to annul the marriage if there existed "natural or incurable impotency of body" when the marriage took place. Divorce was permitted only in cases of fault, such as abandonment, abuse or cruel treatment, and adultery. It did not, however, treat men and women alike when the alleged reason for the divorce was adultery. A wife was permitted to file for divorce if her husband abandoned her and "lived in adultery with another woman." A husband was permitted to divorce his wife if she "shall have been taken in adultery." Thus, a husband's occasional act of adultery was not sufficient justification to obtain a divorce, but a wife's adulterous assignation was sufficient for the husband to act.[42]

The justifications for divorce in Texas changed relatively little between 1841 and 1967. The 1876 legislature added a provision permitting divorce when a spouse was convicted of a felony and imprisoned. Two additional grounds based on something other than fault were later adopted: A couple living apart "without cohabitation" for ten years (later reduced to seven and then in 1967 to three years) could divorce, and a spouse could initiate an action for divorce if the other spouse had been adjudged insane for at least five years before the divorce action was commenced. In 1965 the legislature eliminated the different adultery standard for husband and wife, making "adultery" by either a sufficient ground for the other to initiate a suit for divorce.[43]

The largely fault-based justifications for divorce for over a century reflect a dominant but occasionally contested cultural consensus about marriage and divorce in Texas. Sam Houston's assertion that a marriage was simply a contract was the implicit subject of an intermittent debate in the Texas appellate courts. The dominant view was expressed in 1884 by the Texas Commission of Appeals: "Obviously the validity of the marriage relation is the substructure upon which peace, happiness and perpetuity of society depends; therefore, for the condition or state to be lightly considered, or the bonds of matrimony to be dissolved for slight cause, the effects of which are ephemeral, would be pernicious to society at large."

This debate over the categorization of marriage continued in *Gowin v. Gowin* (1924 and 1927), which discussed whether a wife could sue her husband for breach of a marriage contract caused as a result of his "cruelties." The court of civil appeals reversed a judgment for the wife, declaring that such a lawsuit between husband and wife was not permitted by law. Chief Justice Truman Conner dissented on the ground that the wife's claim should be permitted because of the recent gains in the women's movement in the 1910s and 1920s and on the basis that a marriage was a contract, a breach of which should be cognizable in law. He declared, "That the mutual promises or contract of marriage between a man and woman, when viewed in their individual relations and apart from the interest of the state therein, contain every element of an enforceable agreement, cannot be denied, and the fact that the state in its own interests superimposes a relation to the public that has been termed a status, imposing duties and obligations to the state, does not render the agreement of the individual less a contract as between themselves."

Mrs. Gowin requested that the Texas Supreme Court hear the matter. The supreme court sent the case to the commission of appeals. It affirmed the holding of the court of civil appeals, rejecting the dissenting view of Conner that marriage was largely a contract. The commission of appeals noted the "persistence" of this idea and sought to disabuse the reader of its truth: "[T]he man and the woman, however coincident their minds and desires, may not rescind, novate, or modify, as they might do if the relation were in any just sense contractual. This is so because the thought of mankind (with a discordant view here and there) includes permanency as a necessary element of the estate." Marriage included elements of a contract, but marriage was a status which the state possessed a strong interest in maintaining.[44]

The state's strong interest in marriage prohibited a court from issuing a divorce decree based only on a mutual decision of the husband and wife to divorce. Because state policy favored the continuation rather than dissolution of marriages, many divorce actions were unsuccessful. As noted by the Texas Supreme Court in 1885, "Divorces are not granted for the mere reason that parties cannot live together without quarreling and fighting." A husband sued for divorce on the ground of cruelty. He offered evidence that his wife refused to drink a cup of coffee he brewed, believing it was poisoned. She then moved from their residence to the home of her children. She continued to refuse to live with him for about a year. These acts, the trial and appellate courts concluded, were insufficient to grant a divorce. In general, courts refused to grant a divorce on grounds of cruelty when the plaintiff claimed the defendant hurled invectives, as long as such insults did not charge the plaintiff with adultery.[45]

Despite these cases, a divorce was never made too difficult to obtain in Texas. Texas courts often commented on the liberality of the state's divorce law. In *Bahn v. Bahn* (1884), quoted above, the Texas Commission of Appeals held that the husband had committed an act of cruelty making divorce possible by calling his wife a prostitute in front of his daughter, and later calling her "bad names." However, it cautioned that whether such epithets were an act of cruelty depended on "the social condition of the parties, their mode of life, and all the attending circumstances."

Some circumstances that appear to twenty-first-century minds to make divorce imperative were defenses to a divorce action. Texas barred a divorce if the couple was mutually cruel. However, it allowed a finding of "comparative rectitude," a conclusion that one spouse was less cruel than the other, allowing the spouse less at fault to divorce. If a wife sued for divorce on the ground of adultery, and either committed adultery herself or condoned her husband's "conjugal society or embraces," proof of that fact worked as a "perpetual bar" against a divorce. These defenses existed because the legal paradigm for divorce before 1969 was for a wronged spouse to sue a wrongdoer spouse for a divorce. Condoning otherwise contemptible behavior or engaging in the same behavior (such as adultery) made both parties equal wrongdoers, in which case neither should be permitted a divorce.[46]

REFORMING TEXAS DIVORCE LAW

By the 1960s, Texas divorce law was attacked by those who believed it made divorce too easy and those who believed it made divorce too difficult. What both sides accepted was that the grounds for divorce were mere "artificial technicalities," existing "in a curious world of legalistic make-believe." It was "common knowledge," one writer contended, that "divorce proceedings are nothing but brief rituals of legal hocus-pocus designed to dramatize the defendant's guilt and hence

justify marriage dissolution." The fault-based system was clearly failing. A study of American marriage and divorce stated that 85.3 percent of all 1948 divorces in Texas were granted on the ground of cruelty, one of the highest rates of any state, and well in excess of the national rate of 55 percent. No evidence existed that Texas spouses were more cruel than spouses in any other state. "Cruelty" was simply the "artificial" reason given to begin the divorce process. After remaining steady during the 1950s, divorce became more common nationally in the 1960s. The Texas data explain why fault was perceived by many to be manufactured in a significant number of cases. Because this view was widespread, law reformers, "concerned about the legal system's integrity, pushed for some form of no-fault divorce that avoided perjury or connivance."[47]

During the 1960s the legislature adopted a number of laws providing more legal power to married women. Much of its work was taken from reform proposals of the Family Law Section of the State Bar of Texas. The legislature ended coverture (which legally disabled married women) and granted married women the power to manage and control their separate property. The 1965 divorce amendment equalized the adultery justification for divorce. In 1967 the Marital Community Property Act was adopted. Each of these acts was taken in large part to avoid legislative consideration of an equal rights amendment to the Texas constitution, which had been offered during every legislative session beginning in the 1950s.

Texas's 1969 Family Code was the first unified family law code in the United States. The law regulated the relationship of husband and wife (it adopted provisions concerning parent and child in 1973). The Family Code Project of the Family Law Section of the state bar proposed adding to the usual grounds of abandonment, adultery, and cruelty, divorce "without regard to fault if the marriage has become insupportable because of discord or conflict of personalities that destroys the legitimate ends of the marriage relationship and prevents any reasonable expectation of reconciliation." This "no-fault" provision for divorce followed closely on the heels of California's 1969 no-fault divorce law, although California and not Texas was hailed as the progenitor of no-fault divorce. The difference between the two divorce laws was that California made no-fault incompatibility the sole ground for divorce, while Texas added insupportability to the other grounds justifying a divorce. As noted by Joseph McKnight, director of the project that proposed this change, "A good deal of press coverage has been given to California's recent divorce law reforms, though the equally significant Texas reforms have generated little publicity."[48]

Texas family law reformers understood that the no-fault option might be used to the exclusion of other grounds for divorce. Even so, a strong majority believed that "the law needed to be brought into harmony with the facts of life." McKnight suggested that the members of the section believed that "the *true ground*" of between 90 percent and 95 percent of all divorces was insupportability with no likelihood of reconciliation. Allegations of cruelty, too often based on half-truths offered to obtain a divorce, had brought divorce law "into considerable disrepute with the public."[49]

This integrity-based rationale, one focused on ensuring the integrity of the legal system in judging divorce matters, was intended to be accompanied by a division of property that allowed the divorcing spouses to care for themselves and their dependent children. Marriage was analogized to other types of partnerships. The analogy meant that the key to dissolving a marital partnership was not preventing or slowing its dissolution but providing for an equitable distribution of the assets of the partnership.

The vision that equitable distribution of marital assets would provide for both parties to the divorce has not come to fruition. As noted by Texas Court of Appeals justice Bea Ann Smith, "the partnership theory underlying community property has failed us" in providing for women and children in divorce. One consequence of reform of divorce laws is that "divorce is a major source of poverty in the United States"—poverty largely borne by women. This result occurred in part because most couples possessed relatively little in assets upon divorce. The most valuable "asset" they brought to the marriage was their future earning capacity. However, the Texas Supreme Court refused to recognize professional goodwill as a divisible asset, which worked to the detriment of those spouses, more often than not wives, who did not work outside the home.[50]

ORIGINS AND CONSTITUTIONALIZATION OF COMMUNITY (MATRIMONIAL) PROPERTY IN TEXAS

When the Congress of the Republic of Texas adopted the English common law as the "rule of decision in the Republic," the statute was largely about maintaining the Spanish civil-law concept of community property (through the Louisiana Civil Code of 1825) and rejecting the English common law regarding the status of married women. A single woman in the common law was known as a *feme sole* and possessed legal rights to own and dispose of property as well as to sue or be sued. A married woman was known as a *feme covert*. The marriage of a man and a woman effected a "merger" in their legal identity, an identity controlled entirely by the husband. Under this doctrine of coverture, a husband took ownership of his wife's personal property and controlled the use of any real property she owned. A wife was not permitted to sue anyone without her husband's consent, and if she brought a civil action it had to be brought in both her name and her husband's. The husband's common-law duties to his wife were limited to a legal duty to support her.[51]

The community property system adopted in Texas in 1840 effected some change in the legal identity of married women, including their ownership of property. The property of the husband and wife consisted of two types of property: separate property owned by either and common property owned by both. Separate property was defined as all real property and slaves brought into the marriage, the wife's "paraphernalia" acquired before or during marriage, any increase in slaves through childbirth, and any property either spouse obtained by gift or through an inheritance. Common or community property was all other property brought into the marriage and all property acquired during the marriage. During the marriage, the husband was permitted to sue either by himself or with his wife. The court could grant the wife permission to sue "in her name," contrary to the common law. A betrothed couple was permitted, under strict conditions, to enter into a marriage contract altering some of the conditions of the property of the marriage, although no contract could alter the order of the descent of their property after death or be "contrary to good morals." To avoid the possibility of coercion of the wife by the husband, no such contract was permitted after the marriage was celebrated. But no matrimonial agreement was valid if its effect was "to impair the legal rights of the husband over the person of the wife, or the persons of their common children." This last provision indicated some of the limitations of the community property arrangement. Although the wife retained ownership of her separate real property and slaves, "the husband shall have the sole management of such lands and slaves." He also possessed the sole authority to sell any common property during the marriage. The capacity of the married woman to act was based largely on Louisiana law, and the definition of separate property reflected an 1839 Mississippi statute. Overall, however, what

constituted common and separate property in Texas did not "seem drawn from any particular source. Rather, they appear handmade."[52]

Texas matrimonial property law was adopted at the forefront of a national movement to enact married women's property acts, laws that lessened but did not abolish the harshness of coverture and that protected a married woman from her husband's debt collectors. Arkansas adopted a law in 1835 protecting a wife from her husband's premarital debts. Four years later, Mississippi adopted a broader law "for the protection and preservation of the rights and property of Married Women," which declared as a married woman's property any property owned by the woman before marriage or received by gift or inheritance after marriage. These provisions were adopted by Texas the next year. Maryland adopted two acts in 1841 and 1842 granting a married woman greater protection of her property, particularly from her husband's creditors, and other states adopted laws providing some protection of a married woman's property from debt collection in the first half of the 1840s.[53]

The goal of the 1840 act is not "entirely clear," but the adoption of community property in Texas appears to be related to both the national movement to protect the property of married women and the Panic of 1837. The reliance by Texas on the laws of Mississippi and Louisiana suggests the Texas Congress was influenced by the emerging movement to protect the property of married woman from debt collectors. As a result, congress sheltered from the husband's creditors separate property owned by his wife. The Panic of 1837 made Texas an even more enticing frontier destination for destitute Americans. It also caused economic hardship lasting throughout the republic's existence. The 1839 congress passed a law protecting the homestead of a family from seizure by creditors, which it repealed and then reenacted shortly thereafter. The protection of the homestead, along with the segregation and thus protection of a wife's separate property, limited the ability of creditors to seize the most valuable assets owned by agrarian Texans.[54]

Categorizing property was important to determine what could be seized when debts were not repaid. When a husband contracted debts during the marriage, they were repaid from the property owned in common by the husband and wife or from the husband's separate property. If the husband unlawfully sold his wife's separate real property, the 1840 act provided that she would not be prevented from recovering that land because of the statute of limitations as long as the couple was married. Even after the dissolution of the marriage through death or divorce, the statute of limitations did not begin to run until the children reached the age of majority or married, whichever was first.

The Congress of the Republic provided some legal obstacles to the transfer of a wife's separate property to the community. The wife was to be interviewed privately by the district judge outside of her husband's presence to ensure that she consented to the transfer of her separate property. In the English legal system, equity courts were created in part to avoid the harshness of some common-law rules. In equity, a wife's real property could be placed in trust to prevent the husband from taking ownership under coverture. In Texas, the wife's separate property was hers, and thus the trust device was unnecessary to protect the wife's interests other than through the private interview.[55]

The constitutionalization of community property in the 1845 constitution was broadly supported. Article VII, section 19 provided that "[a]ll property, both real and personal, of the wife, owned or claimed by her before marriage, and that acquired afterwards by gift, devise, or descent, shall be her separate property." Section 19 continued, "[L]aws shall be passed more clearly defining the rights of the wife in relation as well to her separate property as that held in common with her husband. Laws shall also be passed providing for the registration of the wife's separate property." Although the text spoke only of the wife's separate property, Texas courts construed it to apply to both husband and wife. The constitutional definition of separate property was broader than the 1840 statute, for separate property included all real and personal property owned or claimed before the marriage, as well as gifts and inheritances. The remainder of section 19 directed the legislature to craft a community property system. It did so by adopting laws on successive days. The first provided for registration of a wife's separate property, which provided notice to possible purchasers of real property of the validity of any title. The second law followed the 1841 conveyance law. A wife who conveyed any of her separate property, or the homestead or other property exempt by law from execution to satisfy a debt, could do so only after being privately examined by the court and by declaring her action was of her free will. An 1848 act defined as separate property "the increase of all lands or slaves thus acquired."[56]

Texas's 1845 constitutional provision on community property was taken wholesale and included in California's 1849 constitution (Art. XI, § 14). The first legislature of California then adopted the Texas Community Property Act of 1848 to define common property. Although California borrowed its community property law from Texas, its courts interpreted the law differently than did Texas courts. One prominent example was whether rental income from separate real property should be classified as separate or community property. Texas generally held that rental income from separate property was property of the community, following Spanish law. An exception to this rule in Texas was that children born to slaves were separate property if their mother was separate property. The court's justification for this exception was humanitarian: "Although slaves are property, yet in many respects they are persons, and are treated as such." Thus a slave owned by a wife could not be sold by her husband, and because the child of that slave was also the separate property of the wife, the husband was barred from selling the child as well. California was a free state, not a slave state, so this exception was unnecessary. Its supreme court held that all "increases" from separate property remained separate property, adopting the "American" rule.[57]

MARRIED WOMEN'S PROPERTY ACT OF 1913

Texas community property law changed little between the end of the Civil War and the first decade of the twentieth century. The 1876 Texas Constitution adopted the 1845 constitutional provision on community property with but two grammatical changes (Art. XVI, § 15). The only legislative change during this time was quite modest: it allowed a widow to control parts of the community. After the turn of the century, a number of women's organizations began to advocate for prohibition and woman suffrage. They also demanded the law give married women the right to control their separate property and to join their husbands in controlling community property. By 1910 prohibition was the preeminent issue in the state. Many linked prohibition and suffrage, and those favoring both claimed they represented the banner of political reform. These self-proclaimed reformers made the issue of prohibition a fight about the nature of Texas government, not just demon rum. Captured within this broader debate was the narrower issue of the property rights of married women.[58]

The 1911 legislature passed a law permitting a married woman to be declared a *feme sole* "for mercantile and business purposes" as long as her husband consented and joined in her petition to the district court. If the district court granted the married woman's petition, "thereafter the said married woman may, in her

Hortense Sparks Ward, undated. Courtesy Texas State Library and Archives Commission.

own name, contract and be contracted with, sue and be sued . . . as if she were a feme sole." Married women otherwise remained at the sufferance of the economic decisions of their husbands.[59]

In the April 1, 1911, *Houston Chronicle*, Hortense Sparks Ward, one of the first woman lawyers in Texas, wrote an article titled *The Legal Status of Married Women in Texas*. Ward noted the legal disabilities that harmed married women in Texas. The legislature's tepid response in 1911 making married women legally capable to contract for mercantile purposes was insufficient to reformers, and the movement gained momentum. The Texas bar association overwhelmingly adopted in mid-1912 a resolution in favor of the right of a married woman to exclusively manage, control, and dispose of her separate property; to control her earnings independently of her husband; and to contract as if a *feme sole*. Ward reiterated her arguments in a 1912 pamphlet, *Property Rights of Married Women in Texas*, distributed by

The Delineator, a popular women's magazine. Ward's brief pamphlet argued that Texas community property law, by placing in the husband control of both community property and the wife's separate property, failed to protect the married women of Texas. Ward also wrote to reassure those apprehensive about the impact of community property reform on the roles of men and women in marriage. A law adopted along the lines of the state bar's resolution, she wrote, would effect only a modest change, for it "would not force her to assume control of her estate." Granting married women greater control of their separate property and allowing them to contract would simply "protect the helpless woman against the man who does not deserve the rights now held by him under the present laws." This proposed reform was championed by the Texas Federation of Women's Clubs and the Texas Congress of Mothers. At the next session of the Texas legislature, the Married Woman's Act of 1913 was adopted. The caption of the act states it is

> conferring upon the wife, the power to make contracts, authorizing suits on such contracts, giving the wife control over her separate property, placing limitations upon such control, giving her control over the rents from her separate real estate, interest on bonds and notes, and dividends on stock owned by her, and over her personal earnings, exempting the same from debts contracted by the husband, providing that the joinder of the husband shall be necessary to a conveyance or encumbrance of the wife's lands, bonds and stocks, except that upon the order of the district court she may convey the same without the joinder of her husband.

The act was much more limited than indicated by its caption. The act declared in part that "the wife shall have the sole management, control and disposition of her separate property, both real and personal." That right of management and control was limited by the next clause, which required the husband to join in any encumbrance (such as a mortgage) or sale of the wife's separate real estate. Further, a married woman who wished to transfer any stock or bonds owned by her could do so only if her husband also agreed to transfer the property. If her husband refused to join in any encumbrance or conveyance, she was permitted to petition the district court to undertake the transaction. The court granted the petition if it determined the action was "advantageous to the interest of the wife." The act also held that rents from the wife's separate real estate could not be taken by creditors in satisfaction of debts contracted by the husband even though such rents were considered community property in the law of Texas. The act did not provide for any general authority of a married woman to sue or be sued or to make contracts, and it did not give "control" to the married woman of her separate property. Despite the caption, a married woman was not equivalent to a *feme sole*.[60]

The reason the caption and the text differed was a result of the manner in which the Married Woman's Act was adopted. After the bill was adopted by the legislature and sent to Governor Oscar Colquitt, but before he was required to act, the bill was recalled. The legislative recall was precipitated by a message from Colquitt. As recounted by the Texas Supreme Court in *Red River National Bank v. Ferguson* (1918), "[h]e accompanied its return to the House with a message in which emphatic objection was urged to the first clause of the amendment of Article 4624, conferring broadly upon the wife the power to contract as a *feme sole*. The bill was thereupon reconsidered; that clause was stricken out; and the bill was finally passed in the form of the present act. The bill was thus, in a large measure, devitalized, since the powers conferred upon the wife by the stricken clause were its principal feature."

The legislature continued to adopt piecemeal laws regarding control of separate property by married women. In 1915 it declared that money received by a wife as a result of a personal injury remained her separate property. In 1917 it extended the ability of a married woman to sell or encumber her separate real estate by allowing her to do so without her husband's consent if the husband had "permanently" abandoned her or was insane. It also declared that "the rents and revenues derived" from separate property were also separate property. This last law rejected nineteenth-century decisions of the Texas Supreme Court that rents and revenues from separate property were community property in favor of the American rule adopted in California. The 1921 legislature exempted the husband's separate property from debts as a result of the civil wrongs of his wife. It otherwise restated the amendments found in the 1917 act.[61]

This limited emancipation of married women by the act of 1913 was interpreted by the Texas Supreme Court in *Red River National Bank v. Ferguson* (1918). The issue was whether Bessie Ferguson was liable as a surety (a type of guarantor) to her husband's contract with the bank. The court noted that liability was possible only if Mrs. Ferguson's legal disability as a married woman was removed by the act of 1913. The Texas Supreme Court held the act did not give a married woman an unfettered right to make contracts or sue or be sued. A married woman merely possessed the authority to manage her separate property. This limited emancipation was founded on the most beneficent of aims: "This protection of her property from liability for the husband's debts has been an outstanding feature of our system of marital property rights." The cost of that benefit included restrictions in her legal position, including the power to make contracts (and the power to contract as a surety). A married woman had the legal power to contract for debts only "those essentially to her advantage." To agree to act as a surety for her husband was not to her economic advantage, so the bank could not collect

the debt from Mrs. Ferguson. *Red River* made it less likely that a lender would engage in economic transactions with a married woman.[62]

In 1925 the Texas Supreme Court was asked to determine the constitutionality of the statutory community property amendments of 1917 and 1921. The particular issue was whether the legislature could declare that rents and revenues received from separate property were separate property (American rule) rather than community property (Spanish rule), as Texas courts had held. In three companion cases— *Arnold v. Leonard*; *Gohlman, Lester & Co. v. Whittle*; and *Cauble v. Beaver-Electra Refining Co.*—the court declared that, although the legislature was permitted to restructure the rules of management and liability of the community, it lacked the authority to change the constitutional definitions of separate and community property. The community property provision in the 1876 constitution was traceable to the 1840 law concerning separate and community property, and thus the meaning of separate and community property in 1840 declared the meaning of those terms in the 1876 constitution. The 1840 law defined as community property all property that was not specifically declared separate property. The only separate property taken by a married woman was property through gift or inheritance. Rents and revenues from separate property were property taken during the marriage other than through a gift or inheritance. In the court's formalistic view, if the property was not a gift or inheritance it must be community property. Based on the major premise that a constitution may not be changed by legislative action, and on the minor premise that the legislature's declaration that rents and revenues from separate property were also separate property changed the constitutional definitions of separate and community property, the court's syllogistic conclusion in *Arnold* was ineluctable: "Since rents and revenues derived from the wife's separate lands are entirely with out [sic] the constitutional definition of the wife's separate property, and since the Legislature can neither enlarge nor diminish such property, it follows that the portions of the acts of 1917 and 1921, which undertake to make rents and revenues from the wife's separate lands a part of her separate estate, are invalid."[63]

COMMUNITY PROPERTY CODE OF 1967

The legislature avoided making any substantial changes to community property law for nearly thirty years. The legislature's inaction after *Arnold* meant that a married woman was required to obtain her husband's approval (or obtain permission from the district court) to sell her separate property, a legal obstacle anathema to many Texas businesswomen. The Texas Legislative Council, a body charged with assessing needed changes in the law, published a report, *Legal Status of Married Women in Texas* (1956), suggesting community property reform. Demands for reform of community property law in the 1950s were part of a growing women's movement, similar to events in the 1910s. Some proponents of reform of community property, again like their predecessors, also promoted other reform. In the late 1950s that other cause was an equal rights amendment to the Texas Constitution: "Equal rights under the law shall not be denied or abridged because of sex." Most proposed community property reforms failed of legislative adoption through the 1950s. These failures merely led reformers to redouble their efforts.[64]

The legislature ignored the proposed equal rights amendment at each session during the 1960s. It attempted to placate women's rights proponents by offering minor reforms. In 1963 it removed the disabilities of coverture by making a wife the "sole" manager of her separate property. It also gave a married woman "the same powers and capacity as if she were a feme sole" to contract and sue and be sued

regarding her separate property. In 1965 the legislature permitted a married woman to sue alone to recover her separate property. These laws largely remedied the failed legislation of 1913. They were also intended to justify the opposition of the legislature and the State Bar of Texas to an equal rights amendment. In trying to deflect attention from that amendment, the state bar, "almost by inadvertence, . . . became the sponsor of statutory matrimonial property law reform." Joseph W. McKnight nearly completed a proposed reform of Texas community property law by early 1965. In his view, leaders of the State Bar of Texas "saw [community property law reform] as a weapon to blunt the thrust of the advocates of constitutional change," which the bar officially opposed in 1964. A bill substantially changing the law of community property acceptable to both the state bar and the Texas Business and Professional Women's Clubs was sent to the legislature near the end of its 1965 session. Although the legislature adopted a single law allowing married women to sue alone for recovery of separate property, larger reform was proposed too late for adoption.[65]

During the next eighteen months the Family Law Section, led by Dallas lawyer Louise Raggio, and the Real Estate, Probate and Trust Law Section of the state bar, assisted by several law professors, wrote seven successive drafts modernizing Texas community property law. The final draft accepted by the state bar eliminated the provision requiring that marriage contracts not be "contrary to good morals or to some rule of law," provided for equal treatment of spouses by making both responsible to support each other and their children, and eliminated the requirement that a married woman be separately examined to determine whether a transfer of property was made by her free will or as a result of her husband's coercion. To the surprise of some, the bar's bill passed with a few minor amendments in 1967.[66]

Community property law in Texas has since

Louise Ballerstedt Raggio, 1994.
Courtesy of the Raggio family.

of these constitutional amendments is that the individual partners to a marriage can largely arrange and rearrange their separate and community property as they desire.[67]

FAMILY CODE OF 1969 AND 1973

The Family Law Section of the State Bar of Texas was created in 1960 by the bar to examine "the problems of legislation relating to family law." The intensity of interest by the state bar in family law matters grew as the possibility of an equal rights amendment increased. After the adoption of the Matrimonial Property Act of 1967, the Family Law Project continued. In 1969 that part of the Family Code concerning the Law of Husband and Wife, including marriage and divorce, was adopted. The proposed provisions on the subjects of the law of parent and child, including adoption, custody, termination of parental rights, and paternity, were sent back by the legislature for further study. Those code provisions were adopted by the legislature in 1973.[68]

followed the provisions of the 1967 act as reenacted in 1969 and 1973. Married women possess the same rights and duties regarding the community as their husbands, and each controls his or her separate property. An unintended consequence of the reform of the law of community property was that it stymied the development of permanent alimony in Texas, a consequence of increasing importance as the divorce rate rose beginning in the 1960s.

The provision of the Texas Constitution concerning community and separate property (Art. XVI, § 15) has been amended three times since 1980. Among other things, the 1980 amendment effectively overturned *Arnold v. Leonard*. The 1987 and 1999 amendments provide authority for spouses to contract to agree that upon death the community property of the deceased becomes the property of the surviving spouse and that the couple may agree to classify separate property as community property. These amendments to the constitution, in light of related developments in marriage and divorce, again suggest a shift in the understanding of marriage to a contractually based partnership of two distinct individuals with their own life and marital goals. The premise

ALIMONY

One myth of Texas legal history is that Texas has stood alone (although Pennsylvania once joined it) in barring an award of permanent alimony after divorce. James Paulsen notes that permanent alimony was held legally permissible in *Wiley v. Wiley* (1870), which was decided by the hated Semicolon Court (see chapter 2). Paulsen convincingly argues that it was not the court's low reputation that caused subsequent Texas courts to ignore *Wiley*, but its untimely publication. The publication of Texas cases and digests of Texas law was hampered by the politics and economics of Reconstruction. An 1872 digest of Texas law inadequately summarized *Wiley*. An 1881 publication fully reported *Wiley*, including its statement on alimony, but it was less popular among lawyers than the 1872 digest. The result of *Wiley*'s untimely publication was that by 1901, when a well-received treatise on Texas marital rights was published, Texas appellate courts had declared permanent alimony was against public policy without ever citing *Wiley*.[69]

The most persistent policy argument against an award of permanent alimony has been that the law providing for a fair and equitable division of community property permits courts to provide the nonworking spouse (traditionally the wife) sufficient assets to make her way economically after the divorce was ordered. The empirical evidence for this proposition is lacking. Those supporting permanent alimony have anecdotal evidence to support their argument, but also lack empirical evidence. A claim made in the mid-1990s suggested that 40 percent or more of divorced Texas women receive welfare within two or three years of divorce. Subsequent articles also adopt this claim, but its source and empirical basis are uncertain.[70]

The continuing refrain of Texas appellate courts that permanent alimony was not allowed by law focused reformers on remedying this through legislation. From at least the 1971 regular legislative session through the mid-1990s, bills to adopt permanent alimony were routinely offered. Until 1995 the legislature successfully killed each bill without ever formally opposing it. Indeed, as noted by Paulsen, the senate appeared to be on record as supporting the adoption of permanent alimony. Every two years it would adopt a permanent alimony bill and send it to the house, where it would be buried without a vote. The statutory adoption of "spousal maintenance" (not "alimony") in 1995 was a result of fortuitous circumstances. During debate on a welfare bill, Representative Senfronia Thompson, sponsor of an alimony bill in the house, noted that a substantial number of divorced women in Texas were on welfare, and alimony might lessen that percentage. The speaker of the house declared the alimony amendment germane, and the house voted on permanent alimony for the first time. It was

now the senate's turn to bury the bill. Although the alimony bill was successfully killed, Senator Chris Harris obtained a favorable vote in the senate on the Thompson amendment to the welfare bill, which was then signed into law by Governor George W. Bush.[71]

Permanent alimony in Texas remains quite restrictive. With one modest exception, it may be ordered only if the marriage lasted at least ten years. The spouse seeking maintenance must possess insufficient property "to provide for the spouse's minimum reasonable needs" and must show he or she cannot earn a sufficient income to support his or her minimum reasonable needs. Spousal maintenance is limited to a maximum of three years, and the amount is the lesser of twenty-five hundred dollars or 20 percent of the contributing spouse's average monthly gross income. Maintenance ends upon the recipient's death, remarriage, or conjugal cohabitation with another.

Texas has the most restrictive alimony requirements of any state. The legislature has amended the spousal maintenance statute twice since it was adopted, but it has not liberalized the law. Whether Texas's adoption of spousal maintenance has helped keep persons from having to seek welfare assistance is unknown.[72]

EGGEMEYER V. EGGEMEYER (1977)

Eggemeyer v. Eggemeyer decided the extent to which the Family Code altered the authority of judges to apportion separate and community property upon divorce. Virginia and Homer Eggemeyer were farmers with four minor children. A one-third undivided interest in the farm had been given to Homer, making it his separate property. At the trial, District Judge Curt Steib awarded the entire farm to Virginia. He acted based on Section 3.63 of the Family Code, which permitted "a division of the estate of the parties in a manner that the court deems just and right." Before the adoption of Section 3.63, *Hailey v. Hailey* (1960), a court of civil appeals decision, held in part that the district court lacked the authority to divest the husband of his separate real property. The supreme court affirmed *Hailey*.[73]

The initial issue in *Eggemeyer* was one of statutory interpretation. Had the legislature intended to allow a court to divest a divorcing spouse of separate property when it was "just and right" despite *Hailey*? The Family Code was written by an expert drafting committee, and two law professors deeply involved in its making disagreed about the meaning of Section 3.63. Eugene L. Smith interpreted Section 3.63 as it was written, permitting the district court to divide community and separate property as "the court deems right and just." Joseph McKnight disagreed: "In formulating § 3.63 the draftsmen omitted the proviso with respect to the divestiture of title to land. But the commentary on the section which was presented to the legislature, stated that: 'This is a codification of present law.'" The legislature was aware of what Section 3.63 declared and had not amended it. Section 3.63 provided an incentive for the parties to settle any property disputes before trial because any party losing at trial would find it almost impossible to win an appeal claiming the district court's division of property was not "just and right." The unsettled nature of the law and the breadth of the district court's discretion paradoxically created a stability in dividing property by equalizing the power of the spouses. It gave to the nonworking spouse a greater ability to effect a favorable settlement. The *Eggemeyer* court's conclusion was simply, "The legislature believed it was making no change but was carrying forward the law as it then existed." How it knew this was unexplained by the court. One commentator declared the court engaged in a "dubious reading" of the statute.[74]

The supreme court's decision that the district court erroneously interpreted Section 3.63 also relied in part on the Texas Constitution. It held that the constitution prohibited courts

from divesting a spouse of separate real and other property. This conclusion was based on a strained reading of the constitution, that the "nature of property is fixed by the Texas Constitution, and not by what is 'just and right.'"[75]

Eggemeyer's constitutionalization of separate property implied that no separate property, whether real or personal, could be divested of one spouse and given to the other. This settlement of the law perversely rearranged the incentives of divorcing spouses. Because divorce was no longer tied to fault after 1970, and because a court's division of property based on what was just and right was limited to community property, a husband or wife with substantial assets that were arguably separate property was given the incentive to litigate.

Eggemeyer "is a disastrous failure of judicial analysis." It failed as a matter of historical interpretation, as a matter of statutory interpretation, as a matter of constitutional interpretation, and as a matter of societal interpretation. The supreme court's exercise of power to settle the law created legal and social dislocations that continue to reverberate. It was an exercise in hubris, an example that the rush to solve a perceived problem may give rise to other, more serious problems.[76]

THE EQUAL RIGHTS AMENDMENT OF 1972

Despite the state bar's expressed resistance to an equal rights amendment in 1964, and regular efforts to placate women's rights advocates by reforming marital property law, the quest for an equal rights amendment gained momentum through the 1960s. Although legislators claimed support of equal rights for women at each session, in a "game of charades" they never voted as they proclaimed. The Texas equal rights amendment initially focused on banning discrimination on the basis of sex. The final version, adopted by voters at the November 1972 general election, declared, "Equality under the law shall not be denied or abridged because of sex, race, color, creed, or national origin" (Art. I, § 3a). The breakthrough occurred in 1971, when the legislature agreed to send an equal rights amendment to the voters for approval. The catalyst for its adoption is unclear. Women's rights advocates were successful in generating community property reform in 1967 and divorce reform in 1969. That success may have created momentum for the amendment. Broadening the language of the amendment to include race, color, creed, or national origin in addition to sex may have made it easier for more legislators to support it as civil rights became a less divisive issue by 1971. The 1971 Texas legislature was a largely conservative legislature consisting of few female members. Congress had been considering proposing an equal rights amendment to the federal constitution, but it did not do so until March 1972. No state adopted an equal rights amendment before Texas, although fourteen other states adopted such an amendment at about the same time.[77]

The Texas Equal Rights Amendment (ERA) has modestly affected civil rights law. A study of appellate decisions during its first twenty years of existence demonstrates it was used more often by men than women. The most consequential opinion applying the ERA is *In re McLean* (1987). In a five to four decision, the Supreme Court of Texas held unconstitutional a provision of the Family Code on legitimation. A married man fathered a child with an unmarried woman. She gave the child up for adoption. The adoptive parents sued to terminate the parental rights of both parents. The father intervened to legitimate the child as his. The Family Code permitted an unmarried biological father the right to legitimize the child only if this was in the "best interests" of the child. No "best interests" condition existed for the mother to legitimize her child. The court noted that this provision of the Family Code explicitly distinguished between men and

women in determining whether to legitimate the child. Because this law discriminated on the basis of sex, the court was required to decide how stringently to evaluate the law. *McLean* explicitly concluded that the standard of review for cases in which discrimination is on the basis of sex (gender) was strict scrutiny. Strict scrutiny is the most stringent form of constitutional judicial review, and laws subject to that standard are presumed unconstitutional. To overcome that presumption the state must show that it has a compelling interest in the law and "must prove that there is no other manner to protect the state's compelling interest." The law was held unconstitutional. In 2002 the Texas Supreme Court explained that *McLean* does not require the application of strict scrutiny in all cases alleging sex discrimination but only those in which the state discriminated "because of sex." When the state acts in a facially neutral fashion, even if the impact of the law falls disproportionately on one gender, the law is subject to the much more lenient "rational basis" standard. Under that standard the statute is presumed constitutional. Nearly all statutes tested through this standard are held constitutional.[78]

PARENT AND CHILD

The ubiquity of family law cases in state district courts stems almost wholly from the rise of what the Texas Judicial Council categorizes as "other family law matters," cases other than divorce matters. Civil cases increased by 31 percent from 1988 to 2007, a growth rate less than the increase in the Texas population. The modest increase of 3 percent in divorce cases during this same period indicates the easing in the rate of divorce in Texas. In tracking "other family law matters," however, the judicial council found an increase of 282 percent. This extraordinary increase in child support cases, child abuse and neglect cases, and cases involving termination of parental rights reflects the state's increased role in using legal remedies to protect children.[79]

Parent and child provisions were adopted as part of the 1973 Family Code. Codifying the legal relationship between a parent and a minor child required the drafters to enunciate the particular rights and duties between them. Section 12.04 of the 1973 code listed ten rights, privileges, duties, and powers of the parent. Parents continued to possess the common-law right to the "services and earnings of the child," but they also had the duty to support the child by providing food, clothing, shelter, medical care, and education. This duty to support one's children, the Supreme Court of the United States held, forced Texas to require natural fathers to support their illegitimate children, not merely their legitimate children. Parents also possessed the right to the physical custody of the child and to undertake "reasonable discipline" of the child, but also the duty to care for and protect the child.[80]

The code also provided clear guidelines terminating parental rights. Prior Texas law included several statutory provisions on child neglect or dependency, but the Family Code revised these provisions in light of the federal government's 1961 Model Act for the Termination of Parental Rights and Responsibilities and the Adoption of Children. Even though the Family Code provided clarity in the termination of parental rights, the movement in the supreme courts of Texas and the United States was to make termination of parental rights more difficult. In two 1976 cases, the Texas Supreme Court reversed decisions terminating parental rights when the parent suffered from economic or mental health troubles, noting, "The natural right which exists between parents and their children is one of constitutional dimensions." This "natural right" required the courts to "strictly scrutinize" cases of termination of parental rights. In 1980 the Texas court retreated slightly from this declaration, holding that the burden of proof in termination of

parental rights cases was clear and convincing evidence, not evidence beyond a reasonable doubt.[81]

More divorces required the courts to make more decisions about which parent would be awarded legal and physical custody of minor children of the marriage. Through the 1960s Texas courts followed the "tender years" doctrine, which declared that the courts should prefer the mother in determining the custody of young children. The 1973 Family Code barred consideration of the gender of the parent when awarding custody, a direct result of testimony in the legislature that "courts tended to favor mothers when awarding custody." The parent who gained legal custody of the child was called the "managing conservator." In determining who should be named the managing conservator, the district court was required to consider primarily the best interests of the child.[82]

The impact of federal laws on the development of child support laws and lawsuits in the states cannot be overstated. The federal Child Support Enforcement Amendments of 1984 used the spending power of Congress to create better state enforcement and guidelines for child support payments. The law required every state seeking federal funding for public welfare programs to establish guidelines for child support payments. The Child Support Recovery Act of 1988 also used Congress's spending power to encourage states through incentive payments to find ways to ensure that non-custodial parents financially supported their children. Finally, the Child Support Recovery Act of 1992, known as the Deadbeat Dads Act, gave states a strong political incentive to initiate suits to recover child support payments.[83]

ADOPTION

Adoption was unknown in the common law but well established in the civil-law system of continental Europe and existed in Texas during Spanish and Mexican rule. Civil adoption law declared an adopted child a member of the family. Further, a child of an adopted child was a grandchild to the parents of the adopted child. However, for purposes of inheritance, the adoption of a child could not defeat the inheritance claim of a natural child (known as forced heirship). Because Spanish and Mexican law linked adoption with inheritance rights, only males could be adopted.[84]

The 1840 adoption of the common law of England formally ended the Spanish/Mexican law of adoption, although the congress and legislature occasionally passed special acts allowing the adoption of persons as heirs. In 1850 Texas became the third state, following Mississippi and Vermont, to allow adoption for limited purposes. It was a simple law allowing an adopted person to become a legal heir of another. The act did not require the adopted person, if an adult, to consent to the adoption, nor, if a minor, require the consent of the adopted person's legal and natural parents. Under Mexican law, a person could not adopt a "stranger" if the adopting person had a living legitimate child. Modifying this provision, the Texas legislature permitted the adoptee to inherit part of the estate even when the deceased was also the parent of a child "begotten in lawful wedlock."[85]

This modified civil law version of adoption made the adopted person an heir, but not a member of the adopting person's family. The 1850 act created no change in parental rights and duties in the unilateral act of adopting a legal heir.[86]

This modest act was not altered until 1907, when the legislature permitted legal parents to "transfer their parental authority" and "thereafter be barred from exercising any authority, control or custody" over the adopted child. Natural parents could transfer their parental authority only by signing a written document "authenticated or acknowledged as deeds are required to be." A court order was not required to terminate the parental rights of natural par-

ents and award them to adopted parents; the signed, authenticated transfer was sufficient. The act barred the adopting parent to transfer his parental rights, gave the adopted child the "same rights . . . for support and maintenance" as natural children, and allowed a court to take adopted children from their adopted parents if the children were abused, neglected, or poorly treated.[87]

In two decisions released on the same day in 1918, the Texas Supreme Court indicated the limited nature of adoption. Adopting a person did not make a person (or that person's children) a "direct lineal descendant" of the adoptive parent for purposes of inheriting property. Consequently, when an adopted child passed away before her adoptive mother, the children of the adopted child did not take as lawful grandchildren for purposes of Texas law. The second case decided whether the adopted children of Francisco Yturria took real property subject to an inheritance tax when he gave it to them through his will. Direct lineal descendants were not subject to the inheritance tax. The court held that the adopted sons were not Yturria's direct lineal descendants as a matter of Texas law, but "those adopted by him became entitled to the same rights and privileges as children with respect to that which passed to them upon his death without issue of his body." However, the property bequeathed to the natural children of the adopted children of Francisco Yturria was subject to the inheritance tax. Any deleterious consequences that "may result from such construction is not for the courts, but for the Legislature, to take into consideration." The legislature made no changes to the adoption law.[88]

In 1917, Minnesota required a judicial investigation of adoptive parents to determine whether they were fit parents. Texas adopted much of Minnesota's law in 1931. The 1931 law barred the adoption of an adult by another adult, making adoption law more about parental rights and duties than heirship. However, it was not until 1947 that Texas gave the State Department of Public Welfare the authority to use "the best interests of the child" to determine whether to support the adoption petition. Four years later, the legislature required the court to inform the department of any pending adoption to allow it to decide whether to object.[89]

The 1931 adoption law always required the mother to consent to the adoption of her child. If unmarried, however, only the mother's consent was necessary for the termination of parental rights. An unmarried father's consent to the adoption was not required by the Family Code of 1973, for the legislature refused to enact a provision proposed by the state bar on how to determine and possibly terminate a biological father's parental rights. It finally did so in 1975.[90]

Although the end of Jim Crow began after the Supreme Court's decisions in *Brown v. Board of Education* in 1954 and 1955, no Texas court evaluated the constitutionality of laws barring interracial adoption until 1967, when a court of civil appeals held the prohibition on interracial adoption unconstitutional in *In re Gomez*. Walter Strawn, Jr., an African American, married a woman who had borne two children outside of wedlock while living in Mexico. Strawn petitioned the district court to permit him to adopt his wife's two girls. Strawn complied with all statutory requirements necessary to adopt his wife's children. However, because Mrs. Strawn (her first name is unmentioned) was white, as a matter of Texas law, the adoption was prohibited by statute. The court of civil appeals held the statute violated the equal protection clauses of the Texas and federal constitutions.[91]

In 1972 the National Association of Black Social Workers issued a policy paper declaring adoption of black children by white parents a "form of genocide" and concluded that "Black children belong, physically, psychologically and culturally in Black families." The Child Welfare League of America also supported "race matching" by 1972. The Texas Family Code ignored the issue of what was called "transracial" adoption (which ordinarily meant the adoption of an African American child by a white couple). That issue became statewide news in 1992 when a three-year-old African American child was taken by government authorities from the home of his Anglo foster parents. The child had lived with his foster parents since he was five weeks old, and they had sought to adopt him. The Texas Department of Protective and Regulatory Services opposed the adoption petition in favor of placing the child with African American parents, pursuant to the department's policy "to place children with adoptive parents whose race or ethnicity is the same as the child's." The district court ordered the adoption after a public outcry against the department's actions, and an African American legislator successfully introduced a bill in the 1993 legislative session barring the department or a court from considering race when determining whether to approve the adoption of a child or placement of the child with a foster family.[92]

S I X

The Legal Profession, Legal Education, and the Courts

★

AT THE JULY 1918 meeting of the Texas bar association, U.S. Army major John C. Townes, long-time dean of the University of Texas Law Department, reported that a small percentage of Texas lawyers had induced young men subject to the draft to employ them for the purpose of obtaining a falsely granted deferred classification from the local exemption draft board. He urged that the bar association adopt a resolution condemning such action and declaring that those lawyers "be summarily dismissed from this Association, if they be members, and disbarred by competent authority from the further practice of law in Texas."[1]

In the course of the discussion, a member asked, "Haven't we already got a method provided by law to disbar members?" The continuing discussion indicated that, although the Texas legislature had adopted a law to disbar lawyers, "[t]hose statutes are lying there practically unused." The discussion continued the next day, and, like most discussions of the Texas bar association then, eventually devolved into a long-winded, back-and-forth debate whether disbarment was too strong a remedy. For example, was a lawyer who assisted a registrant for a modest fee in making a proper request subject to the resolution? Could a "disproportionate" fee be defined? Was it permissible for the association to seek disbarment of a lawyer for his past action in representing a registrant for a fee, if those efforts occurred after President Woodrow Wilson's request that lawyers assist registrants without pay?[2]

The standards for admission to the practice of law in Texas were slight in 1918. The 1903 law governing the admission of attorneys in Texas required an applicant to (1) have resided in the state for at least six months, (2) be twenty-one years old, and (3) possess a "good reputation for moral character and honorable deportment." A

[181]

John C. Townes, 1905. Reprinted by permission of the Tarlton Law Library, Jamail Center for Legal Research, University of Texas School of Law.

board of law examiners appointed by the court of civil appeals with the jurisdiction to hear cases where the applicant lived was required to give the applicant a written bar exam based on topics listed by the supreme court. The applicant was admitted to the bar if he obtained an overall grade of 75 and not less than a 50 in any subject area. The statute did not declare how the board was to grade, nor did it indicate whether a 75 indicated minimum competence in an era in which those preparing for the bar exam were not law school graduates. If a majority of the three-member board agreed to grant the applicant a permanent license, the applicant was permitted to practice law in any court in the state. Graduates of the University of Texas law department, then the only law school in Texas, were exempt from the bar exam. They were admitted to the bar once they graduated after the 1891 legislature adopted the diploma privilege. No data were kept on the percentage of those who passed and those who failed the written bar exam, which was first required by Texas in 1903.[3]

The 1903 bar licensing statute supplanted statutes from the republic in 1839 and state laws from 1846, 1873, and 1891, but much of the content remained the same. The republic required that the applicant be twenty-one years old and a citizen of the republic and provide "undoubted testimonials of good reputation for moral character and honest and honorable deportment." An applicant in 1839 was examined in open court by three lawyers appointed by the district judge, two of whom had to indicate their satisfaction with his legal qualifications for the applicant to obtain his license. Upon receiving his license, the attorney was permitted to practice law in any district or inferior court in the state. After Texas became a state, an applicant was permitted to practice law in the supreme court, the sole appellate court at the time, only if he applied to it (rather than to the district court) for his permanent license. This limitation on practice was removed in 1873 legislation that permitted all licensed attorneys to appear before the supreme court. Once an attorney was licensed to practice law, revocation of the attorney's authority to practice law occurred only if the attorney was "guilty of any fraudulent or dishonorable conduct, or of any malpractice . . . at the discretion of the court." This nineteenth-century language survived the 1903 changes to the rules of admission.[4]

Admission to the bar throughout the nineteenth century was extraordinarily easy, sometimes in spite of the official rules. The 1877 Rules for the District Court adopted by the Texas Supreme Court included, as rule 106, the requirements of study for those applying for a law license. The court required the applicant to have read a number of treatises on law, including William Blackstone's (English) and James Kent's (American) *Commentaries on the Law*, Simon Greenleaf's *A Treatise on the Law of Evidence* (or older evidence treatises originally written by the Englishmen Thomas Starkie and Samuel Phillipps), and treatises on pleadings, contracts, promissory notes, partnership, and equity. Although actually reading these books would have effected a strong improvement in the learning of most applicants, it seems unlikely many completed this assignment, not only because of the daunting nature of these works (Greenleaf's *Treatise*, for example, was three densely packed volumes), but also because of the relative scarcity of these volumes in frontier Texas.[5]

Charles Coombes was admitted to the Texas bar in 1896. In his memoirs he remembered that "the examination for law license, which was conducted in the district court, was not rigid. It was expected that the lawyer should acquire most of his legal education in actual practice." The notorious gunman John Wesley Hardin spent fifteen years in prison in Texas for murder (one of many he committed), yet just five months after his 1894 pardon by Governor Jim Hogg, Hardin was admitted to the bar, having apparently shown he possessed the requisite good character and sufficient knowledge of the law. (He was killed a year later.) One historian of the Dallas bar noted that only two applicants to the bar were denied admission there before 1890. One of those applicants, J. H. Williams, was black. Despite this apparent racism, a number of African American applicants to the Texas bar were admitted to the practice of law in the nineteenth century. Maxwell Bloomfield notes that the first black lawyer admitted to the practice of law in Texas was W. A. Price, and the first African American lawyer in Dallas was admitted in 1881. In Galveston, eleven black lawyers practiced law between 1895 and 1920, even as Jim Crow laws intensified in Texas. Four of the eleven, a significant percentage in Texas, either graduated from law school or possessed some formal education in law.[6]

In 1919 Texas joined a number of other states interested in increasing standards of admission to the legal profession. The legislature created a five-person board of law examiners with statewide jurisdiction. The legislature delegated to the supreme court the authority to set the rules for eligibility, subject to several baseline requirements. For example, in addition to a good character requirement, the legislature required that the supreme court mandate an applicant have completed "adequate pre–legal study and attainment" and have pursued "adequate study of the Law for a period of at least two years." This mimicked in part the emerging national effort to require applicants to the bar to have spent at least two years in college study before beginning legal studies. The provision that an applicant pursue "adequate study of the Law for a period of at least two years" was an acknowledgment that, in a state with just one university-based law department, most applicants to the bar learned their law through apprenticeships in law offices. Both the 1903 and 1919 statutes on admissions to the bar were largely authored by John C. Townes.[7]

Texas next altered its admissions standards during the Great Depression, as lawyers in the state, consonant with lawyers nationwide, complained regularly of the overcrowding of the bar. The Texas Supreme Court altered its admission rules every other year between 1932 and 1936, and the legislature joined in by abolishing the diploma privilege in 1935. In 1932 an applicant was first required to prove he had graduated from high school, and in 1934 the supreme court expanded the requirements for those applying to the bar after an apprenticeship or law office study. The applicant was required to show he had studied requisite areas of law for twenty-seven months and to submit a certificate indicating that the district court with jurisdiction in his place of residence had approved the applicant's supervising lawyer. The 1934 rules further restricted those applying to take the bar who had avoided attending law school: it required such applicants to spend thirty-six months, at thirty hours per week, studying law (compared with twenty-seven months of study for those enrolled full-time in law school). In 1936 the supreme court made sixty credit hours (about two years as a full-time student) of college study a prerequisite to studying law, joining the majority of states.

Twenty years later, the supreme court increased pre–law study to three years. In 1972, Texas required applicants to the bar to graduate from an ABA-approved law school, thus abolishing the apprenticeship system of studying for the bar examination.[8]

In 1974, Texas joined the majority of states in using the Multistate Bar Examination as part of the bar examination. Texas required bar applicants to pass the Multistate Professional Responsibility Examination, a multiple-choice examination testing applicants on the law of lawyering and ethics, in 1984. In the 1990s Texas adopted the Multistate Performance Test (MPT). The MPT was designed to test an applicant's ability to use legal materials effectively in writing a memorandum or other writing often required of a lawyer. The adoption of the MPT means that half of the Texas bar examination is based on standardized examinations. Only essay questions on Texas law (40 percent of an applicant's score) and questions on Texas civil and criminal procedure (10 percent) remain specific to Texas law.[9]

ETHICAL STANDARDS AND DISCIPLINING LAWYERS

In 1858 the Texas Supreme Court heard an appeal by attorney John Jackson from a jury verdict and a judgment striking him from the roll of attorneys. The court eventually reversed the district court's judgment. In doing so, it offered its understanding of the role and duties of a lawyer:

> It has been truly said that, as a class, attorneys are and have always been the intrepid vindicators of individual rights, and the fearless asserters of the principles of civil liberty, existing where alone they can exist, in a government not of parties or men, but of laws. As a class they well deserve the appellation of an enlightened, chivalrous and honorable profession. Individuals of the class may, and

sometimes do, forfeit their professional franchise by abusing it; and a power to enforce the forfeiture must be lodged somewhere. Such a power is indispensable to preserve the administration of justice.[10]

Disbarment was contemplated by the Congress of the Republic in its 1839 act regulating the practice of law. A lawyer found "in default, or otherwise guilty of any malpractice or misdemeanor" might be suspended or stricken from the roll of attorneys at the discretion of the district court. The first legislature of the state of Texas issued similarly vague standards for the admission of persons to the bar and for their expulsion. Section 8 declared that any lawyer "guilty of any fraudulent or dishonorable conduct, or of any mal-practice, shall be liable to be suspended or stricken from the roll of attorneys at the discretion of the court." The fifth legislature allowed a complaint of fraudulent or dishonorable conduct by a lawyer to be made by two lawyers practicing in the court, and it guaranteed the accused lawyer the right to a trial by jury when disbarment was sought. Although several minor changes were made in phrasing, this modest system of disbarring lawyers remained in effect until the adoption of the State Bar Act of 1939.[11]

Nineteenth-century Texas law on attorney malpractice and expulsion of lawyers from the practice of law was largely nonexistent. Two cases involving former slaves offer desultory tales of lawyer misconduct. Sam Hearne owned several thousand acres of land in Robertson County. He died in 1866, leaving a son he fathered with a former slave, Azeline Hearne. He willed his entire estate to the son, who died in January 1868, making the inheritance the property of Azeline. Now a wealthy woman, Azeline became the target of unscrupulous attorneys, who extracted excessive contingency fee contracts to defend her ownership of the Hearne property. For example, Harvey Prendergast was working as Azeline's lawyer in a case on appeal and was serving as the administrator of Sam Hearne's will, the beneficiary of which was Azeline. Yet, despite his duty of loyalty to his client, he was also suing her for failing to pay him pursuant to a written agreement. Prendergast obtained a judgment in his favor without Azeline's ever answering the complaint or challenging it in court. Azeline was later able to find another attorney to take on a large contingency basis an attorney malpractice case against Prendergast. William Hamman, the attorney who represented Azeline in the (failed) malpractice case, had himself engaged in unprofessional behavior toward her earlier. The same sad story was played out in a case concerning the children of a slave named Sobrina and her white master, John Clark. After the death of the attorney who successfully obtained a judgment making the children the heirs of Clark, a newly appointed second attorney of the heirs cheated them out of much of the land they inherited, buying it for about ten percent of its value.[12]

Article XVI, section 29 of the 1876 constitution required the legislature to adopt a law regulating barratry, the stirring up of quarrels and disputes into lawsuits. The legislature complied by making barratry a misdemeanor. The law did not specifically discuss any limitation on the role of lawyers in stirring up lawsuits for the purpose of harassing others. A quarter-century later the legislature adopted a barratry law applicable to lawyers that limited their ability to solicit clients through personal visits. The intent of the law was to limit lawyer solicitation of prospective clients and was passed after a tremendous increase in personal injury litigation in the last quarter of the nineteenth century. This 1901 law thus limited the ability of personal injury lawyers to "stir up" litigation in order to earn contingent fees, a law that inured in major part to the benefit of the railroads, which spent millions in litigation costs each year.[13]

The barratry statute explicitly applied to "attorneys at law." This narrowness of language allowed a nonattorney named Frank McCloskey to run a business in San Antonio handling personal injury lawsuits as an agent for the injured person. The San Antonio Traction Company sued McCloskey, asking the court to enjoin him from engaging in the business of claims adjuster because he was engaged in barratry. The district court granted the injunction. The court of civil appeals reversed. It held the injunction against McCloskey was invalid because the law barred only an "attorney at law" from seeking or obtaining employment "by means of personal solicitation of such employment." McCloskey was not a lawyer, making the statute inapplicable. The decision of the court of civil appeals was released on February 7, 1917. A month later the legislature amended the barratry statute to include nonlawyers such as McCloskey.[14]

The voluntary Texas Bar Association adopted the 1908 Canons of Ethics of the American Bar Association (ABA) in 1909. This adoption had little effect on Texas lawyers, including members of the association, for in 1923 the association's president, W. A. Wright, suggested that lawyers in the state had "overlooked" that adoption. In 1926, the bar association again adopted the Canons of Ethics. The canons lacked the force of law, and their adoption by the Texas Bar Association was intended to serve to raise voluntarily the standard of professionalism in the practice of law. The canons finally became enforceable law applicable to Texas lawyers after the legislature adopted the State Bar Act of 1939, which created a mandatory bar in Texas, following a national effort championed by the American Judicature Society. Section 4 of the State Bar Act required the supreme court to adopt a code of ethics and a lawyer disciplinary system within six months of its effective date. The supreme court and state bar did so largely by copying the ABA's Canons of Ethics, although a few Texas peculiarities, such as permitting lawyers to pay the expenses of litigation, trumped contrary ABA canons. The Canons of Ethics remained law until late 1971. Only rarely during that time did the supreme court discuss them. A 1966 *Baylor Law Review* article noted that the supreme court had "referred to specific Canons of Ethics only three times since the passage of the State Bar Act and Rules."[15]

Leon Green's 1925 article, *The Courts' Power over Admission and Disbarment*, discussed the history of Texas's unusual disbarment provisions. Green focused in part on the requirement that a lawyer could request a jury trial when subject to disbarment, making unreasonably difficult the regulation of lawyer conduct. One subsequent example was the attempt to disbar S. F. Houtchens, a Fort Worth lawyer. Houtchens was accused by local lawyers of fraudulent conduct. His trial took sixteen days and "developed into one of the most bitterly contested controversies in the history of the county," including "three personal encounters between opposing counsel, with resulting penalties for contempt of court." The trial court disbarred Houtchens after receiving the jury's verdict. The court of civil appeals affirmed. The Texas Commission of Appeals upheld the factual findings that led the jury to conclude that Houtchens should be disbarred. But the trial court's jury instructions were erroneous, and it erroneously admitted in evidence the affidavits of the lawyers who complained about Houtchens's conduct. Therefore, the judgment was reversed three years after the complaint was filed. SMU Law School dean C. S. Potts noted that Texas disbarment law reflected "a small rural community" Texas and was "as much out of place now as ox-carts would be on the boulevards of Houston or Dallas."[16]

The 1939 State Bar Act merely adapted the disbarment system then nearly a century old. Section 5 prohibited the supreme court from adopting any rule abrogating the lawyer's "right of trial by jury in disbarment proceedings." Section 6 provided additional protection to lawyers facing disbarment proceedings: No proceeding to disbar a lawyer could take place other than at the district court in the county of the lawyer's residence, and no suspension of the lawyer from practice could occur until the lawyer was "convicted of the charge pending against him."

This system of regulating the legal profession was joined by the Unauthorized Practice of Law Act of 1933. Like the lawmaking bodies of many other states during the Great Depression, the Texas legislature protected lawyers by adopting a strict prohibition concerning the practice of law by persons not admitted to the bar. In Texas the prohibition was enforceable as a matter of the criminal law. It was reinforced in the State Bar Act of 1939.[17]

The Supreme Court of Texas adopted a variation of the 1970 ABA Code of Professional Responsibility in Texas in late 1971. Texas maintained its rule that a lawyer could forward a case to another and maintain an interest in the fee without any responsibility for the case, contrary to the ABA code. The ABA code was short-lived, and the ABA supplanted it in 1983 with the Model Rules of Professional Conduct. In 1989 the Texas Disciplinary Rules of Professional Conduct, a slight variation of the ABA model rules, were adopted and made effective by the Texas Supreme Court on January 1, 1990. The Texas Rules of Disciplinary Procedure, which controlled the process by which lawyers were disciplined, were adopted in a 1990 referendum of Texas lawyers. The adoption of substantive and procedural rules increased enforcement of discipline. In the last year of the old disciplinary system, May 1, 1991 to April 30, 1992, 228 lawyers were disciplined. In the first year of the new rules, 354 lawyers were disciplined, and in 1993–94, 655 lawyers were disciplined. The number of disciplined lawyers fell by over half in 2006–2007 to 320, of whom 30 (0.037 percent of all lawyers) were disbarred. Between 1994 and 2007, the number of Texas lawyers rose from 59,495 to 79,409, of whom about 90 percent lived in Texas. Whether the decline in disciplinary actions between 1994 and 2007 was evidence of an improvement in the ethical behavior of Texas lawyers or a decline in the enforcement of the disciplinary rules is unclear.[18]

Two additional types of lawyer regulation arose in the 1970s. Texas was on the forefront in the development of Continuing Legal Education (CLE) and the creation of certified specialists in particular areas of law. CLE was intended to promote continuing professionalism by having lawyers learn about different (and often new) legal subjects. Minimum CLE standards became mandatory for all Texas lawyers in 1986, and lawyers were subject to discipline, including disbarment, for failure to attend the required fifteen hours of annual CLE. The first state to approve a formal certification of specialization was California. Right behind it was Texas, which began to certify lawyers as specialists in family law, criminal law, and labor law in 1974. Within three years three additional areas of legal specialization were created. As of 2010, the Texas Board of Legal Specialization certified lawyers in twenty areas of law.[19]

CREATING BAR ASSOCIATIONS

The organization of the Association of the Bar of the City of New York in 1870 and the creation of the ABA in 1878 were but two examples of a nationwide quest to organize in the last third of the nineteenth century. The oldest bar association in Texas was founded in Galveston (1868), arguably the most important city in Texas before 1900, followed closely in time by the Dallas Bar Association (1873), the Houston Bar Association (1870, again in 1901, and finally in 1904), and the Austin Bar Association (1890, becoming the Travis County Bar Association in 1926). The voluntary Texas Bar Association was formed in Galveston in 1882 and modeled on the Galveston Bar Association.[20]

The Galveston Bar Association, home to the most prominent and developed bar in Texas during the nineteenth century, promoted law reform from its inception. Other local bar associations were created for reasons more akin to those of the eating clubs of the Inns of Court in London for barristers: conviviality and social cohesiveness, joined by the possibility that one might obtain some legal business. The stuttering creation of the Houston Bar Association, with three separate dates of creation over a thirty-four-year period, suggests the difficulty in developing a lasting local bar association in the late nineteenth and early twentieth centuries. Similarly, the Dallas Bar Association, formed in 1873, was largely unfunded during its first decade of existence. The Texas Bar Association was both a law reform organization and a social club. Consistent with other large bar associations emerging in most states at that time, the Texas Bar Association comprised a small elite of the bar. In 1900, membership in the Texas Bar Association consisted of fewer than 7 percent of all licensed lawyers.[21]

PRACTICING LAW IN TEXAS IN THE NINETEENTH CENTURY

Many lawyers in mid-nineteenth-century Texas were itinerant businessmen, moving from city to city and from the practice of law to other ventures with remarkable speed, for the practice of law was competitive, and remuneration was often modest. This was particularly true for lawyers working in frontier areas. In 1852, Alfred Howell moved from Virginia to Clarksville, Texas, where he found himself the fifteenth attorney in that small town. Within a year, he moved to Greenville, in which only one other lawyer resided. Even better, that lawyer had a poor reputation for sobriety and abiding by the law. Howell annually traveled hundreds of miles in a circuit of district courts hoping to pick up litigation business. Of the eight lawyers in Dallas in 1850, only two remained in practice there ten years later. Difficult and competitive conditions remained after the Civil War in frontier areas. In 1871, Robert Blake Seay moved to Dallas to practice law. He found thirty lawyers competing for business in a city of approximately three thousand people. It took several years for Seay, who later was elected city and county attorney and district judge in Dallas, to earn a passable living. Lawyers in the Panhandle in the late nineteenth century often came and went, for monetary rewards were often lacking. As cities such as Dallas and Houston grew, joined to a lesser extent by San Antonio and Austin, the work of lawyers became more complex. But even during the first half of the twentieth century, most lawyers in Texas were generalists.[22]

Some lawyers became wealthy men through the practice of law. Galveston lawyer Daniel D. Atchison possessed real estate valued at twenty-five thousand dollars in 1850 and one hundred thousand dollars by 1860, when just 263 Texans had attained such wealth. Of them, 15 were lawyers. Another Galveston lawyer, thirty-five-year-old William Pitt Ballinger, owned property worth over twenty-five thousand dollars by 1860. He annually earned between six thousand and ten thousand dollars by that time, an income "fifteen to twenty times greater than the average skilled worker." Ballinger's talent and reputation helped make him the most sought-after railroad lawyer in the state by the early 1870s. A survey of wealth in Texas in 1870 indicated that of the 58 persons with property worth a hundred thousand dollars or more, 7 were lawyers. Although the number of wealthy lawyers had dropped by more than half, the percentage of lawyers among the wealthiest Texans more than doubled to 12 percent.[23]

Galveston contained the most developed legal community during the last half of the nineteenth century. Both the 1850 and 1860 censuses counted thirty-six lawyers. Half of those thirty-six lawyers were the same in both censuses, indicating a professional stability lacking elsewhere in Texas. By 1900, when the September 8 hurricane nearly destroyed the city, 128 persons practiced law in Galveston. One-quarter had been in practice in the city for at least two decades, and 12 had helped organize the 1868 Galveston Bar Association. Ballinger himself built the best law library in Texas, which he eventually sold to the state.[24]

Most late nineteenth-century lawyers were generalists engaged in civil and criminal litigation, performing title work on contracts for the sale of land, and drafting contracts. The rise of Texas railroads between 1870 and 1900 led both to a tremendous increase in tort litigation for personal injuries and to the rise of the earliest corporate law firms.

THE DEVELOPMENT OF LARGE LAW FIRMS IN TEXAS

What is now known as the law firm of Baker Botts traces its roots to the law partnership in 1840 of Peter Gray and his father in Houston. In 1865, Gray formed a partnership with Walter Browne Botts when both returned to Houston after serving the Confederacy in the Civil War. In 1872 the firm added a third partner, James A. Baker. The firm prospered as it undertook legal work for railroads. By the late 1870s, financiers Jay Gould and Tom Scott were battling over control of the Texas and Pacific Railroad. Gould's victory provided more legal work for lawyers in Texas, including Baker and Botts. Before the end of the nineteenth century, Baker and Botts "was an acknowledged regional leader in railroad law." Shortly thereafter it eschewed much general practice for specialized legal work. Baker and Botts was the first Texas law firm to emulate the practices of large law firms in New York and elsewhere in its growth, its hiring of salaried associates directly from law schools, its antinepotism policy, and its institution of a "firm" concept distinguishable from its individual partners.[25]

In 1917 the Houston law firm of Vinson and Elkins was formed. Founding partner "Judge"

James Elkins opened a bank, the Guaranty Trust Bank, with money of his and other partners in V&E in 1924. Many law firms grew into large, institutional law firms by representing a growing regional bank. Elkins took the additional step of making members of the firm owners of a bank and tying the bank's interests tightly to the interests of the law firm. Elkins also used his increasing contacts with state political heavyweights to develop an extensive client list. By the mid-1920s Elkins was the largest fundraiser for the Texas Democratic Party, and his effective lobbying in the 1930s was crucial in sparing the Pure Oil Company from what it perceived as deleterious orders of the Texas Railroad Commission.[26]

A third large law firm organized in Houston, known today as Fulbright and Jaworski, opened in 1919. Its two founding partners, R. C. Fulbright and John H. Crooker, Sr., divided the work in a manner commonplace to many two-man partnerships of the nineteenth century: one (Fulbright) undertook office work, including railroad and other transactional work, and the other (Crooker), a former district attorney for Harris County, was the firm litigator. Fulbright possessed a B.A. and an M.A. in philosophy from Baylor and a law degree from the University of Chicago. Crooker's formal education had ended at age fourteen; he read law before taking and passing the Texas bar exam. The Fulbright firm was one of the first to open a satellite office in Washington, D.C., doing so in 1927, even before the New Deal made Washington a beacon for lawyers. The firm, and in particular Fulbright, represented a number of clients before the Interstate Commerce Commission. The Fulbright firm represented fewer oil and gas interests than either Baker and Botts or Vinson and Elkins. Its most important client through the 1930s was the Anderson, Clayton and Company cotton business, whose interests expanded into a number of other businesses. Its most famous lawyer was Leon Jaworski, who graduated from the revived Baylor University

Law School before he was twenty. Jaworski was a consummate trial lawyer when lawyers regularly tried cases. One example of both Jaworski's understanding of a lawyer's duty to the law and the respect he possessed in the legal and social community of Houston was his work as a special prosecutor for the United States in the early 1960s in a case against Mississippi governor Ross Barnett. Barnett violated a federal court order to integrate the University of Mississippi by refusing to admit James Meredith. Jaworski's service as special prosecutor at a time when many white Texans opposed civil rights and federal "interference" into state matters had no adverse impact on his practice or standing, for his reputation made his service as special prosecutor unexceptional, though exceptional it was. Jaworski later became famous as the second special prosecutor in the Watergate scandal, work that led to President Richard Nixon's resignation.[27]

The January 1972 issue of the magazine *Juris Doctor* listed all three of these Houston firms among the thirteen largest firms in the country. Only firms from New York (seven), Chicago (two) and San Francisco (one) joined this group. Less than two years later, the same three firms were listed as among the ten largest in the country. The smallest of the three, Baker and Botts, had 160 lawyers. As Griffin Smith noted in 1973, no law firm in Dallas at that time had more than 45 lawyers, and firms in Austin, Fort Worth, and San Antonio "trail far behind" in size. A decade later, each of the three was one of the twenty largest law firms in the nation. Vinson and Elkins remained the largest law firm in Texas and fourth nationally in gross revenues. But much had changed. No Houston firm was in the top ten nationally in size. Of the sixteen law firms in Texas with more than 100 lawyers, ten were primarily located in Dallas, while six were Houston firms. The largest Dallas law firm in 1985, with 160 lawyers, was Johnson and Swanson, a firm not formed until 1970. It was credited and blamed with introducing "a far more aggressive and competitive tone in Dallas" for legal business. By the early 1990s it had 375 lawyers. By 1995 it disbanded, two years after the death of its founder, John Johnson. Jones, Day, Reavis, and Pogue (now Jones Day), a Cleveland law firm, opened a Dallas office in 1981 by merging with a local Dallas firm. Within four years it had 122 lawyers in Dallas alone.[28]

PRACTICING LAW IN MID-TWENTIETH-CENTURY TEXAS: A NOVEL

A Baker and Botts lawyer named Dillon Anderson, later an aide to President Dwight D. Eisenhower, wrote a series of vignettes about the fictional lawyer Richard Billingsley that formed the book *The Billingsley Papers* (1961). The conceit of the novel is that a lawyer and good acquaintance named Gaylord Boswell Peterkin has been asked to comment on an honorary degree to be conferred on Billingsley by State University. Billingsley is a former All-America football player at State, a poker player and sportsman who has stumbled his way to wealth and a successful law practice. Peterkin recounts "the rather amazing sequence of events which propelled Billingsley from professional obscurity to that eminence at the bar which appears to have caught the attention of your committee." Billingsley takes his secretary's husband as a client and invests with him in several businesses. He occasionally represents other individuals. Somehow Billingsley's meager law practice provides enough money to invest in a productive oil well that makes him a millionaire. Billingsley is also involved in a comical series of events with the federal government that leaves him a folk hero. Law practice is not central to *The Billingsley Papers*, for Billingsley possesses enough time to hunt, golf, and pursue other recreational activities. When Anderson wrote these stories, lawyers were in short supply and high demand; it was a golden age for lawyers, as the novel indirectly suggests.[29]

PRACTICING LAW IN MID-TWENTIETH-CENTURY TEXAS: TWO MEMOIRS

Talented and dedicated lawyers in mid-twentieth-century Texas were able not only to find a plethora of opportunities to build a law firm that provided first-rate legal services, but also to find the time to serve as civic leaders aiding in the development of their communities. Wilbur Matthews's memoir of his life as a lawyer in San Antonio presented the richness found in a broad-based legal practice that encompassed both transactional and litigation work. Just three years into the practice of law, Matthews wrote that his experience doing both types of work "set the pattern for my 'general practice of the law' in the years to come." Matthews was intimately involved in the development of San Antonio's medical center, including bringing to the city medical, dental, and nursing schools as well as several hospitals. Paul Carrington's work was largely as a corporate lawyer, but even he undertook some litigation matters. Carrington helped build several Dallas firms. His work in numerous civic projects in the creation of modern Dallas reflects the important work lawyers performed in addition to the practice of law.[30]

INCOME IN THE PRACTICE OF LAW

In 1973 *Texas Monthly* published a sidebar titled "Bricklayers and Attorneys: An Earnings Comparison." The sidebar calculated the hourly wage of a new associate of a large firm at $6.42 (twenty-four hundred hours of work at an annual salary of $15,400). It then compared this pay with that of a hypothetical high school classmate who became a bricklayer at eighteen. It concluded that a lawyer in a big law firm would not likely reach the lifetime earnings of a bricklayer until at least age forty, and "[i]f union pay scales rise faster than lawyers' salaries, he might not catch up until he is in his late forties; perhaps he never would." But it was the pay of lawyers in large law firms that outpaced the pay of bricklayers over the next two decades. By 1985 new lawyers at large Texas law firms were paid $47,000 in Dallas and $40,000 in Houston. The New York law firm of Cravath, Swaine, and Moore increased the salary of its new associates the following year from $48,000 to $65,000. Other large law firms across the country, including those in Texas, quickly followed. By 2008, new lawyers in large Texas law firms were paid $160,000 plus bonuses, when the Great Recession hit.[31]

By the mid-1980s large law firms in Texas began entering into contingent fee agreements, cases in which the firm might reap an extraordinarily large payout or nothing at all. These types of matters had been anathema to those firms a decade earlier. Baker and Botts, along with Houston lawyer Joe Jamail, represented Pennzoil in its suit against Texaco in the mid-1980s, a case that finally settled for $3 billion after the jury awarded Pennzoil over $10 billion (see chapter 8). In 1989, Vinson and Elkins won a civil antitrust case involving over $200 million. *The American Lawyer* noted this amounted to "a spectacular return on the $25–30 million worth of time V&E had devoted to the four-and-one-half-year ETSI case." But not even large firm lawyers made more money than the highest paid plaintiffs' personal injury lawyers in the 1980s and 1990s.[32]

An October 16, 1989, article in *Forbes* magazine estimated the pay of the highest paid lawyers in the United States in 1987 and 1988. The impetus for the article may have been the hundreds of millions (variously reported as between $300 million and $420 million) Jamail received in the Pennzoil-Texaco case. Jamail was ranked first, with an estimated two-year

total of $475 million. Six of the ten highest paid lawyers in the United States were Texas lawyers. Of the sixty-three "trial lawyers" (plaintiffs' personal injury lawyers) listed by *Forbes*, twenty-four, or 38 percent, were Texas lawyers, a consequence of Texas's tort law revolution (see chapter 8). Of the seventy-one other lawyers listed, only three were Texas lawyers. All three practiced at Vinson and Elkins and all were found near the end of the list. Six years later, *Forbes* updated the story. No Texas lawyer made the list of the twenty-five most highly paid corporate lawyers. Of the twenty-five most highly paid trial lawyers in 1994, eight (32 percent) practiced law in Texas. Indeed, the four highest paid lawyers in the United States all practiced law in Texas, led again by Jamail. In 2001, *Forbes* ran a variation of this story for the third time, listing the five highest paid American lawyers. Two of the five were Texas lawyers.[33]

TEXAS WOMEN IN THE PRACTICE OF LAW

The 1900 census listed seventeen women engaged in the practice of law in Texas. That number appears to be wholly erroneous, for the first woman recognized as admitted to the bar in Texas was Edith Locke in 1902, and she left no record of practicing law. Despite the decision of the United States Supreme Court in *Bradwell v. Illinois* (1872) holding constitutionally permissible Illinois's ban on women from the practice of law, by the time the district court for El Paso County admitted Locke to practice, thirty-four other states had already admitted one or more women to the practice of law. The 1910 census listed three women practicing law in the state. Hortense Sparks Ward, admitted to the Texas bar that year, played a consequential role in several areas of law. Ward's writings aided in the adoption of the Married Women's Property Act of 1913 (see chapter 5), and she also played a major role in Texas's adoption of prohibition and in obtaining for Texas women the right to vote.[34]

Ward decided early in her career to avoid the courtroom and its male-only juries and focus on office practice. She worked with her husband, who handled all trial work. Ward's decision to avoid the courtroom was the same as that made by most women lawyers then and later. Data collected from 1920 through 1949 indicate that a majority of women lawyers engaged in general office practice. In both 1939 and 1949, just 1 percent of women lawyers engaged in criminal law practice or "trial work." Where Ward differed from other female lawyers was that she was the mother of three. National data from 1939 indicated 76 percent of women lawyers had no children, while just 3 percent had three or more children.[35]

Although at first Texas lagged behind other states in licensing female lawyers, by 1939 Texas was ninth among states in the percentage of women lawyers. A decade later it was sixth. The first two female law graduates of the University of Texas graduated in 1914, and the following year female law students there created the Texas Women's Law Association. From the late 1910s through the early 1930s a number of proprietary and YMCA law schools opened throughout much of the state, creating greater opportunities for women to enter the legal profession.[36]

Ward is best known in Texas legal history for serving as the chief justice of the all-woman Texas Supreme Court in the case of *Johnson v. Darr* (1925), for which Governor Pat Neff appointed three women, Ward, Hattie Leah Henenberg, and Ruth Virginia Brazzil, as special judges. All three regular members of the Texas Supreme Court had recused themselves from the case because they were members of the Woodmen of the World, a fraternal organization involved in the matter. Ward wrote the opinion of the court, and both Henenberg and Brazzil wrote concurring opinions, affirming

the decision of the court of civil appeals. The all-woman supreme court may have been a stunt, an attempt by Governor Neff to blunt the impact of the inauguration of Miriam "Ma" Ferguson, Texas's first female governor and the wife of impeached and convicted former governor James "Pa" Ferguson. And Neff may also have been tweaking James Ferguson because as governor he opposed suffrage. On the other hand, Neff's appointment of women to judge *Darr* may have been to demonstrate the intellectual qualities of women on Texas political and legal matters or an acknowledgment of the political power wielded by women after they gained the right to vote. Neff would have had little difficulty finding three qualified male lawyers to decide *Darr*. His decision to appoint three women was intentional and designed at least in part to affirm a role for women in public matters.[37]

Nationally, the number of female lawyers rose slightly from the 1930s through the late 1960s, but the overall percentages of women lawyers in the states were slight, between 2.8 percent and 4.0 percent in 1966. Women began to enter the legal profession in much greater numbers beginning in the early 1970s, and the percentage of women graduating from Texas law schools rose quickly and markedly. By 1990 slightly more than 40 percent of Texas law school graduates were women, and by 2004 women constituted 48 percent of the students enrolled in Texas law schools. In 2008–2009 women comprised 32 percent of all lawyers in Texas.[38]

As the number of women entering the legal profession rose substantially, so too did allegations of gender discrimination by law firms. A claim of sex discrimination in the hiring of summer law clerks (from which pool the new law firm associates were usually hired) was made in 1976 by female law students at SMU Law School. The Southern Methodist University Association of Women Law Students and four anonymous female lawyers filed two sepa-

All-Woman Texas Supreme Court, 1925. Courtesy Texas State Library and Archives Commission.

rate suits alleging employment discrimination. The federal district court refused the four lawyers anonymity. Despite this setback, "several out-of-court settlements were agreed to" in the case, providing women more opportunities in the practice of law in Dallas. One female Texas lawyer spoke of her fear that, even if large Texas law firms were forced to hire some female lawyers, "there was no guarantee that anybody was going to treat you like a real lawyer when you got there."[39]

Women lawyers work now in a wide variety of jobs, including criminal law and trial work. Some substantial differences remain between men and women in the practice of law. Women are substantially less likely to work in the private practice of law than men and more likely than men to work for government agencies. Even though fewer women than men are in private practice, a greater percentage of female lawyers than male lawyers practice law in large law firms. The first woman to make partner at Vinson and Elkins, Carol Dinkins, did so in 1980. Although at least one woman made partner each year but one from 1980 through 1995 at Vinson and Elkins, new female partners were greatly outnumbered by new male partners. The reasons for this gender difference in law firms are unclear.[40]

LEGAL EDUCATION IN TEXAS

Texas higher educational institutions made sporadic efforts in the nineteenth century to create law schools or law professorships. Baylor University established the first professorship in law in 1849, with lectures given by Supreme Court justice Abner S. Lipscomb and R. E. B. Baylor. Eight years later, it created a law department consisting of three professors. The law department was closed for the duration of the Civil War and opened briefly in mid-1866, 1870, and 1879. Austin College opened a law department in 1855, which it closed a year later after graduating four students. Trinity University School of Law opened in 1873 and closed five years later after graduating twenty-two students. The only law department in Texas to open in the nineteenth century and remain open was the law department of the University of Texas in Austin, which opened in 1883. Its initial faculty consisted of Oran M. Roberts and Robert Gould. Roberts was a former district and supreme court judge, an elected but unseated U.S. senator after the Civil War, a secessionist nicknamed "Old Alcalde" by his students, and the outgoing governor when he was appointed. Gould was a former Texas Supreme Court justice.[41]

Admission to the University of Texas law department, one of the two departments of the university, required only "a sufficient English education." The study of law was initially an undergraduate undertaking in Texas. A student who passed the first-year examination in law was permitted to enter the law department as a senior, allowing him to graduate in one academic year. The program of legal instruction lasted two years for those students who did not attempt the first-year law examinations. The ability to enter the law department directly from high school created a slight bias in favor of learning law through formal university study rather than learning law as an apprentice in a law office. These incentives were enhanced in 1891 when graduates of the law department were granted the diploma privilege, exempting them from the bar examination.[42]

Between 1883 and 1919, the University of Texas law department was the only educational institution of law in Texas of any size. This contrasted with the rest of the nation, for law schools increased from 31 in 1870 to 124 in 1920. The development nationally of law

schools reflected both a changed understanding of law in the post–Civil War era and the incentives directing would-be lawyers to law schools. Christopher Columbus Langdell, the dean of Harvard Law School from 1870 to 1895, proposed that the law was a science, and "considered as a science, consists of certain principles or doctrines." Langdell's invocation of law as a science was not new with him, but his claim that a "true lawyer" possessed a mastery of those principles or doctrines suggested that those who aspired to the law should be trained in the university.[43]

During the 1920s the number of American law students increased significantly. This was also true in Texas, where the number of law schools increased dramatically. The Houston Law School effectively opened in 1919, as did Jefferson School of Law in Dallas. Baylor University reopened its law school in 1920, now in Waco, adopting the "case method" of teaching first championed by Langdell at Harvard in 1870. South Texas College of Law opened in Houston as a YMCA law school in 1923, and the Dallas School of Law, another YMCA school, and Southern Methodist University School of Law both opened in 1925. The Galveston Institute of Law opened in 1926 and the San Antonio School of Law in 1927. By 1934 the *Annual Review of Legal Education* indicated that fifteen law schools were operating in Texas. Most of them disappeared within a few years, victims of the Great Depression, and by the end of the 1930s Texas had four law schools affiliated with universities—Baylor University School of Law, Southern Methodist University School of Law, St. Mary's University School of Law (founded in 1934), and the University of Texas School of Law—and one independent school, South Texas College of Law. These five law schools were joined shortly after World War II by Texas Southern University School of Law (now the Texas Southern University Thurgood Marshall School of Law).[44]

Heman Marion "Bill" Sweatt, a postal worker in Houston, applied for admission to the University of Texas School of Law for the term beginning in February 1946 but was denied admission solely because he was African American. Sweatt's application was part of the NAACP's effort to attack legal segregation in higher education. In *Missouri ex rel. Gaines v. Canada* (1938), Lloyd Gaines was denied admission to the University of Missouri's law school. It offered him the option of receiving a scholarship to attend law school outside the state or applying to Lincoln University, which would create a law school for blacks in Missouri. The Supreme Court held unconstitutional Missouri's plan.[45]

As World War II neared its end in Europe in spring 1945, Thurgood Marshall of the NAACP and the Texas State Conference of Branches of the NAACP sought a plaintiff to challenge racial segregation at the University of Texas School of Law. The Texas state conference was an engaged and vigorous body of local Texas NAACP branches, energized in part as a result of the 1944 decision of the Supreme Court of the United States declaring unconstitutional the Texas white primary (see chapter 7). While searching for a Texas plaintiff, Oklahoman Ada Lois Sipuel asked for assistance from the NAACP regarding her desire to attend law school at the University of Oklahoma. Sipuel was denied admission there on the ground of race, and NAACP lawyers represented her in her lawsuit. The trial court and Oklahoma Supreme Court dismissed based on insufficient pleadings. The Supreme Court of the United States unanimously reversed, holding that Oklahoma was required to provide Sipuel an education "in conformity with the equal protection clause of the Fourteenth Amendment and provide it as soon as it does for applicants of any other group." The Court's opinion was

Heman Sweatt in registration line, 1947. Courtesy Dolph Briscoe Center for American History, Prints and Photographs Collection, University of Texas at Austin (di 01127).

issued just four days after the January 7–8, 1948, oral arguments. Despite this apparent signal from the Court suggesting that the state admit Sipuel, the Supreme Court did not explicitly order her admission, and Oklahoma quickly fashioned a separate and clearly inadequate law school for her and other possible African American law school applicants, which the Supreme Court refused to hold impermissible. At about the same time as Sipuel applied to law school in Oklahoma, Sweatt volunteered to serve as the plaintiff in the Texas case. This case moved more slowly than *Sipuel*, giving Marshall some time to refine (and alter) the strategy used in *Sipuel*.[46]

The district court in Austin issued an interlocutory order in June 1946, a month after Sweatt filed suit, giving Texas six months to create a "substantially equal" law school. Although it failed to do so during that time, the court issued a final judgment in its favor. It did so based on a promise by the board of Texas A&M University, which supervised Prairie View University, to have Prairie View create a

University of Texas Law School dean Charles T. McCormick, 1949. Reprinted by permission of the Tarlton Law Library, Jamail Center for Legal Research, University of Texas School of Law.

law school upon demand by Texas blacks. In March 1947, by agreement of the parties, the court of civil appeals set aside the judgment and remanded the case to the district court for a hearing on its merits, which took place in May. In the meantime, the legislature passed a law on March 3, 1947, creating the Texas State University for Negroes (now Texas Southern University) by donating land of the Houston College for Negroes and appropriating $2,750,000 to the new university. The immediacy of Sweatt's request led the legislature, in the same bill, temporarily to locate in Austin the law school of the Texas State University for Negroes and to appropriate $100,000 for its operation. Locating the law school in Austin allowed the legislature to "borrow" University of Texas law school faculty, including Dean Charles T. McCormick, who became part-time dean of this separate law school. The new law school for blacks opened for registration on March 10, 1947, a week after the bill was passed, but no students applied, as the NAACP dissuaded prospective applicants from doing so. A month after the conclusion of

the five-day May 1947 hearing, the district court again ruled in favor of Texas. The state's lawyer, Joe Greenhill, noted in his 1986 oral history interview that Marshall "wasn't going to win" in the trial court.[47]

In fall 1947, three African American students enrolled in the new law school in Austin. They were taught by full-time members of the University of Texas law school faculty. The law school was stretched thin because of the massive number of World War II veterans trying to complete law school quickly. McCormick's difficulties were compounded by the law school's inadequate facility, which the university had promised to improve but had failed to do. In addition to the crisis in providing a quality education to veterans (the law school had approximately one thousand students taught by nineteen full-time faculty members), McCormick now faced the problem of being handed operational responsibility for the law school of Texas State University for Negroes. These events were responsible in part for his resignation as dean effective at the end of the 1948–49 academic year.[48]

The court of civil appeals affirmed the district court's judgment on February 25, 1948, justifying segregation in part on *Plessy v. Ferguson* (1896), which set forth the doctrine of "separate but equal." It also surprisingly relied on the Supreme Court's decision a month earlier in *Sipuel*. Marshall made a more direct attack on *Plessy* at both the trial and appellate level than occurred in *Sipuel* (which Marshall did not try). At trial Sweatt testified that his desire was to attend the University of Texas School of Law and that he would not be satisfied with attending a segregated law school, a stance slightly different from statements made by him when he was deposed in 1946. Marshall offered expert evidence that segregation on the basis of race had no scientific justification. This evidence gave Marshall the foundation to make the broad legal argument that racial classifications "have no line of reasonableness," making legalized segregation unconstitutional. Marshall's work at the district court hearing also created a complete factual record of the actual differences between the law schools at the University of Texas and the Texas State University for Negroes, including the number of books in the library and extra- and cocurricular activities (moot court, law review). The court of civil appeals concluded that Marshall implicitly asserted that "race segregation in public schools, at least in the higher and professional fields, inherently is discriminatory within the meaning of the Fourteenth Amendment." The court correctly understood Marshall's assertion. It rejected his claim. The court appended to its opinion a statement from the state favorably comparing the two law schools. The Supreme Court of Texas refused to hear the case, and the NAACP petitioned the Supreme Court of the United States for a writ of certiorari, which the Court granted.[49]

Sweatt was one of three segregation cases argued in early April 1950. *Henderson v. United States* concerned the constitutionality of an order of the Interstate Commerce Commission allowing the Southern Railway to reserve ten tables exclusively for white passengers and one table exclusively for black passengers with a curtain drawn between them. In *McLaurin v. Oklahoma State Regents for Higher Education,* G. W. McLaurin complained that, although admitted to the state university's program to obtain a doctorate in education, he was forced to sit apart from white students in classes (sometimes in an "anteroom adjoining a classroom") and at a designated seat in the library and cafeteria. The brief for the United States in *Henderson* urged the Supreme Court to hold the ICC's decision unconstitutional, and, although it concluded that *Plessy's* "separate but equal" doctrine was not necessarily invoked in the matter, it also urged the Court to overrule *Plessy* should it decide the *Plessy* doctrine was at issue. On June 5, 1950, the Supreme Court released its opinions in *Henderson, McLaurin,*

and *Sweatt.* In each the Court held in favor of the plaintiff, but although it created greater difficulties for states to continue to segregate, it did not overrule *Plessy* and the separate but equal doctrine. In *Sweatt* the Court not only noted that substantial tangible equality was lacking in "terms of number of the faculty, variety of courses and opportunity for specialization, size of the student body, scope of the library, availability of law review and similar activities," but it also noted, "What is more important, the University of Texas Law School possesses to a far greater degree those qualities which are incapable of objective measurement but which make for greatness in a law school. Such qualities, to name but a few, include reputation of the faculty, experience of the administration, position and influence of the alumni, standing in the community, traditions and prestige. It is difficult to believe that one who had a free choice between these law schools would consider the question close."[50]

The law school of Texas State University for Negroes was moved to Houston in August 1948. Its first graduate was Henry Doyle, who in 1978 became the first African American to serve on an appellate court in Texas. Doyle, who passed the bar exam while still enrolled, was extolled as a "fine product of segregated education." He then began filing civil rights lawsuits against the state. In 1951 the legislature changed the name of the school to Texas Southern University, and in 1976 the law school was named in honor of Thurgood Marshall, who became the first Negro (his preferred term) justice of the Supreme Court of the United States. Sweatt entered the University of Texas Law School in fall 1950, but after two years dropped out.[51]

POST–WORLD WAR II EXPANSION OF LAW SCHOOLS IN TEXAS

Three of the four law schools created in Texas after World War II were state law schools. In addition to the law school at Texas Southern University, the University of Houston Law Center was founded in 1947. Texas Tech University School of Law in Lubbock opened in 1967. In 1994, Texas Wesleyan University School of Law became the ninth ABA-approved law school in the state.

Despite the existence of seven ABA-approved law schools in Texas by 1950, the University of Texas School of Law remained the dominant law school in the state, for it was one of the largest law schools in the United States and graduated far more students than any other Texas law school. Its graduates populated all of the largest law firms in Texas, including the state's three largest firms. Indeed, between 1917 and 1994, Vinson and Elkins hired 483 lawyers from the University of Texas.[52]

U.S. News & World Report first created a list ranking law schools in 1987 and began doing so on an annual basis beginning in 1990. That ranking has consistently listed the University of Texas Law School among the nation's top fifteen or so law schools. From the time Heman Sweatt applied to the law school in the late 1940s through the early 1960s, the law school at the University of Texas largely used an open admission policy. The quality of students was assessed not through strict admissions standards, but through strict grading standards during and at the end of the first year of law school. In 1948, one author stated that 30 percent of first-year students at the University of Texas Law School were excluded for poor grades, similar to the 36 percent attrition at full-time ABA law schools nationwide during the 1950s. In the mid-1960s the number of applicants began to exceed "significantly" the number of seats available at the University of Texas. By 1972, attrition nationwide at full-time law schools had dropped to 12 percent as law schools, including the University of Texas, began to institute more stringent admissions standards, in part through widespread adoption and reliance upon the Law School Admission Test (LSAT), the standardized test taken by

St. Mary's University School of Law, 1950s. Courtesy St. Mary's University School of Law Archives.

nearly all law school applicants. Law schools were filled by the early 1970s, to the extent that all 163 ABA-approved law schools admitting students in 1975 were as selective as the top 27 law schools in 1961. By the mid-1980s the competition for seats at all law schools in the country was intense, and that intensity rose in some part because of the use of affirmative action in law school admissions.[53]

HOPWOOD AND AFFIRMATIVE ACTION

The phrase "affirmative action" was coined in 1961 by a lawyer named Hobart Taylor, Jr., a native Texan. It was used by President John Kennedy and Vice President Lyndon Johnson to encourage large federal contractors to increase minority hiring. After the adoption of the 1964 Civil Rights Act, President Johnson signed Executive Order 11246 (1965), which ordered all federal contractors to "take affirmative action to ensure that applicants are employed . . . without regard to their race, creed, color, or national origin."[54]

In 1969, President Richard M. Nixon revived the Philadelphia Plan, which created numerical goals in hiring in trade unions. Congress adopted the plan at the end of that year. The Philadelphia Plan required construction unions in a particular area to set goals and timetables for adding more black members and included quotas based on the area's population demographics.

By the early 1970s affirmative action was used in higher education admissions. The first major lawsuit against its use was filed in 1971 by Marco DeFunis, Jr., against the president of the University of Washington after DeFunis was denied admission to the university's law school. That suit ended without a clear resolution in the Supreme Court.[55]

Allan Bakke was denied admission to the University of California at Davis medical school in 1973 and 1974. Sixteen of the one hundred seats were limited to applicants who were "Black/Afro-American, American Indian, Mexican/American or Chicano, Oriental/Asian-American, Puerto Rican (Mainland), Puerto Rican (Commonwealth), [or] Cuban." Bakke claimed this was an unconstitutional quota. He also claimed that the school's admissions policy violated the Civil Rights Act of 1964. The Supreme Court was very badly split in *Bakke*. Four members of the Court concluded that the university's affirmative action program was constitutionally permissible, and four concluded that the admissions policy violated the Civil Rights Act. The opinion of Justice Lewis F. Powell appeared to split the difference, holding that the Constitution required applying "strict" scrutiny for all race-based programs, a standard the Davis program did not meet in part because of the quota. But Powell also concluded that educational institutions were permitted to use racial minority status as a positive factor to foster diversity in determining admissions.[56]

Instead of resolving the issue, *Bakke* made the debate over affirmative action more bitter and divisive. The Court's subsequent decisions concerning the constitutionality of affirmative action were almost always closely divided. Those opposing affirmative action began efforts in several states to ban the use of affirmative action, particularly in higher public education. In 1992, Cheryl Hopwood and several others applied for admission to the University of Texas School of Law. After their applications were denied, they sued in federal court, claiming that the admissions program of the school violated the Fourteenth Amendment's equal protection clause.

The admissions system then in place used a "Texas Index" (TI), a combination of undergraduate grade point average and LSAT score. To determine which nine hundred applicants would receive letters offering admission (from more than four thousand applications), the admissions committee divided applicants into three categories: presumptive admit, presumptive deny, and a middle "discretionary zone," based on the applicant's TI score. The admissions committee also aspired to admit "a class consisting of 10% Mexican Americans and 5% blacks, proportions roughly comparable to the percentages of those races graduating from Texas colleges." All applicants other than African American and Mexican American applicants were given one set of TI score ranges and placed accordingly in one of the three categories. African American and Mexican American candidates were given a second set of TI score ranges. According to the Fifth Circuit, "In March 1992, for example, the presumptive TI admission score for resident whites and non-preferred minorities was 199. Mexican Americans and blacks needed a TI of only 189 to be presumptively admitted. The difference in the presumptive-deny ranges is even more striking. The presumptive denial score for 'nonminorities' was 192; the same score for blacks and Mexican Americans was 179." This, the Fifth Circuit held, was unconstitutional because the state could not meet the standard of strict scrutiny. It reversed the judgment of the district court, which had upheld the law school's admissions policy. The Supreme Court declined to hear the case.[57]

The law school experienced a large decrease in the number of African American and Mexican American students after *Hopwood*. In fall 1996, thirty-two African American and forty-one Mexican American law students entered the University of Texas. The following year, after the Fifth Circuit's *Hopwood* decision, four African American and twenty-six Mexican American students enrolled, decreases of 87.5 percent and 37 percent, respectively. In 2003 the Supreme Court of the United States held constitutional the use of affirmative action in higher education admissions to achieve a diverse student body in the law school setting, effectively reversing *Hopwood*.[58]

THE TEXAS COURTS

The most unusual aspect of the Texas judicial system is not its byzantine structure, for other states have a plethora of courts with varied, overlapping, and confusing jurisdictional boundaries. It is the creation in 1891 of two supreme courts, the Supreme Court of Texas and the Texas Court of Criminal Appeals, equal in stature and distinguished formally only by jurisdiction. The creation of two such courts, an idea only Oklahoma has followed, is a story of penury. The unwillingness to spend money on the judiciary has resulted in a persistent backlog of cases, a difficulty in keeping judges on the bench, and occasional claims of corruption in the Texas courts.

When Stephen F. Austin drafted a code of laws in 1824, he provided for *alcaldes* with jurisdiction to try matters up to two hundred dollars, then a considerable sum. Appeals went to Austin himself, possibly a surprise to modern readers but sensible in that nearly barren territory with little "law" or law books

to guide anyone. By 1836 the estimated Texas population totaled fifty-two thousand persons, including thirty thousand Texians, dispersed over a broad area often difficult to traverse. The 1836 constitution of the Republic of Texas provided for the selection of judges through a joint ballot of both houses of congress. This joint ballot election required no nomination by the president of the republic of persons for consideration by the houses, nor agreement by the president with the vote of the houses. The joint ballot system for appointing judges existed in Tennessee, from which a number of constitutional delegates emigrated. The affinity for the joint ballot may have resulted from the fact that eighteen of the twenty-five delegates came from states that appointed judges in that manner.[59]

The necessary haste with which the 1836 constitution was written may be shown in the description of the judiciary. Section 1 of Article IV declares, in language nearly identical to that of Article II, section 1 of the Constitution of the United States, that the "[j]udicial powers of the Government shall be vested in one Supreme Court, and such inferior courts as the Congress may, from time to time, ordain and establish." Despite the assertion in section 1 of the 1836 constitution that it created just one mandatory court (the supreme court), section 2 declares, "The Republic of Texas shall be divided into convenient judicial districts, not less than three, nor more than eight. There shall be appointed for each district, a judge. . . ." The constitution of the republic thus constitutionally created at least three district courts, which the congress was permitted to expand to as many as eight.

A willingness to do justice on the cheap began early, for the 1836 constitution made the judges of the district courts the associate justices of the supreme court. This created an unintended difficulty: section 7 of Article IV required a "majority" to constitute a quorum. If congress created only three judicial districts, then the supreme court would consist of a total of four members (a chief justice and three associate justices who also served as district judges). A majority would thus require the presence of at least three justices in any case. Section 8 held that "no judge shall sit in a case in the Supreme Court tried by him in the court below." Thus, if the Texas congress divided the state into three judicial districts, all of the justices other than the associate justice who ruled in the case below had to be present in order to constitute a quorum and to decide the case on appeal. The legislature of the republic solved this by initially dividing Texas into four judicial districts.[60]

The double duty of district judges to try cases and hear appeals was not unusual in the 1830s and early 1840s. All of the members of the Supreme Court of the United States, including the chief justice, spent most of their time riding circuit outside of Washington. One unusual difference between the two courts was that the chief justice of the Texas Supreme Court did not ride circuit between sessions of the court. A second and more important difference was that the associate justices of the Supreme Court of Texas were not aided by sitting district judges when they held sessions of the district court. The judges of the republic were required to do both jobs by themselves. The extent of the burden on the associate judges of the Supreme Court of the Republic of Texas created substantial costs. During the nine years of the republic, twenty-four men served as district judges. The initial creation of four district courts, and thus four district judges, joined by the chief justice, meant the supreme court consisted of five members. In order to obtain a quorum, not only was the presence of the chief justice necessary, but the court could not convene unless a majority of the four district judges (that is, three judges), were present. Because the supreme court did not meet until January 1840, congress remedied this difficulty in part by creating a fifth judicial district in 1838.[61]

When Texas entered the Union in 1845, the judiciary article in the new constitution began,

"The judicial power of this State shall be vested in one supreme court, in district courts, and in such inferior courts as the legislature may from time to time ordain and establish." In section 2 it limited the number of justices in the supreme court to three: one chief justice and two associate justices. Section 5 altered the appointment of supreme court and district court judges: "The governor shall nominate, and, by and with the advice and consent of two-thirds of the Senate, shall appoint the judges of the supreme and district courts, and they shall hold their offices for six years." Although similar to the appointment of judges in the federal system, the two-thirds requirement and the limit of the term in office to six years were major departures from the federal system.[62]

The discussion of the judiciary article in the 1845 constitutional convention was not recorded, but surviving records indicate a division among the delegates concerning direct election of judges, with an amendment to elect judges by a vote of the people failing by a two-thirds majority (19 to 38). Chris Klemme notes that Thomas Jefferson Rusk, who served as chief justice from late 1838 through early 1840, considered the judiciary "the most important branch of the new government, in part because it was the only branch not under the control of the people." This sentiment, however, was contrary to a strong Jacksonian belief in control by the people of all organs of government, including the judiciary. The 1845 constitution exercised control over the judiciary by adoption of two forms of removal of judges: impeachment (Art. IX) and address (Art. IV, § 8). A judge could be removed from office through impeachment, for which no specific reason was required to be given. A judge was to be removed from office "for wilful neglect of duty, or other reasonable cause, which shall not be sufficient ground for impeachment," by the governor upon request of two-thirds of each house of the legislature, as long as "the cause or causes for which such removal shall be required shall be stated at length in such address," and the judge was given notice and an opportunity to be heard before the recorded vote was taken. Both methods of removal remain constitutionally available.[63]

Almost immediately after ratification of the 1845 constitution, a constitutional amendment subjecting judges to election by popular vote was made in the house. It died but was raised again at the next legislative session in 1847–48. (In 1845 only Mississippi—since 1832—provided for popular election of its judges.) A joint resolution proposing this constitutional amendment was then adopted. When Texas voters cast their ballots on this amendment in 1849, New York, Ohio, and Connecticut had made judicial offices elective, and seven other states were considering the issue. The amendment was supported by more than 75 percent of voters. The constitution required a two-thirds approval in each house of any amendment adopted by the people. By the end of December both houses had voted favorably to incorporate the amendment into the constitution, and on January 16, 1850, the Texas Constitution was formally amended to require the election of judges.[64]

The 1861 constitution largely reiterated the provisions of the 1845 constitution, as amended. The 1866 constitution increased the number of justices to five and increased the term of office to ten years. During both presidential and congressional reconstruction, the members of the supreme court were removed from office and replaced by the governor. The 1869 constitution returned to an appointive three-person appellate judiciary serving nine-year terms. An amendment to that constitution, made effective in 1874, increased the number of supreme court justices to five from three. Shortly thereafter, the 1869 constitution was rejected and replaced. The post-Reconstruction 1876 constitution returned to popular election of appellate judges, who served six-year terms. Texas's final constitution also reduced the number of justices to three.

By 1875 the supreme court's docket of pending cases totaled 1,600, and it was growing at the rate of 159 cases per year. The solution of the 1875 constitutional convention was to create a court of appeals, consisting of three members, in addition to the three-member supreme court. The jurisdiction of the court of appeals was limited to appeals in all criminal cases and in any civil case arising from the county courts. Ratification of the 1876 constitution thus permanently divested the supreme court of jurisdiction in criminal cases. But the Texas Court of Appeals did not flatter itself in its decisions. In the July–August 1887 issue of the *American Law Review*, published in Saint Louis, the editors lambasted the court for its record of reversing convictions. The court of appeals had affirmed 882 cases and reversed in 1,604 cases, a reversal rate of 65 percent. Moreover, the editorial noted, the court of appeals had recently decided to "overrule" a decision of the Supreme Court of the United States. This was the same court, the editors pointed out, that reversed a conviction because the verdict stated "guity" instead of "guilty" but affirmed a verdict that read "guilly" instead of "guilty" (see chapter 7).[65]

Divesting the Texas Supreme Court of jurisdiction in criminal cases and cases appealed from county courts failed to ease the court's burden. In 1879 the Texas legislature created a commission of appeals to hear cases upon the consent of the parties. The legislation allowed the governor to appoint three persons "learned in the law," who were permitted to decide civil cases pending in the supreme court or court of appeals. The law was unsuccessfully challenged on the ground that it impermissibly created a court, and in 1881 the act was amended to allow the court to send cases to the commission without the consent of the parties. The Texas Commission of Appeals remained in business (with a two-year exception from 1885 to 1887) until the constitution was amended to restructure the appellate courts of the state. The 1891 amendments to Article V created the

Texas Court of Criminal Appeals to decide all appealed criminal matters. The Texas Court of Appeals was renamed the Texas Court of Civil Appeals. Three courts of civil appeals were mandated by the amendment, and the legislature was empowered to create additional courts. After the 1891 constitutional amendment and 1892 restructuring of the appellate courts, a criminal conviction was appealed directly to the court of criminal appeals. Decisions of the district courts and county courts in all civil matters were appealed as of right to the appropriate court of civil appeals.[66]

The 1891 constitutional amendment was intended in large part to reduce, if not eliminate, the backlog in the supreme court's docket. It did not have this effect in the supreme court, the newly constituted court of criminal appeals, or the courts of civil appeals. Each of these courts consisted of three members, as required by the constitution, and Texas's judicial needs exceeded the ability of those appellate courts to resolve cases in a timely fashion. The court of criminal appeals wrote short opinions and affirmed convictions summarily without opinion in many cases to keep up with its docket. The courts of civil appeals gave a quick summary of the facts and a truncated assessment of the issues on appeal, allowing each to issue several hundred opinions annually. From 1892 through the first decade of the twentieth century, the Texas Supreme Court attempted to keep abreast of its docket by discouraging concurring and dissenting opinions. Stability in the membership of the Texas Supreme Court from 1892 through 1910 (only four persons sat on the three-member court) allowed the court better to winnow its docket. The legislature did its part by limiting the jurisdiction of the court. However, even after issuing more than a hundred opinions each term, the supreme court was sabotaged by newly added courts of civil appeals across the state. The number of courts of civil appeals grew from the three to six by 1907, with two more established in 1911. The increase in the number of decisions issued by the increased number of courts of civil appeals meant more possible requests to the supreme court for a writ of error, creating an overwhelming burden on the court.[67]

The impact of the prohibition movement also indirectly affected the workload of the Texas Supreme Court. In early 1911 the outgoing lame duck prohibitionist governor, Thomas Campbell, made two appointments to the court after the resignation of Chief Justice Reuben Gaines, the first changes to the composition of the court in more than a decade. Campbell appointed Associate Justice Thomas Jefferson Brown as chief justice and named William Ramsey to Brown's seat. Two months later, newly installed governor Oscar Colquitt, an antiprohibitionist, appointed Joseph Dibrell to the court after the resignation of Frank Williams. Although the court rarely decided any case touching on prohibition, Dibrell was perceived by prohibitionists as an "anti." Because all three members of the court had been appointed since the 1910 election, each was required to run for office in the 1912 election. Brown, a well-respected veteran of the court, had no primary opponent. Dibrell was challenged in the Democratic primary by William Hawkins, an ardent prohibitionist. Instead of running for his seat on the court, Ramsey resigned to run for governor as a prohibitionist against the incumbent Colquitt. As a result, Colquitt appointed Nelson Phillips to Ramsey's seat. Phillips, also an anti, was challenged by several pros in the primary. When the primary election results were tallied, Phillips had survived with a plurality of the vote, sufficient because a majority was not required to obtain the nomination. Dibrell had been defeated by Hawkins, becoming the first incumbent justice of the supreme court to lose a primary election, required since 1903 for Democratic Party candidates.[68]

Between 1913 and 1920 the supreme court's output declined substantially, caused by two events: First, the illnesses and later deaths of Chief Justice Brown and Associate Justice

Texas Supreme Court, circa early 1920s. Thomas Benton Greenwood, Nelson Phillips, and William Pierson (from left to right). Courtesy Texas State Library and Archives Commission.

James E. Yantis led to a decline in the number of decided cases. Second, the inability of Justice Hawkins to contribute meaningfully to writing the court's opinions, and his contrary willingness to write lengthy, indeed exhausting, dissenting opinions, left the court years behind in its docket. The legislature attempted to remedy the problem of delay by creating in 1918, as it had in 1879, a commission of appeals to clear much of the court's backlog of cases. It also adopted legislation intended to limit the supreme court's jurisdiction, legislation that had the opposite effect. The court's backlog was reduced after Hawkins's primary defeat in 1920 and stable supreme court membership from 1921 to 1934. In 1927 a proposed amendment to the judiciary article of the constitution, to increase the number of supreme court justices to nine, was soundly defeated (164,036 to 27,949). Despite stability in the supreme court, and despite the existence of the commission of appeals, the court remained substantially behind in its docket through the 1940s.[69]

The commission of appeals attached to the supreme court remained in existence until the court was expanded by constitutional amendment from three members to nine in 1945. Despite the supreme court's efforts, it has consistently fallen behind in its docket in the post–World War II era. This may be a result of the need of members of the court to gain name recognition for election purposes, particularly since such races became competitive and expensive. The time spent traveling, giving speeches, and raising money inevitably leaves less time to write opinions. The supreme court's backlog surely is also a consequence of fourteen courts of appeals deciding several thousand cases annually, which requires the supreme court to spend a substantial amount of time deciding whether to hear or dismiss cases decided by the courts of appeals. Further, a system that encourages litigants to file writs of mandamus to the supreme court while the case is ongoing in the district court also dissipates the court's limited time.[70]

The Texas Court of Criminal Appeals received the assistance of a two-person commission of appeals in 1925 as a result of its own backlog. This commission remained in existence until the adoption in 1966 of a constitutional amendment enlarging the court of criminal appeals to five persons by making the two commissioners its fourth and fifth judges. Continued growth in its caseload led to the addition of two additional commissioners in 1971 to assist the court of criminal appeals. In 1977, another constitutional amendment to Article V, section 4 increased the size of the court of criminal appeals to nine members. Three years later, again by constitutional amendment, the Texas Courts of Civil Appeals were renamed the Texas Courts of Appeals and were given jurisdiction over initial appeals in all criminal cases other than capital cases. This change was necessitated in part by the constitutional criminal procedure revolution of the Supreme Court of the United States in the 1960s and 1970s, which generated more legal issues to be decided by appellate courts.[71]

One example of the unwillingness of the drafters of the Texas constitutions and the Texas legislature to pay for a justice system may be shown through the pay of members of the supreme court. The 1845 constitution set the salary of members of the supreme court at $2,000. That increased in the 1866 constitution to $4,500, which was maintained in the 1869 constitution. When the delegates produced the final product of the penurious 1876 constitution, the salary of justices on the supreme court was reduced to $3,550, despite objection by some delegates. When the appellate judiciary was reorganized in 1891–92, the salary of the members of the supreme court was constitutionally set at $4,000, still $500 less than the salary in the 1866 and 1869 constitutions. That remained the salary of the members of the court for twenty-one years, when the salaries of the members of the court were raised to $5,000. Thus, between 1866 and 1913 the salary of members of the supreme court increased by $500. Even in an era in which deflation was a pernicious if periodic problem, this is astonishing.[72]

THE STRUCTURE OF THE TEXAS JUDICIAL SYSTEM

The complicated structure of the Texas judiciary is found in Article V, section 1 of the 1876 constitution: "The judicial power of this State shall be vested in one Supreme Court, in a Court of Appeals, in District Courts, in County Courts, in Commissioners' Courts, in Courts of Justices of the Peace, and in such other courts as may be established by law." From the simple declaration made in 1836, Texas had six constitutionally created courts by 1876. A two-part 1898 article in the *Quarterly of the Texas State Historical Association* by University of Texas Law Department professor John C. Townes traced the history of the courts in Texas. Townes noted that the 1876 constitution created "two courts of last resort" and "four classes of courts of original jurisdiction, namely, district, county, county commissioners', and justices'." The 1891 constitutional amendment creating the court of criminal appeals for all criminal appellate matters and creating several courts of civil appeals hearing appeals in civil matters, decisions of which might be heard by the Texas Supreme Court, complicated further the Texas judicial branch. The difficulty with this division of labor is that some issues, particularly constitutional issues, may arise either in civil or criminal proceedings. When that happens, and the Texas Supreme Court and the Texas Court of Criminal Appeals differ on the constitutionality of the state's action, which equal supreme court's interpretation is supreme?

This issue of jurisdiction particularly vexed the courts when the politics of prohibition and suppression of vice created more possibilities for conflict. The legislature acted to separate card and billiards games from liquor: "If any person shall play at any game with cards at any house for retailing spirituous liquors, storehouse, tavern, inn . . . ," that person committed a crime. Koenig was charged with the crime of playing cards at a house for retailing spirituous liquors. The "house" was a building in Cuero controlled by a private organization, the Cuero German Turnverein, where members and their guests met, socialized, played billiards and cards, and drank beer and liquor (this being a German community club). The court of criminal appeals held that the house was not in the business of retailing spirituous liquors. A year later, the supreme court heard *State v. Austin Club* (1895). The state sued for nonpayment of an occupation tax on retailers of spirituous liquors. The supreme court held that, because the issue was so closely related to the penal code, "we feel constrained to follow the decision of the court of criminal appeals in this matter."

Less than a decade later, the issue arose again. In 1903 the city of Galveston was governed by a body of commissioners appointed by the governor in the aftermath of the devastating hurricane of 1900. Those commissioners adopted ordinances to operate the city. Was the appointment by the governor of those commissioners to govern Galveston constitutional? In *Ex parte Lewis* (1903) the court of criminal appeals held the law unconstitutional. Three months later, the supreme court, in *Brown v. City of Galveston* (1903) declared the appointment constitutional after noting the contrary conclusion of the court of criminal appeals. A constitutional amendment eventually resolved this conflict.

The most bitter conflict arose when the court of criminal appeals and the supreme court reached contrary conclusions concerning the constitutionality of the "pool hall" law. The legislature adopted a law requiring county commissioners to place on the ballot, once a sufficient number of voters signed a petition for such a referendum, the question whether pool halls should be permitted to operate within the county. In *Ex parte Mitchell*, issued on June 23, 1915, the supreme court held the law unconstitutional. In *Ex parte Mode*, issued on October 13, 1915, the court of criminal appeals reaffirmed its contrary opinion in *Ex parte Francis*, issued on January 7, 1914, which held the "pool hall" law constitutional. The court of criminal appeals raised the stakes two months later in *State ex rel. McNamara v. Clark*, issued

on December 15, 1915. In a twenty-seven-page opinion it excoriated the supreme court's decision in *Mitchell*, claimed *Mitchell* had been negated by a subsequent supreme court opinion, and demanded adherence by the supreme court to its interpretation. All three opinions of the court of criminal appeals were written by Judge Alfred John Harper, and in each case Judge William Davidson dissented, making each case a two-to-one decision (*Mitchell* was also two to one). This impasse was resolved when Harper resigned and was replaced on the court of criminal appeals by Wright Morrow. Morrow authored the court's opinion in *Lyle v. State*, issued on February 28, 1917, which rejected the court's opinions in *Mode*, *Francis*, and *Clark* and joined the supreme court's conclusion in *Mitchell* declaring unconstitutional the pool hall law.[73]

Writing in 1924, Leon Green concluded, "Our court organization is organically diseased, and, therefor, radical treatment will be required." It was organically diseased in large part because the large number of courts created "[q]uestions of jurisdiction that make a wilderness of our procedure." Green's complaint fell on deaf ears.[74]

ELECTING JUDGES IN A ONE-PARTY STATE

Until the late 1970s, Texas was a Democratic Party stronghold, and appellate judges were almost always Democrats. Elections were largely low-key, and the succession of judges occurred more often through resignation and appointment rather than through hard-fought nomination battles within the Democratic Party, although the latter occasionally occurred. In the 1880s two incumbent Texas Supreme Court justices, Robert Gould and Alexander Walker, were not renominated by the party, which at that time nominated its candidates without a primary vote. In 1903 and 1905, after the Democratic Party had successfully defeated the challenge presented by the People's (Populist) Party and were subject to only minor challenge from Republicans, the Terrell Election Laws were adopted, providing for primary elections for any party receiving over one hundred thousand votes in the previous general election (that is, the Democratic Party). Even after adoption of the Terrell Election Laws, a majority of judges reached the appellate courts through appointment rather than election. If a judge resigned or retired before his term was over, the Democratic governor possessed the authority to appoint his replacement. The appointed judge then ran as an incumbent, and usually as an unopposed incumbent, in the Democratic primary.[75]

The battle over Prohibition in Texas created a temporary end to this system beginning with the 1912 elections, when incumbent justice Joseph Dibrell was defeated by William Hawkins in the primary. Hawkins served for the remaining two years of the term and ran unopposed for reelection in 1914. By 1916, Associate Justice Nelson Phillips had been appointed chief justice after the death of T. J. Brown. James Yantis was appointed to serve the seat vacated by Phillips's move. Both Phillips and Yantis were challenged in the primary by prohibitionists. The contest quickly deteriorated after the challengers attacked the character of the incumbents. However, both were renominated. In the 1920 election, both Phillips and Hawkins were on the primary ballot. Phillips easily won renomination. Hawkins was challenged by two court of civil appeals judges and was soundly defeated in the runoff by William Pierson, becoming the second incumbent supreme court justice to lose a primary election.

After the trauma of the 1910s, the pattern of judicial elections largely returned to its previous state: sitting judges and justices were more often than not unopposed for reelection. Consistent population growth created a need for new district courts, giving governors the opportunity to appoint supporters to judicial positions. The expansion of the supreme court to nine members in 1945 and the addition of the final three courts of civil appeals in the 1960s created new appellate positions, allowing for the election of more judges. Finally, judicial positions opened when sitting judges resigned or died, allowing the Democratic governor to make judicial appointments. A majority of judges between 1940 and 1982 initially came to the bench by appointment, not election. Further, the vast majority of incumbents faced no challenger at election time. Between 1952 and 1962, just 4.9 percent of trial judges and 6.6 percent of appellate judges were defeated in election contests. And between 1922 and 1976, no incumbent justice of the supreme court was defeated in an election.[76]

ELECTING JUDGES IN A TWO-PARTY STATE

The combined appointment/election system remained stable into the 1980s, when Texas shifted from a strong Democratic Party state to a politically competitive state. The election of Republican William P. "Bill" Clements as governor in the 1978 election, and the strong support for Republican presidential candidate Ronald Reagan in 1980 was evidence of this political shift. In both Dallas and Harris counties in the late 1970s and early 1980s, a number of Republicans were elected to the district courts, and a number of Democratic judges switched their political affiliation to the Republican Party. By mid-1985, thirty-two of thirty-six district judges in Dallas County were Republicans.[77]

In a 1962 survey the top two reasons that would "always disqualify" an applicant to the bench were, in order, an unsuccessful law practice (21.1 percent) and being "known as a Republican" (20.7 percent). By 1978, that second disqualifying characteristic began to change, in fits and starts. The election of Clements as governor was one harbinger. A second harbinger of change was that in Dallas County three incumbent Democratic judges were defeated in 1978 by their Republican challengers, including two court of civil appeals judges. However, just 14 percent of the 182 judicial elections were contested that year. In 1980, when Ronald Reagan headed the Republican Party ticket, 24 percent of the 173 judicial races were contested, including 38 percent of the appellate court races. But more than half (ten of nineteen) of Republican incumbent judges lost their races, compared with just 31 percent (four of thirteen) of Democratic incumbents. In the off-year election of 1982, Democrats reasserted their hold on the judiciary, winning all of the contested races in which the incumbent was a Democrat and winning nearly 60 percent (23 of 39) of the races in which the incumbent was a Republican. President Reagan's popularity in Texas in 1984 reversed those Democratic gains from two years earlier; just four of twenty incumbent Democrats won their races against Republicans, while all five incumbent Republican judges won against their Democratic opponents.[78]

The rise of a viable two-party system in counties such as Dallas and Harris in the early 1980s did not immediately penetrate the Texas Supreme Court or the Texas Court of Criminal Appeals. In 1979, after Texas Supreme Court justice Sam Johnson was appointed to the United States Court of Appeals for the Fifth Circuit, Governor Clements appointed Republican Will Garwood to replace him. Despite spending an estimated million dollars of his own money, and having Ronald Reagan at the top of the ticket, Garwood lost in 1980 to Democrat C. L. Ray. For the next seven years, even though several Republicans were elected to courts of appeals, all of the members of the two highest courts in Texas were Democrats, including Ruby Kless Sondock, the first female member of the supreme court since the All-Woman Court appointed to hear *Johnson v.*

Darr in 1925. The end of Democratic control began in mid-1987 with the decision of the Texas State Commission on Judicial Conduct to reprimand Associate Justice Ray and to admonish Associate Justice William Kilgarlin. The commission found Ray violated Canon 2 of the Code of Judicial Conduct by transferring cases after a request from Pat Maloney, a San Antonio personal injury lawyer who had contributed money to Ray's election campaign. Ray was also found to have accepted several free trips on private planes, including flights from attorneys with cases pending in the supreme court, in violation of Canon 5C(4). Kilgarlin was admonished by the commission after it found that his law clerks had accepted a trip to Las Vegas from a lawyer who had business before the court. Kilgarlin and Ray filed a defamation suit against an attorney who formerly worked at the supreme court and who testified against them before the Judicial Affairs Committee of the Texas House of Representatives. They sent letters requesting donations to finance the suit. Included among the addressees were attorneys who had cases pending before the supreme court. Not surprisingly, the commission found this action improper. This was the first time the commission had sanctioned any member of the supreme court.[79]

At the national level, Republicans made political headway during the 1980s attacking "judicial activism," an attack echoed in Texas. Republicans charged the Democratic Texas Supreme Court with politicizing the judiciary and creating rather than following the law in its rulings. For some, it was sufficient simply that the Texas Supreme Court had refused to hear the appeal in *Texaco v. Pennzoil*, allowing the $10 billion verdict against Texaco to stand, especially since Pennzoil attorney Joe Jamail had liberally supported the candidacies of several of the court's members. For others it was a perceived shift favoring plaintiffs in tort law that raised their awareness of the court. Finally, the reprimand and admonishment of Ray and

Kilgarlin was offered as evidence of a lack of impartiality on the court. All these events made the 1988 judicial elections transformative.[80]

The call by Republican governor Bill Clements, back in office after a four-year hiatus, for Democrats Ray and Kilgarlin to resign was muted not only because it sounded like a poorly disguised excuse to name more Republicans to the court, but also because it seemed intended to deflect the attention on Clements for his role in improperly paying football players attending his alma mater, Southern Methodist University. Shortly after the sanctions of Ray and Kilgarlin, Chief Justice John Hill announced his resignation, effective January 1, 1988, to promote reform of the Texas judiciary through the adoption of a merit selection system for judges. In December 1987, CBS's *60 Minutes* televised a report provocatively titled "Justice for Sale?" The report, in which correspondent Mike Wallace interviewed several Texas Supreme Court justices as well as Jamail, cast a dark shadow on the Texas judiciary, for a viewer watching the report likely concluded the answer to the question posed in the title was "yes." A month later, a similar report in *Time* magazine was published. National coverage of the Texas Supreme Court followed intense and critical coverage of the court in a number of Texas newspapers, in *Texas Monthly*, and in *Texas Lawyer*.[81]

In late 1987, Clements appointed Tom Phillips to replace Hill as chief justice. Two other Democrats resigned from the court in 1988, and Clements appointed Republicans Barbara Culver and Eugene Cook to replace them. All three ran for election in the November 1988 election. This meant six seats on the supreme court were on the 1988 ballot. Incumbent vice president George H. W. Bush was the Republican presidential nominee that year. Two of the three sitting Republican justices, Phillips and Cook, were elected. An open and contested seat was won by the Democrats, and Democrat Raul Gonzalez, supported by many Republicans and by insurance and other defense interests,

defeated the Republican candidate. The final contested seat was between Republican challenger Nathan Hecht and the incumbent, William Kilgarlin. Hecht defeated Kilgarlin, still tainted by the admonishment given him the year before by the State Commission on Judicial Conduct. Two years later, Republican John Cornyn was elected, making it four Republicans on the supreme court. After the 1992 election, the Texas Supreme Court consisted of a Republican majority. By 1999, all of the members of the Texas Supreme Court were Republicans, as the state became solidly Republican.[82]

The 1988 race for Chief Justice between Phillips and Ted Z. Robertson, then a sitting associate justice, involved raising tremendous amounts of money. Phillips raised over $1 million, and Robertson, $1.9 million. The candidates in the six races for the Texas Supreme Court raised just under $11 million. Their financial support was largely divided along interest group lines. Phillips was supported by business interests and the Texas Medical Association, and Robertson was supported largely by plaintiffs' personal injury lawyers. Phillips won that race but was required to run again in 1990, this time against Oscar Mauzy, an associate justice of the court running for chief justice. Each candidate again received financial support from distinct interest groups, but Phillips now held a commanding financial advantage. At the end of October, Phillips reported receiving campaign contributions of over $2.4 million, while Mauzy declared contributions totaling approximately $950,000. Phillips was reelected.[83]

In 1998, *60 Minutes* returned to Texas, asking whether justice was still for sale. Former chief justice John Hill again spoke with Mike Wallace about Texas judicial politics. Hill concluded that although things had changed only slightly (mentioning that a lawyer was limited to giving no more than five thousand dollars in campaign contributions to any justice), he believed the court was "first-rate." By 1998 only two Democrats remained on the court, one of whom, Raul Gonzalez, was retiring. The *60 Minutes* report noted the close race incumbent Democratic justice Rose Spector found herself in and followed her on the campaign trail. With a popular Republican incumbent, George W. Bush, running for reelection as governor, the major political battles were won by Republicans, including all Republicans running for seats on the supreme court.[84]

The court of criminal appeals also saw contested races, but its jurisdictional limitations made it difficult for candidates to raise money, leaving television advertising out of reach for most candidates. In 1990, Morris Overstreet became the first African American judge to be elected to either of Texas's two highest courts. The first Republican elected to the Texas Court of Criminal Appeals was Lawrence Meyers in 1992. The court of criminal appeals has changed as a result of broader changes in Texas politics.

Since 1999 it, too, has consisted entirely of Republicans.

But the more things change, the more things remain the same. In the 2006 judicial races in Dallas County, no Republican won any of the twenty-eight contested seats. Dallas County also elected the first black district attorney in the state, Craig Watkins. And in 2008, no Republican incumbent district court judge in Dallas County filed for reelection. The 2008 judicial elections in Harris County, encompassing Houston, followed a similar pattern. The strong showing there of Democratic presidential candidate Barack Obama led to a near sweep by Democrats of local judicial races. By 2008, Texas was again a two-party state, but in a different way than in the past. Although statewide it was a Republican stronghold, much of the state was divided into one-party Republican districts and one-party Democratic districts.[85]

SEVEN

Criminal Law and Civil Rights

★

THE STATE possesses a monopoly on defining and prosecuting crime, giving it extraordinary power over the lives and liberties of its residents. That power is meliorated in part by the power of the majority to vote regularly to decide who will serve in the legislative and executive branches, and in Texas, in the judicial branch as well. The state's power is further limited by the federal and Texas constitutions, which bar it from infringing a person's constitutional rights. The state's exercise of its monopoly power is also limited by the cultural norms of the state, values that reflect the manner in which a criminal act is both defined and used or avoided. Finally, when the people believe the state has failed to protect them, they may take extralegal measures to restore or maintain order.

The republic and the state of Texas were founded by men with a conflicted sense of the relation between the state and the individual. Texans justified the revolution against Mexico as necessary to protect their rights against a despotic regime: "Finally, after appeal and remonstrance proved in vain, . . . they raised the standard of independence and took up their arms in defense of their liberties." But this independent streak included a truculence toward authority, a "pronounced individualism" that made enforcing the criminal law hazardous. This was joined by a history of violence in the state from its beginnings.[1]

This chapter combines the close cousins of the criminal law and civil rights. Many of the individual liberties protected in the Bill of Rights of the United States and Texas constitutions, including the right to a trial by jury, the right to confront witnesses, and the right to compel witnesses to come to court to testify on behalf of the defendant, protect a person against the undue exercise of the criminal prosecution power of the state. Civil rights, including the right to vote, are important in limiting the exercise of state power by those entrusted with its use.

THE COMMON LAW OF CRIMES AND THE CODIFICATION OF THE CRIMINAL LAW

The federal government and most states, including Texas, define crime by statute. An act by a person that does not violate an existing criminal statute cannot be punished by the initiation of a criminal prosecution. In eighteenth-century England, however, what constituted a crime was not statutorily defined but defined by judges in deciding cases and known as the common law of crimes. By 1800 the use of the common law of crimes by the federal government was controversial. In the early nineteenth century the adoption of codes of law in France was cited as evidence that the common law was not the only way to organize a legal system. Peter S. Du Ponceau, a Philadelphia lawyer and a native of France, translated and published the French penal code in the *American Review* in 1811. Jeremy Bentham unsuccessfully advocated an end to the common law in England. In America, Bentham's followers, including Edward Livingston, a transplanted Louisianan, took up the cause of codification. Although Livingston's proposed codes were not adopted by Louisiana, his penal codes served as the basis for the 1856 Texas Penal Code and Texas Code of Criminal Procedure.[2]

The first congress of the Republic of Texas created a statutory list of crimes. But Texas legislatures regularly included a provision allowing a person to be charged with any crime punishable under the English common law. For example, the 1836 penal code declared criminal "all offences known to the common law of England as now practised and understood, which are not provided for in this act."[3]

This changed in the 1856 penal code. Article 3 declared that no act was a crime "unless the same is expressly defined and the penalty affixed by the written law of this State." In *Fennell v. State* (1869), the Texas Supreme Court held no indictment could issue except for acts explicitly prohibited in the code. It dismissed an indictment for the common law crime of sodomy, even though an 1860 amendment to the penal code made it a crime for anyone to commit "with mankind or beast the abominable and detestable crime against nature." The statute did not define the act of the "crime against nature," making reference to it legally insufficient.[4]

DEVELOPING THE CRIMINAL LAW IN TEXAS

Stephen F. Austin's 1824 colonization laws included twenty-six articles comprising the criminal laws necessary to protect the "good order" of the colony. The first five articles concerned the relationship of Indians to the colony. Article 6 acknowledged the absence of law enforcement by requiring residents to apprehend those who committed serious crimes. Another five articles concerned issues of slavery. Several criminal regulations concerned proper moral behavior. But the 1824 decree was the merest shell of a criminal code. It assumed a Spanish/Mexican legal system with some engrafted common-law ideas. Mexican Texas was a poverty-stricken colony, and Austin required a convict to pay for the costs of his trial.[5]

The development in Texas of an American-infused society helped lead to writing the constitution of the state of Coahuila and Texas (1827). Article 192 commanded the colonial congress to "establish the trial by jury in criminal cases," a process unknown to the civil law system of Spain (Castile) and Mexico but commonly viewed by Americans as necessary to protect individual liberty from any oppressive government.[6]

Decree 277 (April 1834) reorganized the entire judicial system in Texas, including the criminal justice system. Article 2 expanded the declaration of the 1827 constitution: "All causes civil and criminal shall be tried by juries."

Decree 277 was never operative, but Texians made the absence of trial by jury a justification for the rebellion against Mexico. To quell restless Anglo-Texans, the Mexican government planned a military occupation of Texas by mid-1835 and demanded the arrest of William B. Travis; Samuel May Williams, a land speculator and partner of Stephen Austin; and Lorenzo de Zavala. Once arrested, they were to be tried by the military, not a jury. This demand convinced some Texians that a revolution was both necessary and inevitable.[7]

The 1836 constitution of the Republic of Texas required the legislature as "soon as convenience will permit" to create "a penal code formed on principles of reformation, and not of vindictive justice." The first statute defining crimes and misdemeanors did not meet this goal. In addition to murder, crimes such as arson, theft of a slave, robbery, burglary, and counterfeiting were punishable only by death, a consequence of the absence of any Texas prison and any money to build one. When the punishment was not death, the statute ordinarily assigned whipping, branding, monetary fines, and some jail time as the appropriate punishment.[8]

The state of Texas drafted a penal code in 1848 that tempered the harshness of the 1836 act. Murder was divided into first- and second-degree murder, reserving the death penalty for the former. Manslaughter was punishable by a term of one to ten years at hard labor. Robbery, rape, burglary, arson, and counterfeiting were now punishable by hard labor in the penitentiary. The lenience of the crimes and punishment act of 1848 is best ascribed to the insistence by the framers of the 1845 constitution of the state of Texas that a penitentiary be built "as early as practicable," followed by the adoption of the legislature in both 1846 and 1848 (a week before the penal code was adopted) of laws providing for the development of a penitentiary. The first inmate at the Huntsville penitentiary arrived in late 1849, before it was completed.[9]

Even as the 1854 legislature amended the penal code, it hired three commissioners to arrange a code of the civil and criminal laws. Their proposed penal code and code of criminal procedure was adopted by the legislature in 1856 with just a few modifications. The penal code followed the model proposed by Edward Livingston thirty years earlier—one based on rehabilitation rather than retribution.[10]

The 1856 penal code reflected the principles of reformation suggested in the 1836 constitution. It provided for a chaplain and a physician for the inmates at the penitentiary and required that "[a]ll prisoners confined in the Penitentiary are to be treated with humanity." (This did not include serving prisoners alcoholic beverages.) It provided for the defense of insanity. It also provided that no person be sentenced to death if the crime was committed by the defendant before he was seventeen years old. Further, no child under the age of nine could be convicted of any offense, and no child between nine and thirteen years of age could be convicted unless "it shall appear by proof that he had discretion sufficient to understand the nature and illegality of the act."[11]

The 1856 code was substantially supplemented by acts adopted in 1858 and 1860. The 1858 revision altered or added about 140 articles; the 1860 act amended about 25 provisions. Both expanded the use of the criminal law in relation to the issue of slavery.[12]

THE 1856 CODE OF CRIMINAL PROCEDURE

The code of criminal procedure is a thorough and relatively modern system of criminal procedure. It stated the terms of executing a search warrant, clarified how a grand jury may convene and indict a person for a crime, listed applicable trial rules of evidence and how judges must construe them, and explained how to execute judgments in criminal matters. The Texas Code of Criminal Procedure was a product of the common law and American constitutional law.[13]

FORMALISM IN THE TEXAS COURT OF APPEALS

The awful power of the state to take a person's life or liberty made the framers of both the federal and Texas constitutions wary of its exercise. The framers constitutionally limited the exercise of a government's prosecutorial authority, and a fear of its abuse has often made courts exacting in their requirements for initiating a prosecution and in upholding a guilty verdict. This demand for exactness is a type of legal formalism, for courts ask whether the government met the formal requirements of the law even when the failure to do so is readily characterized as inadvertent or harmless.

Thus, legal formalism, often a term of opprobrium, has an important function in law. But formalism can also take a shape in which form always trumps substance, in "artificially" segregating the law from the lives of the people whom the law serves. In several periods in the legal history of Texas, such formalism has been the predominant understanding of judicial decision making. This has particularly been true in the criminal jurisprudence of Texas.

The Texas Court of Appeals spent much of its existence between 1876 and 1891 crafting artificial legal distinctions that earned it the rebuke of commentators and made it subject to ridicule. It is not coincidental that its decisions were issued when vigilance committees organized in parts of the state as a partial response to the failure of the criminal justice system to reduce lawlessness.[14]

One example of the court's hypertechnical interpretation of the law was its debate whether particular errors in the form of the verdict constituted reversible error. Defendant Shaw appealed a verdict that stated, "We, the jury, the defendant guilty." The court of appeals reversed, holding that the jury's failure to include the word *find* violated a provision of the code of criminal procedure requiring the jury to "find" the defendant guilty or not guilty. The trial court's failure to ask the jury to rectify this error before accepting the verdict required reversal, for "no informality in their verdict can be corrected save with [the jury's] consent." Shortly thereafter, the court of appeals was asked whether a verdict of "guity" was error. Earlier decisions of Texas appellate courts had held a verdict of "gilty" was an inconsequential error. The court concluded that "it may now be stated as a general rule that neither bad spelling nor ungrammatical findings of a jury will vitiate a verdict when the sense is clear." This sensible rule for a semiliterate society was then disregarded by the court, for it decided that "guity" was unclear, requiring reversal of the conviction. Later in 1879 the court was asked whether "guily" was sufficiently clear to withstand the defendant's appeal. It distinguished "guity" from "guily" with the following comment: "[I]n the present case the word 'guily' is followed by the words 'as charged in the indictment;' and by separating the syllables so as to place the first four letters in one syllable, and having the *y* alone for the second, and giving to the letter *i* the short sound, the sound so produced would be, if not identical, at any rate nearly so, with the ordinary pronunciation of the word if written 'guilty.'" Because the verdict was in written form, it is unclear why the pronunciation of the misspelled word "guily" makes any difference; in *Taylor*, in which the court assessed the word "guity," it seems just as possible that the foreman simply spelled the word as he pronounced it, with a swallowed *l*. In neither case does it seem as though the spelling (orthographic) error could possibly make any discernible difference to the jury's intended meaning by its verdict.[15]

The court later revived this debate. In *Walker v. State* (1883), the verdict was, "Wee the jurors finde the defendant gilty and of *mrder* in the first degree." The absence of the *u* in the word "guilty" had already been found unimportant in an 1874 decision. The issue in *Walker* was the apparent misspelling of "murder, also lacking a 'u'." The court of appeals decided the misspelling was insufficient to reverse the verdict. But the court in several other cases maintained its firmness on "guity," declaring it reversible error in several subsequent cases. However, it affirmed a verdict that read "guilly." "Guilly," like "guily" before it, was clear. This was absurd, for the court of appeals offered neither the clarity of a formal rule (for example, "anything spelled other than 'guilty' will be reversible error") nor the sensibility of a rule rooted in a realistic assessment of the society at that time (for example, "because of the lack of educational opportunity and the orthographic difficulties of the English language, 'guily,' 'guilly', and 'guity' will all be treated as equivalent to 'guilty'").[16]

An additional reason to question the court's absurd interpretation was its awareness of the doctrine of *idem sonans*, words that sound alike. In *Goode v. State* (1877) the defendant claimed error because the victim's name was Mary Etta, which was written in the information (the document that charged a defendant with a misdemeanor) as Marietta. The court quoted a criminal law treatise: "'The law does not take notice of orthography.'" This sensible idea was followed two years later. But changes in the membership of the court of appeals altered this approach.[17]

A second issue in which the court's formalism caused a great deal of trouble was the challenge to an indictment, the document that charged a defendant with a felony. Texas constitutions followed the U.S. Constitution in requiring the government to institute a felony criminal prosecution by obtaining an indictment from a grand jury, a body of citizens of the state or local jurisdiction. An indictment will issue only if the prosecutor convinces the grand jury that probable cause exists that the defendant committed the crime alleged by

the government. The 1876 constitution also declared, "All prosecutions shall be carried on in the name and by the authority of 'The State of Texas,' and conclude 'against the peace and dignity of the State,'" language copied from the 1856 code of criminal procedure.[18]

In *Cox v. State* (1880), the defendants were convicted of murder. After the court of appeals heard the appeal, defense counsel moved in rehearing for a disposition on the constitutionality of the indictment, which concluded, "against the peace and dignity of the *statute*" rather than "against the peace and dignity of the *State*." This was the first time defense counsel claimed the indictment was defective. The court held the indictment was fatally defective, and no conviction could stand when based on a fatally defective indictment. More importantly, the court of appeals held this claim "may be availed of at any time," because this was a constitutional right held by the defendant. *Cox* appeared to be based on either a misreading or exaggerated reading of past cases. Further, *Cox* made little practical sense. It encouraged the defendant to make his objection to the indictment as late as possible. If he was acquitted, double jeopardy attached; if he was convicted on a defective indictment, he was guaranteed a new trial on appeal. Finally, if the statute of limitations expired while the case was on appeal, he was a free man. Three years after *Cox*, the court of appeals reaffirmed its strict understanding of this rule. It held that an information that began "In the name and authority of the State" was fatally defective because it failed to include the words "of Texas" at the end of the phrase; it held that an information concluding "against the peace and dignity of State" also was fatally defective for leaving out "the" between "of" and "State"; and it held that an indictment that added "this the third day of November, 1882," after "against the peace and dignity of the State" was also defective.[19]

The court of appeals also required extraordinary specificity in the indictment. The failure

First murder trial in Hale County, Texas, 1892. Courtesy Texas State Library and Archives Commission.

to state specifically all of the elements of the crime and the specifics of the manner in which the crime was allegedly committed made the indictment fatally defective. In *Reed v. State* (1883), the court of appeals declared that the indictment was defective because it failed to allege the money stolen was "*taken from the possession of any one.*" The indictment merely alleged that Reed broke into Simon's house and carried away Simon's money. The indictment was defective because it did not allege that the money was in Simon's possession when it was taken. More astonishingly, the court of appeals held in 1887 that an indictment alleging that "the defendant intended to fraudulently take the personal property of J. W. Bilgen and R. Y. Holman without *their* consent" was defective because it "must allege that the taking was without the consent of *either* of said owners."[20]

Although the code of criminal procedure was based on Edward Livingston's penal code, the Texas drafters did not adopt Livingston's forms for indictments. Instead, they ignored the issue. The technical manner in which the court of appeals viewed indictments led the legislature to adopt the Common Sense Indictment Act of 1881. The act provided that an indictment "shall be deemed sufficient which charges the commission of the offense in ordinary and concise language in such a manner as to enable a person of common understanding to know what is meant." The act offered as "sufficient" twenty-eight separate forms for different crimes using simple language (for example, for the crime of aggravated assault, the proper form was "A.B. did make an aggravated assault on C.D."). The legislature then concluded the standard by which courts were to determine whether the indictment was sufficient: "An indictment shall not be held insufficient . . . which does not prejudice the substantial rights of the defendant."[21]

The court of appeals initially viewed the Common Sense Indictment Act favorably. In two 1882 cases it rejected challenges to indictments that followed the language of the act. These unanimous decisions were written by two of the three members of the court of appeals. The appointment of Samuel Willson to the court after the death of Clinton McKamy

Winkler changed the court's view of the statute. In several cases decided later in 1882, the court held unconstitutional the Common Sense Indictment Act because it violated the right of an individual to an indictment as found in the bill of rights of the 1876 constitution. The defendants had all been indicted by a grand jury. How had the court reached the conclusion that the act was unconstitutional? It held that an "indictment" as meant by the constitution "must charge explicitly all that is essential to constitute the offense." The simple forms provided for in the Common Sense Indictment Act were "mere conclusions of law" and thus constitutionally impermissible. The difficulty of "charging instrument" law was not remedied until constitutional and statutory amendments were adopted in 1985.[22]

THE "UNWRITTEN LAW": ADULTERY AND JUSTIFIABLE HOMICIDE

The authority of a husband to kill a man engaged in adultery with his wife was traceable back to the law of the Visigoths and Roman civil law. It was included in Las Siete Partidas, a code of Spanish law from the thirteenth century descended from Roman civil law that occasionally applied in Mexican Texas. In 1856 the legislature codified this "unwritten law," declaring "justifiable" a homicide "upon one taken in the act of adultery with the wife, provided the killing take place before the parties to the act have separated." In order to avoid any collusion, Article 562 declared an unjustified homicide any killing "where it appears that there has been, on the part of the husband, any connivance in or assent to the adulterous connection." Under English common law, the husband's killing of the adulterer was not justified, but it reduced the husband's crime from murder to manslaughter. The extension of the unwritten law was also permitted in Georgia,

New Mexico, and Utah. Its interpretation in those jurisdictions was either more limited (all of them) or much more rarely invoked (New Mexico and Utah) than in Texas.[23]

The Texas statute was deliberately sexist. The court of criminal appeals held the law inapplicable in the only appellate case in which a wronged wife asserted the statute. From Texas's earliest days, the "rule's primary purpose was to help husbands to cope with infidelity in a society where law enforcement and public surveillance were often nonexistent." A Texas husband who obtained a divorce because of adultery faced a number of legal obstacles in making the divorce financially painful to his former wife. Further, the practical necessity of having a wife as a partner on the frontier made divorce or abandonment a decision fraught with risks for the husband. Finally, self-help fit the culture of honor of the South.[24]

The unwritten law was first interpreted in an appellate court opinion in 1885. Anthony Price shot and killed William Chandler after he found his wife Lucy and Chandler in the corn pen. Chandler's mother testified Chandler had been "playing the fool" with Lucy Price, and witnesses agreed Chandler had given Lucy a number of gifts. Both men were holding Price's gun while Lucy begged her husband not to shoot Chandler: "He, Chandler, then let loose the gun, and I shot him." Price also stated:

> I do not know what they were doing. I did not take time to investigate that. I knew they were there for no good. That was the only time I ever saw them lying down together anywhere. I can't say that I thought they were having connection with each other at the time I called to them at the door of the crib; but by finding them together I supposed that their object was to have connection with each other, and I shot him, Chandler, because I felt that that was the object of their being there together at that time.

Price was convicted of manslaughter. The Texas Court of Appeals reversed. The court broadly interpreted the law, in particular the language "taken in the act of adultery with the wife." It held that the husband did not have to find the wife and murder victim "in the very act of illicit intercourse or copulation." Analogizing to the manner in which the crime of adultery was proven, the court held it sufficient evidence simply to note the time (night), place (corn pen outside of the family home), and circumstances (Lucy Price's initial denial to her husband that anyone was with her in the corn pen). Although the husband might make a mistake of fact, a "party may always act upon reasonable appearances, and his guilt depends upon the reasonableness of the appearances, judged of from his own standpoint."[25]

The breadth of the court's initial interpretation of the law is demonstrated in *Morrison v. State* (1898). Morrison shot his wife's male companion while the deceased and the wife were walking on the street. Morrison's initial statement after the killing was that he wanted to shoot his wife dead, but the deceased got in the way, and he shot in self-defense. At trial, he claimed justification based on the now written "unwritten law." Morrison testified that after hearing the couple copulate while standing outside the room they were in, he waited for them about thirty steps away from the door. When they left the room and began walking, he accosted them. The trial court refused to instruct the jury on Morrison's claim of justifiable homicide, and Morrison was convicted. The court of criminal appeals reversed because Morrison's testimony was sufficient to raise the possible application of the statute, requiring the trial court to instruct the jury on the unwritten law. It also concluded a cuckolded husband was not legally required to shoot the paramour as soon as the latter opened the door.[26]

This broad understanding of the unwritten law may have been influenced by a broad interpretation by the court of criminal appeals

of another statute. A charge of murder could be reduced to manslaughter when a female "under the permanent or temporary protection of the accused at the time of the killing" was insulted by the deceased and the defendant was provoked by a sudden passion to kill the deceased. In *Meyers v. State* (1898), the deceased insulted the madam of a house of prostitution. The defendant responded by killing the deceased. He claimed the trial court erred in refusing to instruct the jury it could find him guilty of manslaughter. The court rejected the claim because the madam was in a house of prostitution and thus not under the defendant's protection. A different result occurred in 1912. The deceased insulted the defendant's mistress, and the defendant killed him. The court held that, although not virtuous, the insulted female was under the care and protection of the defendant.[27]

The unwritten law declared a husband's killing justifiable when committed "upon one taken in the act of adultery with the wife." This language clearly permitted the killing only of the paramour, not the wife. In *Williams v. State* (1914), Williams shot and killed both his wife and her lover. He confessed that he intended to kill his wife, whom he shot first. The court reversed his conviction. In dictum the court rejected as too narrow the trial court's instruction that it was a justifiable homicide if the defendant, while intending to kill the paramour, accidentally killed his wife. A year later the court held in *Cook v. State* (1915) that "where the defendant catches the deceased and his wife in such amorous relations, he would be entitled to kill the wife, as well as the seducer of his wife." This interpretation was contrary both to the traditional unwritten law and the text of the statute.[28]

The court of criminal appeals more strictly interpreted the justifiable homicide statute beginning in the 1920s, as rural Texas became more urbanized. In *Holman v. State* (1922) the defendant saw his wife sitting on the lap of the deceased and saw them enter a hotel together. He shot the companion in the hotel and claimed self-defense. Although the court reversed the conviction, it held the defendant's testimony was insufficient to allow an instruction on justifiable homicide. In *Sensobaugh v. State* (1922), the court upheld the maiming conviction of the defendant, who castrated his wife's lover because he did not want to kill him. In 1925 the court of criminal appeals overruled *Williams* and *Cook*, holding that the aggrieved husband was not permitted to kill his wife: "The right to kill is a matter with which the legislative branch of the government alone ought to deal, and when it confides to the citizen a right so important, it is, we think, the clear duty of this court to follow, but not to extend, such legislative declaration beyond the class clearly stated in the statute."

By the 1930s the court not only restricted the applicability of the justifiable homicide statute, but it also began affirming convictions while so doing. A decade later the court indicated greater willingness to allow a trial court to refuse to instruct the jury on justifiable homicide, and appellate cases on the subject rapidly dwindled. Even though the court of criminal appeals strictly limited this defense, the custom remained, at least on some occasions. A study of homicides in 1969 Houston noted that a husband who killed his wife's lover was not only quickly released from police custody after the murder (the husband had also beaten his wife after shooting the victim), but was not indicted by the grand jury.[29]

The unwritten law was finally repealed in the legislature's 1973 recodification of the penal code. The final appellate case to discuss the law is *Shaw v. State* (1974). The court of criminal appeals affirmed the trial court's decision not to instruct the jury that the defendant's murder of his wife was a justifiable homicide because she had been unfaithful.[30]

REVERSAL RATES IN APPELLATE COURTS IN CRIMINAL CASES

Between 1876 and 1887 the Texas Court of Appeals reversed 1,604 convictions in 2,486 cases, a reversal rate of 65 percent. The *American Law Review* was scandalized, editorializing that "the Texas Court of Appeals seems to have been organized to overrule and reverse." The rate of reversals actually accelerated beginning in 1881. From 1881 through 1886 the court of appeals reversed four cases for every case it affirmed. The court did so as Texas "became notorious for lawlessness and violence." In a largely rural but rapidly populating state (the number of Texans rose from 818,579 in 1870 to 2,235,527 in 1890) where law enforcement was sporadic, this rate of reversals almost beggars belief.[31]

The extent to which the appellate criminal courts reversed convictions was a continuing problem from the late nineteenth century through the first three decades of the twentieth century. Although the newly constituted Texas Court of Criminal Appeals reversed only 61 of 171 appeals (36 percent reversal rate) in 1893, a study by Keith Carter of the court's felony affirmance/reversal rate from 1900 to 1927 showed that 42 percent of all cases were reversed. The Carter study showed interesting trends over that time. In each year from 1900 to 1908, the reversal rate was always over 50 percent and usually at 60 percent or higher. Between 1909 and 1916, reversals never exceeded 47 percent and averaged about 28 percent. This rate jumped again between 1917 and 1921 and fell again between 1922 and 1927. This significant variation in the percentage of cases reversed suggests that the professionalization thesis is wrong. The professionalization thesis is that increasing professionalization of the legal profession, through greater education and access to legal treatises, reduces trial errors and thus increases affirmances on appeal. One explanation for the variation in the percentage of reversals is the membership of the three-man court of criminal appeals. Between 1900 and 1907 the court consisted of the same three men. Only one of those three judges, William L. Davidson, remained on the court after 1909, and a number of judges filtered through the court between 1909 and 1916, when reversals dropped sharply. From 1917 through 1921 there existed some greater court stability, and reversals jumped. From 1922 through 1927 the same three judges were on the court, and reversals dropped. It appears that stability on the court of criminal appeals generally though not always led to an increase in the reversal rate. This is contrary to the course of decision making in the Texas Supreme Court during the same period.[32]

An additional reason for the variation in reversals from 1900 through 1927 is the number of cases decided by the court. As was also true of the Texas Supreme Court, the Texas Court of Criminal Appeals was often behind in clearing its docket, creating a tension between deciding cases and deciding them thoroughly. Between 1900 and 1907 the court of criminal appeals never decided more than 209 cases, averaging about 150 decisions each year. Between 1909 and 1916 the lowest number of cases decided was 198 (1916), and an average of 273 decisions were issued per year, an increase of 82 percent over the earlier period. Between 1917 and 1921, during and after World War I, the number of decisions declined to an average of 219, and between 1922 and 1927 the court issued an average of 334 decisions. The less time the court gave to each case, the better the chances that the conviction would be affirmed.

The reasons why the court reversed convictions during this time varied, but three stood out: (1) errors made in giving or refusing to give jury instructions, (2) errors made in admitting or excluding evidence, and (3) errors made in indictments. Each of these errors suggests a continuing adherence to a kind of legal formalism in the opinions of the court of criminal appeals during the first quarter of the twentieth century, a formalism then under attack in American legal thought. The first two reasons were commonly used by many state appellate courts and caused consternation to legal reformers. At that time model and judicially approved instructions were largely nonexistent, increasing the chances of error when the trial court instructed a jury. This hazard was exacerbated in Texas because a judge was strictly forbidden from commenting on the evidence, a practice intended to enhance the power of the jury to decide the matter. The common law of evidence, which demanded an extraordinary level of accuracy by trial judges, led to the "sporting contest" of trials. This theory of the trial was that a judge acted as a referee between two combatants, and if the referee made some incorrect decisions, the appellate court was to reverse and remand the case for a new trial. In this view the appellate court did not attempt to assess the importance of the evidentiary "errors" made by the trial court; any error was a reversible error. A good lawyer was usually able to elicit some evidentiary error during the trial, for those decisions were made immediately by the trial court in the heat of a trial.[33]

A 1947 comment in the *Texas Law Review*

TABLE 7–1. Reversal Record of the Texas Court of Criminal Appeals, 1900–1927

Years	Cases Decided Annually (Average)	Reversal Rate (Average by Year)	Court Stability
1900–1908	158	59.9%	No change
1909–1916	273	34%	Unstable
1917–1921	219	49%	Mostly stable
1922–1927	334	36.2%	No change

studied homicide prosecutions and appeals of convictions in the Texas Court of Criminal Appeals between 1924 and 1944. It found an overall reversal rate of 37 percent (627 of 1,689), with an annual range of from 24 percent to 52 percent. Just five judges served on the three-member court of criminal appeals during that time. The reversal rate in homicide cases may vary because of regular and confusing changes made by the legislature to the law of homicide, including the degrees of homicide. A survey of volume 147 of the *Texas Criminal Reports* and volumes 191–94 of the *South Western Reporter (Second)* (cases decided in the mid-1940s) found an overall reversal rate of 44.7 percent (114 of 255), still a significant rate of reversals of convictions. This trend did not hold true in death penalty cases. Of the Texans who appealed a death sentence between 1923 and 1971, convictions were upheld in over 90 percent of the cases. Only 6 percent (including just 2 percent of African American and Hispanic men sentenced to die) received new trials. These starkly different percentages suggest that race and ethnicity may have been a significant factor in determining whether to reverse a conviction for first-degree murder.[34]

The rate of appellate reversals in the court of criminal appeals during the third quarter of the twentieth century declined significantly, and the reversal rate between 1976 and 2000 has varied considerably. Changes in reversal rates appear to depend on two factors: (1) with increases in the court's caseload the number of cases reversed decreased, and (2) changes in the court's jurisdiction increased substantially the percentage of reversals. The increase in the number of judges on the court of criminal appeals has not affected the reversal rate. In 1977 the court was expanded to nine members and disposed of 2,551 cases, making serious review nearly impossible. In the period 1977–81, the court disposed of between 2,229 and 2,634 cases annually, affirming between 87 percent and 92 percent of those cases.

A 1980 amendment to the constitution, effective September 1, 1981, changed the courts of civil appeals to the courts of appeals and gave those courts appellate jurisdiction in criminal cases, significantly altering the work of the Texas Court of Criminal Appeals. The court of criminal appeals was required to hear the initial appeal in any case in which the defendant received the death penalty. In all other cases it possessed the discretionary authority to hear any case decided first by a court of appeals. That meant that the court of criminal appeals could, for the first time, hear appeals by the state, not just appeals of convicted defendants. This severe reduction in its caseload gave the court more time to consider each case. More than half its caseload was based on discretionary review, giving the court a better opportunity to correct legal errors, including errors that adversely affected the state. During the last decade of the twentieth century, the court of criminal appeals reversed in about half of all cases. A far greater number of discretionary

TABLE 7–2. Affirmance Record of the Texas Court of Criminal Appeals, 1947, 1956, and 1966–81

Year	Number of Cases Disposed	Affirmance Rate	Number of Judges
1947	325	89%	3
1956	749	85%	3
1966	1,092	95.4%	5
1966–76	Between 1,100 and more than 2,000	90% or more in every year but one (89%)	5
1977–81	2,229–2,634	87–92%	9

Houston and Texas Central locomotive, undated. Courtesy Texas State Library and Archives Commission.

review cases were reversed than direct appeals matters. This increased reversal rate indicates the court of criminal appeals heard discretionary petitions for review often in order to reinstate a guilty verdict or otherwise reverse a court of appeals decision favorable to the convicted defendant.[35]

The 1947 *Texas Law Review* comment also provided an additional piece of information important to understanding the Texas criminal justice system. The percentage of convictions appealed was just 51 percent, a surprisingly low rate. It seems likely that the inability of some defendants to pay a lawyer to appeal the conviction was one reason for that low rate. A second reason concerns race. Booker T. Williams was charged with the murder of a white man in Lufkin in 1924. He was tried and found guilty four days later. The jury sentenced him to death. The people of Lufkin attempted to lynch him, and Governor Pat Neff called on the Texas National Guard to prevent Williams's lynching. Williams did not appeal and was executed just five weeks after the murder occurred.[36]

MORALS OFFENSES

Offenses involving consensual sexual matters, drug and alcohol use, and gambling are often grouped as morals offenses. Texas has an unusual history with regard to such offenses. Fornication, an act of sexual intercourse by an unmarried couple, was a crime in the 1836 Act Punishing Crimes and Misdemeanors. It was not, however, included as a crime in the state's 1848 criminal code, and the 1856 amendments to the penal code merely punished the action of "[e]very man and woman who shall live together in adultery." The words "or fornication" were added to the end of this provision in 1858. In the late 1860s, John Foster was prosecuted for fornication. The district court quashed the indictment. The state appealed to the supreme court. The supreme court held that the language of the statute meant an indictment for simple "adultery or fornication" was not punishable; only such an act combined with evidence that the couple was living together was a crime. Further, because the legislature had not defined "fornication," the 1858 amendment was meaningless, for only specifically defined crimes were punishable. This restrictive reading of the statute was not remedied by the legislature until 1879.[37]

Article 395 of the 1856 penal code expressly declared, "A single act of adultery is not sufficient to bring the offence within the meaning of this Chapter, unless proof be made that the parties live together." The court took this language seriously. "B. Richardson and another" were accused of adultery. The evidence suggested they had engaged in "carnal intercourse" up to six times. The woman was married but no longer lived with her husband. Richardson was unmarried. The court reversed his conviction and dismissed the case. It confessed "our inability to understand what is really meant by" the statute on adultery, but held that these six "occasional and stolen" visits were insufficient to indict the pair. The court also explained why the legislature limited the crime of adultery: "This article provides that where two persons live together in a state of cohabitation, one of them being married, they shall both be regarded as guilty of adultery. This is utterly untrue as a matter of fact, and if it were true would brand half the innocent families of the country with the crime of adultery." "Simple" acts of fornication and adultery were never crimes in Texas, and both crimes were repealed in the 1973 legislature's revision to the penal code.[38]

The history of the criminalization of prostitution is also instructive in assessing Texas history. The 1856 penal code did not criminalize sex for money. Instead, it prohibited the existence of "disorderly houses," defined in Article 396 as a house "kept for the purpose of public prostitution, or as a common resort for prostitutes, vagabonds or free negroes." In the late nineteenth and early twentieth centuries, the legislature permitted municipalities to regulate prostitutes and vagabonds. But prostitution was not made a crime by Texas until 1973.[39]

The crime of sodomy has its own unusual history in Texas. The 1854 penal code criminalized "the abominable and detestable crime against nature." The Penal Code of 1856 omitted this crime. In 1860 the legislature declared that "[i]f any person shall commit with mankind or beast the abominable and detestable crime against nature, he shall be deemed guilty of sodomy." In *Fennell v. State* (1869), the Texas Supreme Court held that the statute did not sufficiently define sodomy. Fourteen years later, the court of appeals held that the act did indeed criminalize sodomy. In 1893 the Texas Court of Criminal Appeals held that sodomy was defined as "carnal knowledge," and carnal knowledge did not include oral sex, but solely anal sex (whether between a man and a woman or two men).[40]

The sodomy statute was revised in 1943. It defined carnal knowledge as oral sex as well as anal sex and was applicable to heterosexual and homosexual couples. The statute was held constitutional by the court of criminal appeals in two early convictions for sodomy. In the late 1960s a professed homosexual was twice arrested for sodomy in Dallas County. He challenged the constitutionality of the statute in a civil action in the federal courts. A married couple intervened, claiming they were threatened with prosecution because they privately engaged in sodomy. The three-judge panel in *Buchanan v. Batchelor* (1970) declared that the statute applied to all persons engaged in sodomy and made no distinction between private and public acts. It also indicated that no married couple had been prosecuted for sodomy in Texas's history and that it was unclear whether "there have been prosecutions of homosexuals for private acts of sodomy." It noted that the number of arrests for sodomy in Dallas between 1963 and 1969 ranged from a low of 35 (1965) to a high of 129 (1966). The court held the sodomy statute void on its face as unconstitutionally overbroad, because it impinged on the private, consensual sexual conduct of married couples. The Supreme Court of the United States vacated the judgment. In 1973, when the legislature repealed its fornication and adultery laws, it amended its sodomy law to prohibit oral or anal sexual contact only between same-sex couples. The amended statute was, like the earlier statute, unenforced for private acts of sodomy. Even so, between 1973 and 2004 the statute's constitutionality was twice challenged and twice held unconstitutional by the Third Court of Appeals in Austin. Both decisions were reversed. The third and successful constitutional challenge involved the sodomy prosecution of John Geddes Lawrence and Tyson Garner.[41]

Houston police were called to an apartment complex to investigate a "weapons disturbance." No weapons were found, but the door

to the apartment shared by Lawrence and Garner was open. Police entered the apartment and
saw Lawrence and Garner engaging in sexual
activity. They were arrested, tried for sodomy,
convicted, and fined two hundred dollars.
The Supreme Court of the United States held
that the Texas sodomy law unconstitutionally
infringed the right to engage in private, consensual sexual activity.[42]

Although the legislature began to criminalize the sale of drugs beginning in 1905, its first
major effort to regulate the possession and
distribution of narcotics through the criminal
law was in 1937, when it adopted the Uniform
Narcotic Drug Act. The act did not differenti-
ate between possession and possession with
intent to sell, which by the late 1960s and early
1970s allowed for extremely long sentences for
possession of modest amounts of marijuana.
Although a person with no previous record
ordinarily received probation in Harris County
for possessing marijuana, Lee Otis Johnson, a
black power advocate, was given a thirty-year
prison sentence in 1968 for selling one marijuana cigarette. Johnson was not freed until
a federal court granted his claim for habeas
corpus relief in 1972. The 1973 legislature
enacted the Texas Controlled Substances Act,
greatly reducing the penalties for the possession and sale of small amounts of marijuana.
Texas was the next to last state to reform its
marijuana laws. It also "took every illicit drug
they recognized, except marijuana, and raised
the possession penalty to life imprisonment for
heroin, speed, and LSD."[43]

FORMALISM IN THE TEXAS COURT
OF CRIMINAL APPEALS REDUX

The "revolt against formalism" in law was
largely accepted as complete by 1937. In Texas,
however, the court of criminal appeals continued to decide cases with extraordinarily
strict regard for the formalities of law, often
without explanation. One set of such cases

was called variance cases, because the indictment varied from some fact of the case. In one
1935 case the indictment mistakenly dated the
offense as October 17, 1934, instead of October
17, 1933. The defendant had, before the trial,
consented to an amendment of the indictment
to reflect the correct date. The court held that
this amendment, despite the defendant's initial
consent (a waiver allowed under the code of
criminal procedure), was impermissible on a
second motion for a rehearing.[44]

The court's variance decisions then moved
farther into the realm of the strange and
unusual. A defendant appealed his conviction for burglary solely on the ground that the
prosecution's identification evidence was insufficient. This claim was rejected. On its own,
the court noted that the indictment alleged the
owner of the house the defendant burglarized
was A. F. Houston. But, the court noted with
a flourish, his actual name (or initials, at least)
was J. F. Houston: "This variance is fatal." In
another case the state claimed the victim was
a "salesman on a bread route." The conviction
was overturned because he "was the seller of
pies, jelly rolls, doughnuts and other sorts of
pastries."[45]

More astonishing than the variance cases
were the drowning and "stomping" cases, a
result of the court's requirement that the state
declare the "means and method" of the crime.
Gragg was on a boat with his wife and two-
year-old stepson, who were found dead at the
bank of the water. The state offered evidence
that Gragg was having an affair with another
woman, whom he falsely told he was divorcing his wife. After the drowning Gragg offered
inconsistent statements about how the tragedy
occurred (one statement was that the child fell
overboard and his mother followed him; a second claimed they slipped into the water from
the bank). He was charged with and convicted
of murdering them by drowning. Gragg moved
to quash the indictment on the ground that it
failed to state in what type of liquid the victims

were drowned ("because it does not allege whether the deceased was drown [*sic*] in water, coffee, tea or what"). The trial court overruled the motion. The court of criminal appeals held the indictment was fatally defective because "[t]here being more than one means by which the drowning may be accomplished, the indictment does not inform the accused with sufficient accuracy of the offense for which he is charged."[46]

The drowning case was topped by the stomping case. The indictment charged Buster Northern with "unlawfully, voluntarily, and with his malice aforethought, kill[ing] Fannie McHenry by then and there kicking and stomping the said Fannie McHenry." He was convicted and sentenced to death. The commission of appeals reversed, holding the indictment defective because it failed to state the means used to cause Fannie McHenry's death. To the contention that "kicking and stomping" could only be done by foot, the commission replied, "We have been unable to find any case so holding, and no text-writer on criminal law, so far as we know, has ever announced such doctrine. To so hold would be a radical departure from the rules of pleading in criminal cases." The court of criminal appeals adopted the commission's opinion.[47]

These decisions were roundly condemned, so much so that the court later refused to acknowledge them and lawyers did not cite them. Although the court almost immediately began backtracking, it avoided the cases for more than fifteen years. It was not until a 1964 case in which a defendant's lawyer had the temerity to cite them that one judge mentioned them. He noted, "[T]his Court is still frequently criticized on account of these two cases and the Court still has them flaunted at it as expressing the philosophy of this Court," and he urged they be overruled. *Gragg* and *Northern*, though disregarded, were not formally overruled until 1980.[48]

What *Gragg* and *Northern* exposed was not a false "philosophy of this Court," but the absence of a philosophy or jurisprudence. Antiformalists (sometimes grouped as "realists") often attacked formalism as falsely "mechanical," as enshrouded in a legal cocoon ignorant of the society in which law applied. But formalism had one great value: it required those who made and enforced the law to follow its established demands before taking a person's life or liberty. Formalism in this sense was a crucial attribute of the rule of law. *Gragg* and *Northern* created a requirement untethered to the demands of the law, one that made true the statement of one of Charles Dickens's characters, "the law is a ass." The negative reverberations of these cases were significant. Long after the court rejected them, they were paraded to criticize the court for its adoption of "technicalities." Those demanding more law and order would use *Gragg* and *Northern* to proclaim criminals were going free on legal technicalities. They could then pressure elected appellate judges to affirm convictions lest more cases like *Gragg* and *Northern* be decided. After all, convicts made for an insignificant interest group.[49]

LYNCHING

Determining that an extralegal killing constitutes a lynching is a difficult task. A lynching is traditionally understood as involving more than one murderer (the NAACP required a minimum of three persons; Texas by an 1897 law required two) often with the tacit or explicit approval of law enforcement or of prominent citizens in the community. The victim of the lynching was usually suspected of committing a crime, although that was not universally so. From the 1880s through the middle of the twentieth century, lynching was also largely tied to racism; cases in Texas in which whites were lynched were rare by 1900. On some occasions lynchings were planned efforts undertaken in the open, demonstrably defiant of law enforcement. In others, lynchings were largely secret and secretive events. In many instances a lynching was an attempt to signal to African Americans and to Mexican Americans in South Texas that violence would be the result of any effort to upend the standing Jim Crow order.

The national and Texas data on lynchings before 1885 are sparse and incomplete, but a number of lynchings occurred in the state before then. Two notorious lynchings were the murder of slaves and their alleged supporters during the claimed slave insurrection of 1860 and the murder of Texas Unionists in August 1862. From the end of the Civil War in 1865 through 1868, 468 freedmen died violently. Ninety percent were killed by whites. How many of these were best described as lynchings is unknown. The best data, though incomplete and occasionally inaccurate, were collected by the Tuskegee Institute and the *Chicago Tribune* from 1889 to 1918 and published by the NAACP. They listed 335 lynchings in Texas, behind only Georgia and Mississippi during that time. Recent work by William Carrigan and Clive Webb confirms 282 lynchings of Mexican Americans between 1848 and 1930. Lawrence Rice believes that at least 500 African Americans were lynched between 1870 and 1900. A 1983 dissertation on lynching in Texas states that 379 persons were killed by lynch mobs between 1889 and 1942, a number the author increased to 468 in a subsequent publication. Most reported lynchings during that time occurred in Texas's so-called Black Belt, and the victims were usually African American. Less well reported were lynchings of Mexican Americans. For example, the murders by Texas Rangers and other law enforcement officers of several hundred Mexican Americans during the "Bandit War" of 1915 were not initially understood as lynchings but should be so classified. The number of murders in Cameron County in deep South Texas were enough "to give this area the bloody prize of America's champion lynching area." As early as 1891, Governor Jim

Hogg decried the regularity of lynching; he noted that 27 persons were hung by law for their murders, while at the same time 140 Texans were lynched.[50]

Texas was the site of several notorious lynchings of African Americans. One, occurring at the height of the national lynching period, was the 1893 lynching in Paris, Texas, of Henry Smith, who allegedly molested a four-year-old girl. Smith was found in Arkansas and transported by rail back to Paris. No effort was made to have Smith tried by law. He was tortured (hot irons were forced down his throat) and burned at the stake in front of a crowd estimated at ten thousand. In the lynching, known as the Waco Horror, of seventeen-year-old Jesse Washington in Waco in 1916, Washington was forcibly removed from the courthouse after he was sentenced to death for murder. He was beaten and hanged from a tree in the center of town before he was burned alive. A large crowd watched and then sought mementos from the lynching. The Sherman lynching and riot of 1930 belied the motto of the Texas Rangers: "One Riot, One Ranger." George Hughes was charged with rape. As the jury was being seated, the mob began to stone the courthouse. The trial was abandoned as the Rangers attempted to prevent the mob from lynching Hughes. Rangers secured Hughes in the courthouse vault, and the courthouse was burned to the ground by the mob. Hughes was dead, but the mob retrieved his body and hanged it from a tree in the African American commercial district.[51]

No one was charged with a crime in the Smith lynching. In 1897, in response to the lynching (and dissemination of photographs memorializing the event) of Robert Hillard, as well as an increase in mob violence, the legislature adopted a law punishing "murder by mob violence" with death or life in prison, following laws adopted in North Carolina, South Carolina, and Georgia. The law may have had some initial effect. Lynchings declined by

Fred Gildersleeve photograph of the Waco Horror (Jesse Washington lynching), 1916. Courtesy the Texas Collection, Baylor Library, Waco, Texas.

half in the five years following the adoption of the law. Eight members of an 1899 lynch mob that killed Jim Humphries and his two sons were convicted of murder, and one widow in the Humphries case won a judgment of ten thousand dollars in a civil suit based on the 1897 law. But the Humphries cases were the exception, not the rule, for Jim Humphries was a white, former Confederate soldier murdered as a result of an East Texas feud. In no case were monetary damages awarded to a widow of an "unjustly" lynched African American. That Jesse Washington was to be lynched was well known: a photographer, Fred Gildersleeve, had the time to set up his camera to take photos of the lynching for later sale. The mayor and chief of police watched the lynching from the mayor's office, yet no one was charged with

murder by mob violence in the Waco Horror. Although fourteen men were indicted for their actions in the Sherman Riot of 1930, none of the charges concerned the lynching itself. Only J. B. McCasland was convicted, and that was for arson (he later pled guilty to one count of rioting). McCasland's conviction was lauded at the time as "the first conviction in Texas in a case growing out of mob violence against a Negro attacker of a white woman."[52]

The last open Texas mob lynching occurred in 1942 in Texarkana. William Vinson was tortured and killed for allegedly committing a rape. The end of the "open mob" meant an end to lynching as a socially approved or accepted method of responding to crime (actual or perceived); it also signaled a shift in the nature of race relations. The end of lynching shifted to the criminal justice system the punishment of African Americans for violations of the law and violations of the social mores of the majority community (for example, by criminalizing as rape consensual sexual relations between a black man and a white woman). What earlier in Texas history might have been a mob lynching became a legal lynching. The death penalty was more often implemented in Texas as lynchings declined, and it was used more often than earlier for offenses other than murder.[53]

THE DEATH PENALTY IN TEXAS BEFORE 1972

The republic and state of Texas have always had a death penalty. Between 1819 and 1972 Texas legally executed 755 persons. Only Virginia (1,277), with a much longer history, executed more persons. Between 1982, when Texas again began to execute convicted murderers, through 2009, it executed 447 persons, more than any other state. This section discusses the death penalty in Texas before the U.S. Supreme Court held it unconstitutional in *Furman v. Georgia* (1972).[54]

Before the 1923 act giving the state control

of executions, executions in Texas were performed by county officials. The 1923 act was both a reaction to lynchings in 1919 and in 1922 (when nine blacks in East Texas were lynched during a two-week span in May), and a progressive effort to reduce the moblike and racially charged atmosphere accompanying public hangings. In adopting the act Texas followed the national trend in closing executions to the public and in altering the manner of execution from hanging to electrocution.[55]

The Supreme Court of the United States currently limits the death penalty to a subset of homicides. Texas historically permitted the death penalty for murder as well as other crimes. However, the crimes for which a person was executed in Texas changed dramatically over time. The vast majority of executions in Texas between 1819 and 1920 were for murder. For example, the first execution for the crime of rape was not until 1875, and of the 385 persons executed through 1920, just over 10 percent were executed for a rape that did not include murder.

Executions for rape, particularly executions of African Americans for rape, increased markedly once lynchings became more rare in the twentieth century. About 80 percent of the persons executed for rape in Texas were African American. Between 1923 and 1964 Texas executed 361 persons. Sixty-three percent of those executed were African American, and 7 percent were Mexican American. Of those executed, 257 were executed for a murder. Of the 99 persons executed for rape, 82 were black. Just 26 persons were executed for rape between 1819 and 1900, and the first execution of a black Texan for rape was not until 1875. The percentage of Texans legally executed for rape between 1890 and 1900, when lynching reached its peak nationally, was much lower than the percentage of Texans executed for rape between 1923 and 1964. These numbers support the view that in some Texas communities in the late nineteenth century a black man accused of rape

did not live long enough to receive a trial. After lynchings declined, the number of executions for rape increased dramatically, particularly for blacks. Executions for rape as a percentage of all executions peaked in Texas in the 1950s, when no Texas lynchings were reported.[56]

The links between racism, rape, and capital punishment are demonstrated in the book *The Rope, the Needle, and the Chair*. The authors note that 443 of the 455 men executed for rape between 1930 and 1972 were executed in former Confederate states. In Texas, a white woman was the victim in 96 percent of the cases in which the death penalty was given for rape. In only one case was the victim black. African Americans were sentenced to death for rape at a rate five to ten times higher than that for whites in Texas.[57]

The willingness of the court of criminal appeals to reverse convictions in homicide cases between 1924 and 1944 and its unwillingness to do so in death penalty cases from 1923 to 1972 again suggest the continuing influence of racism in the criminal justice system. Even when the court of criminal appeals reversed and remanded for a new trial in cases involving black defendants, its impact was often nonexistent. Harry Lacy was accused of shooting and killing a white man, Edgar Womack. Lacy admitted the killing but claimed he was forced to do so by Bosie Beasley, who threatened to kill Lacy if Lacy did not shoot Womack. The jury rejected Lacy's defense and sentenced him to die. Lacy appealed. The court of criminal appeals reversed the conviction because the state offered evidence from Beasley that two grand juries had met since the homicide and neither had indicted him. At the second trial, Lacy was again convicted and sentenced to die. The court of criminal appeals, in a lengthy opinion, rejected Lacy's claims, including his claim that the jury was biased against blacks.

In 1953, Jimmy Richardson was convicted of the rape of a fifteen-year-old white girl. In closing argument, the prosecutor stated, among other things, "Gentlemen, we have tried the restraining influence of religion and the elevating forces of education on this negro in vain. What are we going to do with this unclean creature, who has violated the very cradle to please the lust of his heart? Haven't we promised to give little girls protection from moral destruction? If you turn a deaf ear to the thousand[s] of mothers, who have daughters of her age, haven't you formed a league with Death and a covenant with hell?" The court of criminal appeals reversed, holding Richardson was denied a fair trial. It made no specific comment on the prosecutor's statement. Richardson was retried and again convicted and sentenced to death. The court of criminal appeals affirmed, and Richardson was executed in June 1954.

The limits of the rule of law shine most clearly in the prosecution of Bob White for rape. After a woman was raped in her home by a stranger, White and a number of other black men were picked up and put in the local jail. Apparently because he ate very little in comparison with the other men thrown in jail, White was viewed suspiciously by the sheriff. The victim identified White's voice as the rapist's, but White denied committing the crime. He was taken into the woods by law enforcement and "beaten senseless" until he signed (with an X) a confession dictated by the district attorney. After being convicted and sentenced to death, White appealed, claiming the trial was prejudiced by statements made by the prosecution. The court of criminal appeals reversed and remanded. White was again convicted and sentenced to die. His second appeal was based on the absence of black jurors on the grand jury. The court of criminal appeals rejected White's claim. White then petitioned the Supreme Court of the United States, claiming his confession was coerced, and the Court reversed White's conviction. During jury selection in White's third trial, W. S. Cochran, the husband of the rape victim, shot and killed White. The murder occurred on June 12, 1941. Cochran was tried and acquitted of White's murder on June 19, 1941.[58]

In at least six cases between 1923 and 1972 a sentence of death was either commuted or the person set free after serious doubts were raised about the defendant's guilt. Other convicted prisoners with seemingly strong cases of innocence were not as lucky. Further, a study of capital punishment from 1924 to 1968 concluded that the death penalty did not deter murder in the state. Texas ranked first in total number of murders in 1966 and 1967 and sixth in murder rate.[59]

THE DEATH PENALTY IN TEXAS, 1976 TO THE PRESENT

Elmer Branch was convicted of rape and sentenced to death. He appealed his conviction to the Texas Court of Criminal Appeals, claiming his sentence violated the Eighth Amendment's ban on cruel and unusual punishments. The court affirmed. Branch then petitioned the United States Supreme Court. It issued a writ in Branch's case and joined it with two cases from Georgia. In *Furman v. Georgia* (1972), the Supreme Court, by a 5–4 vote, held the death penalty in Georgia and Texas violated the Eighth Amendment. The brief *per curiam* opinion of the Court did not explain why the death penalty violated the Eighth Amendment. The Court's conclusion was explained in five exhaustive and exhausting separate opinions. Those opinions declared the death penalty unconstitutional because the law was arbitrarily applied in determining who died and who lived.[60]

Within a year, the sixty-third Texas legislature adopted a revised death penalty statute, the key provision of which was "future dangerousness," that is, in the language of the 1973 statute, "whether there is a probability that the defendant would commit criminal acts of violence that would constitute a continuing threat to society." The future dangerousness question was one of three asked of the jury in a death penalty case. It was the first among equals, however, because the other two questions were implicitly answered affirmatively when guilt was decided. Those questions asked (1) whether the crime was committed deliberately and with the expectation that death would result and (2) whether the defendant's conduct was unreasonable. Therefore, the question of future dangerousness was the crucial question in all death penalty cases. The origins of the future dangerousness standard are murky, arising at the very end of the 1973 legislative session.[61]

After Texas readopted the death penalty, Jerry Lane Jurek was tried for the murder of a child. He was convicted and sentenced to death. The Supreme Court of the United States held in *Jurek v. Texas* (1976) that Texas's revised death penalty statute was constitutional, reversing its decision in *Furman*. It favorably compared the discretion available to jurors in Texas's law (on the question of future dangerousness) with the mandatory nature of laws in North Carolina and Louisiana, which the Court held unconstitutional. After *Jurek*, death penalty lawyers focused their attention on the evidence concerning the defendant's future dangerousness. The Supreme Court also exercised a much greater managerial and supervisory role in the administration of the death penalty after 1976.[62]

In *Estelle v. Smith* (1981), the Supreme Court evaluated the constitutionality of the use of statements by the defendant to a psychiatrist to determine future dangerousness. The trial court had, on its own motion, ordered Dr. James Grigson to examine the defendant for mental competency. Grigson found him competent. The examination of the defendant, Ernest Smith, occurred without the knowledge of Smith's lawyer. Grigson was allowed to testify at the sentencing (or penalty) proceeding over defense counsel's objection. He informed the jury that after his ninety-minute examination, he had determined Smith was a sociopath with no regard for another person's life and was a continuing threat to society. The jury sen-

tenced Smith to die. After Texas courts rejected his appeals, Smith attacked his conviction in federal court. The Supreme Court unanimously agreed that Grigson's testimony violated Smith's Fifth Amendment privilege against self-incrimination.[63]

The response to *Estelle v. Smith* was not to eliminate expert testimony on future dangerousness but to ask a psychiatric expert to answer that question based on hypothetical questions. At the penalty phase in the trial of Thomas Barefoot for murdering a police officer, Dr. Grigson, nicknamed "Dr. Death" by death penalty opponents, declared in response to one such question that he was "'100% sure' that an individual with the characteristics of the one in the hypothetical would commit acts of violence in the future." How one could be 100 percent sure about any person's future conduct was unclear. The Court concluded in *Barefoot v. Estelle* (1983) that such expert testimony was neither impermissible nor unreliable. *Barefoot* thus launched the career of Dr. Death, and Grigson became a mainstay in capital punishment cases in Texas through the mid-1990s. He testified that the defendant was a future danger to society and thus a candidate for the death penalty between 150 and 167 times (on eight occasions he testified for the defendant). Several problems existed with Dr. Grigson's testimony: First, it did not appear to be empirically grounded. Second, his testimony violated the law of evidence regarding expert testimony. Third, his predictions were not grounded in the science of psychiatry. Even when *Barefoot* was decided, the American Psychiatric Association, in its amicus brief to the Court, noted, "The unreliability of psychiatric predictions of long-term future dangerousness is by now an established fact within the profession."[64]

The most troublesome death penalty case for both opponents and proponents is that of Johnny Paul Penry. Penry raped and murdered Pamela Moseley Carpenter in 1979 and was tried, convicted, and sentenced to die. The Texas Court of Criminal Appeals affirmed, and his petition for a writ of certiorari to the Supreme Court of the United States was denied. He then began a collateral attack on his sentence. Penry requested and was denied a writ of habeas corpus from the federal district court. The Fifth Circuit affirmed. Penry again petitioned the Supreme Court. This time it heard his case and held that the trial court erred in structuring how the jury was to consider the mitigating circumstances of Penry's alleged mental retardation and evidence of his having suffered abuse as a child. These errors meant the trial court failed to give the jury a way to provide its "reasoned moral response" in sentencing. At the same time, the Supreme Court refused to hold that executing a mentally retarded person was barred by the Eighth Amendment. Penry received another sentencing proceeding in Texas district court. The jury again sentenced him to die. The Texas Court of Criminal Appeals affirmed, and the Supreme Court again denied Penry's petition for a writ of certiorari. Penry again collaterally attacked his sentence by seeking federal relief. The federal district court denied his petition, and the Fifth Circuit denied his motion to certify appealability. The Supreme Court again took his case. It affirmed in part, reversed in part, and remanded for a new penalty phase, declaring that the instructions on the mitigating factors of mental retardation and childhood abuse were constitutionally insufficient. For the third time, the trial court sentenced Penry to death after the jury found the death penalty warranted. Penry again appealed. The court of criminal appeals held that the jury instructions given on the issue of Penry's claimed mental retardation were impermissibly written, and it reversed the death sentence. Then Texas petitioned for a writ of certiorari, but the Supreme Court denied the petition. In February 2008, Penry pleaded guilty and accepted several consecutive sentences of life without parole. Penry's case took twenty-nine years to conclude.[65]

The Texas Defender Service claimed that as of 2000 at least "six men [were] executed by the State of Texas despite substantial and troubling doubts about their guilt" since the reinstitution of the death penalty in 1976. No person executed in the United States has been officially declared innocent of the crime for which he or she was executed. The case of Cameron Todd Willingham, executed in Texas in February 2004 for arson that killed his children, may become the first. Willingham declared his innocence throughout his trial and incarceration. At least two fire science experts later concluded that the evidence offered at trial that the fire was arson was junk science. The advisory Texas Forensic Science Commission was about to evaluate the expert evidence used at Willingham's trial in September 2009 when Governor Rick Perry replaced three members shortly before it was to take up the matter. Through fall 2010, twelve Texans sentenced to death since 1973 have been exonerated and released. The three most well-known cases of actual innocence are those of Randall Dale Adams, Clarence Brandley, and Kerry Max Cook. Adams was accused of murdering a police officer. His death sentence was aided by the notorious Dr. Grigson and was upheld by the Texas Court of Criminal Appeals. In 1980 the Supreme Court vacated his sentence. Adams was subsequently sentenced to life. After the release of Texan Errol Morris's documentary *The Thin Blue Line* (1988), which offered strong evidence that another person had committed the murder, Adams's conviction was set aside, and a new trial was ordered. No new trial took place. That same year, the Texas Court of Criminal Appeals set aside the conviction of Clarence Brandley, a black man accused of the rape and murder of a sixteen-year-old white girl at a high school where Brandley was a janitor. The court noted that the prosecution suppressed exculpatory evidence and engaged in other actions that denied Brandley his right of due process. Again, it appeared clear that another person had committed the murder. Kerry Max Cook was convicted in 1978 of capital murder and sentenced to death. The Supreme Court of the United States vacated the judgment. A second jury trial ended in a mistrial. At the third trial Cook was again convicted of capital murder and sentenced to death. On appeal, the court of criminal appeals reversed on grounds of misconduct by police and the prosecution but held that Cook could be retried. Shortly before the fourth trial, DNA testing on the victim's panties found semen from a former lover of the victim. Cook agreed to a no contest plea in which he made no admission of guilt.[66]

CONFESSIONS

Texas law regulating the admission at trial of a defendant's confession dates from the 1856 Texas Code of Criminal Procedure. Although a confession "freely made without compulsion or persuasion" (Art. 661) was admissible against the accused, any confession made while in custody was admissible *only* if the accused was taken to an examining court and voluntarily confessed or if he confessed "after having been first cautioned that it may be used against him" (Art. 662). These provisions were intended to protect against coerced confessions. This duty to caution long predated the Supreme Court's *Miranda v. Arizona* (1966) decision, which requires law enforcement to caution a person in custody before interrogation. The emphasis that the defendant's confession be voluntary was reinforced in *Cain v. State* (1857): "[Confessions] must not have been obtained by the influence of hope or fear, applied by a third person to the prisoner's mind." Twenty years later, the Texas Court of Appeals, quoting Simon Greenleaf's *Evidence* treatise, stated: "The evidence of verbal confessions of guilt is to be received with great caution," for the defendant "is often influenced by motives of hope or fear to make an untrue confession."[67]

Article 662 was amended in 1860 to allow introduction of a confession if the statement of facts made by the accused corroborated his guilt. That amendment caused no end of problems in interpreting the admissibility of confessions. Although Texas's confession law was not unusual among the states, that it was codified law was exceptional. Texas's skepticism of oral confessions and bias in favor of written confessions was also somewhat unusual among American states. Texas adopted a more stringent statute in 1907 regarding confessions. It specified that the warning must inform the person in custody both that he "does not have to make any statement at all" and that if he did, it could be used against him at his trial. The 1907 act also declared that any written confession was inadmissible if the defendant was illiterate, unless the "mark" made by the defendant was witnessed and signed by someone other than a peace officer. One result of this caution concerning confessions was that law enforcement urged suspects to put their confessions in written form. One unlawful way to accomplish this was by the use of physical violence or the threat of physical violence, called the "third degree," to coerce written confessions.[68]

Despite legal protections intended to ensure that confessions were made voluntarily, confessions during the first half of the twentieth century were often coerced from defendants. Between September 1921 and March 1922 the *Dallas Morning News* published four stories from across the state in which the defendant either testified that his confession was obtained by the third degree or was believed by officials to be false. In late 1921 lurid reports of the use of what was called an "electric monkey" (one end of an electric device was placed against the prisoner's spine, "giving him a needle in the back") led to an investigation of some Dallas police officers. Despite graphic testimony, the officers were exonerated. A 1921 bill admitting confessions only if made in open court in the presence of a representative of the accused failed. It was offered before reports about the electric monkey were made. The 1923 legislature responded to the published claims of torture by adopting an "Anti-Third Degree" law, making it a crime for a peace officer to "torture, torment or punish" a person in police custody "for the purpose of making such prisoner or person . . . confess." Section 3 of the act declared, "The fact that the peace officers in Texas have within the past two years been charged and have admitted that they resorted to the means herein denounced . . . outrage Christian civilization and do violence to the spirit and genius of our government."[69]

Although the Wickersham commission's *Report on Lawlessness in Law Enforcement* (1931) noted that the "electric monkey" was discontinued in 1925, the practice of using coercive tactics to obtain a confession continued. A 1931 book listed 106 third-degree cases taken from the Wickersham commission's report. Nine were from Texas, second in number only to those of Illinois (sixteen). Even so, the news was somewhat positive. In six of the nine cases the Texas Court of Criminal Appeals reversed the conviction; in only one case did it affirm a conviction after finding the third degree was used. This record suggested a stalemate between some in law enforcement and the court of criminal appeals. Although some police used violence to extract confessions, a defendant able to present some proof of that violence found the court ready to reverse the conviction. This was not a true stalemate, however, for an unknown number of cases never made it to the court of criminal appeals.[70]

Through the middle of the twentieth century the court of criminal appeals continued to reverse convictions if the evidence sufficiently showed the confession was coerced. In the last quarter of the century the legislature amended Texas confession law to allow at trial a greater use of statements made by the defendant. Despite these legislative modifications, the admissibility of a defendant's confession remains more difficult in Texas than is required by federal constitutional law.[71]

A stringent requirement of Texas's statutory law of confessions is that custodial confessions must generally be in writing or recorded to be admissible evidence at trial. The requirement can create prosecutorial difficulties when an accused makes an oral but not a written confession. In one well-known case, David Port, a seventeen-year-old, freely told officers he murdered Debra Sue Schatz. However, he refused to confess in writing, and other evidence connecting Port with the murder was slender. The trial court admitted the oral confession, and Port was convicted. The court of appeals reversed on statutory grounds. The court of criminal appeals held that the provision in the statute allowing admission of an oral confession if it "contains assertions of facts or circumstances that are found to be true and which conduce to establish the guilt of the accused, such as the finding of secreted or stolen property or the instrument with which he states the offense was committed," should be interpreted to include any statement in the confession that later aided the state in its prosecution of the defendant. The dissent noted that the court's conclusion altered law existing for "almost one hundred years" and charged that the majority had "implicitly repealed" the statute. The dissent also speculated that "we should soon see a return to those 'good old days' of this century when the norm was taking involuntary confessions from accused persons by law enforcement personnel." A haunting *Texas Monthly* article on the case was titled "Every One a Victim." Oliver Wendell Holmes's aphorism, "hard cases make bad law," fit *Port* all too well.[72]

SENTENCING, PRISONS, AND PRISONERS

Texas has made inviolate the right to trial by jury. Unlike the situation in most states, in Texas the jury not only determines guilt or innocence but also the sentence given to a convicted defendant. It was not until 1966 that judges were given a role in assessing punishment. Because most criminal penalties in Texas are of indeterminate length (a crime might be punishable by imprisonment of from one to thirty years), sentences meted out by one jury could vary tremendously from those given by another jury, even when the crimes were substantially similar. A 1967 study found that more severe sentences were given to those who remained in jail pending the disposition of their cases, to men, and to those whose lawyer was appointed by the court instead of being retained and paid by the defendant. The particular trial court in which the defendant was sentenced was also statistically significant. The study found no statistically significant difference between the sentences determined by a jury and those rendered by a judge. Finally, the authors found that the race of the defendant did not affect the severity of the sentence. However, they cautioned that this did not mean that race was not a factor in sentencing: "[A] more realistic explanation lies in the inability of this study, because of scarcity of information, to account for the effect of the race of the offender's *victim* on predicted sentence severity."[73]

In *Ruiz v. Estelle* (1980), federal district court judge William Wayne Justice held that the overcrowding of prisoners in Texas prisons violated the federal constitution. *Ruiz*, the "longest running prison class action suit in American history," included testimony from 349 witnesses and took a year to try. The case began when David Ruiz sued, complaining about prison conditions. Judge Justice appointed an experienced prisoners' rights attorney, William Bennett Turner, to represent Ruiz and other prisoners. When Justice allowed plaintiffs to amend their complaint, they asked solely for equitable relief, ensuring that the issues would be decided by Judge Justice, not a jury. Justice ordered that the case be heard as a class-action suit, effectively making it a test of the entire Texas prison system. A year after the conclusion of the trial, Judge Justice issued a lengthy opinion. His most well-known conclusion was that overcrowding of the prisons had a "malignant effect" on those incarcerated by the Texas Department of Corrections. After another fifteen months of legal skirmishing, Texas agreed to negotiate an agreement, called a consent decree. In June 1982 the Fifth Circuit affirmed in part and reversed in part Judge Justice's order. It affirmed Justice's conclusion that prisoners unconstitutionally suffered cruel and unusual punishment. A settlement was finally reached in 1987. Five years later the prison system was returned in part to the control of the state.[74]

In March 1996 the Texas Department of Criminal Justice (TDCJ) requested an end to the court's supervision of Texas prisons. The next month, Congress adopted the Prison Litigation Reform Act (PLRA). The PLRA severely restricted lawsuits by prisoners and was intended in part to end *Ruiz*. The TDCJ later moved to vacate the judgment and terminate the district court's jurisdiction based on the PLRA. Judge Justice held the PLRA's termination of supervision provisions unconstitutional. In 2001 the Fifth Circuit reversed. Judge Justice subsequently found several continuing constitutional violations, but the case was largely at an end. Less than two weeks before the litigation turned thirty years old, it was settled.[75]

In 1985, Texas imprisoned 37,281 persons, and total appropriations for the Texas Department of Corrections for its two-year budget were $1 billion. By 1990, shortly before the prison system was returned to the control of the state, Texas imprisoned about 48,000 persons. By 1997, that number had nearly tripled to about 135,000 persons, when the state's overall population had increased by about 17 percent. By 2005, nearly 153,000 persons were incarcerated in Texas prisons, an incarceration rate of 691 per hundred thousand residents, the second highest in the nation, while the rate of violent crime in Texas that year was 530 per hundred thousand residents, twelfth among the states. The 2005 budget for the TDCJ reached $2.6 billion.[76]

LAW ON THE BOOKS AND THE LAW IN ACTION

Whether a criminal justice system provides justice depends much more on the law in action than the law on the books. The most fundamental rights are largely meaningless if law enforcement personnel are permitted to evade them. The requirements of due process mean nothing if a howling mob can interrupt a trial and hang the defendant. The legal system, in particular the appellate legal system, often ignores differences between the law in action and the law on the books. It does so occasionally as a response to powerful social and communal interests; it does so more often because the justness of the legal system depends on the good-faith actions of a number of actors, nearly all of whom are outside the control of the judiciary and whose actions may not come to judicial light.

In May 1930 a man named Turner traveled from New York to conduct business in Dallas. Having to make a phone call, he went to three phone booths to find one in which the phone line was not busy. After entering the third booth, he was taken into custody by a Dallas police officer. He was arrested "on suspicion," the officer believing that Turner was attempting to steal money from the phones. Turner remained incommunicado in his cell for forty-eight hours. After his release, Turner complained to the *Dispatch*, a local paper. A reporter found that in 1930, 1,823 persons were arrested in Dallas "on suspicion," although fewer than 5 percent were charged with any crime. In 1929 an astonishing 8,526 persons were arrested on suspicion. These arrests were barred by Texas law. But the Dallas chief of police justified his officers' actions: "It is not legal. But illegality is necessary to preserve legality."[77]

HUMAN FRAILTY AND THE TEXAS CRIMINAL JUSTICE SYSTEM

In the late 1990s Joe Coleman claimed to be a "deep cover" agent ferreting out drug dealing in Tulia, Texas, a small Panhandle town of about five thousand. His alleged purchases of "eight balls" of cocaine led to the arrest of forty-seven persons. Most were either convicted or agreed to deferred adjudication. Thirty-seven of those arrested were black, of a total of 350 African Americans in Tulia. Despite the early efforts of several (but not all) defense lawyers, the district attorney appeared largely untroubled by Coleman's uncorroborated testimony that every defendant had sold Coleman at least one eight ball, many doing so in a school zone, which would allow a massive increase in the defendant's possible sentence. It was not until a state habeas corpus hearing that the breadth and extent of Coleman's false testimony was revealed, freeing the Tulia defendants. On August 22, 2003, thirty-five of the Tulia defendants were pardoned by Governor Rick Perry. Coleman's false testimony cost the defendants their liberty, cost Coleman his peace officer license and led to his conviction, and cost local residents $6.25 million to settle the wrongful conviction cases.[78]

The Tulia cases were aided not only by the venality of Joe Coleman but also the indifference of the district attorney, the sheer laziness of several defense attorneys in failing adequately to conduct a defense of their clients, the unwillingness of the district judge to assess critically the troubling actions and testimony of a peace officer with a checkered past and a poor reputation for honesty, and even the willingness of juries too often to accept without any second thoughts the evidence offered by the prosecution. Several defense lawyers, including Paul Holloway, Tom Hamilton, Brent Hamilton, and Jeff Blackburn, zealously and professionally represented some Tulia defendants, even at a substantial cost to their legal practice.

Human frailty also affects judging. Deanna Ogg was raped and murdered. Roy Criner was charged with raping her. Criner, an unsympathetic defendant, came to the attention of the police after he told coworkers that he picked up a hitchhiker, had sex with her, and "had to get rough with her." Criner's conviction was reversed by the court of appeals for insufficient evidence. The court of criminal appeals reversed and remanded. In 1997, DNA testing of the semen collected from the body of Deanna Ogg excluded Criner as the source of the semen. Criner moved for a new trial at the court of criminal appeals. It denied the motion, concluding in part that Criner had failed to prove his innocence. One judge surprisingly told an interviewer she voted to deny the motion for a new trial because DNA would not have "made a difference in the verdict." DNA from a cigarette butt collected from the murder scene was later tested. The DNA from the cigarette and the semen were determined to come from the same person, someone other than Criner. Criner was pardoned in 2000. Texas subsequently adopted a limited law allowing some post–conviction DNA testing.[79]

A study of exonerations (official declaration that a person is not guilty of a crime after a conviction) between 1989 and 2003 found that 340 persons were exonerated. DNA evidence led to the exoneration of 144. Texas had the highest number of exonerations during that time, 28. By November 2008 the number of exonerated Texans had reached 36. Dallas County district attorney Craig Watkins created a Conviction Integrity Unit in 2007 to investigate claims of wrongful conviction. In less than two years it found that six men had been wrongly convicted for rape, murder, or robbery in Dallas County.

In 2009, Texas adopted the Tim Cole Act, named after a wrongfully convicted man who died in prison. The act provides for compensation for persons who were shown to have been wrongfully convicted.[80]

Today's criminal justice system depends heavily on the integrity of the crime labs that process forensic evidence used at trials. Whether jurors are subject to a *CSI* effect or not, the work of crime lab personnel is crucial. This makes the problems at the crime lab of the Houston Police Department so troubling: "Since the 2002 exposure of shoddy work and poorly trained personnel, HPD's crime lab has been mired in a forensics controversy that has cast doubt on thousands of cases and led to the exoneration of three men convicted with faulty evidence."[81]

DESEGREGATING TEXAS JURIES

Jim Crow laws infected the Texas criminal justice system through much of the twentieth century. Attacks on discrimination in the criminal justice system were the catalyst for much of the civil rights movement in Texas. One way in which racial discrimination was attacked was to demand that the legal system live up to its promises of due process and equal protection of the laws for all persons.

In *Strauder v. West Virginia* (1880), the Supreme Court declared unconstitutional the exclusion by law of African Americans from the jury. *Strauder* was largely ignored in the South and Texas as Jim Crow and segregation became the order of the day by 1900. However, a series of cases decided by the Supreme Court during the first decade of the twentieth century and again during the 1940s indicated both the strenuous manner in which Texas government officials kept blacks off juries and the conflicted view of the Supreme Court in eradicating racial discrimination in jury selection.[82]

The first Texas jury discrimination case decided by the Supreme Court of the United

States was *Carter v. Texas* (1900). Seth Carter was accused of murder. The grand jury that indicted him consisted solely of white men. Carter was convicted. His appeal and motion for rehearing to the Texas Court of Criminal Appeals both failed, on separate and contradictory grounds. The court first rejected Carter's appeal because he failed to object to the composition of the grand jury in time. On rehearing, the court noted that Carter had not been given an opportunity to object to the membership of the grand jury. Despite recognizing its error, the court of criminal appeals reaffirmed Carter's conviction because it held insufficient his evidence of racial discrimination in the composition of the grand jury, for it was based solely on his own affidavit. As the Supreme Court noted in reversing the court of criminal appeals, Carter was refused the opportunity by the trial court to present any evidence on his claim of racial discrimination. Martin, like Carter, was indicted on a charge of murder. He challenged the composition of both the grand and petit (trial) juries. The Supreme Court declared its readiness to reverse a conviction upon proof of racial discrimination in creating juries. It concluded that Martin failed to offer such proof and upheld his conviction and sentence of death, because the composition of all-white juries was not by itself sufficient to prove evidence of racial discrimination. In a third case, Thomas acknowledged that neither the constitution nor the laws of Texas officially excluded blacks from juries. He claimed that blacks were excluded from jury pools as a factual matter by local jury commissioners. The Supreme Court rejected Thomas's claim. It concluded that it lacked the power to review his factual claim because both the trial court and court of criminal appeals had rejected it.[83]

The difficulty in making a factual claim of racial discrimination was a consequence of the Supreme Court's unwillingness to look behind the curtain drawn by Jim Crow laws, an unwillingness to evaluate not just the formal law, but also the law in action. As a matter of formal law, Texas crafted a system of choosing jurors based on eligibility to vote or citizenship, "good moral character," and the ability to read and write. Whether one possessed good moral character and an ability to read and write was determined by a body of three jury commissioners chosen by the local state district judge. Those jury commissioners in turn selected the members of the grand jury who decided whether the state's evidence was sufficient to indict the accused.[84] African Americans were not excluded by law from jury pools, but the manner in which jurors were selected meant blacks were banned from juries as a matter of fact.

Martin and *Thomas* were two examples of the Supreme Court's unwillingness to intervene in the operation of a racially discriminatory state criminal justice system: "Between 1904 and 1935, the [Supreme] Court did not reverse the conviction of even one black defendant on the ground of race discrimination in jury selection, even though blacks were universally excluded from southern juries." *Norris v. Alabama* (1935), one of the infamous *Scottsboro Boys* cases, was the Court's first occasion in thirty years to reverse a conviction of a black man for reasons of racial discrimination. Shortly after *Norris*, challenges in Texas to racial discrimination in jury selection renewed. The most important effort of the Dallas branch of the NAACP before 1940 was its challenge to the exclusion of blacks from jury service. George Porter had tried to serve on juries in Dallas County in both 1921 and 1935. These attempts "had produced a series of hostile threats, including that of lynching and had ended in Porter's dismissal." He again reported for jury duty in August 1938. After two days of service without incident, he was told by someone to remove himself. When he refused, he was thrown from the building by two white men, causing the sixty-five-year-old Porter permanent injuries.[85]

Porter's injuries led not only to the arrival in Dallas of NAACP lawyer Thurgood Marshall, but also to a concerted local effort to end the jury service ban. Although several district judges ended the ban in their courts, some officials continued to exclude blacks from juries in Dallas County. In 1942 the Supreme Court unanimously reversed the rape conviction of Henry Hill. Hill offered evidence proving racial discrimination in the composition of grand juries. The trial court rejected his contention, and the court of criminal appeals affirmed on the ground that the exclusion of blacks from jury service was a result of a lack of eligible persons, not racial discrimination. The Supreme Court rejected this reasoning, noting that

the 1940 census shows the total population of the county to be 398,564 of whom 61,605 are negroes, and of these 19,133 are males twenty-one years old or more. The census of 1930 showed only 7.5 per cent of the negro population of the county to be illiterate. The census data of 1940 show that of the 17,263 male negroes in the county who were twenty-five years of age or more, 16,107 had attended grade school or higher institutions of learning. Of these 7,979 had attended grade school from five to eight years; 1,970 had attended high school from one to three years, and 1,124 for four years: 466 had attended college from one to three years, and 284 for four years or more.

And yet, no African American had been called for jury service for "so long a period as sixteen years or more." In reversing Hill's conviction the Supreme Court followed its 1940 decision in *Smith v. Texas*, which arose in Harris County. The Court reversed Smith's conviction because Harris County effectively though not formally banned blacks from serving as jurors. The service of African Americans on grand juries by year there was "1931, 1; 1932, 2; 1933, 1; 1934, 1; 1935, none; 1936, 1; 1937, none; 1938, none." On twenty-seven of thirty-two grand juries convened during that time (four grand juries were convened each year), no black person served. On the five grand juries on which a black did serve, the same person served on three. This, the Court unanimously held, violated the defendant's right to the equal protection of the laws.[86]

The response in Dallas County to *Smith* and *Hill* was to allow one and no more than one African American to serve as a grand juror. In 1945, in *Akins v. Texas*, the Supreme Court affirmed the conviction of L. C. Akins, who challenged this arbitrary limitation. It held that, given the reversal of Akins's (then spelled Akens) *initial* conviction by the Texas Court of Criminal Appeals, it appeared that Texas courts were ready to guard against racial discrimination in jury composition. Thus, the Supreme Court accorded great weight to the state court's judgment that Akins did not prove racial discrimination existed in his case. In addition, "[o]n the strictly mathematical basis of population, a grand jury of twelve would have 1.8552 negro members on the average," so having just one was not evidence of racial discrimination. This mathematical claim is not only irrelevant but inaccurate. That the actual number of grand jurors (one) was close to an average (two) was irrelevant to the claim that the jury commissioners set a limit of one, which surely was excluding jurors on the basis of race. Just as importantly, at the beginning of its opinion the Court noted that the one black grand juror seated was one of "sixteen for the term of court at which the indictment against petitioner was found." It was from the list of sixteen persons that a panel of twelve would be chosen to comprise the grand jury that would indict or no-bill the accused. One out of sixteen is 6.25 percent. Based on the Court's own calculation, the mathematical number of black jurors should have been 2.48 (16 × 15.5 percent, the percentage of the African American population in Dallas County).[87]

Akins did not end the Supreme Court's

Gustavo Garcia, Pete Hernandez, and Johnny Herrera, ca. 1953. Courtesy of the Dr. Hector P. García Papers, Special Collections and Archives Department, Texas A&M University–Corpus Christi, Bell Library.

Carlos Cadena during his time as professor, Saint Mary's University School of Law, ca. early 1970s. Courtesy St. Mary's University School of Law Archives.

review of jury seating practices in Texas. In *Cassell v. Texas* (1950), the defendant, like Akins, was charged with murdering a white man. The three white Dallas County jury commissioners testified that they chose for grand jury service only persons with whom they were acquainted. The Supreme Court, reversing the Texas Court of Criminal Appeals, held the grand jury was unconstitutionally constituted. That Dallas County employed a quota for blacks in grand jury service was noted in a concurring opinion by Justice Felix Frankfurter. Between *Hill* and when Cassell was indicted five and one-half years later, twenty-one grand jury panels were impaneled: "On each of these twenty-one consecutive panels there was never more than one Negro."[88]

The most famous Texas jury discrimination case is the Supreme Court's decision in *Hernandez v. Texas* (1954). A group of talented Mexican American lawyers, including Carlos Cadena, Gus Garcia, and Johnny Herrera, argued that the jury commissioners intentionally excluded "persons of Mexican descent" from the grand jury list that indicted Pete

Hernandez for murder. A quarter of a century earlier, a Mexican American named Geronimo "Herman" Ramirez claimed discrimination in the composition of the grand jury and trial jury in his criminal case for the crime of castration. He moved to quash the indictment because no Mexican Americans had been called to serve on either jury. The court of criminal appeals rejected Ramirez's complaint without analysis and reversed his conviction on other grounds. At his retrial, Ramirez was again convicted. He again appealed because Mexican Americans were excluded from the jury pools. Testimony at the hearing on his claim clearly showed that the commissioner who chose the members of the grand jury refused to place on the grand jury any African American or Mexican American and that no African American or Mexican American had been on a grand jury there in recent memory. Despite this unequivocal evidence, the court of criminal appeals rejected Ramirez's claim on the ground that it had been decided in his former appeal. In *Hernandez*, writing for a unanimous Supreme Court, Chief Justice Earl Warren noted that evidence that persons of Mexican descent were treated differently from whites in the community was found in part in the sign above one of the two men's toilets in the courthouse. One was unmarked, and "the other marked 'Colored Men' and 'Hombres Aqui' (Men Here)." The Court's decision, issued two weeks before it issued *Brown v. Board of Education* (1954), both foreshadowed the end of legalized segregation and suggested legal recognition of discrimination against ethnic or racial groups other than blacks.[89]

Castaneda v. Partida (1977) is the Supreme Court's last assessment of racial discrimination in jury selection in Texas. Although the Court did not hold Texas's system of appointing jury commissioners (the "key man" system) facially unconstitutional, it noted that the system could be applied in a racially discriminatory manner. It held that Castaneda's claim that Mexican Americans were systematically denied appointment to the grand jury was sufficient to make a claim of discrimination and reversed Castaneda's conviction. In 1979, Texas amended its laws, providing counties the option of choosing grand jurors through a jury commission (the "key man" approach) or by randomly selecting grand jurors. This did not end charges that the state discriminated in jury selection.[90]

CIVIL RIGHTS AND VOTING (THE WHITE PRIMARY CASES)

By 1900, Texas was a solidly one-party Democratic state. Although the Republican Party fielded statewide candidates, they were invariably defeated. Consequently, elections were a foregone conclusion once Democratic Party candidates were selected. In 1903 and 1905 the election statutes (known as the Terrell Election Law) effectively required a primary for selecting Democratic Party candidates. By the time the first Terrell Election Law was adopted, local primary elections in some areas of Texas were limited to white voters. Although it did not do

so explicitly, the Terrell Election Law implicitly encouraged the exclusion of blacks from the Democratic primary by giving local election bodies the power to reject prospective voters. This encouragement was aided by the adoption in November 1902 of a constitutional amendment requiring all voters to pay a $1.50 poll tax and to provide the receipt for the tax to remain eligible to vote. Violence and intimidation were additional extralegal efforts used to restrict the black vote.[91]

The late nineteenth-century efforts by whites in several Texas counties to limit the vote to white men spread through the state during the early twentieth century. The 1902 poll tax enhanced those efforts, which accelerated after the 1911 prohibition vote. Prohibitionists claimed defeat of the proposed constitutional amendment was because "Antis" had purchased the votes of African Americans and Mexican Americans. By 1920 in most of Texas the all-white Democratic Party primary was the rule, even if not the law. That tacit understanding was insufficient for some. D. A. McAskill of Bexar County demanded that the legislature adopt a statute making the all-white primary official. His demand was a result of losing a race for Bexar County district attorney because his opponent won the black vote. The 1923 legislature adopted such a law, at a time of increased influence of the Ku Klux Klan in Texas (and nationwide), when lynchings of African Americans had again spiked, and when race relations had further deteriorated.[92]

After early unsuccessful efforts to have the white-primary law declared unconstitutional, El Paso resident and medical doctor Lawrence A. Nixon sued local election officials in federal court after he was refused a ballot in the Democratic Party primary. Funded in part by the NAACP, Nixon's lawyer sued for both monetary damages and an injunction to prevent the court from dismissing the case because the election had already occurred. Nixon appealed an adverse decision to the Supreme Court of

Dr. Lawrence A. Nixon, undated. Courtesy of the Texas Western Press Records, MS 366, C. L. Sonnichsen Special Collections Department, University of Texas at El Paso Library.

the United States, which unanimously reversed. Its holding was based on the equal protection clause of the Fourteenth Amendment, not the Fifteenth Amendment right to vote. The legislature responded by amending the law to eliminate any explicit references to the exclusion of African Americans from the Democratic Party primary. A number of lawsuits were initiated, including one by Dr. Nixon. The Supreme Court held this law also violated the Constitution, this time by a 5–4 vote.[93]

Justice Benjamin Cardozo's opinion in *Nixon v. Condon* (1932) focused on the delegation by the state to political parties to decide "who shall be qualified to vote or otherwise participate in such political party." The Democratic Party executive committee then exercised that state-granted power by limiting participation in its primary to white voters. This, Car-

dozo wrote, was not the action of a voluntary organization, for the only body permitted to act for the Democratic Party was the state convention, not the party's executive committee. By granting the executive committee that authority, without any decision from the state convention, Texas had made the party more than just a voluntary organization. The Court noted it was not deciding whether a wholly voluntary organization could discriminate on the basis of race in determining who may vote in something other than a general election.

Democratic Party officials continued their search for ways to refuse to allow blacks to vote. The state convention of the Democratic Party voted in 1928 to limit its primary to white voters. A substantial number of lawsuits challenging this practice failed, with one exception. In 1932 a Bexar County district court ruled that the plaintiff, Booker, an African American, was eligible to vote, a decision overruled the next day by the Fourth Court of Civil Appeals. Nixon again sued and won a victory in federal district court in 1934 which the Democratic Party declined to appeal. It was, according to Darlene Clark Hine, a "pyrrhic victory," for "[i]t had almost no effect on the political status of blacks in Texas." This was due in part to the decision in 1934 of Texas attorney general James V. Allred, a candidate for governor, to issue a legal opinion as attorney general declaring that blacks were forbidden to vote in the Democratic Party primary based on a decision of the Democratic Party state convention. Allred's opinion was challenged. In *Bell v. Hill* (1934), the Texas Supreme Court refused to issue an order allowing the African American petitioners to vote in the Democratic Party primary. Allred's opinion and *Bell v. Hill* inflamed black lawyers and others.[94]

A clever, albeit too clever, response to both decisions was the filing by black Houston lawyers of a lawsuit on behalf of R. R. Grovey against the Harris County clerk, Albert Townsend. Grovey claimed that Townsend had unconstitutionally refused to send him an absentee ballot for the Democratic Party primary. Suing in a justice of the peace court was designed to get the case to the Supreme Court of the United States quickly, for Grovey's lawyers knew that if the justice of the peace rejected Grovey's claim, the only appeal available was to the Supreme Court. The gambit worked. Grovey's claim was rejected, and the Court agreed to hear Grovey's case. But its decision was devastating to black Texans. The Court unanimously ruled the action of the Democratic state convention limiting the primary to white Texans did not constitute state action and was thus constitutional.[95]

Grovey was released the same day as *Norris v. Alabama* (1935), the first case since 1904 in which the Supreme Court upheld a constitutional challenge to the racial composition of a grand jury. These seemingly contrary results made any assessment of the Court's views on civil rights difficult. *Grovey* was taken to the Supreme Court over the objection of the NAACP, making the sting of defeat to black Texas lawyers and other proponents of voting rights reform even greater.[96]

In 1942, the NAACP, through Thurgood Marshall, renewed the battle to end the all-white primary in *Smith v. Allwright* (1944). By this time the Supreme Court appeared more amenable to claims of racial discrimination, for it had decided several jury discrimination cases in favor of the black claimants. Further, just two members of the *Grovey* court remained there when *Smith* was heard. *Smith* held that the Democratic Party was not a voluntary association but possessed a "character as a state agency," and it overruled *Grovey*. Michael Klarman noted that *Grovey* "proved unpalatable to the justices in 1944, not because its legal reasoning was faulty, but because during World War II they found black disfranchisement offensive."

All of Texas did not go gentle into that good night. The Jaybird Democratic Association, created in 1889 in southeast Texas and one of the earliest groups to limit voting to whites, conducted a "pre-primary," an election contest before the primary election, limited to white voters. The Court, in *Terry v. Adams* (1953), held unconstitutional the actions of the Jaybird Democratic Association. Despite deciding the case 8–1, the context of the case fractured the Court. A plurality held the Jaybird primary "has become an integral part, indeed the only effective part, of the elective process that determines who shall rule and govern in the county." The association thus engaged in unconstitutional state action, not merely private action. Another group of four members declared that the actions of the Jaybirds violated the Fifteenth Amendment. Despite this disagreement, *Terry* fit well the Court's clearly emerging civil rights views, for the next year the Court declared unconstitutional legally mandated racial segregation.[97]

CIVIL RIGHTS AND EDUCATION

Blacks and whites in Texas were educated separately as a matter of law from the adoption in 1893 of the Public Free Schools Act until well after *Brown v. Board of Education* (1954). After *Brown* was decided, Texas school boards reacted in a variety of ways to the constitutional duty to desegregate. In some parts of the state segregated schooling remained the norm until courts ordered desegregation; in others, desegregation arrived by the end of the 1960s. A 1982 study found about 12 percent of all Texas school districts were moderately or severely segregated in 1970–71. The continuing existence of "blatant school segregation" in some areas of the state generated a comprehensive legal attack on educational segregation in Texas. The U.S. Department of Justice filed suit in federal district judge William Wayne Justice's court requesting all of Texas be placed under a court order to desegregate its public schools. Texas and the Texas Education Association were two

Texas State Ranger posing with Mansfield High School students during 1956 efforts to prevent racial desegregation of the high school. Courtesy Texas State Library and Archives Commission.

of the numerous defendants. Trial began in September 1970. By November, Judge Justice issued his first order, holding that the education offered in nine black school districts was unconstitutionally inferior to the educational opportunities offered in neighboring white school districts. Justice supplemented his opinion the following spring, ordering the annexation of the black districts into the white districts that abutted them. Justice's order was broad in scope. The state's twofold duties were, "First, to act at once to eliminate by positive means all vestiges of the dual school structure throughout the state; and second, to compensate for the abiding scars of past discrimination." The Fifth Circuit largely affirmed his decision. Because it was aware that federal district judges in

other parts of the state had issued desegregation orders applicable to some (usually large) school districts, the court of appeals added the following: "Nothing herein shall be deemed to affect the jurisdiction of any other district court with respect to any presently pending or future school desegregation suits." This removed from Justice's court the desegregation of the Dallas and Houston school districts, but Justice's order applied to "over one thousand school districts and two-thirds of the Texas student population."[98]

The desegregation of Texas public schools through federal court supervision continued for well over a decade. In 1981 the Fifth Circuit reversed Justice's opinion concerning the desegregation of the public schools in the Gregory-Portland Independent School District in South Texas. Five years later, it reversed Judge Justice's order barring a testing requirement for higher-education students who desired to take professional education courses. This largely ended Judge Justice's oversight of public school desegregation. An early assessment concluded that *United States v. Texas* was a qualified success. By late 2010, only a few school desegregation orders remained. In part driven by demographics and in part by housing patterns, a significant number of Texas public schools have student populations in which the majority are either African American or Hispanic.[99]

The 1893 Public Free Schools Act separated education of the "children of the white and colored races," defining "colored" as "all persons of mixed blood descended from negro ancestry." Ostensibly, this formally left Mexican American students as "white" and not segregated in public schooling. In practice, a number of school districts placed Anglo students in an "American" school and Hispanic students in a "Mexican" school. The initial challenges to segregated education for Mexican American students began in the late 1920s. In 1928, Felipe Vela asked the state superintendent of public instruction to require the Charlotte Independent School District to admit his adopted daughter Amada to the "American" school. Vela argued that Amada spoke English and was not "Mexican" (because she was adopted), making her eligible to attend the American school. The superintendent agreed. The next year the League of United Latin American Citizens (LULAC) was formed as a statewide organization. Shortly thereafter, LULAC initiated the *Salvatierra* case, challenging the segregation of Mexican American school children in Del Rio. The district court issued the injunction requested by LULAC and the parents. The school district appealed. The Fourth Court of Civil Appeals acknowledged that the system in the Del Rio area constituted segregation. However, this was not an "arbitrary segregation." It deferred to the Del Rio superintendent's argu-

ment that segregation in the first three grades was not for reasons of racism, but largely due to differing English language ability, joined by an additional concern that some Mexican American children entered school late because of their parents' migrant work. More arbitrarily, the superintendent also stated, "I have been told that it is true that a Mexican child will reach the puberty stage sooner than an American child." This "English-language speaking" justification was then used to maintain the segregation of Anglo children from Hispanic children for several decades.[100]

The attack on segregation based on alleged linguistic differences was renewed after World War II. In *Mendez v. Westminster School District* (1946), a federal district court held unconstitutional California's maintenance of separate schools for Anglo and Mexican American school children. This decision was upheld on appeal. Less than a week before *Mendez* was affirmed on appeal, Texas attorney general Price Daniel, Sr., issued an opinion declaring impermissible the segregation of Mexican school children from Anglo school children based on race. Daniel concluded that segregation based on "language deficiencies" was allowed through the first three grades. This opinion mimicked the rationale of *Salvatierra*, but subsequent correspondence between Daniel and lawyer Gus Garcia reaffirmed the antidiscrimination emphasis of the opinion. In *Delgado v. Bastrop Independent School District* (1948), the trial court held that the separate education of students of "Mexican or other Latin American descent" violated the equal protection clause of the Fourteenth Amendment. *Delgado* was the beginning of a decade-long fight by LULAC and the more recently founded American G.I. Forum to force school districts to eliminate separate schools for white and Mexican American school children. By 1957 at least fifteen school discrimination cases had been filed by lawyers for these organizations. When *Cisneros v. Corpus Christi Independent School District* (1970) was decided, the desegregation strategy had changed. Plaintiffs, aided by lawyers from the Mexican American Legal Defense and Education Fund (MALDEF) argued that Hispanics should be deemed an identifiable ethnic group and not, as was argued a generation earlier, "other white." The court agreed.[101]

Demetrio Rodriguez and other parents, unhappy with the educational opportunities available to their children in the Edgewood Independent School District in San Antonio, sued in federal court claiming that the Texas system of public school financing violated the equal protection clause of the Fourteenth Amendment. Texas financed public school education largely through property taxes. The value of private property per pupil in Edgewood ISD was $5,960; in the relatively wealthy Alamo Heights Independent School District across town, the value of private property per pupil was more than $49,000. Edgewood contributed $26 in local property tax monies per pupil "above its Local Fund Assignment for the Minimum Foundation Program"; Alamo Heights raised $333 per pupil. The combination of funding from local property taxes, the Minimum Foundation Program, and federal funding totaled $356 per pupil in Edgewood and $594 per pupil in Alamo Heights. About 90 percent of the students in the Edgewood School District were Mexican American, and another 6 percent were black. In Alamo Heights, Mexican American and black students comprised about 19 percent of the student body. Rodriguez's attorney, Arthur Gochman, failed to interest MALDEF in joining the lawsuit. MALDEF instead initiated a separate lawsuit making similar claims in *Guerra v. Smith* (1969). The federal judge hearing *Guerra* dismissed the case. In December 1971 a three-judge panel held unconstitutional Texas's system of public school funding. Texas appealed to the Supreme Court of the United States.[102]

The Supreme Court, by a 5–4 vote, reversed. It addressed two issues in its opinion: First, the Court asked "whether the Texas system

Demetrio Rodriguez, late 1970s.
Courtesy Demetrio Rodriguez.

of financing public education operates to the disadvantage of some suspect class or impinges upon a fundamental right explicitly or implicitly protected by the Constitution." Second, if not, has the Texas approach to funding "rationally furthered some legitimate, articulated state purpose" as required by the equal protection clause? If the Court answered the first question in the negative, the plaintiffs would likely lose, for statutes almost always survived the Court's "rational basis" scrutiny. Thus, the case hinged on whether the Court concluded either that discrimination on the basis of wealth created a suspect classification or that education was a fundamental right. The Court held the claim of wealth discrimination was inadequate. It then concluded that education was not a fundamental right, for it was neither explicitly nor implicitly protected in the U.S. Constitution. The Court then found Texas's funding system rationally furthered a legitimate government purpose.

Rodriguez was just the beginning of the constitutional battle concerning Texas public school financing. Although Texas modified its system of public school financing after *Rodri-*

guez, wide disparities in school district funding led to a lawsuit alleging the funding system violated the Texas Constitution. Edgewood and other school districts sued Commissioner of Education William Kirby. This litigation has generated six substantial opinions by the Supreme Court of Texas concerning the constitutionality of Texas school finance.[103]

Edgewood I (1989) held that the school finance system violated Article VII, section 1 of the Texas Constitution, which makes it "the duty of the Legislature of the State to establish and make suitable provision for the support and maintenance of an efficient system of public free schools." This conclusion followed similar decisions in other state courts. To meet the demands of the constitution, the legislature had to provide to school districts "substantially equal access to similar revenues per pupil at similar levels of tax effort," affording children in poor districts "a substantially equal opportunity" as children in rich districts to "access to educational funds." At the sixth called session, the seventy-first legislature finally agreed to a revised funding approach in Senate Bill 1. In *Edgewood II* (1991), the supreme court affirmed the conclusion of the district court declaring unconstitutional this revised funding program because "Senate Bill 1 leaves essentially intact the same funding system with the same deficiencies we reviewed in *Edgewood I.*" Senate Bill 1 maintained the "vast" inefficiencies in public school financing contrary to the commands of *Edgewood I. Edgewood III* (1992) was decided after the adoption of another bill that attempted to increase revenues for school funding by creating consolidated tax bases that encompassed more than one school district and that limited the ways in which a wealthy school district could use its tax base to generate monies unshared by all districts. The supreme court held that the legislature's attempt to improve equity in the financing of schools was unconstitutional because it violated the prohibition on a statewide *ad valorem* tax (a property tax "according to the value").

The third time for the legislature was a charm. Senate Bill 7 required wealthy districts to reduce their wealth in one of several ways, each of which was intended to recapture some of those funds to give to poorer school districts. Dubbed by its opponents as the "Robin Hood" plan, Senate Bill 7 permitted some funding disparities benefiting wealthier districts, in part because of differences in funding for maintenance and operations and funding for facilities. The court in *Edgewood IV* (1995) held that, despite some inequalities in funding, Senate Bill 7 was constitutional because it met the legislature's constitutional duty to provide for substantially equal funding "necessary for a general diffusion of knowledge." *Edgewood V* (2003) was a challenge by wealthy districts which claimed that the school financing system had created a de facto statewide property tax contrary to the Texas Constitution. The supreme court held that the dismissal of the lawsuit by the district court was procedurally erroneous. *Edgewood VI* (2005) rejected the state's claims that the wealthy school districts challenging public school funding lacked standing and that their claims were nonjusticiable. The court also concluded that the school funding system was again unconstitutional because it constituted a statewide *ad valorem* tax. The legislature has adopted another system of funding which, as one commentator noted, "almost guarantees another Edgewood lawsuit as even wealthy districts run out of funds to run their schools and maintain their advantages over poorer school districts."[104]

AFFIRMATIVE ACTION IN HIGHER EDUCATION

The Fifth Circuit's decision in *Hopwood v. Texas* (1996) barred the use of race as a factor in determining which applicants to admit to public universities in Texas (see chapter 6). The Texas legislature adopted the Top Ten Percent Law the next year, which guaranteed every Texas public high school student graduating in the top 10 percent admission to any state university. As a factual matter the law adversely affected only those non–top-10–percent students interested in enrolling at the University of Texas at Austin. The law was adopted to avoid a decrease in the number of African American and Mexican American students at UT-Austin. The law worked, possibly better than expected. The percentage of African American and Mexican American students at UT-Austin was higher after implementation of the Top Ten Percent Law than when affirmative action was used. The vast majority of African American and Mexican American students at UT-Austin were offered admission through the Top Ten Percent Law. Many of those applicants graduated from predominantly African American or Mexican American high schools. After the Supreme Court of the United States held constitutionally permissible the use of race in educational admissions decisions in 2003, UT-Austin again began using race as a criterion in making admissions decisions. However, the Top Ten Percent Law was used for a substantial majority of its admissions decisions. Two unsuccessful Anglo applicants to UT-Austin sued, claiming the university's use of race in admissions was unconstitutional. The federal district court rejected their claim, a decision affirmed by a three-person panel of the Fifth Circuit on appeal in 2011. The en banc ("in the bench" or entire membership) Fifth Circuit agreed to hear the case in February 2011.[105]

EIGHT

Civil Procedure, Civil Remedies, and Civil Law

★

RULES OF PROCEDURE have always affected the operation of substantive law. An old legal adage is, "I'll take procedural law, you can have the substantive law, and I'll win every time." The separation of procedural and substantive law in civil cases was a modern invention, beginning in the middle of the nineteenth century in the United States. Texas's early rejection of English common law pleading and development of peculiar rules of procedure have affected Texas's substantive law since it became a republic in 1836. One way to change substantive law is to do so directly. Those who prefer the current substantive law may object, making amendments improbable. A second and more subtle way to alter substantive law is to do so indirectly by changing rules of procedure. This indirect approach has often been taken in Texas legal history and has particularly been true in efforts to reshape the substantive law of torts.

PROCEDURE AND PRACTICE BEFORE AND DURING THE REPUBLIC

The Constitution of the Republic of Texas required congress to "introduce, by statute, the common law of England, with such modifications as our circumstances, in their judgment, may require." It did so on December 20, 1836, but only in part. The last section of the statute declared the common law of England applicable to "juries and to evidence." A jury of one's peers, understood in the common law as a bulwark of liberty, was unknown in the civil law system, the legal system of Spain and Mexico. Stephen F. Austin's 1824 Criminal Regulations required trial by jury. Article 192 of the 1827 constitution of the state of Coahuila and Texas commanded the congress to "establish the trial by jury in criminal cases, [and] to extend the same gradually, and even to adopt it in civil cases in proportion as the advantages of this valuable institution become practically known." An 1830 decree of the Coahuila and Texas congress attempted to create a type of jury system, and Decree 277, known as the Chambers Jury Law, adopted in 1834, attempted to put in place a system of trial by jury for both civil and criminal matters. Decree 277 was never operative.[1]

The statute adopting the common law for juries and evidence in inferior courts failed to declare the applicable law of practice and pleading in the trial courts. The result was the continued use of the Spanish and Mexican approach to pleadings, declared in Decree 277: the plaintiff began with a petition and the defendant responded by filing an answer. This system of pleading was much simpler than any existing in the United States, for American states then used the formal, technical, and complicated system of common law pleading. As noted by University of Texas Law Department professor John C. Townes, in Texas the parties were "required to set forth, in a plain and intelligible manner, the facts upon which they respectively relied to sustain their positions before the court; in short, to state to the court the real truth of the matter in controversy, so far as they might be able." The bias toward Spanish/Mexican law in Texas civil procedure extended to the issue of venue, where the lawsuit had to be filed. The common law generally located venue where the act about which the plaintiff complained occurred. In Spanish law, the lawsuit was usually brought where the defendant lived. Section 5 of the December 22, 1836, act organizing the district courts followed the Spanish venue rule.[2]

The 1836 act establishing the jurisdiction of the Supreme Court of the Republic of Texas also granted it the power to prescribe rules of practice and procedure before it. It was not until January 1840 that the first session of the supreme court occurred. The court then issued rules applicable to itself as well as rules applicable to the district courts. Immediately afterward, congress adopted a statute "to regulate the proceedings in Civil Suits."[3]

The rules of practice adopted by the supreme court and applicable to causes in the district courts were modest. The desire to institute a formal culture in the district courts is evident in several rules. Rule 7 required every attorney, upon threat of being held in contempt, to "rise to their feet" when addressing the court or examining a witness. Rule 6 barred an attorney from interrupting his opponent's argument, and Rule 5 prohibited an attorney from arguing after the court had rendered its decision. These rules of "etiquette" in practice in the district courts were important in a country that lacked courthouses, where the members of the bar consisted of some skilled but many marginally qualified members, and whose lawyers and judges possessed few law books.

The 1840 rules of the district courts totaled thirty-four. In addition to the topics noted above, they spoke of issues such as the conduct of counsel and the rules regarding appeals. Only one attorney for each party was allowed to cross-examine a witness, and only two attorneys per side were permitted to make arguments. The rules did not speak of witnesses, nor did they calibrate the extent or limits of rebuttal argument.

On January 20, 1840, the Texas Congress adopted a law providing that "the Common Law of England (so far as it is not inconsistent with the Constitution or the Acts of congress now in force) . . . shall continue in full force until altered or repealed by Congress." Two weeks later, it adopted a law making clear that the adoption of the common law of England did not extend to the common law of pleading. Section 1 of the February 5, 1840, act declared "the adoption of the common law shall not be construed to adopt the common law system of pleading." Instead, congress formally adopted the then-existing Spanish petition-and-answer approach to pleading. This act also offered evidence of the legislature's focus on substance and efficiency over form in pleading and practice. In his answer the defendant was permitted to plead any and all matters of fact or law. A petitioner's "want of form" in his petition did not result in an abatement of the suit, but if a "sufficient matter of substance may appear upon the motion," the court was to hear the merits of the matter.[4]

COMMON-LAW PLEADING AND THE DEVELOPMENT OF EQUITY

Common-law pleading developed in England along with trial by jury and the adversary system. In common-law pleading the parties (adversaries) pled back and forth until "there is ultimately reached a stage where one side has affirmed and the other has denied a single material point in the case," to be resolved by the jury. The back and forth of pleading took place within the writ system, the system that bundled together the procedures, the evidentiary requirements, and the substantive law when one person complained about the actions of another. A plaintiff alleging some harm was limited to using one writ. If he chose the incorrect writ to complain about the defendant's conduct, no matter how wrongful the defendant's conduct, plaintiff lost. This was a harsh system, particularly because the writ system was not altered as England changed, but it had a sound purpose. Common-law pleading was a more rational approach to the resolution of disputes than trial by ordeal (tying a person and placing him in water and determining guilt or innocence depending on whether he sank), trial by wager or compurgation (finding twelve or so persons to swear an oath that the party was trustworthy), or trial by battle. But no additional writs were created after the fourteenth century, leaving lawyers with the choice of the thirty to forty acknowledged common-law writs. If the complainant's facts alleging harm did not fit any of the then existing writs, that was a problem for the complainant, not the sys-

tem. As the common law developed in England, the writ system came to be highly technical and highly formalistic, shorn of practicality and often requiring the pleading of fictional "facts" as required by the writ, unrelated to the dispute which led the parties to court. The writ system was about form, and often about form to the exclusion of substance.[5]

The harshness of the writ system in the common law was ameliorated by the development of equity, created by the king to do justice when the common-law courts failed to do so. A complaint in equity was made to the chancellor, the king's representative. The writ system did not apply in equity; instead, the complainant made his claim through a petition. The chancellor decided the case without a jury, and historically in the absence of a trial. Equity was traditionally more flexible than the common law. But equity also became formal and rigid.[6]

The technicality and formality of common-law pleading led to calls for its revision or abolition in the early nineteenth century. But it was not until 1847 that the New York legislature asked its appointed commissioners to write a code of pleading abolishing the forms of action of the common law. The proposed code, which was adopted by the legislature in 1848, is known as the Field Code after the commission's most energetic and influential member, David Dudley Field. The Field Code abolished the distinction between law and equity and substituted the civil action for the common-law writ system. Although the Field Code is hailed as the first modern system of pleading, Texas's adoption of the law of Spanish pleading applicable to its common-law system significantly predated New York's action.[7]

EQUITY IN TEXAS

The Texas Congress's act of February 5, 1840, did not abolish the distinction between law and equity. Section 12 explicitly required the district courts to act either as a law court or in equity depending on the cause. The supreme court criticized this provision: "A hundred judges, in almost any conceivable case, might differ in some degree as to its interpretation and exact function." The later efforts of the congress of the republic to distinguish between law and equity only "added to the perplexity of the courts in their efforts to harmonize the civil and the common-law systems." The merger of law and equity occurred upon the adoption of the 1845 Texas Constitution. Article IV, section 10 declared that "the District Court shall have original jurisdiction of . . . all suits, complaints and pleas whatever, without regard to any distinction between law and equity." Section 16 gave the parties a right to a trial by jury in all equity matters, a unique approach. The federal court system did not abolish the distinction between law and equity until the adoption in 1938 of the Federal Rules of Civil Procedure.[8]

The Texas Congress's decision to retain the Spanish/Mexican system of petition and answer should not be underestimated. None of the states had departed from common law pleading in 1840, when the Republic of Texas rejected it. And no state went so far as Texas did in creating a right to a trial by jury for matters of equity. These developments suggested a system of civil justice that focused on practicality and pragmatism, rather than on artifice and form. This promise was not, however, always fulfilled in Texas legal history.

PRACTICE ACT OF 1846

The Practice Act of 1846 was the brainchild of Representative Peter Gray, a founder of the firm known today as Baker Botts, and adopted on May 13 by the first legislature of the state of Texas. The Practice Act explicitly repealed the act of February 15, 1840, but retained the petition-and-answer system, requiring the petitioner to give "a full and clear statement of the cause of action and such other allegations pertinent to the case as he may deem necessary

to sustain the suit" and allowing the defendant to "plead as many several matters whether of law or fact as he shall think necessary for his defense." The Practice Act has been regularly amended, but its structure remains in effect today.[9]

THE SUPREME COURT'S RULES OF 1877 AND 1892

Section 25 of Article V of the 1876 constitution granted the supreme court the power "to make rules and regulations for the government of said court, and the other courts of the State, to regulate proceedings and expedite the dispatch of business therein." The court promulgated rules of practice in 1877 for all courts, both trial (district) and appellate courts. Most remained in effect even after the constitutional amendment of the Judiciary Article (Article V) in 1891, which drastically changed the Texas court system (see chapter 6). The 1891 amendment also limited the power of the supreme court to make rules of procedure. Amended section 25 permitted the supreme court to make rules of procedure "not inconsistent with the laws of the State." This gave the legislature the constitutional authority to make any and all rules of practice and procedure. Those rules could be supplemented by rules of the supreme court as long as they were not inconsistent with the rules legislatively adopted. Any rules promulgated by the supreme court could be supplanted at any time by the legislature.[10]

The 1877 Rules of Court marked a major improvement over the 1846 Practice Act in terms of organization and clarity. The supreme court began with pleadings, moved to motions, the call of the trial, and then the trial itself. The rules clearly defined the terms of pleading and practice and the operation of the trial. Substantively, the 1877 rules largely followed the approach in the Practice Act. Just as importantly, the taming of the frontier through rules of the etiquette of practice was reinforced. The formal practice requirements initiated in the era of the republic remained, including requiring counsel to "rise to his feet" (Rule 42) when addressing the court and declaring that "[m]ere personal criticisms by counsel upon each other shall be avoided, and when indulged in, shall be promptly corrected as a contempt of court" (Rule 39). The Rules of the District Court were 122 in number, of which the first 100 concerned civil matters originating in the district courts.

The October 8, 1892, rules adopted by the supreme court in light of the 1891 constitutional amendment followed in major respects the 1877 rules. The 1892 rules continued to insist on proper behavior by attorneys and offered step-by-step directions on civil claims from the filing of the petition to the appeal. The court also adopted rules applicable to appellate practice. These rules of practice were supplemented by a substantial number of rules of procedure adopted by statute.[11]

THE CALCIFICATION OF PROCEDURE AND SPECIAL ISSUES SUBMISSION

In a 1910 address to the Texas Bar Association, Lewis M. Dabney offered a satire of Texas procedure and practice. As a good Texas lawyer, "[b]eing justly proud of our own system of accurate, swift, inexpensive and sure administration of justice," he sought to compare it with the pitiful administration of justice in the mythical land of Canaan, which looked remarkably like Texas. Dabney's knowledge of Canaan came from an old Canaan lawyer residing in an insane asylum. He lived there because he believed that "a court should be a place where God's justice is done on this earth, and that speedily, inflexibly and inexpensively." The combination of elected judges, demonization of out-of-state corporations (particularly railroads), and substitution of emotional appeals for skillful pleading by attorneys made a mockery of the truth-finding function of trials

in Canaan. After a verdict in which the "defendant is soaked," his attorney includes fifty bills of exception and two hundred assignments of error. The court of appeals reverses on one error and declines to hear the rest, and the case is returned to the district court for another trial. "Up and down [the case] goes like a seesaw."[12]

Four years before Dabney's address to the Texas Bar Association, Roscoe Pound, then a little-known professor and dean at the University of Nebraska College of Law, gave a speech at the annual meeting of the American Bar Association in Saint Paul, Minnesota, titled "The Causes of Popular Dissatisfaction in the Administration of Justice." Pound charged lawyers with using procedural devices to turn litigation from a search for the truth into a sporting contest. The address caused a sensation. Although Dabney does not explicitly refer to Pound, he echoes many of Pound's complaints. The trial had devolved into a contest in which both parties attempted to use rhetorical skills and emotional appeals to sway the jury and to use cunning and legal skills to encourage the trial judge to make an error that would guarantee a new trial in case of an adverse verdict. To the horror of legal progressives, procedure had trumped substance, and emotion had trumped rational thought in the American system of justice. Neither was helpful in creating an efficient and effective system of justice.[13]

At that same 1910 meeting the Texas Bar Association voted on two propositions to improve practice and procedure. The first was to amend the law of pleadings in three ways: (1) to require the parties, when requesting affirmative relief, to plead all facts relied on to create an issue of fact for the jury; (2) to abolish the general denial and plea of not guilty by the defendant, used in civil cases in actions for trespass to try title to land; and (3) to assume true all allegations of fact by the plaintiff not specifically denied by the defendant. The second proposition was to amend the law to require the trial judge to use a special verdict unless both parties agreed otherwise. The association adopted both and recommended their adoption by the legislature. Both proposals were intended to streamline the course of the civil justice system, the former by simplifying pleadings and thus the issues of fact for resolution by the jury, and the latter to make appeals of jury verdicts less susceptible to reversal and the "seesaw" effect noted by Dabney. Both were also approved because the Texas Supreme Court and Texas Courts of Civil Appeals were each at least one year behind in deciding cases. Finally, both proposals might make the trial of civil cases more rational and efficient.[14]

Between 1911 and 1925 the number of statutory provisions on civil pleading and practice in trial courts increased from 372 to 458, a stunning increase of 23 percent. For many lawyers the simple and clear rules of pleading and practice adopted when Texas was a republic had been transformed into an uncontrollable Frankenstein's monster. The good-faith proposals of the Texas Bar Association in 1910 seemed only to make the situation worse. The special-issues verdict proposal provides one example. A special verdict asked the jury to decide a number of issues of fact. Based on its answers, the trial court issued a judgment in favor of plaintiff or defendant. If done correctly, the special verdict gave a particular answer to all the questions of fact, leaving lawyers little to argue about other than whether there was sufficient evidence for the jury to decide the case (a legal sufficiency claim), and/or whether the verdict was against the great weight of the evidence (a factual sufficiency claim). Limiting the scope of an appellate court's review of a trial court's judgment would, reformers believed, reduce trial and appellate court congestion, reduce delay in the administration of justice, and eliminate the "sporting contest" of trials. The special-issues submission was initially viewed as a time-saving and justice-promoting device, one that would acknowledge the brevity of life and the search for the truth at trial.[15]

In 1897 the legislature amended a verdict statute because "much inconvenience and intolerable delay accrue to litigants in this State," in part "for want of a law authorizing a simple and expeditious method for the decisions of controverted questions of fact by special verdict." It did so at the suggestion of the Texas Supreme Court, which noted in *Silliman v. Gano* (1897) that a verdict had to embrace all the issues necessary for a judgment, and the failure to include every issue of fact necessary to support a judgment required reversal even when the missing issue of fact was undisputed: "The rule, in our opinion, is therefore technical, arbitrary, and unreasonable, and calculated rather to obstruct, than to promote, the administration of justice." However, the court lacked the constitutional authority to change statutory procedural requirements. In 1899 the legislature declared that the special verdict was not permitted unless all parties agreed to such a submission. It also required a party to request a special issue be submitted before being allowed to complain about its absence on appeal. After the recommendation of the Texas Bar Association in 1910 and again in 1911, the 1913 legislature amended the special verdict rule to require the court to craft a special verdict upon the request of either party. The special issues submission then became the standard: "One marked difference in jury trial practice in the state and federal courts of Texas [between 1913 and 1941] has been that in the state jurisdiction nearly all civil jury cases have been submitted upon special issues."[16]

The difficulty facing a trial judge was crafting a special verdict that both covered the contested factual field and did not overwhelm the jury by asking it to answer a large number of questions. In a 1915 case the issue was whether the defendant railroad had negligently allowed oil from its oil tanks to pool, which then, during a severe rainstorm, coursed through the plaintiff's property, destroying his spinach crop. The railroad claimed the rainstorm was an act of God for which it was not responsible. The trial court crafted a special verdict, and the jury found in favor of the plaintiff. The railroad claimed the jury's findings were indefinite and confusing and moved for a new trial. Its motion was denied by the district court. On appeal, the court of civil appeals noted:

> The findings of the jury in answer to questions 19, 20, 31, 32, 35, 36, 44, and 45 specifically found from the evidence that the rainfall in question both at defendant's oil tanks and track and at appellee's spinach field was extraordinary and unprecedented, such as had never before been known within the memory of living witnesses, and could not have been foreseen or anticipated, thereby establishing that said rainfall was an act of God under the law, and the jury found in answer to questions 22 and 63 submitted by the court, that said rainfall and high water was not an act of God, thus making the latter findings in direct conflict with and contradictory of the findings first set out.

If this fairly simple case resulted in at least sixty-three special verdict questions, ten or more of which were answered in conflicting fashion, then the system of special verdicts was broken nearly as soon as it was mandated. Writing in 1941, lawyer J. B. Dooley noted that in one negligence case in central Texas more than two hundred special issues were submitted to the jury. Charles T. McCormick criticized such actions, concluding that cases such as these "seem to savor rather of the subtle logic of special pleading at the common law than of the spirit of rationalism and practicality of our Texas background and inheritance." Special issues, a progressive reform, had been twisted into a device made for the "technicalities" favored by legal formalists. An approach designed to limit and lessen appeals was used to foster more appeals, particularly by lawyers for defendants, tying up the appellate courts and leading to a more inefficient and cumbersome administration of justice.[17]

The movement toward this technical and formal approach to submitting special issues was in part a consequence of the clogged appellate system and in part a consequence of a jurisprudence emphasizing abstract technicality adopted by Texas courts. In *Texas & N. O. Railway v. Harrington* (1921), the Texas Commission of Appeals, a body legislatively created in 1918 to ease the supreme court's five-year case backlog, heard a case concerning the propriety of the special verdict questions given to the jurors. The plaintiffs were the widow of a man killed, along with their four children, when his automobile was struck by the defendant's train. The sclerotic nature of the state of pleadings even in 1918 may be found in the defendant's pleadings. The defendant made: (1) a general demurrer (even assuming all the plaintiff's facts are true, no liability exists); (2) a special exception (asking the court to require the plaintiff in a negligence case to state more specifically the facts showing negligence); (3) a general denial (refusing to admit any of the plaintiff's claims); (4) a plea of contributory negligence of the deceased (claiming plaintiff was at fault and thus defendant was not liable); and (5) a claim of inevitable accident (claiming no one was negligent, so defendant cannot be liable). The railroad's attorneys requested special issues submissions and requested the court instruct the jury that if it concluded the deceased acted as the defendant claimed, the jury should find he was negligent. Such a finding would bar any recovery by the widow and children. The trial court gave the jury ten questions to decide but refused to make the defendant's requested charge. The jury found in favor of the plaintiffs in the substantial amount of thirty-five thousand dollars. The court of civil appeals reversed, holding that the trial court erred in refusing to instruct the jury as defendant requested. The commission of appeals reversed the court of civil appeals, holding that the railroad's requested instruction to the jury impermissibly commingled a general charge with special issues. The supreme court adopted this opinion.[18]

The next year the supreme court decided *Fox v. Dallas Hotel Co.* (1922), another wrongful death negligence case. Alexander Fox was killed when an elevator, having stopped, started down again after Fox got out and was looking down the elevator shaft. The plaintiffs, Fox's widow and two children, received a workmen's compensation award. She sued the defendant on the ground that it had negligently failed to keep the elevator in good repair. The defendant claimed Fox was contributorily negligent. The trial court instructed the jury to determine whether Fox was "guilty of contributory negligence in his conduct in, around, or about the elevator, or the shaft thereof, prior to or at the time he was injured." The jury answered this question "No." It awarded damages of three thousand dollars to each plaintiff. The court of civil appeals reversed. The Texas Supreme Court affirmed the court of civil appeals, holding that the trial court erred by refusing to give the jury several specific questions of particular actions by Fox that may have constituted contributory negligence. In other words, the decision of the trial court to give the jury just one contributory negligence question was insufficient and reversible error. Because the defendant claimed that several different actions by Fox constituted contributory negligence, the trial court was required to instruct the jury on each one. This was part of the requirement that each issue be "distinctly and separately" given to the jury to decide. This rule gave the defendant several opportunities to have the jury answer a contributory negligence question in the affirmative, any one of which exonerated the defendant from liability. Thus, the defendant enjoyed two advantages in special issues submission: (1) the complexity of special issues submission increased the chance of an error by the trial court that allowed for reversal

on appeal if the plaintiff won at trial; and (2) a defendant was given several chances to claim contributory negligence or otherwise attack the plaintiff's case through an exponential increase in the number of issues submitted for the jury's assessment.[19]

Finally, special issues submission required the trial court to "give such explanation and definition of legal terms as shall be necessary to enable the jury to answer each issue." These legal terms were often couched in the most abstract fashion, legal terminology unknown to most jurors. These "high-level abstractions" did "little to inform the jury of the real problems to be solved in answering the issues." The jury was thus required to answer a number of questions with little understanding of the applicability of the law to the disputed facts in the case. This approach to deciding negligence cases was rejected by most legal progressives writing at the time, for it ignored the pragmatism and practicality shown by earlier Texas courts. No evidence exists that Texas courts were openly biased against plaintiffs at that time, or that they implicitly favored the interests of corporate defendants. But the interpretation of the demands of special issues law favored those defending against claims of negligence by injured plaintiffs.[20]

REFORMING CIVIL PROCEDURE?

In 1924, A. Leon Green, the *enfant terrible* of the University of Texas Law School, attacked the Texas system of civil justice in a short article published in the *Texas Law Review*: "Our court organization is organically diseased, and, therefore, radical treatment will be required. On the other hand, our rules of procedure are basicly [*sic*] sound, but so involved and confused as to defeat their purpose." The rules of civil procedure merely needed to be "simplified and modernized." Eschewing any particular proposal, Green offered four "fundamentals" to consider in revising the civil justice system.

Leon Green, 1921. Reprinted by permission of the Tarlton Law Library, Jamail Center for Legal Research, University of Texas School of Law.

First, Texas needed a "simplified court organization." Second, "the trial judge should be given real power." Third, judges should be selected in a manner other than election. Fourth, "all rules of procedure should be promulgated by the Supreme Court." None of the first three suggestions have ever been adopted in Texas. Green's last suggestion was premised on the antiformalist view that giving the supreme court the power to adopt rules of procedure would result in flexible and efficient rules, contrary to the legislature's rigid and cumbersome rules. Green's plea followed the suggestion in 1922 by Texas lawyer Lewis R. Bryan that "the statutory rules of practice be repealed and the Supreme Court be given the power to make all rules." Although the legislature created a Civil Judicial Council in 1929 to advise it on practice and procedure, no changes were immediately implemented.[21]

The Rules Enabling Act of 1934 gave the Supreme Court of the United States the power to make rules of practice and procedure as well as rules of evidence for federal courts. Three years later, the Court proposed adoption of the Federal Rules of Civil Procedure (FRCP), which went into effect in 1938. As these rules were readied for proposal, a case in the Texas Court of Civil Appeals summed up the rigidity of the Texas system of procedure and proof. Jim Rudd was employed by the Angelina County Lumber Company. Rudd was injured while working in 1931 and later died. His widow applied for workmen's compensation benefits and sued in district court on behalf of herself and their five minor children after the administrative board denied her claim. The widow won a verdict at trial. The insurance carrier for Rudd's employer, Traders & General Insurance Company, appealed the verdict on the ground that the plaintiff widow had "failed to offer proof raising the issue that it [Traders] was the compensation insurance carrier." Everyone agreed that Traders & General was the compensation insurance carrier for Rudd's employer. Had Traders not been the carrier, the case would have been dismissed before trial. And the widow had in fact offered proof that Traders was the compensation carrier. Unfortunately, she (through her woeful attorney) had offered this proof only for *jurisdictional* purposes (a procedural purpose), and not for purposes of *liability* (a substantive purpose). Even though everyone "knew" that Traders was the compensation carrier, the court of civil appeals required proof of this fact for liability purposes at trial, and her lawyer failed at trial to again prove Traders was the carrier. The case was reversed and remanded for a new trial.

The concurring opinion by Justice Combs lamented this result, which he nevertheless believed was required by law. The only important issue at trial was whether Jim Rudd's death was a consequence of the injuries he suffered on the job. Mrs. Rudd's lawyer failed to offer evidence that Traders was the compensation carrier for liability purposes. Traders used this failure to delay payment. This harmed the widow and her children but benefited Traders.

As Justice Combs noted, "The technical errors upon which we are remanding this case have no conceivable bearing upon the correct determination of the only material issue in the case." However, by law "we are compelled, through the necessity of following a mere technical rule, to remand this case, in order that certain proof may be put before the jury which, of itself, cannot possibly change the result and which, after it is introduced, will present no issue of fact for the jury to determine. In the meantime the widow and children must wait another trip through the courts, or else settle for what they can get." The widow had already waited six years for compensation in the midst of the Great Depression. Justice delayed was surely justice denied. Combs continued:

> This writer cannot refrain from remarking, in conclusion, that our courts seem to have lost, in recent years, their power to do justice except as a mere incident of following, meticulously, an elaborate and increasingly more complicated system of rules. In doing that we give the appearance of disregarding the right and justice of the particular case under review. A litigant who thus suffers the remand of his case on such apparently trivial grounds must regard us as devoid of all sense of right. To him it must appear that we operate upon his rights with the calloused indifference of a senior medical student cutting on a cadaver. . . . And, while I appreciate the necessity for rules, as well as our duty to follow them as they are written, I am unwilling to assent to the holding in this case without voicing my protest against a practice which makes it necessary for me to do so.[22]

Traders was often sued. As a "repeat" player in the civil justice system, its counsel used the rules to delay or avoid payment of workmen's compensation claims. A check of the *South Western Reporter* indicates that Traders was often a party in appeals to the Texas Courts of Civil Appeals during the 1930s. It was a named party in nearly eighty cases decided between 1937 and 1940. In 90 percent of those cases it was the appellant, having lost at the trial court level. From 1931 to 1940, Traders & General was a party in an appellate case in at least 125 cases. For a number of compensation carriers, appealing adverse verdicts was a standard approach during the 1930s. Not only did an appeal delay payment of any benefits, but also the unwillingness of the appellate courts to "do justice except as a mere incident of following, meticulously, an elaborate and increasingly more complicated system of rules," to adopt a legal formalism without a sound reason for doing so, made it a rational business decision for Traders & General and other workmen's compensation insurance carriers to appeal adverse judgments at trial.

THE TEXAS RULES OF CIVIL PROCEDURE

The adoption of the FRCP for use in federal district courts encouraged Texas reformers to redouble their efforts to persuade the legislature to give the supreme court the power to write rules of procedure. The Texas Bar Association renewed its efforts to lobby the legislature for procedural reform, and a special committee of the bar association suggested a draft reform bill. The bill failed of adoption in the 1937 session but was enacted two years later. The Rule-making Power Bill was structured similarly to the federal Rules Enabling Act, requiring the Texas Supreme Court to deliver its proposed rules to the legislature, which became effective nine months later "unless disapproved by the Legislature." On October 29, 1940, the Texas Supreme Court issued an order adopting the rules of procedure, which became effective on September 1, 1941.[23]

The 1938 FRCP were premised on simplifying pleading and providing for liberal discovery of the opposing party's case. The FRCP abolished all common law forms of actions and eliminated the distinction between law and equity. Charles E. Clark, the reporter for the committee that prepared the rules for the Supreme Court, noted that the idea of procedural reform was to create "simplicity and uniformity" and urged such reform efforts not become "static." The reforms were completely stated in just eighty-six rules.[24]

The Texas Rules of Civil Procedure were not intended to reform Texas procedure broadly, either in structure or substance, but to provide some modest reform. Instead of 86 rules, the Texas Supreme Court adopted a system consisting of 822 rules, and possibly more, for Rule 819 expressly continued any rules not explicitly repealed. Of those 822 rules, 351 (less several repealed rules), fewer than existed in 1925, concerned pretrial and trial practice. The remainder largely concerned appellate procedure and other topics. The advisory committee, led by Robert W. Calvert, drafted the rules using a "Goldilocks" approach: "We realize that the proposed rules will not satisfy everyone. They will satisfy no one with extreme views. Those who advocate the adoption of the Federal Rules in toto for the control of every justice and county and district court in Texas may consider many of the changes as too meager. On the other hand, those who believe that the technicalities of our present procedure and practice represent the acme of perfection will consider the changes quite radical."[25]

What all agreed was that the Texas Rules of Civil Procedure needed revision to reduce delay and expense to litigants and "unnecessary reversals and new trials upon technical procedural grounds." The president of the Texas Bar Association concluded that adoption of the rules would result in "an abandonment of laborious and super-technical submissions of causes to the juries." The reform of some "technical" rules leading to unnecessary reversals was limited, for the advisory committee understood that the legislature might disapprove of

dramatically altered rules. Consequently, the general denial remained in the rules (Rule 92), even though it had been fingered as one of the causes of delay as early as 1910.[26]

SPECIAL APPEARANCES

University of Texas Law School professor E. Wayne Thode called it the "ultimate in jurisdictional provincialism." The Supreme Court of the United States called it a "peculiar" statute. "It" was a statute giving a Texas court personal jurisdiction over a defendant who came to court challenging the court's assertion of personal jurisdiction over him. In other words, if the defendant believed that the Texas court lacked personal jurisdiction to hale him into court to defend himself, the very act of challenging the assertion of personal jurisdiction gave the Texas court jurisdiction over him. In the federal system and in other states (other than Mississippi), a defendant who believed the court lacked personal jurisdiction over him was permitted to make a "special" appearance, to appear in court solely to challenge the claim of jurisdiction. A special appearance by the defendant did not give a court personal jurisdiction over that defendant. In Texas, a special appearance did not exist. Any appearance before the court by a defendant constituted a general appearance giving the court personal jurisdiction. Once a defendant was subject to the court's jurisdiction, he was required to defend himself to avoid civil liability damages. If he failed to do so, a judgment could be entered and the plaintiff could then execute (collect) on that judgment.[27]

Whether a defendant could be required to travel to Texas to defend a lawsuit was often an important issue for a defendant who was not a Texas resident. Under what circumstances could he be required to defend himself in a Texas court? In *Pennoyer v. Neff* (1878) the Supreme Court of the United States declared that a state possessed jurisdiction over any person or property within the state and lacked "direct jurisdiction" over any person or property outside of the state. If a nonresident defendant found himself in Texas and was served notice there of the plaintiff's lawsuit against him, the defendant had to defend himself to avoid liability. A defendant given notice of the lawsuit while outside of Texas was not required to travel to Texas, hire a lawyer, and obtain the necessary proof to defend himself. What a non-Texas resident could not do was contest the issue of jurisdiction without defending himself against the substantive claim. If the defendant believed that he was not subject to the personal jurisdiction of the Texas court, he had two choices: appear and defend himself against the substantive claims, or not appear, not defend himself, and have the plaintiff take a default judgment against him. When the plaintiff attempted to execute on the default judgment by seizing the defendant's property, the defendant challenged that act by arguing that the judgment was erroneous because he was not subject to the court's jurisdiction (and thus, the court's judgment). Thode noted that the second option was a high-risk strategy, especially if the defendant owned property in Texas: "In most situations a defendant is understandably wary of placing his entire defense on a contention at a later time, and in another forum, that the Texas court lacked jurisdiction over his person." The absence of a Texas special appearance provision dated from the Revised Statutes of 1879.[28]

In *York v. State* (1889) the Texas Supreme Court agreed that defendant York had not been properly served notice of the lawsuit, that he was beyond the jurisdiction of the court as long as he stayed outside of Texas, and that he had made an appearance (through his attorneys) only to plead a lack of personal jurisdiction, not to voluntarily submit himself to the jurisdiction of the court. But pleading a lack of jurisdiction was enough to make him subject to the court's jurisdiction. York claimed error and peti-

tioned the Supreme Court of the United States. It affirmed, holding that the statute did not violate the due process clause of the Fourteenth Amendment. These provisions continued in the 1941 Texas Rules of Civil Procedure.[29]

The end of this subterfuge occurred after the Supreme Court of the United States eased the constitutional requirements for a state to assert jurisdiction over a nonresident defendant. In *International Shoe Co. v. Washington* (1945), the court permitted states to broaden their efforts to obtain jurisdiction against nonresidents by creating a "minimum contacts" rule consonant with "fair play and substantial justice." These vague and broad standards made it much easier for a state to require a nonresident defendant to appear and defend itself. In 1959, Texas adopted a law making a nonresident "doing business" in the state subject to the court's jurisdiction, thus limiting the need for the special appearance issue. In 1962 a modest special appearance rule was adopted by the Texas Supreme Court. If the defendant's motion that the court lacked personal jurisdiction over him was granted, the defendant did not have to defend the claim in Texas court. However, if the defendant's motion was denied, no further notice or process was required. The 1997 legislature ameliorated the rule. It permitted either plaintiff or defendant to file an interlocutory appeal (an appeal while the case was ongoing) on the trial court's decision on whether it possessed personal jurisdiction over the defendant.[30]

The special appearance rule favored Texas plaintiffs against non-Texas defendants. In contrast, venue was a boon to all defendants, some of whom used claims of inappropriate venue to engage in substantial delay in the administration of justice.

VENUE

The Spanish rule of venue that the defendant should ordinarily be sued where he lived (his domicile) was a part of Texas civil procedure from 1836. Even the initial venue statute contained some exceptions to the general rule, most also taken from Spanish law. Beginning in the late nineteenth century the legislature regularly modified the venue rule as railroad injuries increased. However, the legislature's solicitousness was modest. Joseph McKnight concluded that the venue rule "has always been regarded as just in itself, and eminently advantageous to defendants, for whose benefit it was intended." Defendants took full advantage of this benefit.[31]

Article 1995 of the Revised Statutes of 1925 began, "No person who is an inhabitant of this State shall be sued out of the county in which he has his domicile except in the following cases." The "following cases" were numerous. One court noted, "Usually these exceptions, to the general rule, give to the plaintiff, in a case, an additional right to sue the defendant, not only in the county in which he has his domicile, but in some other county." A 1901 statute permitted personal injury suits against railroad companies in either the county where the injury occurred or in the county where the plaintiff resided, although if the railroad neither operated in the plaintiff's county of residence nor employed an agent there, the plaintiff could sue in the county closest to the plaintiff's residence where the railroad operated or employed an agent. Out-of-state corporations could be sued anywhere "the cause of action or a part thereof accrued," or where the corporation had an agent.[32]

The difference between the Spanish civil-law and English common-law venue rules was largely because of the existence of the jury in the common law, which initially selected as jurors only those with a knowledge of the events in dispute. The absence of a jury in the civil-law system lessened any need for the case to be heard where the acts occurred, as required in the common law. Although Texas stringently protected the right of the parties to a jury

trial, Texas venue law was based on civil law. Texas appellate courts declared the venue law was to be interpreted "favorable to the rights and interest of defendants, since experience has demonstrated such right and privilege, so given, to be a valuable one." Other language by Texas courts went farther: "The privilege of the citizen to be sued in the county of his domicile is a fundamental and valuable right, of which he may not be lightly deprived, and the exceptions thereto must be strictly construed and clearly established to be effectual."[33]

In 1953 the legislature amended the venue statute to provide that "[a] suit based upon negligence per se, negligence at common law or any form of negligence, active or passive, may be brought in the county where the act or omission of negligence occurred or in the county where the defendant has his domicile." The former option was the common-law option, while the latter retained the Spanish venue law. If the plaintiff chose a venue other than the defendant's county of residence, the plaintiff had to offer evidence of three facts by a preponderance of the evidence: (1) the act of negligence occurred in the county where the suit was filed; (2) the act was either that of the defendant or an agent of the defendant acting within the scope of the agent's employment; and (3) negligence was the proximate cause of the plaintiff's injuries. A defendant moved to change venue by making a plea of privilege. Once the defendant filed a plea of privilege, the plaintiff responded by filing a plea challenging the defendant's plea of privilege and asking the trial court to hold that the case was filed in the proper venue. Before deciding, the trial court held an evidentiary hearing requiring the plaintiff to prove proper venue. Proving where the act of negligence occurred was usually the plaintiff's least difficult task. If the negligence was committed by an agent (such as an employee) of the defendant, the plaintiff needed to present the testimony of the agent at the hearing or obtain testimony from another employee of the defendant that the absent agent was indeed employed by the defendant and was in fact acting within the scope of his agency. This required the plaintiff to cajole testimony from an employee of the defendant contrary to the defendant's interests. Finally, plaintiff had to prove that the asserted negligence of the defendant was the proximate cause of the plaintiff's injuries. In some respects, the effort to prove proper venue mirrored much of the proof of the substantive trial issues, giving the defendant an early look at the plaintiff's case. Additionally, all of these items of proof cost the plaintiff money. If the defendant lost, Texas law permitted an interlocutory appeal on that decision. The right to take an appeal while the case was pending was rarely allowed in other American states, and almost never when the issue was whether venue was proper. A venue appeal allowed the defendant to delay the case for one to three years and clogged the already overburdened appellate docket. The increase in cost to the plaintiff led to an underfunded plaintiff's "death by a thousand cuts."[34]

This situation changed dramatically when the legislature altered venue practice in 1983. The senate sponsor of the bill, Kent Caperton, wrote a summary of the bill in the March 1984 issue of the *Texas Bar Journal*. He claimed the bill was a "compromise" between the Texas Trial Lawyers Association (representing plaintiffs in tort cases) and the Texas Association of Defense Counsel (representing defendants). The act largely eliminated the interlocutory appeal, eliminated the requirement to prove the facts of the cause of action, barred live testimony and any role for a jury, and barred any rehearing of the court's decision on the motion claiming improper venue. These provisions all benefited the plaintiff. The putative benefit gained by defendants was that a case tried in the wrong venue was harmful error requiring reversal. The value to such defendants was evanescent. As stated by one court, "The new venue statute favors the plaintiff's right to maintain venue in the county in which the action was brought, rather than the defendant's right to transfer venue to its county of residence." One "colossal goof" of the venue law was to allow a plaintiff to sue a railroad in any county. This "catastrophic" error led lawyers to file a "flood of railroad cases" in Matagorda County "since demographically Matagorda County was a plaintiff's shooting gallery against railroads." This mistake was rectified in 1987.[35]

A second procedural change aiding plaintiffs in negligence cases was the Texas Supreme Court's decision in *Cavnar v. Quality Control Parking, Inc.* (1985). *Cavnar* allowed a plaintiff who won a judgment at trial to obtain prejudgment interest at an interest rate much higher than the rate of inflation. *Cavnar* made it economically unattractive for a defendant to delay the resolution of a negligence case. Both changes in the law of procedure were the subject of harsh attacks from self-proclaimed Texas tort reformers.

CIVIL LIABILITY IN TORT

Every first-year law student is taught that a tort is a civil wrong other than a breach of contract. This neatly divides civil wrongs from criminal wrongs and, within civil wrongs, tort from contract. One of the ordinary differences between tort and contract is the relationship of the parties before the event that gave rise to the lawsuit. Contracts are usually voluntary agreements between persons with some acquaintance with one another. In many tort cases the parties were strangers before the event that gave rise to the lawsuit, and the action between the two was involuntary. This distinction quickly breaks down in the messy details of life. Some contracts are involuntary, and some torts begin as voluntary actions involving persons who are well acquainted.

The common law forms of action bundled together the procedural, evidentiary, and substantive requirements for a plaintiff who claimed the defendant harmed him. The Texas petition-and-answer pleading rules avoided some of the problems of the technicalities of common-law pleading, but it is the rise of the railroad that provides much of the impetus of the national development of tort law, which began in the 1870s in Texas.

E. Wayne Thode's 1962 article *Imminent Peril and Emergency in Texas* traces the Texas history of the "imminent peril" doctrine, an area of law "more in need of illumination" than any other area of "personal injury law and practice." Thode begins with *International & G. N. Ry. v. Neff*, an 1894 case creating the doctrine in Texas. In *Neff*, the plaintiff's husband was operating a one-horse wagon. He reached a railroad crossing in downtown San Antonio, stopped, and watched a freight train cross in front of him. He then began to cross the tracks. Tragically, a second train, consisting of an engine and tender, immediately followed the freight train. It did not blow its horn. Neff and his passenger panicked, jumped from the wagon, and were struck and killed by the second train. The defendant railway defended on grounds of contributory negligence, arguing that Neff had jumped into the path of the second train. The supreme court held that whether Neff was negligent in crossing the track after the first train passed or whether the railroad was negligent in failing to signal was a question of fact for the jury. If the jury found that the railroad was negligent, Neff's actions, whether "prudent or imprudent," and "notwithstanding it may turn out that if he had done differently, or had done nothing, he would have escaped injury altogether," were of no consequence. Texas adopted the imminent peril doctrine from the English case of *Jones v. Boyce* (1816) and from *Stokes v. Saltonstall* (1839), a decision of the Supreme Court of the United States. But Texas did so with a twist. It protected a person even when he acted imprudently, unlike *Jones* and *Stokes*. The Texas Supreme Court decided three additional imminent peril cases in a four-

year period after *Neff*. Each case involved a railroad. The imminent peril doctrine expanded the liability of the defendant, similar to the "last clear chance" doctrine (in which a negligent plaintiff might recover against a defendant if the defendant had the "last clear chance" to avoid the accident).[36]

Other tort doctrines arose in cases involving railroads. In *Houston & Texas Central Railroad Co. v. Smith* (1879), the supreme court rejected the doctrine of comparative negligence and in 1880 held that the plaintiff's action of sitting in a baggage car rather than a passenger car of a train was negligence *per se*, that is, negligence as a matter of law. In 1888 the court limited negligence *per se* to either a violation of a statutory duty or an action that "must appear so opposed to the dictates of common prudence that we can say, without hesitation or doubt, that no careful person would have committed it." The Texas Commission of Appeals, in *Houston & Texas Central Railway Co. v. Baker* (1882), held that Texas wrongful death law did not permit the father to sue for exemplary (punitive) damages for the death of his son, allegedly caused by the negligence of a fellow employee. In *Texas & Pacific Railway Co. v. Levi & Bros.* (1883), the supreme court adopted the collateral source rule. The defendant's train allegedly caused a fire that burned the plaintiff's cotton crop stored in a warehouse. The defendant claimed that the amount of its damages owed to plaintiff was limited because the plaintiff's cotton was insured and the insurance company paid on the insurance claim. The court rejected this contention. In *Missouri Pacific Railway Co. v. Shuford* (1888), the court adopted a stringent definition of gross negligence (necessary to permit the jury to award punitive damages) but upheld a judgment awarding the plaintiff four thousand dollars against a claim that the damages were excessive.[37]

One of the earliest negligence cases in Texas is *Bethje v. Houston & Central Texas Railway Company* (1863). Several cattle and pigs owned by Bethje were killed by trains operated by the defendant. Bethje was awarded forty-nine dollars by the justice of the peace. The railroad took the case to the district court, which instructed the jury that the plaintiff was required to prove the death of the animals resulted from the "neglect or want of care" of the engineer of the train. The jury held in favor of the railroad. On appeal to the supreme court, Chief Justice Royall T. Wheeler was "incline[d] to dissent" on the ground that the defendant should be presumed negligent once the plaintiff showed that an injury occurred. Despite his inclination, Wheeler wrote the opinion of the court affirming the judgment on the ground that, though there were some decisions favoring his point of view, "the weight of authorities in this country seems to be the other way." The supreme court's determination to follow the predominant approach to issues of tort law largely continued through the end of the nineteenth century.[38]

Some of the work of the supreme court and the commission of appeals seems to have been to reverse judgments in favor of plaintiffs who sued railroads alleging negligence. In *Houston & T. C. R.R. Co. v. Burke* (1881), a substantial default judgment against the railroad was reversed on the ground that hearsay evidence was erroneously admitted. A number of nineteenth-century cases involved injured railroad employees, who had to sue their employers for damages because workmen's compensation did not exist. In *Robinson v. H. & T. Central Railway Co.* (1877), the supreme court adopted the fellow servant rule. That rule barred recovery by one injured employee (servant) against his employer (master) if the cause of the injury was the negligence of a fellow employee (fellow servant) of the railroad. An employer was liable only if the employer was negligent in hiring the fellow servant. In *H. & T. C. R.R. Co. v. Myers* (1881), the court held plaintiff could not recover damages for personal injuries against his employer because he was aware of the defective

coupling link that he claimed led to his injuries. Texas appellate courts did not always evidence a bias for railroads. In *Watson v. H. & T.C. Ry. Co.* (1883), the commission of appeals reversed a defense verdict on the ground that the use of the disjunctive "or" instead of the conjunctive "and" in giving the jury instructions on when a train car was "out of order" was a material error. However, it also indicated that the injured brakeman's inability to read "out of order" would not suffice to prevent a jury from concluding he had acted in a negligent fashion.[39]

Texas appellate courts generally adopted the law of torts as developed by other states. Some of these doctrines benefited plaintiffs. The fellow servant rule did not eliminate recovery of damages by injured employees, for Texas courts adopted most of the exceptions to the fellow servant rule. A master was liable to an employee for failing to maintain reasonably safe premises, failing to furnish safe tools, hiring fellow servants who were not reasonably competent, and failing to exercise reasonable care in making and enforcing rules regarding the employee's service. Texas courts also adopted the "vice-principal" rule, declaring that the actions of a foreman were the responsibility of the master, making the fellow servant rule inapplicable and the master liable when the foreman's actions caused the plaintiff's injuries. The legislature also passed laws benefiting injured employees. It mandated strict limitations on the fellow servant defense in railroad accident cases beginning in 1891. The 1891 act defined a vice-principal as any employee "with the authority of superintendence" or "with the authority to direct any other employe [*sic*] in the performance of any duty of such employe." An 1893 act applied this rule to insolvent railroads, and an 1897 act expanded the law to street railways and reinforced the abrogation of the fellow servant rule in most railroad personal injury cases.[40]

The extent to which jury verdicts favored

plaintiffs in tort cases against railroads led Edwin A. Parker, a Baker and Botts railroad attorney, to assail the prejudice against railroads in a speech given to the sympathetic Texas Bar Association. Parker's talk, titled "Anti-Railroad Personal Injury Litigation in Texas," offered some interesting (even if incomplete) data on railroad tort litigation. Parker stated that between 1881 and 1899, Texas appellate courts decided 1,283 cases involving personal injuries and railroads, including street cars. Seven out of every eight cases (1,129 of 1,283) were appealed by the railroads. A total of 1,422 personal injury suits were decided on appeal, meaning that 90 percent (1,283 of 1,422) were railroad injury cases. In the 139 other personal injury cases, 35 percent (49 of 139) were appealed by plaintiffs. Of the applications for writs of error to the Texas Supreme Court in personal injury cases, 93.4 percent (354 of 379) involved railroad cases, and 88 percent (311 of 354) of the time the railroads asked for review. This disparity makes some economic sense, given the greater financial resources available to railroads to appeal losses at the trial and intermediate appellate levels. Other data recited by Parker suggest railroads were also effective targets in personal injury litigation by 1900. Parker compared the number of lawsuits and amounts paid per mile of track in Texas in 1899 with comparable numbers in other states in which Texas railroads operated. Outside of Texas, one lawsuit was filed for every forty-nine miles of track, compared with one lawsuit for every fourteen miles in Texas. In states other than Texas, railroads paid $9.48 ($185,418.69) per track mile, while they paid $82.04 per mile ($502,494.43) in Texas.[41]

Parker's address had a slightly discernible impact. In 1901 the legislature amended the venue statute to require a plaintiff who claimed personal injuries from negligence by a railroad to sue either in the county in which the injuries occurred or in the county in which the plaintiff resided when injured, not just anywhere the railroad operated or employed an agent.[42]

Railroad litigation continued to increase in the early twentieth century. In volumes 138 and 139 of the *South Western Reporter* (1910–11), Texas appellate courts published 234 civil case opinions. Fifty-one (21 percent) involved railroads or streetcars. Most involved personal injury claims. The extent of the business of making claims against railroads is indirectly perceived through the legal entanglements of Frank McCloskey. McCloskey began working in San Antonio as an "adjustor and collector" of "claims for unliquidated damages for personal injuries" in 1904 or so. After he had been in business for more than a decade, the San Antonio Traction Company, the owner of a street railway system in San Antonio, sued for injunctive relief, claiming McCloskey was engaged in the unlawful practice of barratry, defined in an 1876 statute as bringing or encouraging the bringing of a lawsuit "in which the party has no interest, with the intent to distress or harass the defendant therein." Soliciting another's legal claims and stirring up vexatious litigation were contrary to the common law in most states. The issue was whether this was unlawful in Texas. An 1895 statute permitted a cause of action for personal injuries to survive the death of the injured party, which Texas courts interpreted as permitting a cause of action for personal injuries to be assigned to a third party. McCloskey's business model was to ask a person injured in an accident involving the San Antonio Traction Company to assign McCloskey part of the claim (between one-third and one-half of the eventual damages paid). In exchange, McCloskey would represent the injured person in settling the case or in having it taken to trial. McCloskey was not a lawyer, but if the case went to trial he was responsible for finding and paying the lawyer from his percentage of the claim.

The district court granted the injunction,

which was reversed on appeal. The Fourth Court of Civil Appeals held that the 1876 barratry statute, joined by the amended barratry statute of 1901, abolished the common law prohibition against soliciting another's legal claim. The injunction against McCloskey was invalid because the 1901 statute barred "any attorney at law" from seeking or obtaining employment "by means of personal solicitation of such employment or by procuring another to solicit for him employment in such cause." McCloskey was not a lawyer and therefore the barratry statute was inapplicable to him. The decision of the Fourth Court was released on February 7, 1917. On March 29, 1917, the legislature amended the barratry statute to apply to nonlawyers such as McCloskey. The Traction Company's suit for injunctive relief against McCloskey claimed the company spent approximately one million dollars annually in "investigating, handling, settling, and defending such claims and suits." It also claimed that 60 percent of the claims presented to it were made by McCloskey. The costs incurred by the Traction Company offer some evidence that personal injury claims were a big business in the early twentieth century.

McCloskey was arrested for soliciting employment to collect claims after adoption of the 1917 law. He asserted that the law violated the Fourteenth Amendment. The Supreme Court of the United States disagreed. Despite this setback, McCloskey spent at least another fifteen years soliciting and adjusting the personal injury claims of others. Between 1920 and 1932 McCloskey was apparently left unmolested in his work. In 1932, the district court enjoined McCloskey from soliciting employment for claims against the San Antonio Public Service Company. The Texas Court of Civil Appeals affirmed and noted that

> appellant has for years made a business of trampling upon the laws as to barratry in

Texas. . . . An office was equipped, agents were employed, attorneys held in readiness, and no accident was reported in which any person was injured, or in the view of the leading spirit of the barratrous concerns should have been injured, but that the emissaries of the guiding spirit were turned loose upon him. He gave advice as to seeking a bed in a hospital or at home, counseled as to what doctors should be employed, and what attorneys should be consulted. According to the court, 57 percent (thirty-eight of sixty-seven) of the personal injury claims against Public Service in 1931 were made by McCloskey.

Despite the court's caustic attack, his work continued. An appellate case from 1935 upheld a judgment in McCloskey's favor against the Yellow Cab Company to recover his 50 percent interest in damages in a case in which Mrs. L. E. Murphy was injured while riding an automobile that collided with a Yellow Cab taxi.[43]

McCloskey's business survived for over thirty years. Although soliciting personal injury claims violated the criminal law by 1917, and despite the injunction against him in 1932, he continued to obtain interests in personal injury and property claims.

A 1915 Texas Supreme Court case suggests the tug between juries and judges in personal injury cases alleging negligence by a railroad. J. W. Petty, a seventy-nine-year-old man whose eyesight "was not good," was riding a horse. The road on which he was traveling went underneath a railroad trestle, which provided about six feet of head room. While walking his horse during daylight hours, he hit his head on the trestle and was injured. Petty sued the railroad. It defended on the ground that Petty could not recover damages because he was negligent. The jury found for Petty. The court of civil appeals reversed on the ground that the instructions to the jury were erroneous and remanded the case for retrial. It refused to decide whether Petty's actions constituted negligence as a matter of law. Petty again won a jury verdict and was awarded twenty-five hundred dollars in damages. The court of civil appeals affirmed, holding that the issue of Petty's contributory negligence was a matter for the jury, not contributory negligence as a matter of law. A majority of the supreme court held that Petty's actions were negligence *per se* and reversed.[44]

As noted by one Texas lawyer in 1917, "While the damage suit lawyer may be responsible for a good many things, the railroad lawyer is responsible for many too, and he is responsible, I expect, for fifty per cent or more of the appeals that are prosecuted in Texas today." Twenty years later, railroad personal injury cases had dwindled to a minuscule few. Accident cases continued to grow, but these usually involved either workplace accidents claiming workmen's compensation or personal injuries for automobile accidents. In volume 131 of *South Western Reporter (Second)*, which published cases from mid-1939, slightly more than two hundred Texas cases were reported, including forty-three cases in which the underlying matter was a claim for damages for personal injuries. Three cases involved alleged negligence by railroads. Two of those concerned collisions between trains and automobiles. The third concerned an injury to the plaintiff while moving a 1,461–pound wheel owned by the railroad. Not one concerned an injured passenger on a train or an injured employee of the railroad. In contrast, fourteen (including the two auto/train collision cases) concerned automobile accidents, and fourteen involved workmen's compensation claims. Appeals by insurance companies in workmen's compensation cases took up much of the work of the Texas Courts of Civil Appeals during the 1930s. Of the fourteen workmen's compensation cases published in volume 131 of the *South Western Reporter (Second)*, twelve were on appeal by the insurer after a judgment in favor of the employee-plaintiff. Of those twelve, four were reversed on appeal.[45]

The post–World War II Texas Supreme Court was viewed by Chief Justice Robert W. Calvert, then its longest-serving member (1950–72), as divided between "law men" and "equity boys." Perhaps Chief Justice Calvert's nomenclature explains why he placed himself in the former camp. The court accepted much of the law first framed in the late nineteenth century, although some changes took place. For example, it overruled *Sun Oil Co. v. Robicheaux* (1930) in *Landers v. East Texas Salt Water Disposal Co.* (1952). Texas had in 1902 required a plaintiff in a nuisance suit to prove the damages caused by each defendant when two or more defendants were separately causing damage: "Where a nuisance results from the acts of several, acting separately and independently of each other, each is responsible only to the extent of the injury inflicted by his own wrong, and can be assessed only for the damages caused by him." In *Robicheaux* several oil companies, acting independently, drained saltwater from the bayou and polluted it, ruining the plaintiff's rice crop. The commission of appeals held that because the defendants had acted independently, "therefore they were not jointly liable; and since such producers were not jointly liable it was a misjoinder of parties and causes of action to seek joint recovery in one suit against the several oil producers for their separate and independent acts." Consequently, plaintiff was required to sue each defendant separately. He then had the burden of proving "the portion of the injury attributable to each defendant." This was impossible when the injury (ruining the rice crops or creating a foul odor) was "in fact but a single indivisible injury," meaning the plaintiff was unable to recover anything even though each defendant had wrongfully caused the plaintiff harm. *Landers* reversed this perverse holding by creating joint and several liability on the part of all of these defendants and rejecting any procedural claim of misjoinder, thus placing the proper economic incentives on the defendants to act with care.[46]

A second case suggested that the severity of the liability rules in Texas would be lessened in some circumstances. Hubert Hamilton was driving a car in which his minor son and married daughter were passengers. Hamilton's car collided with a train. Hamilton was killed instantly; his son lived for seventy-five minutes after the accident. The jury found that Hamilton's negligence was a proximate cause of his injuries. (It also found that the train was speeding and was negligent in its maintenance of the railroad crossing.) As a result, the trial court held in favor of the railroad on the wrongful death action of Hamilton's widow. Ova Hamilton also sued for the wrongful death of her son. The railroad defended on the ground of the community property defense. The community property defense was intended to bar one spouse from profiting from the other's wrongful conduct. A cause of action is property in Texas, and a cause of action for injuries to one spouse is the community property of both. A negligent husband would profit from his wrongful action if his wife could sue for the injuries to their children when he negligently caused those injuries. The trial court held that, because the husband died instantly, and because the wrongful death claim did not arise until the son's death seventy-five minutes later, the cause of action for the wrongful death of the son was separate property of the mother. The appellate court affirmed.[47]

For the most part, however, Texas remained distinctly biased in favor of tort defendants. Several commentators perceived Texas appellate courts before 1970 as tilted toward defense interests: "Up until the abrogation of contributory negligence and similar defenses, and until special issue practice was changed, there was a noticeable 'defense flavor' to Texas tort law." In a 1983 speech Chief Justice Calvert rejected the assertion that "[w]hen Calvert was [on the

court], an oil company, an insurance company, a utility company or a bank could not lose a case." By the late 1960s Texas appellate courts began to alter Texas tort law in ways that benefited plaintiffs in personal injury cases. In doing so, Texas largely followed national trends. But the extent of large damage awards, together with a perceived insurance (particularly medical malpractice) crisis led to a reaction against this extension of liability beginning in the early 1990s, a reaction that continues to the present.[48]

THE TRANSFORMATION OF TEXAS TORT LAW

Since 1960, our modern civil liability regime has experienced a conceptual revolution that is among the most dramatic ever witnessed in the Anglo-American legal system.

Texas joined the conceptual revolution, although it did not do so until the late 1960s, and even then, it did so in fits and starts. In the 1970s the Texas Supreme Court and the Texas legislature modified or eliminated a number of doctrines that circumscribed the liability of defendants in negligence cases. This expansion of liability continued during the first half of the 1980s. Between the mid-1980s and mid-1990s, a battle regarding the proper extent of civil liability occurred in the Texas appellate courts and legislature. Since the mid-1990s both the courts and the legislature have acted to restrict claims of liability and damages amounts. This was accomplished both directly through changes in substantive tort law and indirectly through changes in the law of civil procedure.[49]

In 1965 the American Law Institute (ALI), a national, voluntary body of lawyers, judges, and professors, adopted Restatement (Second) of Torts Section 402A, which dramatically reshaped tort law. The restatement project of the ALI was an effort to restate existing common-law subjects, including torts, beginning in

1923. By the 1950s the second restatement was underway. Section 402A eliminated any finding of fault (negligence) on the part of the defendant in a case in which a plaintiff claimed an injury from a defective product. A defendant was liable in such cases when the product was in a "defective condition unreasonably dangerous to the user or consumer or to his property." Section 402A was largely the creation of William Prosser, the reporter for the Restatement (Second) of Torts. This "strict" liability in tort was fostered by legal academics who believed a negligence standard was too restrictive and by judicial decisions from a few state appellate courts, most notably California. The ALI's status as an elite body of lawyers and judges made it easier for state courts to adopt Section 402A. In *McKisson v. Sales Affiliates, Inc.* (1967), Texas became one of the earliest states to adopt Section 402A. The rapid acceptance of strict liability in products liability matters surprised some on the Texas Supreme Court. Chief Justice Calvert remembered that "products liability—enlargement of liability—took place all over the country, just shortly before I left the Supreme Court. . . . [I]t just really sort of burst upon us." Four years later the supreme court eliminated the doctrine of charitable immunity, making charitable institutions liable for the negligent actions of their agents. It also modified the doctrine of parental immunity, and made parents liable in some instances for negligent acts that caused their children harm. In both instances Texas followed a trend generated elsewhere. Prosser concluded that the shift in tort law "on the whole has been heavily toward the side of the plaintiff, with expanded liability in nearly every area."[50]

The early experience in Texas courts after the adoption of Section 402A was, in the language of one critic of products liability law, "generally sensible and even pragmatic." Strict liability was held inapplicable to a hospital that neither manufactured nor distributed a product, to those who did not sell products,

and in economic loss cases. But suggestions of a broadening of liability could be found even before 1970. In *Darryl v. Ford Motor Co.* (1969), the Texas Supreme Court held that Section 402A was applicable not just to consumers but also to bystanders injured by a product.[51]

The expansion of tort liability by the court from the early 1970s through the 1980s occurred through adoption of additional tort claims, including expanded remedies; abolition or alteration of some defenses to tort liability; and alteration of the appellate standard of review of trial court judgments. In 1973 the court adopted a tort claim for invasion of privacy. In 1975 it adopted claims for wrongful birth and for negligence that caused a person to commit suicide. That same year, the court abolished the defense of assumption of the risk. It also reshaped the law of premises liability, cases in which a person was injured on another's property, again following the lead of other state appellate courts. The court held that landowners owed a duty to avoid acting negligently to "invitees," persons invited by the landowner onto the landowner's premises. This eliminated the defense that an invitee was responsible for all "open and obvious" dangers on the premises. In *Burk Royalty Co. v. Walls* (1981), the Texas Supreme Court held that the court of appeals was to uphold any verdict awarding punitive damages if it found "some evidence" existed of gross negligence by the defendant. This was the converse of the old rule, which required the court of appeals to reverse a judgment awarding punitive damages if some evidence existed that the defendant had exercised some care.[52]

THE 1973 TEXAS LEGISLATIVE SESSION

The legislature also aided the transformation of Texas tort law during the 1970s. Two changes in the 1973 session significantly affected its course and development: First, the legislature, following a number of other states, replaced contributory negligence with comparative negligence. Under the law of contributory negligence, if the plaintiff was even 1 percent negligent, a defendant who was 99 percent negligent was awarded a verdict. By 1973 most states rejected contributory negligence as unfair and contrary to public policy. It was replaced in Texas by a modified form of comparative negligence. If the plaintiff was no more than 50 percent negligent, then the plaintiff could recover a proportionate amount of damages (for example, if the plaintiff and defendant were each 50 percent negligent, and one million dollars in damages was awarded, the plaintiff received half a million dollars). This quickly became more intricate when more than one defendant was sued and when the plaintiff's liability was less than that of some defendants and more than that of others. On a broader scale, the abolition of contributory negligence both increased the number of cases in which it made financial sense for plaintiffs to sue and made it more difficult for defendants to assess the probability they would have to pay damages.[53]

The second 1973 statute transforming Texas tort law was the Deceptive Trade Practices–Consumer Protection Act (DTPA). The DTPA made a defendant liable for "false, misleading, or deceptive acts or practices." Those practices applied to acts related to the sales of goods and services, and if the plaintiff was found to have suffered economic damages or damages for mental anguish from conduct committed knowingly by the defendant, those damages could be trebled. In 1977 the supreme court of Texas held the language of the DTPA mandated a trebling of damages. Fraud claims allowing for damages arising out of contracts were long permitted in Texas. But the DTPA extended the liability of defendants well beyond the bounds of fraud claims. The DTPA also offered a plaintiff the possibility of a much greater award than available in contract law, which also regulated the sales of goods and ser-

vices. In contract law the measure of damages in a "deceptive practice" case was the difference between the good or service as it was promised and as it actually was.

The DTPA also awarded a successful plaintiff-consumer "reasonable and necessary attorneys' fees." Under the American system regarding an attorney's fees, each party was ordinarily responsible for the costs of its own attorney. For most persons unhappy with a good or service, the stringent limits of recovery of damages under contract law and the cost of attorney fees made it uneconomical for them to sue. By altering the measure of damages through a trebling of damages, and by permitting the plaintiff to recoup his attorney fees (thus shifting the cost from the plaintiff to the defendant if the plaintiff won), Texas dramatically changed the incentives regarding the filing of such lawsuits. The courts of appeals spent much of the next twenty years interpreting the DTPA, and the legislature spent part of every regular session changing some aspect of the DTPA. As a historical matter, the DTPA reflected in part a federal law adopted in 1970, the Racketeer Influenced and Corrupt Organizations Act (RICO). RICO was intended to limit the ability of organized crime to move into legitimate organizations, but its provisions could be used in many ordinary civil cases. A successful civil RICO plaintiff was awarded treble damages and attorney fees.[54]

Two changes to the Texas Rules of Civil Procedure by the Texas Supreme Court also benefited plaintiffs. First, on October 3, 1972, the court abolished the necessity of a unanimous verdict by amending rules 291 and 292. Amended Rule 292 permitted a verdict to be rendered by a vote of ten to two, or, in the case of a six-person jury, by a vote of five to one. Second, in May 1973, a month after the legislature adopted the comparative negligence statute, the court amended Rule 277, then titled "Special Verdict." This amendment allowed the trial court in a negligence case to "submit a single question . . . inquiring whether a party was negligent." This amendment returned the general verdict to civil cases in Texas and heralded the end of the special verdict. In *Mobile Chemical v. Bell* (1974), the supreme court held that when several acts of negligence are alleged in a *res ipsa loquitur* ("the thing speaks for itself") case, "the submission of a broad issue inquiring generally whether the defendant was negligent is not error and is not subject to the objection that the single issue inquires about several elements or issues." Lawyers for injured plaintiffs supported the general verdict over the traps found in special-issue submission. In *Burk Royalty* (1981), the court interred the special-issues submission requirement: "We now expressly overrule those cases that arose before the 1973 revision of Rule 277 and which followed the mandate of *Fox v. Dallas Hotel Co.* requiring a submission of 'each issue distinctly and separately, avoiding all intermingling' and stating 'issues should be restricted to specific acts of negligence alleged and proven.'" Special issues submission was still permitted in Rule 277 but all but forgotten.[55]

"AN HISTORIC FLOOD OF TORT LITIGATION"

National media found the drama of the *Texaco v. Pennzoil* case in the mid-1980s reflective of Texas tort law. But it was decisions by the Texas Supreme Court in other cases that more clearly indicated that Texas had become a plaintiff-friendly state. The National Center for State Courts reported that between 1981 and 1989, Texas tort filings increased 70 percent. By 1990, Texas accounted for 10.3 percent of the nation's major product liability suits, even though it constituted just 6.7 percent of the nation's population.[56]

In *Sanchez v. Schindler* (1983), the Texas Supreme Court held a parent could be awarded damages for mental anguish for the death of their child under the Texas Wrongful Death

Act. *Sanchez* was both consonant with the views of other states and "activist" in the sense that it overturned a century-old precedent and reinterpreted a statute that the legislature had refused to amend despite an invitation from the court to do so. Writing in *Texas Monthly*, Paul Burka noted that "Texas law had been clear for a century; parents could only recover a child's lost earnings." James Branton, a well-known personal injury lawyer, saw *Sanchez* differently: "[T]he pecuniary loss rule in the case of a wrongful death of a child was finally overturned, bringing Texas in line with the thirty-five other states that had already discarded the rule of an agrarian society that viewed children solely as economic units." In *Otis Engineering Corp. v. Clark* (1983), an employee was sent home because he was intoxicated. He then killed two women in an automobile accident. Their husbands sued his employer for negligence in failing to prevent the accident. The trial court entered summary judgment in favor of Otis. The court of appeals reversed. The Texas Supreme Court held Otis had a duty to prevent the employee from creating an unreasonable risk of harm to others, and thus was subject to liability. Although the majority couched its decision in part by analogizing to cases decided pursuant to Section 319 of the ALI's Restatement (Second) of Torts, the court was not simply following an established rule declared in case law and the Restatement (Second). In *Otis* the court blazed its own path. The dissent thundered, "No court in any jurisdiction has ever suggested that an employer may be held liable for the off-duty, off-premises torts of an intoxicated employee when the employer has not contributed to the employee's state of intoxication." A third case from 1983, *Corbin v. Safeway Stores, Inc.*, was a slip-and-fall case. The court held that even when the agents of the defendant grocery store lacked actual or constructive knowledge of a danger that a customer might slip and fall, the jury could hold the defendant liable because there existed "known and unusually high risks accompanying customer usage of a self-service display of goods." This decision also followed a national trend to expand liability in slip-and-fall cases.[57]

THE 1983 TEXAS RULES OF EVIDENCE

On November 23, 1982, the Texas Supreme Court promulgated its Rules of Civil Evidence (TRE), effective September 1, 1983. These rules were directly modeled on the 1975 Federal Rules of Evidence (FRE), and both sets of rules marked a change from the common law of evidence. The TRE also affected the development of Texas tort law.[58]

The common law of evidence made it difficult for a plaintiff to prove the person who caused the plaintiff's injuries was an agent of another, usually the employee of a corporation. Common-law evidence also made it difficult to offer evidence of statements made by such an agent to prove liability. For example, in *Big Mack Trucking Co. v. Dickerson* (1973), the Texas Supreme Court held that the out-of-court statements made by an employee of Big Mack to third parties confessing fault were admissible only against the employee and were inadmissible hearsay as applied to his employer. The employee's statements were inadmissible because "[m]ost authorities take the position that a driver's statements after an accident are not authorized by his employer." As a practical matter, an employer never "authorized" the driver to speak as in *Big Mack* because those statements were useful only if they implicated the driver and thus harmed the legal interests of the driver's employer. The TRE rejected this common-law rule by taking the same approach as that of the FRE. Out-of-court statements by an employee-agent were now generally admissible against both the agent and his employer. A second example was *Travelers Insurance Co. v. Smith* (1969). The court of civil appeals held that the statement by an employee to a doctor that

he suffered chest pains while working was sufficient to support the doctor's conclusion that the employee had suffered a heart attack but insufficient to prove the existence, under evidence law, of the heart attack itself. After the employee suffered chest pains, he returned home and was anxious and distressed. He then saw the doctor. He died later in the day of a heart attack. His widow's suit for workmen's compensation failed because of the common law of evidence. The TRE eased these common-law evidence rules.[59]

The TRE went beyond the FRE in admitting evidence favorable to plaintiffs in some cases. A defendant's decision to fix stairs after the plaintiff slipped or fell on them, called a subsequent remedial measure, was inadmissible to show negligence under both the common law of evidence and the TRE. However, TRE 407(a) permitted a plaintiff in a products liability case alleging strict liability to offer evidence of a subsequent change in the design of an allegedly defective product. This new rule favored plaintiffs. Further, under TRE 407(b), evidence of a written notice of any defect of a product by a manufacturer of a product was admissible to prove the product was defective, another change benefiting injured plaintiffs.

CONTINUED CHANGE, THE INSURANCE CRISIS, AND THE TEXAS LEGISLATURE'S 1987 TORT REFORM

The 1983 change in the venue law and the adoption of the TRE offered some procedural mechanisms to assist plaintiffs in making personal injury claims. The Supreme Court of Texas also refashioned legal incentives more favorably to injured plaintiffs. In 1985, the court decided *Cavnar v. Quality Control Parking, Inc. Cavnar* substantively held that in a Wrongful Death Act case all family members listed in the act could receive damages for mental anguish after the death of a child. More importantly, *Cavnar* created a strong incentive for defendants to settle or move for a quick trial: it held that in a personal injury case, the plaintiff should be awarded prejudgment interest if the plaintiff was awarded damages by the jury. Prejudgment interest was permissible in law either by statute or by the "general principles of equity." No statute existed. The court held that equity required the payment by the defendant of prejudgment interest because a plaintiff was entitled to be compensated for her injuries, and "[a] law that denies recovery of prejudgment interest frustrates this goal" of full compensation. *Cavnar* overruled *Watkins v. Junker* (1897), which held prejudgment interest was inappropriate in personal injury matters because the measure of damages was not fixed in such cases before the judgment. *Cavnar* concluded it need not follow *Watkins* because that statement was dictum, not law, since *Watkins* was not a personal injury suit. However, the *Watkins* rationale had been adopted by the Texas Supreme Court in a personal injury case that same year. *Cavnar* declared that interest was calculated beginning "six months after the occurrence of the incident giving rise to the cause of action." That meant that prejudgment interest could begin accruing even before the lawsuit was brought. The interest rate for personal injury damages was determined by reference to statute, and that varied between a minimum of 10 percent and a maximum of 20 percent, depending on the rate of inflation. The creation of a minimum 10 percent prejudgment interest rate, particularly when inflation in 1985 was running at about 3.5 percent, created a great incentive for defendants to move cases more quickly to resolution. The revised venue statute also enhanced the pressure on defendants to move cases quickly to resolution, as certain Texas counties were perceived as very friendly to claims made by plaintiffs.[60]

During the first half of the 1980s, automobile accident matters constituted between 40 percent and 60 percent of all tort cases. The size of the verdicts in these ordinary cases increased just slightly; a study of tort cases in Harris County between 1981 and 1985 found the median verdict in automobile accident cases was $11,140. What grew during the early 1980s were "high stakes" cases, products liability, and malpractice (mostly medical) cases; and mass tort cases, including diethylstilbestrol (DES) cases. In high stakes products liability cases, the median verdict in Harris County was $351,869; in malpractice cases, the median verdict was $455,600. In 1984–85, insurance companies raised the price of coverage and restricted coverage in several states. One claimed reason for this increase was the growth of tort litigation. This claim has been contested since it was made. Even if inaccurate, the perception of an insurance crisis led forty-eight states to enact some type of tort reform between 1985 and 1988, a reform aided in part by a 1986 report issued by the federal Department of Justice. In both the regular session and in a special session in 1987, the Texas legislature adopted a number of provisions intended to produce tort reform in Texas. Part I of a three-part article by Senator John Montford, the principal author of tort reform, listed the laws added and proposals omitted. Among other changes, the 1987 reforms modified the prejudgment interest rule of *Cavnar*, altered comparative negligence to "comparative responsibility," and modified by statute the common law rules on punitive damages.[61]

PENNZOIL V. TEXACO

On April 19, 1987, as the legislature considered tort reform, Texaco filed for bankruptcy, then the largest bankruptcy in American history. The reason was the $10.5 billion judgment won by Pennzoil against Texaco in a Harris County courtroom in November 1985. The dispute was in the form of a claim of tortious interference with contract. Pennzoil claimed that it had an agreement with Getty Oil to purchase it, although both parties recognized no contract for sale had been signed by Getty Oil. Pennzoil claimed that after it reached an agreement with Getty, Texaco wrongfully (tortiously) interfered with the contractual relations of Pennzoil by having Getty Oil agree Texaco would purchase it. The jury awarded Pennzoil $7.53 billion in actual damages and another $3 billion in punitive damages. Because the *Cavnar* rule applied, prejudgment interest was available to Pennzoil—interest accruing at about $3 million every day. Further, the rules of civil procedure required Texaco to post a *supersedeas* bond (a bond sufficient to satisfy the judgment awarded the plaintiff) of about $12 billion to appeal the verdict. As noted by Thomas Petzinger, the worldwide insurance industry had a total of $700 million in bonding capacity. Taking out such a bond would likely trigger covenants with Texaco's creditors, turning Texaco's unsecured debt into secured debt, making its operations more difficult. Finally, entry of the final judgment by the trial court would allow Pennzoil to begin executing the judgment by seizing Texaco's assets.[62]

The extraordinary size of the verdict was in part a consequence of the defense's strategy not to offer evidence on the issue of damages. National reaction to the verdict was twofold: one reaction focused on the size of the verdict, while another focused on the relationship between Pennzoil attorney Joe Jamail and the two trial judges who presided at the trial of the case. Two days after Harris County district judge Anthony Farris was assigned to hear all pretrial matters in the Pennzoil-Texaco case, he received from Jamail a check in the amount of $10,000 to Farris's reelection campaign. Jamail's previous contribution to Farris's campaign coffers was $100. Farris, a Republican fearing Democratic opposition in the November 1984 election, took note of Jamail's contribution. It was, he wrote his campaign manager, "A princely sum." This donation constituted about 30 percent of the $32,710 Jamail gave to all Harris County judges between 1980

and August 1984. For Texaco's lawyers, Jamail's contribution was explicable only as an attempt to influence Farris's pretrial rulings. Although Jamail and Farris were longtime friends, Jamail was a staunch Democrat, and at a time when Republicans were beginning to win more contested judicial races in Texas, his contribution seemed unusual. Texaco lawyer Richard Miller suggested that Jamail's contribution was why Pennzoil seemed to win every pretrial ruling, and Texaco moved to disqualify Farris.

The disqualification hearing was heard in late October 1984, and the court concluded that "mere bias" was insufficient to disqualify any judge as a constitutional matter. In early 1985 the Harris County district courts changed their rules to assign to the trial the judge who heard all pretrial matters. Thus, Judge Farris, whose objectivity had been unsuccessfully challenged by Texaco, was now the trial judge. Farris became ill during the trial and withdrew. He was replaced by visiting judge Solomon Casseb, Jr., from San Antonio. Casseb and Jamail had known each other as children. When Casseb was appointed to complete the case, Texaco's lawyers did not suggest Casseb was biased in favor of Jamail and thus unable objectively to preside in the case. After all, Casseb and Richard Keeton, Richard Miller's law partner, had known and worked with one another in the past. It was only after the jury verdict was rendered and the judgment was signed by Casseb that Texaco suggested impermissible judicial bias by Casseb. It made this suggestion not in Texas courts, but in federal court in New York. Texaco claimed that "Judge Casseb is a close personal friend of plaintiff's lead lawyer," Jamail. No evidence existed indicating that Casseb's judicial conduct was lacking. The largest verdict in American legal history led national media to assume judicial bias when this explanation was flawed and speculative.[63]

On February 12, 1987, the First Court of Appeals of Texas upheld the judgment in favor of Pennzoil but cut the punitive damages award from $3 billion to $2 billion. By mid-1987 the State Commission on Judicial Conduct had issued its decisions condemning the actions of two justices of the Texas Supreme Court, reprimanding Associate Justice C. L. Ray and admonishing Associate Justice William Kilgarlin for violating one or more canons of the Code of Judicial Conduct. Articles in *Texas Monthly, Forbes,* and the *Washington Post* published in May and June 1987 attacked the Texas judiciary and the supreme court in particular for bias in favor of plaintiffs. The title of the *Forbes* article put it bluntly: "The Best Justice Money Can Buy." On November 2, 1987, the Texas Supreme Court denied Texaco's writ of error, concluding no reversible error existed. The next month, a *60 Minutes* exposé titled *Justice for Sale?* aired, asking whether the Texas Supreme Court had been corrupted by the campaign contributions given its members, including large contributions from Jamail. After Texaco declared bankruptcy, the case was settled for $3 billion, and Jamail received a reported fee of between $300 million and $420 million.[64]

MASS TORTS

Mass torts became a national legal phenomenon in the 1980s, but one of the earliest mass tort cases arose out of the Texas City disaster decades earlier. On the morning of April 16, 1947, eight hundred tons of fertilizer-grade ammonium nitrate (FGAN) caught on fire on the SS *Grandcamp* at the port in Texas City. The fire itself was not an extraordinary occurrence, but the massive explosion of the FGAN was. More than a thousand homes in Texas City were destroyed, and at least 576 people were killed. Over 3,000 persons were injured, and property damage was estimated at over $67 million. Tremors from the explosions (a second explosion occurred at one o'clock the next morning) were felt hundreds of miles away. Survivors brought a Federal Tort Claims

Act action against the United States in federal court, alleging the federal government was negligent in its handling of FGAN. In the case selected as determining the results for all the plaintiffs, damages for the death of Henry Dalehite were assessed at $60,000 for his widow and $15,000 for his son. This judgment was reversed on appeal by the Fifth Circuit. The Supreme Court, by a vote of four to three, with two justices not participating, held the Federal Tort Claims Act inapplicable to torts arising from discretionary acts engaged in pursuant to government functions. Because the manufacture, transportation, and handling of FGAN were discretionary governmental functions, plaintiffs recovered nothing. In 1955, Congress adopted the Texas City Explosion Relief Act. The maximum award given to any claimant was $25,000. The commission appointed to distribute funds under the act made 1,394 awards, averaging $12,195.21, approximately $17 million in all. The federal government was assigned the claims of the plaintiffs under the Texas City Explosion Relief Act and sued the Republic of France and the owners of the SS *Grandcamp*. That litigation ended in favor of the defendants in 1962.[65]

The rise of mass tort litigation near the end of the twentieth century involved products with whom thousands, indeed hundreds of thousands, of people came into contact. The first large modern mass tort cases involved Agent Orange, a herbicide used in Vietnam, and the Dalkon Shield intrauterine device to prevent pregnancy. They were followed closely in time by asbestos litigation. Exposure to asbestos could, over time, cause lung disease, and asbestos was used in a substantial number of products (for example, insulation). As noted by Lester Brickman in 1992, "Even though 100,000 claims have already been resolved, 100,000 new claimants now seek compensation. For each claim resolved, two to three new claims are being filed." By early 1992, of sixteen asbestos companies, one had dissolved, and the remainder had filed for bankruptcy protection. Commentators in the early 1990s speculated that the amount to settle asbestos claims would range from $13 billion to $30 billion. In Texas, the asbestos saga known as *Fowler* had become by 1996 "the largest mass products-liability lawsuit in the United States," with more than three thousand plaintiffs and more than three hundred defendants. As the asbestos cases wound their way through the courts, other mass tort claims arose. Did the ingestion by pregnant women of the anti–morning sickness drug Bendectin cause birth defects in their children? Did silicone gel breast implants cause autoimmune diseases? Regarding the latter claim, Texas personal injury lawyers were at the forefront. One Texas lawyer, John O'Quinn, was hired by more than twenty-five hundred clients. Another had more than a thousand breast implant clients.

The difficulty in a number of mass tort cases was not the staggering amount of money involved but whether expert scientific evidence proved a causal connection between the product and the harm alleged by the many plaintiffs. In the Dalkon Shield cases, evidence showed that some women using the device developed pelvic inflammatory disease, and some became infertile. In asbestos cases, plenty of expert evidence existed that asbestos caused malignant injuries to many, but the evidence of injury in nonmalignant asbestos cases was substantially in doubt. Breast implants for cosmetic purposes were forbidden by the Food and Drug Administration in 1992; in 1999 the Institute of Medicine concluded that insufficient evidence existed to determine that either silicone or saline breast implants had caused systemic health problems. In the meantime, Dow Corning, a manufacturer of silicone breast implants, had filed for bankruptcy. In the Bendectin matter, lower courts eventually held that the scientific evidence was insufficient to conclude that Bendectin caused birth defects.[66]

A decline in some mass torts was a result

in part of rulings by courts concerning the standards of admissibility of expert scientific evidence. In *Daubert v. Merrell-Dow Pharmaceuticals* (1993), the Supreme Court of the United States held that scientific evidence was admissible only if it met the standards of Federal Rule of Evidence 702. *Daubert* appeared at first glance to allow a broader admissibility of scientific evidence than existed through prior precedent. However, the guidelines suggested by the Court, along with its admonition to trial courts to act as "gatekeepers" regarding such evidence, made more difficult the admission of all expert evidence, including scientific expert evidence. Texas adopted then-existing FRE 702 in its entirety when it adopted the TRE. In *Du Pont de Nemours v. Robinson* (1995), the Texas Supreme Court followed the *Daubert* standard.[67]

THE TORTS COUNTERREVOLUTION

The 1988 election of three Republicans to the Texas Supreme Court was the first step in the second transformation of Texas tort law. Each Republican was financially supported by self-described tort reformers, including medical doctors and insurance companies, and each was elected in a contest against a Democratic candidate financially supported by personal injury lawyers. An astonishing $11 million was spent by the candidates for the six contested seats on the supreme court in 1988. Chief Justice Tom Phillips, a Republican appointed in late 1987, was required to run in the 1988 election to keep his seat for the remainder of his predecessor's term. He and his opponent, Ted Z. Robertson, raised just under $3 million. After winning the election, Phillips was required to run again in 1990, this time for a new six-year term. He and his new opponent, Oscar Mauzy, raised about $3.4 million. After having been outspent in the 1988 race, Phillips raised significantly more money (about $2.4 million of the total) than

Mauzy. He was again elected. By 1992 a majority of the court was Republican.[68]

The first signs of the torts counterrevolution occurred outside of the civil justice system. On the morning of September 21, 1989, at 7:40 a.m., the brakes of a Valley Coca-Cola truck failed, and it broadsided a Mission Independent School District bus in Alton. The bus tumbled into a caliche pit. Twenty-one children died. As noted by one author:

This was merely the beginning of a nightmarish legal morass. Lawyers swarmed over the grieving town, signing up, and then stealing each other's clients. Members of the community accused each other of trying to profit from its collective tragedy. These events led to even more litigation. The town sued the state for failing to construct guard-rails; the rescue workers sued for the emotional distress incident to their efforts to save children at the scene of the accident; lawyers sued other lawyers, lawyers were prosecuted for barratry, and residents of the town were sued for slander. A tragic accident became just another episode in the seemingly unending saga of America's explosion of litigation.

The final settlement of the cases arising out of this tragedy totaled more than $150 million. The lawyers representing the families of the deceased reportedly charged a contingency fee of between 30 percent and 45 percent and earned between $40 million and $55 million, which in "a conservative estimate of the hourly rate of attorney compensation would be $25,000–$30,000." The availability to lawyers of astonishing amounts of money for work that was nearly without risk made unsurprising the theft of one lawyer's client by another lawyer, the efforts to bribe prospective clients, and charges of barratry. But even more unseemly was the consequence of the litigation on the citizens in Alton. As one reporter stated in a May 1990 story:

[T]he school bus accident that killed 21 children last fall did not simply split the town, but splintered it. First by grief, then by greed. In the eight tumultuous months since the accident, Alton has been jolted by death threats, brawls, a fast-proliferating spate of lawsuits, city financial probes, a mayoral recall drive, charges of ambulance-chasing against prominent Hispanic leaders, the suspension of the entire 30-man volunteer fire department—even accusations of witchcraft.

The barratry conviction of Norma Lopez, a "runner" for a lawyer, and the dismissal of barratry charges against a lawyer, inflamed popular dissatisfaction with the behavior of lawyers. The Alton School Bus Case in part led the Texas legislature to amend the barratry statute, making it the harshest barratry statute in the United States.[69]

The barratry statute has been used occasionally but has made little difference in tamping down illegal case running in personal injury matters. Wilfredo Rogelio Garcia of Mission was a prosecution witness in the barratry cases against three lawyers in the Alton school bus tragedy. He spent the next twenty years "building a reputation as the biggest case runner in Hidalgo County," apparently allowing him to obtain a "personal wealth of $33 million." His work as a case runner did not become public as a result of any criminal barratry action, but as a result of lawsuits filed by lenders claiming that Garcia owed them millions of dollars.[70]

AMENDING WORKERS' COMPENSATION

Texas governor Bill Clements declared the 1989 changes to the Texas workers' compensation system the "most significant piece of legislation to come out of the Texas legislature in twenty years." Even if his words were hyperbolic (Clements had made workers' compensation reform his top legislative priority), the 1989 legislation, which became effective January 1, 1991, constituted a sweeping reform of worker's compensation in Texas.[71]

Workers' compensation costs increased nationally from 1.11 percent of payroll in 1970 to 2.36 percent of payroll in 1990. The amount spent by companies on workers' compensation in 1993 was $60.8 billion, a ten-year increase of 75 percent even after accounting for inflation. In Texas the financial concerns were even greater. Workers' compensation costs were the fifth highest of the states by 1988. Between 1985 and 1989 alone, workers' compensation premiums more than doubled, rising 148 percent.[72]

Statutory changes to workers' compensation law had several effects, one of which was to limit the use of lawyers in the workers' compensation program. As noted by then Fourth Court of Appeals chief justice Phil Hardberger, "If the former workers' compensation system suffered from too many lawyers, the present one suffers from too few lawyers, especially for the seriously injured worker." Changes in the attorney fee structure in workers' compensation cases reduced the number of cases that were economically feasible for a lawyer to take. Indeed, it "all but ended the profitability of this area of business for plaintiffs' lawyers, and most left the field." The unintended consequence of this change was to alter the manner in which lawyers gained clients. Stephen Daniels and Joanne Martin studied the business of Texas personal injury lawyers during the mid-1990s. They found plaintiffs' personal injury lawyers gained clients through client referral, lawyer referral, direct marketing, and other referrals. The end of workers' compensation business left many lawyers with relatively few clients, reducing client referral business and intensifying the use of the other practices to finding clients. Until March 2005 it was ethically permissible for Texas lawyers to forward a case to another lawyer in exchange for a share of the attorney fee without remaining a participant in the case. Lawyers with strong rep-

utations were offered more forwarded cases on the assumption that they would obtain a more favorable result than the forwarding lawyer. This gave lawyers with strong reputations the luxury of greater choice in determining which cases to accept. For the forwarding lawyer, the reduction in clients made it more difficult to remain solely a personal injury lawyer. And then plaintiffs' lawyers faced a double-barreled attack in the mid-1990s: the now Republican majority of the Texas Supreme Court began to roll back some plaintiff-friendly rulings of the 1980s, and the legislature adopted more sweeping tort reform legislation in 1995.[73]

"POURED OUT"

Between 1988 and 1993 relatively little changed in Texas tort law. Tort claims continued to increase, on average 4.9 percent per year between 1989 and 1995, and large verdicts continued to be awarded. In *MBank Abilene v. LeMaire* (1989), five plaintiffs sued MBank for breach of an oral promise to lend $3 million to their oil and gas company. Some officers of the bank (later convicted of multiple criminal charges) made this oral promise contrary to federal banking regulations. The failure to make the loan aided in causing the oil and gas company to go bankrupt, as did the collapse of the oil and gas industry in the early 1980s. The jury awarded the plaintiffs over $100 million in damages, which the trial court reduced to $69 million on the *plaintiffs'* motion. The court of appeals affirmed in part and reversed in part, and reduced the damages to $9.25 million for each of two plaintiffs. One report indicated that over four hundred lender liability lawsuits had been filed in Texas by 1989. In 1990, 25 percent of the nation's largest verdicts were in Texas, and of the nation's ten verdicts of $100 million or more between 1989 and 1991, four came from Texas.[74]

In 1993, when the court consisted of a fragile five-four Democratic majority, it issued its first limitations on expanded liability decisions dating from the 1980s. In 1987 and 1988 the court adopted and established a standard for the tort of good faith and fair dealing owed by an insurer to the insured. In *Lyons v. Millers Casualty Insurance Co. of Texas* (1993), the issue concerned a trial verdict in favor of the plaintiff on the "bad faith" claim. The court of appeals reversed, a conclusion the supreme court agreed with. The supreme court held that the plaintiff had failed to offer any evidence of the unreasonableness of the insurer's action. Two Democrats (Justices Raul Gonzalez and Rose Spector) joined four Republicans in the majority. The supreme court reversed two more large verdicts in bad-faith cases in 1994. Finally, the court held that Texas did not recognize the controversial torts of false light invasion of privacy (falsely portraying a private person, causing emotional harm) and negligent infliction of emotional distress.[75]

A major change occurred in 1995 when the court consisted of six Republicans and three Democrats. Because Democratic justice Raul A. Gonzalez, Jr., the first Mexican American on the supreme court, was perceived as a swing vote and had joined Republicans in several of the cases limiting tort liability, this change in the personnel of the court portended continued major changes to the court's torts jurisprudence.

Two popular articles from 1996 noted this swing. Joseph Calve's *Texas Lawyer* article "Poured Out" examined how the change affected "the workaday PI [personal injury] lawyer" and concluded that many lawyers representing injured persons in tort matters were in "dire straits." A *Wall Street Journal* article listed a number of the changes made by the supreme court in 1995 and 1996. The court limited the use of class-action suits, limited the use of the DTPA, ended "sweetheart" deals (in which an insured settled with the third party and assigned any claims against the insurer to the third party), limited the extent of premises liability, made more strict the standards for

expert testimony, and narrowed bad-faith tort litigation. Trial courts in Dallas and Harris counties seemed less willing to expand notions of duty and proximate cause, and decisions affirming summary judgment in favor of defendants were issued by courts of appeals in those counties. Law review articles criticized the court's seeming disregard for jury verdicts, contrary to longstanding Texas law.[76]

In 1998 the court further limited the legal duty owed by defendants in tort matters. A defendant whose horse, roaming on a rural road, collided with a motorist, did not owe the motorist a duty of care based on a narrow interpretation of a statute. It held a spectator injured by a rock kicked up at a rodeo could not sue the owner because the dirt (which included rocks) could not be unreasonably dangerous as a matter of law. The extent of the court's shift is demonstrated in *City of Tyler v. Likes* (1997). Not only did it hold that the plaintiff-homeowner was barred from recovering for mental anguish caused by damage to her real and personal property, a holding contrary to the decisions in the 1980s extending mental anguish damages in wrongful death cases, but it also did so by a vote of eight to one. Only Justice Spector, one of the court's two remaining Democrats, dissented.[77]

THE TOBACCO LITIGATION: THE LAST HURRAH?

Tobacco litigation in the United States is divided into three waves. The first set of tobacco cases arose between the mid-1950s and the mid-1960s. The second set took place between the mid-1980s and the early 1990s: "In neither period did the cigarette companies pay a cent in compensation." The third wave of litigation resulted in the payment by the tobacco industry of $246 billion to settle all pending cases.[78]

The third wave of litigation began with a lawsuit by the state of Mississippi against tobacco companies in May 1994. The state's lawyers, mostly well-known Mississippi plaintiffs' lawyers, sued in equity claiming that the tobacco companies had been unjustly enriched. They asked the equity chancellor to order that the tobacco companies pay restitution to Mississippi for the costs incurred by it in paying medical costs for those who suffered from illnesses as a result of smoking. The chancellor barred the tobacco industry from offering evidence that Mississippi had prospered through the receipt of excise taxes on tobacco and from alleged savings in medical costs because smokers died prematurely. The pretrial rulings led the tobacco companies in June 1997 to enter into a contingent settlement totaling $368.5 billion. The contingency was an agreement by Congress, which in 1998 rejected the settlement. Mississippi settled its case against tobacco companies for $3 billion.[79]

The Texas case against big tobacco was filed in March 1996. Texas was the seventh state to file a claim and the only one to sue in federal court. Suing in federal court avoided the Republican-dominated Texas Supreme Court; ducked a 1995 law granting immunity to makers of dangerous products, including cigarettes; offered the convenience of a federal judge with time to handle civil cases who knew several of the state's lawyers; and provided the opportunity to use the federal RICO statute. Eighteen months later the case was settled for $15.3 billion, later raised to $17.3 billion. Before the court dismissed the case it held reasonable the 15 percent contingent fee ($2.3 billion) owed to the five private-practice lawyers hired by Attorney General Dan Morales. These five lawyers were well known, "either the Mount Rushmore or the rogues' gallery of the Texas plaintiffs' bar." But Joe Jamail, the most famous personal injury lawyer in Texas, was not among them. The contract between Morales and the Big Five became a central issue in the 1998 election for attorney general. Republican candidate John Cornyn (a member of the Texas Supreme Court) accused Democratic incumbent Morales (who was not running for reelection) of cor-

ruption and aiding lawyers known as strong Democratic Party supporters. Jamail filed an affidavit in May claiming that Morales had solicited a $1 million bribe to get involved in the tobacco case. (Morales claimed the $1 million was how much Jamail would have to pay in up-front expenses.) In addition to the Big Five, a lawyer named Mark Murr claimed a fee based on a contract dated January 31, 1997. A second contract allegedly dated October 1996 gave Murr 3 percent of the total amount awarded ($519 million). An arbitration panel chosen by Murr and Morales rejected that claim but found Murr was owed $260 million. (A fee panel created by the second settlement of the cases gave Murr $1 million.) Cornyn won election and shortly before he took office was told by Morales's assistants that something was wrong with the contracts with Murr. Indeed, the contracts were fraudulent. Murr and Morales were indicted in March 2003 for mail fraud in relation to the tobacco suit, and both later pled guilty. For the Big Five, the $2.3 billion fee was increased to $3.2 billion by the national fee panel deliberating on the fees owed attorneys. Litigation pursued by Cornyn, Texas governor George W. Bush, and others over the amount of the attorney fees was later settled.[80]

In 2000 the Texas Supreme Court heard three cases concerning class-action lawsuits. Two of the lawsuits overturned lower court decisions granting class certification in mass tort cases. The third held that a class certification was impermissible because the class of plaintiffs could not be determined until liability was decided. The "Texas trilogy" made it much more difficult for class actions to be certified, making mass tort cases less likely in Texas.[81]

VENUE REDUX AND TORT REFORM IN THE 1995 LEGISLATURE

A page-one story in the November 30, 1994, issue of the *Wall Street Journal* discussed a securities fraud lawsuit against Prudential Securities and General Electric filed in Maverick County, Texas, by plaintiffs' lawyer Pat Maloney of San Antonio. Maverick County, located on the Texas-Mexico border, "may be the most inconvenient forum possible for this securities fraud case. None of the defendants, and only one of over 2,000 potential plaintiffs, resides there." The article claimed Maloney decided to file the case in Maverick County "even before he had secured a plaintiff from the town" of Eagle Pass, the county seat. Maloney denied so doing. The reason for filing in Maverick County was clear. In the late 1970s Maloney won the then largest verdict in American legal history ($26 million), and, as the *Wall Street Journal* noted, "[s]ince then, he has won many seven-figure awards here and has beaten his old record by negotiating one settlement for $30 million." Under the 1983 venue law, because a Maverick County resident had a plausible claim against the defendants, he could sue there. Once he filed, the district court could allow the 1,999 nonresident plaintiffs to intervene. As stated in another securities fraud case with but tenuous Texas ties, "[I]f it remains the law in Texas, we will be not only the courthouse for the world but the laughingstock of the legal world as well."[82]

The publicity given this case led directly to the changes in the venue rules in 1995: "This change was brought about due to cases like the one currently in Maverick county involving a suit by 2,000 plaintiffs against Prudential Securities, Polaris Investment Management Co., and others." Amending venue rules was only part of the legislature's 1995 tort reform, undertaken "[i]n response to recent outcries about burgeoning litigation and escalating damage awards."[83]

The 1995 legislature adopted several changes in the substantive law of civil remedies: it substantially amended the DTPA, restricting its reach and the availability of mental anguish damages; it limited the amounts and restricted the conditions for awarding punitive damages; it changed the rules on joint and several liabil-ity for the benefit of some defendants; and it altered the liability standard in premises liability cases and the law of medical malpractice.[84]

THE COUNTERREVOLUTION TAKES HOLD

Between 1995 and 2001, the number of new tort cases filed in the Texas trial courts (district and county combined) declined 24.8% (from 65,262 to 49,080), and the rate of filings per thousand population declined 33.7% (from 3.47 to 2.30).

This was a startling trend. The commonplace suggestion connected the decline in filings with the legislature's 1995 tort reform measures. Stephen Daniels and Joanne Martin suggested the decline in filings was less about formal changes in the law and more about cultural changes occurring as a result of sustained public relations efforts demanding tort reform. To prove their case, Martin and Daniels focused on automobile accident case filings, cases not the subject of tort reform public relations efforts. They found that filings had fallen in most years since 1985 and fallen more steeply from 1998 to 2000. This negative trend indicated the efficacy of culture as a catalyst for legal change.[85]

Some changes in filings have been the result of statutory changes. The peak filing year for torts cases was in 1995, when the second legislative reform occurred. Between 1989 and 1995, tort filings rose by 41 percent. Although filings declined to 49,148 in 2001, that figure was still higher in absolute terms (though lower per thousand population) than in 1989. The effect legislative changes have had on the number of tort filings is demonstrated by recent data. In fiscal year 2003, just before medical malpractice reform was scheduled to go into effect, tort filings increased to 63,188, approaching the 1995 record. By fiscal year 2006, Texas tort filings had fallen to 45,865, the lowest number since those records were kept beginning in 1985. Auto accident filings between 1997 and 2006 rose in only two years: 2002 and 2003. The number of auto accident tort filings in 2003 exceeded the number filed in 1995, which Daniels and Martin used as their starting point. Whether these differences reflected changes in the practice of law by personal injury lawyers after the decline in more profitable malpractice and mass tort cases, a result of increased lawyer advertising, or an odd coincidence is unclear.[86]

In 1998, Justice Phil Hardberger wrote a massive article titled "Juries Under Siege." Hardberger, a well-respected judge and former personal injury lawyer, charged the Texas Supreme Court with issuing opinions disregarding jury verdicts contrary to Texas law. For Hardberger "the Phillips/Hecht Court has ignored, trivialized, or written around jury verdicts. In every area of the law, the Phillips/Hecht Court has overturned or limited potential recovery by injured individuals." In his telling the court had engaged in "conservative" judicial activism. Its decisions were less about law than politics, though conservative rather than liberal politics.[87]

A 2003 *Corporate Legal Times* article painted a very different picture of Texas tort reform. It suggested that "the rest of the United States may not be aware of just how much progress has been made in changing the litigious environment [in Texas]" and cited a Texas Department of Transportation study claiming savings of $3 billion in insurance costs between 1996 and 2000. The article also offered tables of the absolute and relative tort filing rates in twenty-one states. In absolute terms Texas was in the middle in 1990, with the tenth highest filing rate, when the court still consisted of a Democratic majority. New Jersey tort filings were quadruple Texas's. By 1999, after the makeover of the Texas Supreme Court, Texas had fallen only three places, despite a 24 percent drop in the rate of tort filings between 1990 and 1999. Texas was far from the only state to undergo tort reform in the 1990s. The

tort crisis in Texas was less about the number and extent of tort cases and more about those relatively few cases in which multimillion-dollar verdicts were rendered.[88]

David Anderson published a compilation of the work of his seminar students on Texas tort law in 2007, arguing that "the court's tort law decisions disproportionately favor defendants and that the disparity cannot be readily explained by factors other than a determination to limit tort liability." Limiting tort liability may simply reflect a policy difference concerning the law. A conclusion that the court's decisions "disproportionately favor defendants" suggests a type of bias that undermines the rule of law. Anderson concluded that decisions of the supreme court in 2004 and 2005 went too far: "[E]vidence of advancing an ideology by adopting congenial legal principles is one thing; advancing an anti-tort ideology simply by refusing to allow plaintiffs to succeed is quite another."[89]

THREE SIGNALS?

Three events from the first decade of the twenty-first century may provide some insight into the current state of Texas tort law. The first jury verdict holding the drug manufacturer Merck liable for the drug Vioxx was rendered in Texas in 2005. It awarded $24,450,000 in compensatory damages and $229 million in punitive damages, reduced by law to $26.1 million. The judgment was reversed on appeal. Second, in a 260–page opinion, Corpus Christi federal district court judge Janis Jack dismissed a multidistrict mass tort case involving claims of silicosis allegedly suffered by over ten thousand plaintiffs. She held that the diagnoses of silicosis were unreliable (indeed, spectacularly unreliable) and ordered plaintiffs' counsel to pay the costs for the expert testimony hearing over which the court had jurisdiction. Third, as if required every eight years, in 2003 Texas adopted yet more tort reform, called "the most comprehensive package of tort reform laws yet." In addition, voters were asked to decide whether to add a proposed constitutional amendment permitting a monetary cap on noneconomic damages. Proposition 12 was adopted in September 2003. Tort reform in Texas has strongly benefited civil defendants. Whether this will lead to another backlash remains to be seen.[90]

After all of this, how is Texas viewed by the tort reform–minded Pacific Research Institute? In its *U.S. Tort Liability Index: 2008 Report*, the authors noted: "Texas is an interesting study in contradictions, because it has low tort costs for its size but also has the specter of great upside risk in individual cases due to its judicial hellholes and runaway jury verdicts. Texas still poses the threat of 'jackpot justice,' which is characterized by reasonable verdicts and awards in most cases but the all too common jackpot, or crackpot, award that can bust a company."[91]

Conclusion

★

THE MOVIE *Charlie Wilson's War* (2007) offers a fictionalized conversation between CIA agent Gust Avrakotos and Texas congressman Charlie Wilson occurring shortly after the Soviet Union leaves Afghanistan in 1989. Avrakotos offers Wilson a parable about a Zen master's response to a village's claim of a boy's fortune and misfortune. When the fourteen-year-old boy receives a horse for his birthday, the people of the village declare, "What a lucky boy!" The Zen master replies, "We'll see." Two years later, the boy falls off the horse and breaks his leg, and the people exclaim, "What an unlucky boy!" The Zen master replies, "We'll see." Soldiers later conscript all able-bodied men in the village. Because his leg is mangled, the boy is left behind. The people cry, "What a lucky boy," and the Zen master, as always, replies, "We'll see." Avrakotos asks Wilson to envision the Soviet departure not as a final victory for the United States, but as the first step in building a nation. The film offers the parable knowing that the viewer is well aware of al Qaeda's subsequent encampment in Afghanistan and the unspoken continuation of the story in the September 11, 2001, attacks. Declaring victory does not make it so.[1]

This is also the story of law in Texas. An individual wins a case in the court system. Victory is declared in part so society can move on, even when the court's decision is the end of the beginning and not the end. A facile understanding of the course of Texas law looks to judge as reactionary or progressive, virtuous or vicious, the manifold decisions of countless legal actors. Those who judge then move on to other judgments. Whether "we won" is permanent or transient is often unknowable. Even when failure is known, an honorable failure may be the best we can ask of our lawmakers, whether legislators or judges, and our law peddlers, lawyers and law enforcement officers. A deeper though paradoxical understanding of events is, "We'll see."

The dramatic legal transformations of Texas are a compelling and continuing story. The breadth of the expansion of law from 1850 to

2010 might be unrecognizable to nineteenth-century Texas lawgivers. This is a two-sided coin, for today's lawgivers might find much of nineteenth-century Texas law uncomprehending and naively and foolishly conclude they know better. A study of the legal history of Texas offers those concerned with how power is exercised a sense of the limits and possibilities of law. It may provide to all students of the law a caution against hubris and an embrace of humility. We may not be condemned to repeat a history we choose not to remember, but an unwillingness to understand the histories of a people and place is folly. More importantly, acknowledging the messiness of life as demonstrated in the history of law is frustrating but ultimately liberating, for this understanding leads to a rejection of the lawgiver as prophet and "the law" as something to idolize. Faith in law creates unrealistic expectations in the ability of human beings to deliver justice.

An overview of the legal history of Texas is necessarily painted in broad strokes. This view misleads, for details always matter. The particular hopes and fears of the vast majority of Texans who have lived and died can only be guessed. The desires of parties in legal matters are often declared in the "legal fictions" of the law, fictions that fail to reflect the emotions of any party. Trial and appellate court accounts of the longings of the parties drain the vibrancy of those human needs in the written opinion and distort the prayer for justice. This distortion may be necessary to shape law within the bounds of the rule of law, but it is a distortion nonetheless. Like the appellate opinion, a general legal history of Texas may distort the hopes and fears of the people it discusses.

The American and Texas legal systems are ponderous. The specialized language of the law both obfuscates and diffuses the responsibility of those charged with its enforcement and interpretation. However, the "law" is much less stable than ordinarily perceived, and the complication of human actors in "operating" this system increases its instability. The contingent meaning of the law may be understood more clearly when evaluated historically, and such contingency may be understood either optimistically or pessimistically (or both). Both what the law is and how it is interpreted suggest to an optimist the possibility for positive change (or "reform"). A pessimist may understand the contingency of the law as demonstrating its all-too-human influences, a law shaped less by reason than by the political and emotional biases of those legal actors and ordinary persons who make it.

The story of law in Texas is a persistently human story, one in which human weaknesses and human strengths appear in equal measure. The quests for liberty and equality, for recompense and vindication, for acknowledgment and acceptance, and for forgiveness and vengeance are central to these stories. A study of the past may inform Texans about who we were, and, more importantly, ask, Who are we?

NOTES

★

NONSTANDARD ABBREVIATIONS

BLR	Baylor Law Review
DMN	Dallas Morning News
HOTO	Handbook of Texas Online
HLR	Houston Law Review
PTBA	Proceedings of the Texas Bar Association
SWHQ	Southwestern Historical Quarterly
STLR	South Texas Law Review
StMLJ	St. Mary's Law Journal
SwLJ	Southwestern Law Journal
TBJ	Texas Bar Journal
TLR	Texas Law Review
TM	Texas Monthly
TTLR	Texas Tech Law Review
WSJ	Wall Street Journal

PREFACE

1. On these two giants, see Gregory L. Ivy, *Publications of Joseph W. McKnight*, 55 SMU L. Rev. 367 (2002), and Basil Markesinis, *Introduction: The Life and Work of Hans Wolfgang Baade*, 36 Tex. Int'l L.J. 403 (2001).

2. The PORTAL TO TEXAS HISTORY is at texas-history.unt.edu/browse/; information about the HANDBOOK OF TEXAS ONLINE (hereafter cited as HOTO) is found at www.tshaonline.org/handbook/about-handbook.

INTRODUCTION

1. *Texas Lawyer's 20th Century in Review*, Tex. Law., Dec. 20, 1999, at § 4; *21 for 21: The Cases That Rocked the Century*, Tex. Law., Dec. 20, 1999, § 4, at 36; in this view I follow Gerald N. Rosenberg, THE HOLLOW HOPE: CAN COURTS BRING ABOUT SOCIAL CHANGE? (1991), as modified in Michael J. Klarman, FROM JIM CROW TO CIVIL RIGHTS: THE SUPREME COURT AND THE STRUGGLE FOR RACIAL EQUALITY (2004); Grant Gilmore, THE AGES OF AMERICAN LAW 110 (1977) ("Law reflects but in no sense determines the moral worth of a society.").

2. Frank E. Vandiver, THE SOUTHWEST: SOUTH OR WEST? (1975); D. W. Meinig, IMPERIAL TEXAS: AN INTERPRETIVE ESSAY IN CULTURAL GEOGRAPHY (1969).

3. On American exceptionalism, see, for example, Daniel J. Boorstin, THE GENIUS OF AMERICAN POLITICS (1953) (largely a good thing); Christopher Lasch, THE CULTURE OF NARCISSISM (1979) (largely bad); and Seymour Martin Lipset, AMERICAN EXCEPTIONALISM: A DOUBLE-EDGED SWORD (1996) (self-explanatory). On the myth of the Texas Rangers, see

Walter Prescott Webb, The Texas Rangers (1935). On exceptional oil wildcatters, see Bryan Burrough, The Big Rich (2009). On Texas exceptionalism and on understanding Texas history I have been greatly influenced by two Texas historiographies, Texas Through Time: Evolving Interpretations (Walter L. Buenger & Robert A. Calvert eds., 1991) and Lone Star Pasts: Memory and History in Texas (Gregg Cantrell & Elizabeth Hayes Turner eds., 2007), and by Randolph B. Campbell, Gone to Texas: A History of the Lone Star State 468–71 (2003).

4. C. W. Raines, *Enduring Laws of the Republic*, 2 Q. Tex. St. Hist. Ass'n 152 (1898); Daffan Gilmer, *Early Courts and Lawyers of Texas*, 12 TLR 435 (1934).

5. Walter A. McDougall, Freedom Just Around the Corner: A New American History, 1585–1828 (2004); Walter A. McDougall, Throes of Democracy: The American Civil War Era, 1829–1877, at xviii (2008).

6. On the "objectivity" question, see Peter Novick, That Noble Lie: The "Objectivity Question" and the American Historical Association (1988).

CHAPTER 1

1. Donald E. Chipman, Spanish Texas, 1521–1821, at 69 (1992) (noting settlement of Corpus Christi de la Isleta in 1682 near present-day El Paso); *id.* ch. 6 (noting permanent settlement of Texas); Jesús F. de la Teja, San Antonio de Béxar: A Community on New Spain's Northern Frontier 8 (1995); Jesús F. de la Teja, *San Fernando de Bexar*, HOTO, www.tshaonline.org/handbook/online/articles/SS/hvs16.html; Alicia V. Tjarks, *Comparative Demographic Analysis of Texas, 1777–1793*, 77 SWHQ 291, 299 (1974) (listing 3,103 persons in Texas in 1777), and Donald E. Chipman, *Spanish Texas, in* Texas Through Time: Evolving Interpretations 130 (Walter L. Buenger & Robert A. Calvert eds., 1991) (noting 3,605 residents in 1804 plus 636 residents of Laredo in a 1795 census); 1860 population, www.census.gov/population/www/documentation/twps0056/tab58.xls.

2. On differences between the civil law and common law systems, see Arthur T. von Mehren & James Gordley, The Civil Law System 3–15 (2d ed. 1977); John Henry Merryman & Rogelio Perez-Perdomo, The Civil Law Tradition (3d ed. 2007).

3. Act of Jan. 20, 1840, 4th Cong., Republic of Texas, 2 The Laws of Texas 177 (H. P. N. Gammel ed., 1898) (hereafter cited as Gammel's). This law

became effective on March 16, 1840 (see Hans W. Baade, *Reflections on the Reception (or Renaissance) of Civil Law*, 55 SMU L. Rev. 59, 60 & n.5 (2002); and Joseph W. McKnight, *The Spanish Legacy to Texas Law*, 3 Am. J. Leg. Hist. 222 *(Part I)*, and 299 *(Part II)* (1959)). On civil procedure, see Joseph W. McKnight, *The Spanish Influence on the Texas Law of Civil Procedure*, 38 TLR 24 (1959), and chapter 8. On community property, see Jean A. Stuntz, Hers, His, and Theirs: Community Property Law in Spain and Early Texas (2005); Kathleen Lazarou, Concealed under Petticoats: Married Women's Property and the Law of Texas (1986); Joseph W. McKnight, *Texas Community Property Law: Its Course of Development and Reform*, 8 Cal. W. L. Rev. 117 (1971); and chapter 5. On water law, see Hans W. Baade, *The Historical Background of Texas Water Law: A Tribute to Jack Pope*, 18 StMLJ 1, 21 (1986), and chapter 3.

4. The information in this section is taken largely from Charles R. Cutter, The Legal Culture of Northern New Spain, 1700–1810 (1995).

5. Quote, Stuntz, at 71; Joseph W. McKnight, *Law Books in the Hispanic Frontier*, 27 J. West 74 (1988), reprinted in Spanish and Mexican Land Grants and the Law 74 (Malcolm Ebright ed., 1989); Joseph W. McKnight, *Law Without Lawyers on the Hispano-Mexican Frontier*, 66 West Tex. Hist. Ass'n Year Book 51, and quotes at 57, 56 (1990).

6. Cutter, at 31–35, 95–102, and quote at 35; McKnight, *Law Books*.

7. Cutter, at 105–24.

8. *Id.* at 125–38.

9. Gregg Cantrell, Stephen F. Austin: Empresario of Texas 110–27 (1999); Eugene C. Barker, *The Government of Austin's Colony, 1821–1831*, 21 SWHQ 223 (1918); Joseph W. McKnight, *Stephen F. Austin's Legalistic Concerns*, 89 SWHQ 239 (1986); Marvin E. Schultz, For the Better Administration of Justice: The Legal Culture of Texas, 1820–1836 (Ph.D. diss., Texas Christian University 1994).

10. Schultz, at 18–19. On Josiah Bell, see Merie Weir, *Bell, Josiah Hughes*, HOTO, www.tshaonline.org/handbook/online/articles/BB/fbe38.html; on John Tumlinson, see Samuel H. Tumlinson, *Tumlinson, John Jackson, Sr.*, HOTO, www.tshaonline.org/handbook/online/articles/TT/ftu29.html.

11. These laws are published in Stephen F. Austin, Establishing Austin's Colony: The First Book Printed in Texas with the Laws, Orders, and Contracts of Colonization 84–89 (David B. Gracy II ed., 1970) (reprinting Stephen Austin's Translation of the Law, Orders, and Contracts of Colonization (1829)), and in Guy M. Bryan, *Official Documents, Laws, Decrees, and*

Regulations Pertaining to Austin's Colonies in 1 A
COMPREHENSIVE HISTORY OF TEXAS 481–92 (2 vols.,
Dudley G. Wooten ed., 1898, repr. 1986). On Texas
civil pleading, see chapter 8.

12. McKnight, *Austin's Legalistic Concerns*, at 255;
"appellate court in Texas," Decree 277, reprinted in
LAWS AND DECREES OF THE STATE OF COAHUILA
AND TEXAS 254 (J. P. Kimball trans., 1839) (hereafter
cited as LAWS AND DECREES), and 1 Gammel's 364;
"Saltillo," Const. of Coahuila and Texas art. 194,
LAWS AND DECREES, at 339, and 1 Gammel's 423, 449;
quote, McKnight, *Austin's Legalistic Concerns*, at 254,
262.

13. Quote, Schultz, at 27; "general safety," *id.* at 28
n.26; Parker case, *id.* at 52–53.

14. Constitutional provisions, 1 Gammel's 423–59,
and LAWS AND DECREES, 313 *et seq.* On the civil-law
tradition, see Merryman, ch. 6; on the common-law
tradition of judging, see Frederick G. Kempin, Jr.,
HISTORICAL INTRODUCTION TO ANGLO-AMERICAN
LAW 102–8 (3d ed. 1990).

15. Constitutional provisions, 1 Gammel's 423 *et
seq.*, and LAWS AND DECREES, at 313 *et seq.*

16. Decree 39 was not published in either
Kimball's translation of the LAWS AND DECREES
or in Gammel's LAWS OF TEXAS, which simply
copied Kimball's translation. A copy was located
in the Bexar Archives of the Dolph Briscoe Center
for American History at the University of Texas at
Austin and was translated into English in 1921 at the
behest of attorney Clarence Wharton, who wished
to use the decree to settle a dispute in favor of his
client (see Clarence Wharton, *Early Judicial History
of Texas*, 12 TLR 311, 318 (1934), recounting finding
Decree 39 in the Bexar Archives; see also Clarence
Wharton, THE JURISDICTION OF THE ALCALDE
COURTS IN TEXAS PRIOR TO THE REVOLUTION:
ARGUMENT FILED IN CONNELY [SIC] V. ABRAMS IN
COURT OF CIVIL APPEALS AT GALVESTON (1927)).

17. Law of Apr. 6, 1830, see Art. 42, EARLY LAWS
OF TEXAS 55 (John Sayles & Henry Sayles comp. &
arr., 1888) (translated into English) (hereafter cited as
Sayles, EARLY LAWS); on the reasons for this decree,
see Alleine Howren, *Causes and Origin of the Decree
of April 6, 1830*, 16 SWHQ 378 (1913); Cantrell, STE-
PHEN F. AUSTIN, at 219–26, and quote at 221; Decree
136, 1 Gammel's 261, and LAWS AND DECREES, at 151.

18. On the "abortive Decree 136" and trial, see
McKnight, *Austin's Legalistic Concerns*, at 258. The
decree was issued on April 19, 1830, and the trial
took place on June 2, 1830. The governor's decision
to return the decree for reformation was given on
September 1, 1830, well after the trial took place (see
LAWS AND DECREES, at 153).

19. McKnight, *Austin's Legalistic Concerns*, at 254.
The defendant was awarded a new trial after showing
the executive department in San Antonio that new
evidence existed that was unavailable at the time of
the trial.

20. Cantrell, STEPHEN F. AUSTIN, at 268, and
quote at 271.

21. Journals of the Consultation, *Plan of Government*, 1 Gammel's 505, 540. On the view that the
Texas Revolution was based in part on a legal revolution melding the Spanish-Mexican civil law system
with the American common-law system, see Gerald
Ashford, *Jacksonian Liberalism and Spanish Law in
Early Texas*, 52 SWHQ 1 (1953).

22. On the Texas Declaration of Independence,
see James K. Greer, *The Committee on the Texas
Declaration of Independence (Part I)*, 30 SWHQ 239
(1927), *(Part II)*, 31 SWHQ 33 (1927), and *(Part III)*, 31
SWHQ 130 (1927). On the Constitution of 1836, see
Rupert N. Richardson, *Framing the Constitution of
the Republic of Texas*, 31 SWHQ 191 (1928), and David
P. Currie, *The Constitution of the Republic of Texas
(Part I)*, 8 Green Bag 2d 145 (2005).

23. Thomas Hobbes, LEVIATHAN ch. 13 (Herbert
W. Schneider ed., 1958); quote, Stanley Siegel, A
POLITICAL HISTORY OF THE TEXAS REPUBLIC 58
(1951); Act of Dec. 15, 1836, 1st Cong., Repub. Tex., 1
Gammel's 1139 (establishing jurisdiction of the Texas
Supreme Court); Act of Dec. 22, 1836, 1st Cong.,
Repub. Tex., 1 Gammel's 1258 (establishing four
district courts).

24. An Act to Establish a General Land Office
for the Republic of Texas, Act of Dec. 22, 1836, 1st
Cong. Repub. Tex., 1 Gammel's 1276, 1284 (creating the Texas General Land Office and noting the
override of Houston's veto); on Houston's veto, see
Siegel, at 62; Act of Dec. 14, 1837, 2d Cong., Repub.
Tex., 1 Gammel's 1404, 1418 (adopting the act again
creating the general land office over Houston's
veto); An Act to Incorporate the Texas Rail Road,
Navigation, and Banking Company, Act of Dec. 16,
1836, 1st Cong., Repub. Tex., 1 Gammel's 1188; An Act
Punishing Crimes and Misdemeanors, Act of Dec.
21, 1836, 1st Cong., Repub. Tex., 1 Gammel's 1247. On
Jackson and the Second Bank, see Robert V. Remini,
ANDREW JACKSON AND THE BANK WAR (1967).

25. See Jodye Lynn Dickson Schilz, *Council House
Fight*, HOTO, www.tshaonline.org/handbook/
online/articles/CC/btc1.html, and John Edward
Weems with Jane Weems, DREAM OF EMPIRE: A
HUMAN HISTORY OF THE REPUBLIC OF TEXAS, 1836–
1845, at 172–80 (1971); quote, Rosalee Morris Curtis,
JOHN HEMPHILL: FIRST CHIEF JUSTICE OF THE STATE
OF TEXAS 33 (1971) (quoting John Henry Brown,

INDIAN WARS AND PIONEERS OF TEXAS 78 (189–?)); "massacre" and quote, Gary Clayton Anderson, THE CONQUEST OF TEXAS: ETHNIC CLEANSING IN THE PROMISED LAND, 1820–1875, at 183 (2005); Woll raid, Spiegel, at 202–4; Woll invasion and Hutchinson capture, see James D. Lynch, BENCH AND BAR OF TEXAS 75 (Nixon-Jones Printing Co. 1885); James W. Paulsen, *The Judges of the Supreme Court of the Republic of Texas*, 65 TLR 305, 336 (1986); Hemphill's service, Curtis, at 40–44; change in supreme court session from January to June, see Act of Feb. 3, 1842, § 1, 6th Cong., Repub. Tex., 2 Gammel's 766.

26. Act of Jan. 26, 1839, 3d Cong., Repub. Tex., 2 Gammel's 125; Joseph W. McKnight, *Protection of the Family Home from Seizure by Creditors: The Sources and Evolution of a Legal Principle*, 86 SWHQ 369 (1983); Brady Cole, *The Homestead Provisions in the Texas Constitution*, 3 TLR 217 (1925); H. Teichmueller, *The Homestead Law*, 11 PTBA 63 (1893); C. W. Raines, *Enduring Laws of the Republic of Texas*, 1 Q. Tex. St. Hist. Assn. 96 (1897); A. E. Wilkinson, *The Author of the Texas Homestead Exemption Law*, 20 SWHQ 35 (1916); Decree 70, Jan. 13, 1829, 1 Gammel's 220; Decree 173, Apr. 8, 1831, 1 Gammel's 289; An Act Concerning Executions, Act of Feb. 5, 1840, 4th Cong., Repub. Tex., 2 Gammel's 267; Act of Dec. 22, 1840, § 7, 5th Cong., Repub. Tex., 2 Gammel's 525, 526; Tex. Const. Art. VII, § 22 (1845), 2 Gammel's 1275, 1294; Tex. Const. Art. XVI, § 50 (1876), 8 Gammel's 779, 832–33; quote, Mark E. Nackman, *Anglo-American Migrants to the West: Men of Broken Fortunes? The Case of Texas, 1821–1846*, 5 W. Hist. Q. 441, 453 (1974).

27. Act of Aug. 19, 1841, 27th Cong., ch. 9, 5 Stat. 440; Act of Jan. 19, 1841, 5th Cong., Repub. Tex., 2 Gammel's 502; reserved goods and land, 5th Cong., Repub. Tex., Rule 4, 2 Gammel's 504. The 1841 bankruptcy law was repealed in 1860 (see Act of Jan. 2, 1860, 8th Leg., ch. 14, 4 Gammel's 1380). See generally Bruce H. Mann, REPUBLIC OF DEBTORS: BANKRUPTCY IN THE AGE OF AMERICAN INDEPENDENCE (2002), and Scott A. Sandage, BORN LOSERS: A HISTORY OF FAILURE IN AMERICA (2005).

28. Act of Jan. 20, 1840, § 1, 4th Cong., Repub. Tex., 2 Gammel's 177 (adopting common law as "rule of decision" and creating a system of community property); Act of Dec. 20, 1836, § 41, 1st Cong., Repub. Tex., 1 Gammel's 1208, 1216–17 (applying common law of England to juries and evidence); Act of Feb. 5, 1840, 4th Cong., Repub. Tex., 2 Gammel's 262 (rejecting common-law pleading and adopting Spanish-Mexican system of pleading); Act of Jan. 28, 1840, 4th Cong., Repub. Tex., 2 Gammel's 306 (on intestate succession); Act of Feb. 5, 1840, 4th

Cong., Repub. Tex., 2 Gammel's 243 (on foreclosure of mortgages); Act of Feb. 5, 1840, 4th Cong., Repub. Tex., 21 Gammel's 327 (on conveying real property). On the use of Spanish law through Louisiana sources, see Peter L. Reich, *Siete Partidas in My Saddlebags: The Transmission of Hispanic Law from Antebellum Louisiana to Texas and California*, 22 Tul. Eur. & Civ. L. F. 79, 81–84 (2007). On the common law in Texas, see J. E. Ericson & Mary P. Winston, *Civil Law and Common Law in Early Texas*, 2 E. Tex. Hist. J. 26 (1964); Ford W. Hall, *An Account of the Adoption of the Common Law by Texas*, 28 TLR 801 (1950); Edward Lee Markham, Jr., *The Reception of the Common Law of England in Texas and the Judicial Attitude toward That Reception*, 29 TLR 904 (1951).

29. The material in this section is taken from James W. Paulsen, *A Short History of the Supreme Court of the Republic of Texas*, 65 TLR 237 (1986); Paulsen, *Judges of the Supreme Court*, 65 TLR 305 (1986); James W. Paulsen ed., *The Missing Cases of the Republic*, 65 TLR 372 (1986); David P. Currie, *The Constitution of the Republic of Texas: The Decisions*, 8 Green Bag 2d 239 (2005); and Joe R. Greenhill, *The Early Supreme Court of Texas and Some of Its Justices*, TBJ, July 1999, at 646.

30. Act of Dec. 15, 1836, 1st Cong., Repub. Tex., 1 Gammel's 1139 (establishing jurisdiction of supreme court); Act of Dec. 22, 1836, 1st Cong., Repub. Tex., 1 Gammel's 1258 (establishing four district courts); Act of May 24, 1838, 2d Cong., 2d Sess., Repub. Tex., 1 Gammel's 1500 (creating a fifth judicial district); Act of Jan. 29, 1840, 4th Cong., Repub. Tex., 2 Gammel's 350 (creating sixth and seventh judicial districts).

31. "Forty-nine cases," Paulsen, *Short History*, at 253–54; Paulsen ed., *Missing Cases*.

32. On Hemphill, see Curtis; Lynch, at 69–73; J. H. Davenport, THE HISTORY OF THE SUPREME COURT OF TEXAS 15–16 (1917); Reuben Reid Gaines, *John Hemphill*, in 4 GREAT AMERICAN LAWYERS 3–26 (8 vols. William D. Lewis ed., 1908); C. S. Potts, *Hemphill, John*, 8 DICTIONARY OF AMERICAN BIOGRAPHY 520 (Dumas Malone ed., 1933); James P. Hart, *John Hemphill—Chief Justice of Texas*, 3 SwLJ 395 (1949); Robert W. Calvert, *John Hemphill*, TBJ, Oct. 1961, at 937; and Timothy S. Huebner, THE SOUTHERN JUDICIAL TRADITION: STATE JUDGES AND SECTIONAL DISTINCTIVENESS, 1790–1890, ch. 4 (1999).

33. "Twenty-six men," see Paulsen, *Judges of the Supreme Court*, App. B at 370–71.

34. The edition of James William Dallam's A DIGEST OF THE LAWS OF TEXAS, CONTAINING A FULL AND COMPLETE COMPILATION OF THE LAND LAWS, TOGETHER WITH THE OPINIONS OF THE SUPREME COURT referenced is the 1883 Gilbert Book

Company printing, which is paginated slightly differently than the 1845 original. Bradley v. McCrabb, Dallam's 504 (1841) and Morton v. Gordon, Dallam's 396 (1841) (right to appeal); Republic v. Smith, Dallam's 407 (1841) (reviewing authority); Republic v. Laughlin, Dallam's 412 (1841), and Nash v. Republic, Dallam's 631 (1844) (congress attempting to extend the court's jurisdiction); Stockton v. Montgomery, Dallam's 473 (1842), and quote at 480; VanHorne's Lessee v. Dorrance, 2 U.S. (2 Dall.) 304 (C.C.D. Pa. 1795); Marbury v. Madison, 5 U.S. (1 Cranch) 137 (1803); Allen v. Scott, Dallam's 615 (1844).

35. McGill v. Delaplain, Dallam's 493 (1843); Bailey v. Haddy, Dallam's 376, 377–78 (1841).

36. Scott v. Maynard, Dallam's 548 (1843), and quotes at 552–53; Mills v. Waller, Dallam's 416, 418 (1841); Garret v. Nash, Dallam's 498 (1844).

37. On the Regulator-Moderator War, see C. L. Douglas, Famous Texas Feuds 1–49 (1936); Wayne Gard, Frontier Justice ch. 2 (1949); C. L. Sonnichsen, Ten Texas Feuds ch. 1 (1957, repr. 2000); James W. Paulsen, *A Short History of the Supreme Court of the Republic of Texas*, 65 TLR 237, 261–63 (1986); Gilbert M. Cuthbertson, *Regulator-Moderator War*, HOTO, www.tshaonline.org/handbook/online/articles/RR/jcr1.html. On Hansford, see *John M. Hansford*, tarlton.law.utexas.edu/justices/spct/hansford.html; Paulsen, *Judges*, at 333–34 (noting Hansford "may be the most infamous judge of the Republic Supreme Court").

38. Sonnichsen, at 39–40.

39. Joe E. Ericson, *Potter, Robert*, HOTO, www.tshaonline.org/handbook/online/articles/PP/fpo31.html; James R. Norvell, *Lewis v. Ames—An Ancient Cause Revisited*, 13 SwLJ 301, 308–10 (1959); Sonnichsen, ch. 2; Douglas, ch. 5.

40. Philip Paxton (pseudonym of Samuel A. Hammett), A Stray Yankee in Texas (Redfield 1853), and quotes at 244, 321, 356 n.* (emphasis in the original); Sonnichsen, at 15. On Hammett, see George Harvey Genzmer, *Hammett, Samuel Adams*, 8 Dictionary of American Biography 201 (Dumas Malone ed., 1933). The lynching of the greatest number of persons in American history at one time occurred in Gainesville and neighboring areas in North Texas in 1862 in the "Great Hanging," in which more than forty Union sympathizers were hung over a period of several weeks (see Richard B. McCaslin, Tainted Breeze: The Great Hanging at Gainesville, Texas, 1862 (1994)). On race-based lynchings, see Arnoldo De León, They Called Them Greasers: Anglo Attitudes toward Mexicans in Texas 80 (1983), and William D. Carrigan, The Making of a Lynching Culture:

Violence and Vigilantism in Central Texas, 1836–1916 (2004).

41. William Ransom Hogan, *Rampant Individualism in the Republic of Texas*, 44 SWHQ 454 (1941); "less than twelve," *id.* at 462; Henderson quote, *id.* at 463; differentiating, *id.* at 463; insecurity on the frontier, McCaslin, at 2. On Jackson and the rule of law, see Jon Meacham, American Lion: Andrew Jackson in the White House 204 (2008) ("Andrew Jackson never allowed anything, much less legal niceties, to stand in his way if he was determined to do something."), and Daniel Walker Howe, What Hath God Wrought: The Transformation of America, 1815–1848, at 411 (2007) ("[Jackson] did not manifest a general respect for the authority of the law when it got in the way of the policies he chose to pursue.").

42. On the 1845 convention and constitution, see Frederic L. Paxson, *The Constitution of Texas, 1845*, 18 SWHQ 386 (1915); Annie Middleton, *The Texas Convention of 1845*, 25 SWHQ 26 (1922); and John Cornyn, *The Roots of the Texas Constitution: Settlement to Statehood*, 26 TTLR 1089, 1124–94 (1995). On the Texas Bill of Rights, see J. E. Ericson, *Origins of the Texas Bill of Rights*, 62 SWHQ 457 (1959). Quote, Middleton, at 37. See generally Chris Klemme, *Jacksonian Justice: The Evolution of the Elective Judiciary in Texas, 1836–1850*, 105 SWHQ 429 (2002) (discussing the evolution of the Texas judiciary).

43. Debates of the Convention, 1845 (July 28, 1845), at 271, http://tarlton.law.utexas.edu/constitutions/pdf/pdf1845debates/indexdebates1845.html#j28.

44. Subcommittee of the Texas Bar Association, *The Blending of Law and Equity*, 30 Am. L. Rev. 813 (1896); George C. Butte, *Early Development of Law and Equity in Texas*, 26 Yale L.J. 699 (1917).

45. On Lipscomb, see Mary J. Highsmith, *Lipscomb, Abner Smith*, HOTO, www.tshaonline.org/handbook/online/articles/LL/fli14.html; Lynch, at 85–90; Davenport, at 30–31; C. S. Potts, *Lipscomb, Abner Smith*, 11 Dictionary of American Biography 289 (Dumas Malone ed., 1933). On Wheeler, see H. Allen Anderson, *Wheeler, Royal T.*, HOTO, www.tshaonline.org/handbook/online/articles/fwh09; Lynch, at 91–96; Davenport, at 22–25; C. S. Potts, *Wheeler, Royall Tyler*, 20 Dictionary of American Biography 53 (Dumas Malone ed., 1933); Paulsen, *Supreme Court Judges*, at 359–61; George W. Paschal, *Preface*, 28 Tex. v–xii (1869) (Paschal was the reporter for volume 28 of the Texas Reports). On Hemphill and nullification, see Curtis, at 15–18; see also chapter 2.

46. Huebner, at 105, quoting letter of Royall T. Wheeler to Oran M. Roberts, Sept. 20, 1849, Oran

M. Roberts Papers, Eugene C. Barker Texas History Collection, University of Texas at Austin; "Wheeler wrote," and "a quarter," *id.*; "only seventy-one," *id.*, citing James W. Paulsen, *The Uncommon Law of Slavery in the Texas Supreme Court* 6 (paper presented at the annual meeting of the Law and Society Association, June 16, 1994); Coles v. Kelsey, 2 Tex. 541, 558–78 (1847) (Wheeler, J., dissenting).

47. Gaines, at 12; Hart, at 405–9; quote, Hart, *John Hemphill*, at 410.

48. Foster v. Van Norman, 1 Tex. 636, 638 (1846); Cocke v. Calkin & Co., 1 Tex. 542, 554 (1846); McCulloch v. Maryland, 4 Wheat. (17 U.S.) 316 (1819); Calkin v. Cocke, 55 U.S. 227 (1853); Benner v. Porter, 50 U.S. 235 (1850) made the collector's argument impossible.

49. Davenport, at 29–30.

50. Wood v. Wheeler, 7 Tex. 19 (1851); Sampson and Keene v. Williamson, 6 Tex. 102 (1851); Cobbs v. Coleman, 14 Tex. 594 (1855); Pryor v. Stone, 19 Tex. 371 (1857); quotes, Paul Goodman, *The Emergence of Homestead Exemption in the United States: Accommodation and Resistance to the Market Revolution, 1840–1880*, 80 J. Am. Hist. 470, 470, 496 (1993); "most significant," Joseph W. McKnight & William A. Reppy, Jr., Texas Matrimonial Property Law 3 (2000). On the desire for protecting assets from creditors that led the republic in 1841 to exempt slaves from a forced sale, see Act of Jan. 27, 1841, 5th Cong., Repub. Tex., 2 Gammel's 515. By the end of the year, congress repealed the law (see Act of Dec. 30, 1841, 6th Cong., Repub. Tex., 2 Gammel's 697).

51. State v. Odum, 11 Tex. 12, 13 (1853). On the Texas Court of Appeals, see chapter 7, section "Formalism in the Texas Court of Appeals."

52. State v. Wuppermann, 13 Tex. 23 (1854); Gehrke v. State, 13 Tex. 568 (1855); White v. State, 16 Tex. 206 (1856).

53. State v. Johnston, 11 Tex. 22 (1853) (intent not alleged, indictment defective); Cain v. State, 18 Tex. 387 (1857); State v. Croft, 15 Tex. 575 (1855) (holding indictment sufficient); Calvin v. State, 25 Tex. 789 (1860) (holding "feloniously" no longer required but reversing conviction on ground that altered indictment was wrongful substantive change).

54. The Laws of Slavery in Texas (Randolph B. Campbell ed., William S. Pugsley & Marilyn P. Duncan comps., 2010); Randolph B. Campbell, An Empire for Slavery: The Peculiar Institution in Texas, 1821–1865 (1989); David Brion Davis, Inhuman Bondage: The Rise and Fall of Slavery in the New World 73–76 (2006); Act of Feb. 5, 1840, 4th Cong., Repub. Tex., 2 Gammel's 325; Proclamation, Dec. 21, 1842, 2 Gammel's 879;

see Code Crim. Proc. Arts. 906–17 (1856) (titled "Of Proceedings Against Free Persons of Color Remaining in the State in Violation of Law"); John E. Fisher, *The Legal Status of Free Blacks in Texas, 1836–1861*, 4 Tex. So. L. Rev. 342 (1977).

55. Jt. Res., June 5, 1837, Repub. Tex., 1 Gammel's 1292; Act of Feb. 5, 1840, 4th Cong., Repub. Tex., 2 Gammel's 325 (forbidding free persons of color from immigrating to Texas); Act of Dec. 14, 1837, 1st Cong., Repub. Tex., 1 Gammel's 1385–86.

56. Act of Mar. 20, 1848, 2d Leg., R.S., ch. 152, § 15, 3 Gammel's 219, 222; Act of Feb. 9, 1854, 5th Leg., R.S., ch. 49, § 4, 3 Gammel's 1502; "high demand," see Earl W. Fornell, *The Abduction of Free Negroes and Slaves in Texas*, 60 SWHQ 369 (1957); "This prohibition," Thomas D. Morris, Southern Slavery and the Law, 1619–1860, at 172 (1996). See also Chandler v. State, 2 Tex. 305, 309 (1847) (upholding the manslaughter conviction of a white man for killing a slave), and on "discipline and punishment," see Alwyn Barr, Black Texans: A History of African Americans in Texas, 1528–1995, at 20–21 (1973, repr. 1996) (noting whipping and other forms of physical punishment meted out to slaves).

57. Act of Feb. 12, 1858, 7th Leg., R.S., ch. 121, 4 Gammel's 1028, 1048–49; Art. 802, *id.* at 1058–60.

58. *Id.* at 1060.

59. Act of Feb. 11, 1860, 8th Leg., R.S., ch. 74, 4 Gammel's 1457, 1461; "eighty slaves," Barr, Black Texans, at 33; "better that ten," William Blackstone, Commentaries on the Law 2:*358, quoted in Coffin v. United States, 156 U.S. 432, 456 (1895); quote, Donald E. Reynolds, Texas Terror: The Slave Insurrection Panic of 1860 and the Secession of the Lower South 214 (2007).

60. Code Crim. Proc. Arts. 644.3 and 906–17; Act of Jan. 27, 1858, ch. 63, 7th Leg., 4 Gammel's 947; Westbrook v. Mitchell, 24 Tex. 560 (1859).

61. Quote, Barr, Black Texans, at 21.

62. Campbell, Empire ch. 5; Huebner, at 118–26; A. E. Keir Nash, *Texas Justice in the Age of Slavery: Appeals Concerning Blacks and the Antebellum State Supreme Court*, 8 HLR 438 (1971); A. E. Keir Nash, *The Texas Supreme Court and Trial Rights of Blacks, 1845–1860*, 58 J. Am. Hist. 622 (1971) (revising and expanding earlier article); Tex. Const. Art. VIII, § 1 (1845); Nels, a slave v. State, 2 Tex. 280 (1847).

63. Chandler v. State, 2 Tex. 305, 309 (1847); Nix v. State, 13 Tex. 575 (1855); State v. Stephenson, 20 Tex. 151, 152 (1857).

64. "Only two," Fisher, at 351; Moore v. Minerva, 17 Tex. 539 (1856); Jones v. Laney, 2 Tex. 342, 349 (1847); Purvis v. Sherrod, 12 Tex. 140 (1854); Huebner, at 122; Hillard v. Franz, 21 Tex. 192 (1858);

see also Armstrong v. Jowell, 24 Tex. 58 (1859) (reaffirming rule of Purvis); Philleo v. Holliday, 24 Tex. 38 (1859) (invalidating bequest); Harold Schoen, *The Free Negro in the Republic of Texas (III): Manumissions*, 40 SWHQ 85 (1936).

65. On Roberts, see *Roberts, Oran Milo*, HOTO, www.tshaonline.org/handbook/online/articles/fro18; 92 Tex. v–xii (1898); Lynch, at 273–84; Davenport, at 49–59; C. S. Potts, Roberts, Oran Milo, 16 DICTIONARY OF AMERICAN BIOGRAPHY 13 (Dumas Malone ed., 1933); James R. Norvell, *A Texas Portrait: Oran M. Roberts*, 23 TBJ 727 (1960). On Bell, see *Bell, James Hall*, HOTO, www.tshaonline.org/handbook/online/articles/fbe36; Lynch, at 293–94; Davenport, at 55–58; 85 Tex. xii (1893).

66. James Marten, TEXAS DIVIDED: LOYALTY AND DISSENT IN THE LONE STAR STATE, 1856–1874, at 20–21 (1990); Wheeler's view, and quote, Paschal, *Preface*, 28 Tex. v. On the Bell-Roberts debate, see William J. Chriss, *Judges as Political Orators: The 1860 Secession Debate between Texas Supreme Court Justices O. M. Roberts and James H. Bell*, works. bepress.com/cgi/viewcontent.cgi?article=1001&context=william_chriss. The speeches are published in O. M. Roberts, THE IMPENDING CRISIS (1860) and James H. Bell, SPEECH OF HON. JAMES H. BELL OF THE TEXAS SUPREME COURT, ON DECEMBER 1ST, 1860 (Intelligencer Book Office 1860). On secession, see Ordinance No. 1, Feb. 1, 1861, Acts of the Texas Convention, 4 Gammel's 1519.

67. Parker v. State, 26 Tex. 204, 207 (1862); James R. Norvell, *The Supreme Court of Texas under the Confederacy—1861–1865*, 4 HLR 46, 59 (1966); David C. Humphrey, *A "Very Muddy and Conflicting" View: The Civil War as Seen from Austin, Texas*, 94 SWHQ 369 (1991).

68. Confederate Conscription Act, see William L. Shaw, *The Confederate Conscription and Exemption Acts*, 6 Am. J. Legal Hist. 368, 374 (1962) (summarizing acts); martial law in Texas, Marten, at 49, 57, and 191 n.37; Paschal, *Preface*, at vii; *Ex parte* Coupland, 26 Tex. 387 (1862); McCulloch v. Maryland, 4 Wheat. (17 U.S.) 316 (1819); *Ex parte* Turman, 26 Tex. 708 (1863) (opinion by Bell following Coupland); *Ex parte* Randle, Robard's Synopses 10 (1863) (holding person released from Army of the Confederacy may be required to serve in the Texas militia); on judicial review in Confederate states, see Marshall L. DeRosa, THE CONFEDERATE CONSTITUTION OF 1861, ch. 6 (1991); on George W. Paschal, see Jane Lynn Scarborough, George W. Paschal, Texas Unionist and Scalawag Jurisprudent (Ph.D. diss., Rice University 1972); on *Ex parte* Coupland, Scarborough, at 72–78; James P. Hart, *George W. Paschal*, 28 TLR 23 (1949);

John T. Vance, *Paschal, George Washington*, 14 DICTIONARY OF AMERICAN BIOGRAPHY 287 (Dumas Malone ed., 1934).

69. *Ex parte* Peebles, Robard's Synopses 17 (1864); Paschal, *Preface*, at vii–viii; Hart, *Paschal*, 28 TLR at 28–29; "five people," Marten, at 61–62. The most detailed account of this incident is Robert Pattison Felgar, TEXAS IN THE WAR FOR SOUTHERN INDEPENDENCE, 1861–1865, ch. 9, and "political prisoners" at 315 (Ph.D. diss., University of Texas 1935). See also State v. Sparks, 27 Tex. 627 (1864); State v. Sparks & Magruder, 27 Tex. 705, 713 (1864).

CHAPTER 2

1. Act of Mar. 30, 1889, 21st Leg., R.S., ch. 117, 9 Gammel's 1169; Act of Apr. 3, 1891, 22d Leg., R.S., ch. 51, 10 Gammel's 57.

2. James Marten, TEXAS DIVIDED: LOYALTY AND DISSENT IN THE LONE STAR STATE, 1856–1874 at 129 (1990); Carl H. Moneyhon, TEXAS AFTER THE CIVIL WAR: THE STRUGGLE OF RECONSTRUCTION 7 (2004).

3. Maria, a Freedwoman v. State, 28 Tex. 698 (1866). Paschal's comments on the applicability of Texas criminal law to Maria are found at 28 Tex. at 699–700.

4. Wilson v. State, 29 Tex. 240 (1867); Presley v. State, 30 Tex. 160 (1867) (following Wilson). Judge Mark Davidson, *The Civil War and Reconstruction in Harris County's Only District Court*, Hous. Law., Nov.–Dec. 1995, at 42, notes that the supreme court erroneously states that Wilson's case was tried in March, *id.* at 43. General Kirby Smith formally surrendered on June 2, 1865, although the partial surrender of the department by Lieutenant Simon Bolivar Buckner on May 26 is often used as the date of surrender. See generally Moneyhon, at 6–7.

5. On the sale cases, see Hall v. Keese (The Emancipation Cases), 31 Tex. 504 (1868); Andrew Kull, *The Enforceability after Emancipation of Debts Contracted for the Purchase of Slaves*, 70 Chi.-Kent L. Rev. 493, 494 n.2 (1994) (listing cases); Robert B. Gilbreath, *The Supreme Court of Texas and the Emancipation Cases*, TBJ, Nov. 2006, at 946; Hans W. Baade, *Chapters in the History of the Supreme Court of Texas: Reconstruction and "Redemption,"* 40 StMLJ 17, 63–66 (2008). The Semicolon Court declared that, had it the opportunity to look at the issue afresh, it inclined to the view of the dissent; see Morris v. Ranney, 37 Tex. 124 (1872).

6. Moneyhon, at 42–44.

7. See John Conger McGraw, The Texas Constitution of 1866, at 72 (Ph.D. diss., Texas Technological

College 1959); Moneyhon, ch. 3. The ordinances are found at 5 Gammel's 887 *et seq.*

8. Quote, Moneyhon, at 42; this argument is attributed to James Throckmorton, see Barry A. Crouch, *"All the Vile Passions": The Texas Black Code of 1866*, 97 SWHQ 13, 21 (1993) (quoting Throckmorton).

9. On the Civil Rights Act of 1866, see Charles Fairman, RECONSTRUCTION AND REUNION, 1864–1888, PART ONE, 1169–1204 (1971); on the congressional debate on the Fourteenth Amendment, *id.* at 1270–1300; Dred Scott v. Sandford, 19 How. (60 U.S.) 393 (1857) (holding Negroes, whether free or slave, cannot be citizens under the Constitution).

10. On the Black Codes, see Theodore Brantner Wilson, THE BLACK CODES OF THE SOUTH (1965); on the Texas Black Code, see Crouch, *Vile Passions*; Barry A. Crouch, *"To Enslave the Rising Generation": The Freedmen's Bureau and the Texas Black Code, in* THE FREEDMEN'S BUREAU AND RECONSTRUCTION ch. 11 (Paul A. Cimbala & Randall M. Miller eds., 1999); Act of Oct. 26, 1866, 11th Leg., ch. 59, 5 Gammel's 977; An Act Establishing a General Apprentice Law, and Defining the Obligations of Master and Mistress and Apprentice, Act of Oct. 27, 1866, 11th Leg., ch. 63, 5 Gammel's 979; An Act Regulating Contracts for Labor, Act of Nov. 1, 1866, 11th Leg., ch. 80, 5 Gammel's 994; Act of Nov. 1, 1866, 11th Leg., ch. 82, 5 Gammel's 998; Act of Nov. 6, 1866, 11th Leg., ch. 102, 5 Gammel's 1015; An Act to Define and Declare the Rights of Persons Lately known as Slaves, and Free Persons of Color, Act of Nov. 10, 1866, 11th Leg., ch. 128, 5 Gammel's 1049; quote, Crouch, *Vile Passions*, at 31. On the Texas rejection of the Fourteenth Amendment, see Joseph B. James, *Southern Reaction to the Proposal of the Fourteenth Amendment*, 22 J. So. Hist. 477, 483–85 (1956).

11. On Reconstruction, see Eric Foner, RECONSTRUCTION: AMERICA'S UNFINISHED REVOLUTION, 1863–1877 (1988).

12. On the Freedmen's Bureau in Texas, see Barry A. Crouch, THE FREEDMEN'S BUREAU AND BLACK TEXANS (1992); "last former Confederate state," *id.* at 12; "by early 1867," *id.* at 30; "Griffin wrote," *id.* (quoting letter of Griffin to Oliver Otis Howard, July 1, 1867, vol. 5, p. 107, of Records of the Bureau of Refugees, Freedmen, and Abandoned Lands in the National Archives); 1865–68 murders, Moneyhon, at 93; "Pease," Marten, at 137; Reynolds letter, Crouch, FREEDMEN'S BUREAU, at 34. On the number of murders, see Ann Patton Barnziger, *The Texas State Police during Reconstruction: A Reexamination*, 72 SWHQ 470, 471 (1969) (citing Committee

on Lawlessness and Violence of the Reconstruction Convention of 1868).

13. Barry A. Crouch, *Black Dreams and White Justice, in* AFRICAN AMERICAN LIFE IN THE POST–EMANCIPATION SOUTH, 1861–1900, at 65, 75 (Donald G. Nieman ed., 1994).

14. William L. Richter, THE ARMY IN TEXAS DURING RECONSTRUCTION, 1865–1870, at 99–102 (1987); William L. Richter, OVERREACHED ON ALL SIDES: THE FREEDMEN'S BUREAU ADMINISTRATORS IN TEXAS, 1865–1868, at 203–7 (1991). Circulars No. 10 and No. 13 are found in the National Archives; I am grateful to Katy Stein for making copies of them at the archives; quotes, Moneyhon, at 70.

15. Moneyhon, at 76–77; J. H. Davenport, THE HISTORY OF THE SUPREME COURT OF THE STATE OF TEXAS 87–89 (1917).

16. Voting registration numbers, Moneyhon, at 82.

17. *Id.* at 95.

18. On ratification, see 6 Gammel's 10–11; Moneyhon, at 118.

19. 74 U.S. (7 Wall.) 700, 725 (1869).

20. On Chase, see John Niven, SALMON P. CHASE: A BIOGRAPHY (1995).

21. On Texas v. White, see Fairman, PART I, at 628–76, and quote at 632 n.39; William Whatley Pierson, Jr., *Texas versus White*, 18 SWHQ 341 (1915) (chs. 1 & 2), and 19 SWHQ 1 (1915) (ch. 3), and at 142 (ch. 4); John J. Templin, *Texas v. White: A Study on the Merits of the Case*, 6 SwLJ 467 (1952); Jane Lynn Scarborough, George W. Paschal: Texas Unionist and Scalawag Jurisprudent ch. 4 (Ph.D. diss., Rice University 1972); Act of Dec. 16, 1851, 4th Leg., ch. 16, § 1, 4 Gammel's 889; Act of Jan. 11, 1862, 9th Leg., ch. 65, 5 Gammel's 489.

22. Fairman, at 648–60; Morgan v. United States, 113 U.S. 476 (1885); *In re* Paschal, 77 U.S. (10 Wall.) 483 (1871); *In re* Chiles, 89 U.S. (22 Wall.) 157 (1875). The end of the story was the court's decision in Merrick's Executors v. Giddings, 115 U.S. 300 (1885), which held that Merrick's acceptance of eight thousand dollars with the option of seeking something better from the Texas legislature was a full relinquishment of his claim, even if done in violation of promises made to counsel that they would obtain their agreed-upon fees.

23. Fairman, at 673–76.

24. Act of June 24, 1870, 12th Leg., C.S., ch. 10, 6 Gammel's 185 (creating militia); Act of July 1, 1870, 12th Leg., C.S., ch. 13, 6 Gammel's 193; John G. Johnson, *State Police*, HOTO, www.tshaonline.org/handbook/online/articles/SS/jls2.html; Barnziger,

at 471–73 (breaking down race of victim and killer); H. V. Redfield, HOMICIDE, NORTH AND SOUTH 77 (1880) (noting 323 murders listed by census); "staggeringly violent," Randolph Roth, AMERICAN HOMICIDE 354 (2009).

25. Act of Apr. 22, 1873, 13th Leg., R.S., ch. 31, 7 Gammel's 493; Barnziger, at 487; number of arrests, Barnziger, at 476, and "40 percent," Barnziger, at 475.

26. On the thirteenth legislature, see Moneyhon, at 188; *Ex parte* Rodriguez, 39 Tex. 706 (1874); on *Ex parte* Rodriguez, see Hans W. Baade, *Chapters*, at 114–21; Lance A. Cooper, *"A Slobbering Lame Thing"? The Semicolon Case Reconsidered*, 101 SWHQ 321 (1998); Carl H. Moneyhon, *Ex parte Rodriguez*, HOTO, www.tshaonline.org/handbook/online/articles/EE/jre1.html; James R. Norvell, *Oran M. Roberts and the Semicolon Court*, 37 TLR 279 (1959); George Shelley, *The Semicolon Court of Texas*, 48 SWHQ 449 (1945); Davenport, at 97–109. Oran M. Roberts, in *The Political, Legislative, and Judicial History of Texas, in* 2 A COMPREHENSIVE HISTORY OF TEXAS, 1685 TO 1897, at 7, 201 (Dudley G. Wooten ed., 1898), wrote about the *Ex parte* Rodriguez court, "So odious has it been in the estimation of the bar of the State, that no Texas lawyer likes to cite any case from the volumes of the Supreme Court reports which contain the decisions of the court that delivered that opinion, and their pages are, as it were, tabooed by the common consent of the legal profession." Roberts was a defender of the "Lost Cause" justifying the secession of Texas. His statement is patently false, both when written and subsequently. As chief justice, Roberts cited with approval cases from the Semicolon Court (see James R. Norvell, *The Reconstruction Courts of Texas 1867–1873*, 62 SWHQ 141, 157 (1958)). Randolph B. Campbell, in *Scalawag District Judges: The E. J. Davis Appointees, 1870–1873*, 14 Hous. Rev. 275 (1992), notes that most district judges appointed between 1870 and 1873 were not carpetbaggers, northerners who traveled to Texas during Reconstruction to obtain wealth and impose "outsider" non-Texan values on Texas, but scalawags, southerners and Texans who were members of the Republican Party and who possessed some Union ties.

27. Act of Mar. 18, 1873, 13th Leg., ch. 14, 7 Gammel's 468 (repealing much of the 1871 militia act); Act of May 19, 1873, 13th Leg., ch. 61, 7 Gammel's 533; quote, Moneyhon, at 190; Act of Mar. 31, 1873, 13th Leg., ch. 19, 7 Gammel's 472; Act of Apr. 1, 1873, 13th Leg., ch. 20, 7 Gammel's 482; Act of May 26, 1873, 13th Leg., ch. 66, 7 Gammel's 552.

28. Act of Mar. 31, 1873, at § 31, *id.* at 481.

29. Cooper (334–38) concludes that a comma instead of a semicolon would likely not have made any interpretive difference. On Walker, see Randolph B. Campbell, *Walker, Moses B.*, HOTO, www.tshaonline.org/handbook/online/articles/WW/fwa21.html. Davenport's *History* offers no portrait of Walker.

30. An essay briefly assessing *Ex parte* Rodriguez and finding it constitutionally sound is Vasan Kesavan & Michael Stokes Paulsen, *Is West Virginia Unconstitutional?*, 90 Cal. L. Rev. 291, 340 (2002).

31. Moneyhon, at 198–99; Baade, at 120–22; Jt. Res. No. 1, 8 Gammel's 235, 234.

32. On the proposed Texas Constitution of 1874, see John Walker Mauer, *State Constitutions in a Time of Crisis: The Case of the Texas Constitution of 1876*, 68 TLR 1615, 1635 (1990).

33. Jt. Res. No. 16, Mar. 13, 1875, 14th Leg., 2d Sess., 8 Gammel's 573; Jt. Res. No. 17, Mar. 15, 1875, 14th Leg., 2d Sess., 8 Gammel's 575.

34. "Thirty-eight," J. E. Ericson, *The Delegates to the Convention of 1875: A Reappraisal*, 67 SWHQ 22, 22 (1963) (noting others have listed more ("about half") or fewer ("37") and that McKay listed only twenty-nine lawyers). On the Constitution of 1876, see John Walker Mauer, Southern State Constitution in the 1870s: A Case Study of Texas (Ph.D. diss., Rice University 1983), and the classic and dated works S. S. McKay, MAKING THE TEXAS CONSTITUTION OF 1876 (1924); S. S. McKay, DEBATES IN THE TEXAS CONSTITUTIONAL CONVENTION OF 1875 (1930); and S. S. McKay, SEVEN DECADES OF THE TEXAS CONSTITUTION OF 1876 (1942). A brief survey is A. J. Thomas, Jr., & Ann Van Wynen Thomas, *The Texas Constitution of 1876*, 35 TLR 907 (1957).

35. "Prolixity," see McCulloch v. Maryland, 4 Wheat. (17 U.S.) 316, 407 (1819).

36. "1,600 appeals pending," see S. S. McKay, DEBATES, at 422 (quoting delegate Jacob Waelder).

37. Tex. Const. Art. V, § 2 (amended 1891); Act of Apr. 7, 1913, 33d Leg., R.S., ch. 155, § 1, 1913 Tex. Gen. Laws 329 (raising salary to $5,000).

38. C. L. Sonnichsen, TEN TEXAS FEUDS 155 (1957, repr. 2000).

39. The initial account of the Salt War is in Walter Prescott Webb, TEXAS RANGERS ch. 16 (1935, 2d ed. 1965); the classic account is C. L. Sonnichsen, THE EL PASO SALT WAR (1961), a reprint of the chapter found in TEN TEXAS FEUDS ch. 6 ("The El Paso Salt War"). A shorter and less helpful account is C. L. Douglas, FAMOUS TEXAS FEUDS 107–25 (1936). A modern appraisal is Robert M. Utley, LONE STAR JUSTICE: THE FIRST CENTURY OF THE TEXAS RANGERS ch. 11 (2002). Revisionist accounts include Mary Romero, *El Paso Salt War: Mob Action or Political*

Struggle?, 16 Aztlan: Int'l J. Chicano Stud. Res. 119 (1985); Note, *Law, Race, and the Border: The El Paso Salt War of 1877*, 117 Harv. L. Rev. 941 (2004); and Paul Cool, SALT WARRIORS: INSURGENCY ON THE RIO GRANDE (2008), a thorough account. The official congressional investigation into the events is found at *El Paso Troubles in Texas*, House Exec. Doc. 93, 45th Cong., 2d Sess. (1878).

40. On the history of the importance of salt, see Mark Kurlansky, SALT: A WORLD HISTORY (2002). On Maverick and Salt Ring and Borrajo's offer, see Cool, at 36–42. On Fountain's election and trial, see Arrell Morgan Gibson, THE LIFE AND DEATH OF COLONEL ALBERT JENNINGS FOUNTAIN 55–56, 84–85 (1965).

41. Cool, at 58–68.

42. Quote, *id.* at 69.

43. *Id.* at 74–81.

44. Sonnichsen, FEUDS, at 127; Cool, at 110.

45. Sonnichsen, FEUDS, at 128; Cool, at 110.

46. Webb, throughout ch. 16; Sonnichsen, FEUDS, at 128, 131, and quote at 124; Romero, at 139, 128; Note, at 949–50, 953; Cool, ch. 10. Cool uses "mob" more regularly when quoting Anglo participants to these events.

47. Cool, at 155.

48. *Id.* at 280, 262–64.

49. Quote, 2 SELECTED WORKS OF MAO TSE-TUNG 224 (4 vols. 1967).

50. *Frontier Echo*, Mar. 24, 1876, quoted in W. C. Holden, *Law and Lawlessness on the Texas Frontier, 1875–1890*, 44 SWHQ 188, 189 (1940).

51. William D. Carrigan, THE MAKING OF A LYNCHING CULTURE: VIOLENCE AND VIGILANTISM IN CENTRAL TEXAS, 1836–1916 (2004); Arnoldo De León, THEY CALLED THEM GREASERS: ANGLO ATTITUDES TOWARD MEXICANS IN TEXAS (1983).

52. Barnziger, at 471–73; Redfield, at 77 (noting 323 murders listed by census); Redfield, at 76 (comparing murders in New York). On census figures, see www.census.gov.

53. "Surge," Barnziger, at 488; Redfield, at 63, 74, 81, 84; Richard Maxwell Brown, STRAIN OF VIOLENCE ch. 8 (1975) (noting violence in Texas between 1860 and 1900).

54. Donald G. Nieman, *Black Political Power and Criminal Justice: Washington County, Texas, 1868–1884*, 55 J. So. Hist. 391, 415, 417–18 (1989), in which Nieman notes that the race of the victim in several cases is unclear, so it is possible that a white person was convicted of murder of a black person; this article is reprinted in AFRICAN AMERICAN LIFE IN THE POST–EMANCIPATION SOUTH, 1861–1900, at 217–46 (Donald G. Nieman ed., 1994). See also Act

of Aug. 1, 1876, 15th Leg., R.S., ch. 76, § 1, 8 Gammel's 914 (providing "an inability to read or write shall be a sufficient cause for challenge").

55. Lawrence Rice, THE NEGRO IN TEXAS, 1874–1900, at 119 (1971), and quote at 250.

56. De León, at 87–92, 96–97; William D. Carrigan & Clive Webb, *Muerto por Unos Desconcidos (Killed by Persons Unknown): Mob Violence against Blacks and Mexicans*, in BEYOND BLACK AND WHITE: RACE, ETHNICITY, AND GENDER IN THE U.S. SOUTH AND SOUTHWEST 35 (Stephanie Cole & Alison M. Parker eds., 2004); Rice, at 252; Hogg's statement, *Crime in Texas*, Illus. Amer., Sept. 26, 1891, at 244.

57. "1897 law," Act of June 19, 1897, 25th Leg., Spec. S., ch. 13, 10 Gammel's 1480; "following," Philip Dray, AT THE HANDS OF PERSONS UNKNOWN: THE LYNCHING OF BLACK AMERICA 262 (2002); Smith lynching, see *Another Negro Burned: Henry Smith Dies at the Stake*, N.Y. Times, Feb. 2, 1893, at 1. Rice, at 253; *Lynching in Texas*, 47 Alb. L.J. 141 (1893), concluded, "[I]t is the worst crime ever committed in America, always excepting the Texarkana affair," which was the 1892 lynching of Edward Coy, who had been involved in a consensual relationship with a white woman and who was lynched after she was coerced into falsely claiming Coy raped her (see Dray, at 73). On the Hillard lynching and the decline in lynchings, see Rice, at 253–54.

58. Lawrence C. Goodwyn, *Populist Dreams and Negro Rights: East Texas as a Case Study*, 76 Am. Hist. Rev. 1435 (1971); a brief mention is made in Rice, at 80–81.

59. Nieman, at 414–15 n.45.

60. *Overruled Their Judicial Superiors*, 21 Am. L. Rev. 610 (1887).

61. Act of July 9, 1879, 16th Leg., Spec. S., ch. 34, 9 Gammel's 62 (creating the Texas Commission of Appeals); Henderson v. Beaton, 52 Tex. 29 (1879) (holding act creating the commission constitutional because it was not a court but a board of arbitrators); Act of Feb. 9, 1881, 17th Leg., R.S., ch. 7, 9 Gammel's 96 (amending 1879 act); Act of Feb. 22, 1879, 16th Leg., R.S., ch. 16, §§ 10–12, 8 Gammel's 1312, 1314 (creating the twenty-eighth, twenty-ninth, and thirtieth judicial districts); Act of Apr. 1, 1885, 19th Leg., R.S., ch. 113, § 5, 9 Gammel's 728 (creating the thirty-ninth judicial district); Act of Mar. 3, 1891, 22d Leg., R.S., ch. 26, § 2, 10 Gammel's 29 (creating the fifty-first judicial district).

62. Sen. Jt. Res. No. 16, 10 Gammel's 199.

63. On the amendment, see *The Judiciary Amendment*, DMN, Aug. 8, 1891, at 4; *Reasons for Rejection*, DMN, Aug. 3, 1891, at 4; *Judicial Amendments*, DMN, Aug. 9, 1891, at 3.

64. Michael Ariens, *The Storm between the Quiet: Tumult in the Texas Supreme Court, 1911–1921*, 38 StMLJ 641 (2007); James T. Worthen, *The Organizational and Structural Development of Intermediate Appellate Courts in Texas, 1892–2003*, 46 STLR 33, 35 (2004) (noting in table 1 the years in which the various courts of civil appeals were created). On the history of the appellate courts in Texas, see Robert W. Higgason, *A History of Texas Appellate Courts: Preserving Rights of Appeal through Adaptations to Growth (Part I)*, Hous. Law., Mar.–Apr. 2002, at 20, and *(Part II)*, July–Aug. 2002, at 12; and Leila Clark Wynn, *A History of the Civil Courts in Texas*, 60 SWHQ 1 (1956).

65. Committee on Jurisprudence and Law Reform, *Report of the Committee on Jurisprudence and Law Reform*, 30 PTBA 12, 16 (1911); Special Committee on Judicial Reform, *Report of the Special Committee on Judicial Reform*, 33 PTBA 17, 18 (1914); "five years behind," see Ariens, *Storm*, at 689, citing Robert W. Stayton & M. P. Kennedy, *A Study of Pendency in Texas Civil Litigation*, 21 TLR 382 (1943).

66. Sen. Jt. Res. No. 3, 1915 Tex. Gen. Laws 278; *Five Amendments Snowed Under by Voters of Texas*, DMN, July 25, 1915, at 1; Act of Mar. 15, 1917, 35th Leg., R.S., ch. 76, 1917 Tex. Gen. Laws 142; Act of Apr. 3, 1918, 35th Leg., 4th C.S., ch. 81, 1918 Tex. Gen. Laws 171.

67. Interstate Commerce Act of 1887, 24 Stat. 379. On the Texas Railroad Commission, see William R. Childs, The Texas Railroad Commission (2005); Alwyn Barr, Reconstruction to Reform: Texas Politics, 1876–1906, ch. 8 (1971, 2000 ed.). A modest personal account is M. M. Crane, *Recollections of the Establishment of the Texas Railroad Commission*, 50 SWHQ 478 (1947). On Hogg, the railroads, and the creation of the commission, see Robert Crawford Cotner, James Stephen Hogg, A Biography chs. 7–9 (1959). On Reagan, see Ben H. Proctor, Not Without Honor (1962) (chs. 17 and 18 discuss his efforts to create the Interstate Commerce Commission, and ch. 20 discusses his work as a member of the Texas Railroad Commission). On Gould's efforts to derail the creation of a commission, see Robert L. Peterson, *Jay Gould and the Railroad Commission of Texas*, 58 SWHQ 422 (1955).

68. Act of Apr. 3, 1891, 22d Leg., R.S., ch. 51, 10 Gammel's 57; Cotner, chs. 7–9; Childs, ch. 2.

69. Reagan v. Farmers' Loan & Trust Co., 154 U.S. 362 (1894); Janet Schmelzer, *Determining the Extent of Power: Farmers' Loan and Trust Company and the Texas Railroad Commission*, in Law in the Western United States 423 (Gordon Morris Bakken ed., 2000). On substantive due process, see Michael

Ariens, *A Thrice Told Tale, or Felix the Cat*, 107 Harv. L. Rev. 620 (1994).

70. Shreveport Rate Cases, 234 U.S. 342 (1914); Act of Mar. 31, 1919, 36th Leg., R.S., ch. 155, Art. 3, 1919 Tex. Gen. Laws 285 (investing the commission with power to regulate oil and gas). On developments leading to 1919 law, see Childs, at 154–55, and ch. 3.

71. Act of Nov. 6, 1866, 11th Leg., ch. 102, 5 Gammel's 1015; Act of Oct. 28, 1871, 12th Leg., ch. 21, § 2, 7 Gammel's 18. On the rise of Jim Crow in Texas, see Rice, ch. 8; Bruce A. Glasrud, *Jim Crow's Emergence in Texas*, 15 Am. Studies 47 (1971); Bruce Alden Glasrud, Black Texans, 1900–1930: A History 91–96 (Ph.D. diss., Texas Tech University 1969). The classic account of the rise of Jim Crow laws across the United States is C. Vann Woodward, The Strange Career of Jim Crow (1955).

72. Civil Rights Act of 1875, 18 Stat. 375; Civil Rights Cases, 109 U.S. 3 (1883); "rarely succeeded," see Rice, at 145–46 (noting that conviction of defendant in one case was dismissed because the property owner possessed no assets on which to execute judgment); United States v. Dodge, 25 Fed. C. 882, 883 (W.D. Tex. 1877) (No. 14,976).

73. Act of Apr. 5, 1889, 21st Leg., R.S., ch 108, 9 Gammel's 1160; Act of Mar. 19, 1891, 22d Leg., R.S., ch. 41, 10 Gammel's 46; Act of Apr. 11, 1891, 22d Leg., R.S., ch. 103, 10 Gammel's 167.

74. Pullman Palace-Car Co. v. Cain, 40 S.W. 220 (Tex. Civ. App. 1897); Plessy v. Ferguson, 163 U.S. 537 (1896).

75. Act of Mar. 22, 1907, 30th Leg., R.S., ch. 36, 1907 Tex. Gen. Laws 58; Act of May 10, 1909, 31st Leg., 2d C.S., 1909 Tex. Gen. Laws 401; August Meier & Elliott Rudwick, *The Boycott Movement against Jim Crow Streetcars in the South, 1900–1906*, 55 J. Am. Hist. 756 (1969).

76. Act of June 5, 1837, 1st Cong., Repub. Tex., § 9, 1 Gammel's 1293; Act of Feb. 9, 1854, 5th Leg., ch. 49, § 38, 3 Gammel's 1502, 1510; Act of Nov. 10, 1866, 11th Leg., ch. 128, § 2, 5 Gammel's 1049; Frasher v. State, 3 Tex. App. 263, 30 Am. Rep. 131 (1877). On Texas laws against interracial marriages before the Civil War, see Mark M. Carroll, Homesteads Ungovernable: Families, Sex, Race, and the Law in Frontier Texas, 1823–1860, at 64–75 (2001). On laws banning interracial marriage in the United States, see Peggy Pascoe, What Comes Naturally: Miscegenation Law and the Making of Race in America (2009).

77. François v. State, 9 Tex. App. 144 (Tex. App. 1880); *Ex parte* François, 3 Woods 367, 9 F. Cas. 699, 700–701 (W.D. Tex. 1879) (No. 5,047); Penal Code Arts. 326–27 (1879).

78. Bell v. State, 25 S.W. 769 (Tex. Crim. App.

1894); Loving v. Virginia, 388 U.S. 1 (1967). Texas formally repealed its miscegenation law in 1969; see Act of May 14, 1969, 61st Leg., ch. 888, § 6, 1969 Tex. Gen. Laws 2733.

79. Strauss v. State, 173 S.W. 663, 665 (Tex. Crim. App. 1915).

80. Barr, at 200–207; Act of Apr. 1, 1903, 28th Leg., R.S., ch. 101, 1903 Tex. Gen. Laws 133; Act of May 1, 1903, 28th Leg., 1st C.S., ch. 8, 12 Gammel's 317; Act of May 15, 1905, 29th Leg., 1st C.S., ch. 11, 1905 Tex. Gen. Laws 520; Carter v. Texas, 177 U.S. 442 (1900); Martin v. Texas, 200 U.S. 316 (1906); Thomas v. Texas, 212 U.S. 278 (1909); for more on these cases, see chapter 7, section "Desegregating Texas Juries."

81. Public Free School Act, Act of May 20, 1893, 23d Leg., R.S., ch. 122, §§ 15, 16, 10 Gammel's 612; Act of Apr. 15, 1905, 29th Leg., R.S., ch. 124, §§ 93–96, 128, 12 Gammel's 1129; Act of Mar. 26, 1907, 30th Leg., R.S., 1907 Tex. Gen. Laws 103; Act of Mar. 5, 1907, 30th Leg., R.S., ch. 14, 1907 Tex. Gen. Laws 21, 22; Act of Mar. 17, 1909, 31st Leg., R.S., ch. 56, Art. 2949, 1909 Tex. Gen. Laws 103, 106.

82. On the lynching of Jesse Washington, see Patricia Bernstein, THE FIRST WACO HORROR: THE LYNCHING OF JESSE WASHINGTON AND THE RISE OF THE NAACP (2005), and James M. SoRelle, The "Waco Horror": The Lynching of Jesse Washington, 86 SWHQ 517 (1983). Two histories of the Waco bar, one from 1940 and the other from 1976, ignore the Waco Horror: William M. Sleeper & Allan D. Sanford, Waco Bar and Incidents of Waco History (1940), and Tony E. Duty, Historical Incidents of the Waco Bar, in THE BENCH AND BAR OF WACO AND MCLENNAN COUNTY, 1849–1976, at 5, 271 (Betty Ann McCartney McSwain ed., 1976).

83. Robert Wooster and Christine Moor Sanders, Spindletop Oilfield, HOTO, www.tshaonline. org/handbook/online/articles/SS/dos3.html; James Anthony Clark & Michel T. Halbouty, SPINDLETOP (1952); and Paul N. Spellman, SPINDLETOP BOOM DAYS (2001). "Eight hundred thousand barrels," Nicholas Malavis, BLESS THE PURE AND HUMBLE: TEXAS LAWYERS AND OIL REGULATION, 1919–1936, at 3 (1996).

84. Act of Mar. 28, 1899, 26th Leg., R.S., ch. 49, 1899 Tex. Gen. Laws 68; Act of May 9, 1905, 29th Leg., R.S., ch. 119, 1905 Tex. Gen. Laws 228; Act of Apr. 2, 1913, 33d Leg., R.S., ch. 111, 1913 Tex. Gen. Laws 212; Act of Mar. 31, 1919, 36th Leg., R.S., ch. 155, Art. 3, 1913 Tex. Gen. Laws 285. On the development of the law of oil and gas, see chapter 3.

85. Act of June 24, 1876, 15th Leg., R.S., ch. 33, 8 Gammel's 862; the vote was 220,627 to 129,270;

quote, Barr, ch. 6; Jt. Res. No. 1, Mar. 4, 1887, 20th Leg., 8 Gammel's 953. On the national prohibition movements, see generally Richard F. Hamm, SHAPING THE EIGHTEENTH AMENDMENT: TEMPERANCE REFORM, LEGAL CULTURE, AND THE POLITY, 1880–1920 (1995), and James H. Timberlake, PROHIBITION AND THE PROGRESSIVE MOVEMENT: 1900–1920 (1963).

86. On the third prohibition movement in Texas, see Ariens, Storm, at 648–55; and Lewis L. Gould, PROGRESSIVES AND PROHIBITIONISTS: TEXAS DEMOCRATS IN THE WILSON ERA ch. 2 (1973, repr. 1992).

87. Ariens, Storm, at 657–65.

88. Act of Mar. 21, 1918, 35th Leg., 4th C.S., ch. 24, 1918 Tex. Gen. Laws 37 (prohibiting the manufacture of intoxicating liquors throughout the state). During the fourth called session the legislature adopted five additional laws regulating the sale and transportation of intoxicating liquors (see chs. 5, 6, 7, 12, and 31 of the 1918 Texas General Laws), and ratified the Eighteenth Amendment to the U.S. Constitution, the prohibition amendment; Tex. H.R.J., Res. 1, 35th Leg., 4th C.S., 1918 Tex. Gen. Laws 200.

89. The material in this section is largely taken from Rodolfo Rocha, The Influence of the Mexican Revolution on the Mexico-Texas Border, 1910–1916 (Ph.D. diss., Texas Tech University 1981); Charles H. Harris III & Louis R. Sadler, THE TEXAS RANGERS AND THE MEXICAN REVOLUTION: THE BLOODIEST DECADE, 1910–1920, chs. 9–10 (2004); and Robert M. Utley, LONE STAR LAWMEN: THE SECOND CENTURY OF THE TEXAS RANGERS chs. 1–3 (2007).

90. Americo Paredes, "WITH A PISTOL IN HIS HAND": A BORDER BALLAD AND ITS HERO (1958); Richard J. Mertz, "No One Can Arrest Me": The Story of Gregorio Cortez, 1 J. S. Tex. 1 (1974), and quote at 9; THE BALLAD OF GREGORIO CORTEZ (1982); "nine," Rocha, at 37.

91. Cortez v. State, 66 S.W. 453 (Tex. Crim. App. 1902) (Gonzales County murder trial); Cortez v. State, 69 S.W. 536 (Tex. Crim. App. 1902) (Karnes County murder trial); Cortez v. State, 74 S.W. 907 (Tex. Crim. App. 1903) (reversing conviction for horse theft); Cortez v. State, 83 S.W. 812 (Tex. Crim. App. 1904) (affirming first-degree murder conviction for Gonzales County killings).

92. "Esparza" and events in July, Rocha, at 262–63, and quotes at 301, 311–12; Utley, at 42–43.

93. Rocha, at 313–14.

94. Minor v. Happersett, 88 U.S. (21 Wall.) 162 (1875). See A. Elizabeth Taylor, The Woman Suffrage Movement in Texas, 17 J. So. Hist. 194 (1951), from which much of the material in this and the follow-

ing paragraphs is derived, and which is reprinted in Citizens at Last: The Woman Suffrage Movement in Texas 13 (Ruthe Winegarten & Judith N. McArthur eds., 1987); and Judith N. McArthur, Creating the New Woman: The Rise of Southern Women's Progressive Culture in Texas, 1893–1918 (1998).

95. Act of Mar. 26, 1918, 35th Leg., 4th C.S., ch. 34, 1918 Tex. Gen. Laws 61 (allowing women to vote in primary); Sen. Jt. Res. No. 7, Feb. 5, 1919, 1919 Tex. Gen. Laws 339 (proposing female suffrage amendment with unanimous vote in both house and senate). On the failed Texas constitutional amendment, see Sara Hunter Graham, Woman Suffrage and the New Democracy 132–36 (1996).

96. Koy v. Schneider, 218 S.W. 479 (1920).

97. On the KKK in Texas in the 1920s, see Charles C. Alexander, Crusade for Conformity: The Ku Klux Klan in Texas, 1920–1930 (1962); on the exclusion of Mexican Americans from juries in South Texas, see Rocha, at 27–28; on the 1919 investigation of the conduct of the Texas Rangers in South Texas, see Utley, ch. 4, and Harris & Sadler, ch. 17; quote, The Report on the Canales Charges, DMN, Feb. 21, 1919, at 10.

98. On the Longview riot, two articles from very different perspectives are Kenneth R. Durham, Jr., The Longview Race Riot of 1919, 18 E. Tex. Hist. J. 13 (1980), and William M. Tuttle, Jr., Violence in a "Heathen" Land: The Longview Race Riot of 1919, 33 Phylon 324 (1972). Durham believes that the riot did not end in more deaths because of the prompt intervention of local public officials, particularly the sheriff and county judge. In Tuttle's view, the actions of the sheriff and county judge contributed to the riots. Durham does not cite Tuttle's earlier article, and the facts they adduce differ considerably, as noted in the text. A short article attempting to place the Longview riot in context is George Ohler, Background Causes of the Longview Race Riot of July 10, 1919, 12 J. Am. Stud. Ass'n of Tex. 46 (1981), which is based on a number of interviews and news stories and which does not cite either article.

CHAPTER 3

1. On the 1821 colonization decree, see Art. 31, Early Laws of Texas 42 (John Sayles & Henry Sayles comp. & arr., 1888) (translated into English; hereafter cited as Sayles, Early Laws); id. at Arts. 32–33 on Moses Austin's colonization grant; and id. at Arts. 31 & 40 on the 1823 and 1824 Mexican decrees.

On the 1825 colonization law of Coahuila and Texas, see Decree 16, 1 Gammel's 99. On the comparable cost of land in the United States and Mexican Texas, see Thomas Lloyd Miller, The Public Lands of Texas, 1519–1970, at 22 (1972). Miller notes that $117 was the cost of 4,428.4 acres but then concludes this amounted to about 38 cents per acre.

2. United States v. Texas, 162 U.S. 1 (1896) (border dispute); United States v. Texas, 339 U.S. 707 (1950) (Tidelands case); Texas v. White, 74 U.S. (7 Wall.) 700 (1869).

3. Thomas Lloyd Miller, at 16–17; number of acres granted by Spain and Mexico, id. at 138; see also Eugene C. Barker, Land Speculation as a Cause of the Texas Revolution, 10 SWHQ 76 (1906) (similar figures).

4. On the Law of Apr. 6, 1830, see Art. 42, Sayles, Early Laws, at 55, and Gregg Cantrell, Stephen F. Austin: Empresario of Texas 219–26 (1999); on repeal of the ban on Americans' settling in Texas by the Law of Apr. 6, see Art. 43, Sayles, Early Laws; "Turning point," Cantrell, at 221; Alleine Howren, Causes and Origin of the Decree of April 6, 1830, 16 SWHQ 378 (1913); Decree 272, Art. 8, 1 Gammel's 357, 358.

5. Quotes, Thomas Lloyd Miller, at 23. On the impact of these speculative land claims in Texas, see Curtis Bishop, Lots of Land 100–101 (1949). The source for most of the information on land speculation in Mexican Texas is Barker, Land Speculation.

6. Quote, Decree 278, reprinted in 1 Gammel's 380; Decree 293, id. at 392; Decree 297, id. at 284. On the impact of these speculative land claims in Texas, see Bishop, at 100–101.

7. Journals of the Consultation, Plan of Government, 1 Gammel's 505, 541–43.

8. Act of June 12, 1837, § 8, 1st Cong., Repub. Tex., 1 Gammel's 1323, 1324–25, and Act of Dec. 14, 1837, § 27, 2d Cong., Repub. Tex., 1 Gammel's 1404, 1413 (allowing suit for lands by empresarios); Houston v. Perry, 3 Tex. 390 (1848); Rose v. Governor, 24 Tex. 496 (1859).

9. Act of Dec. 22, 1836, 1st Cong., Repub. Tex., 1 Gammel's 1276; Act of June 12, 1837, 1st Cong., Repub. Tex., 1 Gammel's 1323; Act of Dec. 14, 1837, 2d Cong., Repub. Tex., 1 Gammel's 1404.

10. Quote, Thomas Lloyd Miller, at 32; Act of Jan. 29, 1840, 4th Cong., Repub. Tex., 2 Gammel's 313; Act of Feb. 5, 1840, 4th Cong., Repub. Tex., 2 Gammel's 337.

11. Act of Jan. 4, 1841, §§ 4–13, 5th Cong., Repub. Tex., 2 Gammel's 554; Act of Feb. 5, 1842, 6th Cong., Repub. Tex., 2 Gammel's 785 (amending initial grant

to Peters); Thomas Lloyd Miller, at 40–44; Aloysius A. Leopold, TEXAS LAND TITLES §§ 2.19–2.20 (3d ed. 2005); Act of Jan. 30, 1844, 8th Cong., Repub. Tex., 2 Gammel's 958 (repealing contracts); Nancy Ethie Eagleton, Mercer Colony in Texas, 1844–1883 (M.A. thesis, University of Texas 1934).

12. An Ordinance in Relation to Colonization Contracts, Aug. 27, 1845, 2 Gammel's 1305; Act of May 11, 1846, § 13, 1st Leg., 2 Gammel's 1512; Act of Feb. 2, 1850, 3d Leg., ch. 108, 3 Gammel's 558; Act of Jan. 24, 1852, 4th Leg., ch. 45, 3 Gammel's 913; Eagleton, at 101–7.

13. Melton v. Cobb, 21 Tex. 539 (1858); Walsh v. Preston, 109 U.S. 297 (1883).

14. Act of Aug. 1, 1856, 6th Leg., ch. 93, 4 Gammel's 432; Act of Jan. 16, 1858, 7th Leg., ch. 43, 4 Gammel's 912; Act of Feb. 7, 1860, 8th Leg., ch. 47, 4 Gammel's 1410; Thomas Lloyd Miller, ch. 8.

15. On the 1844 presidential election and Texas, see Walter A. McDougal, THROES OF DEMOCRACY: THE AMERICAN CIVIL WAR ERA, 1829–1877, at 261–64 (2008); on the 1845 annexation, see Jt. Res., Mar. 1, 1845, 5 Stat. 797; "182 million acres," see Aldon Socrates Lang, FINANCIAL HISTORY OF THE PUBLIC LANDS OF TEXAS 203 (1932) (noting in table I the area of unappropriated public land at various times in the history of Texas and listing 181,965,832 acres in 1845).

16. Act of Dec. 19, 1836, 1st Cong., Repub. Tex., 1 Gammel's 1193; Treaty of Guadalupe Hidalgo, 9 Stat. 922.

17. Act of Feb. 8, 1850, 3d Leg., ch. 122, 3 Gammel's 582; Act of Sept. 4, 1850, 3d Leg., 2d Sess., ch. 19, 3 Gammel's 798. Most of the material on the Miller-Bourland Commission is derived from Galen D. Greaser and Jesús F. de la Teja, *Quieting Title to Spanish and Mexican Land Grants in the Trans-Nueces: The Bourland and Miller Commission, 1850–1852*, 95 SWHQ 445 (1992), and Armando C. Alonzo, TEJANO LEGACY: RANCHEROS AND SETTLERS IN SOUTH TEXAS, 1734–1900, ch. 5 (1998). Alonzo's evaluation is largely reprinted in Armando C. Alonzo, *Mexican-American Land Grant Adjudication*, HOTO, www.tshaonline.org/handbook/online/articles/MM/pqmck.html.

18. Act of Feb. 10, 1852, 4th Leg., ch. 71, 3 Gammel's 941; Act of Feb. 11, 1854, 5th Leg., ch. 65, 3 Gammel's 1533; Act of Feb. 11, 1860, 8th Leg., ch. 78, 4 Gammel's 1471; Act of Aug. 15, 1870, 12th Leg., ch. 83, 6 Gammel's 375; Act of Sept. 3, 1901, 27th Leg., 1st C.S., ch. 4, 1901 Tex. Gen. Laws 4; quote, Michael F. Holt, THE RISE AND FALL OF THE AMERICAN WHIG PARTY: JACKSONIAN POLITICS AND THE ONSET OF THE CIVIL WAR 477 (1999).

19. Holt, chs. 14 & 15, and quote, at 535; Kenneth F. Neighbours, *The Taylor-Neighbors Struggle over the Upper Rio Grande Region of Texas in 1850*, 61 SWHQ 431 (1958) (a biased but thorough discussion).

20. Act of Sept. 9, 1850, 31st Cong., ch. 49, 9 Stat. 446; Act of Nov. 25, 1850, 3d Leg., 2d Sess., ch. 2, 3 Gammel's 832; "33,000 square miles," Holman Hamilton, PROLOGUE TO CONFLICT: THE CRISIS AND COMPROMISE OF 1850, at 179 (1964).

21. Edmund Thornton Miller, A FINANCIAL HISTORY OF TEXAS 117–34 (1916); "twenty-nine cents," Hamilton, at 127; Act of Feb. 11, 1850, 3d Leg., ch. 157, 3 Gammel's 636; Act of Feb. 1, 1856, 6th Leg., ch. 50, 4 Gammel's 47.

22. Berlin B. Chapman, *The Claim of Texas to Greer County (Part I)*, 53 SWHQ 19 (1949), *(Part II)*, at 164, and *(Part III)*, at 404; Treaty, 8 Stat. 252 (1821); Act of Jan. 31, 1885, 48th Cong., ch. 47, 23 Stat. 296; United States v. Texas, 162 U.S. 1 (1896). On the Texas–New Mexico boundary dispute, see J. J. Bowden, *The Texas–New Mexico Boundary Dispute along the Rio Grande*, 63 SWHQ 221 (1959); United States v. Pendell, 185 U.S. 189 (1902) (dispute concerning ownership of land after cession of land from Mexico to United States); New Mexico v. Texas, 275 U.S. 279 (1927) (holding the location of the middle of the Rio Grande on September 9, 1850, as the fixed boundary between states and that the change of flow of the river did not legally change the boundary, making inapplicable legal doctrine that ownership of land may change as the flow and course of a river changes (known as accretion and avulsion)); and Crawford v. White, 25 S.W.2d 629 (Tex. Civ. App. 1930) (following the Supreme Court's conclusion that the boundary of Texas and New Mexico was not subject to accretion and avulsion).

23. Oklahoma v. Texas, 256 U.S. 70 (1921); Oklahoma v. Texas, 258 U.S. 574 (1922); Oklahoma v. Texas, 260 U.S. 606 (1923); Oklahoma v. Texas, 272 U.S. 21 (1926); Oklahoma v. Texas, 273 U.S. 93 (1927); Oklahoma v. Texas, 281 U.S. 694 (1930); Wortham v. Walker, 128 S.W.2d 1138 (Tex. 1939); Act of June 30, 1939, 46th Leg., R.S., ch. 4, 1939 Tex. Gen. Laws 478.

24. Lang, at 203, notes that in 1863 there were 95 million acres of unclaimed public land, reduced in 1868 to 87 million acres. See also Walter Prescott Webb, THE GREAT PLAINS 3–7 (1931).

25. Curtis Bishop, LOTS OF LAND 247 (1949); Thomas Lloyd Miller, at viii, 114–15; "3,050,000 acres," Act of Feb. 20, 1879, 16th Leg., R.S., ch. 13, 8 Gammel's 1309. On the 1873 amendment, Jt. Res. No. 7, 13th Leg., 7 Gammel's 676, and S. G. Reed, A HISTORY OF THE TEXAS RAILROADS 152 (1941, repr. 1981).

26. Hogue v. Baker, 45 S.W. 1004 (Tex. 1898); Art. XIV, § 6 (1876) declared: "To every head of a family without a homestead, there shall be donated one hundred and sixty acres of public land, upon condition that he will select and locate said land, and occupy the same three years and pay the office fees due thereon."

27. Act of July 14, 1879, 16th Leg., Spec. S., ch. 52, 9 Gammel's 80; Act of July 8, 1879, 16th Leg., R.S., ch. 28, 9 Gammel's 55; Act of Apr. 6, 1881, 17th Leg., R.S., ch. 105, 9 Gammel's 211.

28. Act of Apr. 12, 1883, 18th Leg., R.S., ch. 98, 9 Gammel's 391 (State Land Board); Act of Apr. 14, 1883, 18th Leg., R.S., ch. 104, 9 Gammel's 412 (Land Fraud Board); Ernest Wallace, CHARLES DEMORSE, at 209, 212 n.34 (1943, repr. 1985). On the mid-twentieth-century scandal concerning the Veterans' Land Board and the theft and bribery convictions of Bascom Giles, commissioner of the land office, see Patrick L. Cox, Land Commissioner Bascom Giles and the Texas Veteran's Land Board Scandals (M.A. thesis, Southwest Texas State Univ. 1988).

29. Bishop, at 219; quote, John Stricklin Spratt, THE ROAD TO SPINDLETOP: ECONOMIC CHANGE IN TEXAS, 1875–1901, at 16, 17–18, 91 (1955); J. Evetts Haley, CHARLES GOODNIGHT: COWMAN AND PLAINSMAN 312–13 (1936); Frances T. McCallum and James Mulkey Owens, Barbed Wire, HOTO, www.tshaonline.org/handbook/online/articles/BB/aob1.html; Henry D. McCallum, Barbed Wire in Texas, 61 SWHQ 207 (1957); "over 4.3 million," Harley True Burton, A History of the JA Ranch (Part I), 31 SWHQ 89, 97 (1927). On the elimination of Native Americans from the Panhandle, see Gary Clayton Anderson, THE CONQUEST OF TEXAS: ETHNIC CLEANSING IN THE PROMISED LAND, 1820–1875, ch. 22 (2005).

30. Haley, Goodnight, at 312–13.

31. Spratt, at 87; "$512,000," Haley, Goodnight, at 326; "104," Spratt, at 93.

32. Haley, Goodnight, at 321; Spratt, at 12–18.

33. J. E. Ericson, The Delegates to the Convention of 1875: A Reappraisal, 67 SWHQ 22, 22 (1963) (thirty-eight delegates were members of the Grange; others have listed more ("about half" of the ninety delegates) or fewer ("37")); Tex. Const. Art. XVI § 22 (1876); cost of fencing, Spratt, at 124; Act of Aug. 16, 1876, 15th Leg., R.S., ch. 98, 8 Gammel's 986; Act of Mar. 26, 1879, 16th Leg., R.S., ch. 59, 8 Gammel's 1366; Act of Apr. 18, 1879, 16th Leg., R.S., ch. 101, 8 Gammel's 1407.

34. Act of Apr. 12, 1883, 18th Leg., R.S., ch. 98, 9 Gammel's 391; "land boom," Bishop, at 229; "seventeen," Spratt, at 93; J. Evetts Haley, The Grass Lease Fight and Attempted Impeachment of the First Panhandle Judge, 38 SWHQ 1 (1934); Haley, Goodnight ch. 22. The Texas Supreme Court in Smissen v. State, 9 S.W. 112 (Tex. 1888), held that the land board had no authority to raise the minimum lease amount.

35. Quote, Wayne Gard, The Fence-Cutters, 51 SWHQ 1, 8 (1947); Wayne Gard, Fence Cutting, HOTO, www.tshaonline.org/handbook/online/articles/FF/auf1.html; Act of Feb. 6, 1884, 18th Leg., Spec. S., ch. 21, 9 Gammel's 566; Act of Feb. 7, 1884, 18th Leg., Spec. S., ch. 33, 9 Gammel's 600; Harry Sinclair Drago, THE GREAT RANGE WARS: VIOLENCE ON THE GRASSLAND ch. 15 (1970). Gard notes that the prices for cattle increased from seven dollars per head in 1880 to twenty-five dollars by 1883 (Gard, Fence-Cutters, at 2).

36. Quotes, Spratt, at 96, 97.

37. Haley, Grass Lease Fight, at 4 (listing seventy-six indictments); Robert C. Cotner, JAMES STEPHEN HOGG: A BIOGRAPHY 110 (1959) (stating eighty-six indictments were returned); "fifty-four," Cotner, at 112.

38. Haley, Grass Lease Fight, at 8; quote, REPORT OF THE ATTORNEY-GENERAL OF THE STATE OF TEXAS, 1885–1886, at 19 (1886); State ex rel. Templeton v. Goodnight, 11 S.W. 119 (Tex. 1888).

39. Haley, Grass Lease Fight; Cotner, at 107–17.

40. Spratt, at 296 tbl. XI (noting the decline in average price of cattle between 1885 and 1891); "one hundred million," Haley, Grass Lease Fight, at 22; "Clark killed," Haley, Grass Lease Fight, at 22–23; Act of Apr. 1, 1887, 20th Leg., R.S., ch. 99, § 14, 9 Gammel's 881.

41. Quote, Cotner, at 117.

42. Act of Feb. 20, 1879, 16th Leg., R.S., ch. 13, 8 Gammel's 1309; Cotner, at 134; "$3,244,953.45," J. Evetts Haley, THE XIT RANCH OF TEXAS 53 (1953), and quote at 49; Spratt, at 115–19; Ralph Smith, The Farmers' Alliance in Texas, 1875–1900, 48 SWHQ 346 (1945). On British investment in Texas in the 1880s, see Richard Graham, Investment Boom in British-Texan Cattle Companies, 1880–1885, 34 Bus. Hist. Rev. 421 (1960).

43. Spratt, at 115; Thomas Lloyd Miller, at 188; Edmund Thornton Miller, at 336, 338.

44. Cotner, at 340.

45. Act of Apr. 13, 1891, 22d Leg., R.S., ch. 62, 10 Gammel's 84.

46. That Alien Land Law, DMN, July 24, 1891, at 4; Gunter v. Texas Land and Mortgage Co., 17 S.W. 840 (Tex. 1891); State v. Mallinson, 17 S.W. 843 (Tex. 1891); Alien Land Law Void, DMN, Oct. 13, 1891, at 5; Tex. Const. Art. III, § 35.

47. *Hogg's Message*, DMN, Mar. 15, 1892, at 2; Act of Apr. 12, 1892, 22d Leg., 1st C.S., ch. 8, 10 Gammel's 370; "verge of failure," Richard Graham, *Investment Boom in British-Texan Cattle Companies, 1880–1885*, 34 Bus. Hist. Rev. 421, 444–45 (1960); quotes, Worth Robert Miller & Stacy G. Ulbig, *Building a Populist Coalition in Texas, 1892–1896*, 74 J. So. Hist. 255, 265 (2008); Alwyn Barr, RECONSTRUCTION TO REFORM ch. 9 & 139 (1971, repr. 2000) (noting Hogg received 190,486 votes to Clark's 133,395 and Nugent's 108,483 votes).

48. Act of Mar. 24, 1893, 23d Leg., R.S., ch. 38, 10 Gammel's 466; Cotner, at 343; "11,123," Reuben McKitrick, THE PUBLIC LAND SYSTEM OF TEXAS, 1823–1910, at 143 tbl. V & 149 tbl. VI (1918); Note, *Aliens: Right of an Alien to Own Land in Texas*, 7 TLR 607 (1929); Act of Apr. 1, 1921, 37th Leg., R.S., ch. 134, 1921 Tex. Gen. Laws 261.

49. Act of Jan. 20, 1840, § 1, 4th Cong., Repub. Tex., 2 Gammel's 177; Act of Feb. 10, 1852, 4th Leg., ch. 71, 3 Gammel's 941; Cowan v. Hardeman, 26 Tex. 217 (1862); Walace Hawkins, EL SAL DEL REY (1947); Cox v. Robison, 150 S.W. 1149 (Tex. 1912) (recounting history of provision of 1866 constitution releasing ownership of minerals to private landowners).

50. State v. Parker, 61 Tex. 265 (1884); Walace Hawkins, THE CASE OF JOHN C. WATROUS (1950); Act of Jan. 10, 1862, 9th Leg., ch. 8, 5 Gammel's 505; on the ongoing litigation over title to San Salvador del Tule, see State v. Cardenas, 48 Tex. 250 (1877); title to San Salvador del Tule was not settled until 1904 in State v. Rodriguez, see Hawkins, EL SAL DEL REY, at 28 n.24.

51. Robert E. Hardwicke, *Legal History of Conservation of Oil in Texas*, in LEGAL HISTORY OF CONSERVATION OF OIL AND GAS 214, 216 (1939); Maurice Cheek, *Legal History of Conservation of Gas in Texas*, in *id.* at 269; "by 1972," David L. Prindle, PETROLEUM POLITICS AND THE TEXAS RAILROAD COMMISSION 96 (1981). Hardwicke's *Legal History* is elegantly written and an essential starting point in understanding this history. He wrote an update a decade later: Robert E. Hardwicke, *Texas, 1938–1948*, in CONSERVATION OF OIL AND GAS: A LEGAL HISTORY, 1948, at 447 (Blakely M. Murphy ed., 1949, repr. 1972).

52. On the general history of oil, see Daniel Yergin, THE PRIZE (1991); on oil in Texas, see Diana Davids Hinton & Roger M. Olien, OIL IN TEXAS: THE GUSHER AGE, 1895–1945 (2002). An older, more celebratory history is Carl Coke Rister, OIL! TITAN OF THE SOUTHWEST (1949).

53. Act of May 15, 1899, 26th Leg., R.S., ch. 117, 11 Gammel's 202; Act of Mar. 29, 1895, 26th Leg., R.S.,

ch. 49, 11 Gammel's 68; James P. Hart, *Oil, the Courts, and the Railroad Commission*, 44 SWHQ 303, 304 (1941). On the conservation statute, which was promoted by Joseph Cullinan, see John O. King, JOSEPH STEPHEN CULLINAN: A STUDY OF LEADERSHIP IN THE TEXAS PETROLEUM INDUSTRY, 1897–1937, at 68–71 (1970); following Pennsylvania, *id.*, at 69. The 1895 legislature adopted a bill retaining for the state an interest in public lands sold with a mineral classification (Act of Apr. 30, 1895, 24th Leg., R.S., ch. 127, 10 Gammel's 927), and in 1919 the legislature adopted another law allowing for the sale of school and other public lands but reserving ownership of all minerals in the land (Act of Apr. 30, 1919, 36th Leg., R.S., ch. 163, 1919 Tex. Gen. Laws 312).

54. On Spindletop, see James Anthony Clark & Michel T. Halbouty, SPINDLETOP (1952), and Paul N. Spellman, SPINDLETOP BOOM DAYS (2001); "75,000 and 100,000 barrels," Randolph B. Campbell, GONE TO TEXAS 326 (2003); "Before Spindletop," Spratt, at 275, and quote at 276; "In 1902," Thomas Lloyd Miller, at 169; Nicholas Malavis, BLESS THE PURE AND HUMBLE: TEXAS LAWYERS AND OIL REGULATION, 1919–1936, at 3 (1996).

55. Act of Mar. 28, 1899, 26th Leg., R.S., ch. 49, 1899 Tex. Gen. Laws 68; Act of May 9, 1905, 29th Leg., R.S., ch. 119, 1905 Tex. Gen. Laws 228, 229; Act of Apr. 2, 1913, 33d Leg., R.S., ch. 111, 1913 Tex. Gen. Laws 212; "not enforced," William R. Childs, THE TEXAS RAILROAD COMMISSION 152, and (on developments leading to 1919 law) 154–55 (2005); Railroad Commission of Texas, Act of Apr. 3, 1891, 22d Leg., R.S., ch. 51, 10 Gammel's 57.

56. Act of Feb. 20, 1917, 35th Leg., R.S., ch. 30, 1917 Tex. Gen. Laws 48; Sen. Jt. Res. 12, Feb. 23, 1917, 1917 Tex. Gen. Laws 500 (adopted in August by popular vote and found in Art. XVI, § 59a); Act of Mar. 31, 1919, 36th Leg., R.S., ch. 155, Art. 3, 1919 Tex. Gen. Laws 285.

57. "California," Yergin, at 82; "sixth," Lewis L. Gould, PROGRESSIVES AND PROHIBITIONISTS: TEXAS DEMOCRATS IN THE WILSON ERA 35 (1973, repr. 1992); "Oklahoma," W. P. Z. German, *Legal History of Conservation of Oil and Gas in Oklahoma*, in LEGAL HISTORY OF CONSERVATION OF OIL AND GAS 110, 126–27 (1939); Texas Co. v. Daugherty, 176 S.W. 717 (Tex. 1915); for a criticism of Daugherty, see James A. Veasy, *The Struggle of the Oil Industry for the Sanctity of Its Basic Contract—The Oil and Gas Lease*, 39 PTBA 82, 90–91, 105 (1920); Westmoreland Natural Gas Co. v. DeWitt, 18 A. 724 (Pa. 1889); Kelley v. Ohio Oil Co., 49 N.E. 399 (Ohio 1897); "less than 25 percent," Hardwicke, *Legal History*, at 227;

"rule of capture," Robert E. Hardwicke, *The Rule of Capture and Its Implications as Applied to Oil and Gas*, 13 TLR 391, 392 (1935); Herman v. Thomas, 143 S.W. 195 (Tex. Civ. App. 1911) (holding a plaintiff who lacked money to drill an offset well could not demand an accounting from a neighbor whose wells were built near their boundary).

58. Childs, at 157–60.

59. On Rule 37, see Malavis, at 36–37, and on exceptions to the rule, see Prindle, at 47–53; see Childs, at 161–63 (on Butte) and at 166 (on the Yates field); Humble Oil & Refining Co. v. Strauss, 243 S.W. 528 (Tex. Civ. App. 1922); Railroad Comm'n of Texas v. Bass, 10 S.W.2d 586 (Tex. Civ. App. 1928).

60. City of Denison v. Municipal Gas Co., 3 S.W.2d 794 (Tex. 1928); Act of Mar. 29, 1929, 41st Leg., R.S., ch. 313, 1929 Tex. Gen. Laws 694; "issued first," Malavis, at 54; "black giant," Yergin, at 246; oil production, Virginia Knapp and Megan Biesele, *Rusk County*, HOTO, www.tshaonline.org/handbook/online/articles/RR/hcr12.html; Joiner's sale to Hunt, Bryan Burrough, THE BIG RICH 70–73 (2009).

61. Hardwicke, *Legal History*, at 228–33; for a statement of the facts below, see Danciger Oil & Refining Co. v. Railroad Comm'n, 49 S.W.2d 837 (Tex. Civ. App. 1932); Macmillan v. Railroad Comm'n, 51 F.2d 400 (E.D. Tex. 1931). The author of Macmillan and related cases was Joseph C. Hutcheson, Jr.; on Hutcheson, see Charles L. Zelden, *The Judge Intuitive: The Life and Judicial Philosophy of Joseph C. Hutcheson, Jr.*, 39 STLR 905 (1998); Charles L. Zelden, JUSTICE LIES IN THE DISTRICT: THE U.S. DISTRICT COURT, SOUTHERN DISTRICT OF TEXAS, 1902–1960 (1993); Charles Zelden, *Regional Growth and the Federal District Courts: The Impact of Judge Joseph C. Hutcheson, Jr., on Southeast Texas, 1918–1931*, 11 Hous. Rev. 67 (1989).

62. Anti-Market-Demand Act, Act of Aug. 12, 1931, 42d Leg., 1st C.S., ch. 26, 1931 Tex. Gen. Laws 46. A case study of the imposition of martial law is Warner E. Mills, Jr., MARTIAL LAW IN EAST TEXAS (1960).

63. Constantin v. Smith, 57 F.2d 227 (E.D. Tex.), aff'd, 287 U.S. 378 (1932).

64. Danciger, 49 S.W.2d 837; Champlin Refining Co. v. Corporation Comm'n of Oklahoma, 286 U.S. 210 (1932); People's Petroleum Producers, Inc. v. Sterling, 60 F.2d 1041 (E.D. Tex. 1932); People's Petroleum Producers, Inc. v. Smith, 1 F. Supp. 361 (E.D. Tex. 1932); Market Demand Act, Act of Nov. 12, 1932, 42d Leg., 4th C.S., ch. 2, 1942 Tex. Gen. Laws 3; Sterling v. Constantin, 287 U.S. 378 (1932); Nicholas George Malavis, *Sword or Constitution? Martial Law*

in the Oil Patch, in LAW IN THE WESTERN UNITED STATES 373 (Gordon Morris Bakken ed., 2000).

65. On People's Petroleum Producers, Inc. v. Smith, officially unreported, and the commission's increase to 750,000 barrels for the East Texas field, see Hardwicke, *Legal History*, at 241–42; Danciger, 56 S.W.2d 1075 (Tex. 1933); Danciger Oil & Refining Co. v. Smith, 4 F.Supp. 236 (E.D. Tex. 1933).

66. On FDR's first hundred days, see Jonathan Alter, THE DEFINING MOMENT: FDR's HUNDRED DAYS AND THE TRIUMPH OF HOPE (2007); National Industrial Recovery Act, 48 Stat. 195; Exec. Orders 6199, 6204 (implementing hot oil regulations), and 6256 (implementing Code of Fair Competition for petroleum industry); Hardwicke, *Legal History*, at 246–47; Malavis, BLESS ch. 10 and 164–65, and quote at 161.

67. Amazon Refining Corp. v. Railroad Comm'n, 5 F. Supp. 633 (E.D. Tex. 1933) (denying request for injunction); and *id.*, 5 F. Supp. 639 (E.D. Tex. 1933) (granting request for injunction).

68. Ryan v. Amazon Petroleum Corp., 71 F.2d 1 (5th Cir. 1934); Panama Refining Co. v. Ryan, 293 U.S. 388 (1935); Malavis, BLESS ch. 11.

69. Schechter Poultry Corp. v. United States, 295 U.S. 495 (1935) (holding NIRA unconstitutional). On the constitutional crisis of 1937, see Michael Ariens, *A Thrice-Told Tale, or Felix the Cat*, 107 Harv. L. Rev. 620 (1994); NLRB v. Jones & Laughlin Steel Corp., 301 U.S. 1 (1937).

70. Connally Hot Oil Act, 15 U.S.C. § 715 *et seq.*; Griswold v. President of the United States, 82 F.2d 922 (5th Cir. 1936); "ratified," Hardwicke, *Legal History*, at 252, and Malavis, BLESS, at 187; Brown v. Humble Oil & Refining Co., 83 S.W.2d 935 (Tex. 1935).

71. Hardwicke, *Legal History*, at 215; Hardwicke, *Texas, 1938–1948*, at 448, 489; Prindle, at 70; Gulf Land Co. v. Atlantic Refining Co., 131 S.W.2d 73 (Tex. 1939); Gulf Land was reaffirmed in Thomas v. Stanolind Oil & Gas Co., 198 S.W.2d 420 (Tex. 1946), and Trapp v. Shell Oil Co., 198 S.W.2d 424 (Tex. 1946).

72. Rowan & Nichols Oil Co. v. Railroad Comm'n of Texas, 28 F. Supp. 131 (W.D. Tex.), aff'd, 107 F.2d 70 (5th Cir. 1939), rev'd, 310 U.S. 573 (1940); Railroad Comm'n of Texas v. Pullman Co., 312 U.S. 496 (1941).

73. A thorough discussion is found in Robert E. Hardwicke, *Oil-Well Spacing Regulations and Protection of Property Rights in Texas*, 31 TLR 99 (1952); Railroad Commission v. Humble Oil & Refining Co., 193 S.W.2d 824 (Tex. Civ. App. 1946) writ refused no reversible error (Hawkins); Halbouty v. Railroad Comm'n, 357 S.W.2d 364, 376 (Tex. 1962) (Port

Acres); Atlantic Refining Co. v. Railroad Comm'n, 346 S.W.2d 801 (Tex. 1961) (Normanna); Railroad Comm'n v. Shell Oil Co., 380 S.W.2d 556 (Tex. 1964); Act of June 1, 1965, 59th Leg., R.S., ch. 303, 1965 Tex. Gen. Laws 611; Prindle, at 77–81.

74. Act of May 1, 1935, 44th Leg., R.S., ch. 120, 1935 Tex. Gen. Laws 318; Cheek, at 280–86, and quote at 283; Texas Panhandle Gas Co. v. Thompson, 12 F. Supp. 462 (W.D. Tex. 1935); Consolidated Gas Utilities Co. v. Thompson, 14 F. Supp. 318 (W.D. Tex. 1936); Thompson v. Consolidated Gas Utilities Co., 300 U.S. 55 (1937).

75. Prindle, at 63–66; Cheek, at 486–87; Railroad Comm'n v. Shell Oil Co., 206 S.W.2d 235 (Tex. 1947); Railroad Comm'n v. Flour Bluff Oil Co., 219 S.W.2d 506 (Tex. Civ. App. 1949), writ refused.

76. Prindle, at 98–100; Corzelius v. Harrell, 186 S.W.2d 191 (Tex. 1945); National Gas Policy Act, Pub. Law 95–621, Nov. 9, 1978, 92 Stat. 3350.

77. Phillips Petroleum Co. v. Wisconsin, 347 U.S. 672 (1954) (Texas was one of the parties in the Phillips Petroleum case); Northern Natural Gas Co. v. State Corp. Comm'n of Kansas, 372 U.S. 84 (1963); Prindle, at 98–107.

78. A fourth type of water, developed water, "new" water that originated as surface water or groundwater, is discussed in Frank R. Booth, *Ownership of Developed Water: A Property Right Threatened*, 17 StMLJ 1181 (1986).

79. On the history of Texas water law concerning surface water, see Hans Baade, *The Historical Background of Texas Water Law—A Tribute to Jack Pope*, 18 StMLJ 1, 97 (1986), and A. W. Walker, Jr., *Legal History of the Riparian Rights of Irrigation in Texas since 1836, in* PROCEEDINGS OF THE WATER LAW CONFERENCE 41 (University of Texas School of Law, 1959). On groundwater, see Houston & T. C. Ry. Co. v. East, 81 S.W. 279 (Tex. 1904), reaffirmed in Sipriano v. Great Spring Waters of America, Inc., 1 S.W.3d 75 (Tex. 1999) (rule of capture of groundwater), and Dylan O. Drummond, Lynn Ray Sherman & Edmond R. McCarthy, Jr., *The Rule of Capture in Texas: Still So Misunderstood after All These Years*, 37 TTLR 1 (2004).

80. Sturges v. Crowninshield, 17 U.S. 122 (1819) (holding state stay law applicable to all contracts unconstitutional as violative of contracts clause); Ogden v. Saunders, 25 U.S. 213 (1827) (holding constitutional state stay law applied only to contracts made after law adopted).

81. Motl v. Boyd, 286 S.W. 458, 467 (Tex. 1926); "incorrect understanding" and "appeared sincerely," Andrew Walker, *Mexican Law and the Texas Courts*,

55 BLR 225, 257–58 (2003); Peter L. Reich, *Mission Revival Jurisprudence: State Courts and Hispanic Water Law since 1850*, 69 Wash. L. Rev. 869, 914–21 (1994); State v. Valmont Plantations, 346 S.W.2d 853 (Tex. Civ. App. 1961), opinion adopted, 355 S.W.2d 502 (Tex. 1962); *In re* Adjudication of Water Rights in Medina River Watershed of the San Antonio River Basin, 670 S.W.2d 250 (Tex. 1984). In addition to Baade, see Joseph W. McKnight, *The Spanish Watercourses of Texas, in* ESSAYS IN LEGAL HISTORY IN HONOR OF FELIX FRANKFURTER 373, 374 (1966), and Betty Dobkins, THE SPANISH ELEMENT IN TEXAS WATER LAW (1959); a broader survey is Michael C. Meyer, WATER IN THE HISPANIC SOUTHWEST: A SOCIAL AND LEGAL HISTORY, 1550–1850 (1984).

82. Ira P. Hildebrand, *The Rights of Riparian Owners at Common Law in Texas*, 6 TLR 19 (1927); Rhodes v. Whitehead, 27 Tex. 304 (Tex. 1863); Tolle v. Correth, 31 Tex. 362 (Tex. 1868); Fleming v. Davis, 37 Tex. 173 (Tex. 1872); "legislature adopted," Walker, at 48.

83. Act of Mar. 19, 1889, 21st Leg., R.S., ch. 88, 9 Gammel's 1128; Act of Jan. 31, 1887, 20th Leg., R.S., ch. 3, 9 Gammel's 800; Webb, at 431–52 (discussing water law in the arid west); Walker, at 50–51 (discussing reasons for 1889 act). Robert G. Dunbar, FORGING NEW RIGHTS IN WESTERN WATERS 84–85 (1983), noted that Texas adopted the California doctrine of both prior appropriation and riparian right, but in the states that did so, "with the exception of Texas, the courts and the legislatures whittled away that [riparian] right until there is not much left."

84. "borrowed," Baade, at 88; Mud Creek Irrigation Co. v. Vivian, 11 S.W. 1078 (Tex. 1889); Act of Mar. 29, 1893, 23d Leg., R.S., ch. 44, 10 Gammel's 477; Act of Mar. 9, 1895, 24th Leg., R.S., ch. 21, 10 Gammel's 751; Barrett v. Metcalfe, 33 S.W. 758 (Tex. Civ. App. 1896).

85. Watkins Land Co. v. Clements, 86 S.W. 733 (Tex. 1905); *In re* Adjudication of the Water Rights of the Upper Guadalupe Segment of the Guadalupe River Basin, 642 S.W.2d 438 (Tex. 1982).

86. Act of Apr. 9, 1913, 33d Leg., R.S., ch. 171, 1913 Tex. Gen. Laws 358; Act of Mar. 19, 1917, 35th Leg., R.S., ch. 88, 1917 Tex. Gen. Laws 211; Board of Water Eng'rs v. McKnight, 229 S.W. 301 (Tex. 1921); "board continued," Garland F. Smith, *The Valley Water Suit and Its Impact on Texas Water Policy: Some Practical Advice for the Future*, 8 TTLR 577, 582 (1977).

87. Motl v. Boyd, 286 S.W. 458 (Tex. 1926); quotes, *In re* Adjudication, 642 S.W.2d at 441, 439.

88. "Estimated $10 million," Doug Caroom & Paul Elliott, *Water Rights Adjudication—Texas Style*,

TBJ, Nov. 1981, at 1183, 1184; Southern Canal Co. v. State Bd. of Water Eng'rs, 318 S.W.2d 619 (Tex. 1958); Proceedings of the Water Law Conference, Nov. 20–21, 1952, and June 10–11, 1954; Proceedings of the Water Law Conference, June 17–18, 1955; Proceedings of the Water Law Conference, May 25–26, 1956; Proceedings of the Water Law Conference, May 22–23, 1959 (the papers given at each conference were published in four separate volumes); Wilson's paper, 1955 Proceedings, at 38, and White's paper, A. R. White & Will Wilson, *The Flow and Underflow of* Motl v. Boyd *(Part I)*, 9 SwLJ 1, and *(Part II)* at 377 (1955). The Adjudication Act adopted the Oregon system (Dunbar, at 128).

89. 81 S.W. 279, 282 (Tex. 1904); Acton v. Blundell, 152 Eng. Rep. 1223 (Ex. Ch. 1843), cited with approval in East. One nagging issue is that Texas adopted the common law of England in 1840, and Acton was not decided until 1843. Did the legislative adoption of the English common law also adopt prospectively common law rules later declared as part of the English common law? East did not discuss this jurisprudential difficulty.

90. Sen. Jt. Res. 12, Feb. 23, 1917, 1917 Tex. Gen. Laws 500 (adopted in August by popular vote and found in Art. XVI, § 59a); Act of June, 2, 1949, 51st Leg., R.S., ch. 306, 1949 Tex. Gen. Laws 559; "first state," Dunbar, at 188; City of Corpus Christi v. City of Pleasanton, 276 S.W.2d 798 (Tex. 1955); Friendswood Dev. Co. v. Smith-Southwest Indus., Inc., 576 S.W.2d 21 (Tex. 1978); Barshop v. Medina County Underground Water Conservation Dist., 925 S.W.2d 618 (Tex. 1996); Sipriano v. Great Spring Waters of America, Inc., 1 S.W.3d 75 (Tex. 1999). An exhaustive history is Drummond.

91. Sipriano, at 81–83, and, on rejection of rule of capture elsewhere in the West, at 82 n.14, citing Richard S. Harnsberger, *Nebraska Ground Water Problems*, 42 Neb. L. Rev. 721, 727 (1963) ("Almost all of the contiguous seventeen Western states originally accepted the English rule by dictum or decision, but today only Texas appears to follow it.").

92. On Senate Bill 1 and its successors, see Bruce E. Toppin III, *The Path of Least Resistance: The Effects of Groundwater Law's Failure to Evolve with Changing Times*, 38 StMLJ 503 (2007); S. Plains Lamesa R.R. v. High Plains Underground Water Conservation Dist. No. 1, 2 S.W.3d 770 (Tex. App. 2001); Drummond, at 91–93; Tex. Water Code § 36.116(a)(2)(c); Environmental & Natural Resources Law Section, *Environmental Law*, 45 Tex. Prac. § 14.2(c)(2005).

93. Ernest R. Bartley, The Tidelands Oil Controversy: A Legal and Historical Analysis 137

(1953); Exec. Order 9633, Sept. 25, 1945, 10 Fed. Reg. 12,305; United States v. California, 332 U.S. 19 (1947). On Clark, see Mimi Clark Gronlund, Supreme Court Justice Tom C. Clark: A Life of Service (2010).

94. United States v. Texas, 339 U.S. 707 (1950); Sweatt v. Painter, 339 U.S. 629 (1950) (Sweatt won a unanimous decision); white primary cases, see Smith v. Allwright, 321 U.S. 649 (1944).

95. D. B. Hardeman & Donald C. Bacon, Rayburn: A Biography 351–55 (1987); C. Dwight Dorough, Mr. Sam 419 (1962) (they disagree about the exact percentages); Anthony Champagne, Congressman Sam Rayburn (1984), does not discuss the proposed compromise; "another proposal," George Norris Green, The Establishment in Texas Politics: The Primitive Years, 1938–1957, at 142 (1979).

96. United States v. Texas, 339 U.S. at 717; dissenting opinion, *id.* at 722; Frankfurter, *id.* at 724; Bartley, at 203.

97. 43 U.S.C. § 1301 *et seq.*; quote, Green, at 143, and "royalty," at 147.

98. "Over $35 million," Dorough, at 419; "three leagues," United States v. States of Louisiana et al., 363 U.S. 1, 63 (1960).

CHAPTER 4

1. Act of Apr. 24, 1874, 14th Leg., R.S., ch. 97, 8 Gammel's 122; quote, Edmund O. Belsheim, *The Need for Revising the Texas Corporation Statutes*, 27 TLR 659, 694 (1949). Sixty-four of the five hundred largest publicly traded American corporations are headquartered in Texas, more than in any other state; see money.cnn.com/magazines/fortune/fortune500/2009/snapshots/387.html.

2. On Gulf, see Craig Thompson, Since Spindletop: A Human Story of Gulf's First Half-Century 14, 23 (1951); on Texaco, Marquis James, The Texaco Story 17, 41 (1952); quotes, Paul Carrington, *The Texas Business Corporation Act as Enacted and Ten Years Later*, 43 TLR 609, 611 (1965), and Paul Carrington, A *Corporation Code for Texas*, 10 Ark. L. Rev. 28, 28 (1955–56).

3. Walter P. Webb, Divided We Stand: The Crisis of a Frontierless Democracy (1937, rev. ed. 1944); quotes, *id.* at 18 and 27.

4. I agree with Diana Davids Hinton & Roger M. Olien, Oil in Texas: The Gusher Age, 1895–1945, at x (2002), that Texans "exploited outside capitalists and ended up the richer for it"; the general historical

view is that through 1950 "[t]he state was a colonial economy, and its citizens resented it" (Walter L. Buenger & Robert A. Calvert, *Introduction: The Shelf Life of Truth in Texas*, in TEXAS THROUGH TIME: EVOLVING INTERPRETATIONS xix (Walter L. Buenger & Robert A. Calvert eds., 1991)).

5. An Act to Incorporate the Texas Rail Road, Navigation, and Banking Company, Act of Dec. 16, 1836, 1st Cong., Repub. Tex., 1 Gammel's 1188; quote, Herbert Gambrell, ANSON JONES: THE LAST PRESIDENT OF TEXAS 90 (2d ed. 1964). On Archer, see David Minor, *Archer, Branch Tanner*, HOTO, www.tshaonline.org/handbook/online/articles/AA/far2.html, and Eugene C. Barker, *Archer, Branch Tanner*, 1 DICTIONARY OF AMERICAN BIOGRAPHY 338 (Allen Johnson ed., 1933). On James Collinsworth, see Joe E. Ericson, *Collinsworth, James*, HOTO, www.tshaonline.org/handbook/online/articles/CC/fc097.html, and J. H. Davenport, THE HISTORY OF THE SUPREME COURT OF TEXAS 9–10 (1917); the first corporate charter issued in Texas was adopted by the Coahuila and Texas congress in 1830 and awarded to Jim Bowie to establish the Coahuila Manufacturing Company. It was the first of numerous corporate charters issued by the provincial legislature before Texas became a republic (see Ira P. Hildebrand, 1 THE LAW OF TEXAS CORPORATIONS 54 n.3 (4 vols. 1942)).

6. Panic of 1837, see Peter L. Rousseau, *Jacksonian Monetary Policy, Specie Flows and the Panic of 1837*, 62 J. Econ. Hist. 457 (2002); Robert V. Remini, ANDREW JACKSON AND THE BANK WAR (1967); Gambrell, at 92, 105–6. On Sam Houston's involvement, see James L. Haley, SAM HOUSTON 174–75 (2002). In mid-1838, incorporator James Collinsworth, confirmed as chief justice of the supreme court in 1836 and a proposed candidate for president, drowned after apparently jumping from a ship in Galveston Bay.

7. Andrew Forest Muir, *Railroad Enterprise in Texas, 1836–1841*, 47 SWHQ 339 (1947) (citing other acts); Eugene O. Porter, *Railroad Enterprises in the Republic of Texas*, 59 SWHQ 363 (1956); Alan R. Bromberg, *Texas Business Organization and Commercial Law: Two Centuries of Development*, 55 SMU L. Rev. 83, 87–90 (2002) (citing acts creating corporate entities).

8. On vested corporate rights at this time, see Herbert Hovenkamp, ENTERPRISE AND AMERICAN LAW, 1836–1937, ch. 2 (1991).

9. DEBATES OF THE CONVENTION, 1845, Aug. 2, 1845, at 346 (Hogg), and quote at 461 (Rusk), http://tarlton.law.utexas.edu/constitutions/pdf/pdf1845debates/indexdebates1845.html#j28.

10. Frederic L. Paxson, *The Constitution of Texas, 1845*, 18 SWHQ 386, 397–98 (1915); Henry N. Butler, *Nineteenth-Century Jurisdictional Competition in the Granting of Corporate Privileges*, 14 J. Legal Stud. 129, 143 (1985); Tex. Const. Art. XII.

11. Act of May 12, 1846, 1st Leg., 2 Gammel's 1585; "following the trend," see Susan Pace Hamill, *From Special Privilege to General Utility: A Continuation of Willard Hurst's Study of Corporations*, 49 Am. U. L. Rev. 81, 180 (1999) (Appendix D, noting Texas was the twenty-third state to adopt a limited partnership statute).

12. S. G. Reed, A HISTORY OF THE TEXAS RAILROADS 50 (1941, repr. 1981); "fifty-eight," *id.* at 97 and 104.

13. Act of Feb. 7, 1853, 4th Leg., 2d Sess., ch. 46, 3 Gammel's 1339; quote, Charles S. Potts, RAILROAD TRANSPORTATION IN TEXAS 108 (Bulletin of the University of Texas No. 119, 1909); "rescinded," Act of Jan. 26, 1860, 8th Leg., R.S., ch. 29, 4 Gammel's 1389, and Reed, at 120.

14. Act of Jan. 30, 1854, 5th Leg., ch. 15, 3 Gammel's 1455; Act of Aug. 13, 1856, 6th Leg., Adj. S., ch. 103, 4 Gammel's 449; Act of Dec. 19, 1857, 7th Leg., R.S., ch. 30, 4 Gammel's 897; Act of Feb. 8, 1860, 8th Leg., R.S., ch. 51, 4 Gammel's 1422.

15. "Twenty-one," Reed, at 145; "most moved," *id.* at 148; mileage, Bromberg, at 93 n.38. Mileage of Texas railroads from 1853 through 1939 is found in Reed, at 517.

16. "Fewer than twenty" and "only one," Walter L. Buenger & Joseph A. Pratt, BUT ALSO GOOD BUSINESS: TEXAS COMMERCE BANKS AND THE FINANCING OF HOUSTON AND TEXAS, 1886–1986, at 19 (1986).

17. A popular history of the Erie takeover war is John Steele Gordon, THE SCARLET WOMAN OF WALL STREET: JAY GOULD, JIM FISK, CORNELIUS VANDERBILT, AND THE BIRTH OF WALL STREET (1990). Classic contemporaneous accounts are Charles F. Adams, Jr., *The Erie Railroad Row*, 3 Am. L. Rev. 41 (1868), and Charles F. Adams, *A Chapter of Erie*, 109 N. Am. Rev. 30 (1869).

18. On the 1876 constitution, see chapter 2, section "The Constitution of 1876."

19. Curtis Kent Bishop, LOTS OF LAND 247 (1949); Thomas Lloyd Miller, at viii, 114–15; 1873 amendment, Reed, at 152; "2,928 additional miles," Reed, at 160; railroad mileage numbers by decade, Reed, at 517; slightly different numbers are given in Bromberg, at 93 n.38.

20. Act of Dec. 2, 1871, 12th Leg., 2d S., ch. 80, 7 Gammel's 68; Act of Apr. 23, 1873, 13th Leg., R.S., ch. 33, 7 Gammel's 494; Act of Apr. 23, 1874, 14th Leg., R.S., ch. 97, 8 Gammel's 122; "Kansas," Ramsey v.

Tod, 69 S.W. 133 (Tex. 1902); James L. Autry, *The Business Corporation in Texas—Its Formation, If Domestic; Its Admission, If Foreign*, 19 PTBA 101 (1900).

21. Hamill, at 123–27.

22. National Bank of Jefferson v. Texas Inv. Co., 12 S.W. 101 (Tex. 1889); "more than one hundred," Bromberg, at 96.

23. Ramsey v. Tod, 69 S.W. 133 (Tex. 1902).

24. Quote, Bank of Augusta v. Earle, 38 U.S. 519, 588 (1839); Paul v. Virginia, 75 U.S. 168 (1869). On Paul, see Charles Fairman, RECONSTRUCTION AND REUNION, 1864–1888, PART ONE, 1396–1402 (1971).

25. Union Pac. R.R. v. United States, 99 U.S. 700 (1879); Santa Clara County v. S. Pac. R.R. Co., 118 U.S. 394 (1886); Pembina Consol. Silver Mining & Milling Co. v. Pennsylvania, 125 U.S. 181 (1888); Act of Mar. 3, 1875, 18 Stat. 470. A largely favorable interpretation of the Santa Clara and Pembina cases is Charles Fairman, RECONSTRUCTION AND REUNION, 1864–1888, PART TWO, 724–29 (1987). For a strongly contrary view, see Webb, at 36–39. For a critical assessment, see Edward A. Purcell, Jr., LITIGATION AND INEQUALITY: FEDERAL DIVERSITY JURISDICTION IN INDUSTRIAL AMERICA, 1870–1958 (1992).

26. Act of May 4, 1882, 17th Leg., C.S., ch. 17, 9 Gammel's 278; *Ex parte* Asher, 5 S.W. 91, 93 (Tex. App. 1887), *rev'd*, Asher v. Texas, 128 U.S. 129, 131–32 (1888), and quote at 131–32; Robbins v. Taxing Dist., 120 U.S. 489 (1887). On Robbins, see Fairman, PART TWO, at 667–70. In Turner v. State, 55 S.W. 834 (Tex. Crim. App. 1900), the court of criminal appeals refused to alter its view of the Court's conclusion in Asher but accepted the Supreme Court's contrary conclusion.

27. Act of Apr. 2, 1887, 20th Leg., R.S., ch. 128, 9 Gammel's 914; Barron v. Burnside, 121 U.S. 186 (1887); Texas Land & Mort. Co. v. Worsham, 13 S.W. 384 (Tex. 1890); Act of Apr. 3, 1889, 21st Leg., R.S., ch. 78, 9 Gammel's 1115.

28. S. R. Smythe Co. v. Ft. Worth Glass and Sand Co., 142 S.W. 1157 (Tex. 1912); see cases collected in Ira P. Hildebrand, SELECT CASES AND OTHER AUTHORITIES ON THE LAW OF PRIVATE CORPORATIONS TEXAS SUPPLEMENT 489 *et seq.* (1916).

29. Robert C. Cotner, JAMES STEPHEN HOGG: A BIOGRAPHY 117–28 (1959); "approved," *id.* at 125–26.

30. Mileage numbers, Reed, at 517.

31. On the 1880s and changes in agriculture and ranching, see chapters 2 and 3. On changes in prices and capital increase, see John Stricklin Spratt, THE ROAD TO SPINDLETOP 287–302 (1955, repr. 1983) (appendices providing data).

32. Initial quotes, Reed, at 552, 553; final quote, Act of Mar. 28, 1885, 19th Leg., R.S., ch. 67, 9 Gammel's 685 (quoted language in title of act).

33. Quote, Reed, at 556; Gulf, C. & S. F. Ry. Co. v. State, 10 S.W. 81 (Tex. 1888).

34. Charles B. Nutting, *The Texas Anti-trust Law: A Post Mortem*, 14 TLR 293 (1936).

35. Alwyn Barr, RECONSTRUCTION TO REFORM 105–10 (1971, repr. 2000), and quote at 107; "big business," Cotner, at 161; "beef combine" and adoption of law, Tom Finty, Jr., ANTI-TRUST LEGISLATION IN TEXAS 15–17 (1916). In 1883, Alabama passed a law prohibiting railroads from pooling together to set rates for freight (see Allan D. Sanford, *Texas' Million Dollar Anti-Trust Suit*, TBJ, Feb. 1948, at 167, 167), followed by Iowa in 1888 and Maine on March 7, 1889. The latter two were narrower in scope than the Kansas and Texas statutes (see David Millon, *The First Antitrust Statute*, 29 Washburn L.J. 141, 146 & n.23 (1990)).

36. Act of Mar. 30, 1889, 21st Leg., R.S., ch. 117, 9 Gammel's 1169; Sherman Anti-trust Act, Act of July 2, 1890, ch. 647, 26 Stat. 209, codified as amended at 15 U.S.C. § 1 *et seq.*; Hans B. Thorelli, THE FEDERAL ANTITRUST POLICY: ORIGINATION OF AN AMERICAN TRADITION 76–78 (1955), and quote at 78; "controlled," Bruce Bringhurst, ANTITRUST AND THE OIL MONOPOLY: THE STANDARD OIL CASES, 1890–1911, at 1 (1979).

37. Finty, at 15; quote, Queen Ins. Co. v. State, 24 S.W. 397, 402 (Tex. 1893). Sherman did not write the act but was an inspiration for it (Thorelli, at 210–13). On the process of adoption of the Sherman Act, see Thorelli, ch. 4; on the Texas law, see also Cotner, at 160–67.

38. Finty, at 16–17; Anheuser-Busch Brewing Ass'n v. Houck, 30 S.W. 869 (Tex. 1895).

39. Queen Ins. Co. v. State, 24 S.W. 397 (Tex. 1893).

40. Act of Apr. 30, 1895, 24th Leg., R.S., ch. 83, 9 Gammel's 842. The action against Debs began in July 1894 (United States v. Debs, 64 F. 724 (C.C.N.D. Ill. 1894)), and the Supreme Court denied his claim for a writ of habeas corpus on May 27, 1895 (*In re Debs*, 158 U.S. 564 (1895)). The Trusts act was adopted on April 30, 1895. The "conflict" between corporations and labor unions was the subject of the 1894 annual address of the Texas Bar Association; see B. D. Tarlton, *Some Reflections on the Relations of Capital and Labor*, 13 PTBA 51 (1894). On the labor injunction and Debs, see Felix Frankfurter & Nathan Green, THE LABOR INJUNCTION 17–20 (1930).

41. Act of June 5, 1899, 26th Leg., R.S., ch. 146, 11 Gammel's 283; quote, Finty, 18; Act of May 27, 1899, 26th Leg., R.S., ch. 153, 11 Gammel's 299. On the

battle over including the Arkansas affidavit in the 1899 antitrust law, see Charles D. Mathews, *History, Interpretation and Enforcement of Texas Antitrust Laws, in* Proceedings of the 1950 Institute on Antitrust Laws and Price Regulations 19, 33–34 (1950).

42. Connolly v. Union Sewer Pipe Co., 184 U.S. 540, 560 (1902), *overruled in* Tigner v. Texas, 310 U.S. 141 (1940); State *ex rel.* Attorney General v. Shippers' Compress & Warehouse Co., 67 S.W. 1049 (Tex. Civ. App. 1902), *aff'd*, 69 S.W. 58 (Tex. 1902), and quote at 61; State *ex rel.* Attorney General v. Waters-Pierce Oil Co., 67 S.W. 1057 (Tex. Civ. App. 1902); Waters-Pierce Oil Co. v. Texas, 177 U.S. 28 (1900). A Texas federal circuit court held the 1889 Texas act unconstitutional on similar grounds in 1897 (*In re* Grice, 79 F. 297 (C.C.N.D. Tex. 1897), *rev'd on other grounds*, Baker v. Grice, 169 U.S. 284 (1898)). In 1903 the Texas Supreme Court obviated the question of the constitutionality of the 1899 act by holding that the exemption for farmers and stock raisers was not included in Section 14 of the act, making it constitutional (State v. Laredo Ice Co., 73 S.W. 951 (Tex. 1903)).

43. Act of Mar. 31, 1903, 28th Leg., R.S., ch. 94, 1903 Tex. Gen. Laws 119; Arkansas affidavit and foreign corporations, Act of May 16, 1907, 30th Leg., 1st C.S., ch. 22, 1907 Tex. Gen. Laws 500 and Act of Apr. 7, 1909, 31st Leg., 1st C.S., ch. 4, 1909 Tex. Gen. Laws 266; Act of Apr. 25, 1907, 30th Leg., R.S., ch. 173, 1907 Tex. Gen. Laws 322; Act of May 16, 1907, 30th Leg., 1st C.S., ch. 10, 1907 Tex. Gen. Laws 456; Act of Apr. 13, 1909, 31st Leg., 1st C.S., ch. 11, 1909 Tex. Gen. Laws 281. The antitrust exemptions for laborers and farmers and stock raisers were included in the 1911 Revised Penal Statutes and carried forward in the 1925 Revised Penal Statutes, but not the Revised Civil Statutes (State v. Standard Oil Co., 82 S.W.2d 402, 406 (Tex. Civ. App. 1935), *rev'd*, 107 S.W.2d 550 (Tex. 1937)).

44. Jonathan W. Singer, Broken Trusts: The Texas Attorney General versus the Oil Industry, 1889–1909, ch. 1 (2002); "90 percent and 98 percent" and "over five million dollars," Bringhurst, at 42, 48. Singer's excellent study recounts the saga of the Waters-Pierce Oil Company and Texas antitrust law. Other, briefer accounts include Bringhurst, ch. 2; Frederick Upham Adams, The Waters Pierce Case in Texas (1908); Finty, at 21–23; Sanford, at 167; Charles B. Wallace, *Waters-Pierce Oil Company Case Revisited*, TBJ, Mar. 1961, at 221; and John N. Jackson, *Waters-Pierce Cases: Another Visit*, TBJ, June 1975, at 529.

45. Hathaway v. State, 36 S.W. 465 (Tex. Crim. App. 1896).

46. *In re* Grice, 79 F. 627 (C.C.N.D. Tex. 1897),

rev'd on other grounds, Baker v. Grice, 169 U.S. 284 (1898).

47. Baker v. Grice, 169 U.S. 284 (1898).

48. Waters-Pierce Oil Co. v. State, 44 S.W. 936 (Tex. Civ. App. 1898).

49. Waters-Pierce Oil Co. v. Texas, 177 U.S. 28 (1900).

50. The material here and in preceding paragraphs is largely taken from Singer, ch. 1; "3,996," *id.* at 54; "2,747," Wallace, at 273.

51. State *ex rel.* Attorney General v. Waters-Pierce Oil Co., 67 S.W. 1057 (Tex. Civ. App. 1902); on the same day the same court of civil appeals released State *ex rel.* Attorney General v. Shippers' Compress & Warehouse Co., 67 S.W. 1049 (Tex. Civ. App. 1902), *aff'd*, 69 S.W. 58 (Tex. 1902), also declaring the 1899 antitrust act unconstitutional; "three-thousand-dollar payment," Singer, at 96.

52. On Waters-Pierce profits, see Bringhurst, at 57.

53. Steven L. Piott, The Anti-Monopoly Persuasion: Popular Resistance to the Rise of Big Business in the Midwest ch. 6 (1985).

54. The number of days of fines under the 1899 and 1903 acts do not add up, unless the jury was excluding beginning and ending dates. Compounding the error, the supreme court counted 1,480 days of penalties (Waters-Pierce Oil Co. v. Texas, 212 U.S. 86, 96 (1909)). The instructions given by the district court to the jury are likely the cause of the jury's calculations, which modestly benefited Waters-Pierce; "$1,623,900," Waters-Pierce Oil Co. v. State, 106 S.W. 918, 924 (Tex. Civ. App. 1907). On the Texas Supreme Court's reduction of the attorney's fee to $90,000, see Singer, at 190; Sanford states the amount received by the attorneys was $85,000; quote, Singer, at 154.

55. Waters-Pierce Oil Co. v. State, 106 S.W. 918 (Tex. Civ. App. 1907), *aff'd*, 212 U.S. 86 (1909).

56. Singer, at 164–67; Bringhurst, at 65–67.

57. Singer, at 204–6.

58. "three million dollars," Singer, at 210. Wallace, at 274, notes that Pierce spent more than "five million dollars over fifty years on lawyers' fees, court costs, penalties, and other expenses."

59. "Tried to free," Singer, at 208; "control," *id.* at 211; Standard Oil Company of New Jersey v. United States, 221 U.S. 1 (1911). An instant screed on Magnolia and Standard Oil in Texas is John M. Duncan, An Eye Opener: The Standard Oil–Magnolia Compromise: The Whole Truth (1915).

60. Duncan, at unpaginated 4–5; Pierce Oil Corp. v. Weinert, 167 S.W. 808 (Tex. 1914); quotes, Wallace, at 276–77.

61. Finty, at 27, 54; M. S. Breckinridge, *Some Phases of the Texas Anti-trust Law (Part II)*, 4 TLR 129, 153 (1926); Bringhurst, at 68; Singer, at 222; Joseph A. Pratt & Mark E. Steiner, *"An Intent to Terrify": State Antitrust in the Formative Years of the Modern Oil Industry*, 29 Washburn L.J. 270, 289 (1990) (using Finty's language, also adopted by Baker & Botts lawyer Clarence R. Wharton); the same conclusion is found in Joseph A. Pratt, *The Petroleum Industry in Transition: Antitrust and the Decline of Monopoly Control in Oil*, 40 J. Econ. Hist. 815, 831 (1980). See also John O. King, Joseph Stephen Cullinan: A Study of Leadership in the Texas Petroleum Industry, 1897–1937, at 94 (1970) (noting that the absence of Standard Oil from Spindletop "effectively destroyed its monopolistic position within the American petroleum industry well before the U.S. Supreme Court ordered dissolution of the organization in 1911.").

62. State v. Standard Oil Co., 107 S.W.2d 550 (Tex. 1937); "one of four states," James A. Rahl, *Toward a Worthwhile State Antitrust Policy*, 39 TLR 753, 754 (1961); quote, Dan Moody and Charles B. Wallace, *Texas Antitrust Laws and their Enforcement: Comparison with Federal Antitrust Laws*, 11 SwLJ 1, 9 (1957), and "a thousand," at 23; Will Wilson, *The State Antitrust Laws*, ABA J., Feb. 1961, at 160, 162; Act of June 19, 1983, 68th Leg., R.S., ch. 520, 1983 Tex. Gen. Laws 3010, codified at Bus. & Comm. Code § 15.01; J. Michael Weston, *Vertical Distribution Restraints and the Texas Antitrust Laws*, 37 SwLJ 601 (1983). Singer, at 222, notes that Texas filed "at least seven different antitrust suits against one or more firms between 1913 and 1951." Charles Mathews, an assistant attorney general who served as chief of the Antitrust Division, wrote in 1950 that of the twenty-seven lawsuits brought against thirty-five individuals and seventy-five corporations, final judgments had been reached in fourteen cases totaling $300,000 in penalties, "an average of approximately $14,280.00 per suit" (Mathews, at 64); this does not appear to reach the significance Mathews suggests.

63. Act of Apr. 8, 1893, 23d Leg., R.S., ch. 50, 10 Gammel's 486; Mercantile Trust Co. v. Texas & P. Ry. Co., 51 F. 529 (C.C.W.D. Tex. 1892), *rev'd sub nom.* Reagan v. Farmers' Loan & Trust Co., 154 U.S. 362 (1894); E. T. Miller, *The Texas Stock and Bond Law and Its Administration*, 22 Q. J. Econ. 109, 117–18 (1907); Charles Shirley Potts, *Texas Stock and Bond Law*, 53 Annals Amer. Acad. Pol. & Soc. Sci. 162, 164–65 (1914); Cotner, at 328–32; Act of Apr. 15, 1901, 27th Leg., R.S., ch. 91, 1901 Tex. Gen. Laws 257; Act of Apr. 23, 1907, 30th Leg., R.S., ch. 155, 1907 Tex. Gen. Laws 297; Reed, at 712–18.

64. Act of May 15, 1899, 26th Leg., R.S., ch. 117, 1899 Tex. Gen. Laws 209; "one early avenue," see Pratt & Steiner, at 285 n.77. Joseph Pratt notes that Standard Oil built a refinery near Spindletop through the Security Oil Company, making Security "[f]or all practical purposes, itself a Standard subsidiary" (Pratt, at 823, and see generally at 822–27). On the Hogg-Swayne Syndicate sweetheart deals, see James, at 15–16; King, Cullinan, at 99–101; Singer, at 67; Hinton & Olien, at 33. Cotner, ch. 19, and 526, suggests the deal with Guffey was "what seemed then a high figure," with doubtful titles to the real property involved; Cotner is the only chronicler suggesting this was not a sweetheart deal.

65. Texas Company charter, Cotner, at 545, and King, Cullinan, at 131–33.

66. The material in this paragraph is taken from King, Cullinan, at 162–79. On the Kansas investigation, see Piott, at 111–17.

67. Gulf reincorporation, Thompson, at 22–23; Act of Mar. 6, 1915, 34th Leg., R.S., ch. 41, 1915 Tex. Gen. Laws 82; Act of Feb. 20, 1917, 35th Leg., R.S., ch. 31, 1917 Tex. Gen. Laws 54; Act of Feb. 20, 1917, 35th Leg., R.S., ch. 30, 1917 Tex. Gen. Laws 48; "1907 ad," King, Cullinan, at 123, and "eastern investors owned" and "New York ideas," at 189, 194.

68. Texaco reincorporation, James, at 51–53; on Beaty, see *id.* at 38, and King, Cullinan, at 156–57. Humble Oil & Refining Company was incorporated in Texas after the Texas Companies Act of 1917 (Hinton & Olien, at 63). In 1919, Standard Oil of New Jersey purchased a half-interest in Humble and owned a controlling interest by 1920 (Hinton & Olien, at 63, and James A. Clark and Mark Odintz, *Exxon Company, U.S.A.*, HOTO, www.tshaonline. org/handbook/online/articles/EE/doe4.html). John O. King, The Early History of the Houston Oil Company of Texas, 1901–1908, at 30 (1959), quotes the 1901 corporate charter of the Houston Oil Company, which states that it was incorporated "for the purpose of prospecting for, developing, saving, transporting, refining and marketing minerals of whatever kind." Although this combination of purposes was unlawful after Ramsey v. Tod (1902), no change in the corporate charter is noted by King.

69. Spratt, at 128–33; on New York capital, see King, Early History, at 19–24; Buenger & Pratt, at 37–38; Union Bank and local control, Buenger & Pratt, at 38; *Why Texas Should Have Banking Laws*, DMN, Jan. 1, 1903, at 12; "upswing" and charter amounts, Joseph M. Grant & Lawrence L. Crum, The Development of State-Chartered Banking in Texas: From Predecessor Systems until 1970, at 33 (1978); "number of national banks" and

data on operating banks, Grant & Crum, at 34, 49; Jt. Res. Nos. 2 & 5, 28th Leg., R.S., Apr. 1, 1903, 1903 Tex. Gen. Laws 249; Act of May 26, 1905, 29th Leg., 1st C.S., ch. 10, 1905 Tex. Gen. Laws 489; S. J. R. No. 9, 45th Leg., R.S., Mar. 25, 1937, 1937 Tex. Gen. Laws 1495; Act of Mar. 31, 1943, 48th Leg., R.S., ch. 97, 1943 Tex. Gen. Law 127.

70. Act of Apr. 24, 1907, 30th Leg., R.S., ch. 169, 1907 Tex. Gen. Laws 316; quote, James A. Tinsley, *Texas Progressives and Insurance Regulation*, 36 Sw. Soc. Sci. Q. 237 (1955); investment amounts, *id.*, at 239; "$256,675.04," *id.*, at 243; Lewis L. Gould, PROGRESSIVES AND PROHIBITIONISTS: TEXAS DEMOCRATS IN THE WILSON ERA 40–41 (1973, repr. 1992); Act of Mar. 22, 1909, 31st Leg., R.S., ch. 108, 1909 Tex. Gen. Laws 192; Act of Apr. 7, 1909, 31st Leg., 1st C.S., ch. 3, 1909 Tex. Gen. Laws 264; "sharp struggle," Dewey W. Grantham, SOUTHERN PROGRESSIVISM: THE RECONCILIATION OF PROGRESS AND TRADITION 142–59 (1983).

71. Edmund O. Belsheim, *The Need for Revising the Texas Corporation Statutes*, 27 TLR 659, 695 n.181 (1949); a similar call is Edward W. Bailey, *Need for Revision of the Texas Corporation Statutes*, 3 BLR 1 (1950).

72. Hildebrand, 1 TEXAS CORPORATIONS at 160; see Harwell Wells, *The Modernization of Corporation Law, 1920–1940*, 11 U. Pa. J. Bus. L. 573 (2009); Roy Garrett, *Model Business Corporation Act*, 4 BLR 413, 415–19 (1952); and John Ben Shepperd, *Stagecoach Law*, TBJ, Dec. 1950, at 595. As late as 1930, 70 percent of the Texas population depended on cotton to make a living (Grant & Crum, at 221); during World War II, Texas manufacturing increased to $6.5 billion, a 333.3 percent increase, and manufacturing workers more than doubled (Grant & Crum, at 244).

73. *UT Law School Holds Corporation Laws Institute, Honors Justice Tom Clark*, TBJ, May 1950, at 179; Paul J. Bickel, *What a Model Corporation Act Should Contain*, TBJ, May 1950, at 183; Edward W. Bailey, *Texas Corporation Statutes*, TBJ, May 1950, at 185; "drove," Alan R. Bromberg, Byron F. Egan, Dan L. Nicewander & Robert S. Trotti, *The Role of the Business Law Section and the Texas Business Law Foundation in the Development of Texas Business Law*, 41 Tex. J. Bus. L. 41, 45 (2005); "unsatisfactory," TBJ, Aug. 1952, at 424; Paul Carrington et al., *First Draft of Texas Business Corporation Act*, TBJ, May 1951, at 219; "almost immediately proposed," see *Business Corporation Act*, TBJ, Aug. 1951, at 399; *Corporation Act*, TBJ, Nov. 1951, at 653; *Corporation Act*, TBJ, Dec. 1952, at 597. An immediate history is Carrington, *Corporation Code*. On Carrington, see Darwin Payne, AS OLD AS DALLAS ITSELF 194 (1999), and Tory Cox,

Civic Leader-Lawyer Paul Carrington Dies, DMN, May 29, 1988, at 28B; his privately printed memoir is Paul Carrington, A DALLAS LAWYER FOR SIXTY YEARS (1979), a partial copy of which was graciously sent me by his son Paul D. Carrington.

74. "Members asked," Carrington, SIXTY YEARS, at 167; "288" and "39," Carrington, *Ten Years*, at 611 n.5; Act of Apr. 15, 1955, 54th Leg., R.S., ch. 64, 1955 Tex. Gen. Laws 239; Paul Carrington, *Experience in Texas with the Model Business Corporation Act*, 5 Utah L. Rev. 292 (1957); "amateur draftsmen," Garrett, at 427; Paul Carrington, *The History of the Proposed Texas Business Corporation Act*, 4 BLR 428 (1952); Paul Carrington, *Corporation Code*.

75. Bromberg, at 103.

76. Act of May 11, 1959, 56th Leg., R.S., ch. 162, 1959 Tex. Gen. Laws 286; Act of May 24, 1961, 57th Leg., R.S., ch. 205, 1961 Tex. Gen. Laws 408; Act of Apr. 30, 1955, 54th Leg., R.S., ch. 133, 1955 Tex. Gen. Laws 471; Act of May 16, 1961, 57th Leg., R.S., ch. 158, 1961 Tex. Gen. Laws 289; Bromberg, at 105–6.

77. Quote, Byron F. Egan & Curtis W. Huff, *Choice of State of Incorporation—Texas Versus Delaware: Is It Now Time to Rethink Traditional Notions?*, 54 SMU L. Rev. 249, 250 (2001); Act of June 16, 1991, 72d Leg., R.S., ch. 901, 1991 Tex. Gen. Laws 3161; "first state," Byron F. Egan, *Choice of Entity Alternatives*, 39 Tex. J. Bus. L. 379, 385 (2004); Susan Saab Fortney, *Professional Responsibility and Liability Issues Related to Limited Liability Law Partnerships*, 39 STLR 399 (1998); Castleberry v. Branscum, 721 S.W.2d 270, 272–73 (Tex. 1986); "Almost immediately," Glenn D. West & Stacie L. Cargill, *Corporations*, 62 SMU L. Rev. 1057, 1060–61 (2009); see also SSP Partners v. Gladstrong Inv. (USA) Corp., 275 S.W.3d 444 (Tex. 2008) (limiting piercing of corporate veil).

78. Act of May 19, 2003, 78th Leg., R.S., ch. 182, 2003 Tex. Gen. Laws 267; see Egan & Huff, at 323 (favorably comparing Texas to Delaware corporation law); see Curtis W. Huff, *Choice of State of Incorporation-Texas Versus Delaware: Is It Now Time To Rethink Traditional Notions?*, 31 Bull. Bus. L. Sec. St. B. Tex. 9 (Dec. 1994), from which parts are taken in Egan & Huff.

79. "The complaint," Sam Kinch, Jr., & Ben Procter, TEXAS UNDER A CLOUD 26 (1972); Kinch & Procter is an immediate history of the scandal ending before Mutscher's trial and "designed more to influence the elections of 1972 than to provide historical insight" (Kenneth E. Hendrickson, Jr., *Texas Politics since the New Deal*, in TEXAS THROUGH TIME: EVOLVING INTERPRETATIONS 272 (Walter L. Buenger & Robert A. Calvert eds., 1991)). Harvey Katz, SHADOW ON THE ALAMO (1972) also ends before

Mutscher's trial. Charles Deaton, The Year They Threw the Rascals Out (1973) summarizes the events of the scandal, including the Mutscher trial, but focuses on the 1972 election and 1973 legislative session and does not thoroughly analyze the Sharpstown scandal. A. James Reichley, *The Texas Banker Who Bought Politicians*, Fortune, Dec. 1971, at 94, offers a thorough early assessment.

80. Reichley, at 96; Act of Apr. 2, 1913, 33d Leg., R.S., ch. 110, 1913 Tex. Gen. Laws 211; "throughout the 1960s," see, e.g., Chemical Bank & Trust Co. v. Falkner, 369 S.W.2d 427, 432 (Tex. 1963); Chimney Rock Nat'l Bank of Houston v. State Banking Bd., 376 S.W.2d 595 (Tex. Civ. App. 1964); State Banking Bd. v. Airline Nat'l Bank, 398 S.W.2d 805 (Tex. Civ. App. 1966); "our friends in Hooks," see George Norris Green, The Establishment in Texas Politics: The Primitive Years, 1938–1957, at 170 (1979). In 1963 the attorney general was removed from the State Banking Board, replaced by a citizen of the state (see Act of Apr. 23, 1963, 58th Leg., R.S., ch. 442, 1963 Tex. Gen. Laws. 1138, 1142).

81. On Wilson, see *The Fall of Will Wilson*, Reichley, at 99.

82. Quote, SEC v. National Bankers Life Ins. Co., 334 F. Supp. 444 (N.D. Tex. 1971); stock price increase, Katz, at 49.

83. Quotes, Kinch & Procter, at 41; H.B. 72 and H.B. 73, 61st Leg., 2d Spec. S., vetoed Sept. 20, 1969.

84. *Smith Names Dr. Baum to Bank Board*, DMN, Sept. 12, 1969, at 6, and Kinch & Procter, at 1; Act of Apr. 23, 1963, 58th Leg., R.S., ch. 442, 1963 Tex. Gen. Laws. 1138, 1142; timeline, Mutscher v. State, 514 S.W.2d 905, 911 (Tex. Crim. App. 1974); profits, Katz, at 64 (indicating profits of about $60,000 each), and Kinch & Procter, at 30 (indicating profits of $62,500 each); bankruptcy, Katz, at 65. Baum replaced Robert S. Strauss, the well-known Dallas lawyer.

85. Proclamation by the Governor of the State of Texas, No. 41–1378, Sept. 29, 1969, available in Texas State Archives.

86. Kinch & Procter, at 34–36; Katz, at 6–7; Reichley, at 98–99; SEC v. National Bankers Life Ins. Co., 324 F. Supp. 189 (N.D. Tex. 1971) (granting preliminary injunction against all defendants other than Carr), 334 F. Supp. 444 (ordering permanent injunction against all defendants including Carr), aff'd, 477 F.2d 920 (5th Cir. 1973). On Hughes, see Darwin Payne, Sarah Weddington & Barefoot Sanders, Indomitable Sarah: The Life of Sarah T. Hughes (2004); on Shivers's own scandal involving a transaction with Lloyd Bentsen, Sr., giving Shivers a 1,700 percent profit ($425,000) in six months and Bentsen the first water rights permit for Rio Grande

water in twenty years from the State Board of Water Engineers three months after Shivers became governor, see Green, at 153.

87. On Wilson, see Kinch & Procter, at 129–31; Reichley, at 144. Wilson's much later published response was, "I was never implicated, never investigated, and never indicted in the scandal." The affair was one of "guilt by association," which is why he resigned as assistant attorney general (see Will R. Wilson, Sr., A Fool for a Client xi (2000)).

88. Mutscher v. State, 514 S.W.2d 905 (Tex. Crim. App. 1974). Bank examiner Ted Bristol's conviction was also upheld on appeal (United States v. Bristol, 473 F.2d 439 (5th Cir. 1973)).

89. For a different view of the sixty-third legislature, see Hendrickson, at 272.

90. S.J.R. 4, Aug. 26, 1986, 69th Leg., 2d C.S., 1986 Tex. Gen. Laws 100 (proposing constitutional amendment); Act of Sept. 23, 1986, 69th Leg., 2d C.S., ch. 13, § 1, 1986 Tex. Gen. Laws 36, codified in Finance Code § 32.201; Act of June, 16, 1995, 74th Leg., R.S., ch. 914, § 1, 1995 Tex. Gen. Laws 4451, "public necessity," Finance Code § 32.003; Chemical Bank & Trust Co. v. Falkner, 369 S.W.2d 427, 432 (Tex. 1963); requirement eliminated, Act of May 23, 2001, 77th Leg., R.S., ch. 528, §5, 2001 Tex. Gen. Laws 985, 988.

91. Riegle-Neal Interstate Banking and Efficiency Act, Pub. L. No. 103–328, 108 Stat. 2338 (1994) (codified as amended in scattered sections of 12 U.S.C., especially §§ 1831u and 215a-1 (2006)); Act of Apr. 22, 1995, 74th Leg., R.S., ch. 58, § 1, 1995 Tex. Gen. Laws 437.

92. Quote, Dean G. Pawlowic, *Banking Law*, 30 TTLR 425, 432–33 (1999); Ghiglieri v. Nationsbank of Texas, N.A., 1998 WL 241234 (N.D. Tex. 1998) (officially unreported); Interstate Banking Act, Act of May 18, 1999, 76th Leg., R.S., ch. 344, 1999 Tex. Gen. Laws 1255. An extensive history of these events is found in House Comm. on Financial Institutions, Bill Analysis, Tex. H.B. 2066, 76th Leg., R.S. (1999).

CHAPTER 5

1. In both fiscal years 1996–97 and 2006–2007, the number of current divorce actions has hovered at slightly more than 200,000, with about 125,000 divorce cases filed annually. See Texas Judicial Council, 1996–97 data, www.courts.state.tx.us/pubs/AR97/dist/dstot97.htm (210,511 divorce actions); 2006–2007 fiscal year data, www.courts.state.tx.us/pubs/AR2007/dc/4–summary-of-activity-by-case-type-fy07.xls (212,672); *Texas Caseloads Trends by*

Type: All Cases in District and County-Level Courts, Texas Judicial Council 2007 Annual Report, www. courts.state.tx.us/pubs/ar2007/trends/Caseload%20 Trends%20by%20Case%20Type.pdf. The number of "other family law cases" began to exceed divorce filings in the early twenty-first century, *Texas Caseload Trends*, at 3.

2. On marriages and divorces, see U.S. National Center for Health Statistics, Vital and Health Statistics, Ser. 24, no. 21, 100 Years of Marriage and Divorce Statistics, www.cdc.gov/nchs/data/series/ sr_21/sr21_024.pdf; Vital Statistics of the United States, Annual Reports, 1963–1984, www.cdc.gov/ nchs/products/pubs/pubd/vsus/1963/1963.htm; State Data 2000, Centers for Disease Control and Prevention, Marriage Rates by States, 1990–2004, www.cdc. gov/nchs/data/nvss/marriage90_04.pdf; and Divorce Rates by State, 1900–2004, www.cdc.gov/nchs/data/ nvss/divorce90_04.pdf. Historical data, Paul H. Jacobson in collaboration with Pauline F. Jacobson, AMERICAN MARRIAGE AND DIVORCE 43 (marriage), 100 (divorce) (1950) (data 1939–50); James W. Paulsen, *Remember the Alamo[ny]! The Unique Texas Ban on Permanent Alimony and the Development of Community Property*, 56 Law & Contemp. Probs. 7, 31–32 (1993) (noting rise in Texas divorce rate and rank among states between 1870 and 1900); Andrew J. Cherlin, THE MARRIAGE GO-ROUND 212 (2009); DATAPEDIA OF THE UNITED STATES: AMERICAN HISTORY IN NUMBERS 77–79 (3d ed., George Thomas Kurian ed., 2004); Texas Dept. of State Health Servs., tbl. 7, Marriages & Divorces Texas, 1970–2007, www. dshs.state.tx.us/chs/vstat/latest/t07.shtm; Child Support Enforcement Amendments of 1984, 98 Stat. 1304; Family Support Act, 102 Stat. 2343, codified at 42 U.S.C. § 667 (2000); Child Support Recovery Act of 1992, 18 U.S.C. § 228 (1992), as amended by the Deadbeat Parents Punishment Act of 1998.

3. Lawrence M. Friedman, THE CULTURE OF CHOICE: LAW, AUTHORITY AND CULTURE 178 (1990); Mary Ann Glendon, ABORTION AND DIVORCE IN WESTERN LAW 63 (1987) (The changes in family law beginning in the 1960s were its "most fundamental shift since family law had begun to be secularized at the time of the Protestant Reformation."); Hendrik Hartog, MAN AND WIFE IN AMERICA: A HISTORY (2000); Glenda Riley, DIVORCE: AN AMERICAN TRADITION (1991).

4. James L. Haley, SAM HOUSTON 98 (2002); Maynard v. Hill, 125 U.S. 190, 211 (1888).

5. Stephen F. Austin, ESTABLISHING AUSTIN'S COLONY: THE FIRST BOOK PRINTED IN TEXAS WITH THE LAWS, ORDERS AND CONTRACTS OF COLONIZA-TION 84–89 (David B. Gracy II ed., 1970) (Art. 9); Hans W. Baade, *The Form of Marriage in Spanish North America*, 61 Cornell L. Rev. 1 (1975); Bennett Smith, MARRIAGE BY BOND IN COLONIAL TEXAS (1972); "forfeitures" and "larger land grant," Mark M. Carroll, HOMESTEADS UNGOVERNABLE: FAMILIES, SEX, RACE AND THE LAW IN FRONTIER TEXAS, 1823–1860, at 113 and 116 (2001).

6. Ordinance and Decree of Jan. 16, 1836, § 9, 1 Gammel's 1039, 1041–42; Act of June 5, 1837, 1st Cong., Repub. Tex., 1 Gammel's 1293; Act of Feb. 5, 1841, 5th Cong., Repub. Tex., 2 Gammel's 640.

7. Act of June 5, 1837, 1st Cong., Repub. Tex., § 9, 1 Gammel's 1293; Act of Feb. 9, 1854, 5th Leg., ch. 49, § 38, 3 Gammel's 1502, 1510; "unconstitutional," Loving v. Virginia, 388 U.S. 1 (1967); Tex. Penal Code Art. 386 (1856); Act of Feb. 12, 1858, 7th Leg., R.S., ch. 121, 4 Gammel's 1028, 1037–38. Texas repealed its antimiscegenation law in its codification of family law in 1969; see Act of May 14, 1969, 61st Leg., ch. 888, § 6, 1969 Tex. Gen. Laws 2733.

8. Act of Aug. 15, 1870, 12th Leg., C.S., ch. 77, 6 Gammel's 301.

9. Bonds v. Foster, 36 Tex. 68 (1871–72).

10. Honey v. Clark, 37 Tex. 686 (1872–73). A thorough study is Jason A. Gillmer, *Base Wretches and Black Wenches: A Story of Sex and Race, Violence and Compassion, during Slavery Times*, 59 Ala. L. Rev. 1501 (2008), from which these facts are taken. See also Hans W. Baade, *Chapters in the History of the Supreme Court of Texas: Reconstruction and "Redemption" (1866–1882)*, 40 StMLJ 17, 99 (2008). Although the children, and Sobrina's children by a previous relationship, took this large estate, Clark's long-lost heirs at law continued the litigation, and the attorney for the children purchased much of the land at a fraction of its value. Other cases concerning the estate include Treasurer of the State v. Wygall, 51 Tex. 621 (1879), and Treasurer of the State v. Wygall, 46 Tex. 447 (1877). Another similar tale is Dale Baum, COUNTERFEIT JUSTICE: THE JUDICIAL ODYSSEY OF TEXAS FREEDWOMAN AZELINE HEARNE (2009), discussed in chapter 6.

11. Clements v. Crawford, 42 Tex. 601 (1875).

12. Oldham v. McIver, 49 Tex. 556 (1878).

13. Ashworth v. State, 9 Tex. 490 (1853); Act of Dec. 21, 1836, 1st Cong., Repub. Tex., § 23, 1 Gammel's 1247, 1250; Act of Feb. 9, 1854, 5th Leg., ch. 49, § 38, 3 Gammel's 1502, 1510; Carroll, at 64–75.

14. Act of Nov. 10, 1866, 11th Leg., ch. 128, § 2, 5 Gammel's 1049; Smelser v. State, 31 Tex. 96 (1869). The "military court" existed from 1867 until the ratification and implementation of the 1869 constitu-

tion and was followed by the "Semicolon Court"; see James R. Norvell, *The Reconstruction Courts of Texas 1867–1873*, 62 SWHQ 141, 148 (1958).

15. Frasher v. State, 3 Tex. App. 263, 30 Am. Rep. 131 (1877); Moore v. State, 7 Tex. App. 608 (1880).

16. François v. State, 9 Tex. App. 144 (1880); *Ex parte* François, 3 Woods 367, 9 F. Cas. 699, 700–701 (W.D. Tex. 1879) (No. 5,047).

17. On the story of Calvin and Katie Bell, see Charles F. Robinson II, *Legislated Love in the Lone Star State: Texas and Miscegenation*, 108 SWHQ 65 (2004); Bell v. State, 25 S.W. 163 (Tex. Crim. App. 1894).

18. Stewart v. Profit, 146 S.W. 563 (Tex. Civ. App. 1912).

19. Robinson, at 82, 85–86 tbls. I & II.

20. Fenton v. Reed, 4 Johns. 52 (N.Y. 1809); Tarpley v. Poage's Adm'r, 2 Tex. 139 (1847); Katherine S. Vaughn, Comment, *The Recent Changes to the Texas Informal Marriage Statute: Limitation or Abolition of Common-Law Marriage?*, 28 HLR 1131, 1150–69 (1991); Grigsby v. Reib, 153 S.W. 1124 (Tex. 1913). On the English law of marriage, J. H. Baker, AN INTRODUCTION TO ENGLISH LEGAL HISTORY ch. 23 (2d ed. 1979).

21. Jack Pope, *Common Law Marriages in Modern Society*, *in* REPORT OF THE INTERIM STUDY COMMITTEE ON DIVORCE TO THE 58TH LEGISLATURE 55, 63 (1963); Tex. Fam. Code § 1.91 (1969 and 1973); Act of June 14, 1989, 71st Leg., R.S., ch. 369, § 9, 1989 Tex. Gen. Laws 1458, 1461; Act of Apr. 17, 1997, 75th Leg., R.S., ch. 7, § 1, 1997 Tex. Gen. Laws 8, 15.

22. Stevens v. State, 243 S.W.2d 162 (Tex. Crim. App. 1951).

23. Act of Dec. 21, 1836, § 54, 1st Cong., Repub. Tex., 1 Gammel's 1247, 1255; Republic of Texas v. Mumford, Dallam's 374 (Tex. 1840).

24. Act of Mar. 20, 1848, 2d Leg., ch. 152, 3 Gammel's 219; Act of Feb. 9, 1854, 5th Leg., ch. 49, § 36, 3 Gammel's 1502, 1509; Gorman v. State, 23 Tex. 646 (1859).

25. Act of Dec. 21, 1836, 1st Cong., Repub. Tex., § 22, 1 Gammel's 1247, 1250; Act of Feb. 9, 1854, 5th Leg., ch. 49, § 36, 3 Gammel's 1502, 1509. For an excellent discussion, see Carroll, at 123–29.

26. Smith v. Smith, 1 Tex. 621 (1846); Yates v. Houston, 3 Tex. 433 (1848).

27. Carroll v. Carroll, 20 Tex. 731 (1858).

28. Bigamy, Michael Grossberg, GOVERNING THE HEARTH: LAW AND FAMILY IN NINETEENTH-CENTURY AMERICA 120–21 (1985); Nichols case, see Carroll, at 109–11, and Nichols v. Stewart, 15 Tex. 226 (1855); Act of Jan. 28, 1840, § 15, 4th Cong., Repub.

Tex., 2 Gammel's 306; Act of Mar. 18, 1848, 2d Leg., ch. 103, § 10, 2 Gammel's 129; Hartwell v. Jackson, 7 Tex. 576 (1852) (holding that, even if a marriage were legally invalid, children took their share of the estate by statute).

29. Quotes, Carroll, at 128; on Hemphill, see chapter 1.

30. Penal Code Art. 392 (1856); quote, Halbadier v. State, 220 S.W. 85 (Tex. Crim. App. 1920); Hafley v. State, 224 S.W. 1099 (Tex. Crim. App. 1920) (listing cases in which multiple acts of sexual intercourse did not constitute habitual intercourse); Cohron v. State, 242 S.W.2d 776 (Tex. Crim. App. 1951); Cadle v. State, 235 S.W. 894 (Tex. Crim. App. 1921); Compton v. State, 13 Tex. App. 271, 44 Am. Rep. 703 (1882) (incest); Thomas v. State, 14 Tex. App. 70 (1883) and Hall v. State, 188 S.W.2d 388 (Tex. Crim. App. 1945) (adultery).

31. Tex. Penal Code Art. 562 (1856).

32. Robert A. Weninger, *Factors Affecting the Prosecution of Rape: A Case Study of Travis County, Texas*, 64 Va. L. Rev. 357 (1978), and quote at 363; case law, *id.* at 363 nn.19–21 (citing cases all dating from 1933 or earlier); Act of May 15, 1975, 64th Leg., R.S., ch. 203, § 3, 1975 Tex. Gen. Laws 476, 477–78.

33. Act of June 16, 1991, 72d Leg., R.S., ch. 662, 1991 Tex. Gen. Laws 2412. On the marital rape reform movement begun in the late 1970s, see Rebecca M. Ryan, *The Sex Right: A Legal History of the Marital Rape Exemption*, 20 L. & Soc. Inq. 941 (1995). Quote, Gerald S. Reamey, CRIMINAL OFFENSES AND DEFENSES IN TEXAS 420 (3d ed. 2000).

34. Murray v. State, 86 S.W. 1024 (Tex. Crim. App. 1905) and Purdy v. State, 97 S.W. 480 (Tex. Crim. App. 1906); Hawkins v. United States, 358 U.S. 74 (1958); Trammel v. United States, 445 U.S. 40 (1980) (reversing Hawkins and granting the witness spouse the privilege to decide whether to testify against defendant spouse); Stewart v. State, 587 S.W.2d 148 (Tex. Crim. App. 1979).

35. Act of May 11, 1995, 74th Leg., R.S., ch. 67, 1995 Tex. Gen. Laws 446 (amending Code of Criminal Procedure § 38.10); Fielder v. State, 756 S.W.2d 309 (Tex. Crim. App. 1988) (allowing the defendant wife to offer expert evidence on battered woman syndrome in a murder case in which the husband was the victim); Tex. Code Crim. Proc. Art. 38.36(b)(2) (codifying Fielder).

36. Whitlesey v. Miller, 572 S.W.2d 665, 666 (Tex. 1978); Garrett v. Reno Oil Co., 271 S.W.2d 764 (Tex. Civ. App. 1954). For the history of Texas law on consortium, see Reagan v. Vaughn, 804 S.W.2d 463 (Tex. 1990).

37. Quote, American Law Institute, RESTATE-
MENT OF THE LAW OF TORTS § 685 (1933); Kelsey-
Seybold Clinic v. Maclay, 466 S.W.2d 716 (Tex. 1971)
(alienation of affections); Felsenthal v. McMillan, 493
S.W.2d 729 (Tex. 1973) (criminal conversation).

38. Family Code §§ 1.106–1.107; Smith v. Smith,
126 S.W.3d 660 (Tex. App. 2004). On the tort of
alienation of affections in Texas, see Norris v. Stone-
ham, 46 S.W.2d 363 (Tex. Civ. App. 1932) (allowing a
wife to sue in her name for alienation of affections),
and Smith v. Smith, 25 S.W.2d 1001 (Tex. Civ. App.
1950) (same, and discussing history of tort in Texas).

39. Twyman v. Twyman, 855 S.W.2d 619 (Tex.
1993).

40. Nickerson v. Nickerson, 65 Tex. 281 (1886)
(adopting interspousal immunity in tort); Bounds
v. Caudle, 560 S.W.2d 925 (Tex. 1977) (intentional
torts); Price v. Price, 732 S.W.2d 316 (Tex. 1987) (all
torts).

41. William Blackstone, COMMENTARIES ON THE
LAW 1:*442–43, quoted in Hartog, at 106.

42. Houston divorce, see Paulsen, Remember the
Alamo[ny], at 9–12; Act of Dec. 18, 1837, 2d Cong.,
Repub. Tex., § 2, 1 Gammel's 1436, 1437; Act of
Jan. 6, 1841, 5th Cong., Repub. Tex., 2 Gammel's 483;
adultery, § 2 at 484; "copied," Joseph W. McKnight &
William A. Reppy, Jr., TEXAS MATRIMONIAL PROP-
ERTY LAW 5 (2000).

43. Act of May 27, 1876, 15th Leg., R.S., ch. 25, 8
Gammel's 852; Act of Apr. 1, 1913, 33d Leg., R.S., ch.
97, 1913 Tex. Gen. Laws 183; Act of May 9, 1941, 47th
Leg., R.S., ch. 214, 1941 Tex. Gen. Laws 383; Act of
June 18, 1965, 59th Leg., R.S., ch. 701, 1965 Tex. Gen.
Laws 1634.

44. Bahn v. Bahn, 62 Tex. 518, 520 (1884), and for
a similar statement nearly a century later, Ex parte
Rodriguez, 636 S.W.2d 844 (Tex. App. 1981) ("Marriage and family law are areas of the law of such great
importance to the structure of our society that we,
as judges, are mandated by society to assure their
stability and finality."); Gowin v. Gowin, 264 S.W.
529 (Tex. Civ. App. 1924), aff'd, 292 S.W. 211 (Tex.
Com. App. 1927); quote, 264 S.W. at 540 (Conner, J.,
dissenting); "persistence," 292 S.W. at 213.

45. Beck v. Beck, 63 Tex. 34 (1885); Sapp v. Sapp, 9
S.W. 258 (Tex. 1888); Bingham v. Bingham, 149 S.W.
214 (Tex. Civ. App. 1912).

46. "Comparative rectitude," see McFadden v.
McFadden, 213 S.W.2d 71 (Tex. Civ. App. 1948).

47. Initial quotes, William L. Morrow, Comment,
Divorce Reform in Texas—The Path of Reason, 18
SwLJ 86, 86 (1964); "more common nationally," J.
Thomas Oldham, Changes in the Economic Conse-
quences of Divorces, 1958–2008, 42 Fam. L.Q. 419,

420 (2008), and Datapedia, at 77; "85.3 percent,"
Jacobson, at 123; final quote, Bea Ann Smith, The
Partnership Theory of Marriage: A Borrowed Solution
Fails, 68 TLR 689, 695 (1990).

48. "First unified," The Codification Binge, Tex.
Law., Dec. 20, 1999, at S31; Act of May 14, 1969, 61st
Leg., R.S., ch. 888, § 3.01, 1969 Tex. Gen. Laws 2707,
2721; quote, Joseph W. McKnight, Recodification
and Reform of the Law of Husband and Wife: A
Recodification of Familiar Statute and Case Law with
Changes Demanded by 20th Century Conditions, TBJ,
Jan. 1970, at 34, 38.

49. McKnight, Recodification and Reform, at 38.

50. Bea Ann Smith, Why the Community Property
System Fails Divorced Women and Children, 7 Tex.
J. Women & L. 135, 144 (1998); professional goodwill,
Nail v. Nail, 486 S.W.2d 761 (Tex. 1972).

51. Act of Jan. 20, 1840, 4th Cong., Repub. Texas,
2 Gammel's 177; on the common law of husband
and wife, see Hartog, esp. ch. 4; the husband also
possessed a right to "moderate" physical correction
of his wife (see Hartog, at 116). On Texas coverture,
see Joseph W. McKnight, Texas Community Property
Law: Conservative Attitudes, Reluctant Change, 56
Law & Contemp. Probs. 71 (1993), Joseph McKnight,
Spanish Law for the Protection of Surviving Spouses in
North America, 57 Anuario de Historia del Derecho
Español 365 (1987), and Thomas M. Featherston, Jr.,
& Julie A. Springer, Marital Property in Texas: The
Past, Present and Future, 39 BLR 861 (1987).

52. Kathleen Lazarou, CONCEALED UNDER PET-
TICOATS: MARRIED WOMEN'S PROPERTY AND THE
LAW OF TEXAS, 1840–1913 (1986); "based largely on
Louisiana law," Ray August, The Spread of Commu-
nity-Property Law to the Far West, 3 W. Leg. Hist. 35,
50 (1990), and Joseph W. McKnight, Texas Commu-
nity Property Law—Its Course of Development and
Reform, 8 Cal. W. L. Rev. 117, 119 (1971), quote at 119.

53. August, at 44–48; Lazarou, at 28. Other states
included New York, Alabama, Maine, Michigan,
Florida, Vermont, and Pennsylvania.

54. Quote, McKnight, Course of Development,
at 119; Act of Jan. 26, 1839, 3d Cong., Repub. Tex., 2
Gammel's 125; An Act Concerning Executions, Act
of Feb. 5, 1840, 4th Cong., Repub. Tex., 2 Gammel's
267; Act of Dec. 22, 1840, § 7, 5th Cong., Repub. Tex.,
2 Gammel's 525, 526. On the economic ailments of
those who immigrated to Texas, see Mark E. Nackman, Anglo-American Migrants to the West: Men of
Broken Fortunes? The Case of Texas 1821–1846, 5 W.
Hist. Q. 441 (1974).

55. Act of Feb. 3, 1841, 5th Cong., Repub. Tex., 2
Gammel's 608; equity, Lazarou, at 19–23.

56. James W. Paulsen, Community Property and

the *Early American Women's Rights Movement: The Texas Connection*, 32 Idaho L. Rev. 641 (1996); Act of Apr. 29, 1846, 1st Leg., 2 Gammel's 1460; Act of Apr. 30, 1846, 1st Leg., 2 Gammel's 1462; Act of Mar. 13, 1848, 2d Leg., 2 Gammel's 77; Act of Aug. 26, 1856, 6th Leg., Adj. S., ch. 123, 4 Gammel's 469 (stating duties of surviving husband); William O. Huie, *The Texas Constitutional Definition of the Wife's Separate Property*, 35 TLR 1054 (1957).

57. California, August, at 53; Bea Ann Smith, *Partnership Theory*, at 703; and George v. Ransom, 15 Cal. 322 (1860); increase in slaves, Cartwright v. Cartwright, 18 Tex. 626, 635 (1857); rents, Carr v. Tucker, 42 Tex. 330 (1875); Thomas R. Andrews, *Income from Separate Property: Towards a Theoretical Foundation*, 56 Law & Contemp. Probs. 171 (1993). On the impact of Texas's law on the laws of New York and Wisconsin, see Paulsen, *Community Property*, at 660–79.

58. On prohibition in Texas, see Lewis L. Gould, Progressives and Prohibitionists: Texas Democrats in the Wilson Era ch. 2 (1973, repr. 1992), and on the link between prohibition and woman suffrage, *id.* at 24–25. See also Michael Ariens, *The Storm between the Quiet: Tumult in the Texas Supreme Court, 1911–1921*, 38 StMLJ 641, 648–55 (2007).

59. Act of Aug. 9, 1876, 15th Leg., R.S., ch. 134, § 116, 8 Gammel's 929, 961; Act of Mar. 13, 1911, 32d Leg., R.S., ch. 52, 1911 Tex. Gen. Laws 92.

60. Judith N. McArthur, Creating the New Woman: The rise of Southern Women's Progressive culture in Texas, 1893–1918, at 102 and 179 n.16 (1998) (citing Houston Chronicle article); 31 PTBA 148–49 (1912); Hortense Ward, Property Rights of Married Women in Texas (The Delineator undated but from 1912); quotes, unnumbered page 5; Act of Mar. 21, 1913, 33d Leg., R.S., ch. 32, 1913 Tex. Gen. Laws 61.

61. Act of Mar. 15, 1915, 34th Leg., R.S., ch. 54, 1915 Tex. Gen. Laws 103; Act of Apr. 4, 1917, 35th Leg., R.S., ch. 194, 1917 Tex. Gen. Laws 436; Act presented Mar. 12, 1921, 37th Leg., R.S., ch. 130, 1921 Tex. Gen. Laws 251.

62. Red River National Bank v. Ferguson, 206 S.W. 923 (Tex. 1918).

63. Arnold v. Leonard, 273 S.W. 799 (Tex. 1925); Gohlman, Lester & Co. v. Whittle, 273 S.W. 808 (Tex. 1925); Cauble v. Beaver-Electra Refining Co., 274 S.W. 120 (Tex. 1925); quote, 273 S.W. at 803.

64. Texas Legislative Council, Legal Status of Married Women in Texas: A Report to the 55th Legislature (1956); on the minor change to the law in 1929 after Arnold, see McKnight, *Course of Development*, at 126–27; on changes from the 1950s through 1970, McKnight, at 127–32; failures, Act of

June 6, 1957, 55th Leg., R.S., ch. 407, 1957 Tex. Gen. Laws 1233.

65. 1963 changes, see Eugene L. Smith, *Legislative Note: 1963 Amendments Affecting Married Women's Rights in Texas*, 18 SwLJ 70 (1964); quotes, McKnight, *Course of Development*, at 129; Joseph W. McKnight, *Recodification of Texas Matrimonial Law*, Tex B. J., Dec. 1966, at 1000; Act of June 16, 1965, 59th Leg., R.S., ch. 495, 1965 Tex. Gen. Laws 1010.

66. McKnight, *Recodification of Texas Matrimonial Law*, at 1001–2; Act of May 27, 1967, 60th Leg., R.S., ch. 309, 1967 Tex. Gen. Laws 735. On Raggio's view of the adoption of the Marital Property Act of 1967, see Louise Ballerstedt Raggio with Vivian Anderson Castleberry, Texas Tornado ch. 13 (2003), and "surprise" at 180–81.

67. For a discussion, see Pamela E. George, Texas Marital Property Rights: Cases and Materials 52–55 (2009).

68. Morgan A. Jones, *History of the Family Code*, 5 TTLR 267, 267 (1974); Act of June 14, 1973, 63d Leg., R.S., ch. 543, 1973 Tex. Gen. Laws 1411.

69. "Pennsylvania once," Joseph W. McKnight, *Family Law: Husband and Wife*, 32 SwLJ 109, 128 (1978); Wiley v. Wiley, 33 Tex. 358 (1870). James W. Paulsen, *The History of Alimony in Texas and the New "Spousal Maintenance" Statute*, 7 Tex. J. Women & L. 151, 152 (1998), declares the Texas Supreme Court's claim that the 1841 divorce statute "is a public policy prohibiting alimony is an historical falsehood." Writing in 1993, James W. Paulsen, *Remember the Alamo[ny]*, at 8 notes, "Texas now stands alone among U.S. jurisdictions in its absolute ban on permanent, court-ordered alimony."

70. "40 percent," Paulsen, *History of Alimony*, at 155 (citing State Rep. Senfronia Thompson that "43 percent of Texas homemakers are on welfare within two or three years after divorce," but not citing where Thompson obtained this information); Bea Ann Smith, *Why*, at 145 n.45 (citing an article that cites the Displaced Homemakers Network estimate that 57 percent of "displaced homemakers earn income at or near the poverty line" without explaining the source of that datum); and Lauren F. Redman, *Domesticity and the Texas Community Property System*, 16 Buff. Women's L.J. 23, 23 n.1 (2008) ("Forty percent of American women live in poverty after divorce," citing a 2000 book but not stating whether the national statistic is mirrored in Texas).

71. Paulsen, *History of Alimony*, at 154–55; Act of June 13, 1995, 74th Leg., R.S., ch. 655, § 10.02, 1995 Tex. Gen. Laws 3543, 3578, codified at Tex. Fam. Code § 8.001 (amended in 2001 and continued at Tex. Fam. Code § 8.051 *et seq.*).

72. Paulsen, *History of Alimony*, at 156.

73. Eggemeyer v. Eggemeyer, 535 S.W.2d 425 (Tex. Civ. App. 1976), *aff'd*, 554 S.W.2d 137 (Tex. 1977); Paulsen, *Remember the Alamo[ny]*, at 42–51; Hailey v. Hailey, 331 S.W.2d 299 (Tex. 1960).

74. Eugene L. Smith, *Family Law*, 26 SwLJ 50, 55 (1972); Joseph W. McKnight, *Commentary to Texas Family Code*, 5 TTLR 281, 337 (1973); quote, 554 S.W.2d at 139; "dubious reading," Paulsen, *Remember the Alamo[ny]*, at 43.

75. 554 S.W.2d at 140.

76. Paulsen, *Remember the Alamo[ny]*, at 46. For the legal community's reaction to Eggemeyer, see *id.* at 43.

77. S.J.R. 16, May 5, 1971, 62d Leg., R.S., 1971 Tex. Gen. Laws 4129; "no state," Susan Crump, *An Overview of the Equal Rights Amendment in Texas*, 11 HLR 136, 137 n.9 (1973); "fourteen other states," Linda J. Wharton, *State Equal Rights Amendments Revisited: Evaluating Their Effectiveness in Advancing Protection against Sex Discrimination*, 36 Rutgers L.J. 1201, 1201 n.1 (2005); Raggio, at 176.

78. Wolfgang P. Hirczy de Miño, *Does an Equal Rights Amendment Make a Difference?*, 60 Alb. L. Rev. 1581 (1997); Rodric B. Schoen, *The Texas Equal Rights Amendment in the Courts, 1972–1977: A Review and Proposed Principles of Interpretation*, 15 HLR 537 (1978); Rodric B. Schoen, *The Texas Equal Rights Amendment after the First Decade: Judicial Developments 1978–1982*, 20 HLR 1321 (1983); William Wayne Kilgarlin & Banks Tarver, *The Equal Rights Amendment: Governmental Action and Individual Liberty*, 68 TLR 1545 (1990); *In re McLean*, 725 S.W.2d 696 (Tex. 1987); Bell v. Low Income Women of Texas, 95 S.W.3d 253 (Tex. 2002).

79. *Texas Caseloads Trends by Case Type: All Cases in District and County-Level Courts*, Texas Judicial Council, 2007 Annual Report, www.courts. state.tx.us/pubs/AR2007/trends/Caseload%20 Trends%20by%20Case%20Type.pdf.

80. Eugene L. Smith, *Commentary to Title II: Parent and Child*, 5 TTLR 389 (1974); Gomez v. Perez, 409 U.S. 535 (1973).

81. Eugene L. Smith, *Commentary*, at 437; quote, Wiley v. Spartlan, 543 S.W.2d 349, 352 (Tex. 1976); Holley v. Adams, 544 S.W.2d 367 (Tex. 1976); In the Interest of G. M., 596 S.W.2d 846 (Tex. 1980).

82. Herrera v. Herrera, 409 S.W.2d 395 (Tex. 1966); Spitzmiller v. Spitzmiller, 429 S.W.2d 557 (Tex. Civ. App. 1968); quote, Eugene L. Smith, *Commentary*, at 425; Raymon Zapata, *Child Custody in Texas and the Best Interest Standard: In the Best Interest of Whom?*, 6 Scholar 197 (2003).

83. 98 Stat. 1304; 102 Stat. 2343; Child Support Recovery Act of 1992, 18 U.S.C. § 228 (1992). Texas's statutory response to some of these incentives is found at Tex. Fam. Code ch. 231.

84. "Common law," Eckford v. Knox, 2 S.W. 372 (Tex. 1886); on civil law and adoption, see E. Wayne Carp, FAMILY MATTERS: SECRECY AND DISCLOSURE IN THE HISTORY OF ADOPTION 11 (1998); "only males," Jean A. Stuntz, HERS, HIS, AND THEIRS: COMMUNITY PROPERTY LAW IN SPAIN AND EARLY TEXAS 39 (1986).

85. "Third state," Grossberg, at 271; Act of Jan. 18, 1845, 9th Cong., Repub. Tex., 2 Gammel's 1065 (allowing Henry Smith to change his name to Henry West and become "adopted son and legal heir of George West and Mary West"); Act of Jan. 16, 1850, 3d Leg., ch. 39, 3 Gammel's 474; Mexican law, see Teal v. Sevier, 26 Tex. 520 (1863); Stuntz, at 139 & 160.

86. Eckford, at 374.

87. Act of Mar. 26, 1907, 30th Leg., R.S., ch. 47, 1907 Tex. Gen. Laws 103. The Texas legislature also allowed parental rights to be terminated if the parents voluntarily abandoned a child for three or more years; Act of June 19, 1920, 36th Leg., 3d C.S., 1920 Tex. Gen. Laws 115.

88. Harle v. Harle, 204 S.W. 317 (Tex. 1918); State v. Yturria, 204 S.W. 315 (Tex. 1918).

89. Minnesota, Carp, at 21; Act of May 23, 1931, 42d Leg., R.S., ch. 177, 1931 Tex. Gen. Laws 300; Act of June 19, 1947, 50th Leg., R.S., ch. 424, 1947 Tex. Gen. Laws 1005; Act of May 18, 1951, 52d Leg., R.S., ch. 249, 1951 Tex. Gen. Laws 388; "adoption of an adult," see Grant v. Marshall, 280 S.W.2d 559 (Tex. 1955).

90. In Stanley v. Illinois, 405 U.S. 605 (1972), the Supreme Court held an unwed father's parental rights could not constitutionally be terminated by Illinois after the mother's death without holding a hearing on the father's fitness to act as a parent; Gomez v. Perez, 409 U.S. 535 (1973); Ernest E. Smith, *Illegitimate Children and Their Fathers: Some Problems with Title 2*, 5 TTLR 613, 614 (1974); Act of June 2, 1975, 64th Leg., R.S., ch. 476, 1975 Tex. Gen. Laws 1253.

91. Brown v. Board of Educ., 347 U.S. 483 (1954), and 349 U.S. 294 (1955); Loving, 388 U.S. 1; *In re* the Adoption of Gomez, 424 S.W.2d 656 (Tex. Civ. App. 1967).

92. Quotes, Jo Beth Eubanks, *Transracial Adoption in Texas: Should the Best Interests Standard Be Color-Blind?*, 24 StMLJ 1225, 1238 and 1227 (1993); "ordered the adoption," *id.* at 1226 n.3; Act of May 19, 1993, 73d Leg., R.S., ch. 189, 1993 Tex. Gen. Laws 375; 42 U.S.C. § 671(a)(18).

CHAPTER 6

1. 37 PTBA 52–66, and quote at 59.

2. *Id.* at 108–39.

3. A 1903 statute eliminated the diploma privilege but was an apparent oversight remedied by its readoption in 1905; Act of Mar. 19, 1903, 28th Leg., R.S., ch. 42, 1903 Tex. Gen. Laws 59; Act of Apr. 15, 1905, 29th Leg., R.S., ch. 100, 1905 Tex. Gen. Laws 150; Act of Mar. 19, 1891, 22d Leg., R.S., ch. 22, 10 Gammel's 25; "the only law school in Texas": Although the Houston Law School was formed in 1912 as a "coaching school" to prepare students to take the bar examination, its founding as a law school is 1919 (see Mark E. Steiner, *The Secret History of Proprietary Legal Education: The Case of the Houston Law School, 1919–45*, 47 J. Legal Educ. 341, 343 (1997)).

4. Act of Jan. 26, 1839, Repub. Tex., 2 Gammel's 136; Act of May 12, 1846, 2 Gammel's 1551; Act of Apr. 18, 1873, 13th Leg., R.S., ch. 28, 7 Gammel's 491. Stephen K. Huber & James E. Myers, *Admission to the Practice of Law in Texas: An Analytical History*, 15 HLR 485 (1978), is a very helpful guide. An attack on the licensure and disciplinary systems in Texas is Leon Green, *The Courts' Power over Admission and Disbarment*, 4 TLR 1 (1925). A modest essay on the history of Texas bar admission is Ralph W. Yarborough, *A History of Law Licensing in Texas in* Centennial History of the Texas Bar, 1882–1982, at 181 (1981).

5. Rule 106, Rules for the District Court, 47 Tex. 615, 636 (1877); the same reading requirements were listed in Rule 71 of the Rules of the Supreme Court, 47 Tex. 597, 614 (1877).

6. "John Wesley Hardin," Roger Roots, *When Lawyers Were Serial Killers: Nineteenth Century Visions of Good Moral Character*, 22 N. Ill. U. L. Rev. 19 (2001); without the pardon Hardin was ineligible for admission to the bar (see Act of May 12, 1846, § 5, 1st Leg., R.S., 2 Gammel's 1551, 1552); "the examination," Huber & Myers, at 495 (citing Charles Coombes, The Prairie Dog Lawyer (1945)); admission to the bar in Dallas up to 1890, Berry H. Cobb, A History of Dallas Lawyers 16 (1933) (noting one case arising in 1870); "J. H. Williams," "first African American lawyer in Dallas," Darwin Payne, As Old as Dallas Itself: A History of the Lawyers of Dallas, the Dallas Bar Association, and the City They Helped Build 58, 56 (1999). On black lawyers in Galveston, see Maxwell Bloomfield, *From Deference to Confrontation: The Early Black Lawyers of Galveston, Texas, 1895–1920, in* The New High Priests: Lawyers in Post–Civil War America 154 (Gerard W. Gawalt ed., 1984).

7. Huber & Myers, at 509; Act of Mar. 19, 1903, 28th Leg., R.S., ch. 42, 1903 Tex. Gen. Laws 59; Act of Mar. 7, 1919, 36th Leg., R.S., ch. 38, 1919 Tex. Gen. Laws 63.

8. *Bar Section*, 10 TLR 324, 327–28 (1932); B. Eugene Gilbert, *Fitness for the Bar*, 12 TLR 453 (1934); Huber & Myers, at 513–15. On the national efforts in the 1930s to limit entry into the legal profession, see Michael Ariens, *American Legal Ethics in an Age of Anxiety*, 40 StMLJ 343, 410–20 (2008). On elimination of the diploma privilege, see Act of May 8, 1935, 44th Leg., R.S., ch. 176, 1935 Tex. Gen. Laws 438.

9. Multistate examinations, see Michael Ariens, *Law School Branding and the Future of Legal Education*, 34 StMLJ 301 (2003); *Rules Governing Admission to the Bar of Texas*, 1974, 1979, 1985, and 1995 editions.

10. Jackson v. State, 21 Tex. 668, 673 (1858).

11. Act of Jan. 26, 1839, § 5, 2 Gammel's 136, 137; Act of May 12, 1846, § 8, 1st Leg., 2 Gammel's 1551, 1553; Act of Feb. 11, 1854, 5th Leg., ch. 89, 3 Gammel's 1562; Act of Jan. 18, 1860, 8th Leg., ch. 24, 4 Gammel's 1385.

12. Dale Baum, Counterfeit Justice: The Judicial Odyssey of Texas Freedwoman Axeline Hearne, at 126–30 and chs. 7 & 8 (2009); Jason A. Gillmer, *Base Wretches and Black Wenches: A Story of Sex and Race, Violence and Compassion, during Slavery Times*, 59 Ala. L. Rev. 1501, 1550–52 (2008).

13. Act of Aug. 21, 1876, 15th Leg., R.S., ch. 135, 8 Gammel's 1063; Act of Apr. 10, 1901, ch. 57, 27th Leg., R.S., 1901 Tex. Gen. Laws 125.

14. McCloskey v. San Antonio Traction Co., 192 S.W. 1116 (Tex. Civ. App. 1917) (for more on McCloskey, see chapter 8); Act of Mar. 29, 1917, ch. 133, 35th Leg., R.S., 1917 Tex. Gen. Laws 336. See Penal Code 38.12, making barratry a felony, adopted in the aftermath of the Alton School Bus Tragedy and discussed in chapter 8.

15. 28 PTBA 47, 85 (1909) (adopting ABA Canons of Ethics); "overlooked," 42 PTBA 18 (1923); readoption of canons in 1926, 45 PTBA 193 (1926); readoption in 1939, TBJ, July 1938, at 191, and *Proposed Rules of Conduct for the State Bar of Texas*, TBJ, Nov. 1939, at 362, 369; State Bar Act, Act of Apr. 26, 1939, 46th Leg., R.S., ch. 1, § 4, 1939 Tex. Gen. Laws 64; *Bar Should Study Four Omitted Canons*, TBJ, Nov. 1940, at 304 (noting adoption by Texas Supreme Court of all but four ABA Canons of Ethics); Cullen Smith, *The Texas Canons of Ethics Revisited*, 18 BLR 183, 191 (1966).

16. Green, *The Courts' Power*; Houtchens v. State, 63 S.W.2d 1011 (Tex. Com. App. 1933); C. S. Potts, *Inadequacy of Disbarment Machinery: Houtchens v. State,* 12 TLR 127 (1934).

17. Act of May 31, 1933, 43d Leg., R.S., ch. 238, 1933 Tex. Gen. Laws 835; this statute was repealed in 1949, Act of May 19, 1949, 51st Leg., R.S., ch. 301, 1949 Tex. Gen. Laws 548; State Bar Act, § 3, 1939 Tex. Gen. Laws at 65. See generally *In re* Nolo Press/Folk Law, 991 S.W.2d 768 (Tex. 1999); Rodney Gilstrap & Leland C. de la Garza, *UPL: Unlicensed, Unwanted, and Unwelcome*, TBJ, Oct. 2004, at 798.

18. "Increased enforcement of discipline," Timothy W. Floyd, *How You Can Get into Trouble (and What Happens When You Do): Lawyer Disciplinary Procedures, in* A GUIDE TO THE BASICS OF LAW PRACTICE 171, 178 (3d ed., W. Frank Newton ed., 1996); *Commission for Lawyer Discipline Annual Report, June 1, 2006–May 31, 2007*, at 11 (2007). Thanks to Cory Squires of the Research and Analysis Department of the State Bar of Texas for providing the number of licensed Texas lawyers in the 1990s.

19. *Minimum Continuing Legal Education Rules: Supreme Court Orders Referendum*, TBJ, July 1985, at 768; *MCLE Referendum Passes*, TBJ, Jan. 1986, at 33; *Minimum Continuing Legal Education Rules and Regulations*, TBJ, Dec. 1986, at 1187. On certification in Texas, see www.tbls.org.

20. See Maxwell Bloomfield, *The Texas Bar in the Nineteenth Century*, 32 Vand. L. Rev. 261, 286 (1979) (Galveston); Payne, at 45 (Dallas); William B. Carssow, *Organization and Activity of the Texas Bar Association, in* CENTENNIAL HISTORY 1; Mark E. Steiner, *"If We Don't Do Anything But Have an Annual Dinner": The Early History of the Houston Bar Association*, 11 Hous. Rev. 95 (1989); Robert L. Dabney, Jr., *A Dugout Canoe, A Bottle Gourd of Whiskey, and the Pursuit of "Right": The Origins of the Houston Bar Association*, Hous. Law., Sept.–Oct. 1999, at 46; Julia A. Woods, Ashley Craddock, and Regan Marie Brown, AUSTIN LAWYERS: A LEGACY OF LEADERSHIP AND SERVICE 85 (2005). On the Association of the Bar of the City of New York, see George Martin, CAUSES AND CONFLICTS: THE CENTENNIAL HISTORY OF THE ASSOCIATION OF THE BAR OF THE CITY OF NEW YORK, 1870–1970, at 8 (1970). On the ABA, see John A. Matzko, *"The Best Men of the Bar": The Founding of the American Bar Association, in* NEW HIGH PRIESTS 75.

21. Bloomfield, *Texas Bar*, at 268–69 (noting just 315 members in a state with about 4,000 lawyers).

22. Payne, at 39; Bloomfield, *Texas Bar*, at 269–73. On Texas lawyers in the late nineteenth century through World War II, see J. F. Hulse, TEXAS LAWYER: THE LIFE OF WILLIAM H. BURGES (1982) (biography of a well-known El Paso lawyer); E. F. Smith, A SAGA OF TEXAS LAW (1940) (autobiography of a lawyer who eventually joined Baker & Botts); Thomas F. Turner, *Prairie Dog Lawyers*, 2 Panhandle-Plains Hist. Rev. 104, 111 (1929). On mythologizing the law and lawyers in the West, see Maxwell Bloomfield, *Western Lawyers and Judges: Image and Reality*, 24 J. West 15 (1985). On the nature of law practice in Mexican Texas, see THE DIARY OF WILLIAM BARRET TRAVIS: AUGUST 30, 1833–JUNE 26, 1834 (Robert E. Davis ed., 1966).

23. Bloomfield, *Texas Bar*, at 264, 267, 274–75; "263 Texans," Ralph A. Wooster, *Wealthy Texans, 1860*, 71 SWHQ 163 (1967), and "fifteen to twenty" at 164; John Anthony Moretta, WILLIAM PITT BALLINGER: TEXAS LAWYER, SOUTHERN STATESMAN, 1825–1888, at 96–97, 106–7 (2000); "7 were lawyers," Ralph A. Wooster, *Wealthy Texans, 1870*, 74 SWHQ 24, 29 (1970).

24. Bloomfield, *Texas Bar*, at 267, 274–75; Moretta, at 186–90. Ballinger also financially supported George Paschal's seminal work, *A Digest of Texas Laws*.

25. Kenneth J. Lipartito & Joseph A. Pratt, BAKER & BOTTS IN THE DEVELOPMENT OF MODERN HOUSTON, at 19, 21–22 (1991). On railroads and the southern legal profession, William Thomas, LAWYERING FOR THE RAILROAD: BUSINESS, LAW, AND POWER IN THE NEW SOUTH (1999).

26. "Bank," Harold M. Hyman, CRAFTSMANSHIP AND CHARACTER: A HISTORY OF THE VINSON & ELKINS LAW FIRM OF HOUSTON, 1917–1997, at 69–70 (1998), and "political heavyweights" at 106. On lobbying for Pure Oil, see Nicholas George Malavis, BLESS THE PURE AND HUMBLE: TEXAS LAWYERS AND OIL REGULATION, 1919–1936, at 65–74 (1996).

27. On Fulbright & Jaworski, see John H. Crooker, Jr., & Gibson Gayle, Jr., FULBRIGHT & JAWORSKI: 75 YEARS (1919–1994) (1994). Jaworski coauthored two unsatisfactory memoirs, Leon Jaworski with Mickey Herskowitz, CONFESSION AND AVOIDANCE (1979), and Leon Jaworski with Dick Schneider, CROSSROADS (1981).

28. "Alexis de Tocqueville,"*Money Talks: Why It Shouts to Some Lawyers and Whispers to Others*, Juris Doctor, Jan. 1972, at 54, 56; Griffin Smith, Jr., *Empires of Paper*, TM, Nov. 1973, at 53; Peter W. Bernstein, *Profit Pressures on the Big Law Firms*, Forbes, Apr. 19, 1982, at 84, 87; Peter Elkins, *The Hustlers*, TM, Nov. 1985, at 55, 268; Payne, at 272–74.

29. Dillon Anderson, THE BILLINGSLEY PAPERS

(1961). On Anderson, see Lipartito & Pratt, at 187, and Joyce Glover Lee, *Anderson, Dillon*, HOTO, www.tshaonline.org/handbook/online/articles/AA/fan31.html.

30. Wilbur L. Matthews, SAN ANTONIO LAWYER: MEMORANDA OF CASES AND CLIENTS 6 (1983); Paul Carrington, A DALLAS LAWYER FOR SIXTY YEARS (1979).

31. Smith, *Empires of Paper*, at 63; 1985 Texas salaries, Elkins, *The Hustlers*, at 150; 1986 Cravath increase, John R. Kramer, *Will Legal Education Remain Affordable, By Whom, and How?*, 1987 Duke L.J. 240, 248. On associate salaries at large law firms, see NALP Associate Salary Survey, an annual publication.

32. Gay Jervey, *Grumbling All the Way to the Bank*, The American Lawyer, July–Aug. 1989; Hyman, at 507–8.

33. *The Best-Paid Trial Lawyers*, Forbes, Oct. 16, 1989, at 204; Brigid McMenamin, *The Best Paid Lawyers*, Forbes, Nov. 6, 1995, at 145; Michael Freedman, *Judgment Day*, Forbes, May 14, 2001, at 132 (the two Texas lawyers were Jamail and Fred Baron).

34. The facts in this paragraph are taken from Betty Trapp Chapman, ROUGH ROAD TO JUSTICE: THE JOURNEY OF WOMEN LAWYERS IN TEXAS, at 9–10 and 27 nn.2, 8 (2008); "seventeen women," *id.* at 27 n.2; Bradwell v. Illinois, 83 U.S. 130 (1872); "thirty-four other states," Chapman, at 8 n.12, *citing* Virginia Drachman, SISTERS IN LAW, at 251–53 tbl. 1 (1998). Drachman listed Hortense Ward as the first female Texas lawyer in 1910, which would have made Texas the forty-first state to license a female lawyer. On Hortense Ward, see Barbara Bader Aldave, *Women in the Law in Texas: The Stories of Three Pioneers*, 25 StMLJ 289 (1993).

35. "Avoid the courtroom," Janelle D. Scott, *Hortense Sparks Ward*, HOTO, www.tshaonline.org/handbook/online/articles/WW/fwa83.html; Drachman, at 257 tbl. 10 & 259 tbl. 13.

36. Drachman, at 255 tbl. 5; "graduated" and "Association," Chapman, at 12.

37. Alice G. McAfee, *The All-Woman Texas Supreme Court: The History behind a Brief Moment on the Bench*, 39 StMLJ 467 (2008). Two other women initially appointed as special justices of the court, Nellie Gray Robertson and Edith E. Wilmans, later resigned because they did not meet the requirement that a supreme court justice have practiced law for seven years (*id.* at 473; Johnson v. Darr, 272 S.W. 1098 (Tex. 1925)).

38. National data, Richard L. Abel, AMERICAN LAWYERS 284 tbl. 26 & 285 tbl. 27 (1989); Texas data,

Nils Greger Olsson & Greg Hammond, *Annual Report on the Status of Women in the State Bar of Texas (2003–2004)*, www.texasbar.com/AM/Template.cfm?Section=Archives&Template=/CM/ContentDisplay.cfm&ContentID=11497; "By 1990," Elizabeth York Enstam, *Women and the Law*, HOTO, www.tshaonline.org/handbook/online/articles/WW/jsw2.html.

39. Southern Methodist University Ass'n of Women Law Students v. Wynne & Jaffe, 599 F.2d 707 (5th Cir. 1979); Payne, at 277; Hyman, at 394 (quoting Melinda Harmon).

40. Olsson & Hammond, at 4; "Dinkins," Hyman, at 399, and "substantially," at 546 (App. 13).

41. On Baylor, see Charles Alfred Mackenzie, A History of the Baylor University School of Law from the Lectures of Abner S. Lipscomb through the Deanship of Abner V. McCall (M.A. thesis, Baylor University 1988), and Nancy Newton with Frances Carrington, *Baylor School of Law*, in THE BENCH AND BAR OF WACO AND MCLENNAN COUNTY, 1849–1976, at 293 (Betty Ann McCartney McSwain ed., 1976); on Trinity, see Mark W. Lambert, *The Trinity University School of Law, 1873–1878, and the Jurisprudence of Texas*, Hous. Law., Nov.–Dec. 2003, at 34; on the origins of the University of Texas law department, see Hans W. Baade, *Law at Texas: The Roberts-Gould Era (1883–1893)*, 86 SWHQ 161 (1982); Steiner, *Secret History*, at 343. See generally W. Frank Newton & Nancy J. Sewell Newton, *Legal Education in Texas*, in CENTENNIAL HISTORY 161 (1981).

42. Baade, *Law at Texas*, at 166–67.

43. "Any size," see Ann Arnold, HISTORY OF FORT WORTH LEGAL COMMUNITY 21–23 & 34–43 (2000), which notes that Fort Worth University had a law school from 1893 until 1911, when the university closed, and that Texas Christian University opened a law department in 1915, which closed in 1920. Much has been written about Langdell's development of the Harvard system of legal education, including Robert Stevens, LAW SCHOOL chs. 3–4 (1983); Joel Seligman, THE HIGH CITADEL: THE INFLUENCE OF HARVARD LAW SCHOOL ch. 2 (1978); William P. LaPiana, LOGIC AND EXPERIENCE: THE ORIGIN OF MODERN AMERICAN LEGAL EDUCATION ch. 2 (1994); and Bruce A. Kimball, THE INCEPTION OF MODERN PROFESSIONAL EDUCATION: C. C. LANGDELL, 1826–1906, chs. 3–8 (2009). On law schools then, see Alfred Zantzinger Reed, TRAINING FOR THE PUBLIC PROFESSION OF THE LAW 442 tbl. 1 (1921).

44. Baylor reopened, see Mackenzie, at 22–28; Houston Law School, Steiner, *Secret History*; Jefferson School of Law and others in Dallas, Payne,

at 147–51; South Texas, Christopher Anglim, *South Texas College of Law: Houston's Gateway to Opportunity in Law*, 39 STLR 919 (1998); YMCA law schools, Dorothy E. Finnegan, *Raising and Leveling the Bar: Standards, Access, and the YMCA Evening Law Schools, 1890–1940*, 55 J. Legal Educ. 208 (2005). On the history of Texas Southern University School of Law, see Vonceil Jones, *Texas Southern University School of Law—The Beginning*, 4 Tex. S. U. L. Rev. 197 (1977), and Marguerite L. Butler, *The History of Texas Southern University, Thurgood Marshall School of Law: "The House that* Sweatt *Built,"* 23 T. Marshall L. Rev. 45 (1997).

45. On the Sweatt case, see Michael L. Gillette, *Blacks Challenge the White University*, 86 SWHQ 321 (1982). On Heman Sweatt, see Gary Lavergne, BEFORE BROWN: HEMAN MARION SWEATT, THURGOOD MARSHALL, AND THE LONG ROAD TO JUSTICE (2010); a list of secondary materials on Sweatt v. Painter is available at tarltonguides.law.utexas.edu/heman-sweatt.

46. "White primary," Smith v. Allwright, 321 U.S. 649 (1944); Sipuel v. Oklahoma State Board of Regents, 332 U.S. 631 (1948); in addition to Lavergne, see Richard Kluger, SIMPLE JUSTICE ch. 12 (1975) (titled "The Spurs of Texas Are Upon You"); Mark V. Tushnet, THE NAACP'S LEGAL STRATEGY AGAINST SEGREGATED EDUCATION, 1925–1950, ch. 8 (1987); Mark V. Tushnet, MAKING CIVIL RIGHTS LAW, ch. 9 (1994); Michael J. Klarman, FROM JIM CROW TO CIVIL RIGHTS 204–12 (2004). See also Michael J. Gillette, *Heman Marion Sweatt: Civil Rights Plaintiff*, in BLACK LEADERS: TEXANS FOR THEIR TIMES 161 (Alwyn Barr & Robert Calvert eds., 1981); Gillette, *Blacks Challenge*.

47. The initial timeline and events of Sweatt v. Painter are recounted in the opinion of the court of civil appeals, 210 S.W.2d 442 (Tex. Civ. App. 1948). The Greenhill quote is from 2 A TEXAS SUPREME COURT TRILOGY: ORAL HISTORY INTERVIEW WITH THE HONORABLE JOE R. GREENHILL, JR. 16 (1998); Greenhill also noted that he believed it was a "very fair trial."

48. One thousand students and nineteen faculty, Gillette, *Blacks Challenge*, at 330. The Texas Court of Civil Appeals and the State of Texas suggested the law school consisted of 850 students, sixteen full-time professors, and three part-time professors.

49. Sweatt, 210 S.W.2d at 445; Plessy v. Ferguson, 163 U.S. 537 (1896); Sweatt v. Painter, 339 U.S. 629, 634 (1950).

50. Henderson v. United States, 339 U.S. 816 (1950); McLaurin v. Oklahoma State Regents for Higher Education, 339 U.S. 637 (1950); Brief for United States at 9 (summary of argument), Henderson v. United States; quotes, Sweatt, at 633–34.

51. Butler, at 52; Gillette, *Blacks Challenge*, at 344.

52. "483 lawyers," Hyman, at 541 (Appendix 7); Crooker & Gayle; Smith, *Empires of Paper*, at 53.

53. On rankings, see U.S. News & World Report, ANNUAL GUIDE TO LAW SCHOOLS (annual publication); Richard Abel, AMERICAN LAWYERS, at 60 (selectivity) and 61 (attrition); "significantly" exceeded number of seats, Hopwood v. Texas, 861 F. Supp. 2d 551, 557 (W.D. Tex. 1994).

54. The scholarship on affirmative action is massive. One excellent summary is Terry H. Anderson, THE PURSUIT OF HAPPINESS: A HISTORY OF AFFIRMATIVE ACTION (2004). Much of the following general information is taken from my self-published constitutional law book, Michael Ariens, 2 AMERICAN CONSTITUTIONAL LAW AND HISTORY (annually published).

55. DeFunis v. Odegaard, 82 Wash.2d 11, 507 P.2d 1169 (1973), *dismissed as moot*, 416 U.S. 312 (1974).

56. Bakke v. Regents of the University of California, 438 U.S. 265 (1978); see also Howard Ball, THE BAKKE CASE: RACE, EDUCATION, AND AFFIRMATIVE ACTION (2000).

57. Hopwood v. Texas, 78 F.3d 932, 936 (5th Cir.), *cert. denied*, 518 U.S. 1033 (1996).

58. Grutter v. Bollinger, 539 U.S. 244 (2003); on changes in minority enrollment at the University of Texas School of Law, see tarltonguides.law.utexas.edu/content.php?pid=98968&sid=742812.

59. Marvin E. Schultz, For the Better Administration of Justice: The Legal Culture of Texas, 1820–1836 (Ph.D. diss., Texas Christian University, 1994); Clarence Wharton, *Early Judicial History of Texas*, 12 TLR 311 (1934); Chris Klemme, *Jacksonian Justice: The Evolution of the Elective Judiciary in Texas, 1836–1850*, 105 SWHQ 429 (2002).

60. Act of Dec. 22, 1836, § 1, Repub. Tex., 1 Gammel's 1258 (1898) (establishing four district courts); Act of Dec. 15, 1836, Repub. Tex., 1 Gammel's 1139 (1898) (establishing jurisdiction of supreme court).

61. James W. Paulsen, *A Short History of the Supreme Court of the Republic of Texas*, 65 TLR 237 (1986); James W. Paulsen, *The Judges of the Supreme Court of the Republic of Texas*, 65 TLR 305, 307 (1986) (listing four chief justices and twenty-four associate judges); Act of May 24, 1838, Repub. Tex., 1 Gammel's 1500 (creating fifth judicial district).

62. Tex. Const. Art. IV (1845).

63. Quote, Klemme, at 437; Susan G. Douglass, Note, *Selection and Discipline of State Judges in*

Texas, 14 HLR 672 (1977); Lance A. Cooper, *An Historical Overview of Judicial Selection in Texas*, 2 Tex. Wesleyan L. Rev. 317 (1995); J. H. Davenport, THE HISTORY OF THE SUPREME COURT OF THE STATE OF TEXAS (1917).

64. Klemme, at 445. Klemme notes that 59 percent of all eligible voters (26,760) voted in favor of the amendment (*id.* at 446).

65. "Totaled 1,600," S. S. McKay, DEBATES IN THE TEXAS CONSTITUTIONAL CONVENTION OF 1875, at 379, 422 (1930) (quoting delegate Jacob Waelder); D. W. Ogletree, *Establishing the Texas Court of Appeals, 1875–1876*, 47 SWHQ 5, 9 (1943); see also Deborah D. Powers, THE COURT OF APPEALS AT AUSTIN, 1892–1992, at 2 (1992); *Overruled Their Judicial Superiors*, 21 Am. L. Rev. 610 (1887); *Ex parte* Asher, 5 S.W. 91 (Tex. App. 1887), purporting to overrule, Robbins v. Taxing Dist., 120 U.S. 489 (1887); "guity," Harwell v. State, 2 S.W. 606 (Tex. App. 1886), following Taylor v. State, 5 Tex. App. 569 (Tex. App. 1879); Shaw v. State, 2 Tex. App. 487 (Tex. App. 1877) (holding verdict stating "We, the jury, the defendant guilty" reversible error due to the absence of word "find"); "guilly," Partain v. State, 2 S.W. 854 (Tex. App. 1886); Curry v. State, 7 Tex. App. 91 (Tex. App. 1879); Walker v. State, 13 Tex. App. 618 (Tex. App. 1883) (affirming verdict stating "Wee the jurors finde the defendant gilty and of *mrder* in the first degree" by concluding "mrder" is "murder").

66. Act of July 9, 1879, 16th Leg., Spec. S., ch. 34, 9 Gammel's 62 (creating commission of appeals); Act of Feb. 9, 1881, 17th Leg., R.S., ch. 7, 9 Gammel's 96 (amending 1879 act); Act of Mar. 20, 1883, 18th Leg., R.S., ch. 36, 9 Gammel's 331 (extending life of commission); Act of Mar. 30, 1887, 20th Leg., R.S., ch. 95, 9 Gammel's 872 (recreating commission); Act of Mar. 26, 1889, 21st Leg., R.S., ch. 55, 9 Gammel's 1077 (extending life of commission); Acts of Apr. 13, 1892, 22d Leg., 1st C.S., chs. 14, 15, 16, 10 Gammel's 383 *et seq.* (organizing the supreme court, court of civil appeals, and court of criminal appeals); Henderson v. Beaton, 52 Tex. 29 (1879) (holding act creating commission constitutional because it was not a court but a board of arbitrators).

67. Michael Ariens, *The Storm between the Quiet: Tumult in the Texas Supreme Court, 1911–1921*, 38 StMLJ 641 (2007); James T. Worthen, *The Organizational and Structural Development of Intermediate Appellate Courts in Texas, 1892–2003*, 46 STLR 33, 35 (2004) (noting when courts of civil appeals created); history of Texas appellate courts, Robert W. Higgason, *A History of Texas Appellate Courts: Preserving Rights of Appeal through Adaptations to Growth (Part I)*, Hous. Law., Mar.–Apr. 2002, at 20, and *(Part II)*, July–Aug. 2002, at 12; Leila Clark Wynn, *A History of the Civil Courts in Texas*, 60 SWHQ 1 (1956); Ogletree, *Establishing*.

68. Ariens, *Storm*; Act of Apr. 3, 1918, 35th Leg., 4th C.S., ch. 81, 1918 Tex. Gen. Laws 171 (creating the Texas Commission of Appeals); vote totals, S. D. Myres, Jr., *Mysticism, Realism, and the Texas Constitution of 1876*, 9 Sw. Pol. & Soc. Sci. Q. 166, 167 n.2 (1928).

69. On the failed 1927 amendment, see Sen. Jt. Res. No. 24, 40th Leg., R.S., 1927 Tex. Gen. Laws 468.

70. On increasing membership in the Texas Supreme Court to nine, see Sen. Jt. Res. No. 8, 49th Leg., R.S., 1945 Tex. Gen. Laws 1043.

71. Act of Mar. 19, 1925, 39th Leg., R.S., ch. 95, 1925 Tex. Gen. Laws 269; 1966 amendment, Sen. Jt. Res. No. 26, § 1, 59th Leg., R.S., 1965 Tex. Gen. Laws 2200; 1977 amendment, Sen. Jt. Res. No. 18, 1977 Tex. Gen. Laws 3359; expanding membership of the Court of Criminal Appeals and granting criminal appellate jurisdiction to the renamed Court of Appeals, 1981 Tex. Gen. Laws 4229 (reprinting adopted 1980 constitutional amendment); Carl E. F. Dally & Patricia A. Brockway, *Changes in Appellate Review in Criminal Cases following the 1980 Constitutional Amendment*, 13 StMLJ 211 (1981); Joe R. Greenhill, *The Constitutional Amendment Giving Criminal Jurisdiction to the Texas Courts of Appeals and Recognizing the Inherent Power of the Texas Supreme Court*, 33 TTLR 377 (2002).

72. Tex. Const. Art. IV, § 7 (1845); Tex. Const. Art. IV, § 2 (1866); Tex. Const. Art. V, § 13 (1869); Tex. Const. Art. V, § 2 (1876); Tex. Const. Art. V, § 2 (amended 1891); McKay, DEBATES, at 442 (quoting William Pitt Ballinger); Act of Apr. 7, 1913, 33d Leg., R.S. ch. 155, § 1, 1913 Tex. Gen. Laws 329 (raising salary to five thousand dollars).

73. John C. Townes, *Sketch of the Development of the Judicial System in Texas (Part I)*, 2 Q. Tex. St. Hist. Ass'n 29 (1898), and *(Part II)*, at 134; Koenig v. State, 26 S.W. 835 (Tex. Crim. App. 1894); State v. Austin Club, 33 S.W. 113 (Tex. 1895); *Ex parte* Lewis, 73 S.W. 811 (Tex. Crim. App. 1903); Brown v. City of Galveston, 75 S.W. 488 (1903); *Ex parte* Mitchell, 109 Tex. 11, 177 S.W. 953 (Tex. 1915) (holding act unconstitutional); *Ex parte* Francis, 165 S.W. 147 (Tex. Crim. App. 1914); *Ex parte* Mode, 180 S.W. 708 (Tex. Crim. App. 1915); State *ex rel.* McNamara v. Clark, 187 S.W. 760 (Tex. Crim. App. 1915) (holding law constitutional); Lyle v. State, 193 S.W. 680 (Tex. Crim. App. 1917).

74. Leon Green, *Suggestions for Improving Court Procedure in Texas*, 2 TLR 464, 466, 467 (1924).

75. "Resignation and appointment," Bancroft C. Henderson & T. C. Sinclair, *The Selection of Judges in Texas*, 5 HLR 430, 441 (1968); Bancroft C. Henderson & T. C. Sinclair, THE SELECTION OF JUDGES IN TEXAS: AN EXPLORATORY STUDY (1964); Anthony Champagne, *The Selection and Retention of Judges in Texas*, 40 SwLJ 53, 66 (1986) (updating the work of Henderson & Sinclair). On Gould and Walker, see Ariens, *Storm*, at 658 n.100. On the Terrell election laws of 1903 and 1905, see O. Douglas Weeks, *The Texas Direct Primary System*, 13 Sw. Soc. Sci. Q. 95 (1932).

76. Henderson & Sinclair, *Selection of Judges*.

77. Anthony Champagne, *Judicial Reform in Texas*, 72 Judicature 146 (Oct.–Nov. 1988); Champagne, *Judicial Selection*, at 67; Anthony Champagne, *Coming to a Judicial Election Near You: The New Era in Texas Judicial Elections*, 43 STLR 9, 26–27 (2001).

78. "Always disqualify," Henderson & Sinclair, *Selection of Judges*, at 467–68; 1978 to 1984 elections, Champagne, *Judicial Selection*, at 67–71.

79. On Ray and Kilgarlin, see Orrin W. Johnson & Laura Johnson Urbis, *Judicial Selection in Texas: A Gathering Storm?*, 23 TTLR 525, 540–41 & nn.81–83 (1992); "Las Vegas," Champagne, *New Era*, at 11.

80. On the history of the term "judicial activism," see Keenan D. Kmiec, *The Origin and Current Meanings of "Judicial Activism,"* 92 Cal. L. Rev. 1441 (2004). A conservative attack on the Texas Supreme Court is Robert D'Agostino, *The Decline of the Law in Texas*, 2 Benchmark 171 (1986). On changes in Texas tort law, see chapter 8, and J. Caleb Rackley, *A Survey of Sea-Change on the Supreme Court of Texas and Its Turbulent Toll on Texas Tort Law*, 48 STLR 733 (2007). On the Texaco-Pennzoil case, see chapter 8, and John Petzinger, OIL AND HONOR: THE TEXACO-PENNZOIL WARS (1987), and Texaco, Inc. v. Pennzoil Co., 729 S.W.2d 768, 833–34 (Tex. App. 1987), *cert. dism'd*, 485 U.S. 994 (1988).

81. Stephen J. Adler, *The Texas Bench: Anything Goes*, Am. Lawyer, Apr. 1986, at 11; Ken Case, *Blind Justice*, TM, May 1987, at 137; Paul Burka, *Heads, We Win, Tails, You Lose: How a Group of Trial Lawyers Took Over the Texas Supreme Court and Rewrote State Law*, TM, May 1987, at 138; William P. Barrett, *The Best Justice Money Can Buy*, Forbes, June 1, 1987, at 122; Sheila Kaplan, *What Price Justice? Oh, About $10,000*, Wash. Post, May 17, 1987, at C4; *60 Minutes: Justice for Sale?* (CBS television broadcast Dec. 6, 1987); Richard Woodbury, *Is Texas Justice for Sale?* Time, Jan. 11, 1988, at 74.

82. Champagne, *Selection and Retention*; Anthony Champagne, *Judicial Reform in Texas*, in JUDICIAL POLITICS IN TEXAS (Anthony Champagne & Kyle Cheek eds., 2005); Johnson & Johnson Urbis, *Judicial Selection in Texas*; Paul D. Carrington, *Big Money in Texas Judicial Elections: The Sickness and Its Remedies*, 53 SMU L. Rev. 263 (2000).

83. Phillips-Robertson race, Kyle D. Cheek & Anthony Champagne, *Partisan Judicial Elections: Lessons from a Bellwether State*, 39 Willamette L. Rev. 1357, 1359 (2003); "just under $11 million," Anthony Champagne & Kyle Cheek, *The Cycle of Judicial Elections*, 29 Fordham Urban L.J. 907, 914 (2002); Texans for Public Justice, Checks and Imbalances: How Texas Court Justices Raised $11 Million (2000), www.tpj.org/reports/checks/toc.html; Phillips-Mauzy campaign amounts, see Janet Elliott, *There's Joy in Mudville over Battle of the Giants*, Tex. Law., Nov. 5, 1990, at 5.

84. *60 Minutes: Justice for Sale?*; Mary Flood, *Justice Still for Sale? Clock is Ticking on the Answer*, WSJ, June 24, 1998, at T1; Janet Elliott, *"60 Minutes" Visit Finds Court's Defenders in Hiding*, Tex. Law., Aug. 24, 1998, at 1.

85. On Dallas County, see W. Wendell Hall & Mark Emery, *The Texas Hold Out: Trends in the Review of Civil and Criminal Jury Verdicts*, 49 STLR 539, 549 & nn.49–50 (2008); on Harris County, see Nathan Koppel, *Democrats in Houston Take Aim at GOP Judges*, WSJ, Nov. 1–2, 2008, at A5.

CHAPTER 7

1. Quote, Nelson Phillips, *Historical Introduction*, in 1 Tex. Jur. xxvii, xlix (1929). See also William Ransom Hogan, *Rampant Individualism in the Republic of Texas*, 44 SWHQ 454 (1941) (discussing "pronounced individualism" that "marked Texas as a region apart"). On violence, see Richard E. Nisbett & Dov Cohen, CULTURE OF HONOR: THE PSYCHOLOGY OF VIOLENCE IN THE SOUTH (1996); William D. Carrigan, THE MAKING OF A LYNCHING CULTURE: VIOLENCE AND VIGILANTISM IN CENTRAL TEXAS, 1836–1916 (2004); Richard Maxwell Brown, STRAIN OF VIOLENCE ch. 8 (1975); W. C. Holden, *Law and Lawlessness on the Texas Frontier, 1875–1890*, 44 SWHQ 188 (1940); Bill O'Neal, *Violence in Texas History*, in TEXAS: A SESQUICENTENNIAL CELEBRATION 353 (1984); and Bill Neal, GETTING AWAY WITH MURDER ON THE TEXAS FRONTIER: NOTORIOUS KILLINGS AND CELEBRATED TRIALS (2006).

2. Julius Goebel, Jr., ANTECEDENTS AND BEGINNINGS TO 1801, at 608–51 (1971); George Lee Haskins & Herbert A. Johnson, FOUNDATIONS OF POWER:

JOHN MARSHALL, 1801–15, at 633–46 (1981); Peter S. du Ponceau, *Penal Code of the French Empire*, 2 Am. Rev. of Hist. & Pol. app. 1 (1811), *cited in* Charles M. Cook, THE AMERICAN CODIFICATION MOVEMENT: A STUDY OF ANTEBELLUM LEGAL REFORM 92 (1981). On Bentham and codification, see "LEGISLATOR OF THE WORLD": WRITINGS ON CODIFICATION, LAW, AND EDUCATION: THE COLLECTED WORKS OF JEREMY BENTHAM (Philip Schofield & Jonathan Harris eds., 1998); A. E. Wilkinson, *Edward Livingston and the Penal Codes*, 1 TLR 25 (1922); Tex. Penal Code § 1.03 (a).

3. Act of Dec. 21, 1836, 1st Cong., Repub. Tex., § 54, 1 Gammel's 1247, 1255; Act of Feb. 9, 1854, 5th Leg., R.S., ch. 49, § 58, 3 Gammel's 1502, 1512 (adopting similar provision).

4. Tex. Penal Code Art. 3 (Galveston News Office 1857); Fennell v. State, 32 Tex. 378 (1869); Act of Feb. 11, 1860, 8th Leg., ch. 74, 4 Gammel's 1457, 1459; Act of Feb. 12, 1858, 7th Leg., ch. 121, 4 Gammel's 1028; 1879 amendment to Article 3, Keith Carter, *The Texas Court of Criminal Appeals (Part II)*, 11 TLR 185, 187 (1933); Robinson v. State, 11 Tex. App. 309 (1881) (noting amendment).

5. See Stephen F. Austin, ESTABLISHING AUSTIN'S COLONY: THE FIRST BOOK PRINTED IN TEXAS WITH THE LAWS, ORDERS AND CONTRACTS OF COLONIZATION 84–89 (David B. Gracy II ed., 1970), and Guy M. Bryan, *Official Documents, Laws, Decrees, and Regulations Pertaining to Austin's Colonies*, *in* 1 A COMPREHENSIVE HISTORY OF TEXAS 481–92 (2 vols., Dudley G. Wooten ed., 1898, repr. 1986); Joseph W. McKnight, *Stephen Austin's Legalistic Concerns*, 89 SWHQ 239 (1986).

6. Art. 192, Const. Coahuila and Texas (1827), 1 Gammel's 44.

7. Decree 277, 1 Gammel's 364; "never operative," Charles T. McCormick, *The Revival of the Pioneer Spirit in Texas Procedure*, 18 TLR 426, 430 (1940). On the proposed military trial of Travis and others, see Randolph B. Campbell, GONE TO TEXAS: A HISTORY OF THE LONE STAR STATE 129 (2003).

8. Tex. Const. Gen. Prov. § 7 (1836), 1 Gammel's 1079; An Act Punishing Crimes and Misdemeanors, Act of Dec. 21, 1836, § 54, 1st Cong., Repub. Tex., 1 Gammel's 1247, 1255. On the "absence of any Texas prison," see Herman Lee Crow, A Political History of the Texas Penal System, 1829–1951, at 21 (Ph. D. diss., University of Texas 1964).

9. Act of Mar. 20, 1848, 2d Leg., ch. 152, 3 Gammel's 219; Art. 7, § 14 of the 1845 Tex. Const., 2 Gammel's 1293 (building penitentiary); Act of May 11, 1846, 1st Leg., 2 Gammel's 1527; Act of Mar. 13, 1848, 2d Leg., ch. 80, 3 Gammel's 79; "first inmate," Robert Perkinson, TEXAS TOUGH: THE RISE OF AMERICA'S PRISON EMPIRE 76 (2010).

10. Act of Feb. 10, 1854, 5th Leg., ch. 55, 3 Gammel's 1520; Tex. Penal Code (Galveston News Office 1857); Wilkinson, *Edward Livingston*.

11. Tex. Penal Code at Art. 158 ("humanity"); *id.* at Art. 41 ("insanity"); *id.* at Art. 47 ("mistake of fact"); *id.* at Art. 37 (under 17); *id.* at Art. 36 (under 9 and between 9 and 13).

12. Act of Feb. 12, 1858, 7th Leg., ch. 121, 4 Gammel's 1028; Act of Feb. 11, 1860, 8th Leg., ch. 74, 4 Gammel's 1457.

13. Robert W. Stayton, *Texas' Approaches to the Parker Ideal and Her Shortcomings*, 37 TLR 845, 847 (1959).

14. *Overruled Their Judicial Superiors*, 21 Am. L. Rev. 610 (1887). On vigilance committees and lawlessness at that time, see David M. Horton & Ryan Kellus Turner, LONE STAR JUSTICE: A COMPREHENSIVE OVERVIEW OF THE TEXAS CRIMINAL JUSTICE SYSTEM 15–27 (1999).

15. Shaw v. State, 2 Tex. App. 487 (1877); Taylor v. State, 5 Tex. App. 569 (1879) ("guity"), *distinguishing* Koontz v. State, 41 Tex. 570 (1874) ("gilty"); Curry v. State, 7 Tex. App. 91 (1879) ("guily").

16. Walker v. State, 13 Tex. App. 618 (1883); Wilson v. State, 12 Tex. App. 481 (1882) ("guity"); Harwell v. State, 2 S.W. 606 (Tex. App. 1886) ("guity"); Partain v. State, 2 S.W. 854 (Tex. App. 1886) ("guilly").

17. Goode v. State, 2 Tex. App. 520 (Tex. App. 1877); Henry v. State, 7 Tex. App. 388 (Tex. App. 1879).

18. Tex. Const. Declaration of Rights Art. 6 (1836); Tex. Const. Art. 1, § 8 (1845); Tex. Const. Declaration of Rights Art. 1, § 10 (1876) and Art. V, § 12 (taken from Tex. Const. Art. IV, § 4 (1836) and Tex. Const. Art. IV, § 9 (1845)); Code Crim. Proc. Art. 395 (Galveston News Office 1857).

19. Cox v. State, 8 Tex. App. 254 (1880); Saine v. State, 14 Tex. App. 144 (1883); Thompson v. State, 15 Tex. App. 39 (1883) Haun v. State, 13 Tex. App. 383 (1883).

20. Webster v. State, 9 Tex. App. 75 (1880) ("The particular felony or theft intended to be committed must be described with all its statutory ingredients."); Reed v. State, 14 Tex. App. 662 (1883) (emphasis in the original); Taylor v. State, 5 S.W. 141 (Tex. App. 1887) (emphasis added).

21. Act of Mar. 26, 1881, 17th Leg., R.S., ch. 57, 9 Gammel's 155; Arnold v. State, 11 Tex. App. 472 (1882).

22. Arnold v. State, 11 Tex. App. 472 (1882) (holding the act permissible but reversing because it

was not in effect when the indictment was issued); White v. State, 11 Tex. App. 476 (1882) (approving the indictment based on the act but reversing on another ground); Williams v. State, 12 Tex. App. 395 (1882) (holding the act unconstitutional); Rodriguez v. State, 12 Tex. App. 552 (1882) (same); Huntsman v. State, 12 Tex. App. 619 (1882) (same). On the 1985 changes, see Gerald S. Reamey, *Charging Instruments*, in Gerald S. Reamey & Walter W. Steele, Jr., TEXAS CRIMINAL PROCEDURE (2d ed. 1991).

23. "Visigoths and Roman civil law" and "Las Siete Partidas," Mark M. Carroll, HOMESTEADS UNGOVERNABLE: FAMILIES, SEX, RACE, AND THE LAW IN FRONTIER TEXAS, 1841–1860, at 209 n.52 (2001); "English common law," C. S. Potts, *Is Husband's Act in Killing Wife Taken in Act of Adultery Justifiable Homicide in Texas?*, 2 TLR 111, at 111 n.3 (1923) (quoting William Blackstone, 4 COMMENTARIES ON THE LAW 135); George Wilfred Stumberg, *Defense of Person and Property under Texas Criminal Law*, 21 TLR 17 (1942); William M. Ravkind, Comment, *Justifiable Homicide in Texas*, 13 SwLJ 508 (1959); Jeremy D. Weinstein, Note, *Adultery, Law, and the State: A History*, 38 Hastings L.J. 195 (1986); Paul Kens, *Don't Mess Around in Texas: Adultery and Justifiable Homicide in the Lone Star State*, in LAW IN THE WESTERN UNITED STATES 114 (Gordon Morris Bakken ed., 2000); Bill Neal, SEX, MURDER, AND THE UNWRITTEN LAW: GENDER AND JUDICIAL MAYHEM, TEXAS STYLE (2009).

24. Carroll, at 152; Barr v. State, 172 S.W.2d 322 (Tex. Crim. App. 1943).

25. State v. Price, 18 Tex. App. 474 (1885).

26. Morrison v. State, 47 S.W. 369 (Tex. Crim. App. 1898).

27. Meyers v. State, 46 S.W. 817 (Tex. Crim. App. 1898); Gaines v. State, 148 S.W. 717 (Tex. Crim. App. 1912).

28. Williams v. State, 165 S.W. 583 (Tex. Crim. App. 1914); Cook v. State, 180 S.W. 254 (Tex. Crim. App. 1915); R. C. W., *Homicide-Justification-Cook v. State*, 180 S. W. (Tex.) 254, 25 Yale L.J. 678 (1916) (noting case).

29. Holman v. State, 243 S.W. 1093 (Tex. Crim. App. 1922); Sensobaugh v. State, 244 S.W. 379 (Tex. Crim. App. 1922); Billings v. State, 27 S.W. 687 (Tex. Crim. App. 1925) (overruling Williams and Cook); Jimenez v. State, 280 S.W. 829 (Tex. Crim. App. 1925) (same); Jordan v. State, 294 S.W. 1109 (Tex. Crim. App. 1927) (same); Steadman v. State, 43 S.W.2d 944 (Tex. Crim. App. 1931) (same); Burton v. State, 86 S.W.2d 768 (Tex. Crim. App. 1935) (affirming conviction); Zimmerman v. State, 51 S.W.2d 327 (Tex.

Crim. App. 1932) (same); Ryan v. State, 55 S.W.2d 829 (Tex. Crim. App. 1932) (same); McFarland v. State, 196 S.W.2d 829 (Tex. Crim. App. 1946); Halbert v. State, 137 S.W.2d 1010 (Tex. Crim. App. 1940); "1969 Houston," Henry P. Lundsgaarde, MURDER IN SPACE CITY 106–9 (1977).

30. Shaw v. State, 510 S.W.2d 926 (Tex. Crim. App. 1974).

31. *Overruled Their Judicial Superiors*, 21 Am. L. Rev. 610 (1887); "became notorious," Campbell, at 304, and census numbers at 290.

32. "61 of 171 appeals," Lawrence Friedman, CRIME AND PUNISHMENT IN AMERICAN HISTORY 257 (1993); 1900 through 1927 data, Keith Carter, *The Texas Court of Criminal Appeals (Part II)*, 11 TLR 185, 191 tbl. A (1933). Carter's four-part series on the Texas Court of Criminal Appeals, found at 11 TLR 1 at 1 *(Part I)*, at 185 *(Part II)*, at 301 *(Part III)*, and at 455 *(Part IV)*, is an excellent study.

33. On the history of the law of evidence and the sporting contest theory of the trial, see Michael Ariens, *Progress Is Our Only Product: Legal Reform and the Codification of Evidence*, 17 Law & Soc. Inq. 213, 219–26 (1992); Roscoe Pound, *The Causes of Popular Dissatisfaction in the Administration of Justice*, 29 A.B.A. Rep. 395 (1906).

34. John Davenport, Comment, *Twenty Years of Homicide in Texas*, 25 TLR 634 (1947); Charles B. McGregor, *Homicide Charge in Texas*, 6 BLR 40 (1953); "death penalty cases from 1923–1971," James W. Marquart, Sheldon Ekland-Olson, & Jonathan R. Sorenson, THE ROPE, THE NEEDLE, AND THE CHAIR 96 (1994); A. R. Stout, *Criminal Procedure in Texas Should Be Revised: An Address*, 25 TLR 613, 622 (1947). Stout noted that of the 174 written opinions published in 147 Texas Criminal Reports, 17 affirmed cases presented "nothing" for review, leaving 70 reversals and 87 (rather than 104) affirmances.

35. Much of this data comes from the Annual Reports of the Texas Judicial Council, which began reporting criminal docket data in 1974; material before 1974 was collected by Ryan Cox, a research assistant, and all interpretations of these data are mine.

36. Indigent defendants did not constitutionally receive appellate counsel until Douglas v. California, 372 U.S. 353 (1963); "Booker T. Williams," Marquart, at 92–93.

37. State v. Foster, 31 Tex. 578 (1869); Penal Code Art. 337 (1879); Act of Feb. 12, 1858, 7th Leg., R.S., ch. 121, 4 Gammel's 1028, 1037; Act of Dec. 21, 1836, 1st Cong., Repub. Tex., § 23, 1 Gammel's 1247, 1250.

38. Richardson v. State, 37 Tex. 346 (1872); forni-

cation and adultery repealed in 1973, see Act of June 14, 1973, 63d Leg., R.S., ch. 399, § 3, 1973 Tex. Gen. Laws 883, 992.

39. Art. 396, Tex. Penal Code (1856); Act of Feb. 12, 1858, 7th Leg., R.S., ch. 121, 4 Gammel's 1028, 1037 (adding "or slaves" to Article 396 and increasing the fine in Article 398 from a maximum of one hundred dollars to between one hundred and five hundred dollars); Act of June 14, 1973, 63d Leg., ch. 399, 1973 Tex. Gen. Laws 883, 958–59 (making prostitution a crime).

40. Act of Feb. 9, 1854, 5th Leg., R.S., ch. 49, § 40, 3 Gammel's 1502, 1510; Act of Feb. 11, 1860, 8th Leg., R.S., ch. 74, 4 Gammel's 1457, 1459; Fennell v. State, 32 Tex. 378 (1869); *Ex parte* Bergen, 14 Tex. App. 52 (1883); Prindle v. State, 21 S.W. 360 (Tex. Crim. App. 1893).

41. Act of May 11, 1943, 48th Leg., R.S., ch. 112, § 1, 1943 Tex. Gen. Laws 194; Buchanan v. Batchelor, 308 F.Supp. 729 (N. D. Tex. 1970), *judgment vacated sub nom.* Wade v. Buchanan, 401 U.S. 989 (1971); Act of June 14, 1973, 63d Leg., R.S., ch. 399, 1973 Tex. Gen. Laws 883, 917; "unenforced," State v. Morales, 869 S.W.2d 941, 943 (Tex. 1994); "twice held," City of Dallas v. England, 846 S.W.2d 957 (Tex. App. 1993); Morales, 826 S.W.2d 201 (Tex. App. 1992), *rev'd on other grounds*, 869 S.W.2d 941 (Tex. 1994).

42. Lawrence v. Texas, 539 U.S. 559 (2004); Bowers v. Hardwick, 478 U.S. 186 (1986); Lawrence v. State, 41 S.W.3d 349 (Tex. App. 2001); James W. Paulsen, *The Significance of Lawrence v. Texas*, Hous. Law., Jan.–Feb. 2004, at 32.

43. Act of Mar. 23, 1905, 29th Leg., R.S., ch. 35, 1905 Tex. Gen. Laws 45 (criminalizing sale of cocaine and morphine); Uniform Narcotic Drug Act, Act of Apr. 16, 1937, 45th Leg., R.S., ch. 169, 1937 Tex. Gen. Laws 333; Texas Controlled Substances Act, Tex. Rev. Civ. Stats. art. 4476–15 (1974); John W. Sayer & Daniel L. Rotenberg, *Marijuana in Houston: A Second Report and a Proposal*, 8 HLR 209, 215 (1970); Johnson v. State, 447 S.W.2d 927 (Tex. Crim. App. 1969); Johnson v. Beto, 337 F.Supp. 1371 (S.D. Tex. 1972); John Schwartz, *Lee Otis, Free*, TM, Aug. 2002, at 46; Dick J. Reavis, *Why I Turned in Lee Otis Johnson*, TM, July 1980, at 107; quote, Griffin Smith, Jr., *How the New Drug Law was Made*, TM, Sept. 1973, at 67, 68; Charles P. Bubany, *The Texas Penal Code of 1974*, 28 SwLJ 292, 335, 339 (1974); Jones v. State, 502 S.W.2d 771 (Tex. Crim. App. 1974) (holding that a defendant charged with possession of two ounces before the act was adopted but tried on the date the act was effective cannot be charged with a felony).

44. Morton White, SOCIAL THOUGHT IN AMER-ICA: THE REVOLT AGAINST FORMALISM (1957); Jeter v. State, 82 S.W.2d 150 (Tex. Crim. App. 1935). On the challenge to formalism in law in the first decades of the twentieth century, see Neil Duxbury, PATTERNS OF AMERICAN JURISPRUDENCE ch. 1 (1995). On the court's switch in time, see Michael Ariens, *A Thrice-Told Tale, or Felix the Cat*, 107 Harv. L. Rev. 620 (1994).

45. Newsome v. State, 151 S.W.2d 225, 226 (Tex. Crim. App. 1941); Adams v. State, 163 S.W.2d 410, 411 (Tex. Crim. App. 1941) ("seller of pies").

46. Gragg v. State, 186 S.W.2d 243 (Tex. Crim. App. 1945); "because it does not," Stout, at 618. Gragg was reindicted, retried, and again convicted, and a divided Court of Criminal Appeals upheld the conviction (Gragg v. State, 214 S.W.2d 292 (Tex. Crim. App. 1948)).

47. Northern v. State, 203 S.W.2d 206 (Tex. Crim. App. 1947); no subsequent appellate opinion in the case is given.

48. Riley v. State, 379 S.W.2d 79 (Tex. Crim. App. 1964) (McDonald, J., concurring); Vaughn v. State, 607 S.W.2d 914 (Tex. Crim. App. 1980).

49. On attacks on legal formalism, see Edward A. Purcell, Jr., THE CRISIS OF DEMOCRATIC THEORY: SCIENTIFIC NATURALISM AND THE PROBLEM OF VALUE ch. 5 (1973); "the law is a ass," Charles Dickens, OLIVER TWIST ch. 51 (1970 ed.) (Mr. Bumble).

50. Robert W. Shook, *The Battle of the Nueces, August 10, 1862*, 66 SWHQ 31 (1962); Richard B. McCaslin, TAINTED BREEZE: THE GREAT HANGING AT GAINESVILLE, TEXAS, 1862 (1994); "468," Barr, BLACK TEXANS, at 43; "335," Marquart et al., at 5; "282," William D. Carrigan & Clive Webb, *Muerto por Unos Desconcidos (Killed by Persons Unknown): Mob Violence against Blacks and Mexicans, in* BEYOND BLACK AND WHITE: RACE, ETHNICITY, AND GENDER IN THE U.S. SOUTH AND SOUTHWEST 63 (Appendix B) (Stephanie Cole & Alison M. Parker eds., 2004); "at least 500," Lawrence Rice, THE NEGRO IN TEXAS, 1874–1900, at 250 (1971); "379," Ross, at 255. Ross is the author of the HOTO entry on lynching, in which he states that there were "468 victims in Texas between 1885 and 1942" of lynching (John Ross, *Lynching*, HOTO, www.tshaonline.org/handbook/online/articles/LL/jgl1.html). On the Bandit War of 1915, see Robert M. Utley, LONE STAR LAWMEN: THE SECOND CENTURY OF THE TEXAS RANGERS ch. 2 (2007), Charles H. Harris III & Louis R. Sadler, THE TEXAS RANGERS AND THE MEXICAN REVOLUTION: THE BLOODIEST DECADE, 1910–1920, chs. 9–10 (2004), and Rodolfo Rocha, The Influence of the Mexican Revolution on the Mexico-Texas

Border, 1910–1916, ch. 6 (Ph.D. diss., Texas Tech Univ. 1981); quote, Ross, at 134; Hogg quote, *Crime in Texas*, Illus. Amer., Sept. 26, 1891, at 244. On lynchings before the Civil War, see Thomas North, Five Years in Texas ch. 7 (1871); Philip Paxton (pseudonym of Samuel Hammett), A Stray Yankee in Texas (1853); Wayne Gard, Frontier Justice 199 (1949); John Raymond Ross, At the Bar of Judge Lynch: Lynching and Lynch Mobs in America (Ph.D Diss., Texas Tech Univ. 1983). A chronology on lynching in Texas is found in Horton & Turner, at 32–51; NAACP, Thirty Years of Lynching in the United States, 1889–1918 (1919, Arno Press repr. 1969) (collecting some data on lynchings). Brown, ch. 8, discusses violence and vigilantism in Texas between 1860 and 1900.

51. Smith lynching, *Another Negro Burned: Henry Smith Dies at the Stake*, N.Y. Times, Feb. 2, 1893, at 1; Rice, at 253; *Lynching in Texas*, 47 Alb. L.J. 141 (1893) (concluding "it is the worst crime ever committed in America, always excepting the Texarkana affair," which was the murder by lynching of Edward Coy in 1892); Jesse Washington lynching, James M. SoRelle, *The "Waco Horror": The Lynching of Jesse Washington*, 86 SWHQ 517 (1983), and Patricia Bernstein, The First Waco Horror: The Lynching of Jesse Washington and the Rise of the NAACP (2005); Carrigan, Lynching Culture; lynching of George Hughes, Edward Hake Phillips, *The Sherman Courthouse Riot of 1930*, 25 E. Tex. Hist. J. 12 (1987), and Arthur F. Raper, The Tragedy of Lynching ch. 16 (1933). Neither history of the Waco bar discusses the Waco Horror (William M. Sleeper & Allan D. Sanford, *Waco Bar and Incidents of Waco History* (1940) and Tony E. Duty, *Historical Incidents of the Waco Bar* in The Bench and Bar of Waco and McLennan County, 1849–1976, at 5 & 271 (Betty Ann McCartney McSwain ed., 1976)).

52. Act of June 19, 1897, 25th Leg., Spec. S., ch. 13, 10 Gammel's 1480; "following," Philip Dray, At the Hands of Persons Unknown: The Lynching of Black America 262 (2002); "lynching declined," Rice, at 254; McCasland and quote, Phillips, at 16. On the Humphries case, see *Horror in Henderson*, DMN, May 29, 1899, at 1; *Accept the Penalty*, DMN, Aug. 22, 1900, at 1; *Humphries Lynching Suits*, DMN, Sept. 29, 1899, at 1. Rice states incorrectly that "George" Humphries was a Negro.

53. Ross, At the Bar, at 151, citing James A. Burran, *Transforming a Tradition: "Streamlined" Lynching in the New South*, paper presented at the Citadel Conference on the South, Charleston, S.C., Apr. 19–21, 1979.

54. "755 persons," Death Penalty Information Center, Executions in the U.S., 1608–2002: The Espy File, www.deathpenaltyinfo.org/executions-us-1608–2002–espy-file; "447 persons," Texas Department of Criminal Justice, Executed Offenders, www.tdcj.state.tx.us/stat/executedoffenders.htm; Furman v. Georgia, 408 U.S. 238 (1972). No executions took place in Texas from 1965 through 1981.

55. Act of June 4, 1923, 38th Leg., 2d C.S., ch. 51, 1923 Tex. Gen. Laws 111; "reaction," Marquart, at 13.

56. Marquart, at 20 tbl. 2.1. I have calculated the percentages from the Espy Files organized by state.

57. The information in this paragraph is taken from Marquart, ch. 3.

58. Lacy v. State, 111 S.W.2d 264 (Tex. Crim. App. 1937); Lacy v. State, 128 S.W.2d 1165 (Tex. Crim. App.), *cert. denied*, 308 U.S. 551 (1939); Richardson v. State, 257 S.W.2d 308 (Tex. Crim. App. 1953); Richardson v. State, 266 S.W.2d 129 (Tex. Crim. App. 1953); White v. State, 117 S.W.2d 450 (Tex. Crim. App. 1938); White v. State, 128 S.W.2d 51 (Tex. Crim. App. 1939), *rev'd and remanded*, 309 U.S. 631 (1940). On White's coerced confession and his death, see Marquart, at 61–62.

59. Marquart, at 110–15; Rupert C. Koeninger, *Capital Punishment in Texas, 1924–1968*, 15 Crime & Delinquency 132 (1969).

60. Branch v. State, 447 S.W.2d 932 (Tex. Crim. App. 1969), *rev'd sub nom.* Furman v. Georgia, 408 U.S. 238 (1972).

61. Act of June 14, 1973, 63d Leg., R.S., ch. 426, 1973 Tex. Gen. Laws 1122; "crucial question," see Tex. Defender Service, Deadly Speculation: Misleading Texas Capital Juries with False Predictions of Future Dangerousness 46 n.217 (2004) (http://o2f2fd4.netsolhost.com/tds/images/publications/DEADLYSP.pdf). On the legislative history of future dangerousness, see Eric F. Citron, Note, *Sudden Death: The Legislative History of Future Dangerousness and the Texas Death Penalty*, 25 Yale L. & Pol'y Rev. 143 (2006).

62. Jurek v. Texas, 429 U.S. 875 (1976). A thorough review of the death penalty in Texas from the mid-1970s to 2000 is Guy Goldberg & Gena Bunn, *Balancing Fairness and Finality: A Comprehensive Review of the Texas Death Penalty*, 5 Tex. Rev. L. & Pol. 49 (2000); see also Andrea Keilen & Maurie Levin, *Moving Forward: A Map for Meaningful Habeas Reform in Texas Capital Cases*, 34 Am. J. Crim. L. 207 (2007). The legislature permitted the application of the death penalty in multiple murder cases after 1984 (Gary M. Lavergne, Worse Than

DEATH: THE DALLAS NIGHTCLUB MURDERS AND
THE TEXAS MULTIPLE MURDER LAW ch. 14 (2003)).

63. Estelle v. Smith, 451 U.S. 454 (1981); Smith v.
Estelle, 445 F.Supp. 647 (N.D. Tex. 1977), aff'd, 602
F.2d 694 (5th Cir. 1979). On the original appeal, see
Smith v. State, 540 S.W.2d 693 (Tex. Crim. App.
1976) (affirming conviction and sentence), cert.
denied, 430 U.S. 922 (1977).

64. Barefoot v. Estelle, 463 U.S. 880, 905 n.11
(1983). "Dr. Death" is used in the documentary
movie The Thin Blue Line (MGM 1988). On Grigson,
see Paul C. Giannelli, Ake v. Oklahoma: The Right
to Expert Assistance in a post-Daubert, post-DNA
World, 89 Cornell L. Rev. 1305, 1309–10 (2004); Ron
Rosenbaum, TRAVELS WITH DR. DEATH AND OTHER
UNUSUAL INVESTIGATIONS (1991); Bruce Vincent, A
Dearth of Work for "Dr. Death," Tex. Law., Dec. 4,
1995, at 4; DEADLY SPECULATION, at 16–19. As the
noted physicist Neils Bohr said, "Prediction is very
difficult, especially of the future," David I. C. Thomson, LAW SCHOOL 2.0 xii (2009).

65. Penry v. State, 691 S.W.2d 636 (Tex. Crim.
App. 1985), cert. denied, 474 U.S. 1073 (1986); Penry
v. Lynaugh, 832 F.2d 915 (5th Cir. 1986), rev'd and
remanded, 492 U.S. 302 (1989); Penry v. State, 903
S.W.2d 715 (Tex. Crim. App.), cert. denied, Penry v.
Johnson, 516 U.S. 977 (1995); Penry v. Johnson, 215
F.3d 504 (5th Cir. 2000), aff'd in part, rev'd in part,
and remanded, 532 U.S. 782 (2001); Penry v. State,
178 S.W.3d 782 (Tex. Crim. App. 2005), cert. denied,
547 U.S. 1200 (2006); Atkins v. Virginia, 536 U.S. 304
(2002).

66. Quote, Texas Defender Service, A STATE OF
DENIAL: TEXAS JUSTICE AND THE DEATH PENALTY
136 (2000); on Willingham's case, see David Grann,
Trial by Fire: Did Texas Execute an Innocent Man?,
New Yorker, Sept. 7, 2009, at 42, and the television
documentary Death by Fire (PBS television broadcast
Oct. 19, 2010); "twelve Texans," www.deathpenal-
tyinfo.org/innocence-and-death-penalty#inn-st;
Adams v. State, 577 S.W.2d 717 (Tex. Crim. App.
1979), aff'd, Adams v. Texas, 448 U.S. 38 (1980); Ex
parte Adams, 768 S.W.2d 281 (Tex. Crim. App. 1989)
(setting aside conviction); see Randall Adams et al.,
ADAMS V. STATE (1992); on Brandley, see Brandley
v. State, 691 S.W.2d 699 (Tex. Crim. App. 1985); Ex
parte Brandley, 781 S.W.2d 886 (Tex. Crim. App.
1989) (setting conviction aside); Nick Davies, WHITE
LIES: RAPE, MURDER, AND JUSTICE TEXAS STYLE
(1991); Cook v. State, 741 S.W.2d 928 (Tex. Crim.
App. 1987), vacated, 488 U.S. 807 (1988), rev'g conviction on rehearing, 821 S.W.2d 600 (Tex. Crim. App.
1991); Cook v. State, 940 S.W.2d 623 (Tex. Crim.

App. 1996) (setting aside conviction); Kerry Max
Cook, CHASING JUSTICE (2007). A book excoriating
the criminal justice system in Texas is Thomas Cahill,
A SAINT ON DEATH ROW: THE STORY OF DOMIN-
IQUE GREEN (2009).

67. Texas Code of Crim. Proc. Arts. 661–62 (1857)
(Article 663 barred the use of a confession by a slave
if made after "whipping or other chastisement");
Miranda v. Arizona, 384 U.S. 436 (1966); Cain v.
State, 18 Tex. 387 (1857); quote, Gay v. State, 2 Tex.
App. 127, 132 (1877) (quoting Simon Greenleaf, 1
EVIDENCE § 214 (1848)).

68. "Was unusual," Bram v. United States, 168
U.S. 532 (1897); Act of Apr. 16, 1907, 30th Leg., R.S.,
ch. 118, 13 Gammel's 229. The origins of the term
"third degree" are traced in Ernest Jerome Hopkins,
OUR LAWLESS POLICE: A STUDY OF THE UNLAWFUL
ENFORCEMENT OF THE LAW 191 (1931, repr. 1972).

69. Campbell Jury, Out More Than 30 Hours,
Dismissed, DMN, Sept. 11, 1921, at 5; Negro Claims
Klan Threat Forced His Confession, DMN, Oct. 12,
1921; Negro Is Given Death Penalty, DMN, Jan. 18,
1922, at 1; Officers Believe Negro's Alleged Confession False, DMN, Mar. 18, 1922, at 5; Try Officers on
Cruelty Charges, DMN, Feb. 2, 1922, at 9; "giving him
a needle," Hopkins, at 220; Witness Tells of "Electric
Monkey," DMN, Feb. 3, 1922, at 6; Charges against
Officers Dropped By Commissioners, DMN, Feb. 7,
1922; Bills in the House, DMN, Jan. 14, 1921, at 3; Act
of Mar. 23, 1923, 38th Leg., R.S., ch. 129, 1923 Tex.
Gen. Laws 269.

70. Hopkins, at 220; White v. State, 248 S.W. 690
(Tex. Crim. App. 1923); Floyd v. State, 246 S.W. 1040
(Tex. Crim. App. 1923); Rains v. State, 252 S.W. 558
(Tex. Crim. App. 1923); Hoobler v. State, 24 S.W.2d
413 (Tex. Crim. App. 1930); Hernandez v. State, 8
S.W.2d 947 (Tex. Crim. App. 1928); Berry v. State,
281 S.W. 1058 (Tex. Crim. App. 1926) (all reversing
conviction); Kelley v. State, 269 S.W. 796 (Tex. Crim.
App. 1925) (affirming conviction).

71. Cavazos v. State, 160 S.W.2d 260 (Tex. Crim.
App. 1942); Cavazos v. State, 172 S.W.2d 348 (Tex.
Crim. App. 1943); Melendez v. State, 314 S.W.2d 104
(Tex. Crim. App. 1958). On changes to confession
law, see George E. Dix, Texas "Confession" Law and
Oral Self-Incriminating Statements, 41 BLR 1, 8–16
(1989).

72. Tex. Code Crim. Proc. Art. 38.22(3)(c); Port v.
State, 791 S.W.2d 103 (Tex. Crim. App. 1990); Briddle
v. State, 742 S.W.2d 379 (Tex. Crim. App. 1987); Gary
Cartwright, Every One a Victim, TM, Nov. 1987, at
140.

73. Ex parte Marshall, 161 S.W. 112 (Tex. Crim.

App. 1913) (declaring legislature has power to vest sentencing in jury or judge); Walter E. Barnett, *Criminal Punishment in Texas*, 36 TLR 63 (1957) (discussing history); George William Baab & William Royal Furgeson, Jr., *Texas Sentencing Practices: A Statistical Study*, 45 TLR 471, 478, 498–99 (1967).

74. Ruiz v. Estelle, 503 F.Supp. 1265 (E.D. Tex. 1980), *aff'd in part and rev'd in part*, 679 F.2d 1115 (5th Cir. 1982), *amended in part and vacated in part*, 688 F.2d 266 (5th Cir. 1982); Horton & Turner, at 235–37. On the case through 1987, see Steve J. Martin & Sheldon Ekland-Olson, TEXAS PRISONS: THE WALLS CAME TUMBLING DOWN (1987). On Judge Justice and the Ruiz case, see Frank R. Kemerer, WILLIAM WAYNE JUSTICE ch. 15 (1991). For an early assessment of Ruiz, see James W. Marquart & Ben M. Crouch, *Judicial Reform and Prisoner Control: The Impact of Ruiz v. Estelle on a Texas Penitentiary*, 19 Law & Soc'y Rev. 557 (1985).

75. Ruiz v. Estelle, 161 F.3d 814 (5th Cir. 1998); Ruiz v. Johnson, 37 F.Supp.2d 855 (S.D. Tex. 1999), *rev'd*, 243 F.3d 941 (5th Cir. 2001), *remanded*, 154 F.Supp.2d 975 (S.D. Tex. 2001); Perkinson, at 326.

76. Data on numbers of incarcerated, see Horton & Turner, at 243–44 (1990 and 1997 numbers); www.pewcenteronthestates.org/uploadedFiles/TX%20 State%20Profile%202-22-07.pdf (1985 and 2005 numbers); 1985 budget, Martin & Ekland-Olson, at 238; Perkinson, at 365.

77. Hopkins, at 64.

78. Nate Blakeslee, TULIA: RACE, COCAINE, AND CORRUPTION IN A SMALL TEXAS TOWN (2005).

79. *Frontline: The Case for Innocence: Four Cases* (PBS television), www.pbs.org/wgbh/pages/frontline/ shows/case/cases/; Criner v. State, 816 S.W.2d 137 (Tex. App. 1991), *rev'd and remanded*, 860 S.W.2d 84 (Tex. Crim. App. 1992), *aff'd*, 868 S.W.2d 29 (Tex. App. 1994); postconviction DNA testing, Code Crim. Proc. § 64.03 (2007).

80. Samuel R. Gross, Kristen Jacoby, Daniel J. Matheson, Nicholas Montgomery & Sujata Patil, *Exonerations in the United States 1989 through 2003*, 95 J. Crim. L. & Criminology 523 (2005); "36" and "six," Jennifer S. Forsyth & Leslie Eaton, *The Exonerator: The Dallas D.A. Is Reviewing Old Cases, Freeing Prisoners—and Riling His Peers*, WSJ, Nov. 15–16, 2008, at A1; Tim Cole Act, 81st Leg., R.S., ch. 180, 2009 Gen. Laws 532 (codified in scattered sections of Tex. Civ. Prac. & Rem. Code § 103.000 and Tex. Gov't Code § 501.91).

81. *Problems Persisted at Reformed Crime Lab*, Hous. Chron., Feb. 21, 2008, www.chron.com/disp/ story.mpl/front/5561236.html; "CSI effect," Wendy Brickell, *Is It the CSI Effect or Do We Just Distrust Juries?*, 23 Crim. Just. 10 (2008).

82. Strauder v. West Virginia, 100 U. S. 303 (1880).

83. Carter v. Texas, 177 U.S. 442 (1900); Carter v. State, 46 S.W. 236 (Tex. Crim. App. 1898); on rehearing, 48 S.W. 508 (Tex. Crim. App. 1898); Martin v. Texas, 200 U.S. 316 (1906); Thomas v. Texas, 212 U.S. 278 (1909).

84. Act of Aug. 1, 1876, 15th Leg., R.S., ch. 76, § 1, 8 Gammel's 914.

85. "Between 1904 and 1935," Michael J. Klarman, FROM JIM CROW TO CIVIL RIGHTS: THE SUPREME COURT AND THE STRUGGLE FOR RACIAL EQUALITY 43 (2004); Norris v. Alabama, 294 U.S. 587 (1935). On the Scottsboro Boys case, see Dan T. Carter, SCOTTSBORO: A TRAGEDY OF THE AMERICAN SOUTH (1969). On George Porter, see Michael L. Gillette, *The Rise of the NAACP in Texas*, 81 SWHQ 393, 398 (1981).

86. Marshall and end on jury service ban, Gillette, at 399; Hill v. Texas, 316 U.S. 400, 403–4 (1942); Smith v. Texas, 311 U.S. 128, 129 (1940).

87. Akens v. State, 167 S.W.2d 758 (Tex. Crim. App. 1943) (reversing conviction); Akins v. Texas, 182 S.W.2d 723 (Tex. Crim. App. 1944), *aff'd*, 325 U.S. 398 (1945). Akins's death sentence was commuted to life imprisonment by Governor Coke Stevenson after a national campaign and a petition signed by fifteen thousand Dallas residents (see Klarman, at 283, 285; George Clifton Edwards, *White Justice in Dallas*, Nation, Sept. 15, 1945, at 253–55).

88. Cassell v. Texas, 339 U.S. 282 (1950), and quote at 293 (Frankfurter, J., concurring in the judgment).

89. Hernandez v. Texas, 347 U.S. 475 (1954); COLORED MEN AND HOMBRES AQUÍ: HERNANDEZ V. TEXAS AND THE EMERGENCE OF MEXICAN AMERICAN LAWYERING (Michael A. Olivas ed. 2006); Ignacio M. Garcia, WHITE BUT NOT EQUAL: MEXICAN AMERICANS, JURY DISCRIMINATION AND THE SUPREME COURT (2009); Clare Sheridan, *"Another White Race": Mexican Americans and the Paradox of Whiteness in Jury Selection*, 21 Law & Hist. Rev. 109 (2003); Ariela J. Gross, *"The Caucasian Cloak": Mexican Americans and the Politics of Whiteness in the Twentieth-Century Southwest*, 95 Geo. L.J. 337 (2007); Brown v. Board of Educ., 347 U.S. 483 (1954). A documentary on Hernandez is *A Class Apart* (PBS television broadcast Feb. 23, 2009). The first case formally to recognize Mexican Americans as a distinct ethnic group is Cisneros v. Corpus Christi Indep. Sch. Dist., 324 F.Supp. 599 (S.D. Tex. 1970).

90. Castaneda v. Partida, 430 U.S. 482 (1977); Ciudadanos Unidos de San Juan v. Hidalgo County Grand Jury Comm'rs, 622 F.2d 807, 810 (5th Cir. 1980) (noting 1979 change in law).

91. Act of Apr. 1, 1903, 28th Leg., R.S., ch. 101, 1903 Tex. Gen. Laws 133; Act of May 15, 1905, 29th Leg.,

1st C.S., ch. 11, 1905 Tex. Gen. Laws 520; Ralph W. Steen, TWENTIETH CENTURY TEXAS 331–32 (1942); O. Douglas Weeks, *The Texas Direct Primary System*, 13 Sw. Soc. Sci. Q. 95, 96 (1932); poll tax, see Sen. Jt. Res. 3, 11 Gammel's 1029; "extralegal efforts," see Charles L. Zelden, THE BATTLE FOR THE BLACK BALLOT: *SMITH V. ALLWRIGHT* AND THE DEFEAT OF THE ALL-WHITE PRIMARY 37–39 (2004); Darlene Clark Hine, BLACK VICTORY: THE RISE AND FALL OF THE WHITE PRIMARY IN TEXAS (1979, new ed. 2003).

92. Bruce Alden Glasrud, Black Texans, 1900–1930: A History 91–96 (Ph.D. diss., Texas Tech. University 1969); Alwyn Barr, RECONSTRUCTION TO REFORM, at 203–8; Zelden, ch. 2; 1911 prohibition election, Michael S. Ariens, *The Storm between the Quiet: Tumult in the Texas Supreme Court, 1911–21*, 38 StMLJ 641, 651–55 (2007); *Will Hold Two Primaries*, DMN, Mar. 9, 1902, at 2; *White Man's Primary*, DMN, Mar. 3, 1903, at 2; *Politics at Terrell*, DMN, Mar. 2, 1903, at 7; Act of May 10, 1923, 38th Leg., 2d C.S., ch. 32, § 1, 1923 Tex. Gen. Laws 74.

93. Nixon v. Herndon, 273 U.S. 536 (1927); Act of June 7, 1927, 40th Leg., 1st C.S., ch. 67, 1927 Tex. Gen. Laws 193; Nixon v. Condon, 286 U.S. 73 (1932).

94. Zelden, at 63–64; Darlene Clark Hine, *The Elusive Ballot: The Black Struggle against the Texas Democratic White Primary, 1932–1945*, 81 SWHQ 371, 375 (1978) (noting adoption of Huggins plan); County Democratic Exec. Comm. in and for Bexar County v. Booker, 53 S.W.2d 123 (Tex. Civ. App. 1932); quote, Hine, at 378; Bell v. Hill, 74 S.W.2d 113 (Tex. 1934).

95. Grovey v. Townsend, 295 U.S. 45 (1935).

96. Norris v. Alabama, 294 U.S. 587 (1935).

97. Smith v. Allwright, 321 U.S. 649 (1944); quote, Klarman, at 448; Terry v. Adams, 345 U.S. 461 (1953).

98. Act of Apr. 15, 1905, 29th Leg., R.S., ch. 124, §§ 93–96, 128, 12 Gammel's 1129; "moderately or severely," see SCHOOL DESEGREGATION IN TEXAS: THE IMPLEMENTATION OF U.S. v. TEXAS 33 (Policy Research Report No. 51, Lyndon Baines Johnson School of Public Affairs, University of Texas at Austin 1982); United States v. Texas, 321 F. Supp. 1043 (E.D. Tex. 1970), opinion supplemented, 330 F.Supp. 235 (E.D. Tex. 1971), *aff'd as modified*, 447 F.2d 441, 442–43 (5th Cir. 1971), *cert. denied sub nom.* Edgar v. United States, 404 U.S. 1016 (1972); quote, Kemerer, at 118, 124.

99. United States v. Gregory-Portland Indep. Sch. Dist., 654 F.2d 989 (5th Cir. 1981); United States v. LULAC, 793 F.2d 636 (5th Cir. 1986); "qualified success," SCHOOL DESEGREGATION IN TEXAS, at 53–54. Not all consent decrees ended at this time; the consent decree for the Uvalde Independent School District finally ended in September 2008, after thirty-eight years (Graeme Zielinski, *Desegregation Case in Uvalde Is Settled*, San Antonio Express-News, Sept. 19, 2008, at B1), and a statewide school desegregation order was lifted after thirty-nine years in late 2010 (Terry Wallace, *Districts Released from Desegregation Order*, San Antonio Express-News, Oct. 2, 2010, at 10B).

100. Public Free School Act, Act of May 20, 1893, 23d Leg., R.S., ch. 122, §§ 15, 16, 10 Gammel's 612, modified and reenacted in 1905 (Act of Apr. 15, 1905, 29th Leg., R.S., ch. 124, §§ 93–96, 128, 12 Gammel's 1129; Indep. Sch. Dist. v. Salvatierra, 33 S.W.2d 790 (Tex. App. 1930), *cert. denied*, 284 U.S. 580 (1931). On the history of Mexican-Americans and segregated education in Texas, see Guadalupe San Miguel, Jr., "LET THEM ALL TAKE HEED": MEXICAN AMERICANS AND THE CAMPAIGN FOR EDUCATIONAL EQUAL-ITY IN TEXAS, 1910–1981 (1987, repr. 2001). On the Amada Vela case, see San Miguel, at 76–77. See also Steven H. Wilson, Brown *over "Other White": Mexican Americans' Legal Arguments and Litigation Strategy in School Desegregation Lawsuits*, 21 Law & Hist. Rev. 145 (2003).

101. Mendez v. Westminster Sch. Dist., 64 F.Supp. 544 (S.D. Cal. 1946), *aff'd*, 161 F.2d 774 (9th Cir. 1947); Delgado case, San Miguel, at 123–26; "fifteen," San Miguel, at 133; Cisneros v. Corpus Christi Indep. Sch. Dist., 324 F.Supp. 599 (S.D. Tex. 1970), opinion supplemented, 330 F.Supp. 1377 (S.D. Tex. 1971), *aff'd in part, modified in part, and remanded*, 467 F.2d 142, 144 (5th Cir. 1972) (affirming conclusion identifying Mexican Americans as ethnic group).

102. Paul A. Sracic, SAN ANTONIO v. RODRIGUEZ AND THE PURSUIT OF EQUAL EDUCATION: THE DEBATE OVER DISCRIMINATION AND SCHOOL FUND-ING (2006); Rodriguez v. San Antonio Indep. Sch. Dist., 337 F.Supp. 280 (W.D. Tex. 1971), *rev'd*, 411 U.S. 1 (1973); Guerra v. Smith, No. 71–2857, *aff'd*, 474 F.2d 1399 (5th Cir. 1973).

103. Albert H. Kauffman, *The Texas School Finance Litigation Saga: Great Progress, then Near Death by a Thousand Cuts*, 40 StMLJ 511 (2008). Kauffman was counsel for MALDEF during the first four Edgewood cases.

104. Edgewood Indep. Sch. Dist. v. Kirby, 777 S.W.2d 391 (Tex. 1989) (Edgewood I); Edgewood Indep. Sch. Dist. v. Kirby, 804 S.W.2d 491 (Tex. 1991) (Edgewood II); Carrollton-Farmers Branch Indep. Sch. Dist. v. Edgewood Indep. Sch. Dist., 826 S.W.2d 489 (Tex. 1992) (Edgewood III); Edgewood Indep. Sch. Dist. v. Meno, 917 S.W.2d 717 (Tex. 1995) (Edgewood IV); W. Orange-Cove Consol. Indep. Sch. Dist. v. Alanis, 107 S.W.3d 558 (Tex. 2003) (Edgewood V); W. Orange-Cove Consol. Indep. Sch. Dist. v. Neeley, 176 S.W.3d 746 (Tex. 2003) (Edgewood VI); Act of

June 7, 1990, 71st Leg., 6th C.S., ch. 1, 1990 Tex. Gen. Laws 1; Act of Apr. 11, 1991, 72d Leg., R.S., ch. 20, 1991 Tex. Gen. Laws 381, amended by Act of May 27, 1991, 72d Leg., R.S., ch. 391, 1991 Tex. Gen. Laws 1475; Act of May 28, 1993, 73d Leg., R.S., ch. 347, 1993 Tex. Gen. Laws 1479; Act of May 26, 2006, 79th Leg., 3d C.S., ch. 5, 2006 Tex. Gen. Laws 45, amended by Act of May 4, 2007, 80th Leg., R.S., ch. 19, 2007 Tex. Gen. Laws 16; quote, Kauffman, at 552.

105. Codified as amended at Tex. Educ. Code § 51.803 (2009); Brian T. Fitzpatrick, *Strict Scrutiny of Facially Race-Neutral State Action and the Texas Ten Percent Plan*, 53 BLR 289 (2001); Fisher v. Texas, 556 F.Supp.2d 603 (W.D. Tex. 2008), and Fisher v. University of Texas at Austin, 645 F.Supp.2d 587 (W.D. Tex. 2009), *aff'd*, 631 F.3d 213, 2011 WL 135813 (5th Cir. 2011), rev. granted.

CHAPTER 8

1. Tex. Const. Art. IV, § 13 (1836); Act of Dec. 20, 1836, § 41, 1st Cong., Repub. Tex., 1 Gammel's 1208, 1216–17; Art. 192, Const. Coahuila and Texas, 1 Gammel's 449; Decree 136, Laws and Decrees of Coahuila and Texas, 1 Gammel's 262; Decree 277, Laws and Decrees of Coahuila and Texas, 1 Gammel's 364, 365, Arts. 2, 7; "never operative," Charles T. McCormick, *The Revival of the Pioneer Spirit in Texas Procedure*, 18 TLR 426, 430 (1940). On receiving the common law of England, see Edward Lee Markham, Jr., *The Reception of the Common Law of England in Texas and the Judicial Attitude toward That Reception, 1840–1859*, 29 TLR 904 (1951).

2. Decree 277, Art. 94 (on filing a petition), 1 Gammel's 375, and Art. 100 (on answering petition by defendant) and Art. 101 (on replica and duplica), 1 Gammel's 376; John C. Townes, PLEADING IN THE DISTRICT AND COUNTY COURTS OF TEXAS 84 (2d ed. 1913); Joseph Webb McKnight, *The Spanish Influence on the Texas Law of Civil Procedure*, 38 TLR 24 (1959); Sandra Williams & David Harrell, *Civilized Procedure: The Practice Act of 1846*, Hous. Law., Jan.–Feb. 1999, at 21. On adopting the common law, see Ford W. Hall, *An Account of the Adoption of the Common Law by Texas*, 28 TLR 801 (1950). On venue, see Act of Dec. 22, 1836, § 5, 1 Gammel's 1260, and Joseph W. McKnight, *The Spanish Legacy to Texas Law (Part II)*, 3 Am. J. Leg. Hist. 299, 299–305 (1959).

3. Act of Dec. 15, 1836, 1st Cong., Repub. Tex., 1 Gammel's 1139 (establishing jurisdiction of the supreme court); James W. Paulsen, *Rules of Procedure in Early Texas Courts*, 65 TLR 451, 453–68

(1986) (reprinting 1840 and 1846 rules of the supreme court and district courts); 1 Tex. R. 848–49 (1841 ed.) (reprinting supreme court and district court rules); Act of Feb. 5, 1840, 4th Cong., Repub. Tex., 2 Gammel's 262 (regulating proceedings in civil matters); Act of Jan. 20, 1840, 4th Cong., Repub. Tex., 2 Gammel's 177 (adopting the common law of England as the "rule of decision").

4. Act of Feb. 5, 1840, §§ 1, 10, 11 & 16, 4th Cong., Repub. Tex., 2 Gammel's 262; see generally Markham, and McKnight, *Spanish Influence*.

5. Quote, Charles E. Clark, *History, Systems, and Functions of Pleading*, 11 Va. L. Rev. 517, 526 (1925); "thirty to forty common law writs," Joseph H. Koffler & Alison Reppy, COMMON LAW PLEADING 35 n.11 (1969). On other forms of trial, see T. F. T. Plucknett, A CONCISE HISTORY OF THE COMMON LAW 113–19 (5th ed. 1956).

6. Clark, at 528–29; Stephen N. Subrin, *How Equity Conquered Common Law: The Federal Rules of Civil Procedure in Historical Perspective*, 135 U. Pa. L. Rev. 909 (1987); Subcommittee of the Texas Bar Association, *The Blending of Law and Equity*, 30 Am. L. Rev. 813 (1896); George C. Butte, *Early Development of Law and Equity in Texas*, 26 Yale L.J. 699 (1917).

7. Daun Van Ee, DAVID DUDLEY FIELD AND THE RECONSTRUCTION OF THE LAW (1986).

8. *Blending*; "A hundred judges," Whiting v. Turley, Dallam's 453 (Tex. Rep. 1842); "perplexity," Butte, at 703; Tex. Const. Art. IV, § 10 (1845).

9. Act of May 13, 1846, 1st Leg., 2 Gammel's 1669.

10. Tex. Const. Art. V, § 25 (1876); Rules for the Courts of Texas, 47 Tex. 597 (1877); Jt. Res. 16, Apr. 28, 1891, 10 Gammel's 199, 203.

11. Texas Court Rules, adopted October 8, 1892, 20 S.W. v–xix (1892); Tex. Rev. Civ. Stats. arts. 1177–1504f (1895).

12. Lewis M. Dabney, *Pleading and Practice in the Land of Canaan*, 29 PTBA 140 (1910), and quotes at 140, 143, 147 & 148.

13. Roscoe Pound, *The Causes of Popular Dissatisfaction in the Administration of Justice*, 29 A.B.A. Rep. 395 (1906); John Henry Wigmore, *The Spark That Kindled the White Flame of Progress*, 20 J. Am. Jud. Soc'y 176 (1937); Michael Ariens, *The Storm between the Quiet: Tumult in the Texas Supreme Court, 1911–21*, 38 StMLJ 641 (2007).

14. 29 PTBA 103–4 (1910); *id.* at 84 (at least one year behind).

15. Tit. 37, Tex. Rev. Stats. Arts. 1812–2183 (1911); Tit. 42, Tex. Rev. Stats. Arts. 1971–2328 (1925); Practice Act § 108. On factual and legal sufficiency claims, see W. Wendell Hall & Mark Emery, *The Texas Hold*

Out: Trends in the Review of Civil and Criminal Jury Verdicts, 49 STLR 539, 549–51 (2008).

16. Silliman v. Gano, 39 S.W. 559, 561 (Tex. 1897); Act of June 18, 1897, 25th Leg., Spec. S., ch. 7, 10 Gammel's 1455; Act of May 12, 1899, 26th Leg., R.S., ch. 111, 1899 Tex. Gen. Laws 190; Act of Mar. 29, 1913, 33d Leg., R.S., ch. 59, 1913 Tex. Gen. Laws 113; 29 PTBA 103–4 (1910); 30 PTBA 75–76 (1911); quote, J. B. Dooley, *The Use of Special Issues under the New State and Federal Rules*, 20 TLR 32, 32 (1941).

17. Houston & T. C. R. Co. v. Walsh, 183 S.W. 18 (Tex. Civ. App. 1915); Dooley, at 34; McCormick, at 432.

18. Texas & N. O. Ry. Co. v. Harrington, 235 S.W. 188 (Tex. Com. App. 1921).

19. Fox v. Dallas Hotel Co., 240 S.W. 517 (Tex. 1922); Note, 23 TLR 190 (1945).

20. Gus M. Hodges, SPECIAL ISSUE SUBMISSION IN TEXAS 27 (1959); Guthrie v. Texas Pac. Coal & Oil Co., 122 S.W.2d 1049 (Tex. Comm. App. 1939) (holding general charge requires reversal).

21. Quotes, Leon Green, *Suggestions for Improving Court Procedure in Texas*, 2 TLR 464, 466–69 (1924); McCormick, at 433, quoting Bryan; Act of May 23, 1929, 41st Leg., 1st C.S., ch. 19, 1929 Tex. Gen. Laws 51.

22. Traders & General Ins. Co. v. Rudd, 102 S.W.2d 457 (Tex. App. 1937); no further official report of Mrs. Rudd's travails exists.

23. Act of May 12, 1939, ch. 25, 46th Leg., R.S., 1939 Tex. Gen. Laws 201; Roy W. McDonald, *The Background of the Texas Procedural Rules*, 19 TLR 229 (1941).

24. Charles E. Clark, *The Texas and Federal Rules of Civil Procedure*, 20 TLR 4 (1941).

25. As drafted, 3 TBJ 525 *et seq.* (1940); as amended in 1941, 4 TBJ 487 *et seq.* (1941); *Letter of September 16, 1940 from Advisory Committee to Texas Supreme Court*, 3 TBJ 522, 524 (1940), and 4 TBJ 620, 621 (1941).

26. "unnecessary reversals," Act of May 15, 1939, ch. 25, 46th Leg., R.S., 1939 Tex. Gen. Laws 201, 202; "abandonment," Gordon Simpson, *The Task Still Challenges*, TBJ, Oct. 1941, at 485.

27. E. Wayne Thode, *In Personam Jurisdiction: Article 2031B, the Texas "Long Arm" Jurisdiction Statute, and the Appearance to Challenge Jurisdiction in Texas and Elsewhere*, 42 TLR 279, 293 (1964); York v. Texas, 137 U.S. 15, 16 (1890).

28. Pennoyer v. Neff, 95 U.S. 714 (1878).

29. York v. State, 11 S.W. 869 (Tex. 1889), *aff'd*, York v. Texas, 137 U.S. 15 (1890).

30. International Shoe Co. v. Washington, 326 U.S. 310 (1945); Act of Apr. 1, 1959, 56th Leg., R.S., ch. 43, § 4, 1959 Tex. Gen. Laws 85, codified

as amended at Tex. Civ. Prac. & Rem. § 17.042; W. Frank Newton & Jeremy C. Wicker, *Personal Jurisdiction and the Appearance to Challenge Jurisdiction in Texas*, 38 BLR 491 (1986). On the 1997 act, see Richard E. Flint & L. Wayne Scott, TEXAS CIVIL PROCEDURE: PRETRIAL 246 (2007).

31. McKnight, *Spanish Influence*, at 40.

32. Act of Mar. 27, 1901, ch. 27, 26th Leg., R.S., 1901 Tex. Gen. Laws 31; Art. 1194, § 25, Batts' Ann. Tex. Civ. Stats. (1895), at 650; Fox v. Cone, 13 S.W.2d 65 (Tex. 1929).

33. McKnight, *Spanish Influence*, at 40, and Joseph W. McKnight, *A Century of Development in Texas Law*, TBJ, Nov. 1973, at 1051, 1052 (tracing venue rule to thirteenth-century Castilian law and noting the absence of a jury as the reason for the rule's existence in Castile); Fox, at 66; Amberson v. Anderson, 43 S.W.2d 120, 122 (Tex. Civ. App. 1931).

34. Act of May 8, 1953, ch. 107, 53d Leg., R.S., 1953 Tex. Gen. Laws 390; Kent Caperton, Alan Schoenbaum & Art Anderson, *Anatomy of the Venue Bill*, TBJ, Mar. 1984, at 244.

35. Act of Apr. 28, 1983, 68th Leg., R.S., ch. 385, 1983 Tex. Gen. Laws 2119; Tenneco, Inc. v. Salyer, 739 S.W.2d 448, 449 (Tex. App. 1987); Dan R. Price, *New Texas Venue Statute: Legislative History*, 15 StMLJ 855 (1984). On the railroad venue error, see John T. Montford & Will G. Barber, *1987 Texas Tort Reform: The Quest for a Fairer and More Predictable Texas Civil Justice System (Part III)*, 25 HLR 1005, 1033–34 (1988).

36. E. Wayne Thode, *Imminent Peril and Emergency in Texas*, 40 TLR 441 (1962); International & G. N. Ry. v. Neff, 28 S.W. 283 (Tex. 1894); Jones v. Boyce, 171 Eng. Rep. 540 (N.P. 1816); Stokes v. Saltonstall, 38 U.S. 161 (1839); Texas & P. Ry. v. Watkins, 29 S.W. 232 (Tex. 1895); Jackson v. Galveston, H. & S. A. Ry., 38 S.W. 745 (Tex. 1897); Missouri, K. & T. Ry. v. Rogers, 40 S.W. 956 (Tex. 1897).

37. Houston & Texas Cent. Railroad Co. v. Smith, 52 Tex. 178 (1879); H. & T. C. R.R. Co. v. Clemmons, 55 Tex. 88 (1881) (although not using the word *negligence* per se, court holds the evidence insufficient and reverses judgment for $2,200 in favor of plaintiff); Gulf, C. & S. F. Ry. Co. v. Gascamp, 7 S.W. 227 (Tex. 1888) (holding the decision of plaintiff to ride a horse over a dangerous bridge negligently kept by the railroad not negligence per se); Houston & Texas Cent. Ry. Co. v. Baker, 57 Tex. 419 (1882); Texas & Pac. Ry. Co. v. Levi & Bros., 59 Tex. 674 (1883); Missouri Pacific Railway Co. v. Shuford, 10 S.W. 408 (Tex 1888). On railroads and tort law, see James W. Ely, Jr., RAILROADS AND AMERICAN LAW ch. 9 (2001), and John Fabian Witt, THE ACCIDENTAL REPUBLIC:

CRIPPLED WORKINGMEN, DESTITUTE WIDOWS, AND THE REMAKING OF AMERICAN LAW ch. 2 (2004). See generally Mark Aldrich, DEATH RODE THE RAILS: AMERICAN RAILROAD ACCIDENTS AND SAFETY, 1828–1965 (2006).

38. Bethje v. Houston & Central Texas Railway Co., 26 Tex. 604 (1863).

39. Houston & T. C. R.R. Co. v. Burke, 55 Tex. 323 (1881); Robinson v. H. & T. Central Railway Co., 46 Tex. 540 (1877); H. & T. C. R.R. Co. v. Myers, 55 Tex. 110 (1881); Watson v. H. & T. C. Ry. Co., 58 Tex. 434 (1883).

40. Houston and Texas Central Railway Co. v. Dunham, 49 Tex. 181 (1878); International and Great Northern Railroad Co. v. Doyle, 49 Tex. 190 (1878) (safe tools); Dallas v. Gulf, Col. & S. F. Ry. Co., 61 Tex. 196 (1884) (employing reasonably competent fellow servants); International & G. N. Ry. Co. v. Hinzie, 18 S.W. 681 (Tex. 1891) (making and enforcing rules); Missouri Pacific Railway Co. v. Williams, 12 S.W. 835 (Tex. 1889) (vice-principal); Act of Mar. 10, 1891, 22d Leg., R.S., ch. 24, 10 Gammel's 27; Act of May 4, 1893, 23d Leg., R.S., ch. 91, 10 Gammel's 550; Act of June 18, 1897, 25th Leg., Spec. S., ch. 6, 10 Gammel's 1454.

41. Edwin A. Parker, *Anti-Railroad Personal Injury Litigation in Texas*, 19 PTBA 165, 167–70 (1900).

42. Act of Mar. 27, 1901, 27th Leg., R.S., ch. 27, 1901 Tex. Gen. Laws 31. Parker complained that "[u]nder our Texas practice, railroad companies are suable in any county through which their lines run or in which they have an agent, irrespective of where the plaintiff resides or where the cause of action arises" (Parker, at 181).

43. Railroad cases data, Ariens, *Storm*, at 677; McCloskey v. San Antonio Traction Co., 192 S.W. 1116 (Tex. Civ. App. 1917); *Ex parte* McCloskey, 199 S.W. 1101 (Tex. Crim. App. 1917); McCloskey v. Tobin, 252 U.S. 107 (1920); McCloskey v. San Antonio Public Service Co., 51 S.W.2d 1088 (Tex. Civ. App. 1932); Yellow Cab Co., Inc. v. McCloskey, 82 S.W.2d 1042 (Tex. Civ. App. 1935); Act of Aug. 21, 1876, ch. 135, 15th Leg., R.S., 8 Gammel's 1063; Act of May 4, 1895, ch. 89, 24th Leg., R.S., 10 Gammel's 873; Act of Apr. 10, 1901, ch. 57, 27th Leg., R.S., 1901 Tex. Gen. Laws 125; Act of Mar. 29, 1917, ch. 133, 35th Leg., R.S., 1917 Tex. Gen. Laws 336.

44. Marshall & E. T. Ry. Co. v. Petty, 134 S.W. 406 (Tex. Civ. App. 1911); Marshall & E. T. Ry. Co. v. Petty, 145 S.W. 1195 (Tex. Civ. App. 1912), *rev'd*, Marshall & E. T. Ry. Co. v. Petty, 180 S.W. 105 (Tex. 1915).

45. *Report of the Committee on Judicial Administration and Remedial Procedure*, 36 PTBA 16, 32 (1917); Gross v. Dallas Ry. & Terminal Co., 131 S.W.2d 113 (Tex. Civ. App. 1939); Texas & P. Ry. Co. v. Jefferson, 131 S.W.2d 175 (Tex. Civ. App. 1939); Figula v. Fort Worth & D. C. Ry. Co., 131 S.W.2d 998 (Tex. Civ. App. 1939).

46. Robert W. Calvert, HERE COMES THE JUDGE 164 (1977); Sun Oil Co. v. Robicheaux, 23 S.W.2d 713 (Tex. Com. App. 1930); Landers v. East Texas Salt Water Disposal Co., 248 S.W.2d 731 (Tex. 1952); Neville v. Mitchell, 66 S.W. 579 (Tex. Civ. App. 1902).

47. Missouri-Kansas-Texas R.R. v. Hamilton, 314 S.W.2d 114 (Tex. Civ. App 1958).

48. "Up until," Terry L. Jacobson & Kevin L. Wentz, *A Lawyer Has to Know His/Her Limitations: The Statute of Limitations in Medical Malpractice Cases—A Constitutional Compromise*, 23 TTLR 769, 834 (1992); "[w]hen Calvert," Robert W. Calvert, *Remarks to the Texas Association of Defense Counsel* 7 (Sept. 30, 1983), quoted in L. Wayne Scott, *Robert Wilburn Calvert, the Prudentialist*, 26 StMLJ 905, 910 (1995).

49. George L. Priest, *The Invention of Enterprise Liability: A Critical History of the Intellectual Foundations of Modern Tort Law*, 14 J. Legal Stud. 461, 461 (1985).

50. G. Edward White, TORT LAW IN AMERICA (1985); David G. Owen, *The Evolution of Products Liability Law*, 26 Rev. Litig. 955 (2007); Herbert W. Titus, *Restatement (Second) of Torts Section 402A and the Uniform Commercial Code*, 22 Stan. L. Rev. 713 (1970); Gary T. Schwartz, *The Vitality of Negligence and the Ethics of Strict Liability*, 15 Ga. L. Rev. 963 (1981), and Gary T. Schwartz, *The Beginning and the Possible End of the Rise of Modern American Tort Law*, 26 Ga. L. Rev. 601 (1992), among many others; Decker & Sons, Inc. v. Capps, 164 S.W.2d 828 (Tex. 1942) (creating strict liability in unfit food cases); quote, McKisson v. Sales Affiliates, Inc., 416 S.W.2d 787, 788 (Tex. 1967) (quoting and adopting §402A(1)); quote of Calvert, see 1 A TEXAS SUPREME COURT TRILOGY: ORAL HISTORY INTERVIEW WITH THE HONORABLE ROBERT W. CALVERT 64 (1998); Howle v. Camp Amon Carter, 470 S.W.2d 629 (Tex. 1971) (eliminating charitable immunity); Felderhoff v. Felderhoff, 473 S.W.2d 928 (Tex. 1971) (modifying doctrine of parental immunity); final quote, William B. Prosser, HANDBOOK OF THE LAW OF TORTS xxi (4th ed. 1971).

51. Quote, Warren Freedman, *The Texas Politics of Today's Products Liability*, 5 StMLJ 16, 22 (1973); Shivers v. Good Shepherd Hosp., 417 S.W.2d 104 (Tex. Civ. App. 1968) (hospital); O. M. Franklin Serum Co. v. C. A. Hoover & Son, 410 S.W.2d 272 (Tex. Civ. App. 1967) (inapplicable to those not sell-

ers); Melody Home Mfg. Co. v. Morrison, 455 S.W.2d 825 (Tex. Civ. App. 1970) (economic loss); Darryl v. Ford Motor Co., 440 S.W.2d 630 (Tex. 1969).

52. J. Caleb Rackley, *A Survey of Sea-Change on the Supreme Court of Texas and Its Turbulent Toll on Texas Tort Law*, 48 STLR 733 (2007); Meredith B. Parenti & Susanna Dokupil, TEXAS-SIZED TRANSFORMATION: THE CONSERVATIVE COUNTERREVOLUTION ON THE TEXAS SUPREME COURT (Federalist Society 2006); Billings v. Atkinson, 489 S.W.2d 858 (Tex. 1973); Jacobs v. Theimer, 519 S.W.2d 846 (Tex. 1975); Exxon Corp. v. Brecheen, 526 S.W.2d 519 (Tex. 1975); Farley v. MM Cattle Co., 529 S.W.2d 751 (Tex. 1975); Parker v. Highland Park, Inc., 565 S.W.2d 512 (Tex. 1978); Burk Royalty Co. v. Walls, 616 S.W.2d 911 (Tex. 1981), *rev'g* Sheffield Div., Armco Steel Corp. v. Jones, 376 S.W.2d 825 (Tex. 1964); James L. Branton, *Franklin S. Spears: A Proud Legacy to Texas Jurisprudence*, 28 StMLJ 329, 333 (1997) (stating that the "end result [of *Burk*] was not the adoption of a 'liberal' rule, but rather the return to the hundred-year-old rule written in a decision in 1888.").

53. Proportionate Responsibility Act, Act of Apr. 9, 1973, ch. 28, 63d Leg., R.S., 1973 Tex. Gen. Laws 41.

54. Deceptive Trade Practices–Consumer Protection Act, Act of May 21, 1973, ch. 143, 63d Leg., R.S., 1973 Tex. Gen. Laws 322; Woods v. Littleton, 554 S.W.2d 662 (Tex. 1977); Racketeer Influenced and Corrupt Organizations Act, 18 U.S.C. § 1961 *et seq.* Treble damages for civil harms were permitted in the Sherman Anti-trust Act, Act of July 2, 1890, ch. 647, 26 Stat. 209, codified as amended at 15 U.S.C. § 1 *et seq.*

55. Original version, *Rules of Practice and Procedure in Civil Actions*, 4 TBJ 487, 532 (1941); Rules 291 and 292 amended in 1972, effective February 1, 1973, see *Civil Procedure Rules Amended*, TBJ, Nov. 1972, at 1037, 1045; amended Rule 277, see 36 TBJ 495, 495–96 (1973); Mobile Chemical v. Bell, 517 S.W.2d 245 (Tex. 1974); quote, Burk Royalty, at 925. L. Wayne Scott notes that the Supreme Court amended Rule 277 to preempt any action by the legislature on this issue.

56. Subhead, Rackley, at 760; Michael D. Weiss, *America's Queen of Torts*, Pol'y Rev., Fall 1992, at 62 (citing data from the National Center for State Courts and the American Insurance Association).

57. Sanchez v. Schindler, 651 S.W.2d 249 (Tex. 1983); Paul Burka, *Heads, We Win, Tails, You Lose: How a Group of Trial Lawyers Took Over the Texas Supreme Court and Rewrote State Law*, TM, May 1987, at 138, 206; Branton, at 333; Otis Engineering Corp. v. Clark, 668 S.W.2d 307 (Tex. 1983); Corbin v. Safeway Stores, Inc., 648 S.W.2d 292, 295 (Tex. 1983).

58. Kent Caperton & Erwin McGee, *Background, Scope and Applicability of the Texas Rules of Evidence*, 20 HLR 49, 57 (1983); FRE, Pub. L. 93–595, 88 Stat. 1926.

59. Big Mack Trucking Co. v. Dickerson, 497 S.W.2d 283, 288 (Tex. 1973); Olin Guy Wellborn III, *Article VIII: Hearsay*, 20 HLR 477, 501–2 (1983) (listing criticisms of Big Mack); Travelers Ins. Co. v. Smith, 448 S.W.2d 541 (Tex. Civ. App. 1969).

60. Cavnar v. Quality Control Parking, Inc., 696 S.W.2d 549 (Tex. 1985); Watkins v. Junker, 90 Tex. 584, 40 S.W. 11 (Tex. 1897); Texas & N.O. R. Co. v. Carr, 43 S.W. 18 (Tex. 1897) (following Watkins).

61. On the division of cases, see Joseph Sanders & Craig Joyce, *"Off to the Races": The 1980s Tort Crisis and the Law Reform Process*, 27 HLR 207, 230 (1990), citing D. Hensler et al., TRENDS IN TORT LITIGATION: THE STORY BEHIND THE STATISTICS (Rand Corp. 1987). For median award data, see Sanders & Joyce, at 231, citing Stephen Daniels & Joanne Martin, *Jury Verdicts and the "Crisis" in Civil Justice*, 11 Just. Sys. J. 321, 340–42 (1986). On the insurance crisis and its relation to tort law, see Sanders & Joyce, at 212–23; REPORT OF THE TORT POLICY WORKING GROUP ON THE CAUSES, EXTENT AND POLICY IMPLICATIONS OF THE CURRENT CRISIS IN INSURANCE AVAILABILITY AND AFFORDABILITY (U.S. Gov't Printing Office Feb. 1986). On 1987 Texas tort reform, see John T. Montford & Will G. Barber, *1987 Texas Tort Reform: The Quest for a Fairer and More Predictable Texas Civil Justice System (Part I)*, 25 HLR 59 (1988), *(Part II)* at 245, *(Part III)* at 1005. For citations to 1987 Acts, see Montford, *Part I*, at 64 n.24, and on proposals, *Part I*, at 66–67.

62. Thomas Petzinger, Jr., OIL AND HONOR: THE TEXACO-PENNZOIL WARS, at 406, 411 (1987); "executing judgment," *id.* at 422; Roger M. Baron & Ronald J. Baron, *The Pennzoil-Texaco Dispute: An Independent Analysis*, 38 BLR 253 (1986) (concluding damages incorrectly determined). On Jamail's views, see Joe Jamail with Mickey Herskowitz, LAWYER: MY TRIALS AND JUBILATIONS 137–67 (2003).

63. Jamail contributions, Petzinger, at 278–79; disqualification, *id.* at 285–87; "as children," *id.* at 372; "close personal friend," *id.* at 446.

64. Texaco, Inc. v. Pennzoil Co., 729 S.W.2d 768 (Tex. App. 1987); Texaco, Inc. v. Pennzoil Co., 626 F. Supp. 250 (S.D.N.Y. 1986), *aff'd in part and rev'd in part*, 784 F.2d 1133 (2d Cir. 1986), *rev'd*, 481 U.S. 1 (1987); Ken Case, *Blind Justice*, TM, May 1987, at 137; Burka, at 138; William P. Barrett, *The Best Justice Money Can Buy*, Forbes, June 1, 1987, at 122; Sheila Kaplan, *What Price Justice? Oh, About $10,000*, Wash. Post, May 17, 1987, at C4; Richard Wood-

bury, *Is Texas Justice for Sale?*, Time, Jan. 11, 1988, at 74; Jamail fee, Herbert M. Kritzer, *Advocacy and Rhetoric vs. Scholarship and Evidence in the Debate over Contingency Fees: A Reply to Professor Brickman*, 82 Wash. U. L.Q. 477, 505 (2004) (noting reports of fee between $300 million and $400 million); *The Best Paid Trial Lawyers*, Forbes, Oct. 16, 1989, at 204 ($420 million); Michael Freedman, *Judgment Day*, Forbes, May 14, 2001, at 132 ($345 million); Jean Fleming Powers, *What the Market Will Bear: Questions about Limits on Attorneys' Fees*, Hous. Law., Nov.–Dec. 1998, at 23 ($400 million).

65. *In re* Texas City Disaster Litigation, 197 F.2d 771 (5th Cir. 1952); Dalehite v. United States, 346 U.S. 15 (1953); Texas City Explosion Relief Act, 69 Stat. 707; "1,394 awards," Bill Minutaglio, CITY ON FIRE 264 (2004); Petition of Republic of France, 171 F.Supp. 497 (S.D. Tex. 1959), *rev'd*, Republic of France v. United States, 290 F.2d 395 (5th Cir. 1961), *cert. denied*, 369 U.S. 804 (1962).

66. Peter H. Schuck, AGENT ORANGE ON TRIAL (1987); Richard B. Sobol, BENDING THE LAW: THE STORY OF THE DALKON SHIELD BANKRUPTCY (1991); Lester Brickman, *The Asbestos Litigation Crisis: Is There a Need for an Administrative Alternative?*, 13 Cardozo L. Rev. 1819, 1819 n.2, 1820 & n.3 (1992); "more than three thousand," Skip Hollandsworth, *The Lawsuit from Hell*, TM, June 1996, at 106; "twenty-five hundred clients" and "more than a thousand," Joseph Nocera & Henry Goldblatt, *Dow Corning Succumbs*, Fortune, Oct. 30, 1995, at 137; Joseph Nocera & Henry Goldblatt, *Fatal Litigation*, Fortune, Oct. 16, 1995, at 60; "nonmalignant," Lester Brickman, *On the Applicability of the Silica MDL Proceeding to Asbestos Litigation*, 36 Conn. Ins. L.J. 35, 36 (2006) (concluding "a substantial percentage of these nonmalignant claimants had no disease caused by asbestos exposure as recognized by medical science and no loss of lung function."); Institute of Medicine, SAFETY OF SILICONE BREAST IMPLANTS (1999); Bendectin, see Daubert v. Merrell Dow Pharm., Inc., 727 F.Supp. 570, 575–76 (S.D. Cal. 1989), *aff'd*, 43 F.3d 1311 (1995), on remand from 509 U.S. 579 (1993); Merrell Dow Pharmaceuticals, Inc. v. Havner, 953 S.W.2d 706 (Tex. 1997) (reversing judgment in favor of plaintiff in Bendectin case).

67. Daubert v. Merrell Dow Pharm., Inc., 509 U.S. 579 (1993); Frye v. United States, 293 F. 1013 (D.C. Cir. 1923); Du Pont de Nemours & Co., Inc v. Robinson, 923 S.W.2d 549 (Tex. 1995).

68. "$11 million," Anthony Champagne & Kyle Cheek, *The Cycle of Judicial Elections*, 29 Fordham Urban L.J. 907, 914 (2002); money in Phillips-Robertson race, Kyle D. Cheek & Anthony Champagne, *Partisan Judicial Elections: Lessons from a Bellwether State*, 39 Willamette L. Rev. 1357, 1359 (2003); Phillips-Mauzy campaign amounts, Janet Elliott, *There's Joy in Mudville over Battle of the Giants*, Tex. Law., Nov. 5, 1990, at 5.

69. Quote, Austin Sarat, *Exploring the Hidden Domains of Civil Justice: "Naming, Blaming, and Claiming" in Popular Culture*, 50 DePaul L. Rev. 425, 425 (2000); "totaled more than $150 million," Tony McAdams, *Blame and The Sweet Hereafter*, 24 Legal Stud. F. 599, 607 (2000); "conservative estimate," Lester Brickman, *Effective Hourly Rates of Contingency-Fee Lawyers: Competing Date and Non-Competitive Fees*, 81 Wash. U. L.Q. 653, 694 (2003); Lisa Belkin, *Where 21 Youths Died, Lawyers Wage a War*, N.Y. Times, Jan. 18, 1990, at A1 (stating more than fifteen lawyers were being investigated for the possibility they represented clients in a case only after "misleading or bribing families"); barratry, Lopez v. State, 846 S.W.2d 90 (Tex. App. 1992) (affirming conviction of runner); State v. Sandoval, 842 S.W.2d 782 (Tex. App. 1992) (affirming dismissal of suit); Act of June 14, 1989, 71st Leg., R.S., ch. 866, 1989 Tex. Gen. Laws 3855, as amended codified at Tex. Penal Code § 38.12; final quote, Paul Weingarten, *Lawsuits, Greed Tear Grieving Texas Town*, Chi. Trib., May 27, 1990, at A23. The Alton event became the basis for the novel THE SWEET HEREAFTER (1991) by Russell Banks and was the subject of an ABC News documentary, *Day One: From Grief to Greed* (ABC television broadcast June 7, 1993). A twenty-year retrospective is Lynn Brezosky, *School Bus Tragedy Still Hurts*, San Antonio Express-News, Sept. 21, 2009, at A1.

70. John MacCormack, *Story of South Texas "Case Runner" Reads Like a Novel*, San Antonio Express-News, Dec. 6, 2009, at 1A, 24A. A novel about personal injury law and lawyers in South Texas is Carlos Cisneros, THE CASE RUNNER (2008).

71. Act of Dec. 12, 1989, 71st Leg., 2d C.S., ch. 1, § 17.16, 1989 Tex. Gen. Laws 122 (effective January 1, 1991); quote, Jill Williford, *Reformers' Regress: The 1991 Texas Workers' Compensation Act*, 22 StMLJ 1111, 1112 (1992); Phil Hardberger, *Texas Workers' Compensation: A Ten-Year Survey—Strengths, Weaknesses, and Recommendations*, 32 StMLJ 1 (2000).

72. Martha T. McCluskey, *The Illusion of Efficiency in Workers' Compensation "Reform,"* 50 Rutgers L. Rev. 657, 684–85 (1998); "fifth highest," Hardberger, at 4; "148 percent," Williford, at 1122.

73. Hardberger, at 64; quote, Stephen Daniels & Joanne Martin, *"It's Darwinism—Survival of the Fittest": How Markets and Reputations Shape the Ways in Which Plaintiffs' Lawyers Obtain Clients*, 21

Law & Pol'y 377, 384 (1999); Tex. Disc. R. Prof. Cond. 1.04(f), effective March 1, 2005, limits division of fees to proportion of "the professional services performed by each lawyer."

74. *New Tort Cases Filed in Texas District and County-level Courts, Fiscal Years 1987 to 2006* (Texas Judicial Council 2006), www.courts.state.tx.us/pubs/ar2006/trends/torts-87-06.pdf; MBank v. LeMaire, 1989 WL 30995 (Tex.App. 1989) (officially unreported); four hundred lawsuits, $100 million verdicts, Weiss, *America's Queen of Torts*; Eugene H. Methvin, *Texas on Trial*, Nat'l Rev., Dec. 31, 1990, at 32 (noting changes in the Texas Supreme Court from the late 1980s).

75. Arnold v. National County Mut. Fire Ins. Co., 725 S.W.2d 165 (Tex. 1987); Aranda v. Insurance Co. of North America, 748 S.W.2d 210 (Tex. 1988); Lyons v. Millers Cas. Ins. Co. of Texas, 866 S.W.2d 597 (Tex. 1993); Transportation Ins. Co. v. Moriel, 879 S.W.2d 10, 25 (Tex. 1994) (reversing punitive damages award of $1 million); American Physicians Ins. Exch. v. Garcia, 876 S.W.2d 842 (Tex. 1994) (reversing $2 million award); Cain v. Hearst Corp., 878 S.W.2d 577 (Tex. 1994); Boyles v. Kerr, 855 S.W.2d 593 (Tex. 1993).

76. Joseph Calve, *Poured Out: Times Have Never Been Tougher for the Plaintiffs Personal-Injury Bar: The Civil-Justice System May Never Be the Same*, Tex. Law., Dec. 16, 1986, at 1; Michael Totty, *Defense Rests: Texas' High Court Pounded Plaintiffs in Past Year*, WSJ, July 17, 1996, at T1; Timothy D. Howell, *So Long "Sweetheart"—State Farm Fire & Casualty Co. v. Gandy Swings the Pendulum Further to the Right as the Latest in a Line of Setbacks for Texas Plaintiffs*, 29 StMLJ 47 (1997); De los Santos v. Occidental Chem. Corp., 933 S.W.2d 493 (Tex. 1996) (limiting enlarging class actions); Amstadt v. United States Brass Corp., 919 S.W.2d 644 (Tex. 1996) (limiting use of DTPA); State Farm Fire & Cas. Co. v. Gandy, 925 S.W.2d 696 (Tex. 1996); Motel 6 G.P., Inc. v. Lopez, 929 S.W.2d 1 (Tex. 1996) (premises liability); Du Pont De Nemours v. Robinson, 923 S.W.2d 549 (Tex. 1995) (standards for admissibility of scientific expert testimony); May v. United Services Ass'n of America, 844 S.W.2d 666 (Tex. 1996) (reversing verdict in favor of plaintiffs and limiting common law duty of agent in advising about and procuring insurance); Saenz v. Fidelity Ins. Underwriters, 925 S.W.2d 607 (Tex. 1996) (reversing bad faith claim and holding that plaintiff take nothing); Jay D. Reeve, Note, *Judicial Tort Reform: Bad Faith Cannot Be Predicated upon the Denial of a Claim for an Invalid Reason If a Valid Reason Is Later Shown: Republic Insurance Co. v. Stoker, 903 S.W.2d 338 (Tex. 1995)*, 27 TTLR 351

(1996) (listing bad faith cases); Hartsfield v. McRee Ford, Inc., 893 S.W.2d 148 (Tex. App. 1995); Lawson v. B Four Corp., 888 S.W.2d 31 (Tex. App. 1994); Way v. Boy Scouts of Amer., 856 S.W.2d 230 (Tex. App. 1993); Vineyard v. Kraft, 828 S.W.2d 248 (Tex. App. 1992) (affirming trial court decisions granting defendant summary judgment); William Powers, Jr., *Judge and Jury in the Texas Supreme Court*, 75 TLR 1699 (1997); Phil Hardberger, *Juries Under Siege*, 30 StMLJ 1 (1998).

77. Gibbs v. Jackson, 990 S.W.2d 745 (Tex. 1999); Johnson County Sheriff's Posse, Inc. v. Endsley, 926 S.W.2d 284 (Tex. 1996); Schlueter v. Schlueter, 975 S.W.2d 584 (Tex. 1998); City of Tyler v. Likes, 962 S.W.2d 489 (Tex. 1997).

78. Martha A. Derthick, UP IN SMOKE: FROM LEGISLATION TO LITIGATION IN TOBACCO POLITICS 27 (2d ed. 2005); "$246 billion," Mark Curriden, *Up in Smoke*, 6 ABA J. E-Rep. 3 (Mar. 2, 2007) (noting reduction of original settlement of $369 billion to $246 billion payable over twenty-five years).

79. Derthick, at 72–77; barred evidence, *id.* at 77–78; "settlement," *id.* at 253.

80. Texas v. Real Parties in Interest, 259 F.3d 387 (5th Cir. 2001) recounts some events of the case; "seventh state," Curriden, *Up in Smoke*; "Suing in federal court," Mark Curriden, *Texas-Sized Fight Crystallizes Contingency Fee Issues in High-Stakes Litigation*, 19 Of Counsel 1 (Sept. 11, 2000); "raised to $17.3 billion," Skip Hollandsworth, *Up in Smoke*, TM, Aug. 1999, at 25; quote, Gregory Curtis, *Up in Smoke*, TM, Mar. 1998, at 9; "Jamail," Lou Dubose, *"Dime con Quien Andas, y Te Dire Quien Eres,"* TM, Mar. 2002, at 92 (noting conflicting accounts of Jamail and Morales). On Murr's fee claim, see Hollandsworth, *Up in Smoke*.

81. Southwestern Refining Co. v. Bernal, 960 S.W.2d 293 (Tex. 2000); Ford Motor Co. v. Sheldon, 965 S.W.2d 65 (Tex. 2000); Intratex Gas Co. v. Beeson, 22 S.W.3d 398 (Tex. 2000).

82. Laurie P. Cohen, *Southern Exposure: Lawyer Gets Investors to Sue GE, Prudential in Poor Border Town: Out of State Plaintiffs Hope for a Sympathetic Judge and Texas-Size Awards—"The Jurors Are Bountiful,"* WSJ, Nov. 30, 1994, at A1; Polaris Inv. Management Corp. v. Abascal, 890 S.W.2d 486 (Tex. App. 1994) (Rickhoff, J., concurring); quote, "21" International Holdings, Inc. v. Westinghouse Elec. Corp., 856 S.W.2d 479, 486 (Tex. App. 1993) (Peeples, J., concurring).

83. Act of May 18, 1995, 74th Leg., R.S., ch. 138, 1995 Tex. Gen. Law 978; Masonite Corp. v. Garcia, 951 S.W.2d 812, 817–18 (Tex. App. 1997) (quoting House Comm. on State Affairs, Bill Analysis, Tex.

S.B. 32, 74th Leg., R.S. at 26 (1995)); quote, A. Erin Dwyer, Donald Colleluori & Thomas A. Graves, *Texas Civil Procedure*, 49 SMU L. Rev. 1371, 1375 (1996).

84. *Tort Reform*, TBJ, Oct. 1995, at 936 (summarizing legislation); Stephen Daniels & Joanne Martin, *The Strange Success of Tort Reform*, 53 Emory L.J. 1225, 1232–33 (2004).

85. Epigraph, Daniels & Martin, at 1225; on the falling rate of auto accident filings from 1986–2000, *id.* at 1235 (fig. 2).

86. *New Tort Cases*, www.courts.state.tx.us/pubs/ ar2006/trends/torts-87-06.pdf.

87. Hardberger, at 141; *60 Minutes: Justice for Sale?* (CBS television broadcast Nov. 1, 1998) (noting influence of defense interests in Texas Supreme Court elections).

88. Christopher O'Leary, *Lone Star Litigation: Are Huge Jury Awards in Texas a Relic?*, Corp. Legal Times, May 2003, at 43, and quote at 46. The tort reform group Citizens for a Sound Economy alleged savings of over $10.4 billion in 2000 alone, of which $7.63 billion was attributable to "reforms and related factors in Texas" (The Perryman Group, *The Impact of Judicial Reforms on Economic Activity in Texas* 1 (August 2000), www.cse.org/reports/perryman_ texas_study.pdf, on file with author).

89. David A. Anderson, *Judicial Tort Reform in Texas*, 26 Rev. Lit. 1, 7, 46 (2007).

90. Merck & Co. v. Ernst, 296 S.W.3d 81 (Tex. App. 2009); *In re* Silica Products Liability Litigation, 398 F.Supp.2d 563 (S.D. Tex. 2005); quote, Anderson, at 4; Act of June 11, 2003, 78th Leg., R.S., ch. 204, 2003 Tex. Gen. Laws 847. On H.B. 4 and Proposition 12, Michael S. Hull et al., *House Bill 4 and Proposition 12: An Analysis with Legislative History, Part One*, 36 TTLR 1 (2005), *Part Two*, 36 TTLR 51 (2005); Lucas v. United States, 757 S.W.2d 687 (Tex. 1988) (holding statutory limitation on damages in medical malpractice cases violates Texas constitution).

91. Lawrence J. McQuillan & Hovannes Abramyan, U.S. TORT LIABILITY INDEX: 2008 REPORT (Pacific Research Institute 2008).

CONCLUSION

1. CHARLIE WILSON'S WAR (Universal Pictures 2007). CHARLIE WILSON'S WAR (2003), by George Crile, the nonfiction book on which the movie is based, lacks any such account (at 505). Wilson wrote a note to Avrakotos stating, "We won" (Crile, at 504); Crile's *Epilogue: Unintended Consequences* ends, "Epilogues indicate that the story has been wrapped up, the chapter finished. This one, sadly, is far from over" (at 520).

BIBLIOGRAPHY

★

BOOKS

Abel, Richard L., AMERICAN LAWYERS (1989).

Adams, Frederick Upham, THE WATERS PIERCE CASE IN TEXAS (1908).

Adams, Randall, et al., ADAMS V. TEXAS (1992).

Aldrich, Mark, DEATH RODE THE RAILS: AMERICAN RAILROAD ACCIDENTS AND SAFETY, 1828–1965 (2006).

Alexander, Charles C., CRUSADE FOR CONFORMITY: THE KU KLUX KLAN IN TEXAS, 1920–1930 (1962).

Alonzo, Armando C., TEJANO LEGACY: RANCHEROS AND SETTLERS IN SOUTH TEXAS, 1734–1900 (1998).

Alter, Jonathan, THE DEFINING MOMENT: FDR'S HUNDRED DAYS AND THE TRIUMPH OF HOPE (2007).

American Law Institute, RESTATEMENT OF THE LAW OF TORTS (1933).

Anderson, Dillon, THE BILLINGSLEY PAPERS (1961).

Anderson, Gary Clayton, THE CONQUEST OF TEXAS: ETHNIC CLEANSING IN THE PROMISED LAND, 1820–1875 (2005).

Anderson, Terry H., THE PURSUIT OF FAIRNESS: A HISTORY OF AFFIRMATIVE ACTION (2004).

Ariens, Michael, AMERICAN CONSTITUTIONAL LAW AND HISTORY (annual publication).

Arnold, Ann, HISTORY OF FORT WORTH LEGAL COMMUNITY (2000).

Baker, J. H., AN INTRODUCTION TO ENGLISH LEGAL HISTORY (2d ed. 1979).

Bakken, Gordon Morris, ed., LAW IN THE WESTERN UNITED STATES (2000).

Ball, Howard, THE BAKKE CASE: RACE, EDUCATION, AND AFFIRMATIVE ACTION (2000).

Banks, Russell, THE SWEET HEREAFTER (1991).

Barr, Alwyn, BLACK TEXANS: A HISTORY OF AFRICAN AMERICANS IN TEXAS, 1528–1995 (1973, repr. Univ. of Oklahoma Press 1996).

———, RECONSTRUCTION TO REFORM: TEXAS POLITICS, 1876–1906 (1971, repr. 2000).

———, & Robert Calvert, eds., BLACK LEADERS: TEXANS FOR THEIR TIMES (1981).

Bartley, Ernest R., THE TIDELANDS OIL CONTROVERSY: A LEGAL AND HISTORICAL ANALYSIS (1953).

Baum, Dale, COUNTERFEIT JUSTICE: THE JUDICIAL ODYSSEY OF TEXAS FREEDWOMAN AZELINE HEARNE (2009).

Bell, James H., SPEECH OF HON. JAMES H. BELL OF THE TEXAS SUPREME COURT, ON DECEMBER 1ST, 1860 (Intelligencer Book Office 1860).

Bernstein, Patricia, THE FIRST WACO HORROR: THE LYNCHING OF JESSE WASHINGTON AND THE RISE OF THE NAACP (2005).

BIENNIAL REPORT OF ATTORNEY GENERAL: TEXAS, 1914–1916 (1916).

Bishop, Curtis Kent, LOTS OF LAND (1949).

Blackstone, William, COMMENTARIES ON THE LAW OF ENGLAND (4 vols. 1765–69).

Blakeslee, Nate, TULIA: RACE, COCAINE, AND CORRUPTION IN A SMALL TEXAS TOWN (2005).

Bloomfield, Maxwell, *From Deference to Confrontation: The Early Black Lawyers of Galveston, Texas, 1895–1920, in* THE NEW HIGH PRIESTS: LAWYERS IN POST–CIVIL WAR AMERICA (Gerard W. Gawalt ed., 1984).

Boorstin, Daniel J., THE GENIUS OF AMERICAN POLITICS (1953).

Bringhurst, Bruce, ANTITRUST AND THE OIL MONOPOLY: THE STANDARD OIL CASES, 1890–1911 (1979).

Brown, John Henry, INDIAN WARS AND PIONEERS (1890).

Brown, Richard Maxwell, STRAIN OF VIOLENCE: HISTORICAL STUDIES OF AMERICAN VIOLENCE AND VIGILANTISM (1975).

Buenger, Walter L., & Joseph A. Pratt, BUT ALSO GOOD BUSINESS: TEXAS COMMERCE BANKS AND THE FINANCING OF HOUSTON AND TEXAS, 1886–1986 (1986).

Buenger, Walter L., & Robert A. Calvert, eds., TEXAS THROUGH TIME: EVOLVING INTERPRETATIONS (1991).

Burrough, Bryan, THE BIG RICH: THE RISE AND FALL OF THE GREATEST TEXAS OIL FORTUNES (2009).

Cahill, Thomas, A SAINT ON DEATH ROW: THE STORY OF DOMINIQUE GREEN (2009).

Calvert, Robert W., HERE COMES THE JUDGE (1977).

Campbell, Randolph B., AN EMPIRE FOR SLAVERY: THE PECULIAR INSTITUTION IN TEXAS, 1821–1865 (1989).

———, GONE TO TEXAS: A HISTORY OF THE LONE STAR STATE (2003).

———, ed., THE LAWS OF SLAVERY IN TEXAS (William S. Pugsley & Marilyn P. Duncan comps., 2010).

Cantrell, Gregg, STEPHEN F. AUSTIN: EMPRESARIO OF TEXAS (1999).

———, & Elizabeth Hayes Turner, eds., LONE STAR PASTS: MEMORY AND HISTORY IN TEXAS (2007).

Carp, E. Wayne, FAMILY MATTERS: SECRECY AND DISCLOSURE IN THE HISTORY OF ADOPTION (1998).

Carrigan, William D., THE MAKING OF A LYNCHING CULTURE: VIOLENCE AND VIGILANTISM IN CENTRAL TEXAS, 1836–1916 (2004).

———, & Clive Webb, *Muerto por Unos Desconcidos (Killed by Persons Unknown): Mob Violence against Blacks and Mexicans, in* BEYOND BLACK AND WHITE: RACE, ETHNICITY, AND GENDER IN THE U.S. SOUTH AND SOUTHWEST (Stephanie Cole & Alison M. Parker eds., 2004).

Carrington, Paul, A DALLAS LAWYER FOR SIXTY YEARS (1979).

Carroll, Mark M., HOMESTEADS UNGOVERNABLE: FAMILIES, SEX, RACE, AND THE LAW IN FRONTIER TEXAS, 1823–1860 (2001).

Carter, Dan T., SCOTTSBORO: A TRAGEDY OF THE AMERICAN SOUTH (1969).

CENTENNIAL HISTORY OF THE TEXAS BAR, 1882–1982 (1981).

Champagne, Anthony, CONGRESSMAN SAM RAYBURN (1984).

———, & Kyle Cheek, eds., JUDICIAL POLITICS IN TEXAS: PARTISANSHIP, MONEY, AND POLITICS IN STATE COURTS (2005).

Chapman, Betty Trapp, ROUGH ROAD TO JUSTICE: THE JOURNEY OF WOMEN LAWYERS IN TEXAS (2008).

Cherlin, Andrew J., THE MARRIAGE GO-ROUND: THE STATE OF MARRIAGE AND THE FAMILY IN AMERICA TODAY (2009).

Childs, William R., THE TEXAS RAILROAD COMMISSION: UNDERSTANDING REGULATION IN AMERICA TO THE MID-TWENTIETH CENTURY (2005).

Chipman, Donald E., SPANISH TEXAS, 1521–1821 (1992).

Cimbala, Paul A., & Randall M. Miller, eds., THE FREEDMEN'S BUREAU AND RECONSTRUCTION (1999).

Cisneros, Carlos, THE CASE RUNNER (2008).

Clark, James Anthony, & Michel T. Halbouty, SPINDLETOP (1952).

Cobb, Berry H., A HISTORY OF DALLAS LAWYERS (1933).

COMMISSION FOR LAWYER DISCIPLINE ANNUAL REPORT JUNE 1, 2006–MAY 31, 2007 (2007).

Cook, Charles M., THE AMERICAN CODIFICATION MOVEMENT: A STUDY OF ANTEBELLUM LEGAL REFORM (1981).

Cook, Kerry Max, CHASING JUSTICE: MY STORY OF FREEING MYSELF AFTER TWO DECADES ON DEATH ROW FOR A CRIME I DIDN'T COMMIT (2007).

Cool, Paul, SALT WARRIORS: INSURGENCY ON THE RIO GRANDE (2008).

Coombes, Charles, THE PRAIRIE DOG LAWYER (1945).

Cotner, Robert Crawford, JAMES STEPHEN HOGG, A BIOGRAPHY (1959).

Crile, George, CHARLIE WILSON'S WAR (2003).

Crooker, John H., Jr., & Gibson Gayle, Jr., FULBRIGHT & JAWORSKI: 75 YEARS (1919–1994) (1994).

Crouch, Barry A., THE FREEDMEN'S BUREAU AND BLACK TEXANS (1992).

——, *"To Enslave the Rising Generation": The Freedman's Bureau and the Texas Black Code, in* THE FREEDMAN'S BUREAU AND RECONSTRUCTION (Paul A. Cimbala & Randall M. Miller, eds., 1999).

Curtis, Rosalee Morris, JOHN HEMPHILL: FIRST CHIEF JUSTICE OF THE STATE OF TEXAS (1971).

Cutter, Charles R., THE LEGAL CULTURE OF NORTHERN NEW SPAIN, 1700–1810 (1995).

Dallam, James Wilmer, A DIGEST OF THE LAWS OF TEXAS, CONTAINING A FULL AND COMPLETE COMPILATION OF THE LAND LAWS, TOGETHER WITH THE OPINIONS OF THE SUPREME COURT (1845, repr. 1883).

Davenport, J. H., THE HISTORY OF THE SUPREME COURT OF TEXAS (1917).

Davies, Nick, WHITE LIES: RAPE, MURDER AND JUSTICE TEXAS STYLE (1991).

Davis, David Brion, INHUMAN BONDAGE: THE RISE AND FALL OF SLAVERY IN THE NEW WORLD (2006).

Davis, Robert E., ed., THE DIARY OF WILLIAM BARRET TRAVIS: AUGUST 30, 1833–JUNE 26, 1834 (1966).

Deaton, Charles, THE YEAR THEY THREW THE RASCALS OUT (1973).

de la Teja, Jesús, SAN ANTONIO DE BÉXAR: A COMMUNITY ON NEW SPAIN'S NORTHERN FRONTIER (1995).

De León, Arnoldo, THEY CALLED THEM GREASERS: ANGLO ATTITUDES TOWARD MEXICANS IN TEXAS (1983).

DeRosa, Marshall L., THE CONFEDERATE CONSTITUTION OF 1861 (1991).

Derthick, Martha A., UP IN SMOKE: FROM LEGISLATION TO LITIGATION IN TOBACCO POLITICS (2d ed. 2005).

Dickens, Charles, OLIVER TWIST (1970 ed.).

DICTIONARY OF AMERICAN BIOGRAPHY (Allen Johnson & Dumas Malone eds., 1933 *et seq.*).

Dobkins, Betty, THE SPANISH ELEMENT IN TEXAS WATER LAW (1959).

Dorough, C. Dwight, MR. SAM (1962).

Douglas, C. L., FAMOUS TEXAS FEUDS (1936).

Drachman, Virginia, SISTERS IN LAW: WOMEN LAWYERS IN MODERN AMERICAN HISTORY (1998).

Drago, Harry Sinclair, THE GREAT RANGE WARS: VIOLENCE ON THE GRASSLAND (1970).

Dray, Philip, AT THE HANDS OF PERSONS UNKNOWN: THE LYNCHING OF BLACK AMERICA (2002).

Dunbar, Robert G., FORGING NEW RIGHTS IN WESTERN WATERS (1983).

Duncan, John M., AN EYE OPENER: THE STANDARD OIL-MAGNOLIA COMPROMISE: THE WHOLE TRUTH (1915).

Duxbury, Neil, PATTERNS OF AMERICAN JURISPRUDENCE (1995).

EARLY LAWS OF TEXAS (Sayles, John, and Henry Sayles comp. & arr. 1888 ed.).

Ebright, Malcolm ed., SPANISH AND MEXICAN LAND GRANTS AND THE LAW 74 (1989).

Ely, James W., Jr., RAILROADS AND AMERICAN LAW (2001).

Fairman, Charles, RECONSTRUCTION AND REUNION, 1864–1888, PART ONE (1971); PART TWO (1987).

Finty, Tom, Jr., ANTI-TRUST LEGISLATION IN TEXAS (1916).

Flint, Richard E., & L. Wayne Scott, TEXAS CIVIL PROCEDURE: PRETRIAL (2007).

Frankfurter, Felix, & Nathan Green, THE LABOR INJUNCTION (1930).

Friedman, Lawrence, CRIME AND PUNISHMENT IN AMERICAN HISTORY (1993).

——, THE REPUBLIC OF CHOICE: LAW, AUTHORITY AND CULTURE (1990).

Foner, Eric, RECONSTRUCTION: AMERICA'S UNFINISHED REVOLUTION, 1863–1877 (1988).

Gambrell, Herbert, ANSON JONES: THE LAST PRESIDENT OF TEXAS (2d ed. 1964).

Gammel, H. P. N., ed., THE LAWS OF TEXAS, 1822–1897 (10 vols., Gammel Book Co. 1898).

Garcia, Ignacio M., WHITE BUT NOT EQUAL: MEXICAN AMERICANS, JURY DISCRIMINATION AND THE SUPREME COURT (2009).

Gard, Wayne, FRONTIER JUSTICE (1949).

George, Pamela E., TEXAS MARITAL PROPERTY RIGHTS: CASES AND MATERIALS (2009).

Gibson, Arrell Morgan, THE LIFE AND DEATH OF COLONEL ALBERT JENNINGS FOUNTAIN (1965).

Gilmore, Grant, THE AGES OF AMERICAN LAW (1977).

Goebel, Julius J., ANTECEDENTS AND BEGINNINGS TO 1801 (1971).

Gordon, John Steele, THE SCARLET WOMAN OF WALL STREET: JAY GOULD, JIM FISK, CORNELIUS VANDERBILT, AND THE BIRTH OF WALL STREET (1990).

Gould, Lewis L., PROGRESSIVES AND PROHIBITIONISTS: TEXAS DEMOCRATS IN THE WILSON ERA (1973, repr. 1992).

Gracy, David B., II, ed., ESTABLISHING AUSTIN'S COLONY: THE FIRST BOOK PRINTED IN TEXAS WITH THE LAWS, ORDERS AND CONTRACTS OF COLONIZATION (1970).

Graham, Sara Hunter, WOMAN SUFFRAGE AND THE NEW DEMOCRACY (1996).

Grant, Joseph M., & Lawrence L. Crum, THE DEVELOPMENT OF STATE-CHARTERED BANKING IN TEXAS: FROM PREDECESSOR SYSTEMS UNTIL 1970 (1978).

Grantham, Dewey W., SOUTHERN PROGRESSIVISM: THE RECONCILIATION OF PROGRESS AND TRADITION (1983).

Green, George Norris, THE ESTABLISHMENT IN TEXAS POLITICS: THE PRIMITIVE YEARS, 1938–1957 (1979).

Greenleaf, Simon, EVIDENCE (Little, Brown 1848).

Gronlund, Mimi Clark, SUPREME COURT JUSTICE TOM C. CLARK: A LIFE OF SERVICE (2010).

Grossberg, Michael, GOVERNING THE HEARTH: LAW AND FAMILY IN NINETEENTH-CENTURY AMERICA (1985).

Haley, J. Evetts, CHARLES GOODNIGHT: COWMAN AND PLAINSMAN (1936).

———, THE XIT RANCH OF TEXAS (1953).

Haley, James L., SAM HOUSTON (2002).

Hamilton, Holman, PROLOGUE TO CONFLICT: THE CRISIS AND COMPROMISE OF 1850 (1964).

Hamm, Richard F., SHAPING THE EIGHTEENTH AMENDMENT: TEMPERANCE REFORM, LEGAL CULTURE, AND THE POLITY, 1880–1920 (1995).

Hardeman, D. B., & Donald C. Bacon, RAYBURN: A BIOGRAPHY (1987).

Hardwicke, Robert E. *Texas, 1938–1948, in* CONSERVATION OF OIL AND GAS: A LEGAL HISTORY, 1948 (Blakely M. Murphy ed., 1949, repr. 1972).

Harris, Charles H., III, & Louis R. Sadler, THE TEXAS RANGERS AND THE MEXICAN REVOLUTION: THE BLOODIEST DECADE, 1910–1920 (2004).

Hartog, Hendrik, MAN AND WIFE IN AMERICA: A HISTORY (2000).

Haskins, George Lee, & Herbert A. Johnson, FOUNDATIONS OF POWER: JOHN MARSHALL, 1801–1815 (1981).

Hawkins, Walace, THE CASE OF JOHN C. WATROUS, UNITED STATES JUDGE FOR TEXAS: A POLITICAL STORY OF HIGH CRIMES AND MISDEMEANORS (1950).

———, EL SAL DEL REY (1947).

Henderson, Bancroft C., & T. C. Sinclair, THE SELECTION OF JUDGES IN TEXAS: AN EXPLORATORY STUDY (1964).

Hensler, D., et al., TRENDS IN TORT LITIGATION: THE STORY BEHIND THE STATISTICS (1987).

Hildebrand, Ira P., THE LAW OF TEXAS CORPORATIONS (4 vols., 1942).

———, SELECT CASES AND OTHER AUTHORITIES ON THE LAW OF PRIVATE CORPORATIONS: TEXAS SUPPLEMENT (1916).

Hine, Darlene Clark, BLACK VICTORY: THE RISE AND FALL OF THE WHITE PRIMARY IN TEXAS (1979, new ed. 2003).

Hinton, Diana Davids, & Roger M. Olien, OIL IN TEXAS: THE GUSHER AGE, 1895–1945 (2002).

Hobbes, Thomas, LEVIATHAN (Herbert W. Schneider ed. 1958).

Hodges, Gus M., SPECIAL ISSUE SUBMISSION IN TEXAS (1959).

Holt, Michael F., THE RISE AND FALL OF THE AMERICAN WHIG PARTY: JACKSONIAN POLITICS AND THE ONSET OF THE CIVIL WAR (1999).

Hopkins, Ernest Jerome, OUR LAWLESS POLICE: A STUDY OF THE UNLAWFUL ENFORCEMENT OF THE LAW (1931, repr. 1972).

Horton, David M., & Ryan Kellus Turner, LONE STAR JUSTICE: A COMPREHENSIVE OVERVIEW OF THE TEXAS CRIMINAL JUSTICE SYSTEM (1999).

Hovenkamp, Herbert, ENTERPRISE AND AMERICAN LAW, 1836–1937 (1991).

Howe, Daniel Walker, WHAT HATH GOD WROUGHT: THE TRANSFORMATION OF AMERICA, 1815–1848 (2007).

Huebner, Timothy S., THE SOUTHERN JUDICIAL TRADITION: STATE JUDGES AND SECTIONAL DISTINCTIVENESS, 1790–1890 (1999).

Hulse, J. F., TEXAS LAWYER: THE LIFE OF WILLIAM H. BURGES (1982).

Hyman, Harold M., CRAFTSMANSHIP AND CHARACTER: A HISTORY OF THE VINSON & ELKINS LAW FIRM OF HOUSTON, 1917–1997 (1998).

Institute of Medicine, SAFETY OF SILICONE BREAST IMPLANTS (1999).

Jacobson, Paul H., with Pauline F. Jacobson, AMERICAN MARRIAGE AND DIVORCE (1950).

Jamail, Joe, with Mickey Herskowitz, LAWYER: MY TRIALS AND JUBILATIONS (2003).

James, Marquis, THE TEXACO STORY (1952).

Jaworski, Leon, with Dick Schneider, CROSSROADS (1981).

Jaworski, Leon, with Mickey Herskowitz, CONFESSION AND AVOIDANCE: A MEMOIR (1979).

Katz, Harvey, SHADOW ON THE ALAMO: NEW HEROES FIGHT OLD CORRUPTION IN TEXAS POLITICS (1972).

Kemerer, Frank R., WILLIAM WAYNE JUSTICE (1991).

Kempin, Frederick G., Jr., HISTORICAL INTRODUCTION TO ANGLO-AMERICAN LAW (3d ed. 1990).

Kimball, Bruce A., THE INCEPTION OF MODERN PROFESSIONAL EDUCATION: C. C. LANGDELL, 1826–1906 (2009).

Kinch, Sam, Jr., & Ben Procter, TEXAS UNDER A CLOUD (1972).

King, John O., THE EARLY HISTORY OF THE HOUSTON OIL COMPANY OF TEXAS, 1901–1908 (1959).
——, JOSEPH STEPHEN CULLINAN: A STUDY OF LEADERSHIP IN THE TEXAS PETROLEUM INDUSTRY, 1897–1937 (1970).

Klarman, Michael J., FROM JIM CROW TO CIVIL RIGHTS: THE SUPREME COURT AND THE STRUGGLE FOR RACIAL EQUALITY (2004).

Kluger, Richard, SIMPLE JUSTICE: THE HISTORY OF BROWN V. BOARD OF EDUCATION AND BLACK AMERICA'S STRUGGLE FOR EQUALITY (1975).

Koffler, Joseph H., & Alison Reppy, COMMON LAW PLEADING (1969).

Kulansky, Mark, SALT: A WORLD HISTORY (2002).

Kurian, George Thomas, ed., DATAPEDIA OF THE UNITED STATES: AMERICAN HISTORY IN NUMBERS (2004).

Lang, Aldon Socrates, FINANCIAL HISTORY OF THE PUBLIC LANDS OF TEXAS (1932).

LaPiana, William P., LOGIC AND EXPERIENCE: THE ORIGIN OF MODERN AMERICAN LEGAL EDUCATION (1994).

Lasch, Christopher, THE CULTURE OF NARCISSISM (1979).

Lavergne, Gary, BEFORE BROWN: HEMAN MARION SWEATT, THURGOOD MARSHALL, AND THE LONG ROAD TO JUSTICE (2010).

Lavergne, Gary M., WORSE THAN DEATH: THE DALLAS NIGHTCLUB MURDERS AND THE TEXAS MULTIPLE MURDER LAW (2003).

LAWS AND DECREES OF THE STATE OF COAHUILA AND TEXAS (J. P. Kimball trans., 1839).

Lazarou, Kathleen, CONCEALED UNDER PETTICOATS: MARRIED WOMEN'S PROPERTY AND THE LAW OF TEXAS (1986).

LEGAL HISTORY OF CONSERVATION OF OIL AND GAS (1939).

Leopold, Aloysius A., TEXAS LAND TITLES (3d ed. 2005).

Lewis, William D., ed., GREAT AMERICAN LAWYERS (8 vols. 1908).

Lipartito, Kenneth J., & Joseph A. Pratt, BAKER & BOTTS IN THE DEVELOPMENT OF MODERN HOUSTON (1991).

Lipset, Seymour Martin, AMERICAN EXCEPTIONALISM: A DOUBLE-EDGED SWORD (1996).

Lundsgaarde, Henry P., MURDER IN SPACE CITY: A CULTURAL ANALYSIS OF HOUSTON HOMICIDE PATTERNS (1977).

Lynch, James D., BENCH AND BAR OF TEXAS (Nixon-Jones Printing Co. 1885).

Malavis, Nicholas, BLESS THE PURE AND HUMBLE: TEXAS LAWYERS AND OIL REGULATION, 1919–1936 (1996).

Mann, Bruce H., REPUBLIC OF DEBTORS: BANKRUPTCY IN THE AGE OF AMERICAN INDEPENDENCE (2002).

Marquart, James W., Sheldon Ekland-Olson & Jonathan R. Sorensen, THE ROPE, THE CHAIR, AND THE NEEDLE: CAPITAL PUNISHMENT IN TEXAS, 1923–1990 (1994).

Marten, James, TEXAS DIVIDED: LOYALTY AND DISSENT IN THE LONE STAR STATE, 1856–1874 (1990).

Martin, George, CAUSES AND CONFLICTS: THE CENTENNIAL HISTORY OF THE ASSOCIATION OF THE BAR OF THE CITY OF NEW YORK, 1870–1970 (1970).

Martin, Steve J., & Sheldon Ekland-Olson, TEXAS PRISONS: THE WALLS CAME TUMBLING DOWN (1987).

Matthews, Wilbur L., SAN ANTONIO LAWYER: MEMORANDA OF CASES AND CLIENTS (1983).

McArthur, Judith N., CREATING THE NEW WOMAN: THE RISE OF SOUTHERN WOMEN'S PROGRESSIVE CULTURE IN TEXAS, 1893–1918 (1998).

McCaslin, Richard B., TAINTED BREEZE: THE GREAT HANGING AT GAINESVILLE, TEXAS 1862 (1994).

McDougall, Walter A., FREEDOM JUST AROUND THE CORNER: A NEW AMERICAN HISTORY, 1585–1828 (2004).
——, THROES OF DEMOCRACY: THE AMERICAN CIVIL WAR ERA, 1829–1877 (2008).

McKay, S. S., DEBATES IN THE TEXAS CONSTITUTIONAL CONVENTION OF 1875 (1930).
——, MAKING THE TEXAS CONSTITUTION OF 1876 (1924).
——, SEVEN DECADES OF THE TEXAS CONSTITUTION OF 1876 (1942).

McKitrick, Reuben, THE PUBLIC LAND SYSTEM OF TEXAS, 1823–1910 (1918).

McKnight, Joseph W., The Spanish Watercourses of Texas, in ESSAYS IN LEGAL HISTORY IN HONOR OF FELIX FRANKFURTER (1966).
——, & William A. Reppy, Jr., TEXAS MATRIMONIAL PROPERTY LAW (2000).

McQuillan, Lawrence J., & Hovannes Abramyan, U.S. TORT LIABILITY INDEX: 2008 REPORT (2008).

McSwain, Betty Ann McCartney, ed., THE BENCH AND BAR OF WACO AND MCLENNAN COUNTY, 1849–1976 (1976).

Meacham, Jon, AMERICAN LION: ANDREW JACKSON IN THE WHITE HOUSE (2008).

Meinig, D. W., IMPERIAL TEXAS: AN INTERPRETIVE ESSAY IN CULTURAL GEOGRAPHY (1969).

Merryman, John Henry, & Rogelio Perez-Perdomo, THE CIVIL LAW TRADITION (3d ed. 2007).

Meyer, Michael C., WATER IN THE HISPANIC SOUTH-
WEST: A SOCIAL AND LEGAL HISTORY, 1550–1850
(1984).

Miller, Edmund Thornton, A FINANCIAL HISTORY
OF TEXAS (1916).

Miller, Thomas Lloyd, THE PUBLIC LANDS OF TEXAS,
1919–1970 (1972).

Mills, Warner E., Jr., MARTIAL LAW IN EAST TEXAS
(1960).

Minutaglio, Bill, CITY ON FIRE: THE EXPLOSION
THAT DEVASTATED A TEXAS TOWN AND IGNITED
A HISTORIC LEGAL BATTLE (2004).

Moneyhon, Carl H., TEXAS AFTER THE CIVIL WAR:
THE STRUGGLE OF RECONSTRUCTION (2004).

Moretta, John Anthony, WILLIAM PITT BALL-
INGER: TEXAS LAWYER, SOUTHERN STATESMAN,
1825–1888 (2000).

Morris, Thomas D., SOUTHERN SLAVERY AND THE
LAW, 1619–1860 (1996).

NAACP, THIRTY YEARS OF LYNCHING IN THE
UNITED STATES, 1889–1918 (1919, repr. 1969).

Neal, Bill, GETTING AWAY WITH MURDER ON THE
TEXAS FRONTIER: NOTORIOUS KILLINGS AND
CELEBRATED TRIALS (2006).

——— SEX, MURDER, AND THE UNWRITTEN LAW:
GENDER AND JUDICIAL MAYHEM, TEXAS STYLE
(2009).

Newton, W. Frank, ed., A GUIDE TO THE BASICS OF
LAW PRACTICE (3d ed. 1996).

Nieman, Donald G., ed., AFRICAN AMERICAN LIFE
IN THE POST–EMANCIPATION SOUTH, 1861–1900
(1994).

Nisbet, Richard E., & Dov Cohen, CULTURE OF
HONOR: THE PSYCHOLOGY OF VIOLENCE IN THE
SOUTH (1996).

Niven, JOHN, SALMON P. CHASE: A BIOGRAPHY
(1995).

North, Thomas, FIVE YEARS IN TEXAS (1871).

Novick, Peter, THAT NOBLE LIE: THE "OBJECTIVITY
QUESTION" AND THE AMERICAN HISTORICAL
ASSOCIATION (1988).

Olivas, Michael A., ed., "COLORED MEN" AND "HOM-
BRES AQUÍ": HERNANDEZ V. TEXAS AND THE
EMERGENCE OF MEXICAN-AMERICAN LAWYER-
ING (2006).

O'Neal, Bill, Violence in Texas History, in TEXAS: A
SESQUICENTENNIAL CELEBRATION (1984).

Paredes, Americo, "WITH A PISTOL IN HIS HAND": A
BORDER BALLAD AND ITS HERO (1958).

Parenti, Meredith B., & Susanna Dokupil, TEXAS-
SIZED TRANSFORMATION: THE CONSERVATIVE
COUNTERREVOLUTON ON THE TEXAS SUPREME
COURT (2006).

Pascoe, Peggy, WHAT COMES NATURALLY: MISCE-
GENATION LAW AND THE MAKING OF RACE IN
AMERICA (2009).

Paxton, Philip (pseudonym of Samuel A. Hammett),
A STRAY YANKEE IN TEXAS (Redfield 1853).

Payne, Darwin, AS OLD AS DALLAS ITSELF: A HIS-
TORY OF THE LAWYERS OF DALLAS, THE DALLAS
BAR ASSOCIATION, AND THE CITY THEY HELPED
BUILD (1999).

———, Sarah Weddington & Barefoot Sanders,
INDOMITABLE SARAH: THE LIFE OF SARAH T.
HUGHES (2004).

Perkinson, Robert, TEXAS TOUGH: THE RISE OF
AMERICA'S PRISON EMPIRE (2010).

Petzinger, John, OIL AND HONOR: THE TEXACO-
PENNZOIL WARS (1987).

Plucknett, T. F. T., A CONCISE HISTORY OF THE
COMMON LAW (5th ed. 1956).

Potts, Charles S., RAILROAD TRANSPORTATION
IN TEXAS (Bulletin of the University of Texas
No. 119, 1909).

Powers, Deborah D., THE COURT OF APPEALS AT
AUSTIN, 1892–1992 (1992).

Prindle, David L., PETROLEUM POLITICS AND THE
TEXAS RAILROAD COMMISSION (1981).

PROCEEDINGS OF THE 1950 INSTITUTE ON ANTITRUST
LAWS AND PRICE REGULATIONS (1950).

PROCEEDINGS OF THE WATER LAW CONFERENCE
(University of Texas School of Law, 1959).

Proctor, Ben H., NOT WITHOUT HONOR: THE LIFE
OF JOHN H. REAGAN (1962).

Prosser, William B., HANDBOOK OF THE LAW OF
TORTS (4th ed. 1971).

Purcell, Edward A., Jr., THE CRISIS OF DEMOCRATIC
THEORY: SCIENTIFIC NATURALISM AND THE
PROBLEM OF VALUE (1973).

———, LITIGATION AND INEQUALITY: FEDERAL
DIVERSITY JURISDICTION IN INDUSTRIAL
AMERICA, 1870–1958 (1992).

Raggio, Louise Ballerstedt, with Vivian Anderson
Castleberry, TEXAS TORNADO: THE LIFE OF A
CRUSADER FOR WOMEN'S RIGHTS AND FAMILY
JUSTICE (2003).

Raper, Arthur F., THE TRAGEDY OF LYNCHING (1933).

Reamey, Gerald S., CRIMINAL OFFENSES AND
DEFENSES IN TEXAS (3rd ed. 2000).

———, & Walter W. Steele, Jr., TEXAS CRIMINAL
PROCEDURE (2d ed. 1991).

Redfield, H. V., HOMICIDE, NORTH AND SOUTH
(1880).

Reed, Alfred Zantzinger, TRAINING FOR THE PUBLIC
PROFESSION OF THE LAW (1921).

Reed, S. G., A History of the Texas Railroads (1941, repr. 1981).

Remini, Robert V., Andrew Jackson and the Bank War (1967).

Report of the Attorney-General of the State of Texas, 1885–1886 (1886).

Report of the Interim Study Committee on Divorce to the 58th Legislature (1963).

Report of the Tort Policy Working Group on the Causes, Extent, and Policy Implications of the Current Crisis in Insurance Availability and Affordability (Feb. 1986).

Reynolds, Donald E., Texas Terror: The Slave Insurrection Panic of 1860 and the Secession of the Lower South (2007).

Rice, Lawrence, The Negro in Texas, 1874–1900 (1971).

Richter, William L., The Army in Texas during Reconstruction, 1865–1870 (1987).

———, Overreached on All Sides: The Freedmen's Bureau Administrators in Texas, 1865–1868 (1991).

Riley, Glenda, Divorce: An American Tradition (1991).

Rister, Carl Coke, Oil! Titan of the Southwest (1949).

Roberts, O. M., The Impending Crisis (1860).

Rosenbaum, Ron, Travels with Dr. Death and Other Unusual Investigations (1991).

Rosenberg, Gerald N., The Hollow Hope: Can Courts Bring About Social Change? (1991).

Roth, Randolph, American Homicide (2009).

Rules Governing Admission to the Bar of Texas (1974, 1979, 1985 and 1995 eds.).

Sandage, Scott A., Born Losers: A History of Failure in America (2005).

San Miguel, Guadalupe, Jr., "Let Them All Take Heed": Mexican Americans and the Campaign for Educational Equality in Texas, 1910–1981 (1987, repr. 2001).

Schofield, Philip, & Jonathan Harris, eds., "Legislator of the World": Writings on Codification, Law, and Education: The Collected Works of Jeremy Bentham (1998).

School Desegregation in Texas: The Implementation of U.S v. Texas (Policy Research Report No. 51, Lyndon Baines Johnson School of Public Affairs, University of Texas at Austin, 1982).

Schuck, Peter H., Agent Orange on Trial (1987).

Selected Works of Mao Tse-Tung (4 vols. 1967).

Seligman, Joel, The High Citadel: The Influence of Harvard Law School (1978).

Singer, Jonathan W., Broken Trusts: The Texas Attorney General versus the Oil Industry, 1889–1909 (2002).

Sleeper, William M., & Allan D. Sanford, Waco Bar and Incidents of Waco History, in The Bench and Bar of Waco and McLennan County, 1849–1976 (Betty Ann McCartney McSwain ed., 1976).

Smith, Bennett, Marriage by Bond in Colonial Texas (1972).

Smith, E. F., A Saga of Texas Law (1940).

Sobel, Richard B., Bending the Law: The Story of the Dalkon Shield Bankruptcy (1991).

Sonnichsen, C. L., The El Paso Salt War (1961).

———, Ten Texas Feuds (1957, repr. 2000).

Spellman, Paul N., Spindletop Boom Days (2001).

Spratt, John Stricklin, The Road to Spindletop: Economic Change in Texas, 1875–1901 (1955).

Sracic, Paul A., San Antonio v. Rodriguez and the Pursuit of Equal Education: The Debate over Discrimination and School Funding (2006).

Steen, Ralph W., Twentieth Century Texas (1942).

Stevens, Robert, Law School: Legal Education in America from the 1850s to the 1980s (1983).

Stuntz, Jean A., Hers, His, and Theirs: Community Property Law in Spain and Early Texas (1986).

Texas Defender Service, Deadly Speculation: Misleading Texas Capital Juries with False Predictions of Future Dangerousness (2004).

———, A State of Denial: Texas Justice and the Death Penalty (2000).

Texas Legislative Council, Legal Status of Married Women in Texas: A Report to the 55th Legislature (1956).

A Texas Supreme Court Trilogy: Oral History Interviews with the Honorable Robert W. Calvert, Joe R. Greenhill Sr., and Jack Pope (3 vols. 1998).

Thomas, William, Lawyering for the Railroad: Business, Law, and Power in the New South (1999).

Thompson, Craig, Since Spindletop: A Human Story of Gulf's First Half-Century (1951).

Thomson, David I. C., Law School 2.0: Legal Education for the Digital Age (2009).

Thorelli, Hans B., The Federal Antitrust Policy: Origination of an American Tradition (1955).

Timberlake, James H., PROHIBITION AND THE PRO-GRESSIVE MOVEMENT: 1900–1920 (1963).

Townes, John C., PLEADING IN THE DISTRICT AND COUNTY COURT OF TEXAS (2d ed. 1913).

Tushnet, Mark V., MAKING CIVIL RIGHTS LAW (1994).

U.S. News and World Report, ANNUAL GUIDE TO LAW SCHOOLS (annual publication).

Utley, Robert M., LONE STAR JUSTICE: THE FIRST CENTURY OF THE TEXAS RANGERS (2002).

———, LONE STAR LAWMEN: THE SECOND CENTURY OF THE TEXAS RANGERS (2007).

Vandiver, Frank E., THE SOUTHWEST: SOUTH OR WEST? (1975).

Van Ee, Daun, DAVID DUDLEY FIELD AND THE RECONSTRUCTION OF THE LAW (1986).

von Mehren, Arthur T., & James Gordley, THE CIVIL LAW SYSTEM (2d ed. 1977).

Wallace, Ernest, CHARLES DEMORSE: PIONEER EDITOR AND STATESMAN (1943, repr. 1985).

Ward, Hortense, PROPERTY RIGHTS OF MARRIED WOMEN IN TEXAS (The Delineator 1912).

Webb, Walter P., DIVIDED WE STAND: THE CRISIS OF A FRONTIERLESS DEMOCRACY (1937, rev. ed. 1944).

———, THE GREAT PLAINS (1931).

———, TEXAS RANGERS: A CENTURY OF FRONTIER DEFENSE (1935, 2d ed. 1965).

Weems, John Edward, with Jane Weems, DREAM OF EMPIRE: A HUMAN HISTORY OF THE REPUBLIC OF TEXAS, 1836–1845 (1971).

Wharton, Clarence, THE JURISDICTION OF THE ALCALDE COURTS IN TEXAS PRIOR TO THE REVOLUTION: ARGUMENT FILED IN CONNELY [SIC] V. ABRAMS IN COURT OF CIVIL APPEALS AT GALVESTON (1927).

White, Morton, SOCIAL THOUGHT IN AMERICA: THE REVOLT AGAINST FORMALISM (1957).

Wilson, Theodore Brantner, THE BLACK CODES OF THE SOUTH (1965).

Wilson, Will R., Sr., A FOOL FOR A CLIENT: HOW PRESIDENT NIXON COULD HAVE AVOIDED IMPEACHMENT (2000).

Winegarten, Ruth, & Judith N. McArthur, eds., CITIZENS AT LAST: THE WOMAN SUFFRAGE MOVEMENT IN TEXAS (1987).

Witt, John Fabian, THE ACCIDENTAL REPUBLIC: CRIPPLED WORKINGMEN, DESTITUTE WIDOWS, AND THE REMAKING OF AMERICAN LAW (2004).

Woods, Julia A., Ashley Craddock, and Regan Marie Brown, AUSTIN LAWYERS: A LEGACY OF LEADERSHIP AND SERVICE (2005).

Woodward, C. Vann, THE STRANGE CAREER OF JIM CROW (1955).

Wooten, Dudley G., ed., A COMPREHENSIVE HISTORY OF TEXAS (2 vols. 1898, repr. 1986).

Yergin, Daniel, THE PRIZE: THE EPIC QUEST FOR OIL, MONEY, AND POWER (1991).

Zelden, Charles L., THE BATTLE FOR THE BLACK BALLOT: SMITH V. ALLWRIGHT AND THE DEFEAT OF THE ALL-WHITE PRIMARY (2004).

———, JUSTICE LIES IN THE DISTRICT: THE U.S. DISTRICT COURT, SOUTHERN DISTRICT OF TEXAS, 1902–1960 (1993).

JOURNAL ARTICLES

Adams, Charles F., *A Chapter of Erie*, 109 N. Am. Rev. 30 (1869).

———, *The Erie Railroad Row*, 3 Am. L. Rev. 41 (1868).

Aldave, Barbara Bader, *Women in the Law in Texas: The Stories of Three Pioneers*, 25 StMLJ 289 (1993).

Alexander, James P., *The New Bar Examination Rules*, TBJ, Apr. 1943, at 90.

Anderson, David A., *Judicial Tort Reform in Texas*, 26 Rev. Lit. 1 (2007).

Andrews, Thomas R., *Income from Separate Property: Towards a Theoretical Foundation*, 56 Law & Contemp. Probs. 171 (1993).

Anglim, Christopher, *South Texas College of Law: Houston's Gateway to Opportunity in Law*, 39 STLR 919 (1998).

Ariens, Michael, *American Legal Ethics in an Age of Anxiety*, 40 StMLJ 343 (2008).

———, *Law School Branding and the Future of Legal Education*, 34 StMLJ 301 (2003).

———, *Progress Is Our Only Product: Legal Reform and the Codification of Evidence*, 17 L. & Soc. Inq. 213 (1992).

———, *The Storm between the Quiet: Tumult in the Texas Supreme Court, 1911–1921*, StMLJ 641 (2007).

———, *A Thrice Told Tale, or Felix the Cat*, 107 Harv. L. Rev. 620 (1994).

Ashford, Gerald, *Jacksonian Liberalism and Spanish Law in Early Texas*, 52 SWHQ 1 (1953).

August, Ray, *The Spread of Community-Property Law to the Far West*, 3 W. Leg. Hist. 35 (1990).

Autry, James L., *The Business Corporation in Texas—Its Formation, If Domestic; Its Admission, If Foreign*, 19 PTBA 101 (1900).

Baab, William, & William Royal Furgeson, Jr., *Texas*

Sentencing Practices: A Statistical Study, 45 TLR 471 (1967).

Baade, Hans W., *Chapters in the History of the Supreme Court of Texas: Reconstruction and "Redemption,"* 40 StMLJ 17 (2008).

———, *The Form of Marriage in Spanish North America*, 61 Cornell L. Rev. 1 (1975).

———, *The Historical Background of Texas Water Law: A Tribute to Jack Pope*, 18 StMLJ 1 (1986).

———, *Law at Texas: The Roberts-Gould Era (1883–1893)*, 86 SWHQ 161 (1982).

———, *Reflections on the Reception (or Renaissance) of Civil Law*, 55 SMU L. Rev. 59 (2002).

Bailey, Edward W., *Need for Revision of the Texas Corporation Statutes*, 3 BLR 1 (1950).

———, *Texas Corporation Statutes*, TBJ, May 1950, at 185.

Bar Section, 10 TLR 324 (1932).

Bar Should Study Four Omitted Canons, TBJ, July 1940, at 304.

Barker, Eugene C., *The Government of Austin's Colony, 1821–1831*, 21 SWHQ 223 (1918).

———, *Land Speculation as a Cause of the Texas Revolution*, 10 SWHQ 76 (1906).

Barnett, Walter E., *Criminal Punishment in Texas*, 36 TLR 63 (1957).

Barniziger, Ann Patton, *The Texas State Police during Reconstruction: A Reexamination*, 72 SWHQ 470 (1969).

Baron, Roger M., & Ronald J. Baron, *The Pennzoil-Texaco Dispute: An Independent Analysis*, 38 BLR 253 (1986).

Belsheim, Edmund O., *The Need for Revising the Texas Corporation Statutes*, 27 TLR 659 (1949).

Bickel, Paul J., *What a Model Corporation Act Should Contain*, TBJ, May 1950, at 183.

Bloomfield, Maxwell, *Western Lawyers and Judges: Image and Reality*, 24 J. West 15 (1985).

———, *The Texas Bar in the Nineteenth Century*, 32 Vand. L. Rev. 261 (1979).

Booth, Frank R., *Ownership of Developed Water: A Property Right Threatened*, 17 StMLJ 1181 (1986).

Bowden, J. J., *The Texas-New Mexico Boundary Dispute along the Rio Grande*, 63 SWHQ 221 (1959).

Branton, James L., *Franklin S. Spears: A Proud Legacy to Texas Jurisprudence*, 28 StMLJ 329 (1997).

Breckinridge, M. S., *Some Phases of the Texas Anti-Trust Law (Part II)*, 4 TLR 129 (1926).

Brickell, Wendy, *Is It the CSI Effect or Do We Just Distrust Juries?*, 23 Crim. Just. 10 (2008).

Brickman, Lester, *Effective Hourly Rates of Contingency-Fee Lawyers: Competing Data and Non-Competitive Fees*, 81 Wash. U. L.Q. 653 (1003).

———, *On the Applicability of the Silica MDL Proceeding to Asbestos Litigation*, 36 Conn. Ins. L.J. 35 (2006).

———, *The Asbestos Litigation Crisis: Is There a Need for an Administrative Alternative?*, 13 Cardozo L. Rev. 1819 (1992).

Bromberg, Alan R., *Texas Business Organization and Commercial Law: Two Centuries of Development*, 55 SMU L. Rev. 83 (2002).

———, Byron F. Egan, Dan L. Nicewander & Robert S. Trotti, *The Role of the Business Law Section and the Texas Business Law Foundation in the Development of Texas Business Law*, 41 Tex. J. Bus. L. 41 (2005).

Bubany, Charles P., *The Texas Penal Code of 1974*, 28 SwLJ 292 (1974).

Burton, Harley True, *A History of the JA Ranch (Part I)*, 31 SWHQ 89 (1927).

Butler, Henry N., *Nineteenth-Century Jurisdictional Competition in the Granting of Corporate Privileges*, 14 J. Legal Stud. 129 (1985).

Butler, Marguerite L., *The History of Texas Southern University, Thurgood Marshall School of Law: "The House that Sweatt Built,"* 23 T. Marshall L. Rev. 45 (1997).

Butte, George C., *Early Development of Law and Equity in Texas*, 26 Yale L.J. 699 (1917).

Calvert, Robert W., *John Hemphill*, TBJ, Oct. 1961, at 937.

Campbell, Randolph B., *Scalawag District Judges: The E. J. Davis Appointees, 1870–1873*, 14 Hous. Rev. 275 (1992).

Cantú, Charles E., *An Essay on the Tort of Negligent Infliction of Emotional Distress in Texas: Stop Saying It Does Not Exist*, 33 StMLJ 455 (2002).

Caperton, Kent, Alan Schoenbaum & Art Anderson, *Anatomy of the Venue Bill*, TBJ, Mar. 1984, at 244.

Caperton, Kent, & Erwin McGee, *Background, Scope and Applicability of the Texas Rules of Evidence*, 20 HLR 49 (1983).

Caroom, Doug, & Paul Elliott, *Water Rights Adjudication—Texas Style*, TBJ, Nov. 1981, at 1183.

Carrington, Paul, *A Corporation Code for Texas*, 10 Ark. L. Rev. 28 (1955–56).

———, *Experience in Texas with the Model Business Corporation Act*, 5 Utah L. Rev. 292 (1957).

———, *First Draft of Texas Business Corporation Act*, TBJ, May 1951, at 219.

———, *The History of the Proposed Texas Business Corporation Act*, 4 BLR 428 (1952).

———, *The Texas Business Corporation Act as Enacted and Ten Years Later*, 43 TLR 609 (1965).

Carrington, Paul D., *Big Money in Texas Judicial Elections: The Sickness and Its Remedies*, 53 SMU L. Rev. 263 (2000).

Carter, Keith, *The Texas Court of Criminal Appeals (Part I)*, 11 TLR 1 (1933); *Part II, id.* at 186; *Part III, id.* at 301; *Part IV, id.* at 455.

Champagne, Anthony, *Coming to a Judicial Election Near You: The New Era in Texas Judicial Elections*, 43 STLR 9 (2001).

———, *Judicial Reform in Texas*, 72 Judicature 146 (Oct.–Nov. 1988).

———, *The Selection and Retention of Judges in Texas*, 40 SwLJ 53 (1986).

———, & Kyle Cheek, *The Cycle of Judicial Elections*, 29 Fordham Urban L.J. 907 (2002).

Chapman, Berlin B., *The Claim of Texas to Greer County (Part I)*, 53 SWHQ 19 (1949); *Part II, id.* at 164; *Part III, id.* at 404 (1950).

Cheek, Kyle D., & Anthony Champagne, *Partisan Judicial Elections: Lessons from a Bellwether State*, 39 Willamette L. Rev. 1357 (2003).

Citron, Eric F., Note, *Sudden Death: The Legislative History of Future Dangerousness and the Texas Death Penalty*, 25 Yale L. & Pol'y Rev. 143 (2006).

Civil Procedure Rules Amended, TBJ, Nov. 1972, at 1037.

Clark, Charles E., *History, Systems and Functions of Pleading*, 11 Va. L. Rev. 517 (1925).

———, *The Texas and Federal Rules of Civil Procedure*, 20 TLR 4 (1941).

Cole, Brady, *The Homestead Provisions on the Texas Constitution*, 3 TLR 217 (1925).

Committee on Jurisprudence and Law Reform, *Report of the Committee on Jurisprudence and Law Reform*, 30 PTBA 12 (1911).

Cooper, Lance A., *An Historical Overview of Judicial Selection in Texas*, 2 Tex. Wesleyan L. Rev. 317 (1995).

———, *"A Slobbering Lame Thing"? The Semicolon Case Reconsidered*, 101 SWHQ 321 (1998).

Cornyn, John, *The Roots of the Texas Constitution: Settlement to Statehood*, 26 TTLR 1089 (1995).

Crane, M. M., *Recollections of the Establishment of the Texas Railroad Commission*, 50 SWHQ 478 (1947).

Crouch, Barry A., *"All the Vile Passions": The Texas Black Code of 1866*, 97 SWHQ 13 (1993).

Crump, Susan, *An Overview of the Equal Rights Amendment in Texas*, 11 HLR 136 (1973).

Curriden, Mark, *Texas-Sized Fight Crystallizes Contingency Fee Issues in High-Stakes Litigation*, 19 Of Counsel 1 (Sept. 11, 2000).

———, *Up in Smoke*, 6 ABA J. E-Rep. 3 (Mar. 2, 2007).

Currie, David P., *The Constitution of the Republic of Texas (Part I)*, 8 Green Bag 2nd 145 (2005).

Dabney, Lewis M., *Pleading and Practice in the Land of Canaan*, 29 PTBA 140 (1910).

Dabney, Robert L., Jr., *A Dugout Canoe, A Bottle Gourd of Whiskey, and the Pursuit of "Right": The Origins of the Houston Bar Association*, Hous. Law., Sept.–Oct. 1999, at 46.

D'Agostino, Robert, *The Decline of the Law in Texas*, 2 Benchmark 171 (1986).

Dally, Carl E. F., & Patricia Brockway, *Changes in Appellate Review in Criminal Cases Following the 1980 Constitutional Amendment*, 13 StMLJ 211 (1981).

Daniels, Stephen, & Joanne Martin, *"It's Darwinism—Survival of the Fittest": How Markets and Reputations Shape the Ways in Which Plaintiffs' Lawyers Obtain Clients*, 21 Law & Pol'y 377 (1999).

———, *Jury Verdicts and the "Crisis" in Civil Justice*, 11 Just. Sys. J. 321 (1986).

———, *The Strange Success of Tort Reform*, 53 Emory L.J. 1225 (2004).

Davenport, John, Comment, *Twenty Years of Homicide in Texas*, 25 TLR 634 (1947).

Davidson, Mark, *The Civil War and Reconstruction in Harris County's Only District Court*, Hous. Law., Nov.–Dec. 1995, at 42.

"de Tocqueville, Alexis," *Money Talks: Why It Shouts to Some Lawyers and Whispers to Others*, Juris Doctor, Jan. 1972, at 54.

du Ponceau, Peter S., *Penal Code of the French Empire*, 2 Am. Rev. of Hist. & Pol. (1811), app. 1.

Dix, George E., *Texas "Confession" Law and Oral Self-Incriminating Statements*, 41 BLR 1 (1989).

Dooley, J. B., *The Use of Special Issues under the New State and Federal Rules*, 20 TLR 32 (1941).

Douglass, Susan G., Note, *Selection and Discipline of State Judges in Texas*, 14 HLR 672 (1977).

Drummond, Dylan O., Lynn Ray Sherman & Edmond R. McCarthy, Jr., *The Rule of Capture in Texas: Still So Misunderstood after All These Years*, 37 TTLR 1 (2004).

Durham, Kenneth R., *The Longview Race Riot of 1919*, 18 E. Tex. Hist. J. 13 (1980).

Dwyer, A. Erin, Donald Colleluori & Thomas A. Graves, *Texas Civil Procedure*, 49 SMU L. Rev. 1371 (1996).

Egan, Byron F., *Choice of Entity Alternatives*, 39 Tex. J. Bus. L. 379 (2004).

———, & Curtis W. Huff, *Choice of State Incorpora-*

tion—*Texas Versus Delaware: Is It Now Time to Rethink Traditional Notions?*, 54 SMU L. Rev. 249 (2001).

Environmental and Natural Resources Law Section, *Environmental Law*, 45 Tex. Prac. § 14.2(c) (2005).

Ericson, J. E., *The Delegates to the Convention of 1875: A Reappraisal*, 67 SWHQ 22 (1963).

———, *Origins of the Texas Bill of Rights*, 62 SWHQ 457 (1959).

———, & Mary P. Winston, *Civil Law and Common Law in Early Texas*, 2 E. Tex. Hist. J. 26 (1964).

Eubanks, Jo Beth, Comment, *Transracial Adoption in Texas: Should the Best Interests Standard Be Color-Blind?*, 24 StMLJ 1225 (1993).

Featherson, Thomas M., Jr., & Julie A. Springer, *Marital Property in Texas: The Past, Present, and Future*, 39 BLR 861 (1987).

Finnegan, Dorothy E., *Raising and Leveling the Bar: Standards, Access, and the YMCA Evening Law Schools, 1890–1940*, 55 J. Legal Educ. 208 (2005).

Fisher, John E., *The Legal Status of Free Blacks in Texas, 1836–1861*, 4 Tex. So. L. Rev. 342 (1977).

Fitzpatrick, Brian T., *Strict Scrutiny of Facially Race-Neutral State Action and the Texas Ten Percent Plan*, 53 BLR 289 (2001).

Fornell, Earl W., *The Abduction of Free Negroes and Slaves in Texas*, 60 SWHQ 369 (1957).

Fortney, Susan Saab, *Professional Responsibility and Liability Issues Related to Limited Liability Law Partnerships*, 39 STLR 399 (1998).

Freedman, Warren, *The Texas Politics of Today's Products Liability*, 5 StMLJ 16 (1973).

Gard, Wayne, *The Fence-Cutters*, 51 SWHQ 1 (1947).

Garrett, Roy, *Model Business Corporation Act*, 4 BLR 415 (1952).

Giannelli, Paul C., *Ake v. Oklahoma: The Right to Expert Assistance in a Post–Daubert, Post–DNA World*, 89 Cornell L. Rev. 1305 (2004).

Gilbert, B. Eugene, *Fitness for the Bar*, 12 TLR 453 (1934).

Gilbreath, Robert B., *The Supreme Court of Texas and the Emancipation Cases*, TBJ, Nov. 2006, at 946.

Gillette, Michael L., *Blacks Challenge the White University*, 86 SWHQ 321 (1982).

———, *The Rise of the NAACP in Texas*, 81 SWHQ 393 (1981).

Gillmer, Jason A., *Base Wretches and Black Wenches: A Story of Sex and Race, Violence, and Compassion during Slavery Times*, 59 Ala. L. Rev. 1501 (2008).

Gilmer, Daffan, *Early Courts and Lawyers of Texas*, 12 TLR 435 (1934).

Gilstrap, Rodney, & Leland C. de la Garza, *UPL: Unlicensed, Unwanted, and Unwelcome*, TBJ, Oct. 2004, at 798.

Glasrud, Bruce A., *Jim Crow's Emergence in Texas*, 15 Am. Studies 47 (1971).

Goldberg, Guy, & Gena Bunn, *Balancing Fairness & Finality: A Comprehensive Review of the Texas Death Penalty*, 5 Tex. Rev. L. & Pol. 49 (2000).

Goodman, Paul, *The Emergence of Homestead Exemption in the United States: Accommodation and Resistance to the Market Revolution, 1840–1880*, 80 J. Am. Hist. 470 (1993).

Goodwin, Lawrence C., *Populist Dreams and Negro Rights: East Texas as a Case Study*, 76 Am. Hist. Rev. 1435 (1971).

Graham, Richard, *Investment Boom in British-Texan Cattle Companies, 1880–1885*, 34 Bus. Hist. Rev. 421 (1960).

Greaser, Galen D., and Jesús F. de la Teja, *Quieting Title to Spanish Mexican Land Grants in the Trans-Nueces: The Bourland and Miller Commission, 1850–1852*, 95 SWHQ 445 (1992).

Green, Leon, *The Courts' Power Over Admission and Disbarment*, 4 TLR 1 (1925).

———, *Suggestions for Improving Court Procedure in Texas*, 2 TLR 464 (1924).

Greenhill, Joe R., *The Constitutional Amendment Giving Criminal Jurisdiction to the Texas Courts of Appeals and Recognizing the Inherent Power of the Texas Supreme Court*, 33 TTLR 377 (2002).

———, *The Early Supreme Court of Texas and Some of Its Justices*, TBJ, July 1999, at 646.

Greer, James K., *The Committee on the Texas Declaration of Independence (Part I)*, 30 SWHQ 239 (1927); *Part II*, 31 SWHQ 33 (1927); *Part III*, id. at 130.

Gross, Ariela J., *"The Caucasian Cloak": Mexican Americans and the Politics of Whiteness in the Twentieth-Century Southwest*, 95 Geo. L.J. 337 (2007).

Gross, Samuel R., Kristen Jacoby, Daniel J. Matheson, Nicholas Montgomery & Sujata Patil, *Exonerations in the United States, 1989 Through 2003*, 95 J. Crim. L. & Criminology 523 (2005).

Haley, J. Evetts, *The Grass Lease Fight and Attempted Impeachment of the First Panhandle Judge*, 38 SWHQ 1 (1934).

Hall, Ford W., *An Account of the Adoption of the Common Law by Texas*, 28 TLR 801 (1950).

Hall, W. Wendell, & Mark Emery, *The Texas Hold Out: Trends in the Review of Civil and Criminal Jury Verdicts*, 49 STLR 539 (2008).

Hamill, Susan Pace, *From Special Privilege to General Utility: A Continuation of Willard Hurst's Study of Corporations*, 49 Am. U. L. Rev. 81 (1999).

Hardberger, Phil, *Juries Under Siege*, 30 StMLJ 1 (1998).

———, *Texas Workers' Compensation: A Ten-Year Survey—Strengths, Weaknesses, and Recommendations*, 32 StMLJ 1 (2000).

Hardwicke, Robert E., *Oil-Well Spacing Regulations and Protection of Property Rights in Texas*, 31 TLR 99 (1952).

———, *The Rule of Capture and Its Implications as Applied to Oil and Gas*, 13 TLR 391 (1935).

Harnsberger, Richard S., *Nebraska Ground Water Problems*, 42 Neb. L. Rev. 721 (1963).

Hart, James P., *George W. Paschal*, 28 TLR 23 (1949).

———, *John Hemphill—Chief Justice of Texas*, 3 SwLJ 395 (1949).

———, *Oil, the Courts, and the Railroad Commission*, 44 SWHQ 303 (1941).

Henderson, Bancroft C., & T. C. Sinclair, *The Selection of Judges in Texas*, 5 HLR 430 (1968).

Higgason, Robert W., *A History of Texas Appellate Courts: Preserving Rights of Appeal through Adaptations to Growth*, Hous. Law., Mar.–Apr. 2002, at 20; *Part II, id.*, July–Aug. 2002, at 12.

Hildebrand, Ira P., *The Rights of Riparian Owners at Common Law in Texas*, 6 TLR 19 (1927).

Hine, Darlene Clark, *The Elusive Ballot: The Black Struggle Against the Texas Democratic White Primary, 1932–1945*, 81 SWHQ 371 (1978).

Hirczy de Miño, Wolfgang P., *Does an Equal Rights Amendment Make a Difference?*, 60 Alb. L. Rev. 1581 (1997).

Hogan, William Ransom, *Rampant Individualism in the Republic of Texas*, 44 SWHQ 454 (1941).

Holden, W. C., *Law and Lawlessness on the Texas Frontier, 1875–1890*, 44 SWHQ 188 (1940).

Howell, Timothy D., *So Long "Sweethearts": State Farm Fire & Casualty Co. v. Gandy Swings the Pendulum Further to the Right as the Latest in a Line of Setbacks for Texas Plaintiffs*, 29 StMLJ 47 (1997).

Howren, Alleine, *Causes and Origin of the Decree of April 6, 1830*, 16 SWHQ 378 (1913).

Huber, Stephen K., & James E. Myers, *Admission to the Practice of Law in Texas: An Analytical History*, 15 HLR 485 (1978).

Huff, Curtis W., *Choice of State Incorporation—Texas Versus Delaware: Is It Now Time to Rethink Traditional Notions?*, 31 Bull. Bus. L. Sec. St. B. Tex 9 (Dec. 1994).

Huie, William O., *The Texas Constitutional Definition of the Wife's Separate Property*, 35 TLR 1054 (1957).

Hull, Michael, et al., *House Bill 4 and Proposition 12: An Analysis with Legislative History, Part One*, 36 TTLR 1 (2005); *Part Two, id.* at 51.

Humphrey, David C., *A "Very Muddy and Conflicting" View: The Civil War As Seen from Austin, Texas*, 94 SWHQ 369 (1991).

Ivy, Gregory L., *Publications of Joseph W. McKnight*, 55 SMU L. Rev. 367 (2002).

Jackson, John N., *Waters-Pierce Cases: Another Visit*, TBJ, June 1975, at 529.

Jacobson, Terry L., & Kevin L. Wentz, *A Lawyer Has to Know His/Her Limitations: The Statute of Limitations in Medical Malpractice Cases—A Constitutional Compromise*, 23 TTLR 769 (1992).

James, Joseph B., *Southern Reaction to the Proposal of the Fourteenth Amendment*, 22 J. So. Hist. 477 (1956).

Johnson, Orrin W., & Laura Johnson Urbis, *Judicial Selection in Texas: A Gathering Storm?*, 23 TTLR 525 (1992).

Jones, Morgan A., *History of the Family Code*, 5 TTLR 267 (1974).

Jones, Vonceil, *Texas Southern University School of Law: The Beginning*, 4 Tex. So. U. L. Rev. 197 (1977).

Kauffman, Albert H., *The Texas School Finance Litigation Saga: Great Progress, Then Near Death by a Thousand Cuts*, 40 StMLJ 511 (2008).

Keilen, Andrea, & Maurie Levin, *Moving Forward: A Map for Meaningful Habeas Reform in Texas Capital Cases*, 34 Am. J. Crim. L. 207 (2007).

Kesavan, Vasan, & Michael Stokes Paulsen, *Is West Virginia Unconstitutional?*, 90 Cal. L. Rev. 291 (2002).

Kilgarlin, William Wayne, & Banks Tarver, *The Equal Rights Amendment: Governmental Action and Individual Liberty*, 68 TLR 1545 (1990).

Klemme, Chris, *Jacksonian Justice: The Evolution of the Elective Judiciary in Texas, 1836–1850*, 105 SWHQ 429 (2002).

Kmiec, Keenan D., *The Origin and Current Meanings of "Judicial Activism,"* 92 Cal. L. Rev. 1441 (2004).

Koeninger, Rupert C., *Capital Punishment in Texas*, 15 Crime & Delinquency 132 (1969).

Kramer, John R., *Will Legal Education Remain Affordable, by Whom and How?*, 1987 Duke L.J. 240.

Kritzer, Herbert M., *Advocacy and Rhetoric vs. Scholarship and Evidence in the Debate over Contingency Fees: A Reply to Professor Brickman*, 82 Wash. U. L.Q. 477 (2004).

Kull, Andrew, *The Enforceability after Emancipation of Debts Contracted for the Purchase of Slaves*, 70 Chi.-Kent L. Rev. 493 (1994).

Lambert, Mark W., *The Trinity University School of Law, 1873–1878, and the Jurisprudence of Texas*, Hous. Law., Nov.–Dec. 2003, at 34.

Letter of September 16, 1940, from Advisory Committee to Texas Supreme Court, 3 TBJ 522 (1940); *id.* at 4 TBJ 620 (1941).

Lynching in Texas, 47 Alb. L.J. 141 (1893).

Markesinis, Basil, *Introduction: The Life and Work of Hans Wolfgang Baade*, 36 Tex. Int'l L.J. 403 (2001).

Markham, Edward Lee, Jr., *The Reception of the Common Law of England in Texas and the Judicial Attitude Toward That Reception*, 29 TLR 904 (1951).

Marquardt, James W., & Ben M. Crouch, *Judicial Reform and Prisoner Control: The Impact of Ruiz v. Estelle on a Texas Penitentiary*, 19 Law & Soc'y Rev. 557 (1985).

Mauer, John Walker, *State Constitutions in a Time of Crisis: The Case of the Texas Constitution of 1876*, 68 TLR 1615 (1990).

McAdams, Tony, *Blame and The Sweet Hereafter*, 24 Legal Stud. F. 599 (2000).

McAfee, Alice G., *The All-Woman Texas Supreme Court: The History Behind a Brief Moment on the Bench*, 39 StMLJ 467 (2008).

McCallum, Henry D., *Barbed Wire in Texas*, 61 SWHQ 207 (1957).

McCluskey, Martha T., *The Illusion of Efficiency in Workers' Compensation "Reform,"* 50 Rutgers L. Rev. 657 (1998).

McCormick, Charles T., *The Revival of the Pioneer Spirit in Texas Procedure*, 18 TLR 426 (1940).

McDonald, Roy W., *The Background of the Texas Procedural Rules*, 19 TLR 229 (1941).

McGregor, Charles B., *Homicide Charge in Texas*, 6 BLR 40 (1953).

McKnight, Joseph W., *A Century of Development in Texas Law*, TBJ, Nov. 1973, at 1051.

———, *Commentary to Texas Family Code*, 5 TTLR 281 (1973).

———, *Law Without Lawyers on the Hispano-Mexican Frontier*, 66 W. Tex. Hist. Ass'n Year Book 51 (1990).

———, *Protection of the Family Home from Seizure by Creditors: The Sources and Evolution of a Legal Principle*, 86 SWHQ 369 (1983).

———, *Recodification of Texas Matrimonial Law*, TBJ, Dec. 1966, at 1000.

———, *Spanish Law for the Protection of Surviving Spouses in North America*, 57 Annuario de Historia del Derecho Español 365 (1987).

———, *Stephen Austin's Legalistic Concerns*, 89 SWHQ 239 (1986).

———, *The Spanish Influence on Texas Law of Civil Procedure*, 38 TLR 24 (1959).

———, *Texas Community Property Law: Its Course of Development and Reform*, 8 Cal. W. L. Rev. 117 (1971).

———, *The Spanish Legacy to Texas Law (Part I)*, 3 Am. J. Leg. Hist. 222 (1959); *Part II, id.* at 299.

MCLE Referendum Passes, TBJ, Jan. 1986, at 33.

Meier, August, & Elliott Rudwick, *The Boycott Movement Against Jim Crow Streetcars in the South, 1900–1906*, 55 J. Am. Hist. 756 (1969).

Mertz, Richard J., *"No One Can Arrest Me": The Story of Gregorio Cortez*, 1 J. S. Tex. 1 (1974).

Middleton, Annie, *The Texas Convention of 1845*, 25 SWHQ 26 (1922).

Miller, E. T., *The Texas Stock and Bond Law and Its Administration*, 22 Q.J. Econ. 109 (1907).

Miller, Robert Worth, & Stacy G. Ulbig, *Building a Populist Coalition in Texas, 1892–1896*, 74 J. So. Hist. 255 (2008).

Millon, David, *The First Antitrust Statute*, 29 Washburn L.J. 141 (1990).

Minimum Continuing Legal Education Rules: Supreme Court Orders Referendum, TBJ, July 1986, at 768.

Minimum Continuing Legal Education Rules and Regulations, TBJ, Dec. 1986, at 1187.

Montford, John T., & Will G. Barber, *1987 Texas Tort Reform: the Quest for a Fairer and More Predictable Texas Civil Justice System (Part III)*, 25 HLR 1005 (1988).

Moody, Dan, & Charles B. Wallace, *Texas Antitrust Laws and Their Enforcement: Comparison with Federal Antitrust Laws*, 11 SwLJ 1 (1957).

Morrow, William L., Comment, *Divorce Reform in Texas: The Path of Reason*, 18 SwLJ 86 (1964).

Muir, Andrew Forest, *Railroad Enterprise in Texas, 1836–1841*, 47 SWHQ 339 (1947).

Myres, S. D., Jr., *Mysticism, Realism, and the Texas Constitution of 1876*, 9 Sw. Pol. & Soc. Sci. Q. 166 (1928).

Nackman, Mark E., *Anglo-American Migrants to the West: Men of Broken Fortunes? The Case of Texas, 1821–1846*, 5 W. Hist. Q. 441 (1974).

Nash, A. E. Keir, *Texas Justice in the Age of Slavery: Appeals Concerning Blacks and the Antebellum State Supreme Court*, 8 HLR 438 (1971).

———, *The Texas Supreme Court and Trial Rights of Blacks, 1845–1860*, 58 J. Am. Hist. 622 (1971).

Neighbours, Kenneth F., *The Taylor-Neighbors Struggle over the Upper Rio Grande Region of Texas in 1850*, 61 SWHQ 431 (1958).

Newton, W. Frank, & Jeremy C. Wicker, *Personal Jurisdiction and the Appearance to Challenge Jurisdiction in Texas*, 38 BLR 491 (1986).

Nieman, Donald G., *Black Political Power and Criminal Justice: Washington County, Texas, 1868–1884*, 55 J. So. Hist. 391 (1989).

Norvell, James R., *Lewis v. Ames—An Ancient Cause Revisited*, 13 SwLJ 301 (1959).

——, *Oran M. Roberts and the Semicolon Court*, 37 TLR 279 (1959).

——, *The Reconstruction Courts of Texas, 1867–1873*, 62 SWHQ 141 (1958).

——, *The Supreme Court of Texas under the Confederacy, 1861–1865*, 4 HLR 46 (1966).

——, *A Texas Portrait: Oran M. Roberts*, TBJ, Nov. 1960, at 727.

Note, *Aliens: Right of an Alien to Own Land in Texas*, 7 TLR 607 (1929).

Note, *Law, Race, and the Border: The El Paso Salt War of 1877*, 117 Harv. L. Rev. 941 (2004).

Note, 23 TLR 190 (1945).

Nutting, Charles B., *The Texas Anti-trust Law: A Post Mortem*, 14 TLR 293 (1936).

Ogletree, D. W., *Establishing the Texas Court of Appeals, 1875–1876*, 47 SWHQ 5 (1943).

Ohler, George, *Background Causes of the Longview Race Riot of July 10, 1919*, 12 J. Am. Stud. Ass'n of Tex. 46 (1981).

Oldham, J. Thomas, *Changes in the Economic Consequences of Divorces, 1958–2008*, 42 Fam. L.Q. 419 (2008).

Overruled Their Judicial Superiors, 21 Am. L. Rev. 610 (1887).

Parker, Edwin A., *Anti-Railroad Personal Injury Litigation in Texas*, 19 PTBA 165 (1900).

Paschal, George W., *Preface*, 28 Tex. v (1869).

Paulsen, James W., *Community Property and the Early American Women's Rights Movement: The Texas Connection*, 32 Idaho L. Rev. 641 (1996).

——, *The History of Alimony in Texas and the New "Spousal Maintenance" Statute*, 7 Tex. J. Women & L. 151 (1998).

——, *The Judges of the Supreme Court of the Republic of Texas*, 65 TLR 305 (1986).

——, *Remember the Alamo[ny]! The Unique Texas Ban on Permanent Alimony and the Development of Community Property*, 56 Law & Contemp. Probs. 7 (1993).

——, *Rules of Procedure in Early Texas Courts*, 65 TLR 451 (1986).

——, *A Short History of the Supreme Court of the Republic of Texas*, 65 TLR 237 (1986).

——, *The Significance of Lawrence v. Texas*, Hous. Law., Jan.–Feb. 2004, at 32.

——, ed., *The Missing Cases of the Republic of Texas*, 65 TLR 372 (1986).

Pawlowic, Dean G., *Banking Law*, 30 TTLR 425 (1999).

Paxson, Frederic L., *The Constitution of Texas, 1845*, 18 SWHQ 386 (1915).

Peterson, Robert L., *Jay Gould and the Railroad Commission of Texas*, 58 SWHQ 422 (1955).

Phillips, Edward Hake, *The Sherman Courthouse Riot of 1930*, 25 E. Tex. Hist. J. 12 (1987).

Phillips, Nelson, *Historical Introduction*, 1 Tex. Jur. xxvii (1929).

Pierson, William Whatley, Jr., *Texas versus White*, 18 SWHQ 341 (1915).

Porter, Eugene O., *Railroad Enterprises in the Republic of Texas*, 59 SWHQ 363 (1956).

Potts, Charles S., *Inadequacy of Disbarment Machinery: Houtchens v. State*, 12 TLR 127 (1934).

Potts, Charles Shirley, *Texas Stock and Bond Law*, 53 Annals Amer. Acad. Pol. & Soc. Sci. 162 (1914).

Potts, C. S., *Is Husband's Act in Killing Wife Taken in Act of Adultery Justifiable Homicide in Texas?*, 2 TLR 111 (1923).

Pound, Roscoe, *The Causes of Popular Dissatisfaction in the Administration of Justice*, 29 A.B.A. Rep. 395 (1906).

Powers, Jean Fleming, *What the Market Will Bear: Questions about Limits on Attorneys' Fees*, Hous. Law., Nov.–Dec. 1998, at 23.

Powers, William, Jr., *Judge and Jury in the Texas Supreme Court*, 75 TLR 1699 (1997).

Pratt, Joseph A., *The Petroleum Industry in Transition: Antitrust and the Decline of Monopoly Control in Oil*, 40 J. Econ. Hist. 815 (1980).

——, & Mark E. Steiner, *"An Intent to Terrify": State Antitrust in the Formative Years of the Modern Oil Industry*, 29 Washburn L.J. 270 (1990).

Price, Dan R., *New Texas Venue Statute: Legislative History*, 15 StMLJ 855 (1984).

Priest, George L., *The Invention of Enterprise Liability: A Critical History of the Intellectual Foundations of Modern Tort Law*, 14 J. Legal Stud. 461 (1985).

Proposed Rules of Conduct for the State Bar of Texas, TBJ, Nov. 1939, at 361.

Rackley, J. Caleb, *A Survey of Sea-Change on the Supreme Court of Texas and Its Turbulent Toll on Texas Tort Law*, 48 STLR 733 (2007).

Rahl, James A., *Toward a Worthwhile State Antitrust Policy*, 39 TLR 753 (1961).

Raines, C. W., *Enduring Laws of the Republic of Texas (Part I)*, 1 Qtrly. Tex. St. Hist. Ass'n 96 (1897).

Ravkind, William M., Comment, *Justifiable Homicide in Texas*, 13 SwLJ 508 (1959).

Redman, Lauren F., *Domesticity and the Texas Community Property System*, 16 Buff. Women's L.J. 23 (2008).

Reeve, Jay D., Note, *Judicial Tort Reform: Bad Faith Cannot Be Predicated upon the Denial of a Claim for an Invalid Reason If a Valid Reason Is Later Shown: Republic Insurance Co. v. Stoker, 903 S.W.2d 338 (Tex. 1995)*, 27 TTLR 351 (1996).

Reich, Peter L., *Mission Revival Jurisprudence: State Courts and Hispanic Water Law Since 1850*, 69 Wash L. Rev. 869 (1994).

———, *Siete Partidas in My Saddlebags: The Transmission of Hispanic Law from Antebellum Louisiana to Texas and California*, 22 Tul. Eur. & Civ. L. F. 79 (2007).

Report of the Committee on Judicial Administration and Remedial Procedure, 36 PTBA 16 (1917).

Richardson, Rupert N., *Framing the Constitution of the Republic of Texas*, 31 SWHQ 191 (1928).

Robinson, Charles F., II, *Legislated Love in the Lone Star State: Texas and Miscegenation*, 108 SWHQ 65 (2004).

Romero, Mary, *El Paso Salt War: Mob Action or Political Struggle?*, 16 Aztlan: Int'l J. Chicano Stud. Res. 119 (1985).

Roots, Roger, *When Lawyers Were Serial Killers: Nineteenth Century Visions of Good Moral Character*, 22 N. Ill. U. L. Rev. 19 (2001).

Rousseau, Peter L., *Jacksonian Monetary Policy, Specie Flows and the Panic of 1837*, 62 J. Econ. Hist. 457 (2002).

Rules of Practice and Procedure in Civil Actions, TBJ, Oct. 1941, at 487.

Ryan, Rebecca M., *The Sex Right: A Legal History of the Marital Rape Exemption*, 20 L. & Soc. Inq. 941 (1995).

Sanders, Joseph, & Craig Joyce, *"Off to the Races": The 1980s Tort Crisis and the Law Reform Process*, 27 HLR 207 (1990).

Sanford, Allan D., *Texas' Million Dollar Anti-Trust Suit*, TBJ, Feb. 1948, at 167.

Sarat, Austin, *Exploring the Hidden Domains of Civil Justice: "Naming, Blaming, and Claiming" in Popular Culture*, 50 DePaul L. Rev. 425 (2000).

Sayer, John W., & Daniel L. Rotenberg, *Marijuana in Houston: A Second Report and a Proposal*, 8 HLR 209 (1970).

Schoen, Harold, *The Free Negro in the Republic of Texas (III): Manumissions*, 40 SWHQ 85 (1936).

Schoen, Rodric B., *The Texas Equal Rights Amendment in the Courts, 1972–1977: A Review and Proposed Principles of Interpretation*, 15 HLR 537 (1978).

———, *The Texas Equal Rights Amendment After the First Decade: Judicial Developments 1978–1982*, 20 HLR 1321 (1983).

Schwartz, Gary T., *The Beginning and the Possible End of the Rise of Modern American Tort Law*, 26 Ga. L. Rev. 601 (1992).

———, *The Vitality of Negligence and the Ethics of Strict Liability*, 15 Ga. L. Rev. 963 (1981).

Scott, L. Wayne, *Robert Wilburn Calvert, the Prudentialist*, 26 StMLJ 905 (1995).

Shaw, William L., *The Confederate Conscription and Exemption Acts*, 6 Am. J. Legal Hist. 368 (1962).

Shelley, George, *The Semicolon Court of Texas*, 48 SWHQ 449 (1945).

Sheridan, Clare, *"Another White Race": Mexican Americans and the Paradox of Whiteness in Jury Selection*, 21 Law & Hist. Rev. 109 (2003).

Shook, Robert W., *The Battle of the Nueces, August 10, 1862*, 66 SWHQ 31 (1962).

Simpson, Gordon, *The Task Still Challenges*, TBJ, Oct. 1941, at 485.

Smith, Bea Ann, *The Partnership Theory of Marriage: A Borrowed Solution Fails*, 68 TLR 689 (1990).

———, *Why the Community Property System Fails Divorced Women and Children*, 7 Tex. J. Women & L. 135 (1998).

Smith, Cullen, *The Texas Canons of Ethics Revisited*, 18 BLR 183 (1966).

Smith, Ernest E., *Illegitimate Children and Their Fathers: Some Problems with Title 2*, 5 TTLR 613 (1974).

Smith, Eugene L., *Commentary to Title II: Parent and Child*, 5 TTLR 389 (1974).

———, *Family Law*, 26 SwLJ 50 (1972).

———, *Legislative Note: 1963 Amendments Affecting Married Women's Rights in Texas*, 18 SwLJ 70 (1964).

Smith, Garland F., *The Valley Water Suit and Its Impact on Texas Water Policy: Some Practical Advice for the Future*, 8 TTLR 577 (1977).

Smith, Ralph, *The Farmers' Alliance in Texas, 1875–1900*, 48 SWHQ 346 (1945).

SoRelle, James M., *The "Waco Horror": The Lynching of Jesse Washington*, 86 SWHQ 517 (1983).

Special Committee on Judicial Reform, *Report of the Special Committee on Judicial Reform*, 33 PTBA 17 (1914).

Stayton, Robert W., *Texas' Approaches to the Parker Ideal and Her Shortcomings*, 37 TLR 845 (1959).

———, & M. P. Kennedy, *A Study of Pendency in Texas Civil Litigation*, 21 TLR 382 (1943).

Steiner, Mark E., *The Secret History of Proprietary Legal Education: The Case of the Houston Law School, 1919–45*, 47 J. Legal Educ. 341 (1997).

———, *"If We Don't Do Anything But Have an Annual Dinner": The Early History of the Houston Bar Association*, 11 Hous. Rev. 95 (1989).

Stout, A. R., *Criminal Procedure in Texas Should Be Revised: An Address*, 25 TLR 613 (1947).

Stumberg, George Wilfred, *Defense of Person and Property under Texas Criminal Law*, 21 TLR 17 (1942).

Subcommittee of the Texas Bar Association, *The Blending of Law and Equity*, 30 Am. L. Rev. 813 (1896).

Subrin, Stephen N., *How Equity Conquered Common Law: The Federal Rules of Civil Procedure in Historical Perspective*, 135 U. Pa. L. Rev. (1987).

Tarlton, B. D., *Some Reflections on the Relations of Capital and Labor*, 13 PTBA 51 (1894).

Taylor, A. Elizabeth, *The Woman Suffrage Movement in Texas*, 17 J. So. Hist. 194 (1951).

Teichmueller, H., *The Homestead Law*, 11 PTBA 63 (1893).

Templin, John J., *Texas v. White: A Study on the Merits of the Case*, 6 SwLJ 467 (1952).

Thode, E. Wayne, *Imminent Peril and Emergency in Texas*, 40 TLR 441 (1962).

———, *In Personam Jurisdiction: Article 2031B, the Texas "Long Arm" Jurisdiction Statute, and the Appearance to Challenge Jurisdiction in Texas and Elsewhere*, 42 TLR 279 (1964).

Thomas, A. J., & Ann Van Wynen Thomas, *The Texas Constitution of 1876*, 35 TLR 907 (1957).

Tinsley, James A., *Texas Progressives and Insurance Regulation*, 36 Sw. Soc. Sci. Q. 237 (1955).

Titus, Herbert W., *Restatement (Second) of Torts Section 402A and the Uniform Commercial Code*, 22 Stan. L. Rev. 713 (1970).

Tjarks, Alicia V., *Comparative Demographic Analysis of Texas, 1777–1793*, 77 SWHQ 291 (1974).

Toppin, Bruce E., III, *The Path of Least Resistance: The Effects of Groundwater Law's Failure to Evolve with Changing Times*, 38 StMLJ 503 (2007).

Tort Reform, TBJ, Oct. 1995, at 936.

Townes, John C., *Sketch of the Development of the Judicial System in Texas (Part I)*, 2 Qtrly. Tex. St. Hist. Ass'n 29 (1898); *Part II, id.* at 134.

Turner, Thomas F., *Prairie Dog Lawyers*, 2 Panhandle-Plains Hist. Rev. 104 (1929).

Tuttle, William M., Jr., *Violence in a "Heathen" Land: The Longview Race Riot of 1919*, 33 Phylon 324 (1972).

UT Law School Holds Corporation Laws Institute, Honors Justice Tom Clark, TBJ, May 1950, at 179.

Vaughn, Katherine S., Comment, *The Recent Changes to the Texas Informal Marriage Statute: Limitation or Abolition of Common-Law Marriage?*, 28 HLR 1131 (1991).

Veasy, James A., *The Struggle of the Oil Industry for the Sanctity of its Basic Contract—The Oil and Gas Lease*, 39 PTBA 82 (1920).

W., R. C., *Homicide-Justification-Cook v. State, 180 S.W. (Tex) 254*, 25 Yale L.J. 678 (1916).

Walker, Andrew, *Mexican Law and the Texas Courts*, 55 BLR 225 (2003).

Wallace, Charles B., *Waters-Pierce Oil Company Case Revisited*, TBJ, Mar. 1961, at 221.

Weeks, O. Douglas, *The Texas Direct Primary System*, 13 Sw. Soc. Sci. Q. 95 (1932).

Weinstein, Jeremy D., Note, *Adultery, Law, and the State: A History*, 38 Hastings L.J. 195 (1986).

Weiss, Michael D., *America's Queen of Torts*, Pol'y Rev., Fall 1992.

Wellborn, Olin Guy, III, *Article VIII: Hearsay*, 20 HLR 477 (1983).

Wells, Harwell, *The Modernization of Corporation Law, 1920–1940*, U. Pa. J. Bus. L. 573 (2009).

Weninger, Robert A., *Factors Affecting the Prosecution of Rape: A Case Study of Travis County, Texas*, 64 Va. L. Rev. 357 (1978).

West, Glenn D., & Stacie L. Cargill, *Corporations*, 62 SMU L. Rev. 1057 (2009).

Weston, J. Michael, *Vertical Distribution Restraints and the Texas Antitrust Laws*, 37 SwLJ 601 (1983).

Wharton, Clarence, *Early Judicial History of Texas*, 12 TLR 311 (1934).

Wharton, Linda J., *State Equal Rights Amendments Revisited: Evaluating Their Effectiveness in Advancing Protection against Sex Discrimination*, 36 Rutgers L.J. 1201 (2005).

White, A. R., & Will Wilson, *The Flow and Underflow of Motl v. Boyd (Part I)*, 9 SwLJ 1 (1955); *Part II, id.* at 377.

Wigmore, John Henry, *The Spark That Kindled the White Flame of Progress*, 20 J. Am. Jud. Soc'y 176 (1937).

Wilkinson, A. E., *The Author of the Texas Homestead Exemption Law*, 20 SWHQ 35 (1916).

———, *Edward Livingston and the Penal Codes*, 1 TLR 25 (1922).

Williams, Sandra, & David Harrell, *Civilized*

Procedure: *The Practice Act of 1846*, Hous. Law., Jan.–Feb. 1999, at 21.

Williford, Jill, *Reformers' Regress: The 1991 Texas Workers' Compensation Act*, 22 StMLJ 1112 (1992).

Wilson, Steven H., *Brown over "Other White": Mexican Americans' Legal Arguments and Litigation Strategy in School Desegregation Lawsuits*, 21 Law & Hist. Rev. 145 (2003).

Wilson, Will, *The State Antitrust Laws*, ABA J., Feb. 1961, at 160.

Wooster, Ralph A., *Wealthy Texans, 1860*, 71 SWHQ 163 (1967).

———, *Wealthy Texans, 1870*, 74 SWHQ 24 (1970).

Worthen, James T., *The Organizational and Structural Development of Intermediate Appellate Courts in Texas, 1892–2003*, 46 STLR 33 (2004).

Wynn, Leila Clark, *A History of Civil Courts in Texas*, 60 SWHQ 1 (1956).

Zapata, Raymon, *Child Custody in Texas and the Best Interest Standard: In the Best Interest of Whom?*, 6 Scholar 197 (2003).

Zelden, Charles L., *The Judge Intuitive: The Life and Judicial Philosophy of Joseph C. Hutcheson, Jr.*, 39 STLR 905 (1998).

———, *Regional Growth and the Federal District Courts: The Impact of Judge Joseph C. Hutcheson, Jr., on Southeast Texas, 1918–1931*, 11 Hous. Rev. 67 (1989).

NEWSPAPER AND MAGAZINE ARTICLES

Accept the Penalty, DMN, Aug. 22, 1900.

Adler, Stephen J., *The Texas Bench: Anything Goes*, Am. Law., Apr. 1986.

Alien Land Law Void, DMN, Oct. 13, 1891.

Another Negro Burned: Henry Smith Dies at the Stake, N.Y. Times, Feb. 2, 1893.

Barrett, William P., *The Best Justice Money Can Buy*, Forbes, June 1, 1987.

Belkin, Lisa, *Where 21 Youths Died, Lawyers Wage A War*, N.Y. Times, Jan. 18, 1990.

Bernstein, Peter W., *Profit Pressures on the Big Law Firms*, Forbes, Apr. 19, 1982.

The Best Paid Trial Lawyers, Forbes, Oct. 16, 1989.

Bills in the House, DMN, Jan. 14, 1921.

Brezosky, Lynn, *School Bus Tragedy Still Hurts*, San Antonio Express-News, Sept. 21, 2009.

Burka, Paul, *Heads, We Win, Tails, You Lose: How a Group of Trial Lawyers Took Over the Texas Supreme Court and Rewrote State Law*, TM, May 1987.

Calve, Joseph, *Poured Out: Times Have Never Been Tougher for the Plaintiffs' Personal-Injury Bar: The Civil-Justice System May Never Be the Same*, Tex. Law., Dec. 16, 1986.

Campbell Jury, Out More Than 30 Hours, Dismissed, DMN, Sept. 11, 1921.

Cartwright, Gary, *Every One a Victim*, TM, Nov. 1987.

Case, Ken, *Blind Justice*, TM, May 1987.

Charges against Officers Dropped by Commissioners, DMN, Feb. 7, 1922.

Cohen, Laurie P., *Southern Exposure: Lawyer Gets Investors to Sue GE, Prudential in Poor Border Town: Out of State Plaintiffs Hope for a Sympathetic Judge and Texas-Size Awards: "The Jurors Are Bountiful,"* WSJ, Nov. 30, 1994.

Cox, Tory, *Civic Leader-Lawyer Paul Carrington Dies*, DMN, May 29, 1988.

Crime in Texas, Illus. Amer., September 26, 1891.

Curtis, Gregory, *Up in Smoke*, TM, Mar. 1998.

Dubose, Lou, *Dime con Quien Andas, y Te Dire Quien Eres*, TM, Mar. 2002.

Edwards, George Clifton, *White Justice in Dallas*, Nation, Sept. 15, 1945.

Elkins, Peter, *The Hustlers*, TM, Nov. 1985.

Elliott, Janet, *"60 Minutes" Visit Finds Court's Defenders in Hiding*, Tex. Law., Aug. 24, 1998.

———, *There's Joy in Mudville over Battle of the Giants*, Tex. Law., Nov. 5, 1990.

Five Amendments Snowed Under by Voters of Texas, DMN, July 25, 1915.

Flood, Mary, *Justice Still for Sale? Clock is Ticking on the Answer*, WSJ, June 24, 1998.

Forsyth, Jennifer S., & Leslie Eaton, *The Exonerator: The Dallas D.A. is Reviewing Old Cases, Freeing Prisoners—and Riling His Peers*, WSJ, Nov. 15–16, 2008.

Freedman, Michael, *Judgment Day*, Forbes, May 14, 2001.

Grann, David, *Trial by Fire: Did Texas Execute an Innocent Man?*, New Yorker, Sept. 7, 2009.

Hogg's Message, DMN, Mar. 15, 1892.

Hollandsworth, Skip, *The Lawsuit from Hell*, TM, June 1996.

———, *Up in Smoke*, TM, Aug. 1999.

Horror in Henderson, DMN, May 29, 1899.

Humphries Lynching Suits, DMN, Sept. 29, 1899.

Jervey, Gay, *Grumbling All the Way to the Bank*, Am. Law., July–Aug. 1989.

Judicial Amendments, DMN, Aug. 9, 1891.

The Judiciary Amendment, DMN, Aug. 8, 1891.

Kaplan, Sheila, *What Price Justice? Oh, About $10,000*, Wash. Post, May 17, 1987.

Koppel, Nathan, *Democrats in Houston Take Aim at GOP Judges*, WSJ, Nov. 1–2, 2008.

MacCormack, John, *Story of South Texas "Case Runner" Reads Like a Novel*, San Antonio Express-News, Dec. 6, 2009.

McMenamin, Brigid, *The Best Paid Lawyers*, Forbes, Nov. 6, 1995.

Methvin, Eugene H., *Texas on Trial*, Nat'l Rev., Dec. 31, 1990.

Negro Claims Klan Threat Forced His Confession, DMN, Oct. 12, 1921.

Negro is Given Death Penalty, DMN, Jan. 18, 1922.

Nocera, Joseph, & Henry Goldblatt, *Dow Corning Succumbs*, Fortune, Oct. 30, 1995.

———, & Henry Goldblatt, *Fatal Litigation*, Fortune, Oct. 16, 1995.

Officers Believe Negro's Alleged Confession False, DMN, Mar. 18, 1922.

O'Leary, Christopher, *Lone Star Litigation: Are Huge Jury Awards in Texas a Relic?*, Corp. Legal Times (May 2003).

Politics at Terrell, DMN, Mar. 2, 1903.

Reasons for Rejection, DMN, Aug. 3, 1891.

Reavis, Dick J., *Why I Turned in Lee Otis Johnson*, TM, July 1980.

Reichley, A. James, *The Texas Banker Who Bought Politicians*, Fortune, Dec. 1971.

———, *The Fall of Will Wilson*, Fortune, Dec. 1971.

The Report on the Canales Charges, DMN, Feb. 21, 1919.

Schwartz, John, *Lee Otis, Free*, TM, Aug. 2002.

Smith, Griffin, Jr., *Empires of Paper*, TM, Nov. 1973.

———, *How the New Drug Law was Made*, TM, Sept. 1973.

Smith Names Dr. Baum to Bank Board, DMN, Sept. 12, 1969.

Texas Lawyer's 20th Century in Review, Tex. Law., Dec. 20, 1999.

That Alien Land Law, DMN, July 24, 1891.

Totty, Michael, *Defense Rests: Texas' High Court Pounded Plaintiffs in Last Year*, WSJ, July 17, 1996.

Try Officers on Cruelty Charges, DMN, Jan. 14, 1921.

21 for 21: The Cases That Rocked the Century, Tex. Law., Dec. 20, 1999.

Vincent, Bruce, *A Dearth of Work for "Dr. Death,"* Tex. Law., Dec. 4, 1995.

Wallace, Terry, *Districts Released from Desegregation Order*, San Antonio Express-News, Oct. 2, 2010.

Weingarten, Paul, *Lawsuits, Greed Tear Grieving Texas Town*, Chi. Trib., May 27, 1990.

White Man's Primary, DMN, Mar. 3, 1903.

Why Texas Should Have Banking Laws, DMN, Jan. 1, 1903.

Will Hold Two Primaries, DMN, Mar. 9, 1902.

Witness Tells of "Electric Monkey," DMN, Feb. 3, 1922.

Woodbury, Richard, *Is Texas Justice for Sale?*, Time, Jan. 11, 1988.

Zielinski, Graeme, *Desegregation Case in Uvalde Is Settled*, San Antonio Express-News, Sept. 19, 2008.

DISSERTATIONS, THESES, AND PAPERS

Burran, James A., Transforming a Tradition: "Streamlined" Lynching in the New South (Paper presented at The Citadel Conference on the South, Charleston, S.C., Apr. 19–21, 1979).

Calvert, Robert W., Remarks to the Texas Association of Defense Counsel, Sept. 30, 1983.

Cox, Patrick L., Land Commissioner Bascom Giles and the Texas Veteran's Land Board Scandals (M.A. thesis, Southwest Texas State Univ. 1988).

Crow, Herman Lee, A Political History of the Texas Penal System, 1829–1951 (Ph.D. diss., University of Texas 1964).

Eagleton, Nancy Ethie, Mercer Colony in Texas, 1844–1883 (M.A. thesis, University of Texas 1934).

Felgar, Robert Pattison, Texas in the War for Southern Independence, 1861–1865 (Ph.D. diss., University of Texas 1935).

Glasrud, Bruce Alden, Black Texans, 1900–1930: A History (Ph.D. diss., Texas Tech University 1969).

Mackenzie, Charles Alfred, A History of the Baylor University School of Law from the Lectures of Abner S. Lipscomb through the Deanship of Abner V. McCall (M.A. thesis, Baylor University 1988).

Mauer, John Walker, Southern State Constitutions in the 1870s: A Case Study of Texas (Ph.D. diss., Rice University 1983).

McGraw, John Conger, The Texas Constitution of 1866 (Ph.D. diss., Texas Technological College 1959).

Rocha, Rodolfo, The Influence of the Mexican Revolution on the Mexico-Texas Border, 1910–1916 (Ph.D. diss., Texas Tech University 1981).

Ross, John Raymond, At the Bar of Judge Lynch: Lynching and Lynch Mobs in America (Ph.D diss., Texas Tech University 1983).

Scarborough, Jane Lynn, George W. Paschal, Texas Unioʼist and Scalawag Jurisprudent (Ph.D. diss., Rice University 1972).

Schulz, Marvin E., For the Better Administrations of Justice: The Legal Culture of Texas, 1820–1836 (Ph.D. diss., Texas Christian University 1994).

SELECTED INTERNET SOURCES

Alonzo, Armando C., *Mexican-American Land Grant Adjudication*, HOTO, www.tshaonline.org/handbook/online/articles/MM/pqmck.html.

Anderson, H. Allen, *Wheeler, Royal T.*, HOTO, www.tshaonline.org/handbook/lonline/articles/WW/fwh9_print.html.

Bell, James Hall, HOTO, www.tshaonline.org/handbook/online/articles/BB/fbe36.html.

Campbell, Randolph B., *Walker, Moses B.*, HOTO, www.tshaonline.org/handbook/online/articles/WW/fwa21.html.

Centers for Disease Control and Prevention, *Marriage Rates by State, 1990, 1995, and 1999–2004*, www.cdc.gov/nchs/data/nvss/marriage90_04.pdf.

Changes in Minority Enrollment at University of Texas School of Law, tarltonguides.law.utexas.edu/content.php?pid=98968&sid=742751.

Chriss, William J., *Judges as Political Orators: The 1860 Secession Debate between Texas Supreme Court Justices O. M. Roberts and James H. Bell*, works.bepress.com/cgi/viewcontent.cgi?article=1001&context=william_chriss.

Clark, James A., and Mark Odintz, *Exxon Company, U.S.A.*, HOTO, www.tshaonline.org/handbook/online/articles/EE/doe4.html.

Constitution of 1876, HOTO, www.tshaonline.org/handbook/online/articles/CC/mhc7.html.

Cuthbertson, Gilbert M., *Regulator-Moderator War*, HOTO, www.tshaonline.org/handbook/online/articles/RR/jcr1.html.

DEATH PENALTY FOCUS, deathpenalty.org/.

de la Teja, Jesús F., *San Fernando de Bexar*, HOTO, www.tshaonline.org/handbook/online/articles/SS/hvs16.html.

Debates of the Convention, 1845, http://tarlton.law.utexas.edu/constitutions/pdf/pdf1845debates/indexdebates1845.html#j28

Dixon, Ford, *Roberts, Oran Milo*, HOTO, www.tshaonline.org/handbook/online/articles/RR/fro18.html.

Enstam, Elizabeth York, *Women and the Law*, HOTO, www.tshaonline.org/handbook/online/articles/WW/jsw2.html.

Ericson, Joe E., *Collinsworth, James*, HOTO, www.tshaonline.org/handbook/online/articles/CC/fc097.html.

———, *Potter, Robert*, HOTO, www.tshaonline.org/handbook/online/articles/PP/fp031.html.

Frontline: The Case for Innocence: Four Cases (PBS television), pbs.org/wgbh/pages/frontline/shows/case/cases/.

Gard, Wayne, *Fence Cutting*, HOTO, www.tshaonline.org/handbook/online/articles/auf01.

Highsmith, Mary J., *Lipscomb, Abner Smith*, HOTO, www.tshaonline.org/handbook/online/articles/LL/fli14.html.

John M. Hansford, tarlton.law.utexas.edu/justices/spct/hansford.html.

Johnson, John G., *State Police*, HOTO, www.tshaonline.org/handbook/online/articles/SS/jls2.html.

Knapp, Virginia, and Megan Biesele, *Rusk County*, HOTO, www.tshaonline.org/handbook/online/articles/RR/hcr12.html.

Lee, Joyce Glover, *Anderson, Dillon*, HOTO, www.tshaonline.org/handbook/online/articles/AA/fan31.html.

McCallum, Frances T., and James Mulkey Owens, *Barbed Wire*, HOTO, www.tshaonline.org/handbook/online/articles/BB/aob1.html.

Minor, David, *Archer, Branch Tanner*, HOTO, www.tshaonline.org/handbook/online/articles/AA/far2.html.

Moneyhon, Carl H., *Ex parte Rodriguez*, HOTO, www.tshaonline.org/handbook/online/articles/EE/jre1.html.

New Tort Cases Filed in Texas District and County-Level Courts Fiscal Years 1987–2006 (Texas Judicial Council 2006), www.courts.state.tx.us/pubs/ar2006/trends/torts-87-06.pdf.

Olsson, Nils Gregor, & Greg Hammond, *Annual Report on the Status of Women in the State Bar of Texas (2003–2004)*, www.texasbar.com/AM/Template.cfm?Section=Archives&Template=/CM/ContentDisplay.cfm&ContentID=11497.

Perryman Group, *The Impact of Judicial Reforms on Economic Activity in Texas* (August 2000), www.cse.org/reports/perryman_texas_study.pdf

PORTAL TO TEXAS HISTORY, texashistory.unt.edu/browse/.

Ross, John R., *Lynching*, HOTO, www.tshaonline.org/handbook/online/articles/LL/jgl1.html.

Schilz, Jodye Lynn Dickson, *Council House Fight*, HOTO, www.tshaonline.org/handbook/online/articles/CC/btc1.html.

Scott, Janelle D., *Hortense Sparks Ward*, HOTO, www.tshaonline.org/handbook/online/articles/WW/fwa83.html.

Sweatt v. Painter, tarltonguides.law.utexas.edu/heman-sweatt.

Texans for Public Justice, *Checks and Imbalances: How Texas Supreme Court Justices Raised $11 Million* (2000), www.tpj.org/reports/checks/toc.html.

Texas Defender Service, www.texasdefender.org/.

Texas Department of Criminal Justice, *Executed Offenders*, www.tdcj.state.tx.us/stat/executedoffenders.htm.

Texas Judicial Counsel, www.courts.state.tx.us/tjc/.

Tumlinson, Samuel H., *Tumlinson, John Jackson, Sr.*, HOTO, www.tshaonline.org/handbook/online/articles/TT/ftu29.html.

U.S. Census Bureau, Census Information, www.census.gov/.

Vital Statistics of the United States, Annual Reports 1963–1984, www.cdc.gov/nchs/products/vsus.htm.

Weir, Merie, *Bell, Josiah Hughes*, HOTO, www.tshaonline.org/handbook/online/articles/BB/fbe38.html.

Wooster, Robert, and Christine Moor Sanders, *Spindletop Oilfield*, HOTO, www.tshaonline.org/handbook/online/articles/SS/dos3.html.

MOVIES AND TELEVISION

The Ballad of Gregorio Cortez (MGM 1982).

Charlie Wilson's War (Universal Pictures 2007).

A Class Apart (PBS television broadcast Feb. 23, 2009).

Day One: From Grief to Greed (ABC television broadcast June 7, 1993).

Death by Fire (PBS television broadcast Oct. 19, 2010).

60 Minutes: Justice for Sale? (CBS television broadcast Dec. 6, 1987).

60 Minutes: Justice for Sale? (CBS television broadcast Nov. 1, 1998).

The Thin Blue Line (MGM 1988).

INDEX

★

200, 239; nineteenth-century practice of, 187–88; in Northern New Spain, 5–7; requirements for admission to the bar, 181–84; specialization of, 187, 197; twentieth-century practice of, 190. *See also Sweatt v. Painter*

league (measure of land), 15, 71, 72, 73, 74, 110–12

League of United Latin American Citizens. *See* LULAC

Legal Status of Married Women in Texas, The (Ward), 170

Legal Status of Married Women in Texas (Texas Legislative Council), 173

Lewis, Ex parte, 206

liberty, concept of, 2, 8, 13, 284

Lightfoot, Jewel, 136, 137

Lincoln, Abraham, 32

Lincoln University, 195

Ling & Co., 146

Lipscomb, Abner S., 19, 24–26, 29, 32, 193

Livingston, Edward, 212, 213

Locke, Edith, 191

London, 90, 187

Longview riot, 69–70

Looney, Benjamin F., 137

Lopez, Norma, 276

López de Santa Anna, Antonio, 12

Louisiana, 142, 230; adoption of civil law in, 13; codification of law in, 13; influencing development of Texas law, 13, 61, 167–68

Loving v. Virginia, 62

Lubbock (TX), 198

Lucas, Anthony, 93

LULAC, 244

Lyle v. State, 206

lynchings: in antebellum Texas, 22; condoning of, 227; defined, 225; extent of, compared with other states, 226; in late-nineteenth-century Texas, 53–54; legislative efforts to limit, 54; of Mexican Americans, 67, 226; and race, 225–26, 240; supplanted by death penalty, 227; in twentieth-century Texas, 228, 240; used as intimidation tactic, 36, 52; used in lieu of legal execution, 54. *See also* Hillard, Robert; Smith, Henry; Washington, Jesse

lynch law, 22, 30, 52

Lyons v. Millers Casualty Insurance Co. of Texas, 278

Macmillan v. Railroad Commission, 97–98

Magnolia Petroleum Company, 136–37

Magruder, John, 35

Malavis, Nicholas, 99

MALDEF (Mexican American Legal Defense and Education Fund), 245

Maloney, Pat, 208, 280

Manifest Destiny, 78. *See also* frontier, end of

Marbury v. Madison, 20

Maria (a slave), 37

marital property. *See* community property, law of

Market Demand Act, 98

marriage, 8; by bond, 152–53; ceremonial, 159; common law, 156–58; limitations on, 40, 42, 61–62, 153–56 (*see also* bigamy; miscegenation); legal presumptions concerning, 164–65, 167; legal understanding of (status versus contract), 152; married women's property acts and, 168; Mexican law of, 154; religious, 152, 153; same-sex, 158

Married Women's Property Act of 1913, 170–73, 191

Marshall, John, 20, 25, 26, 47

Marshall, Thurgood, 195–97, 238, 242

Martin, Crawford, 148

Martin, Joanne, 277, 280–81

Maryland, 168

Mason, Alexander, 53

Mason, John T., 15, 24, 73, 74

Massachusetts, 53

mass tort cases, 272, 274–75, 279, 281

Matagorda County (TX), 261

Matrimonial Property Act of 1967. *See* community property, 1967 code of

Matthews, Wilbur, 190

Mauer, John, 47

Mauzy, Oscar, 209, 275–76

Maverick, Samuel, 48

Maverick County (TX), 280

Maynard v. Hill, 152

MBank Abilene v. LeMaire, 277

McAskill, D. A., 240

McBride, John, 50, 51, 52

McCasland, J. B., 227

McCloskey, Frank, 185, 264–65

McCormick, Charles T., 195, 254

McCulloch v. Maryland, 26, 34, 47

McDonald, J. G., 54–55

McDougall, Walter A., 2

McGill v. Delaplain, 20

McGinty, Rush, 148

McHenry, Fannie, 225

McKisson v. Sales Affiliates, 268

McKnight, Joseph W., 5, 8, 17, 104, 167, 173, 176, 260

McLaurin, G. W., 197

McLaurin v. Oklahoma State Regents for Higher Education, 197

McLean, In re, 177

Melish map, 82–83

Melton v. Cobb, 76

Mendez v. Westminster School District, 244

Mercer, Charles, 75–76

Mercer Colony, 76–77

Meredith, James, 189

Merck, 281

Mexican American Legal Defense and Education Fund. *See* MALDEF

Mexican-American War, 22, 78, 79, 80

Mexican Cession, 79–80

Mexico: law of, 4, 5, 212, 248; Texas as part of, 13–15, 18, 213

Mexico City, 4, 73

Meyers, Lawrence, 210

Meyers v. State, 218

Michigan, 129, 142

Miller, Edmund, 138

Miller, James B., 78, 79

Miller, Richard, 273

Miller, Thomas Lloyd, 73, 75, 77

Miller-Bourland Commission, 79, 91

Mills v. Waller, 21

Minnesota, 179

Minor v. Happersett, 68

Miranda v. Arizona, 232

miscegenation: abolition of, 62; crime of, 62–63, 154, 155; enforcement of law against, 156. *See also* marriage

Mission San Antonio de Valero, 4

Mississippi, 142, 168, 179, 189, 202, 226, 258, 278–79

Missouri, 142, 168, 179, 189, 202, 226, 258, 278–79

Missouri Compromise of 1850, 79

Missouri ex rel. Gaines v. Canada, 185

Missouri Pacific Railway Co. v. Shuford, 262

Mitchell, Ex parte, 206

Mobile Chemical v. Bell, 270

Model Act for the Termination of Parental Rights and Responsibilities and the Adoption of Children, 178

Mode, Ex parte, 206

Model Business Corporation Act, 142

ABOUT THE AUTHOR

★

Michael Ariens is professor of law at St. Mary's University of San Antonio,
where he teaches courses in legal history, constitutional law, and the legal profession.
Lone Star Law is an effort to provide a different lens for viewing the unique history of Texas.